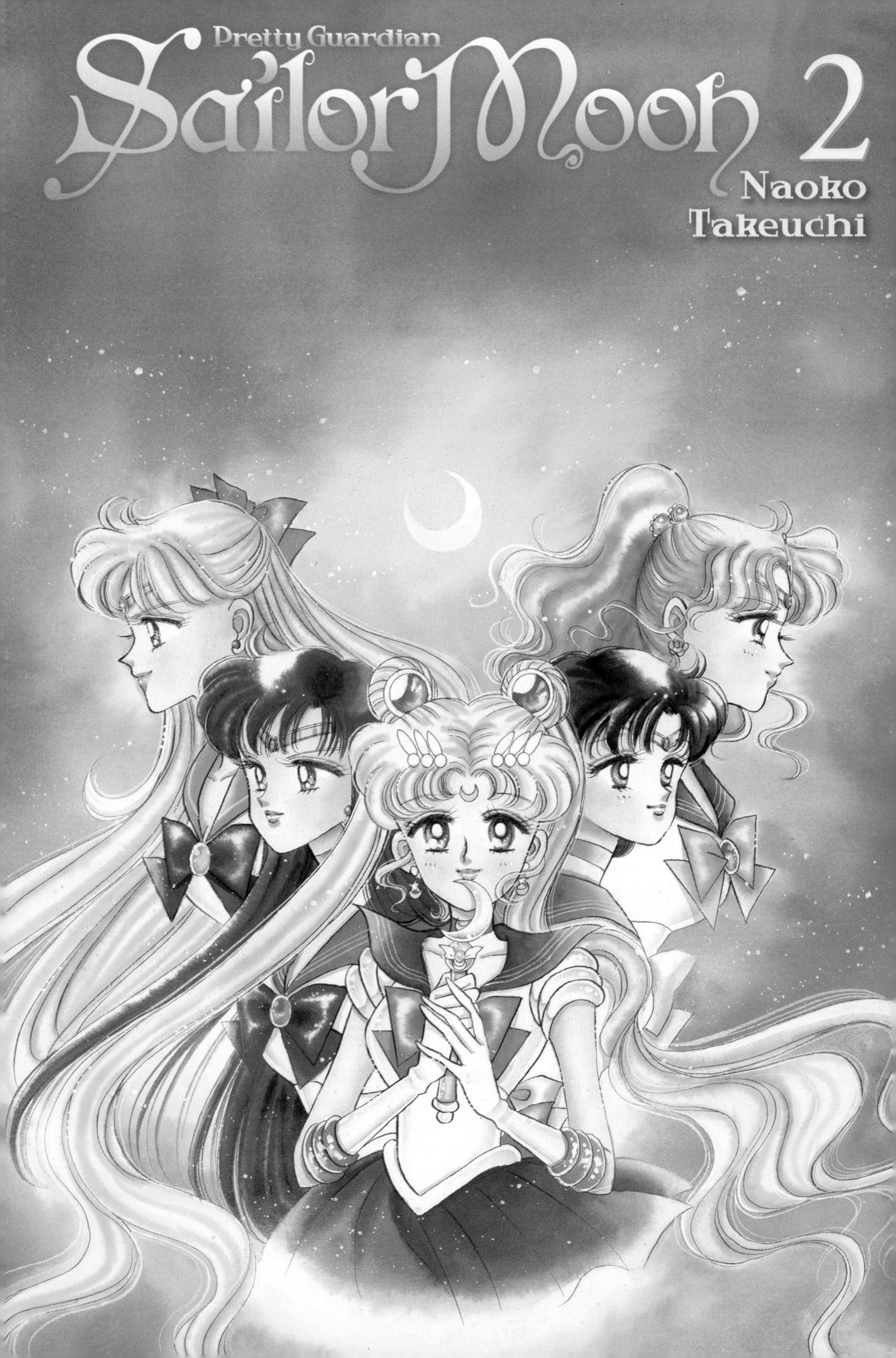
Pretty Guardian
Sailor Moon 2
Naoko
Takeuchi

# CONTENTS

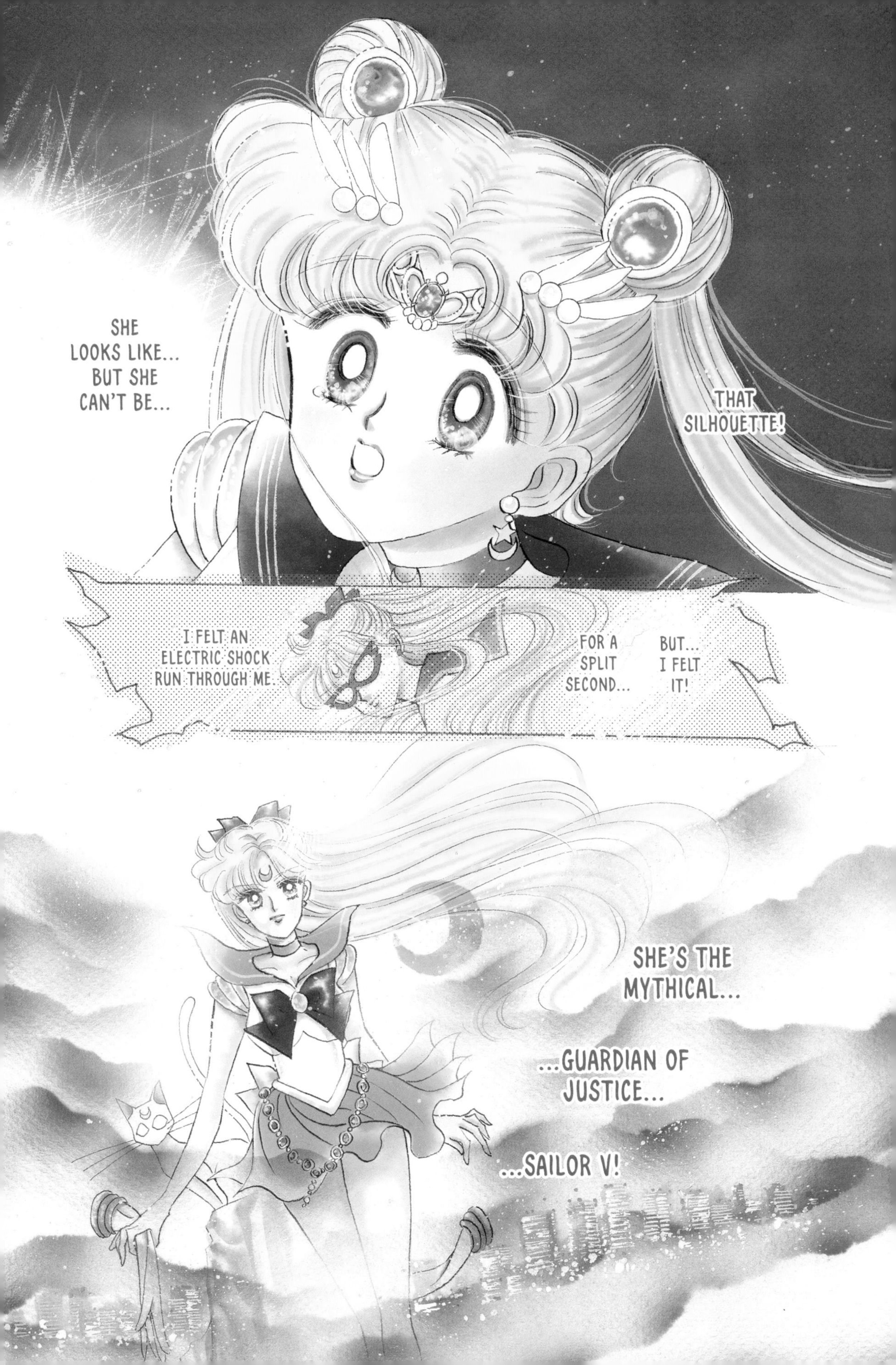
THAT SILHOUETTE!
SHE LOOKS LIKE... BUT SHE CAN'T BE...
BUT... I FELT IT!
FOR A SPLIT SECOND...
I FELT AN ELECTRIC SHOCK RUN THROUGH ME.
SHE'S THE MYTHICAL...
...GUARDIAN OF JUSTICE...
...SAILOR V!

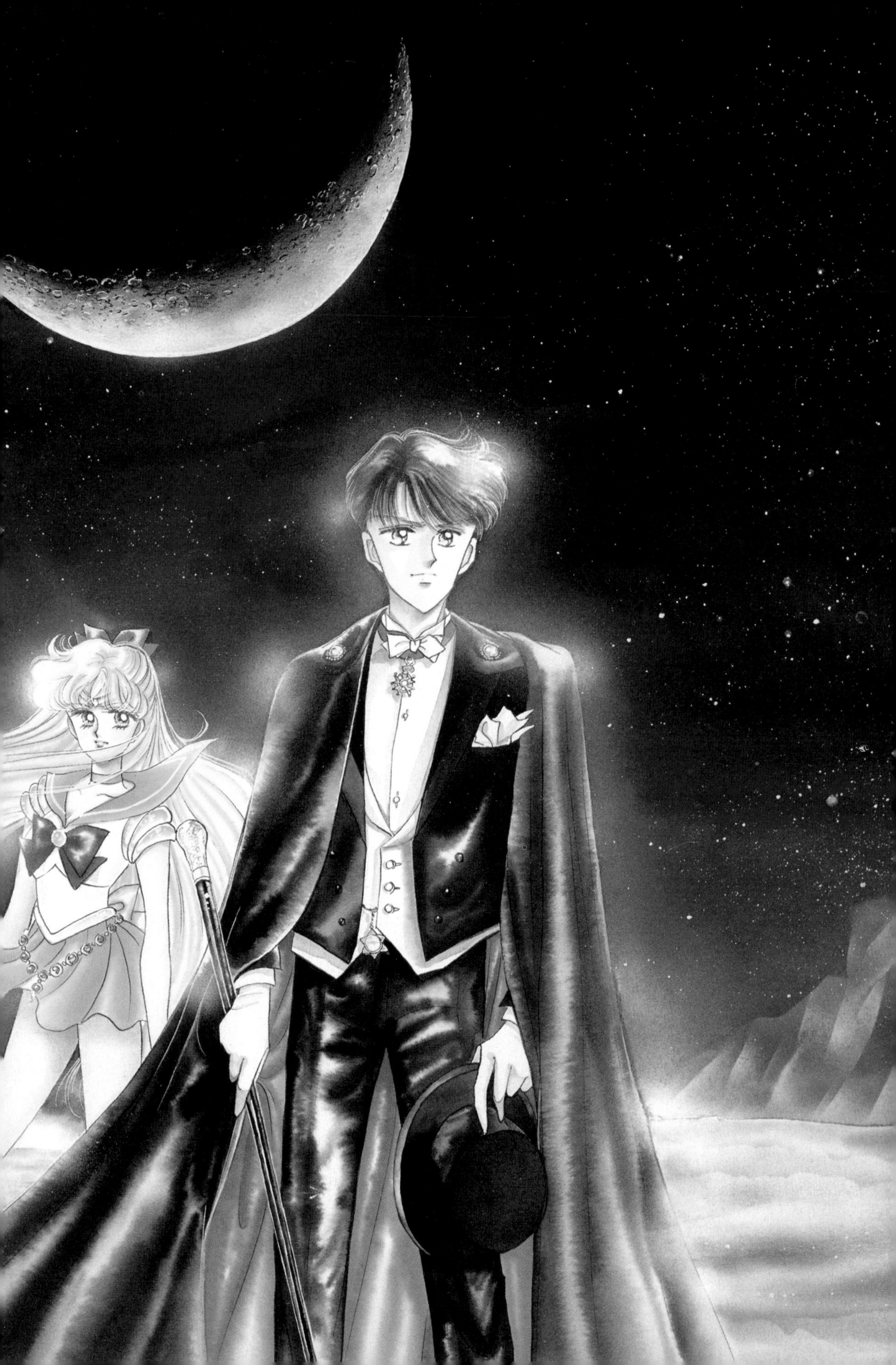

# Act. 8 Minako: Sailor V

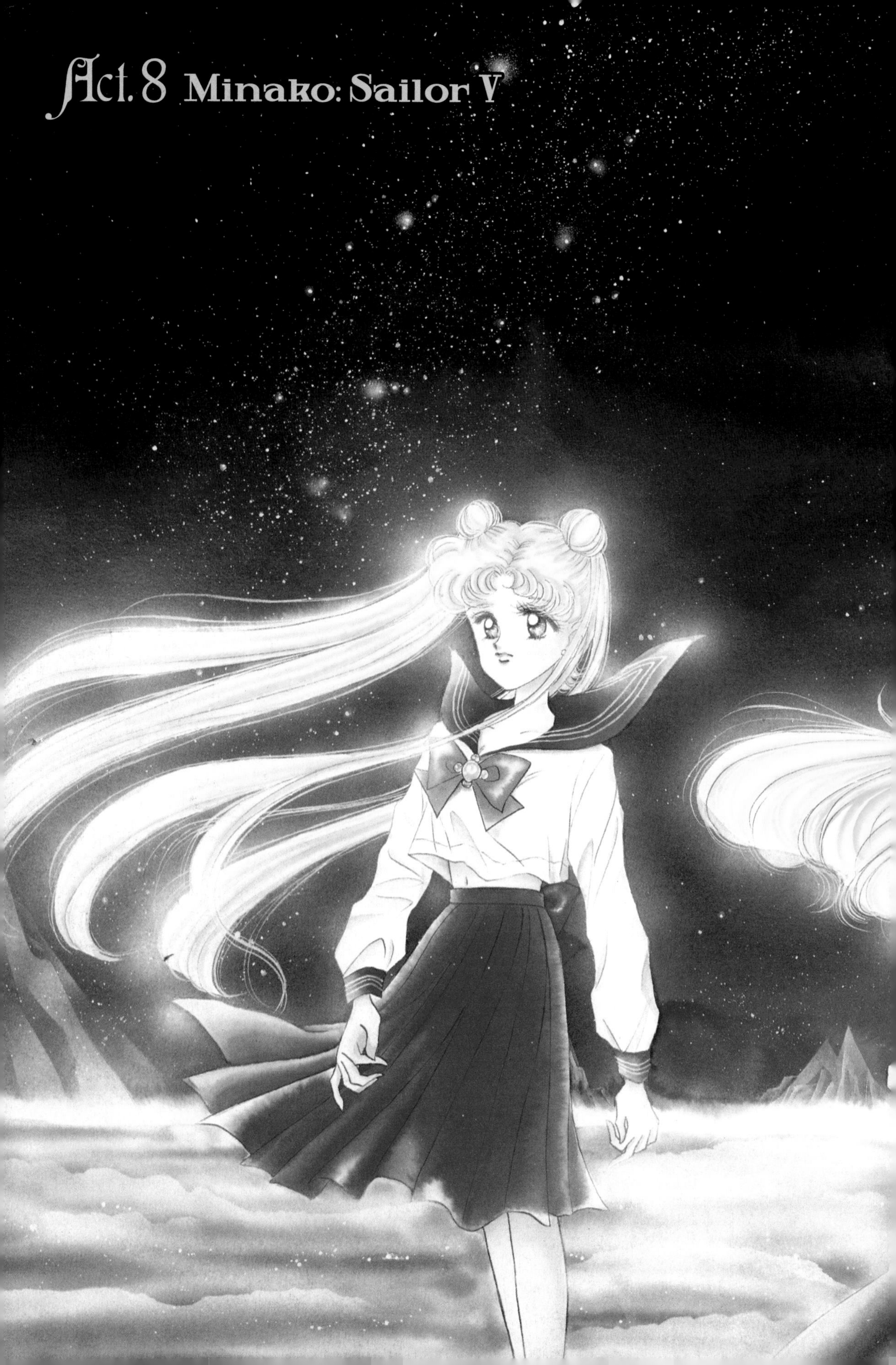

Pretty Guardian Sailor Moon

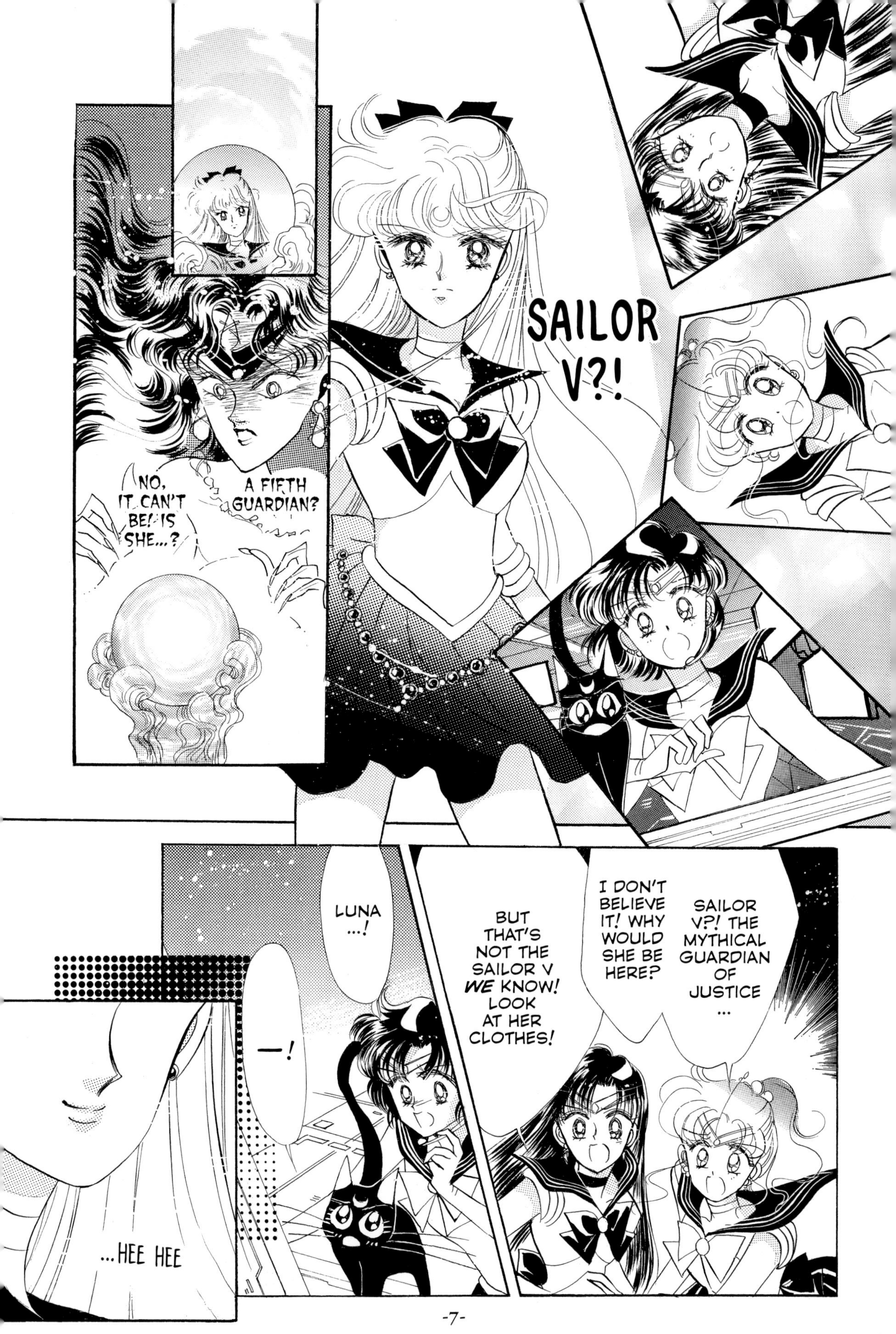
SAILOR V?!
A FIFTH GUARDIAN?
NO, IT CAN'T BE! IS SHE...?
SAILOR V?! THE MYTHICAL GUARDIAN OF JUSTICE ...
I DON'T BELIEVE IT! WHY WOULD SHE BE HERE?
BUT THAT'S NOT THE SAILOR V *WE* KNOW! LOOK AT HER CLOTHES!
LUNA ...!
—!
...HEE HEE

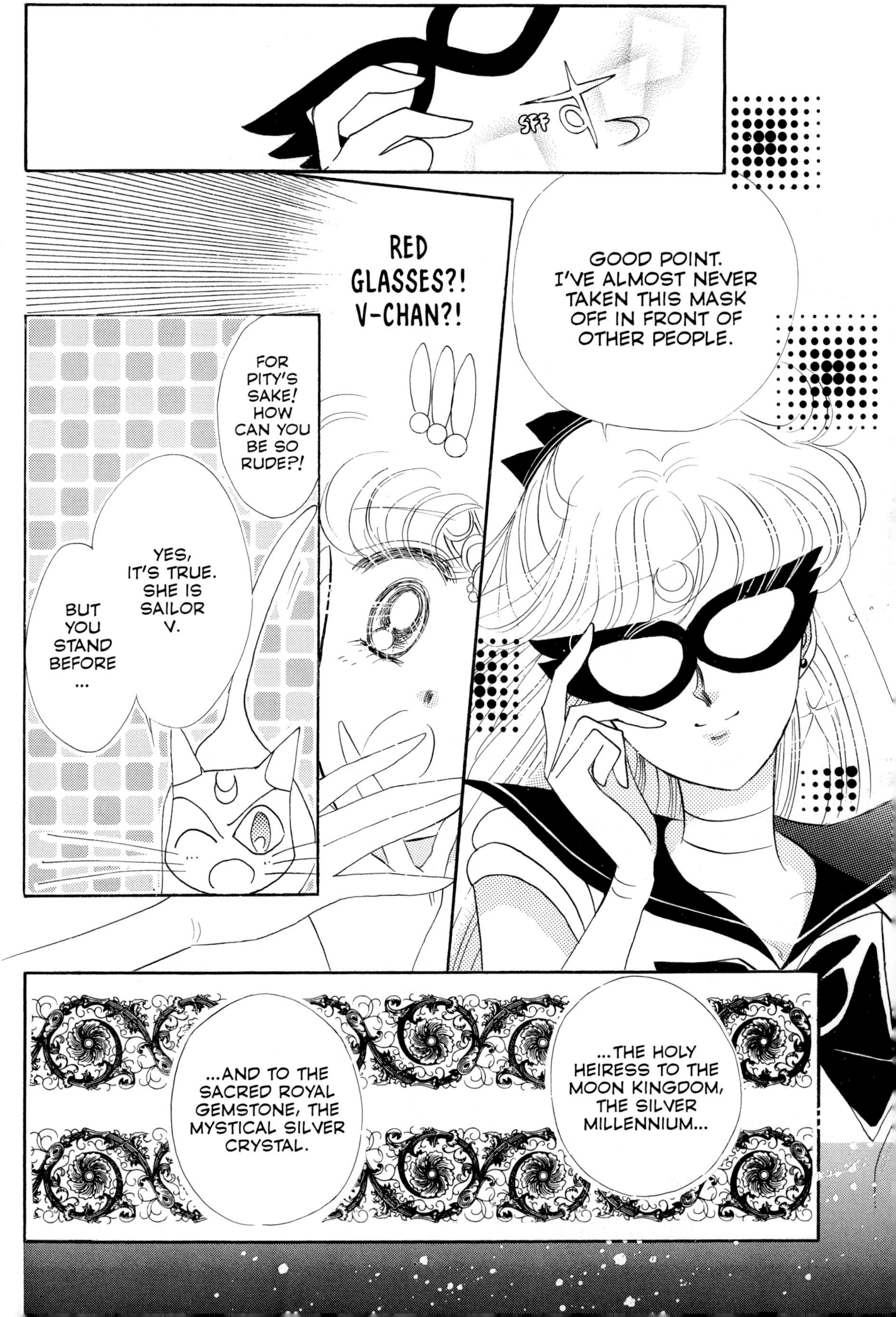
SFF
GOOD POINT. I'VE ALMOST NEVER TAKEN THIS MASK OFF IN FRONT OF OTHER PEOPLE.
RED GLASSES?! V-CHAN?!
FOR PITY'S SAKE! HOW CAN YOU BE SO RUDE?!
YES, IT'S TRUE. SHE IS SAILOR V.
BUT YOU STAND BEFORE ...
...THE HOLY HEIRESS TO THE MOON KINGDOM, THE SILVER MILLENNIUM...
...AND TO THE SACRED ROYAL GEMSTONE, THE MYSTICAL SILVER CRYSTAL.

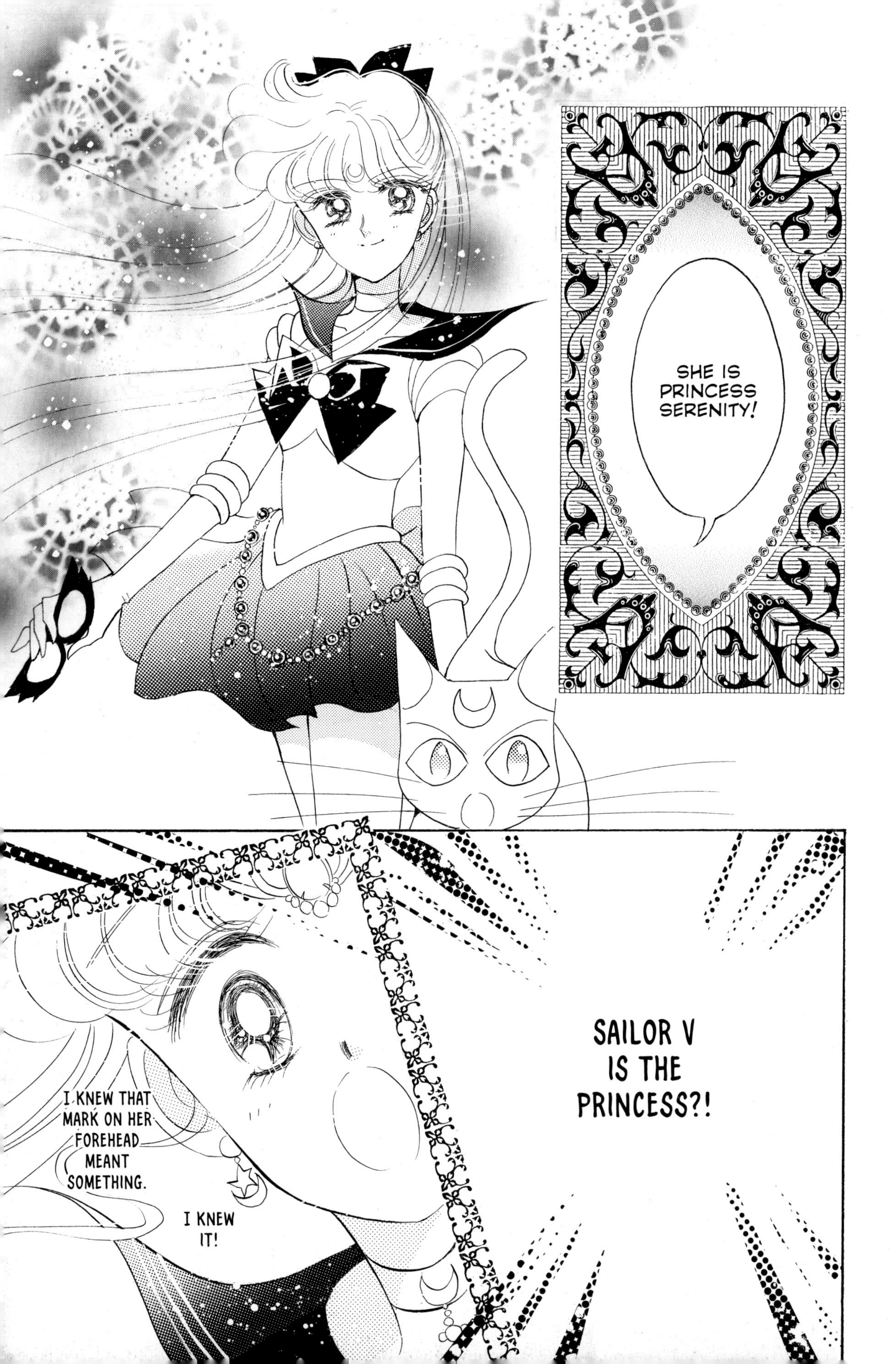
SHE IS PRINCESS SERENITY!
SAILOR V IS THE PRINCESS?!
I KNEW THAT MARK ON HER FOREHEAD MEANT SOMETHING.
I KNEW IT!

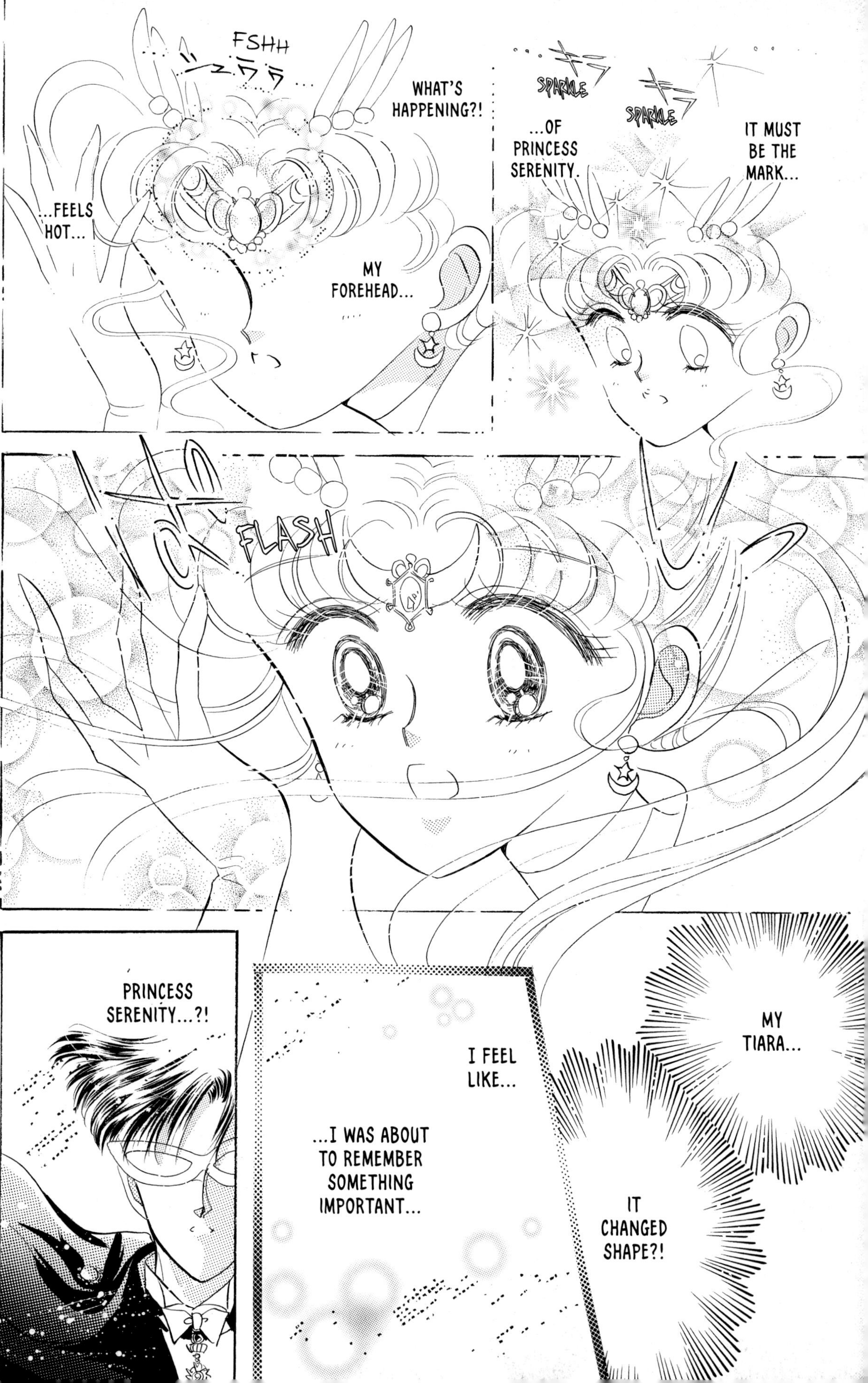
IT MUST BE THE MARK...
SPARKLE
SPARKLE
...OF PRINCESS SERENITY.
WHAT'S HAPPENING?!
FSHH
MY FOREHEAD...
...FEELS HOT...
FLASH
MY TIARA...
IT CHANGED SHAPE?!
I FEEL LIKE...
...I WAS ABOUT TO REMEMBER SOMETHING IMPORTANT...
PRINCESS SERENITY...?!

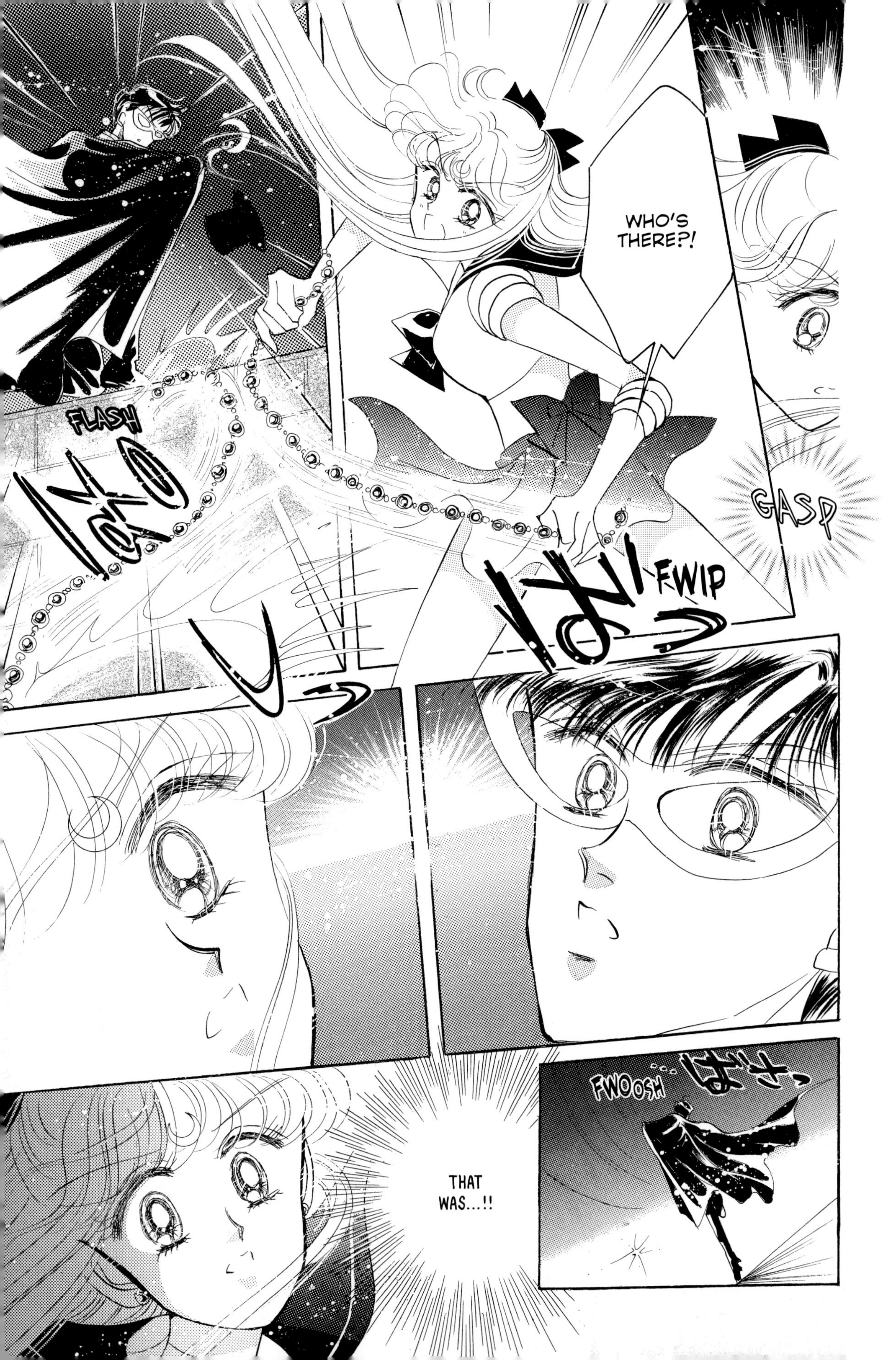
GASP
WHO'S THERE?!
FWIP
FLASH
FWOOSH
ばさっ
THAT WAS...!!

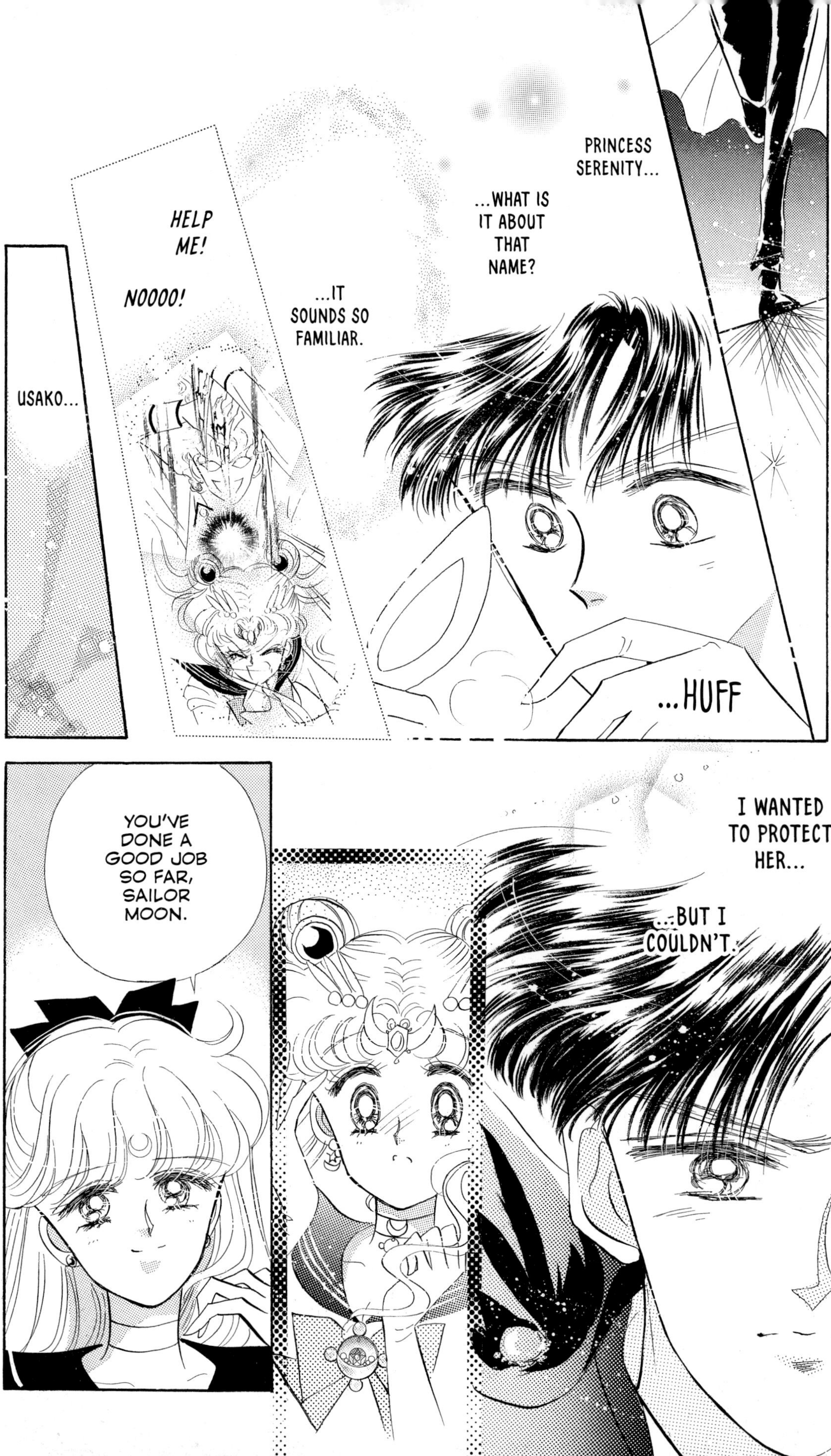
PRINCESS SERENITY...
...WHAT IS IT ABOUT THAT NAME?
...IT SOUNDS SO FAMILIAR.
...HUFF
HELP ME!
NOOOO!
USAKO...
I WANTED TO PROTECT HER...
...BUT I COULDN'T.
YOU'VE DONE A GOOD JOB SO FAR, SAILOR MOON.

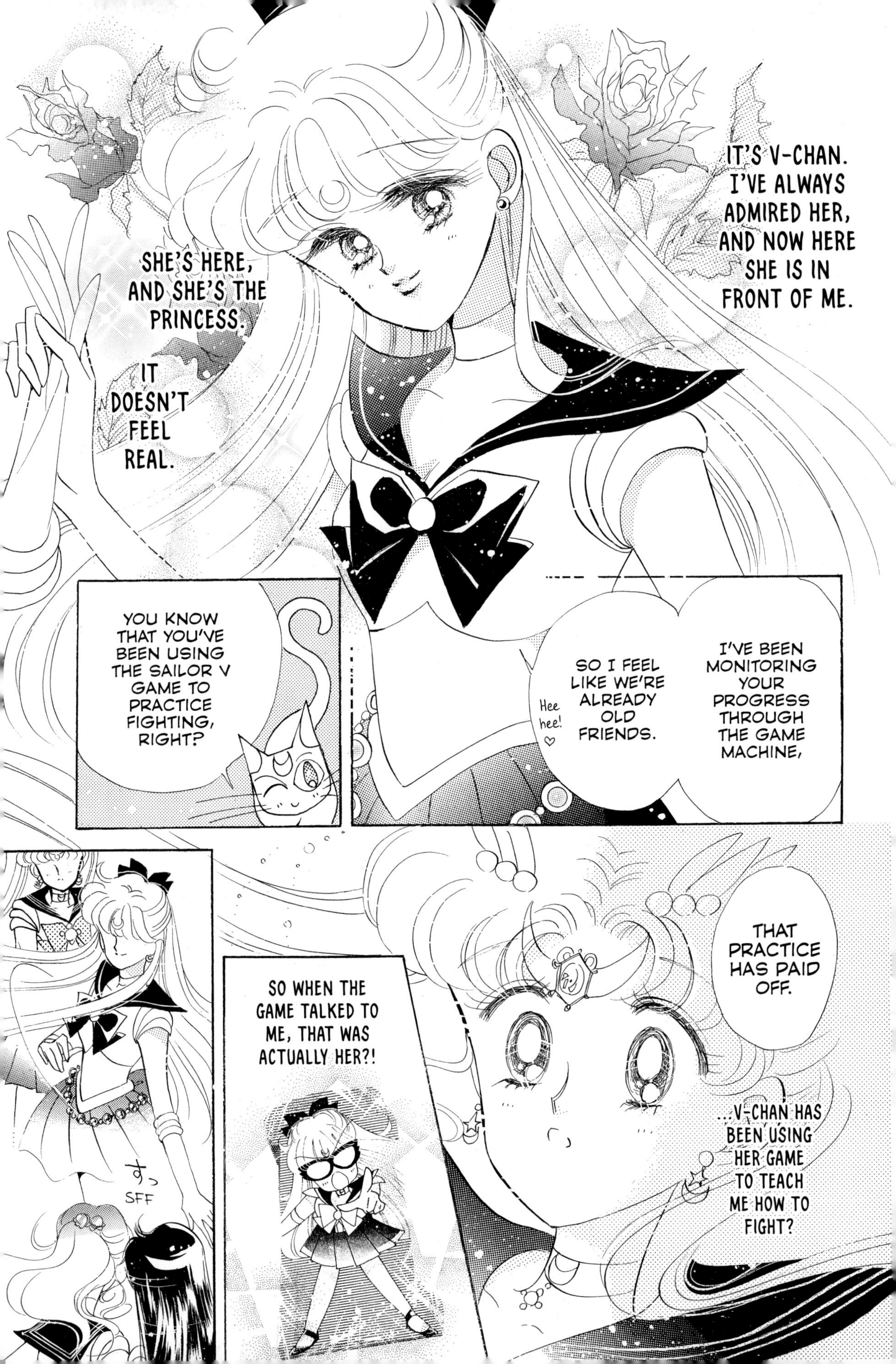
IT'S V-CHAN. I'VE ALWAYS ADMIRED HER, AND NOW HERE SHE IS IN FRONT OF ME.
SHE'S HERE, AND SHE'S THE PRINCESS.
IT DOESN'T FEEL REAL.
I'VE BEEN MONITORING YOUR PROGRESS THROUGH THE GAME MACHINE,
SO I FEEL LIKE WE'RE ALREADY OLD FRIENDS.
Hee hee! ♡
YOU KNOW THAT YOU'VE BEEN USING THE SAILOR V GAME TO PRACTICE FIGHTING, RIGHT?
THAT PRACTICE HAS PAID OFF.
...V-CHAN HAS BEEN USING HER GAME TO TEACH ME HOW TO FIGHT?
SO WHEN THE GAME TALKED TO ME, THAT WAS ACTUALLY HER?!
すっ
SFF

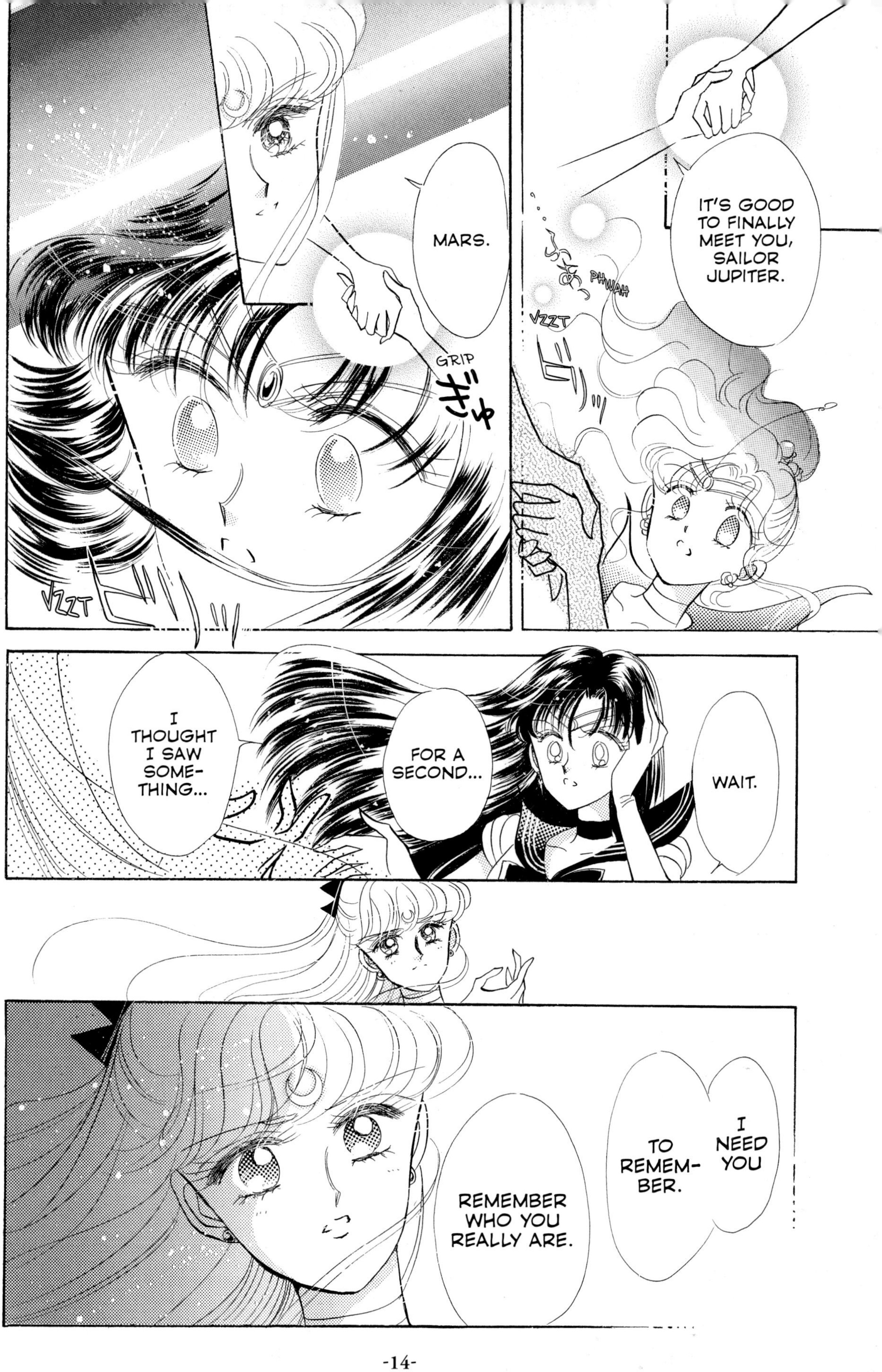
IT'S GOOD TO FINALLY MEET YOU, SAILOR JUPITER.
PHWAH
VZZT
MARS.
GRIP
ぎゅ
VZZT
WAIT.
FOR A SECOND...
I THOUGHT I SAW SOME-THING...
I NEED YOU
TO REMEM-BER.
REMEMBER WHO YOU REALLY ARE.

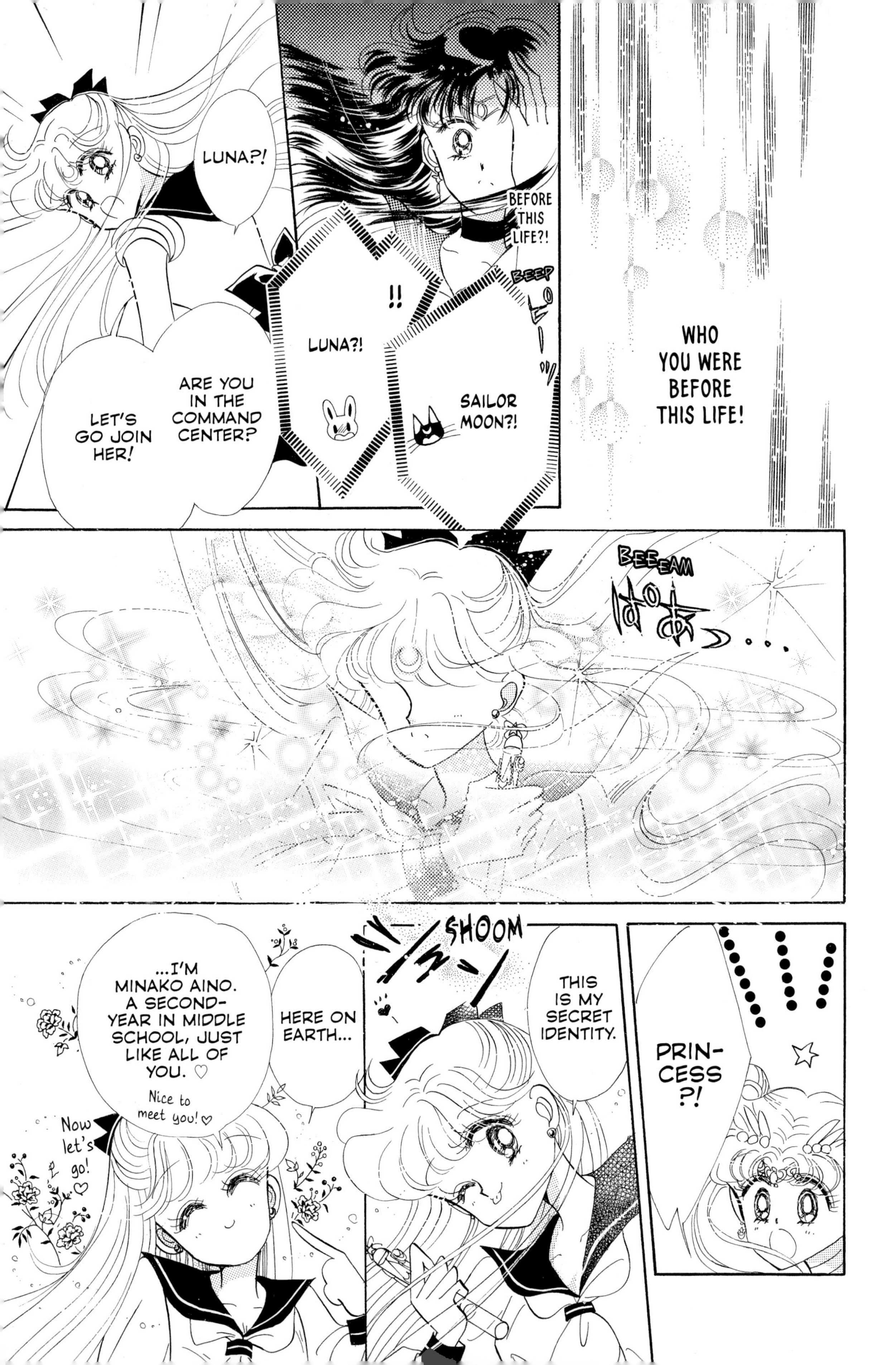
WHO YOU WERE BEFORE THIS LIFE!
BEFORE THIS LIFE?!
BEEP
SAILOR MOON?!
!!
LUNA?!
LUNA?!
ARE YOU IN THE COMMAND CENTER?
LET'S GO JOIN HER!
BEEEAM
はあっ…
PRIN-CESS?!
SHOOM
THIS IS MY SECRET IDENTITY.
HERE ON EARTH...
...I'M MINAKO AINO. A SECOND-YEAR IN MIDDLE SCHOOL, JUST LIKE ALL OF YOU. ♡
Nice to meet you! ♡
Now let's go! ♡

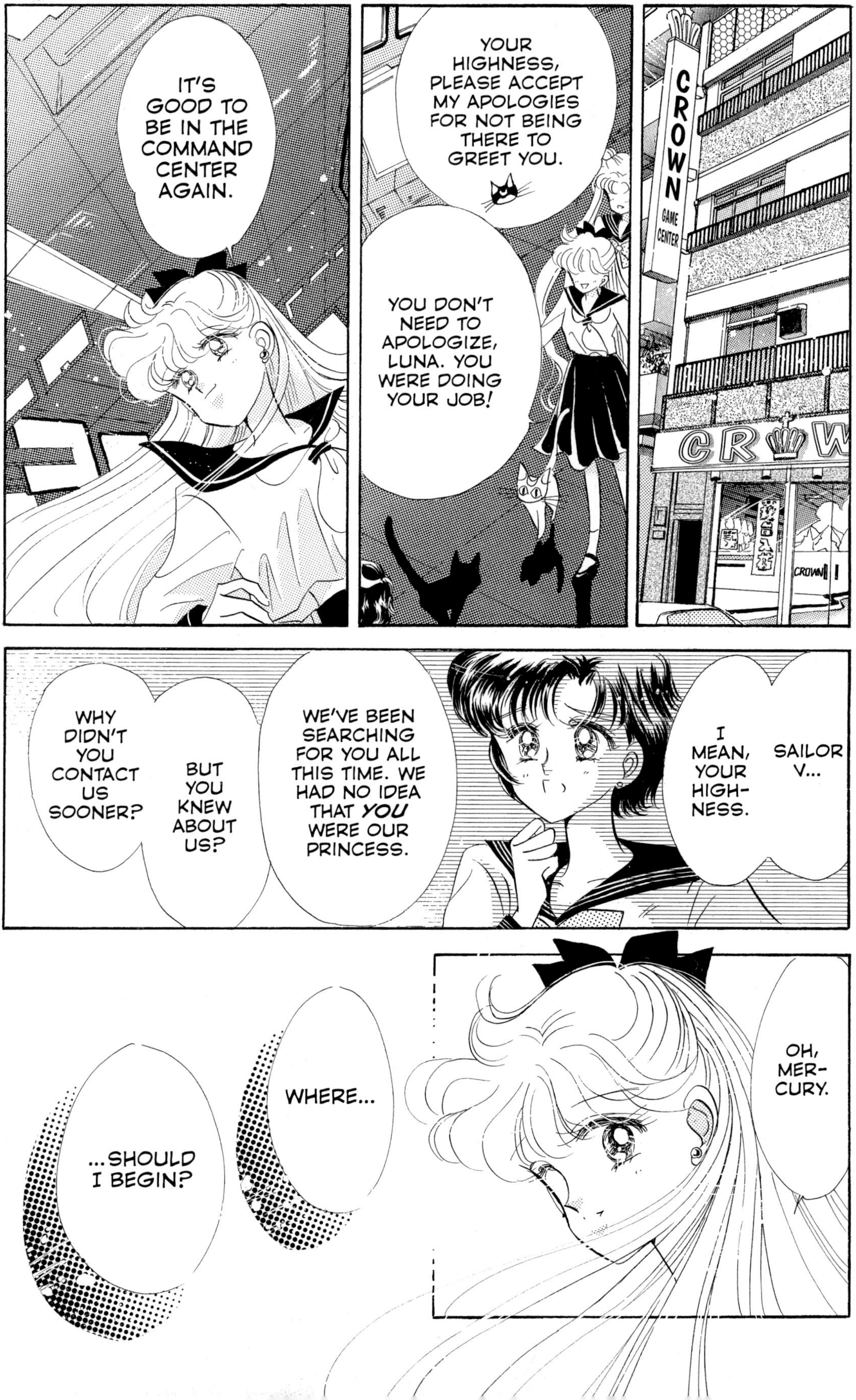
CROWN GAME CENTER
YOUR HIGHNESS, PLEASE ACCEPT MY APOLOGIES FOR NOT BEING THERE TO GREET YOU.
YOU DON'T NEED TO APOLOGIZE, LUNA. YOU WERE DOING YOUR JOB!
IT'S GOOD TO BE IN THE COMMAND CENTER AGAIN.
SAILOR V...
I MEAN, YOUR HIGHNESS.
WE'VE BEEN SEARCHING FOR YOU ALL THIS TIME. WE HAD NO IDEA THAT *YOU* WERE OUR PRINCESS.
BUT YOU KNEW ABOUT US?
WHY DIDN'T YOU CONTACT US SOONER?
OH, MERCURY.
WHERE...
...SHOULD I BEGIN?

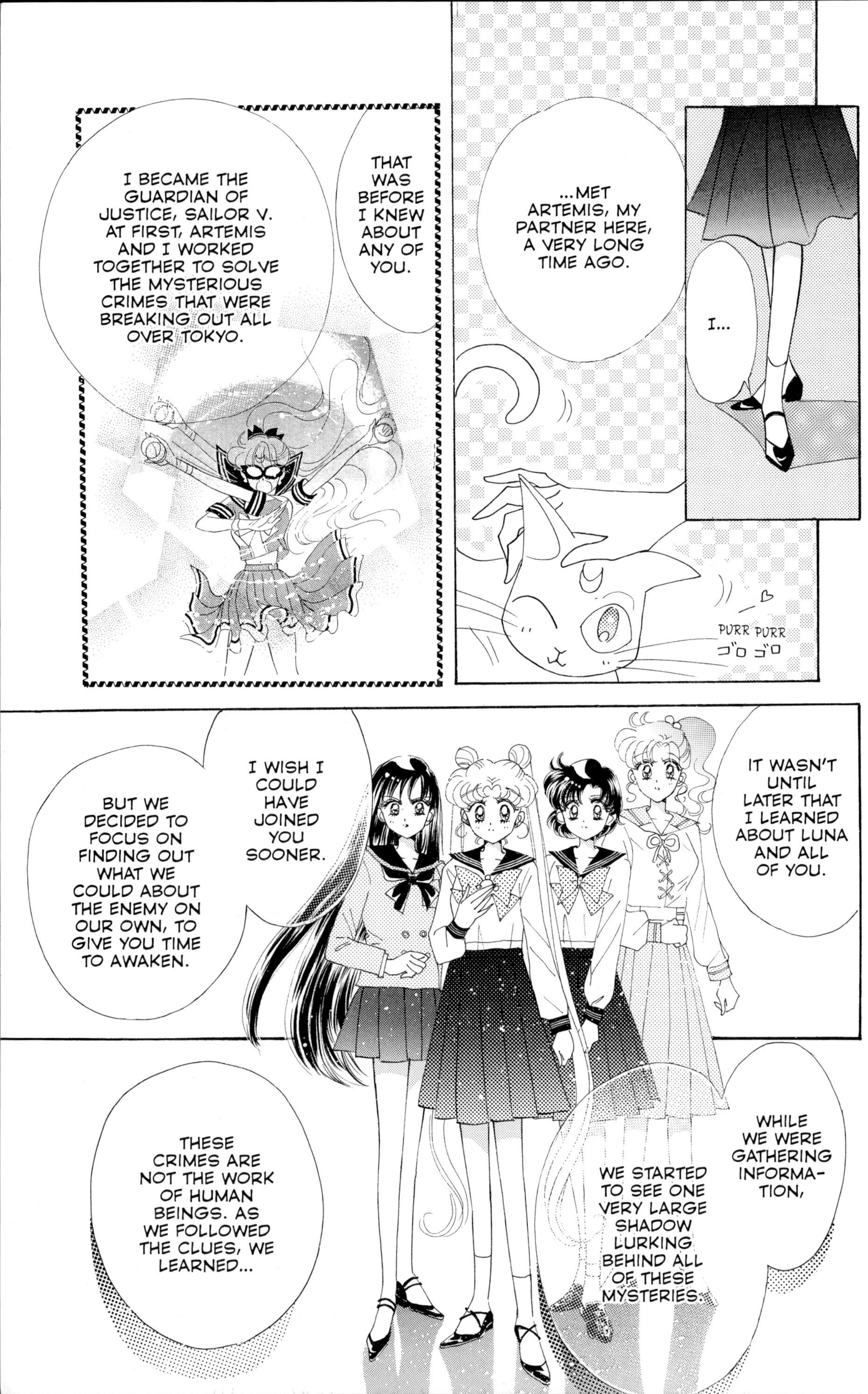
I...
...MET ARTEMIS, MY PARTNER HERE, A VERY LONG TIME AGO.
PURR PURR
ゴロゴロ
THAT WAS BEFORE I KNEW ABOUT ANY OF YOU.
I BECAME THE GUARDIAN OF JUSTICE, SAILOR V. AT FIRST, ARTEMIS AND I WORKED TOGETHER TO SOLVE THE MYSTERIOUS CRIMES THAT WERE BREAKING OUT ALL OVER TOKYO.
IT WASN'T UNTIL LATER THAT I LEARNED ABOUT LUNA AND ALL OF YOU.
I WISH I COULD HAVE JOINED YOU SOONER.
BUT WE DECIDED TO FOCUS ON FINDING OUT WHAT WE COULD ABOUT THE ENEMY ON OUR OWN, TO GIVE YOU TIME TO AWAKEN.
WHILE WE WERE GATHERING INFORMATION,
WE STARTED TO SEE ONE VERY LARGE SHADOW LURKING BEHIND ALL OF THESE MYSTERIES.
THESE CRIMES ARE NOT THE WORK OF HUMAN BEINGS. AS WE FOLLOWED THE CLUES, WE LEARNED...

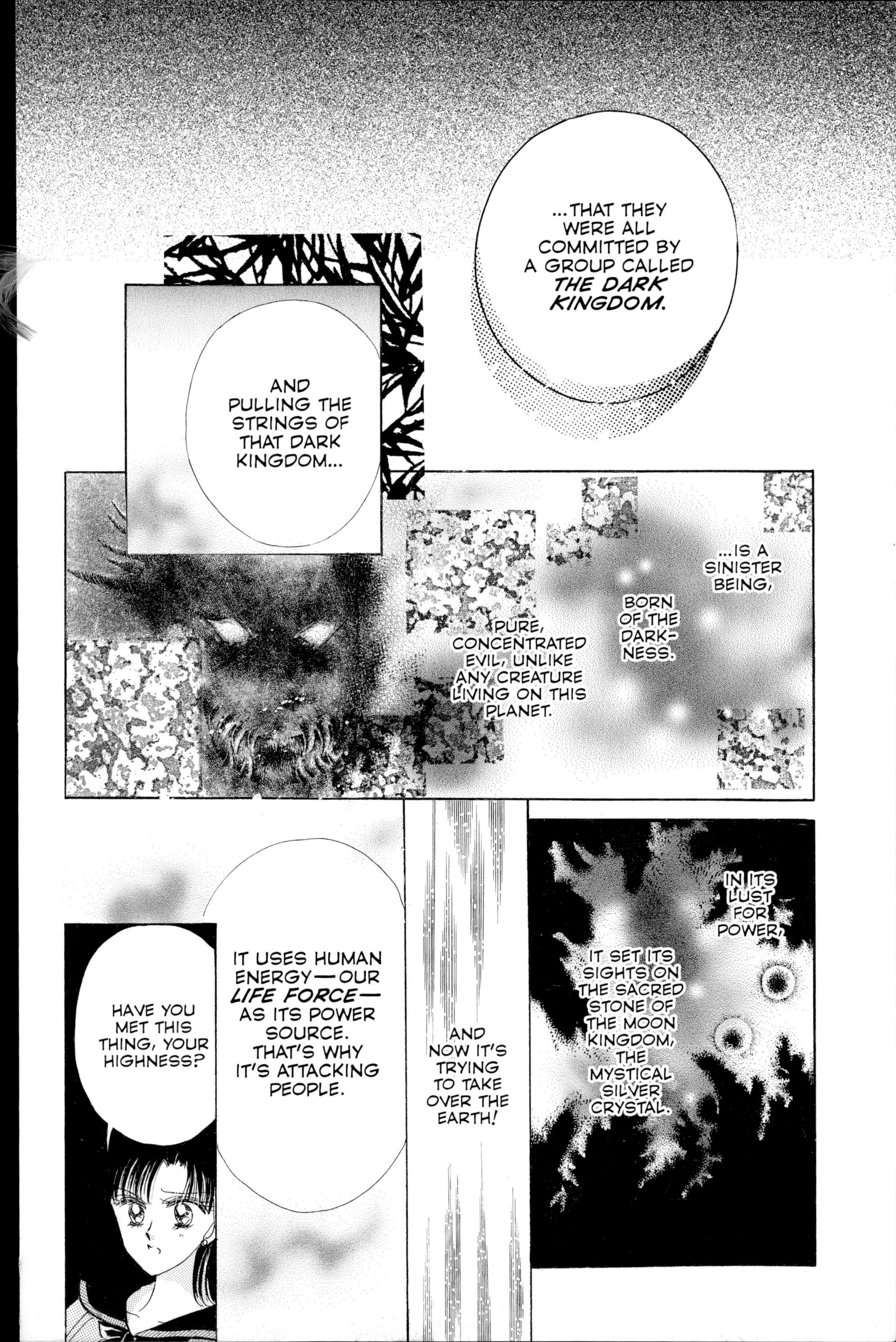
...THAT THEY WERE ALL COMMITTED BY A GROUP CALLED *THE DARK KINGDOM.*
AND PULLING THE STRINGS OF THAT DARK KINGDOM...
...IS A SINISTER BEING,
BORN OF THE DARK-NESS.
PURE, CONCENTRATED EVIL, UNLIKE ANY CREATURE LIVING ON THIS PLANET.
IN ITS LUST FOR POWER,
IT SET ITS SIGHTS ON THE SACRED STONE OF THE MOON KINGDOM, THE MYSTICAL SILVER CRYSTAL.
AND NOW IT'S TRYING TO TAKE OVER THE EARTH!
IT USES HUMAN ENERGY—OUR *LIFE FORCE*—AS ITS POWER SOURCE. THAT'S WHY IT'S ATTACKING PEOPLE.
HAVE YOU MET THIS THING, YOUR HIGHNESS?

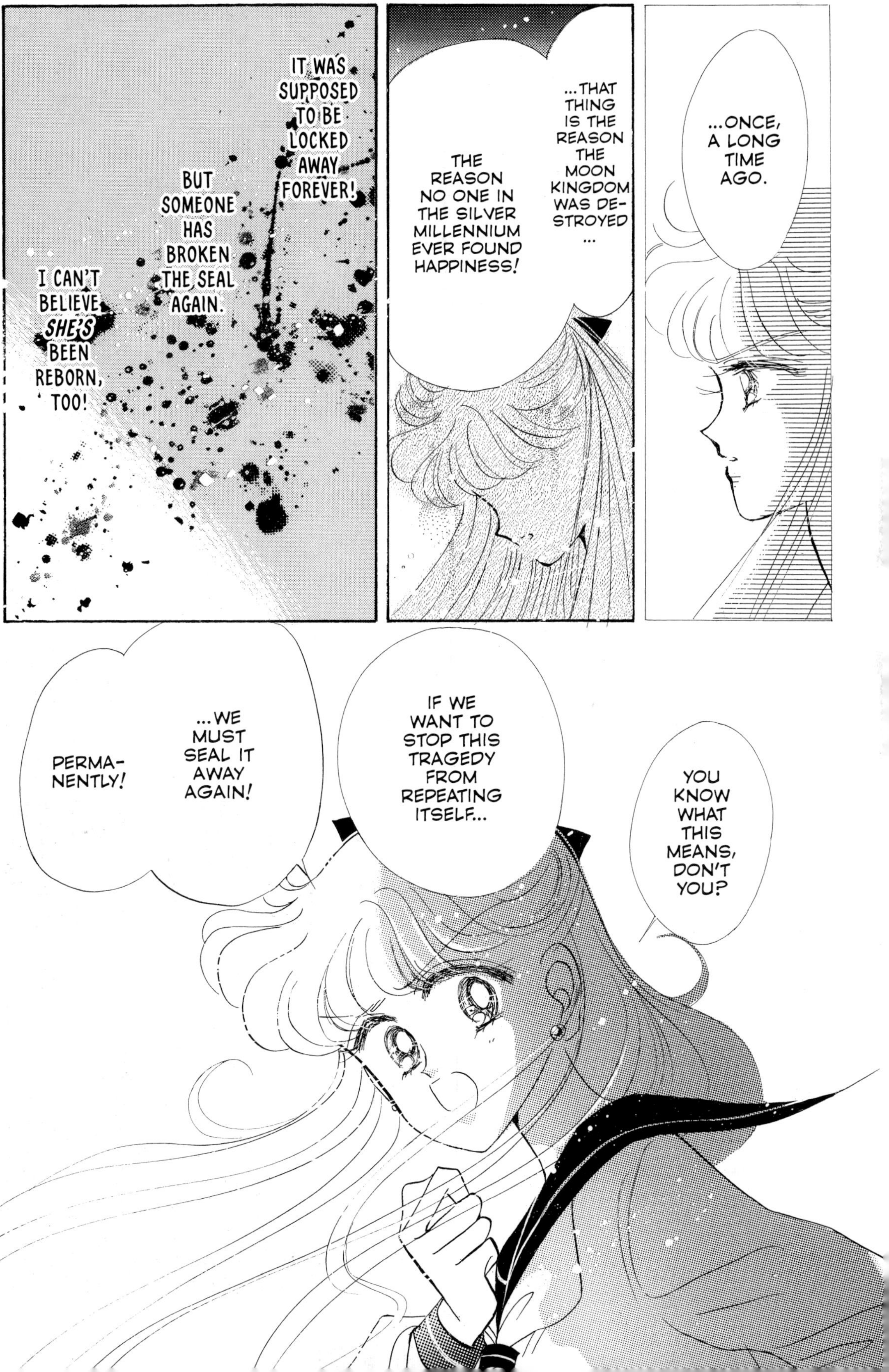
...ONCE, A LONG TIME AGO.
...THAT THING IS THE REASON THE MOON KINGDOM WAS DE-STROYED ...
THE REASON NO ONE IN THE SILVER MILLENNIUM EVER FOUND HAPPINESS!
IT WAS SUPPOSED TO BE LOCKED AWAY FOREVER!
BUT SOMEONE HAS BROKEN THE SEAL AGAIN.
I CAN'T BELIEVE *SHE'S* BEEN REBORN, TOO!
YOU KNOW WHAT THIS MEANS, DON'T YOU?
IF WE WANT TO STOP THIS TRAGEDY FROM REPEATING ITSELF...
...WE MUST SEAL IT AWAY AGAIN!
PERMA-NENTLY!

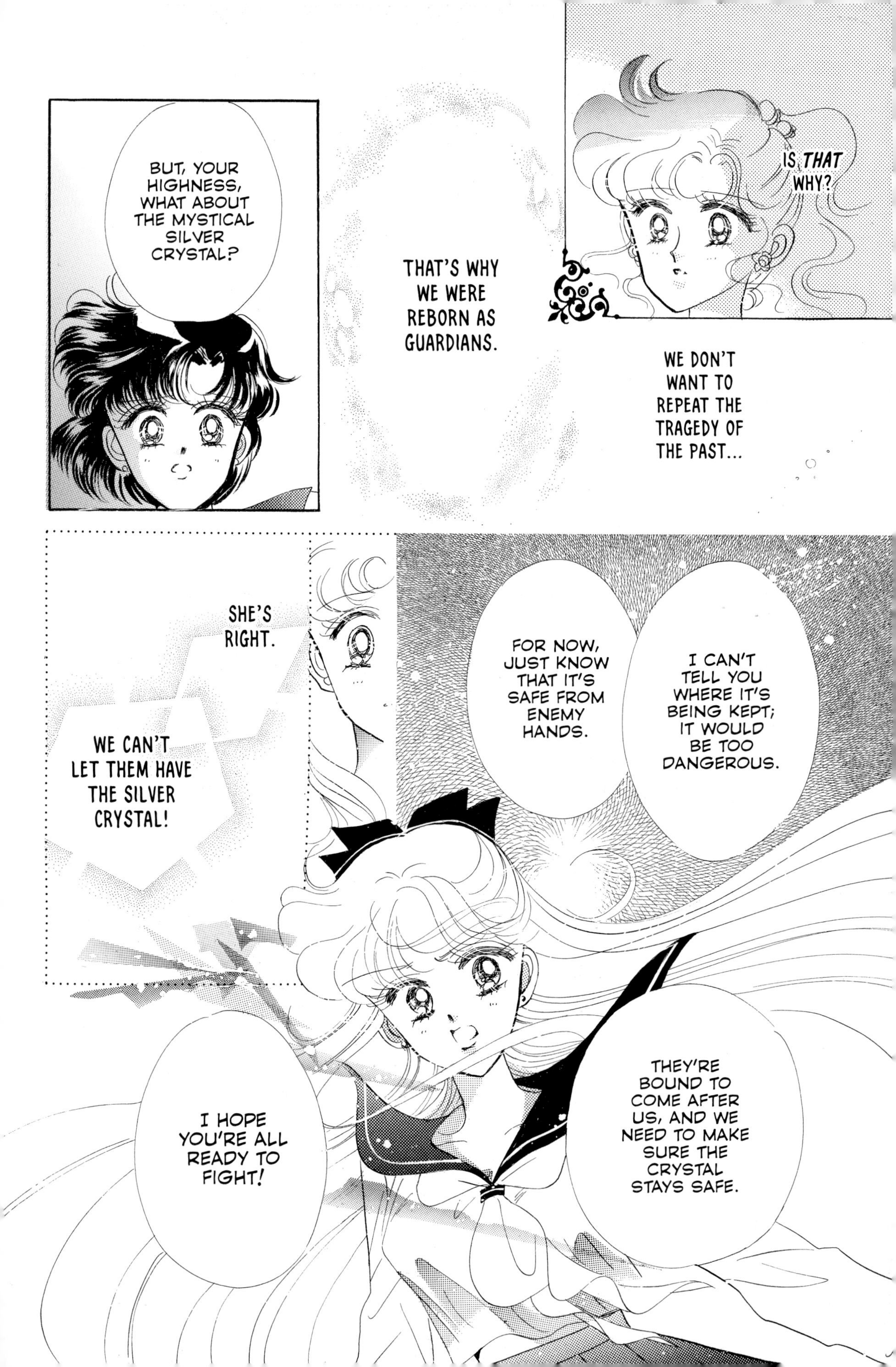

WE DON'T WANT TO REPEAT THE TRAGEDY OF THE PAST...
THAT'S WHY WE WERE REBORN AS GUARDIANS.
IS *THAT* WHY?
BUT, YOUR HIGHNESS, WHAT ABOUT THE MYSTICAL SILVER CRYSTAL?
I CAN'T TELL YOU WHERE IT'S BEING KEPT; IT WOULD BE TOO DANGEROUS.
FOR NOW, JUST KNOW THAT IT'S SAFE FROM ENEMY HANDS.
SHE'S RIGHT.
WE CAN'T LET THEM HAVE THE SILVER CRYSTAL!
THEY'RE BOUND TO COME AFTER US, AND WE NEED TO MAKE SURE THE CRYSTAL STAYS SAFE.
I HOPE YOU'RE ALL READY TO FIGHT!

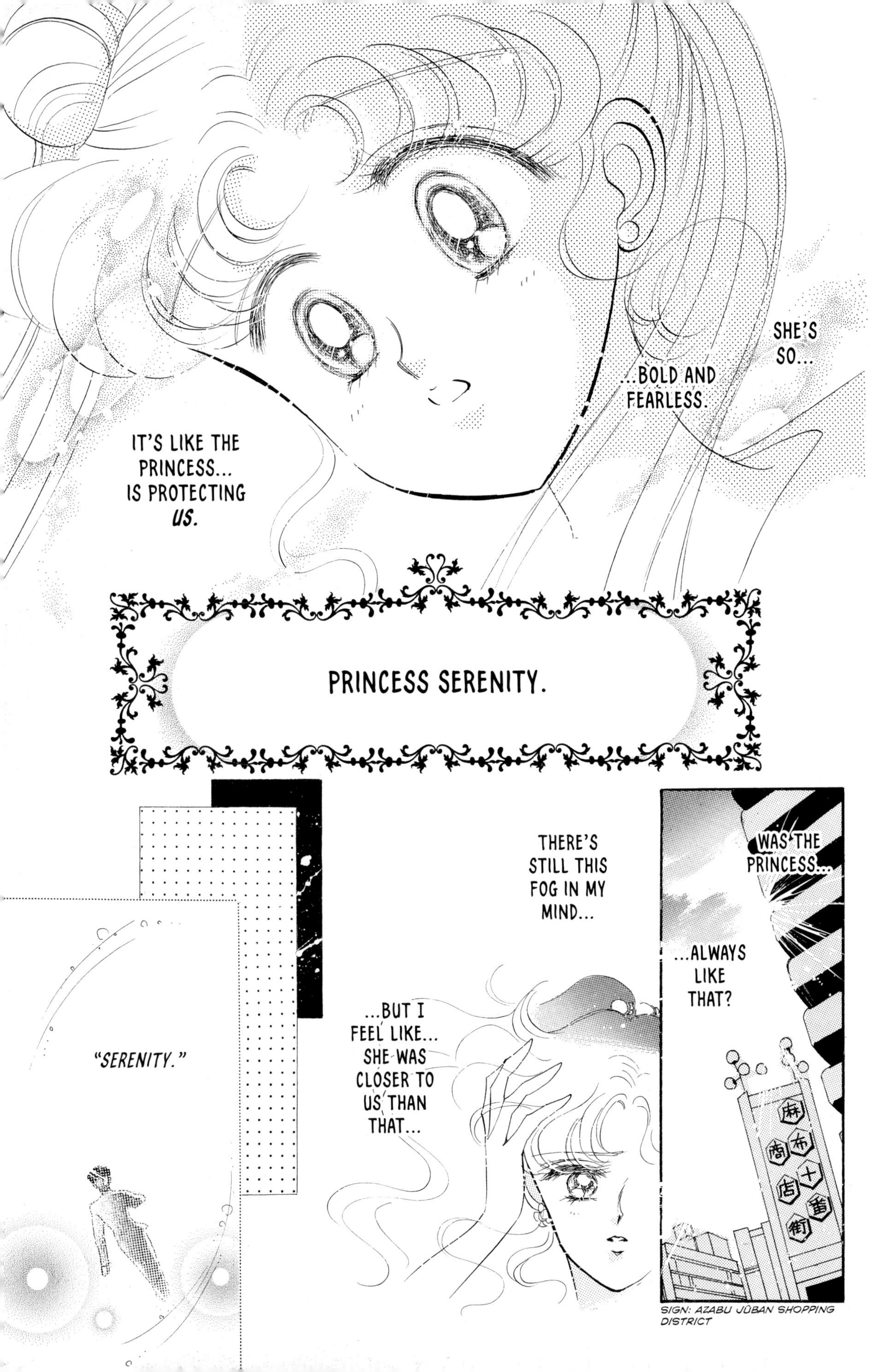
SHE'S SO...
...BOLD AND FEARLESS.
IT'S LIKE THE PRINCESS... IS PROTECTING *US.*
PRINCESS SERENITY.
WAS THE PRINCESS...
...ALWAYS LIKE THAT?
麻布十番
商店街
THERE'S STILL THIS FOG IN MY MIND...
...BUT I FEEL LIKE... SHE WAS CLOSER TO US THAN THAT...
*"SERENITY."*

*SIGN: AZABU JŪBAN SHOPPING DISTRICT*

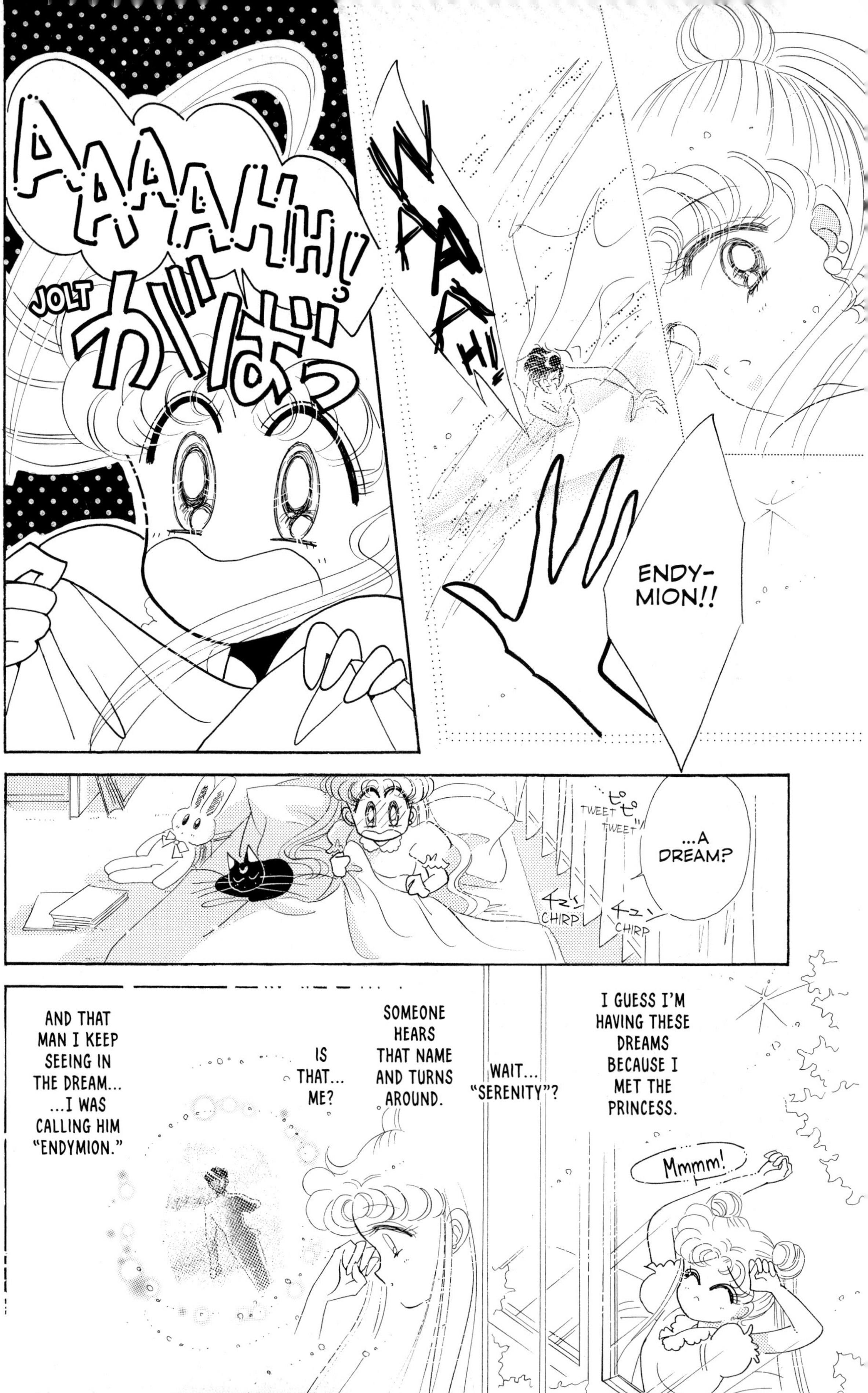
WAPAAH!
ENDY-MION!!
AAAAHH!
JOLT
がばっ
...A DREAM?
ピピ
TWEET TWEET
チュン
CHIRP
チュン
CHIRP
Mmmm!
I GUESS I'M HAVING THESE DREAMS BECAUSE I MET THE PRINCESS.
WAIT... "SERENITY"?
SOMEONE HEARS THAT NAME AND TURNS AROUND.
IS THAT... ME?
AND THAT MAN I KEEP SEEING IN THE DREAM...
...I WAS CALLING HIM "ENDYMION."

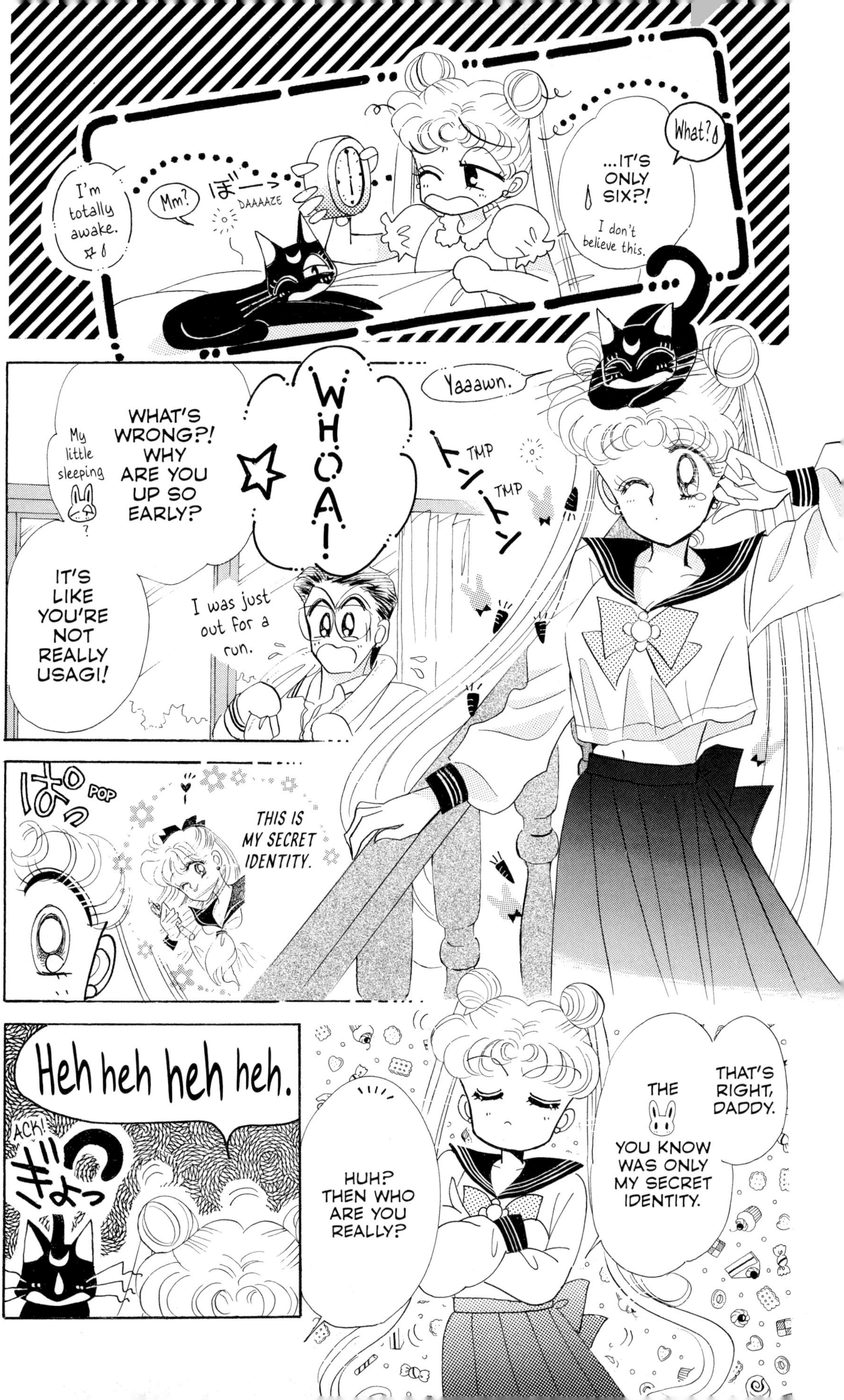
What?!
...IT'S ONLY SIX?!
I don't believe this.
ぼー DAAAAZE
Mm?
I'm totally awake.
Yaaawn.
トン トン TMP TMP
WHOA!
WHAT'S WRONG?! WHY ARE YOU UP SO EARLY?
My little sleeping ?
I was just out for a run.
IT'S LIKE YOU'RE NOT REALLY USAGI!
THIS IS MY SECRET IDENTITY.
ぱっ POP
THAT'S RIGHT, DADDY.
THE YOU KNOW WAS ONLY MY SECRET IDENTITY.
HUH? THEN WHO ARE YOU REALLY?
Heh heh heh heh.
ぎょっ ACK!

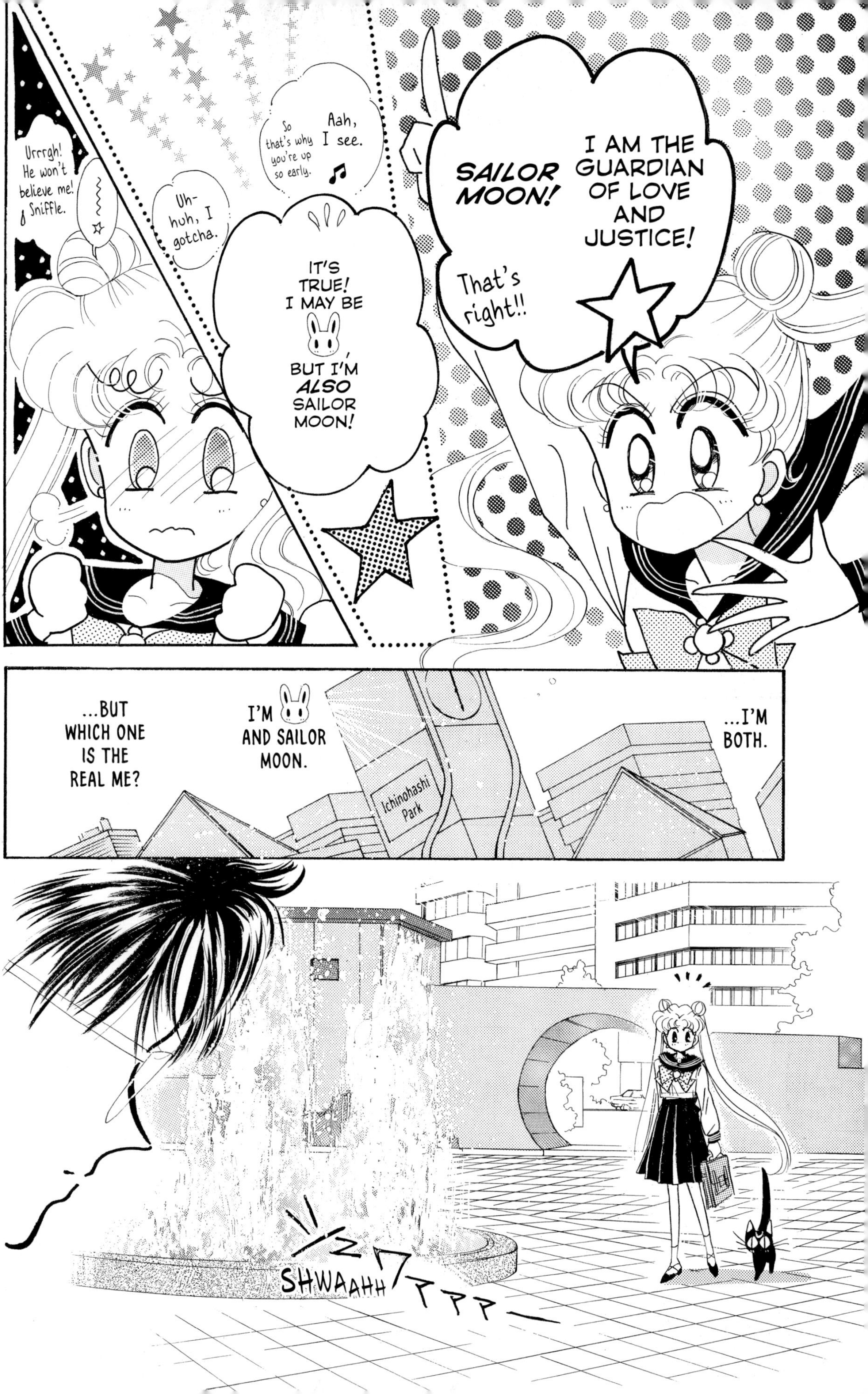

I AM THE GUARDIAN OF LOVE AND JUSTICE!
SAILOR MOON!
That's right!!
Aah, I see. ♪
So that's why you're up so early.
Uh-huh, I gotcha.
IT'S TRUE! I MAY BE BUT I'M ALSO SAILOR MOON!
Urrrgh! He won't believe me! Sniffle.
...I'M BOTH.
I'M AND SAILOR MOON.
...BUT WHICH ONE IS THE REAL ME?
Ichinohashi Park
SHWAAHH

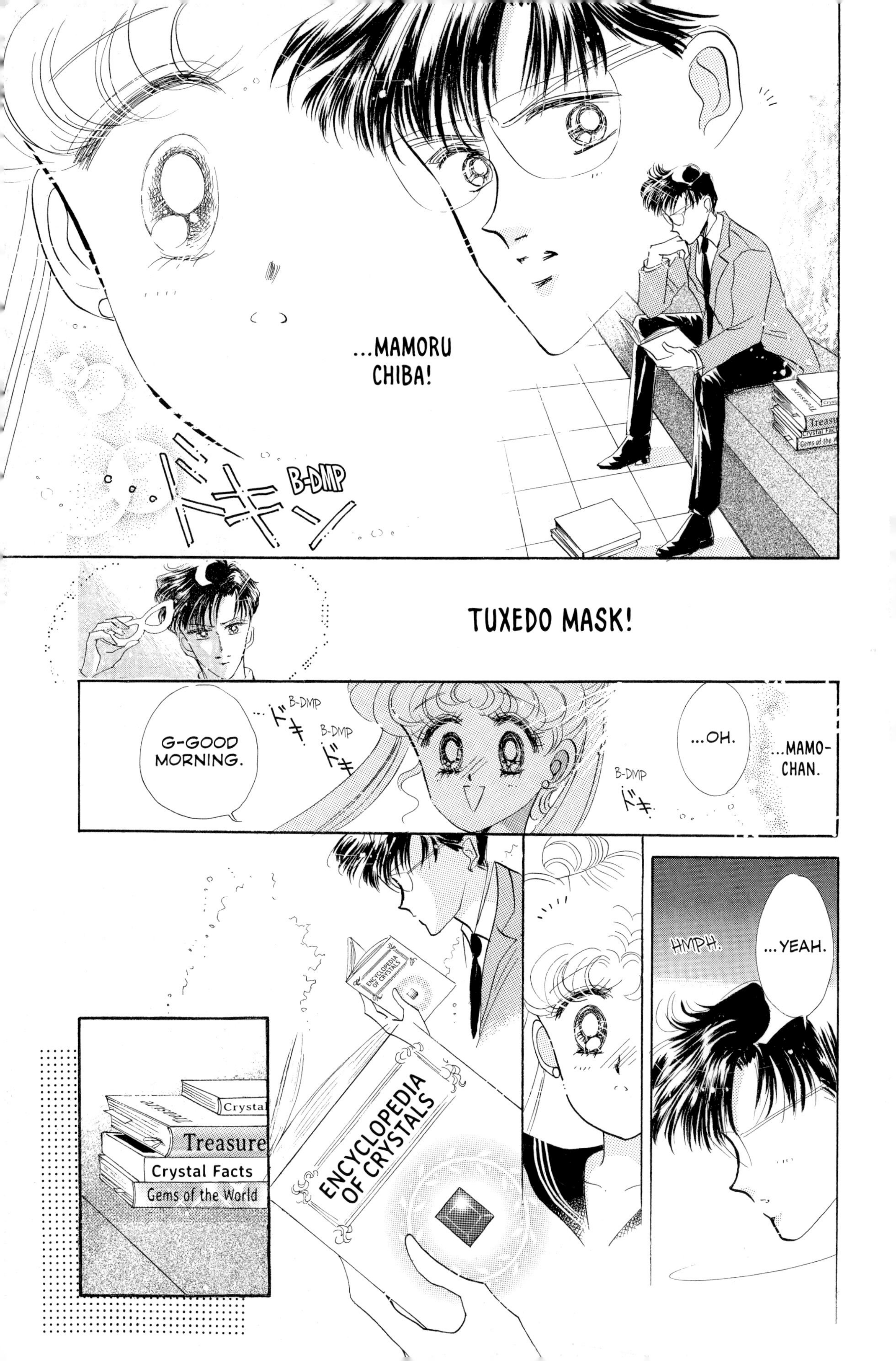

...MAMORU CHIBA!
ドキン
B-DMP
TUXEDO MASK!
...MAMO-CHAN.
...OH.
B-DMP
ドキ
B-DMP
ドキ
B-DMP
ドキ
G-GOOD MORNING.
...YEAH.
HMPH.
ENCYCLOPEDIA OF CRYSTALS
Crystal
Treasure
Crystal Facts
Gems of the World

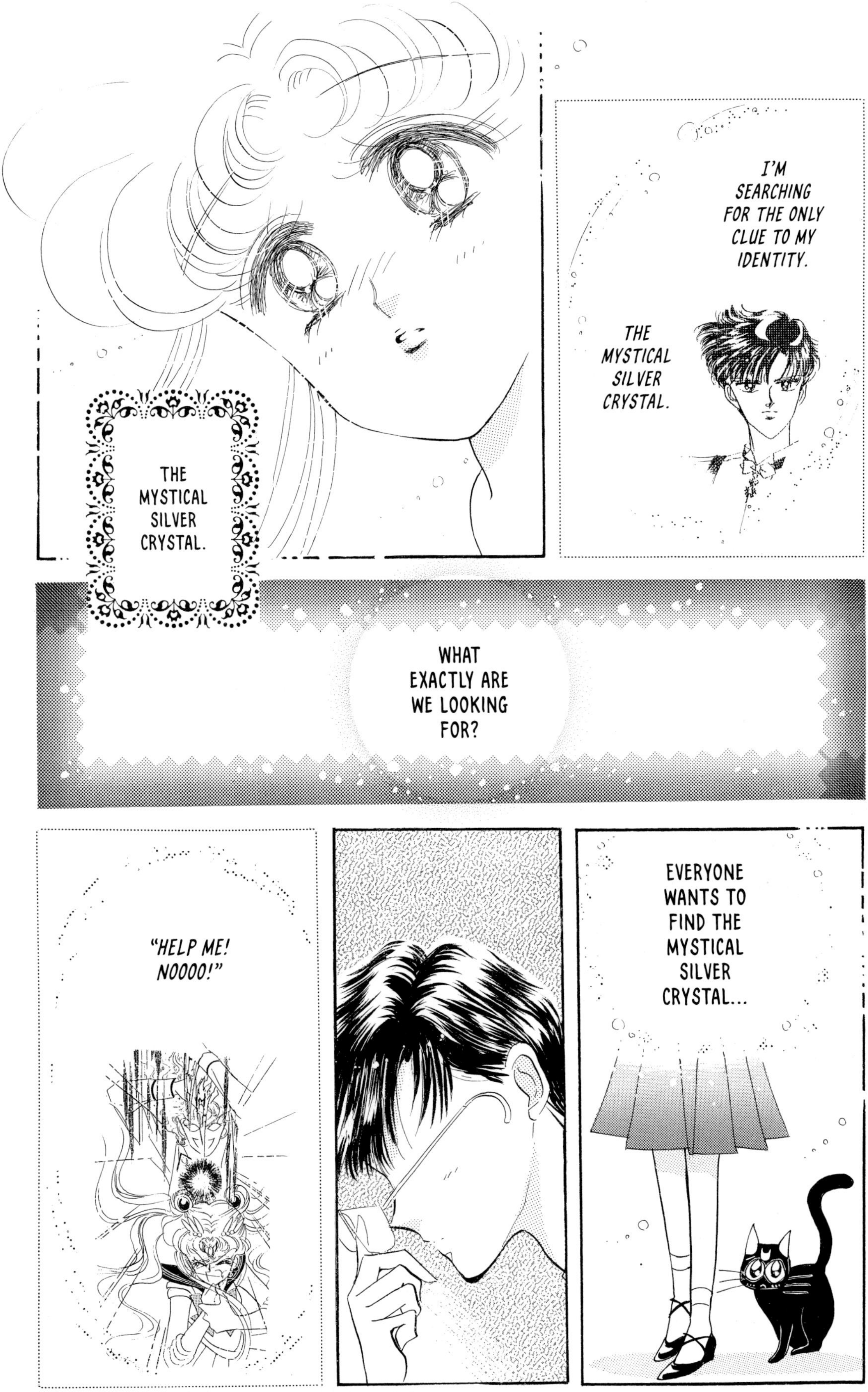
I'M SEARCHING FOR THE ONLY CLUE TO MY IDENTITY.
THE MYSTICAL SILVER CRYSTAL.
THE MYSTICAL SILVER CRYSTAL.
WHAT EXACTLY ARE WE LOOKING FOR?
EVERYONE WANTS TO FIND THE MYSTICAL SILVER CRYSTAL...
"HELP ME! NOOOO!"

...EVEN WHEN I FEEL LIKE I DON'T HAVE THE RIGHT TO TALK TO YOU,

DESTINY WANTS ME TO SEE YOU ANYWAY, USAKO.

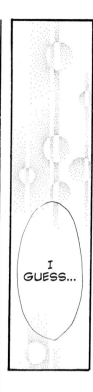

I GUESS...

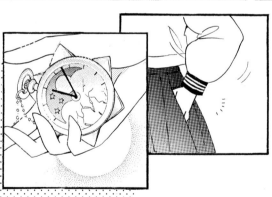

DESTINY WANTS US TO SEE EACH OTHER...

B-DMP "Usako"!
ドキ
ドキ
B-DMP B-DMP

...YEAH. I GUESS SO.

THIS WATCH.

IT'S YOURS, ISN'T IT? I'VE BEEN MEANING TO GIVE IT BACK TO YOU.

...SO, UM.

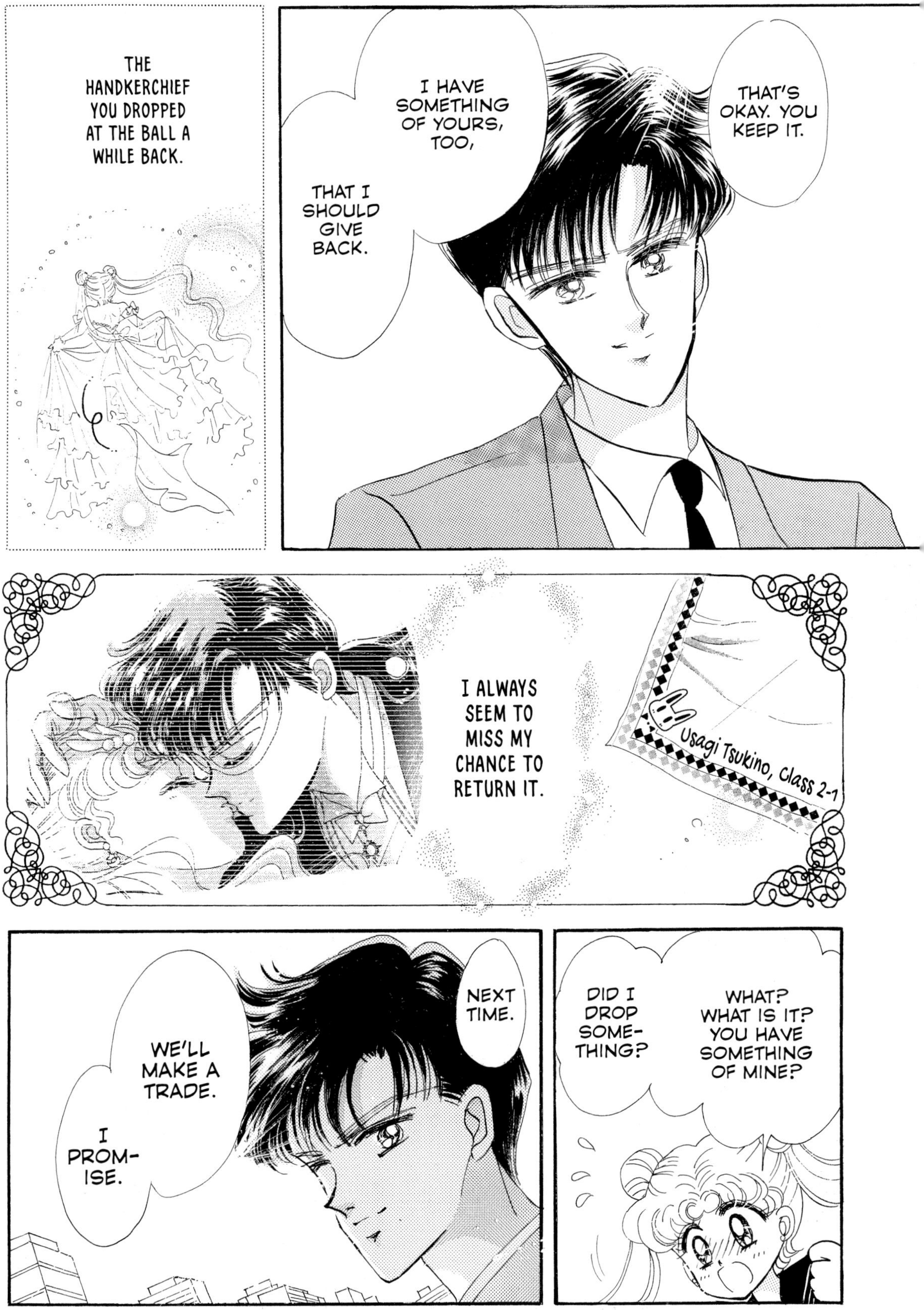
THAT'S OKAY. YOU KEEP IT.
I HAVE SOMETHING OF YOURS, TOO,
THAT I SHOULD GIVE BACK.
THE HANDKERCHIEF YOU DROPPED AT THE BALL A WHILE BACK.
Usagi Tsukino, Class 2-1
I ALWAYS SEEM TO MISS MY CHANCE TO RETURN IT.
WHAT? WHAT IS IT? YOU HAVE SOMETHING OF MINE?
DID I DROP SOME-THING?
NEXT TIME.
WE'LL MAKE A TRADE.
I PROMISE-ISE.

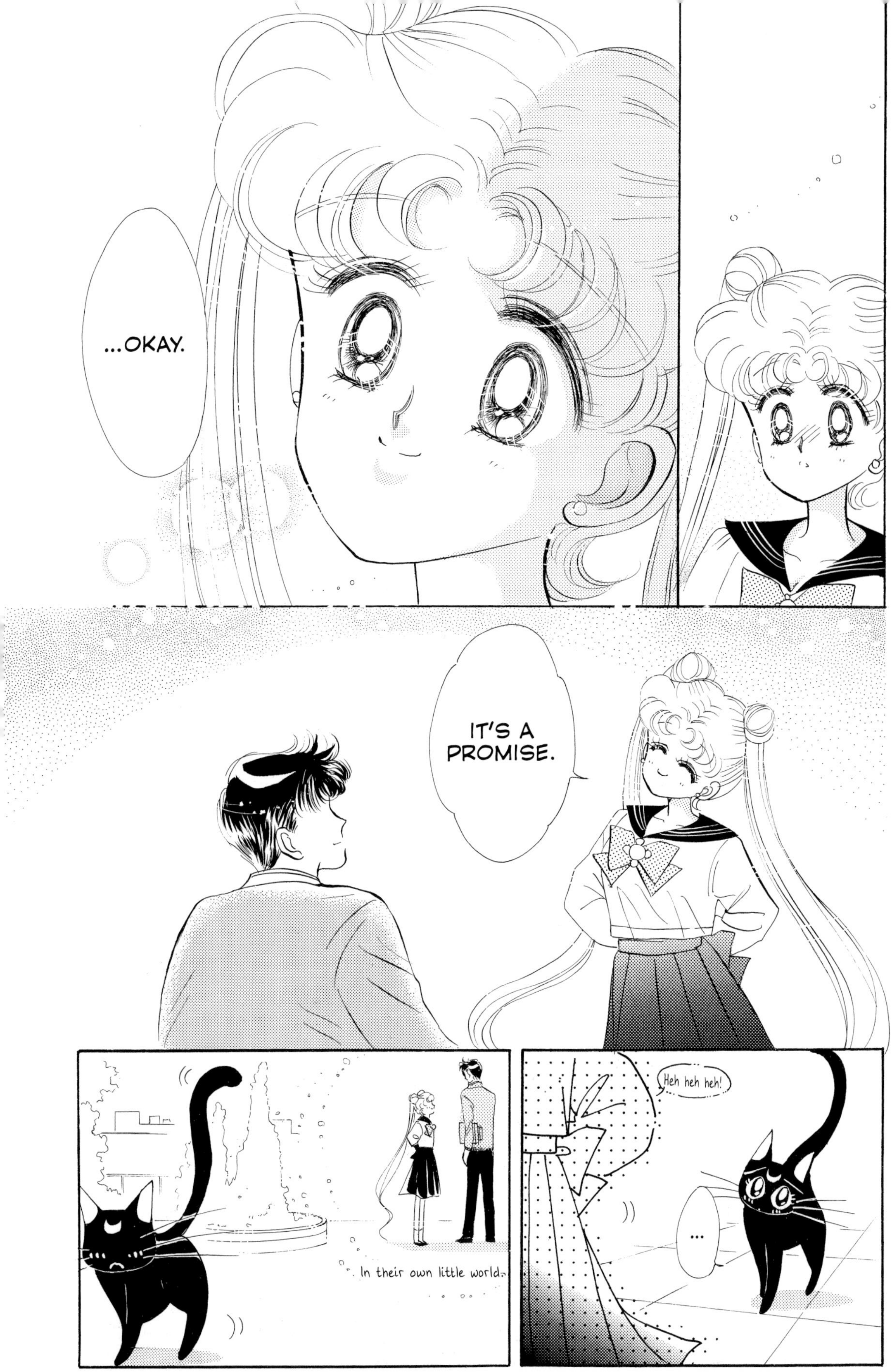
...OKAY.
IT'S A PROMISE.
Heh heh heh!
...
In their own little world.

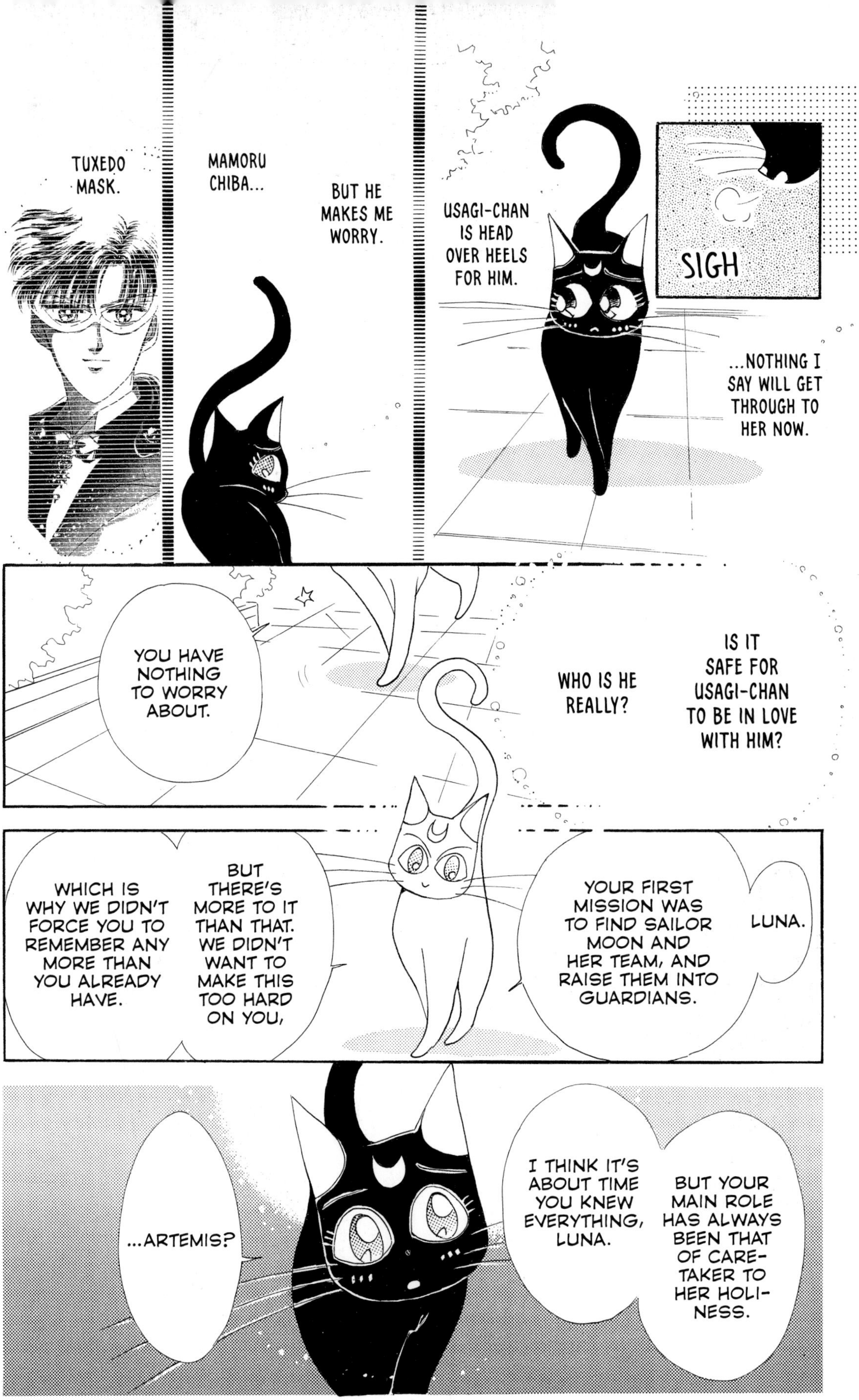
SIGH
USAGI-CHAN IS HEAD OVER HEELS FOR HIM.
...NOTHING I SAY WILL GET THROUGH TO HER NOW.
BUT HE MAKES ME WORRY.
MAMORU CHIBA...
TUXEDO MASK.
IS IT SAFE FOR USAGI-CHAN TO BE IN LOVE WITH HIM?
WHO IS HE REALLY?
YOU HAVE NOTHING TO WORRY ABOUT.
LUNA.
YOUR FIRST MISSION WAS TO FIND SAILOR MOON AND HER TEAM, AND RAISE THEM INTO GUARDIANS.
BUT THERE'S MORE TO IT THAN THAT. WE DIDN'T WANT TO MAKE THIS TOO HARD ON YOU,
WHICH IS WHY WE DIDN'T FORCE YOU TO REMEMBER ANY MORE THAN YOU ALREADY HAVE.
BUT YOUR MAIN ROLE HAS ALWAYS BEEN THAT OF CARE-TAKER TO HER HOLI-NESS.
I THINK IT'S ABOUT TIME YOU KNEW EVERYTHING, LUNA.
...ARTEMIS?

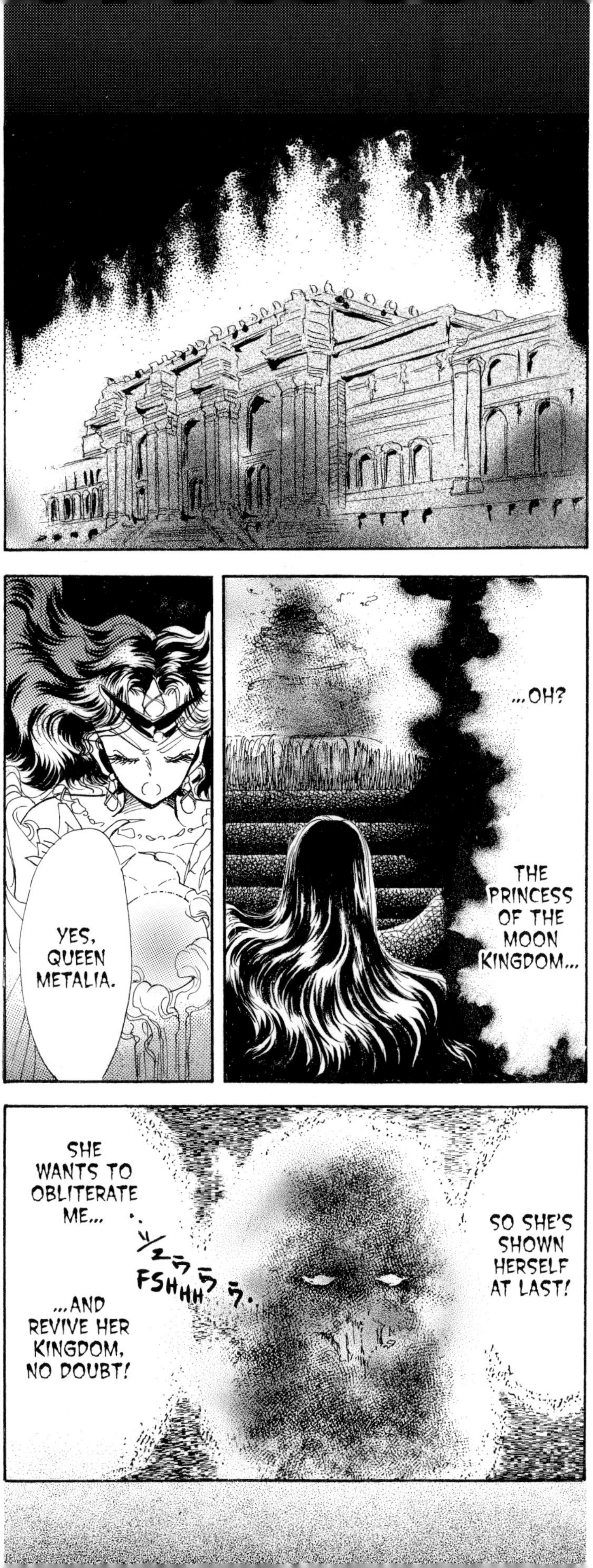
...OH?
THE PRINCESS OF THE MOON KINGDOM...
YES, QUEEN METALIA.
SO SHE'S SHOWN HERSELF AT LAST!
SHE WANTS TO OBLITERATE ME...
FSHHH
...AND REVIVE HER KINGDOM, NO DOUBT!

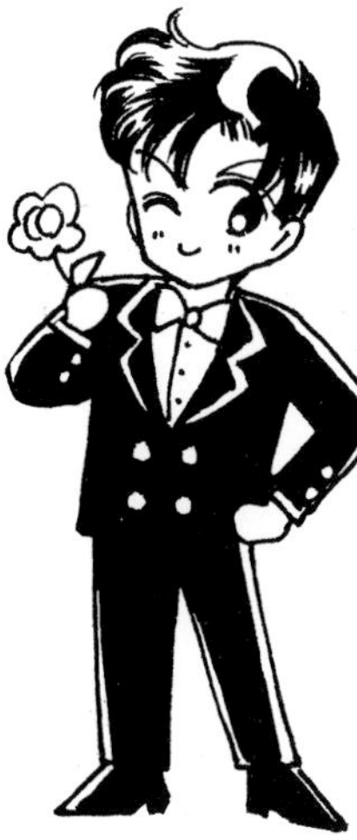

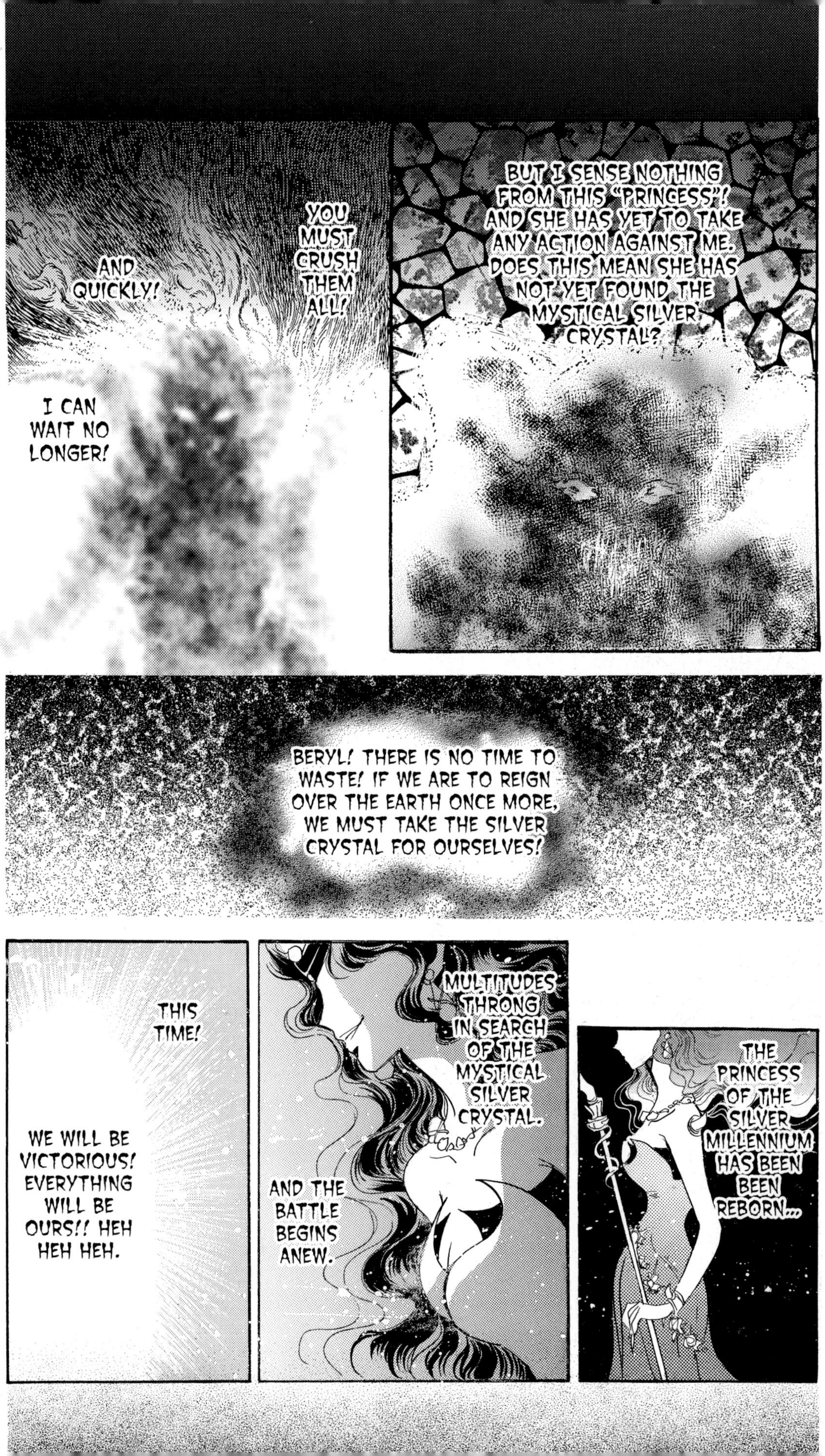
BUT I SENSE NOTHING FROM THIS "PRINCESS"! AND SHE HAS YET TO TAKE ANY ACTION AGAINST ME. DOES THIS MEAN SHE HAS NOT YET FOUND THE MYSTICAL SILVER CRYSTAL?
YOU MUST CRUSH THEM ALL!
AND QUICKLY!
I CAN WAIT NO LONGER!
BERYL! THERE IS NO TIME TO WASTE! IF WE ARE TO REIGN OVER THE EARTH ONCE MORE, WE MUST TAKE THE SILVER CRYSTAL FOR OURSELVES!
THE PRINCESS OF THE SILVER MILLENNIUM HAS BEEN BEEN REBORN...
MULTITUDES THRONG IN SEARCH OF THE MYSTICAL SILVER CRYSTAL.
AND THE BATTLE BEGINS ANEW.
THIS TIME!
WE WILL BE VICTORIOUS! EVERYTHING WILL BE OURS!! HEH HEH HEH.

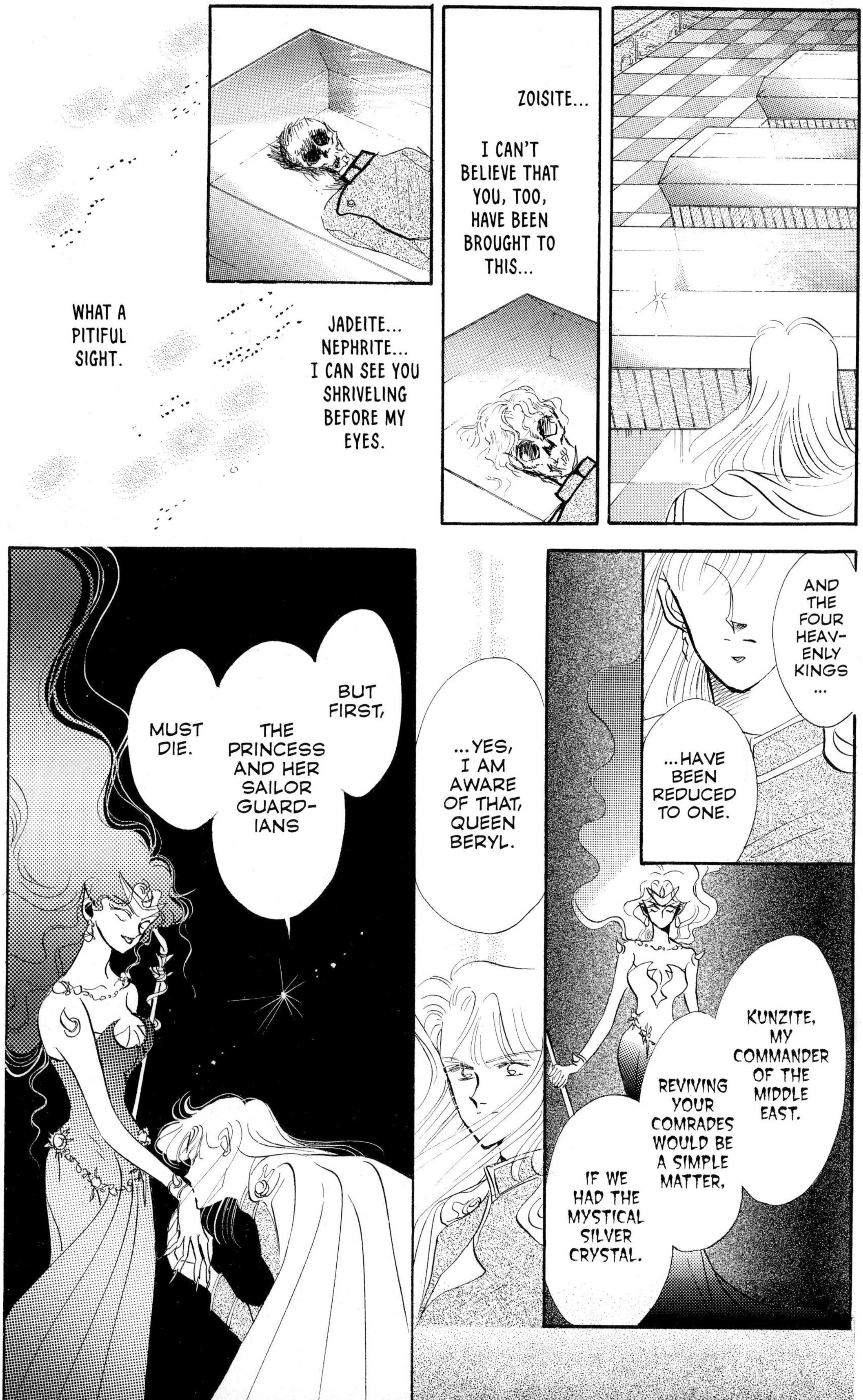
ZOISITE...
I CAN'T BELIEVE THAT YOU, TOO, HAVE BEEN BROUGHT TO THIS...
JADEITE... NEPHRITE... I CAN SEE YOU SHRIVELING BEFORE MY EYES.
WHAT A PITIFUL SIGHT.
AND THE FOUR HEAVENLY KINGS...
...HAVE BEEN REDUCED TO ONE.
KUNZITE, MY COMMANDER OF THE MIDDLE EAST.
REVIVING YOUR COMRADES WOULD BE A SIMPLE MATTER,
IF WE HAD THE MYSTICAL SILVER CRYSTAL.
...YES, I AM AWARE OF THAT, QUEEN BERYL.
BUT FIRST,
THE PRINCESS AND HER SAILOR GUARDIANS
MUST DIE.

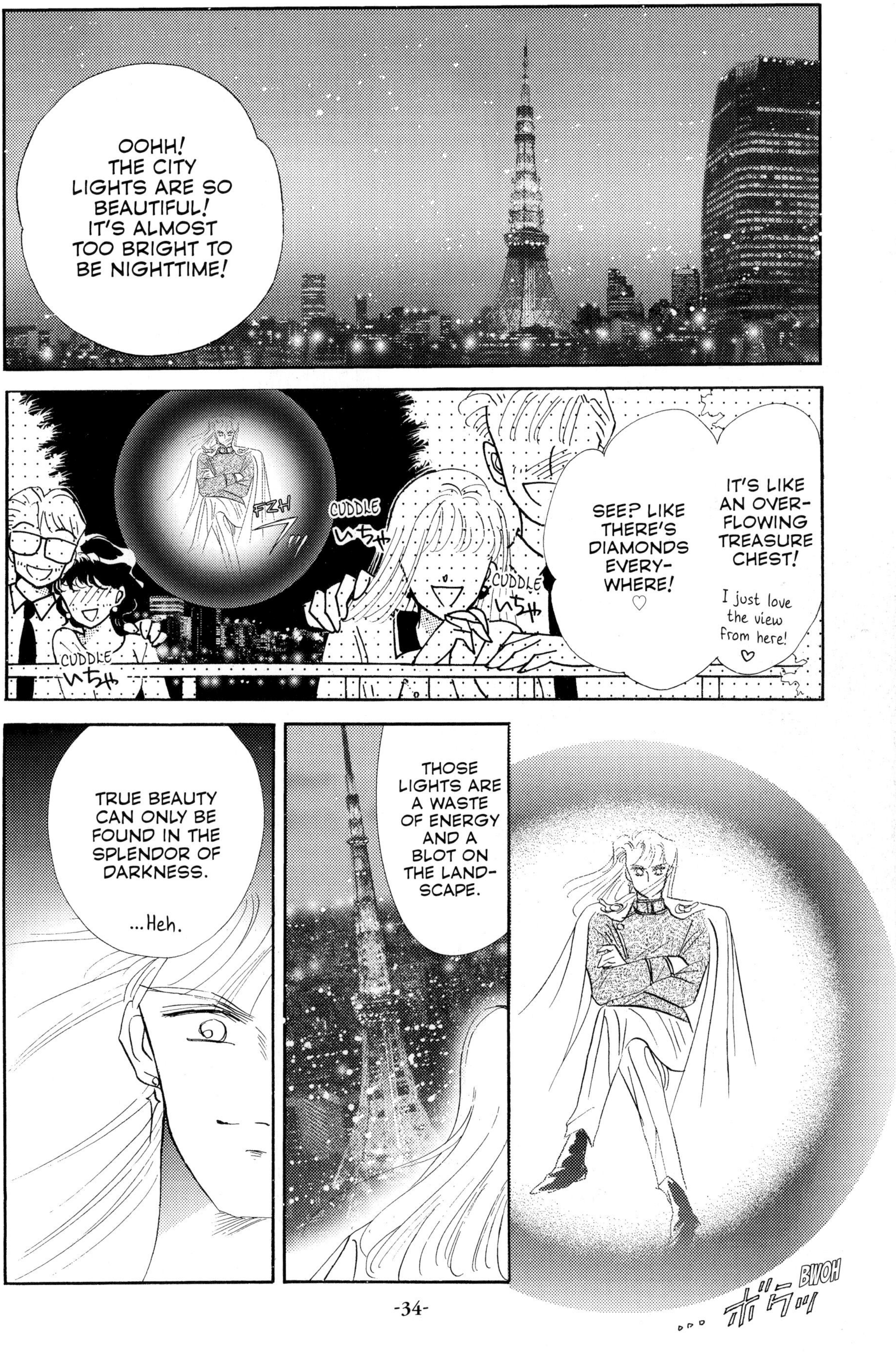
OOHH! THE CITY LIGHTS ARE SO BEAUTIFUL! IT'S ALMOST TOO BRIGHT TO BE NIGHTTIME!
IT'S LIKE AN OVER-FLOWING TREASURE CHEST!
I just love the view from here! ♡
SEE? LIKE THERE'S DIAMONDS EVERY-WHERE! ♡
CUDDLE
CUDDLE
FZH
CUDDLE
BWOH
THOSE LIGHTS ARE A WASTE OF ENERGY AND A BLOT ON THE LAND-SCAPE.
TRUE BEAUTY CAN ONLY BE FOUND IN THE SPLENDOR OF DARKNESS.
...Heh.

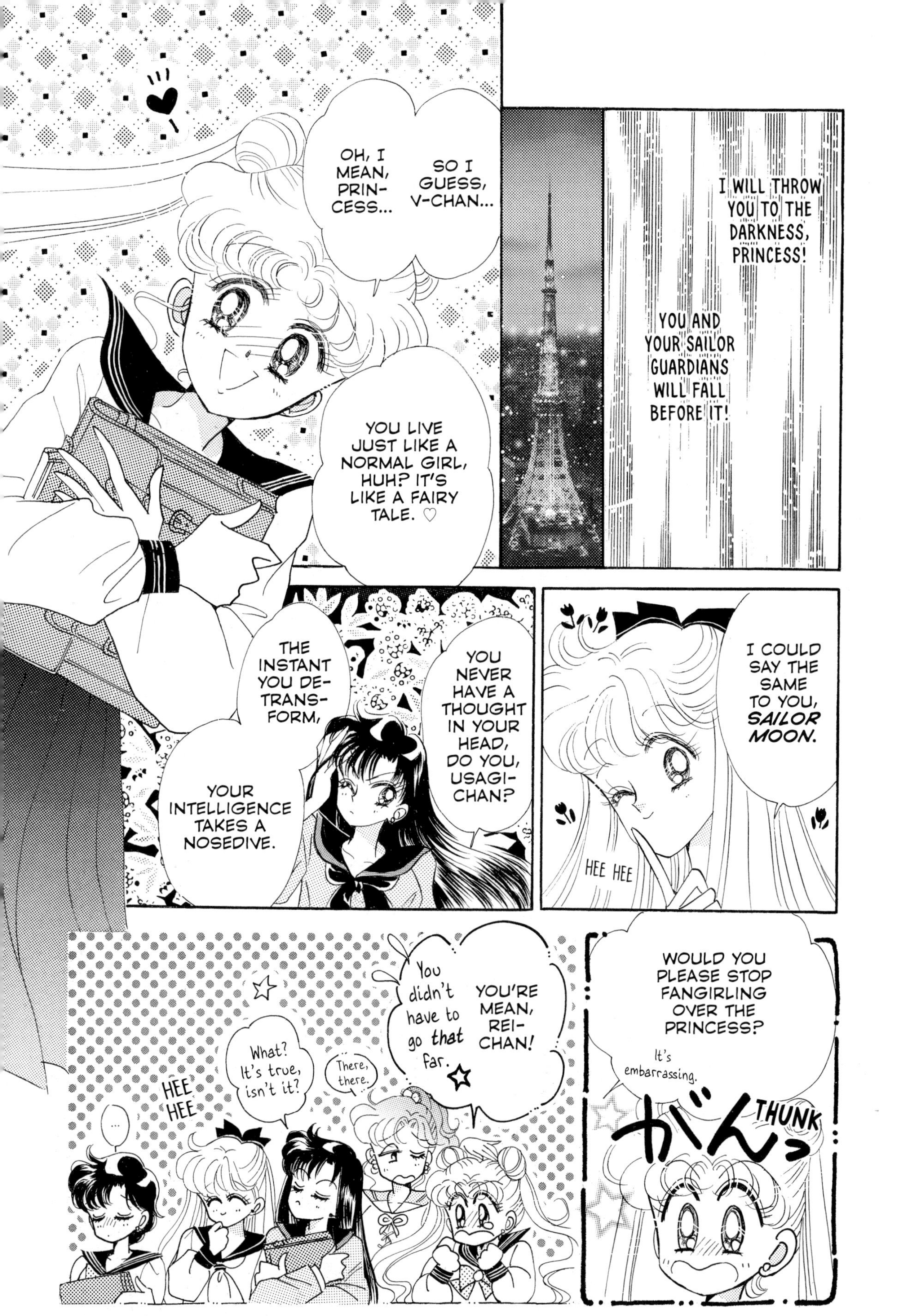
I WILL THROW YOU TO THE DARKNESS, PRINCESS!
YOU AND YOUR SAILOR GUARDIANS WILL FALL BEFORE IT!
SO I GUESS, V-CHAN...
OH, I MEAN, PRIN-CESS...
YOU LIVE JUST LIKE A NORMAL GIRL, HUH? IT'S LIKE A FAIRY TALE. ♡
I COULD SAY THE SAME TO YOU, ***SAILOR MOON.***
HEE HEE
YOU NEVER HAVE A THOUGHT IN YOUR HEAD, DO YOU, USAGI-CHAN?
THE INSTANT YOU DE-TRANS-FORM,
YOUR INTELLIGENCE TAKES A NOSEDIVE.
WOULD YOU PLEASE STOP FANGIRLING OVER THE PRINCESS?
It's embarrassing.
THUNK
YOU'RE MEAN, REI-CHAN!
You didn't have to go *that* far.
There, there.
What? It's true, isn't it?
HEE HEE
...

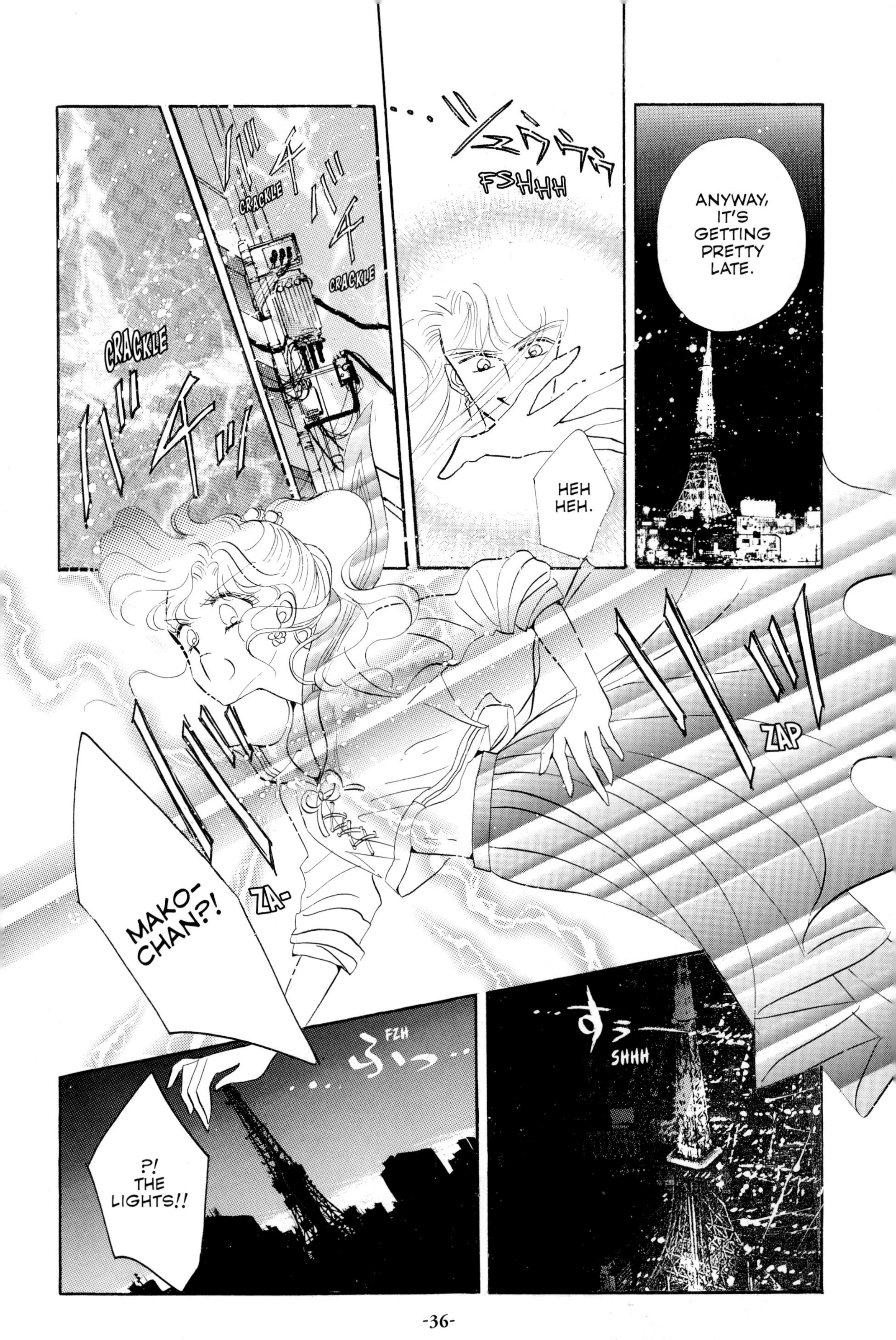
ANYWAY, IT'S GETTING PRETTY LATE.
FSHHH
HEH HEH.
CRACKLE
CRACKLE
CRACKLE
ZAP
ZA-
MAKO-CHAN?!
SHHH
FZH
?! THE LIGHTS!!

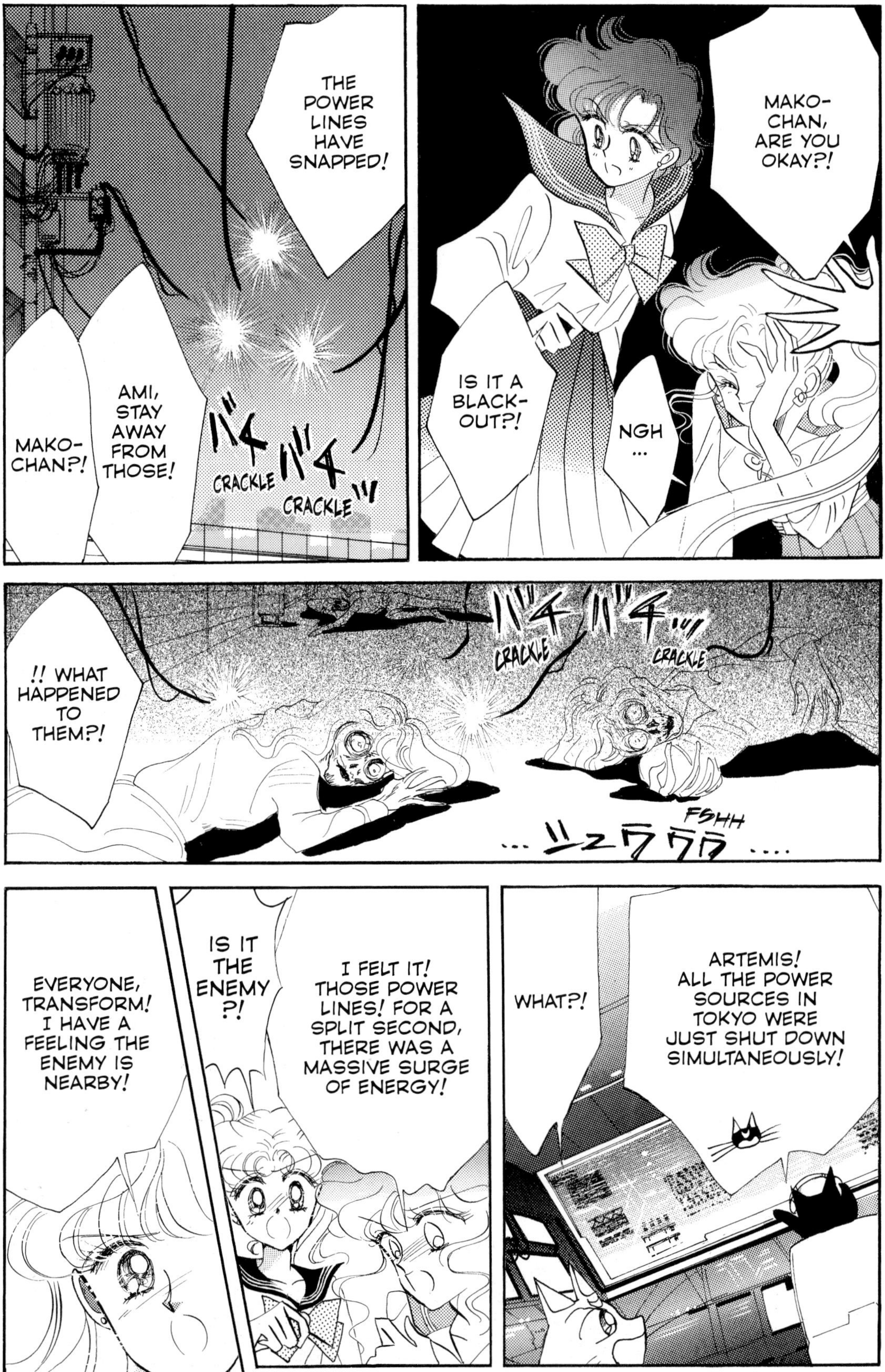
MAKO-CHAN, ARE YOU OKAY?!
NGH ...
IS IT A BLACK-OUT?!
THE POWER LINES HAVE SNAPPED!
CRACKLE CRACKLE
AMI, STAY AWAY FROM THOSE!
MAKO-CHAN?!
CRACKLE CRACKLE
!! WHAT HAPPENED TO THEM?!
FSHH
ARTEMIS! ALL THE POWER SOURCES IN TOKYO WERE JUST SHUT DOWN SIMULTANEOUSLY!
WHAT?!
I FELT IT! THOSE POWER LINES! FOR A SPLIT SECOND, THERE WAS A MASSIVE SURGE OF ENERGY!
IS IT THE ENEMY?!
EVERYONE, TRANSFORM! I HAVE A FEELING THE ENEMY IS NEARBY!

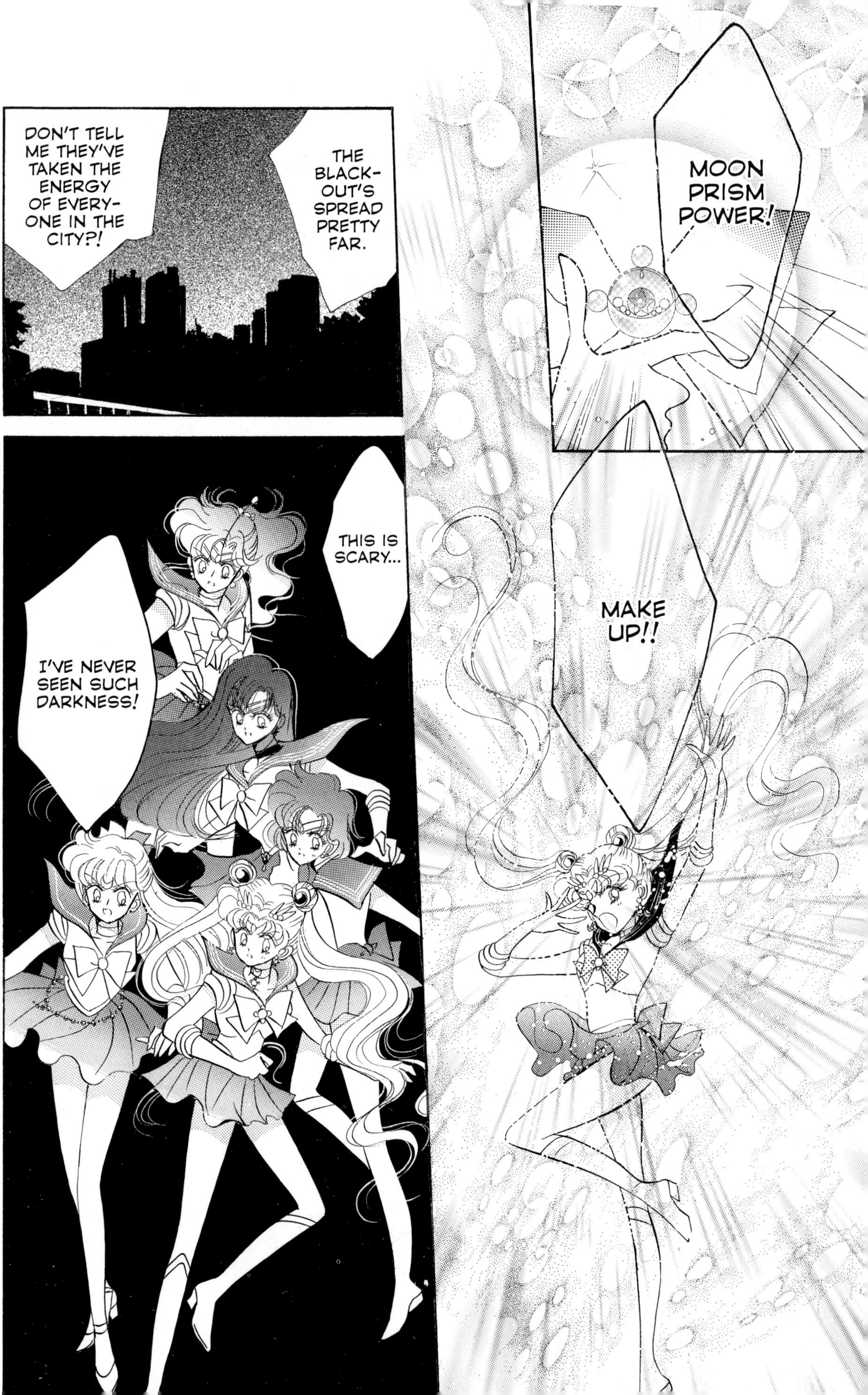
MOON PRISM POWER!
MAKE UP!!
THE BLACK-OUT'S SPREAD PRETTY FAR.
DON'T TELL ME THEY'VE TAKEN THE ENERGY OF EVERY-ONE IN THE CITY?!
THIS IS SCARY...
I'VE NEVER SEEN SUCH DARKNESS!

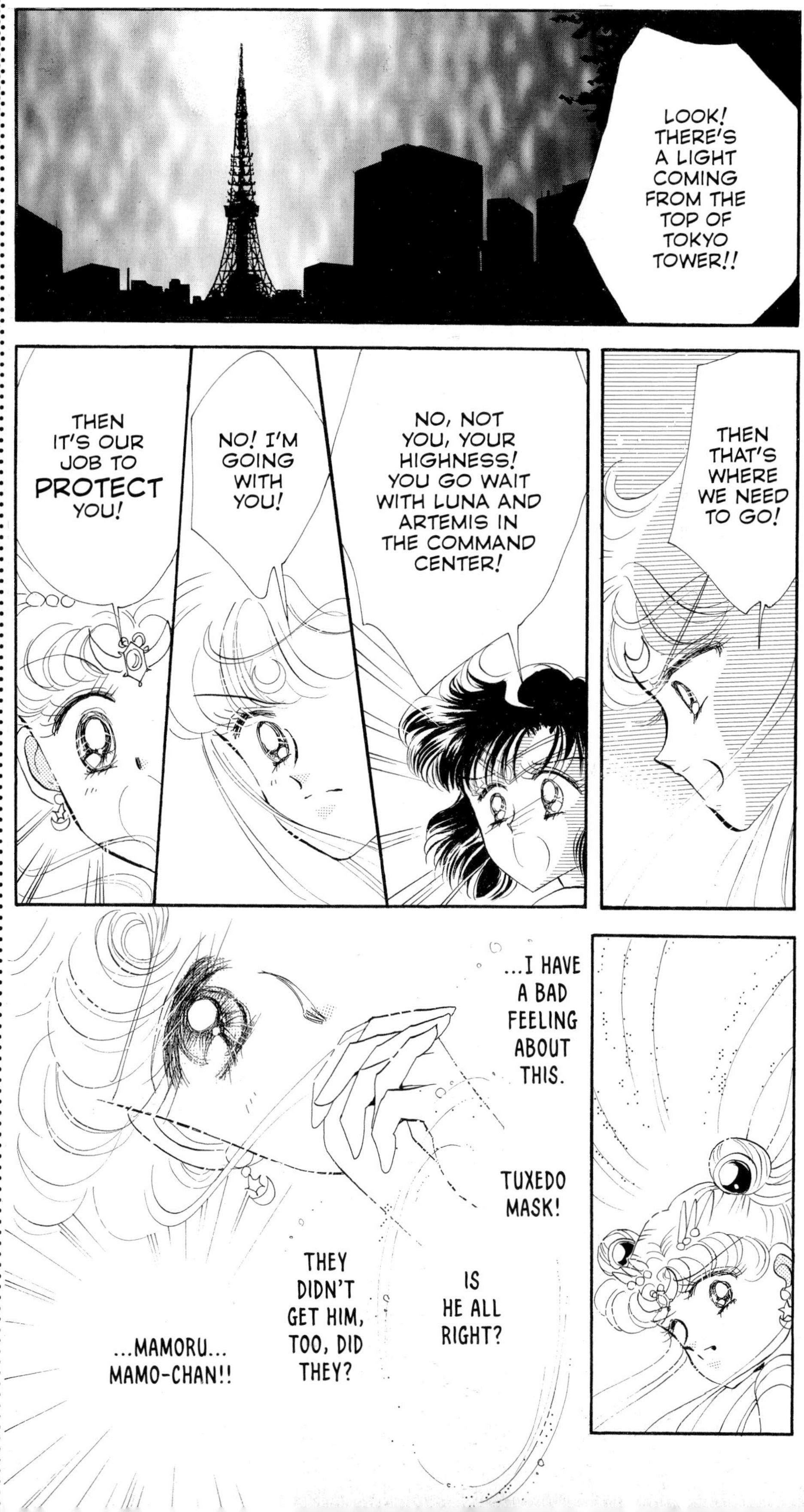
LOOK! THERE'S A LIGHT COMING FROM THE TOP OF TOKYO TOWER!!
THEN THAT'S WHERE WE NEED TO GO!
NO, NOT YOU, YOUR HIGHNESS! YOU GO WAIT WITH LUNA AND ARTEMIS IN THE COMMAND CENTER!
NO! I'M GOING WITH YOU!
THEN IT'S OUR JOB TO PROTECT YOU!
...I HAVE A BAD FEELING ABOUT THIS.
TUXEDO MASK!
IS HE ALL RIGHT?
THEY DIDN'T GET HIM, TOO, DID THEY?
...MAMORU... MAMO-CHAN!!

ENDYMION!!

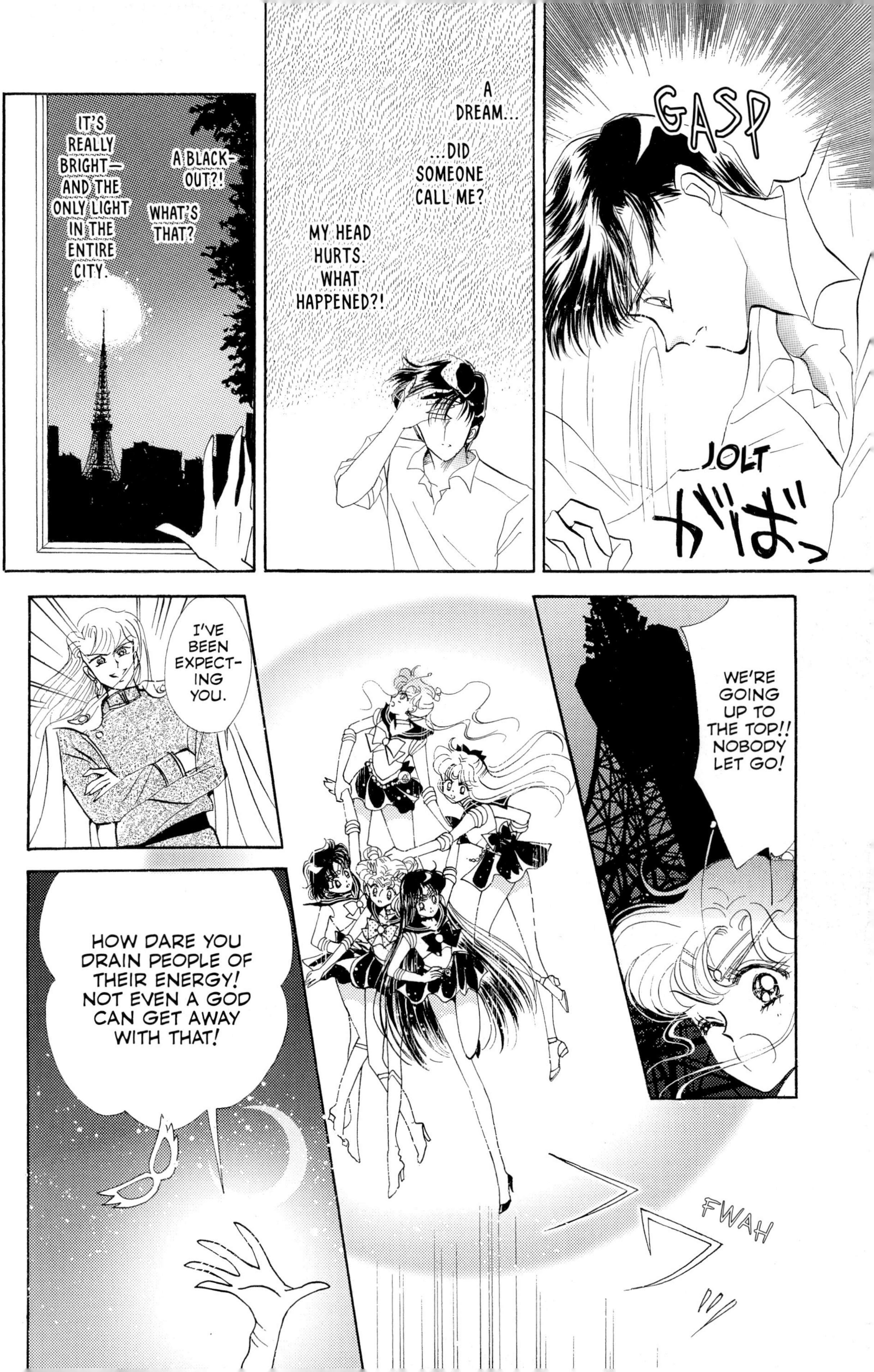
GASP
JOLT
がばっ
A DREAM...
...DID SOMEONE CALL ME?
MY HEAD HURTS. WHAT HAPPENED?!
A BLACK-OUT?!
WHAT'S THAT?
IT'S REALLY BRIGHT—AND THE ONLY LIGHT IN THE ENTIRE CITY.
WE'RE GOING UP TO THE TOP!! NOBODY LET GO!
FWAH
I'VE BEEN EXPECT-ING YOU.
HOW DARE YOU DRAIN PEOPLE OF THEIR ENERGY! NOT EVEN A GOD CAN GET AWAY WITH THAT!

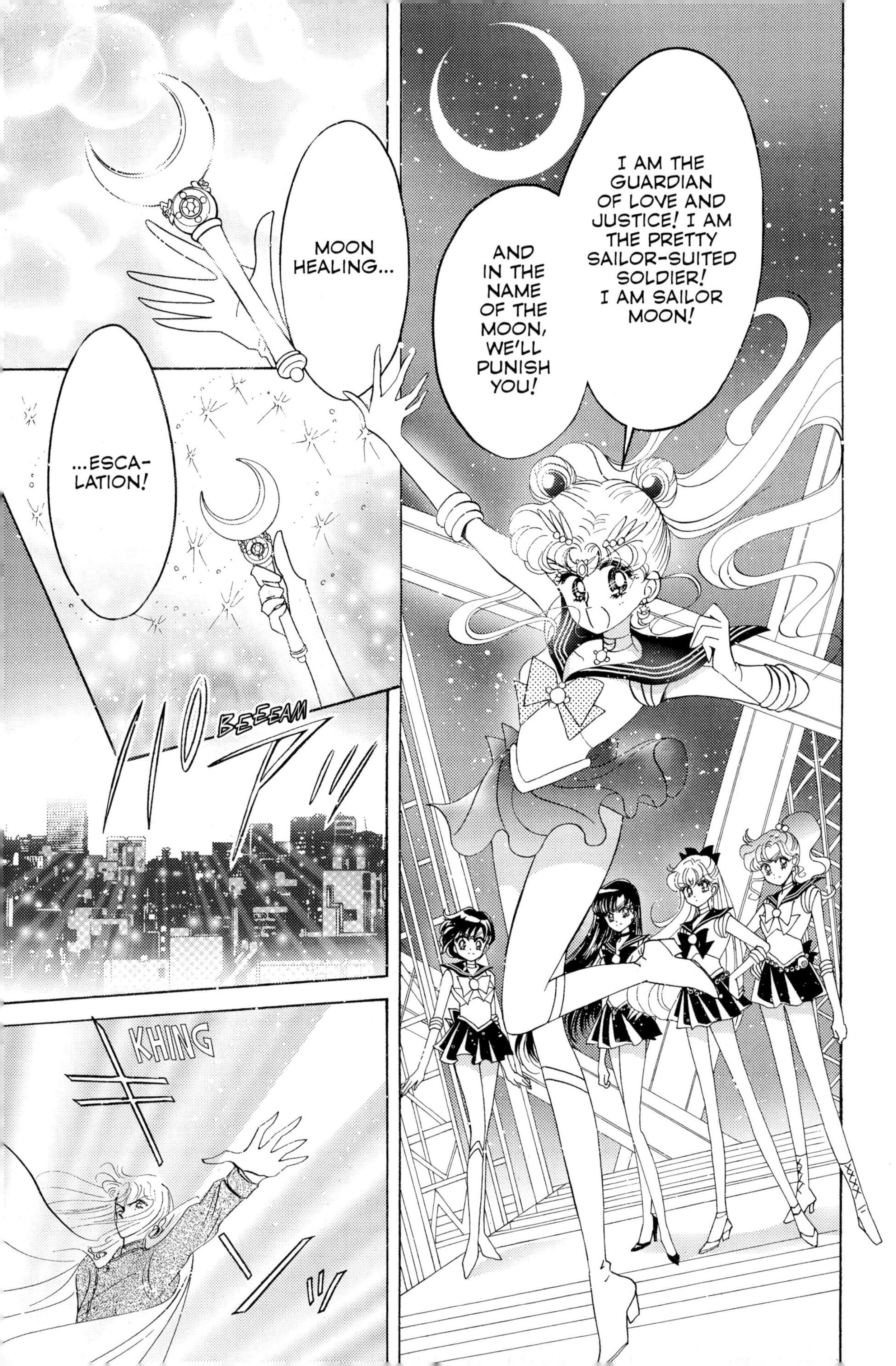
I AM THE GUARDIAN OF LOVE AND JUSTICE! I AM THE PRETTY SAILOR-SUITED SOLDIER! I AM SAILOR MOON!
AND IN THE NAME OF THE MOON, WE'LL PUNISH YOU!
MOON HEALING...
...ESCA-LATION!
BEEEAM
KHING

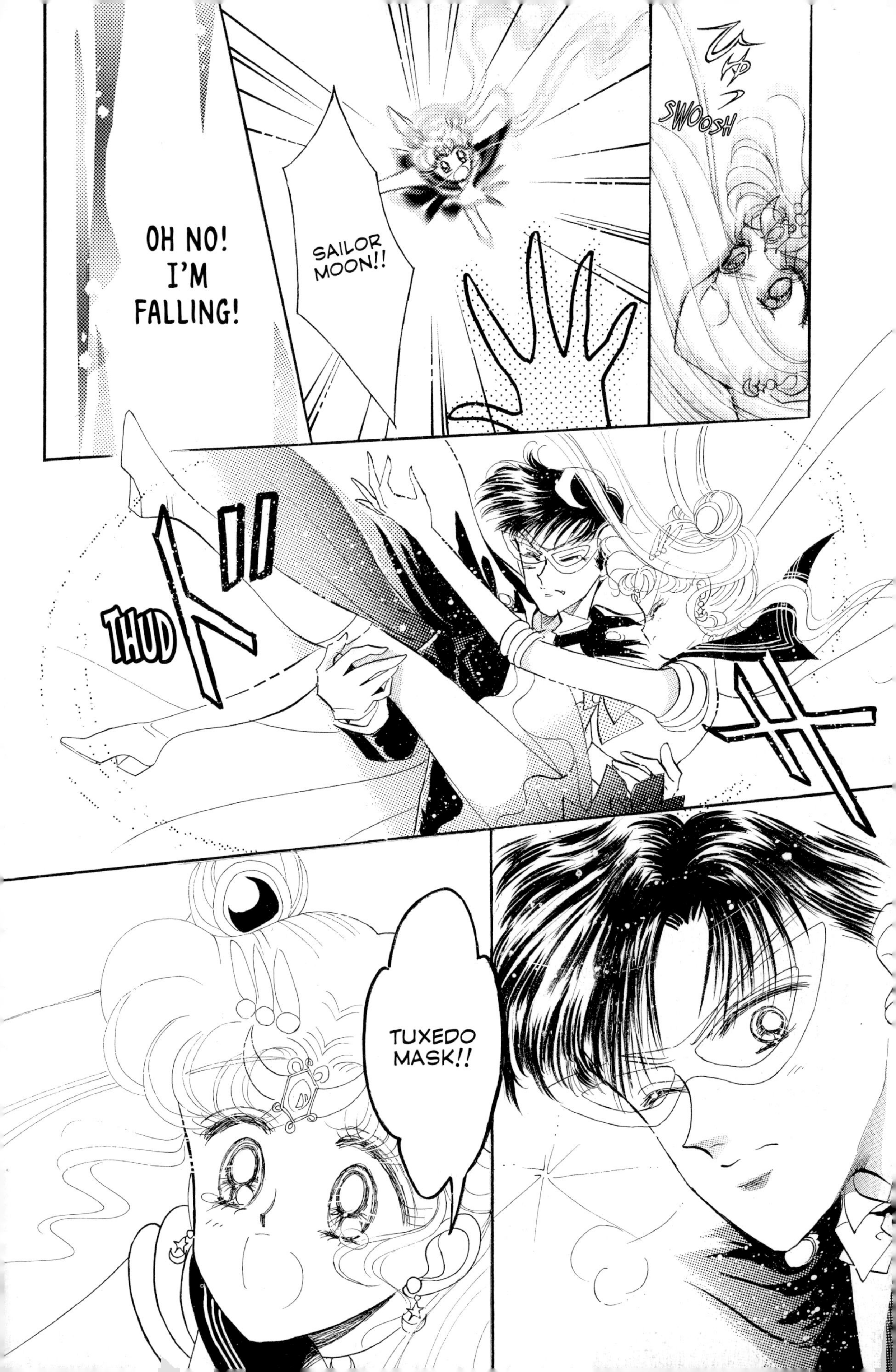
SWOOSH
SAILOR MOON!!
OH NO! I'M FALLING!
THUD
TUXEDO MASK!!

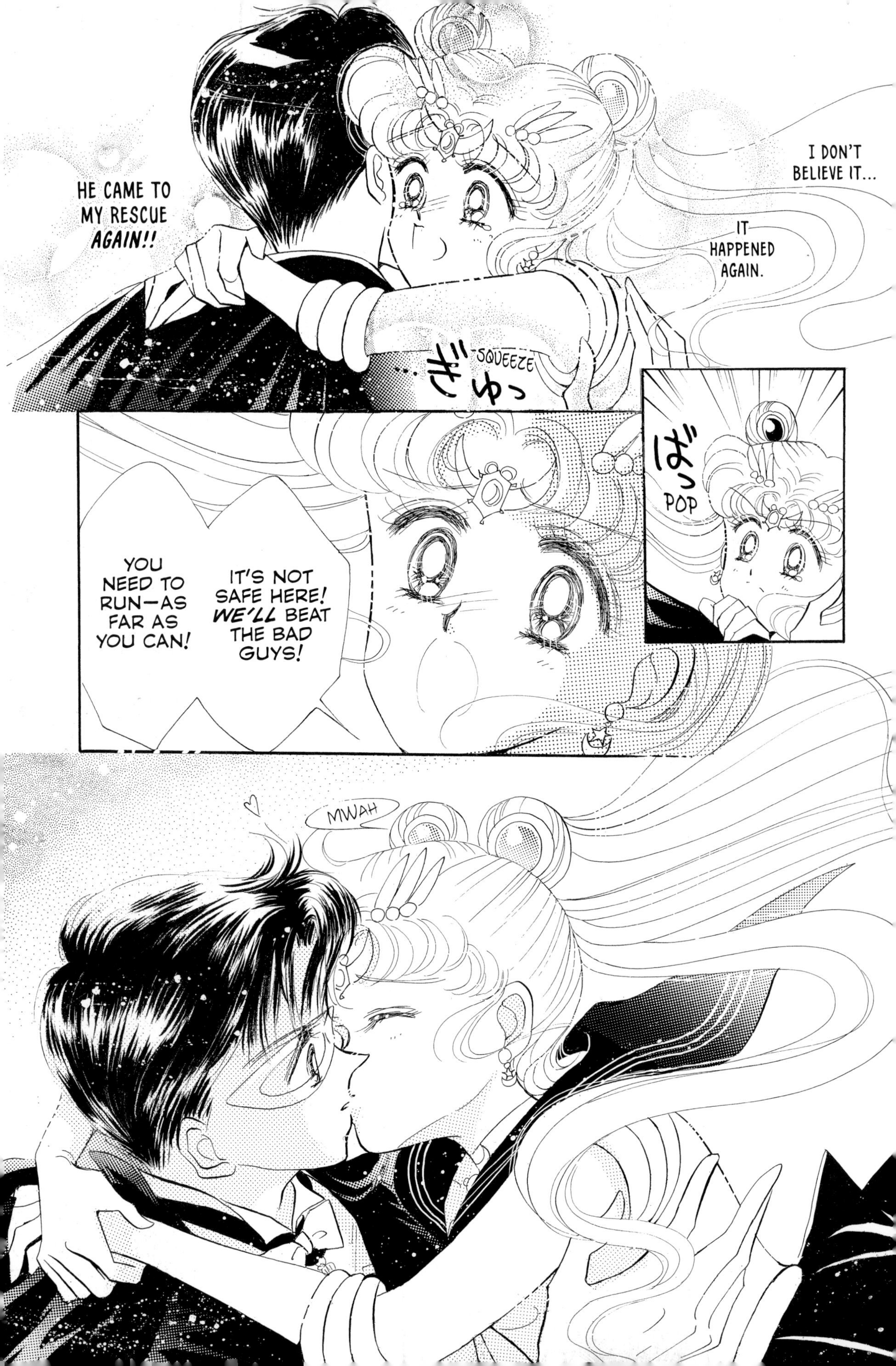
I DON'T BELIEVE IT...
IT HAPPENED AGAIN.
HE CAME TO MY RESCUE *AGAIN!!*
ぎゅっ
SQUEEZE
ばっ
POP
IT'S NOT SAFE HERE! *WE'LL* BEAT THE BAD GUYS!
YOU NEED TO RUN—AS FAR AS YOU CAN!
MWAH

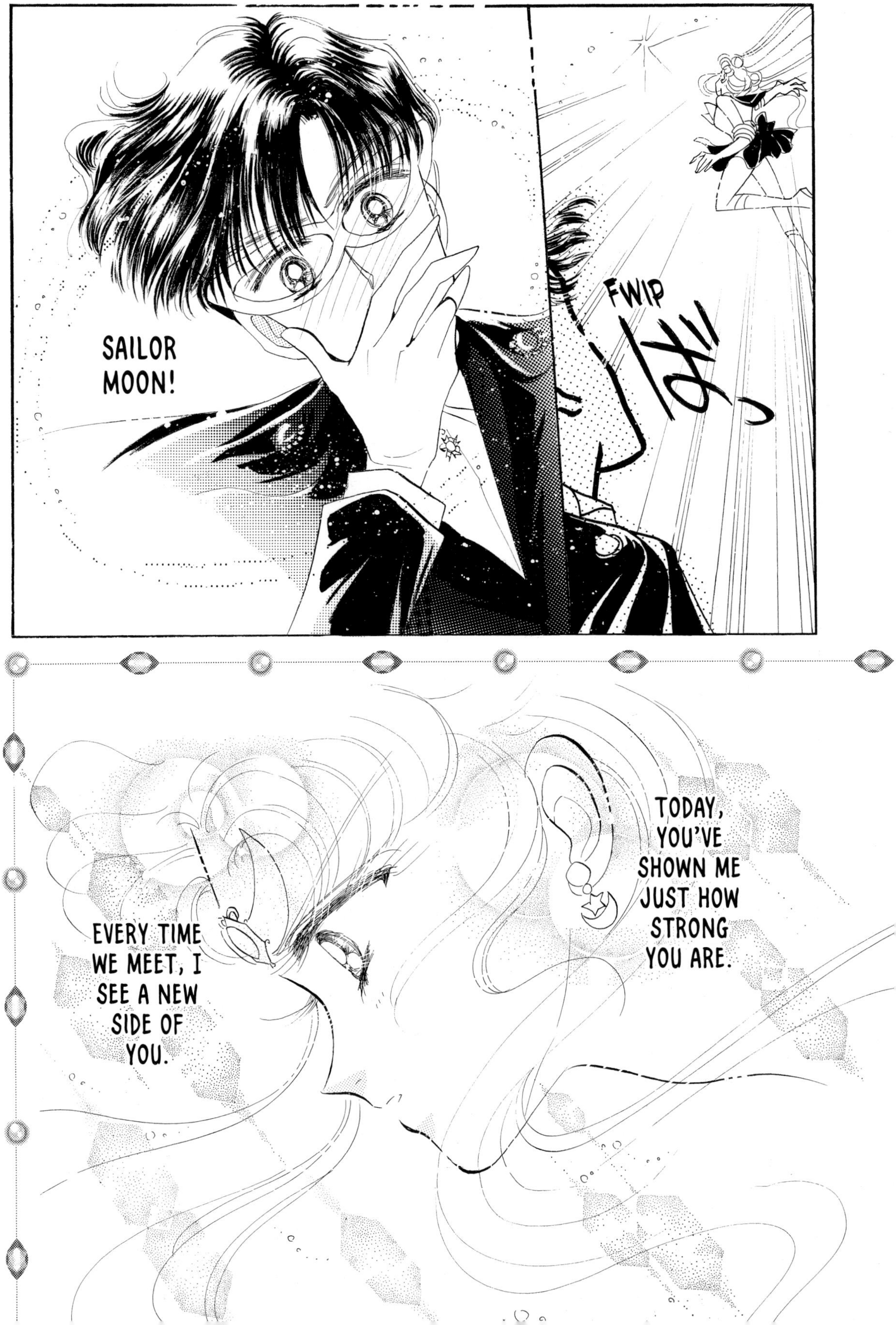
FWIP
SAILOR MOON!
TODAY, YOU'VE SHOWN ME JUST HOW STRONG YOU ARE.
EVERY TIME WE MEET, I SEE A NEW SIDE OF YOU.

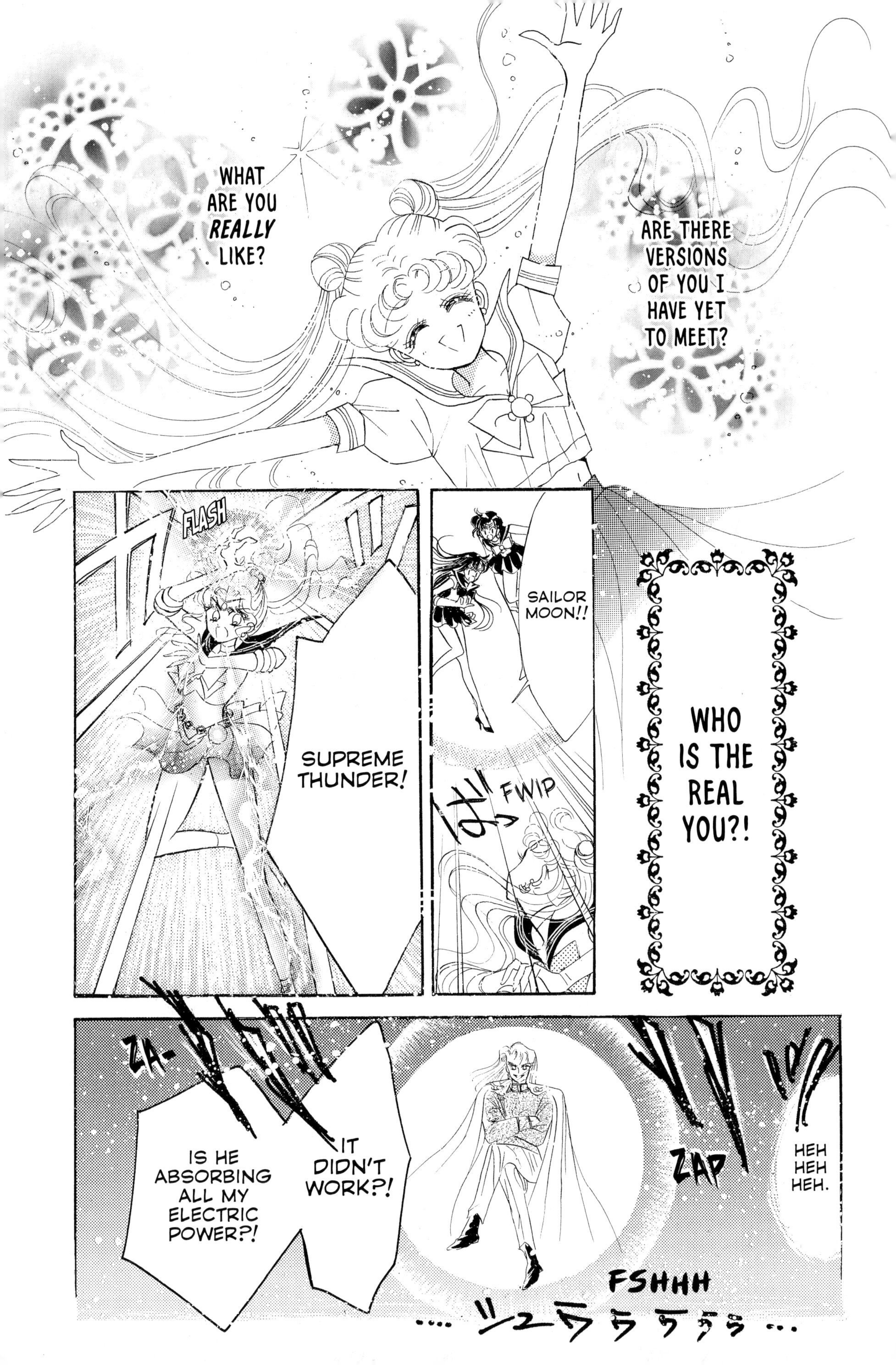
WHAT ARE YOU *REALLY* LIKE?
ARE THERE VERSIONS OF YOU I HAVE YET TO MEET?
WHO IS THE REAL YOU?!
SAILOR MOON!!
FWIP
FLASH
SUPREME THUNDER!
HEH HEH HEH.
ZAP
FSHHH
IT DIDN'T WORK?!
IS HE ABSORBING ALL MY ELECTRIC POWER?!
ZA-

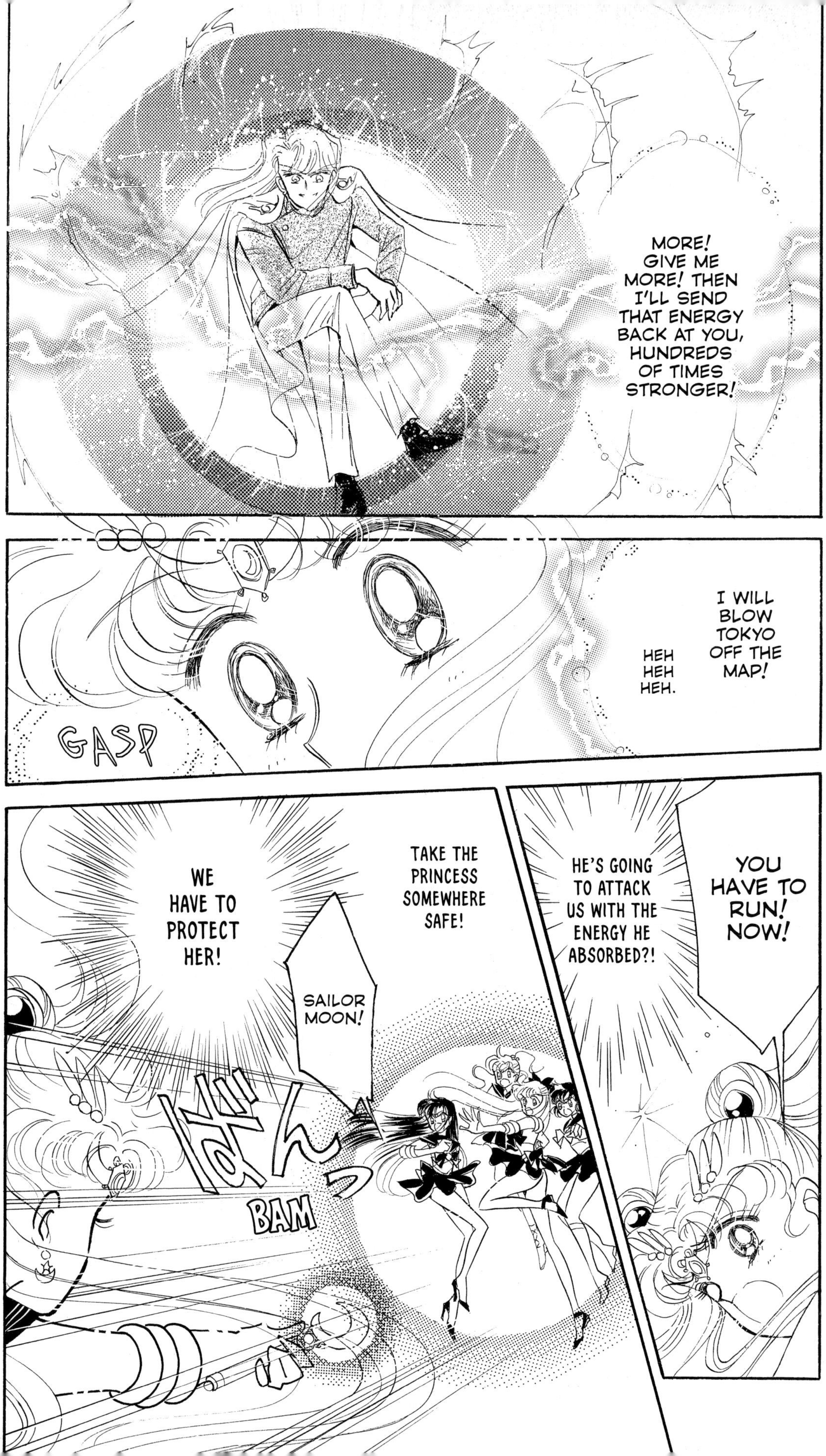
MORE! GIVE ME MORE! THEN I'LL SEND THAT ENERGY BACK AT YOU, HUNDREDS OF TIMES STRONGER!
I WILL BLOW TOKYO OFF THE MAP!
HEH HEH HEH.
GASP
YOU HAVE TO RUN! NOW!
HE'S GOING TO ATTACK US WITH THE ENERGY HE ABSORBED?!
TAKE THE PRINCESS SOMEWHERE SAFE!
WE HAVE TO PROTECT HER!
SAILOR MOON!
ばんっ
BAM

WHAT HAVE I DONE?!

SAILOR MOON!!

WE HAVE TO PROTECT SAILOR MOON! HURRY!

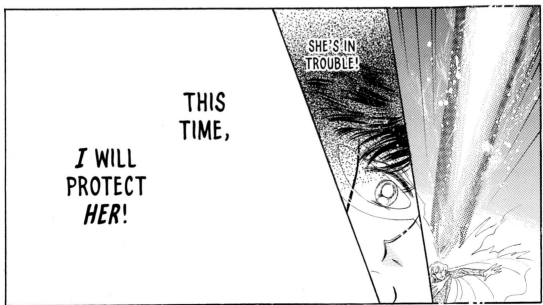

SHE'S IN TROUBLE!

THIS TIME, *I* WILL PROTECT *HER*!

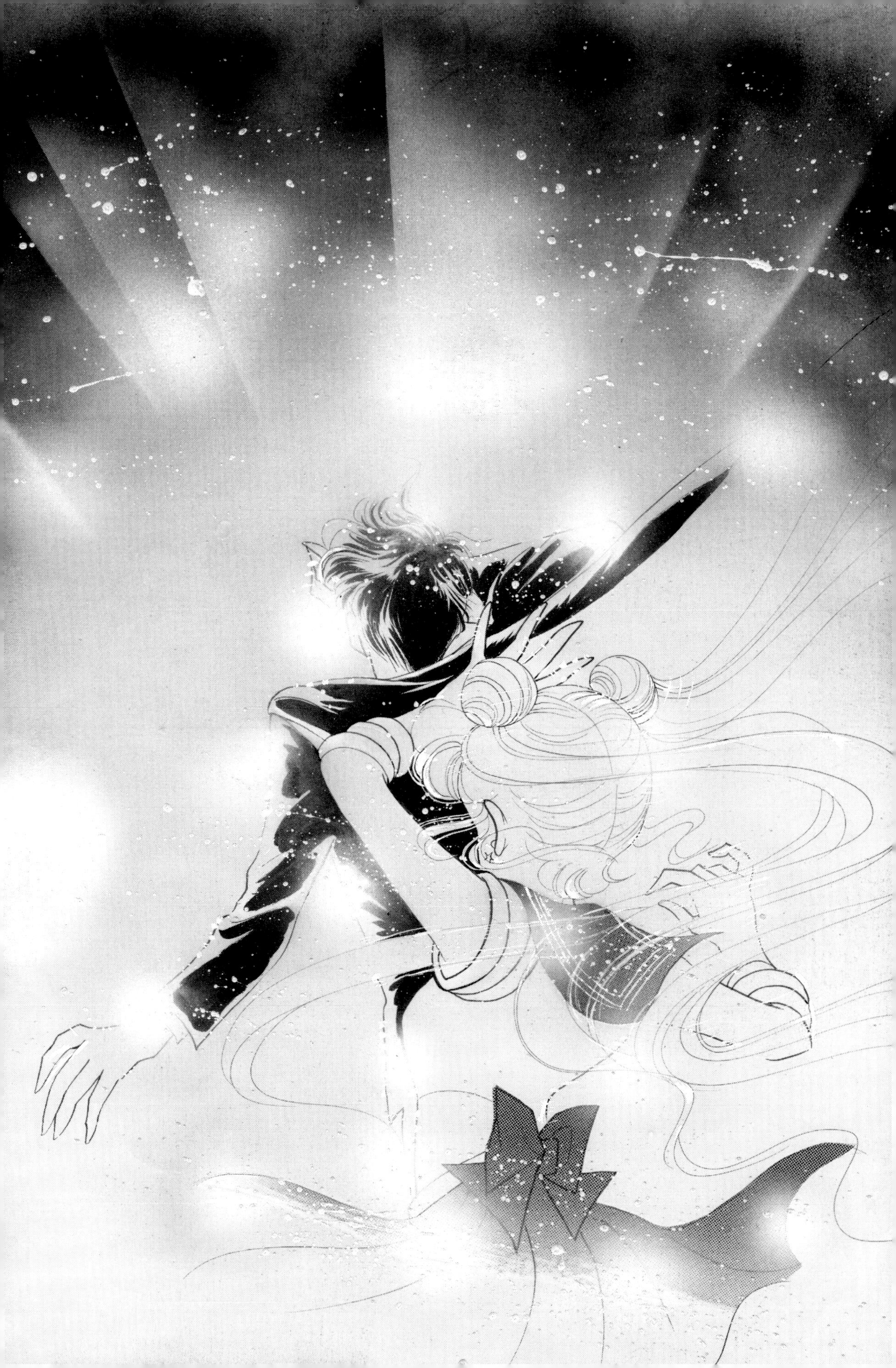

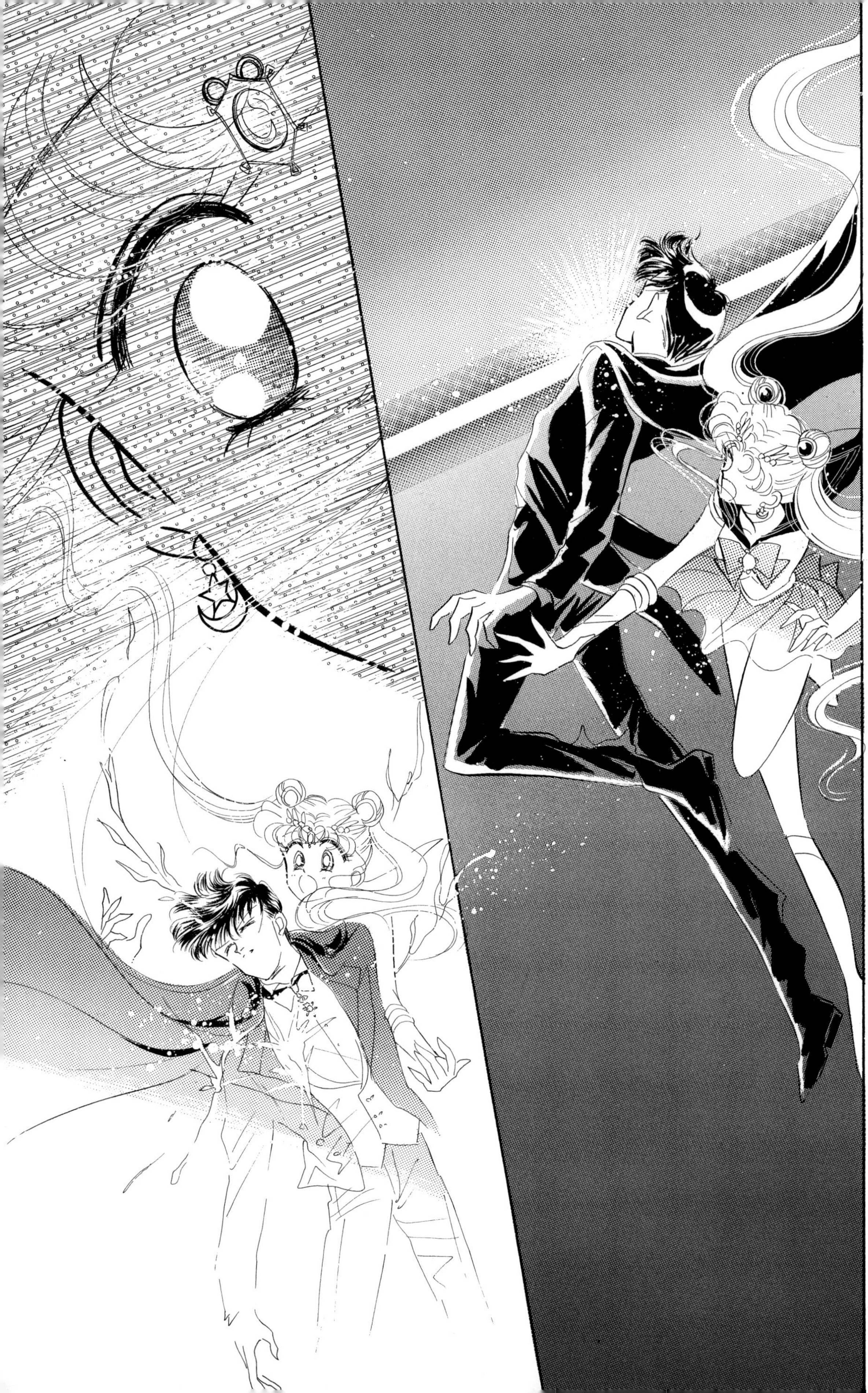

Pretty Guardian
Sailor Moon

# Act.9 Serenity: Princess

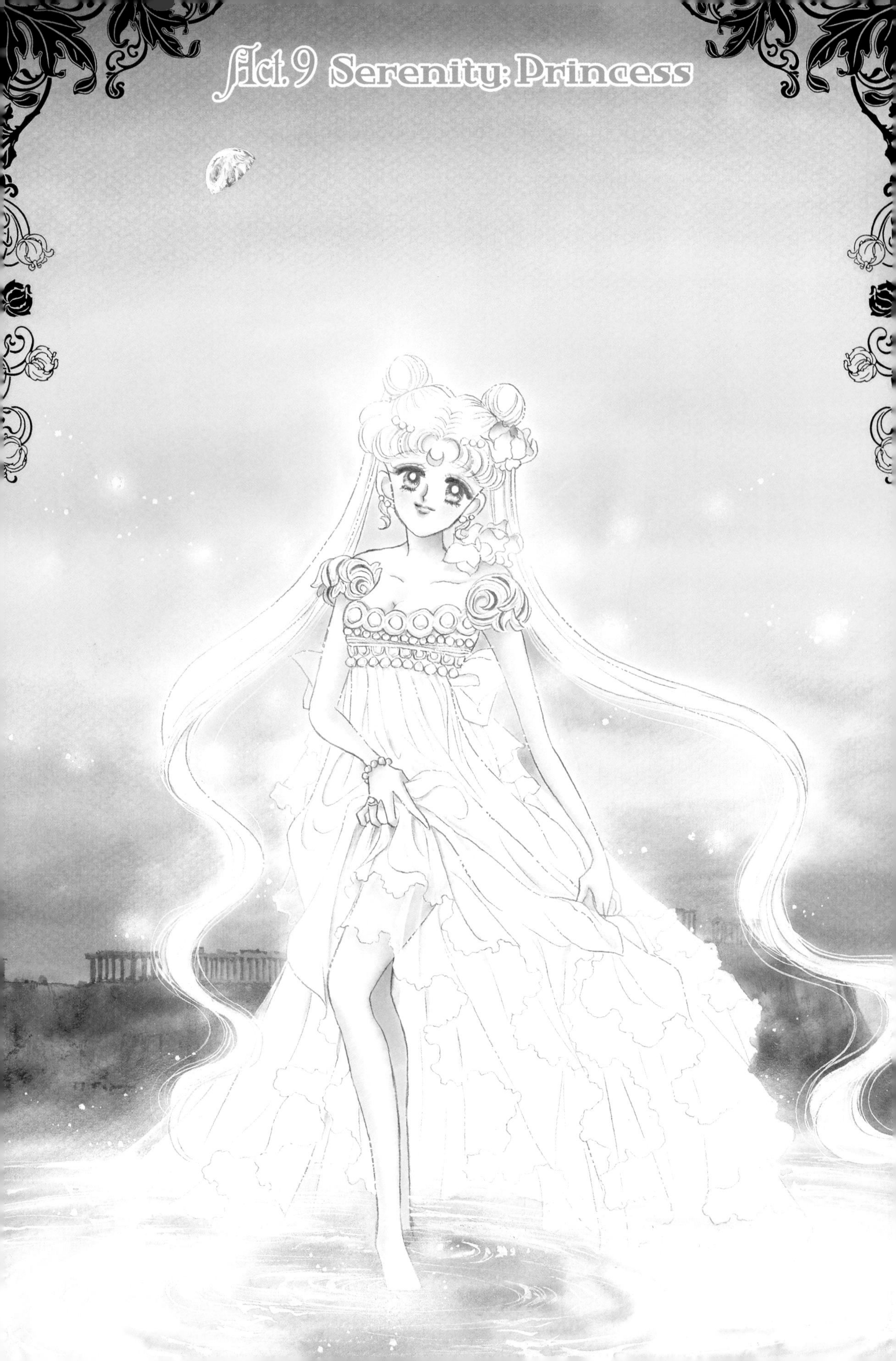

Pretty Guardian Sailor Moon

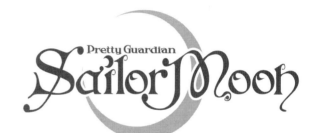

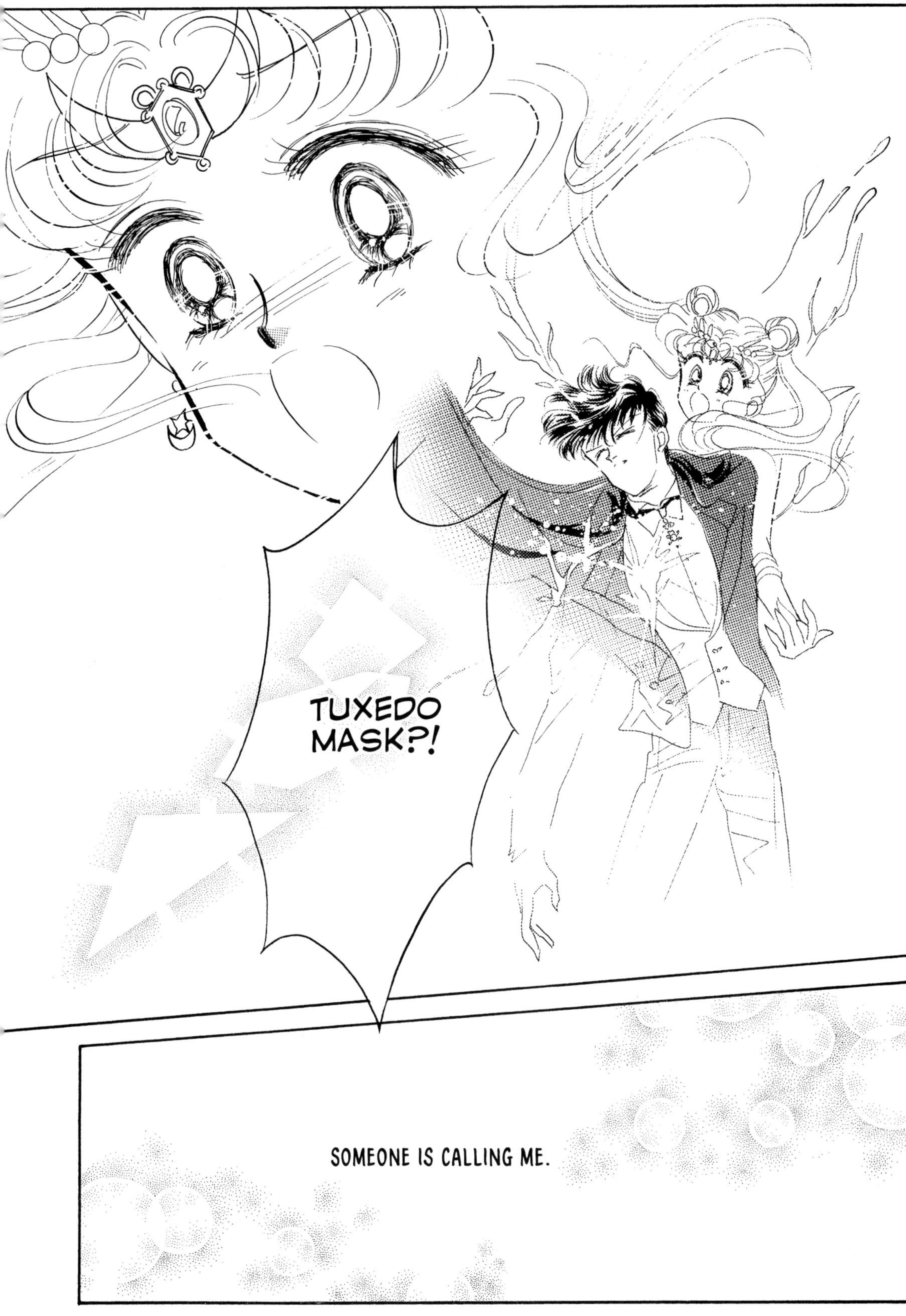
TUXEDO MASK?!
SOMEONE IS CALLING ME.

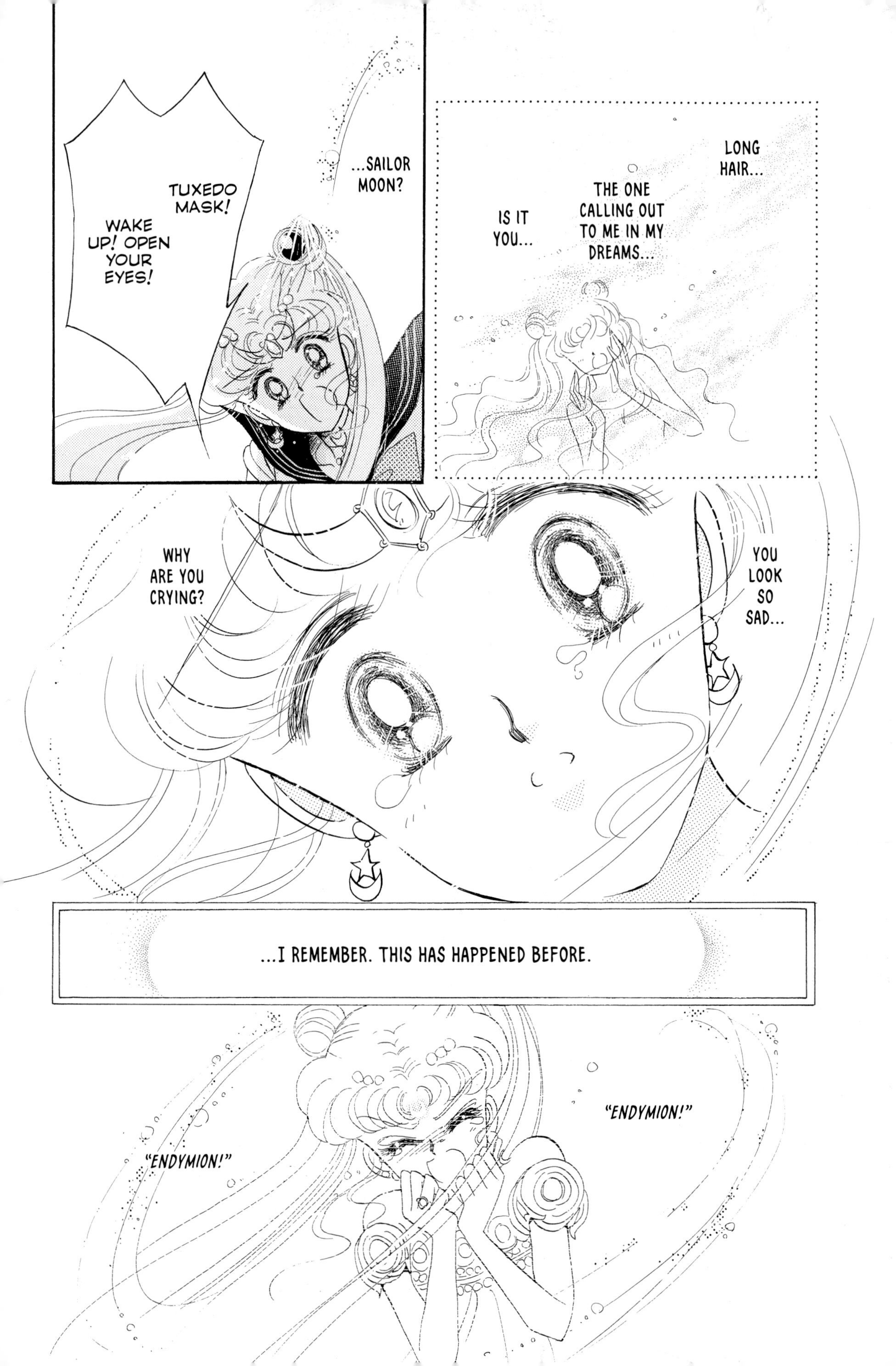

LONG HAIR...
THE ONE CALLING OUT TO ME IN MY DREAMS...
IS IT YOU...
...SAILOR MOON?
TUXEDO MASK!
WAKE UP! OPEN YOUR EYES!
YOU LOOK SO SAD...
WHY ARE YOU CRYING?
...I REMEMBER. THIS HAS HAPPENED BEFORE.
"ENDYMION!"
"ENDYMION!"

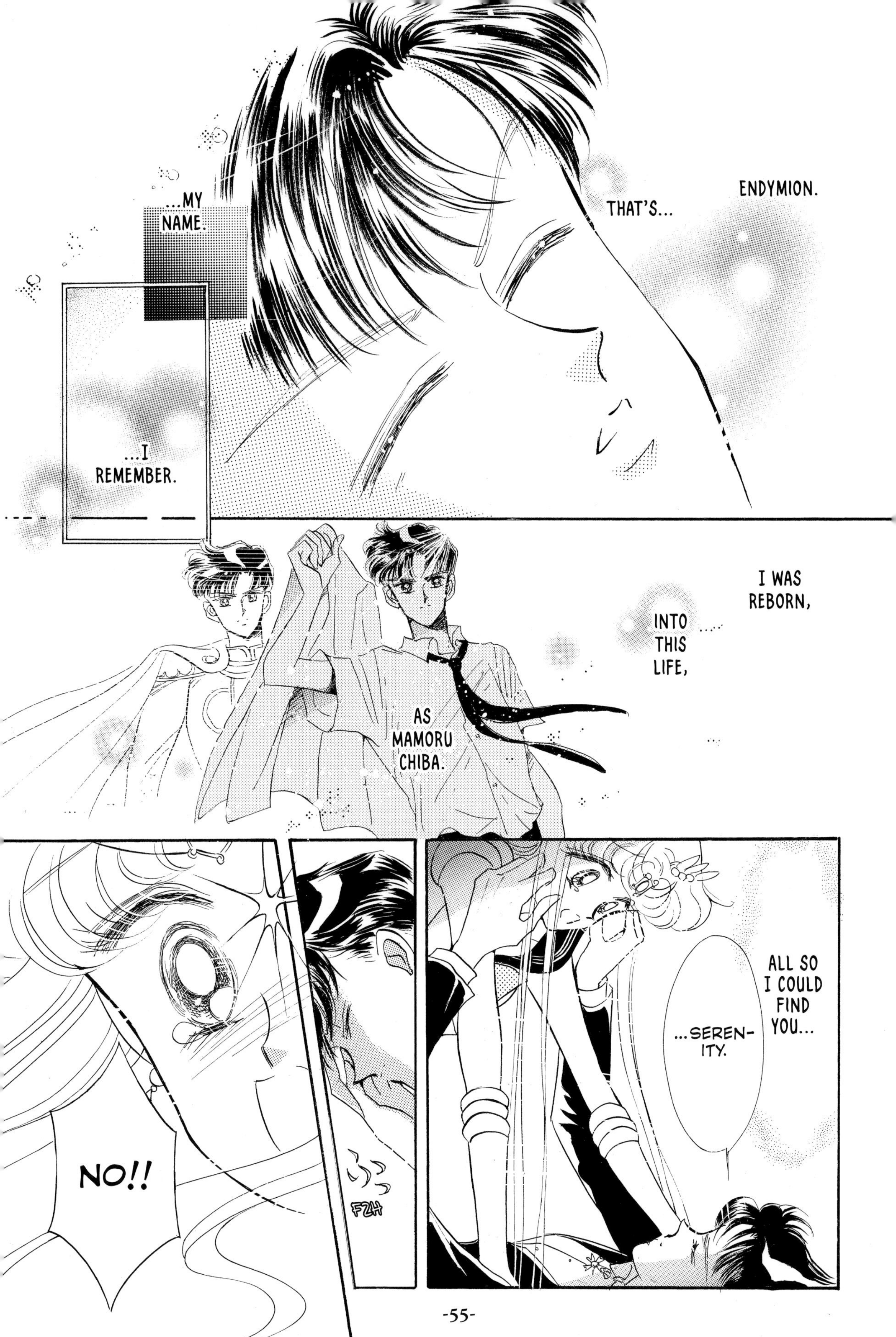
ENDYMION.
THAT'S...
...MY NAME.
...I REMEMBER.
I WAS REBORN,
INTO THIS LIFE,
AS MAMORU CHIBA.
ALL SO I COULD FIND YOU...
...SEREN-ITY.
FZH
NO!!

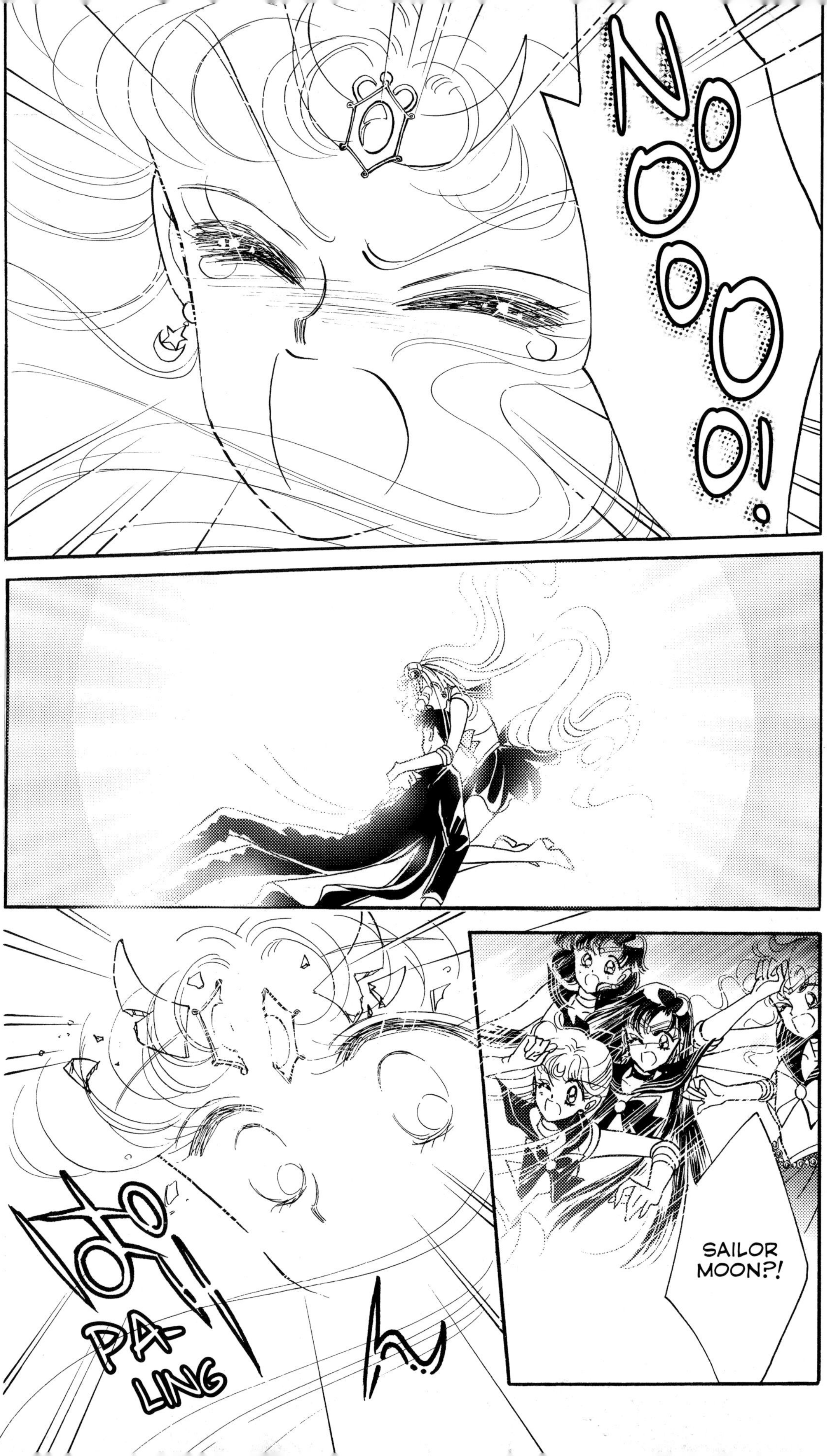
NOOOOO!
SAILOR MOON?!
PA-LING

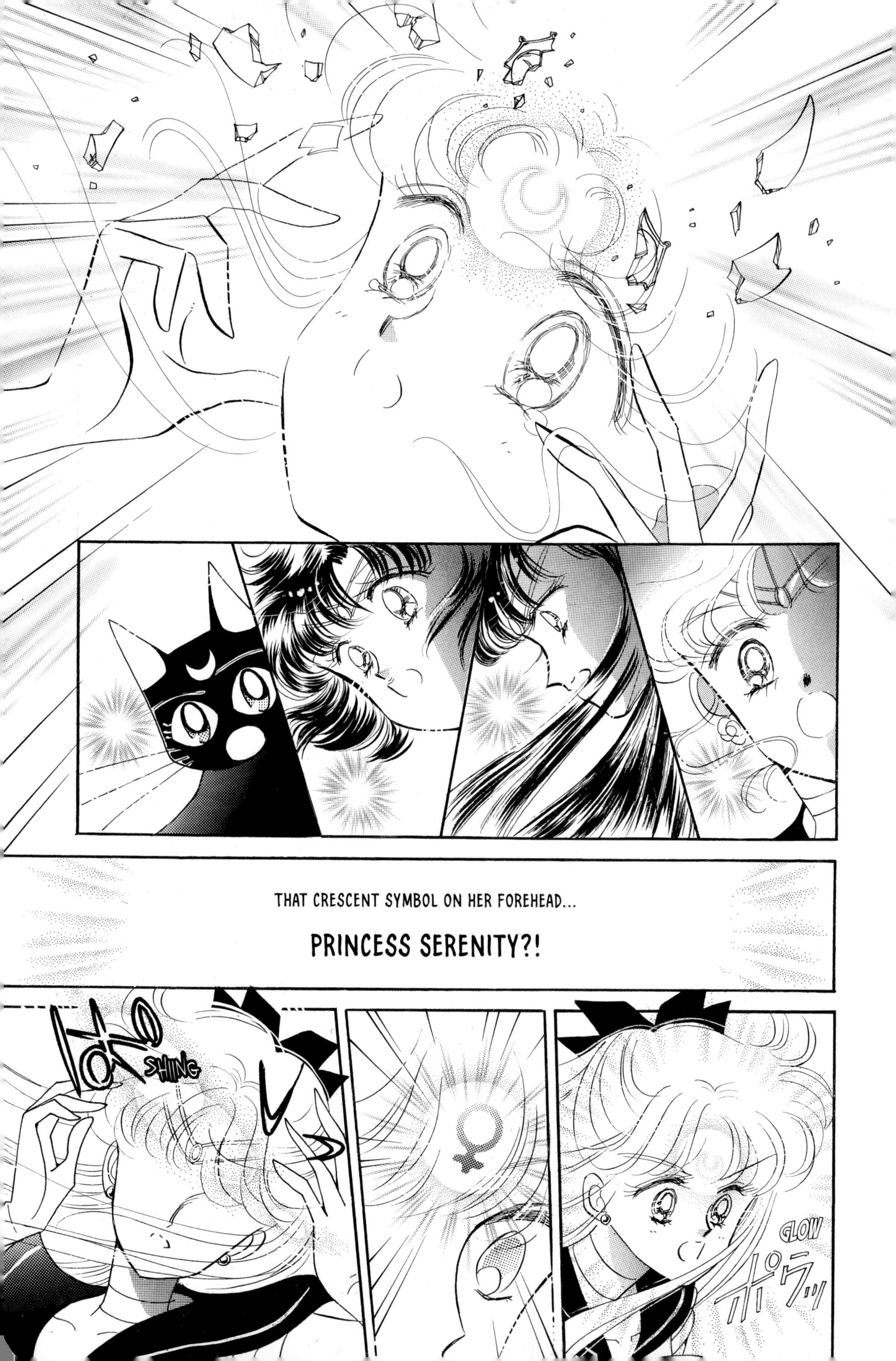
THAT CRESCENT SYMBOL ON HER FOREHEAD...
PRINCESS SERENITY?!
GLOW
SHING

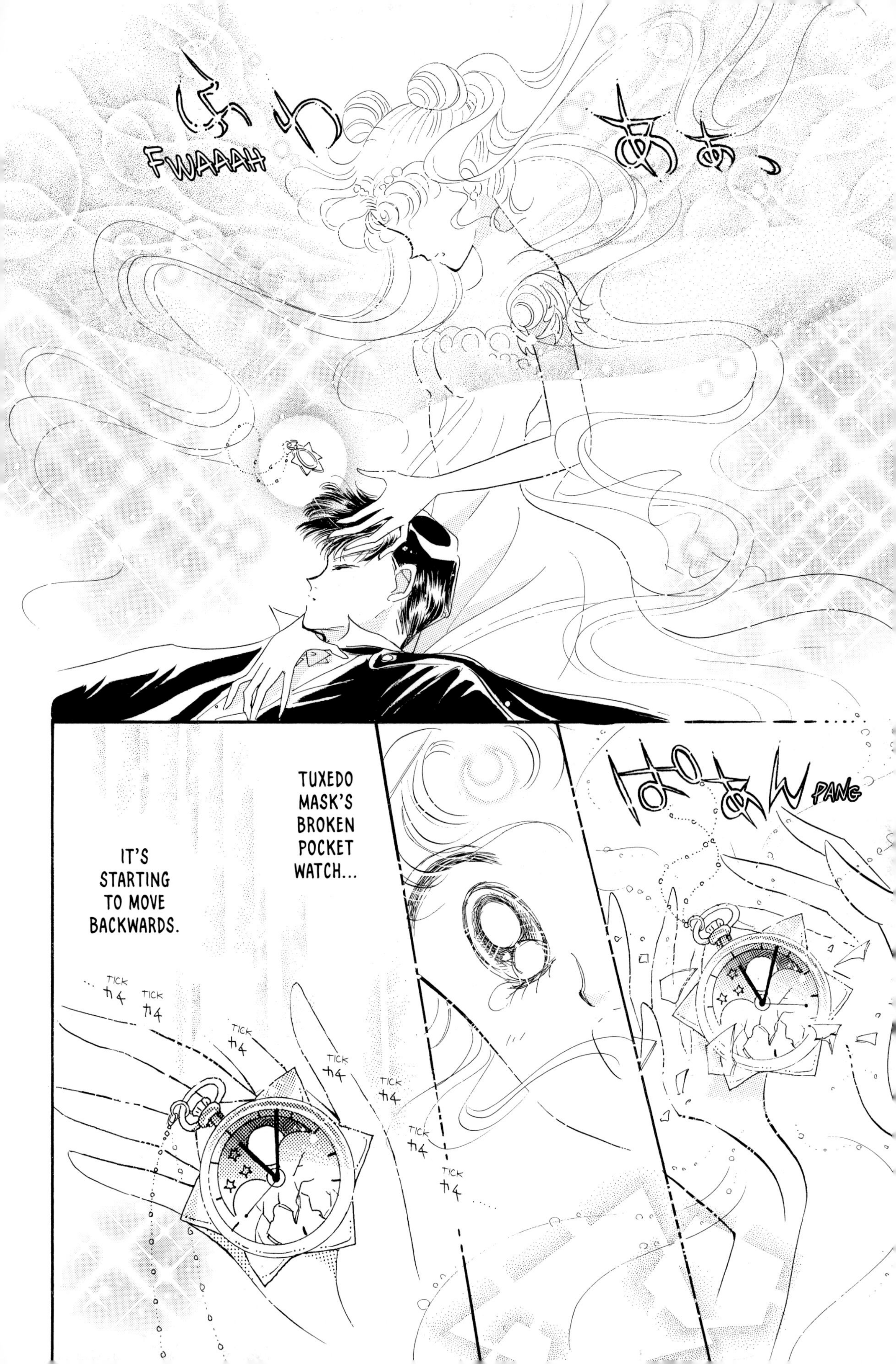
FWAAAH
PANG
TUXEDO MASK'S BROKEN POCKET WATCH...
IT'S STARTING TO MOVE BACKWARDS.
TICK
TICK
TICK
TICK
TICK
TICK
TICK

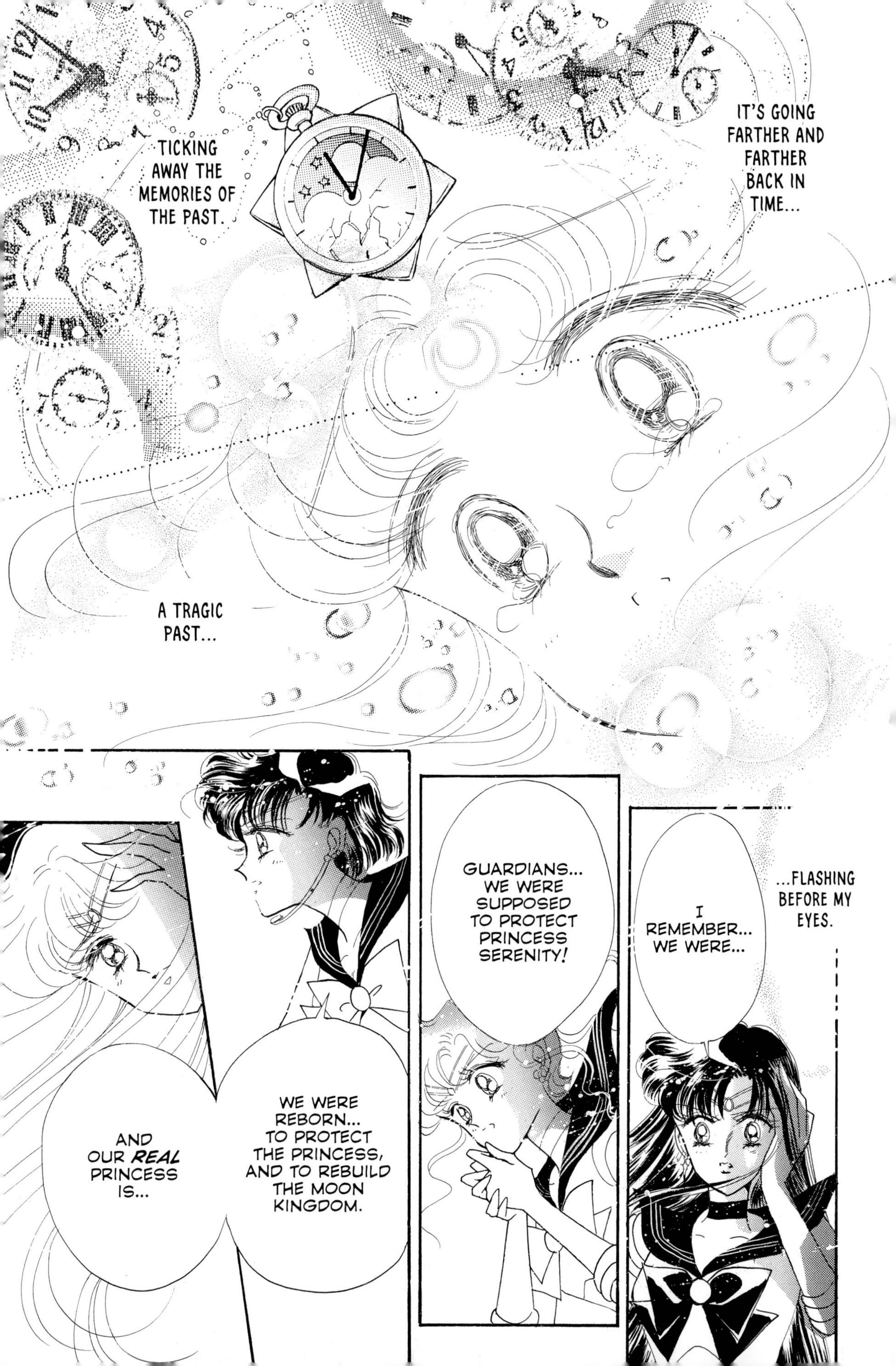
IT'S GOING FARTHER AND FARTHER BACK IN TIME...
TICKING AWAY THE MEMORIES OF THE PAST.
A TRAGIC PAST...
...FLASHING BEFORE MY EYES.
I REMEMBER... WE WERE...
GUARDIANS... WE WERE SUPPOSED TO PROTECT PRINCESS SERENITY!
WE WERE REBORN... TO PROTECT THE PRINCESS, AND TO REBUILD THE MOON KINGDOM.
AND OUR *REAL* PRINCESS IS...

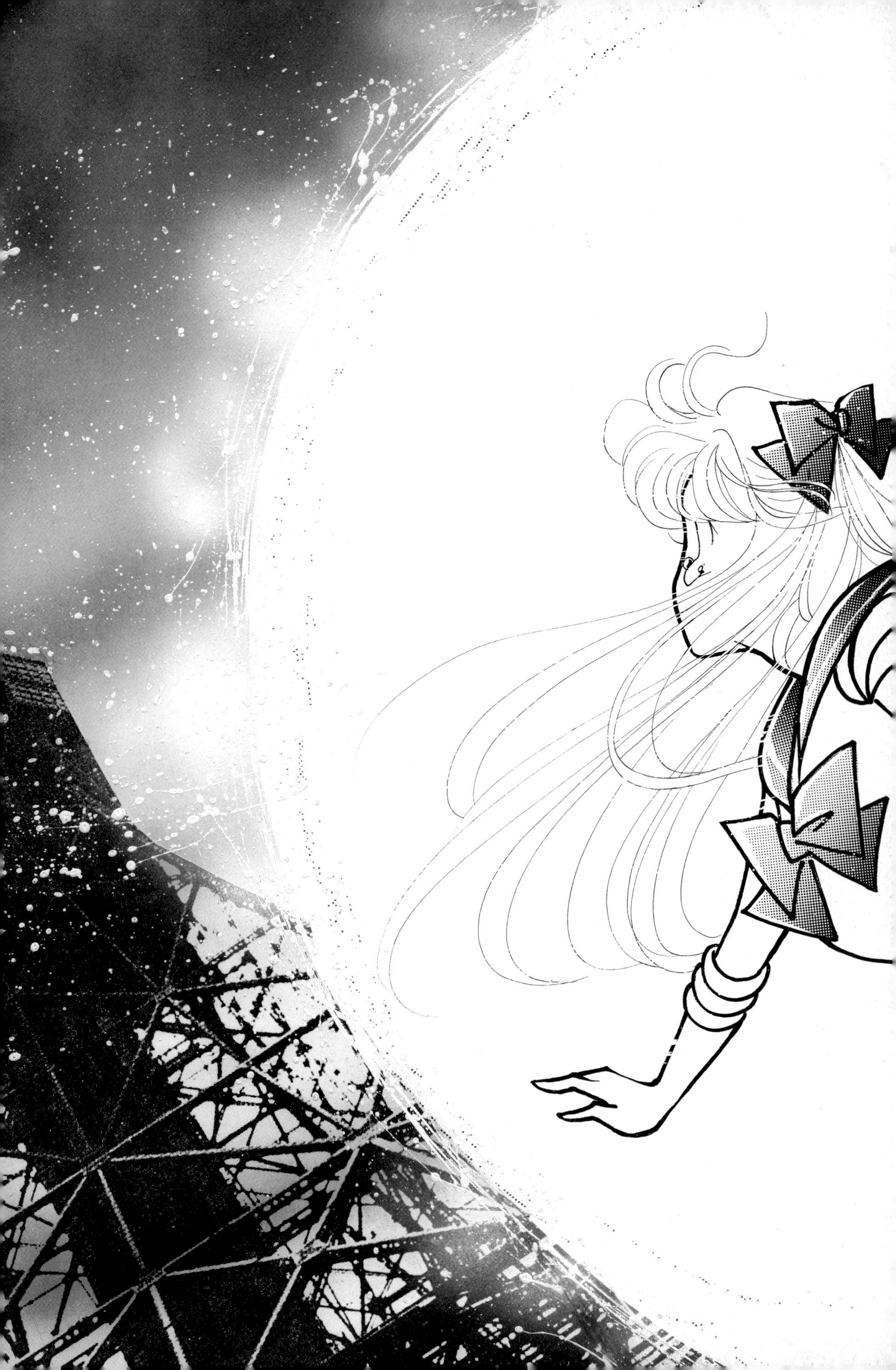

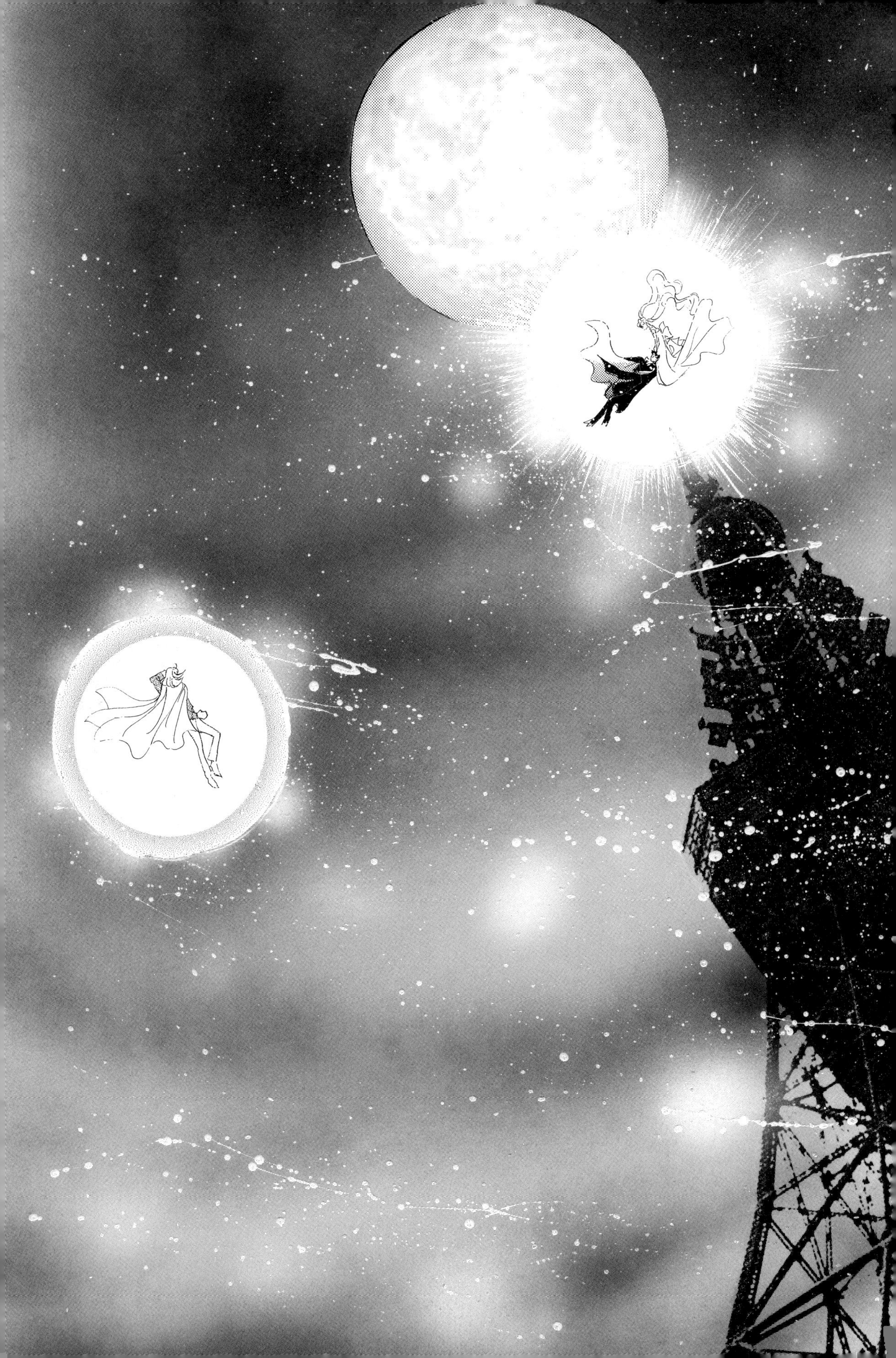

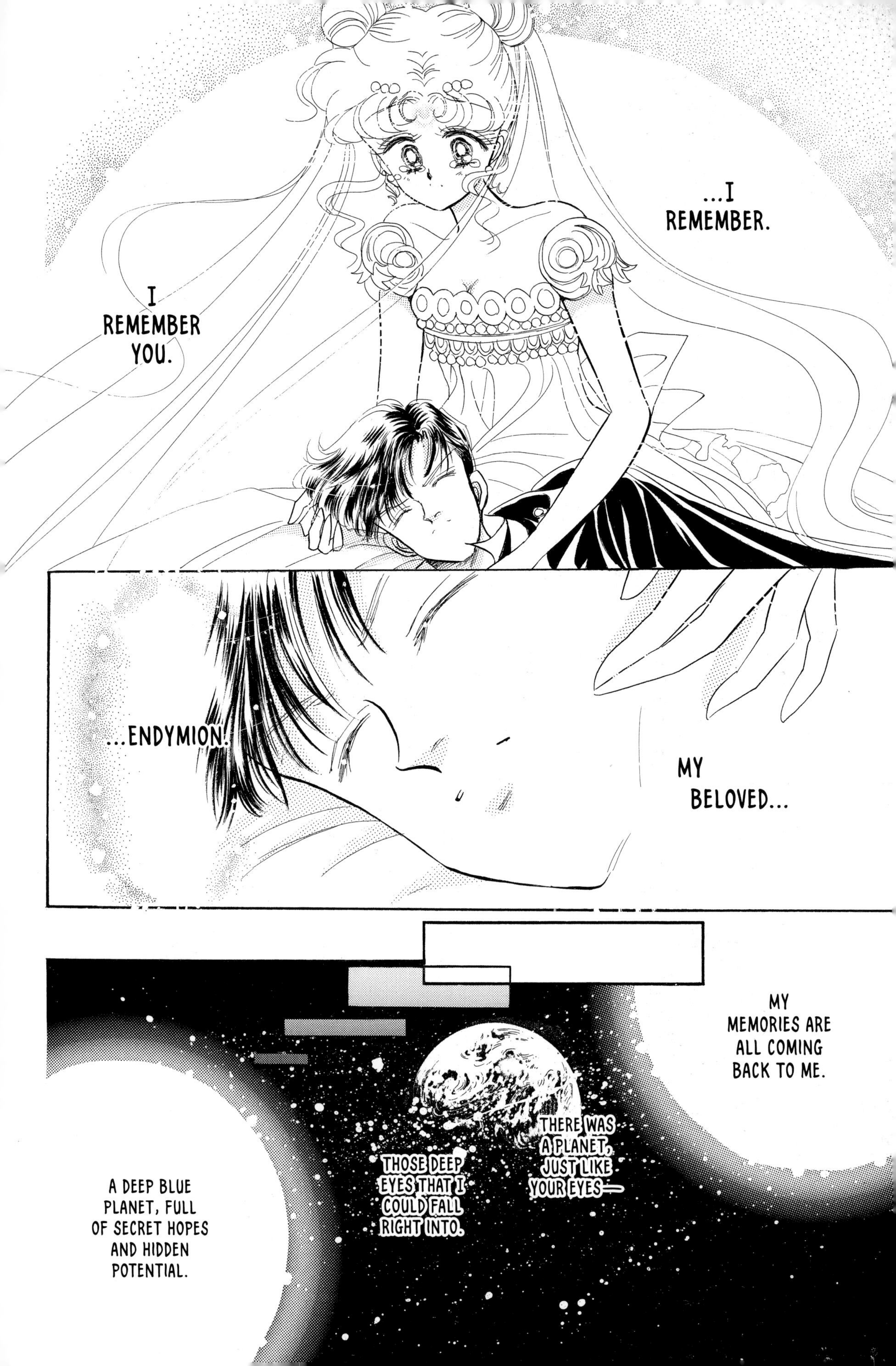
...I REMEMBER.
I REMEMBER YOU.
MY BELOVED...
...ENDYMION.
MY MEMORIES ARE ALL COMING BACK TO ME.
THERE WAS A PLANET, JUST LIKE YOUR EYES—
THOSE DEEP EYES THAT I COULD FALL RIGHT INTO.
A DEEP BLUE PLANET, FULL OF SECRET HOPES AND HIDDEN POTENTIAL.

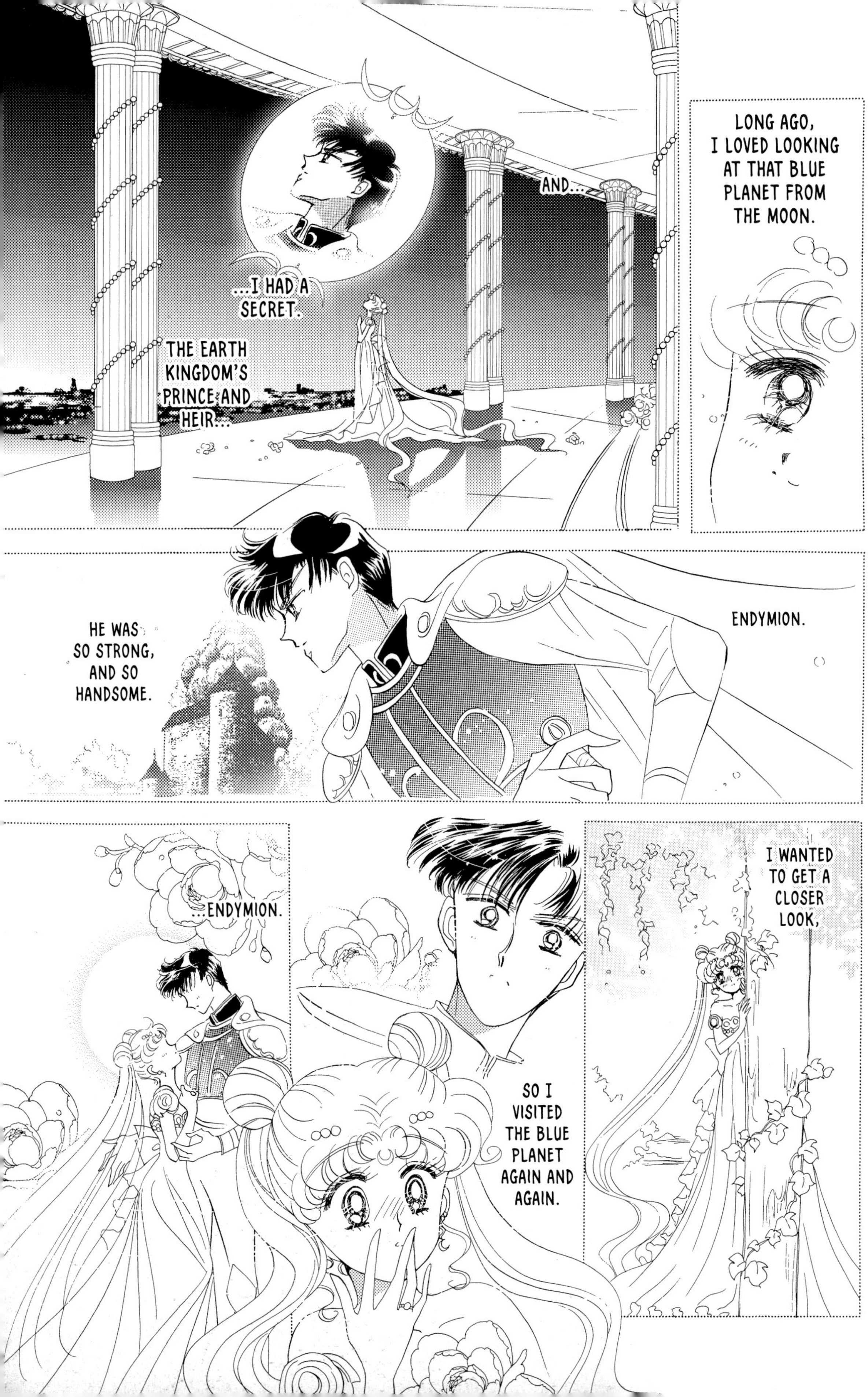
LONG AGO, I LOVED LOOKING AT THAT BLUE PLANET FROM THE MOON.
AND...
...I HAD A SECRET.
THE EARTH KINGDOM'S PRINCE AND HEIR...
ENDYMION.
HE WAS SO STRONG, AND SO HANDSOME.
I WANTED TO GET A CLOSER LOOK,
SO I VISITED THE BLUE PLANET AGAIN AND AGAIN.
...ENDYMION.

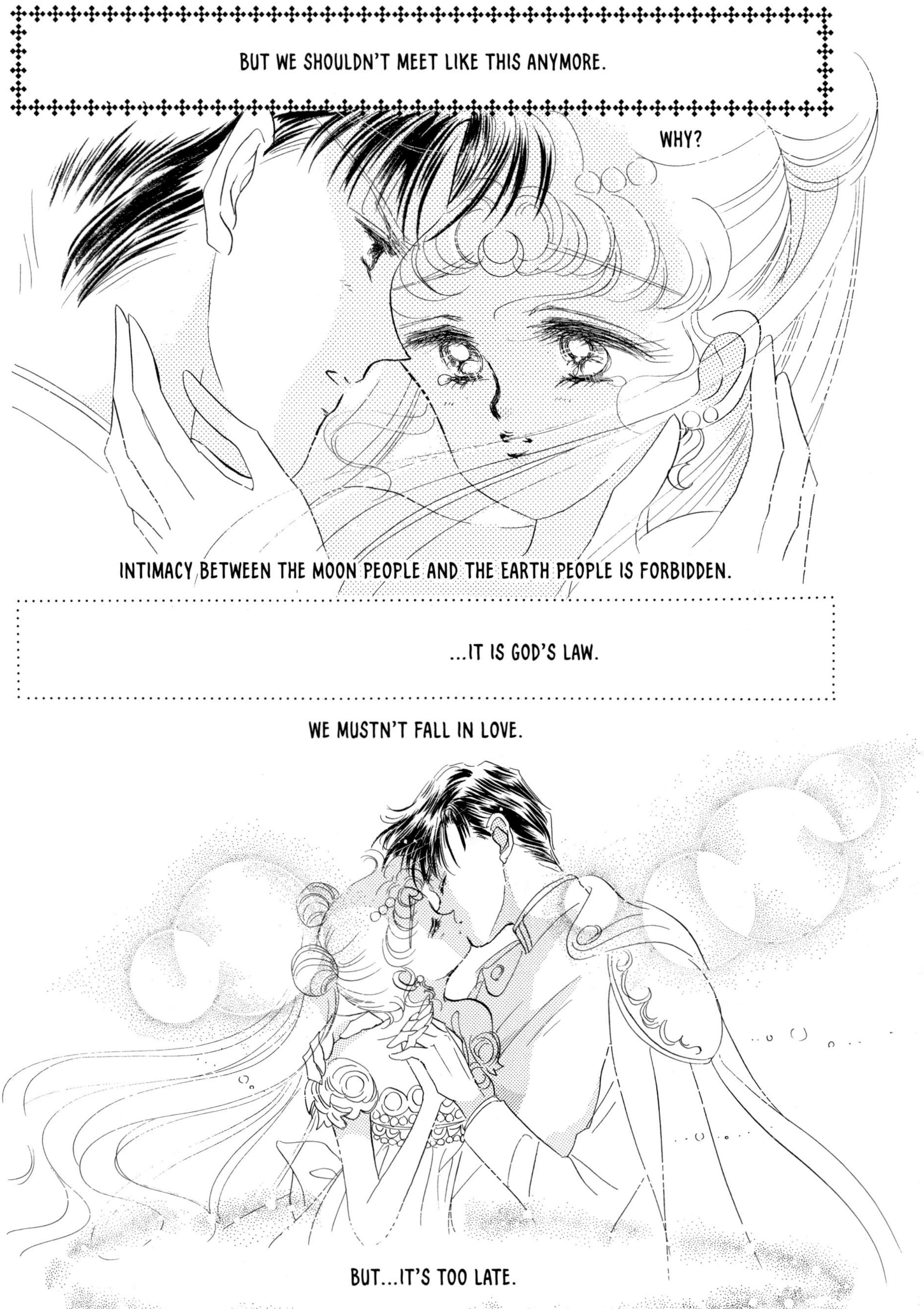
BUT WE SHOULDN'T MEET LIKE THIS ANYMORE.
WHY?
INTIMACY BETWEEN THE MOON PEOPLE AND THE EARTH PEOPLE IS FORBIDDEN.
...IT IS GOD'S LAW.
WE MUSTN'T FALL IN LOVE.
BUT...IT'S TOO LATE.

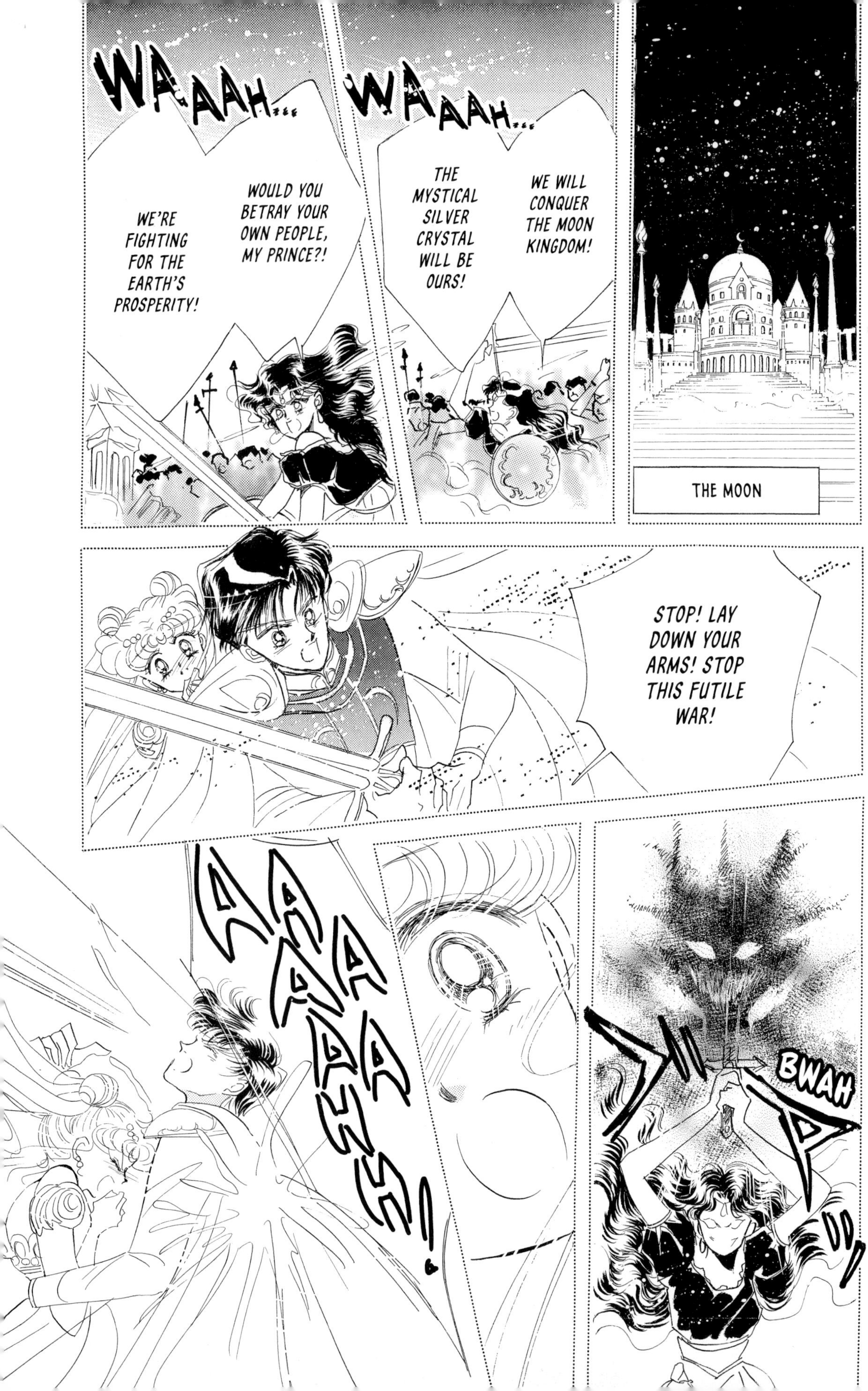
THE MOON
WAAAH...
WE WILL CONQUER THE MOON KINGDOM!
THE MYSTICAL SILVER CRYSTAL WILL BE OURS!
WAAAH...
WOULD YOU BETRAY YOUR OWN PEOPLE, MY PRINCE?!
WE'RE FIGHTING FOR THE EARTH'S PROSPERITY!
STOP! LAY DOWN YOUR ARMS! STOP THIS FUTILE WAR!
BWAH
WAAAAAHH!

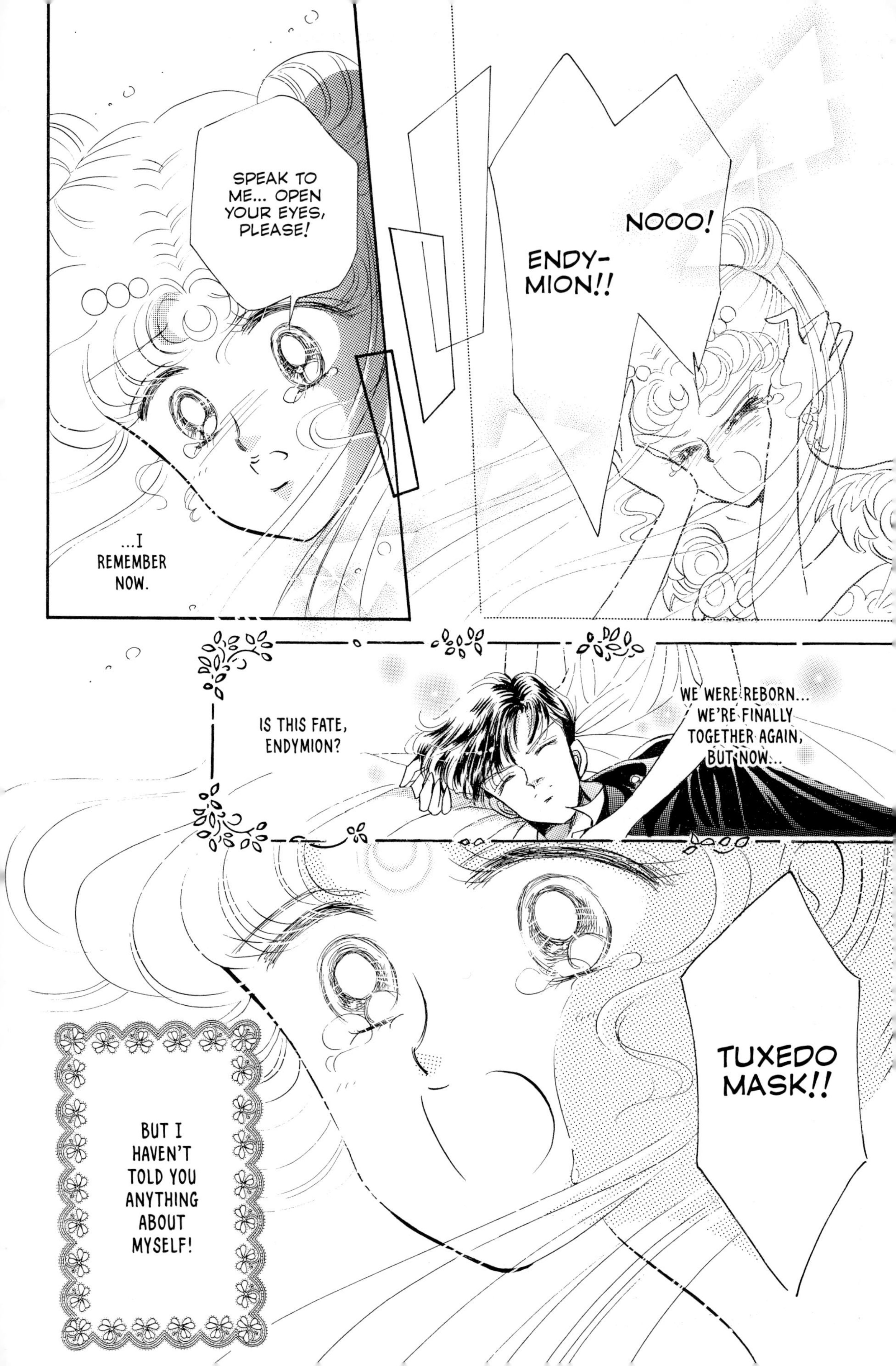
NOOO!
ENDY-MION!!
SPEAK TO ME... OPEN YOUR EYES, PLEASE!
...I REMEMBER NOW.
WE WERE REBORN... WE'RE FINALLY TOGETHER AGAIN, BUT NOW...
IS THIS FATE, ENDYMION?
TUXEDO MASK!!
BUT I HAVEN'T TOLD YOU ANYTHING ABOUT MYSELF!

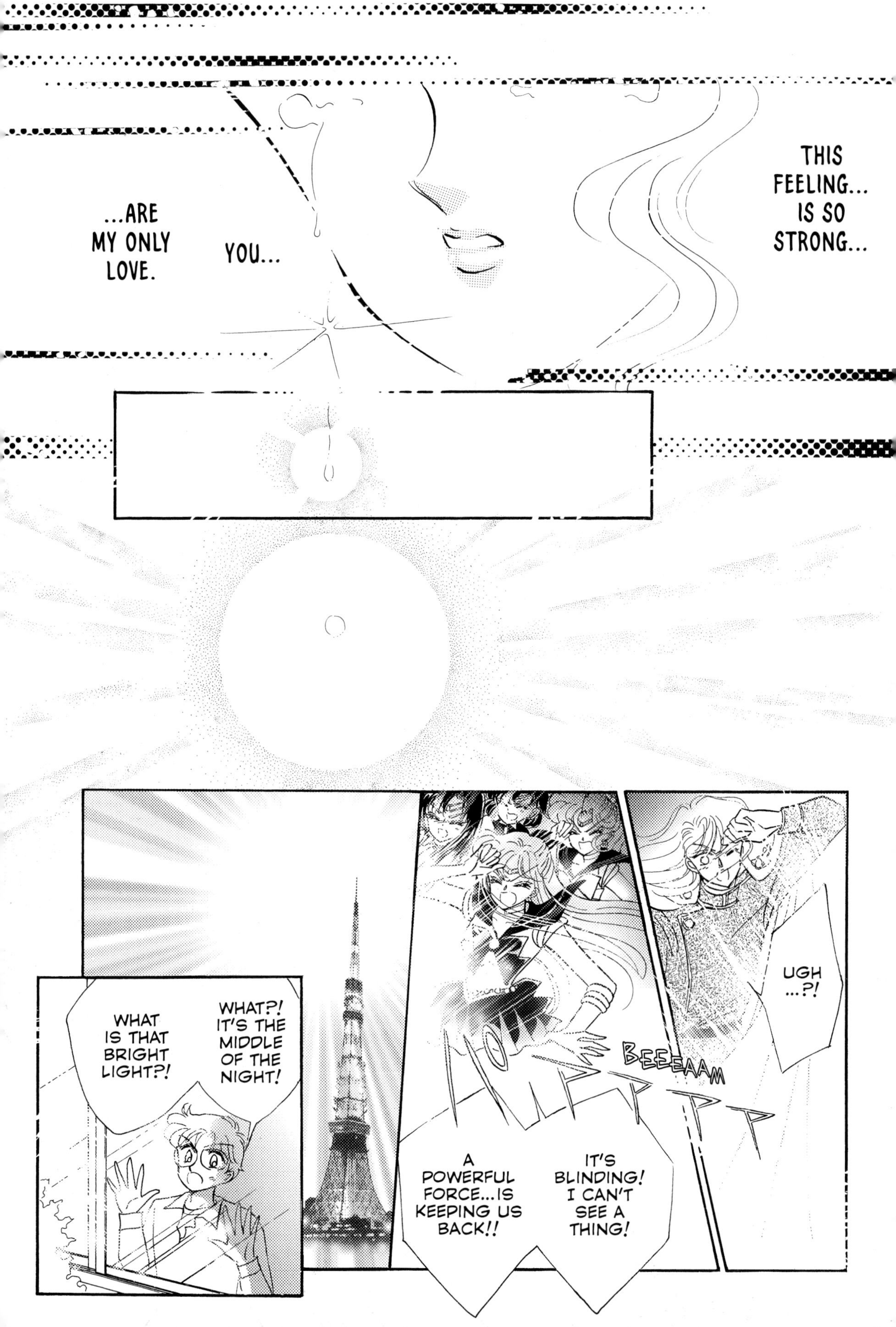
THIS FEELING... IS SO STRONG...
YOU...
...ARE MY ONLY LOVE.
UGH ...?!
BEEEAAM
IT'S BLINDING! I CAN'T SEE A THING!
A POWERFUL FORCE...IS KEEPING US BACK!!
WHAT?! IT'S THE MIDDLE OF THE NIGHT!
WHAT IS THAT BRIGHT LIGHT?!

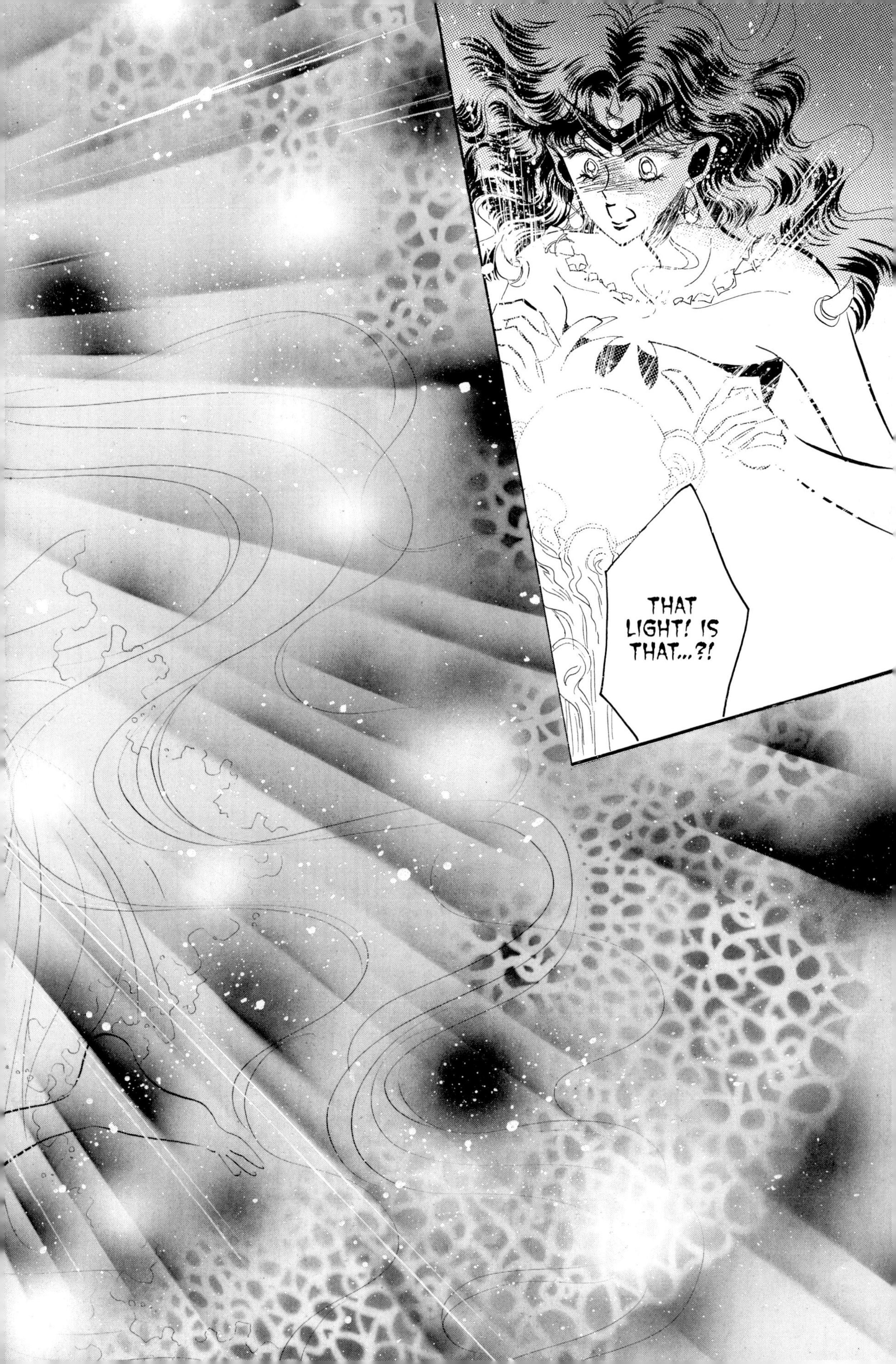
THAT LIGHT! IS THAT...?!

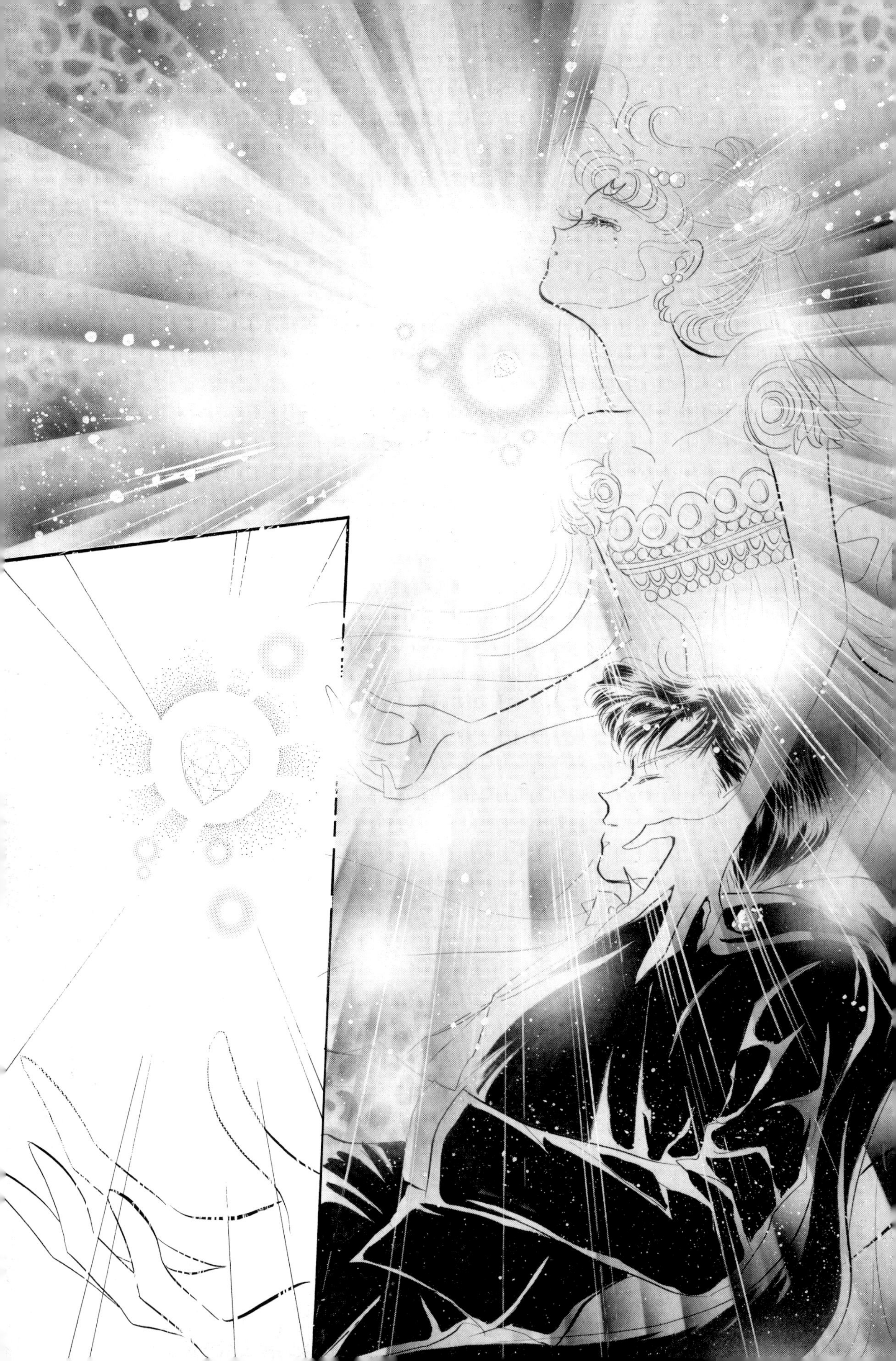

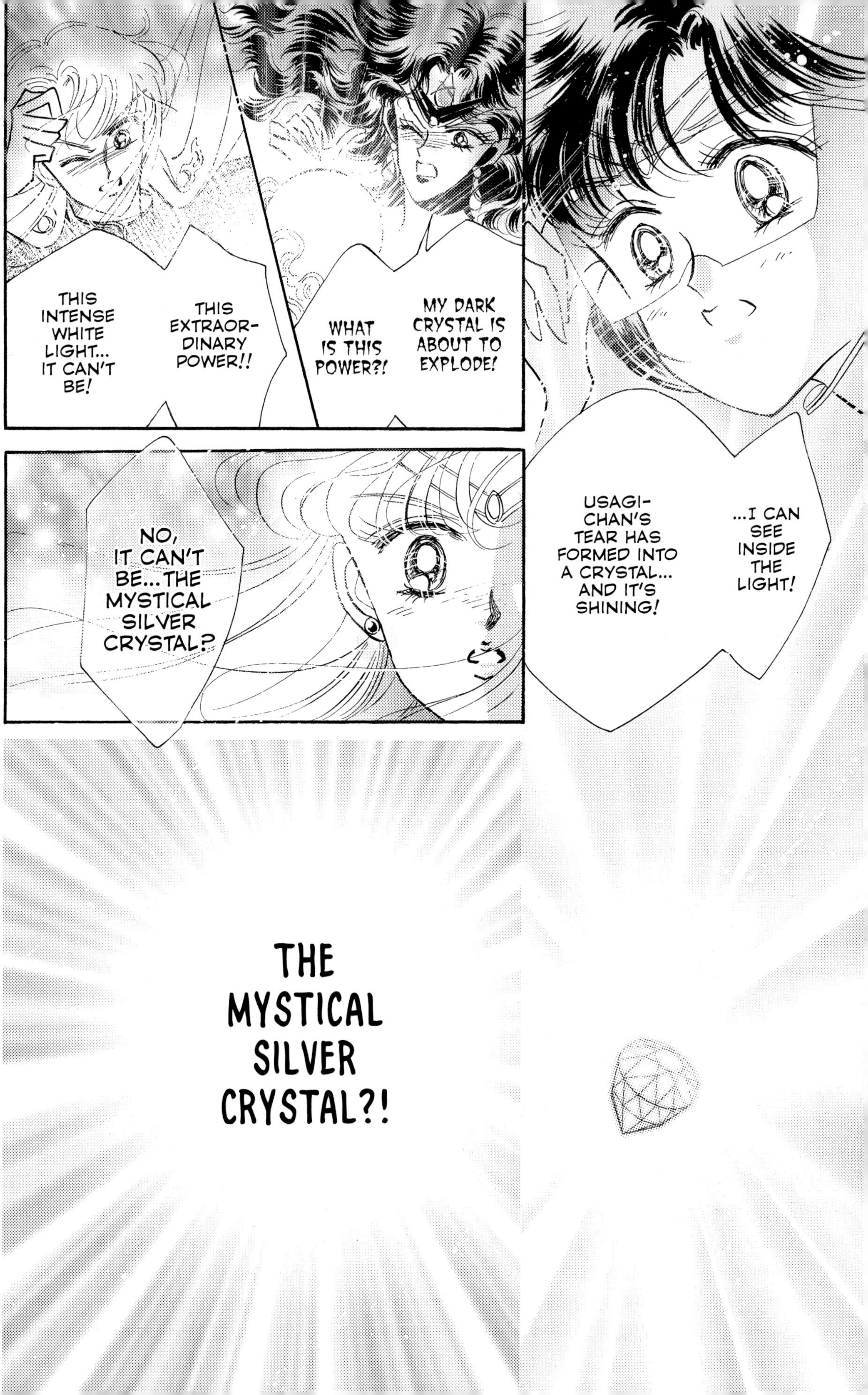
USAGI-CHAN'S TEAR HAS FORMED INTO A CRYSTAL... AND IT'S SHINING!
...I CAN SEE INSIDE THE LIGHT!
MY DARK CRYSTAL IS ABOUT TO EXPLODE!
WHAT IS THIS POWER?!
THIS EXTRAORDINARY POWER!!
THIS INTENSE WHITE LIGHT... IT CAN'T BE!
NO, IT CAN'T BE...THE MYSTICAL SILVER CRYSTAL?
THE MYSTICAL SILVER CRYSTAL?!

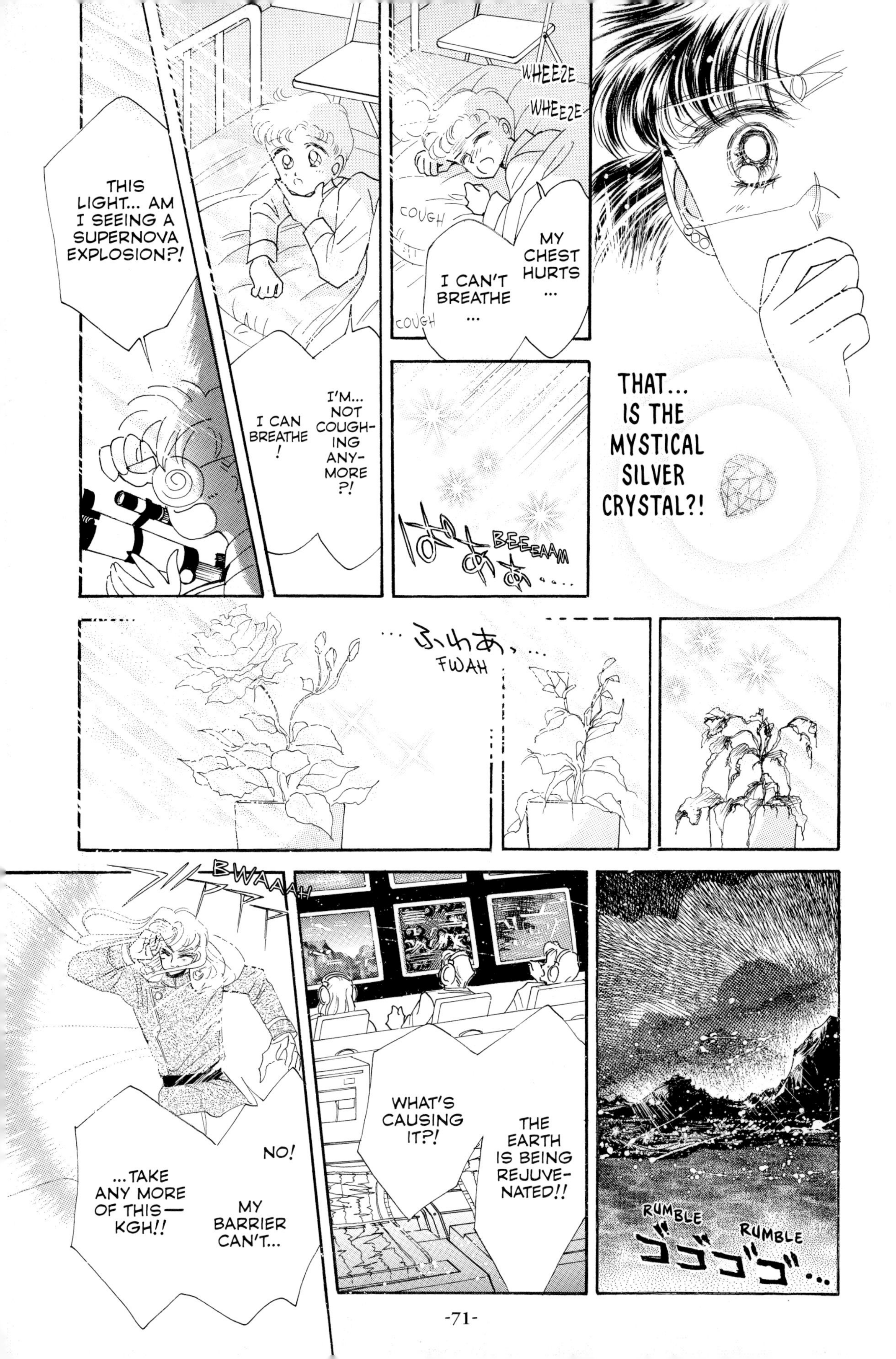

THAT... IS THE MYSTICAL SILVER CRYSTAL?!
WHEEZE
WHEEZE
COUGH
COUGH
MY CHEST HURTS...
I CAN'T BREATHE...
BEEEAAM
I'M... NOT COUGH-ING ANY-MORE?!
I CAN BREATHE!
THIS LIGHT... AM I SEEING A SUPERNOVA EXPLOSION?!
...ふわあ...
FWAH
ゴゴゴゴ...
RUMBLE
RUMBLE
THE EARTH IS BEING REJUVE-NATED!!
WHAT'S CAUSING IT?!
BWAAAAH
NO!
MY BARRIER CAN'T...
...TAKE ANY MORE OF THIS—KGH!!

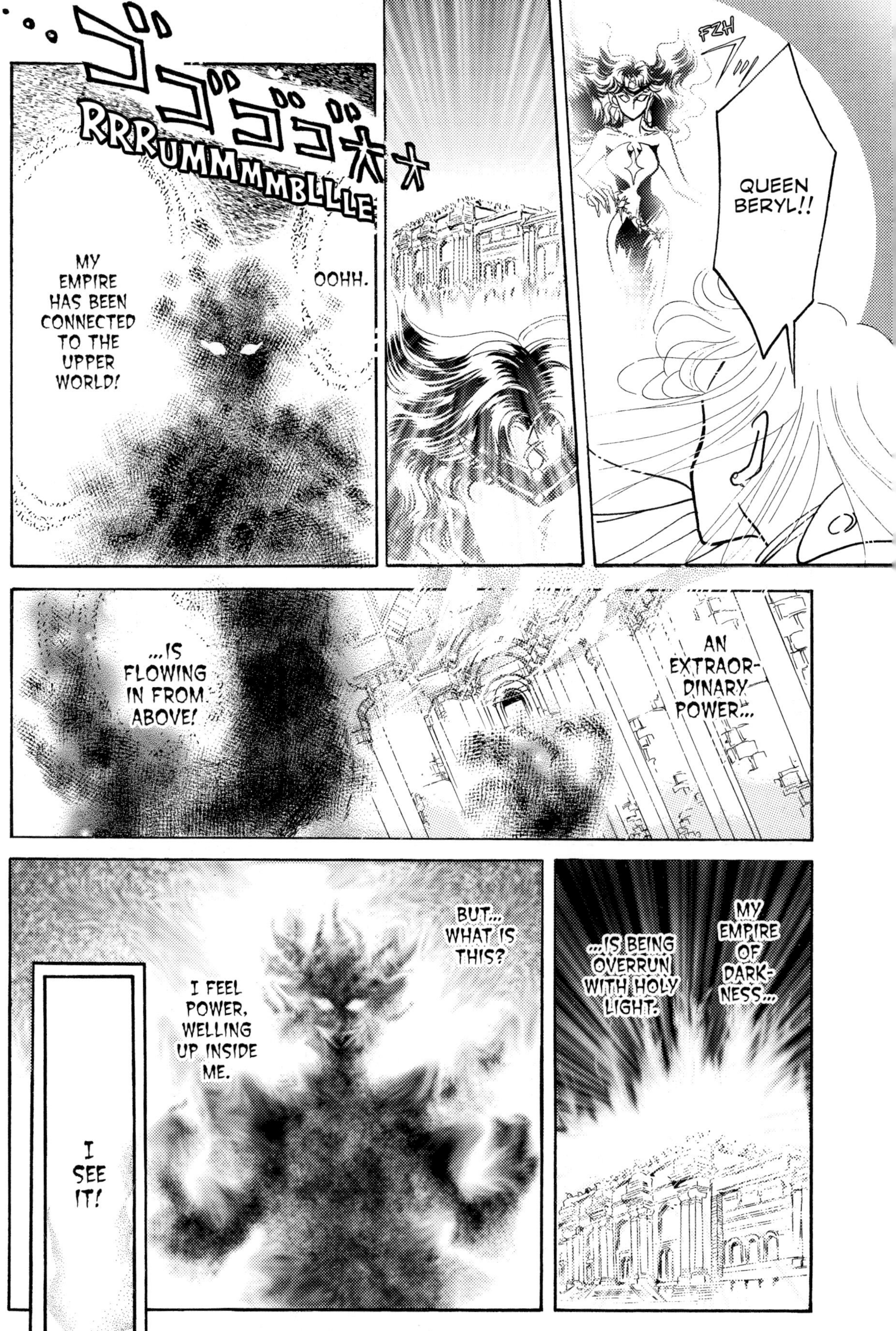
FZH
QUEEN BERYL!!
OOHH.
...ゴゴゴゴォォ
RRRUMMMMBLLLE
MY EMPIRE HAS BEEN CONNECTED TO THE UPPER WORLD!
AN EXTRAOR-DINARY POWER...
...IS FLOWING IN FROM ABOVE!
MY EMPIRE OF DARK-NESS...
...IS BEING OVERRUN WITH HOLY LIGHT.
BUT... WHAT IS THIS?
I FEEL POWER, WELLING UP INSIDE ME.
I SEE IT!

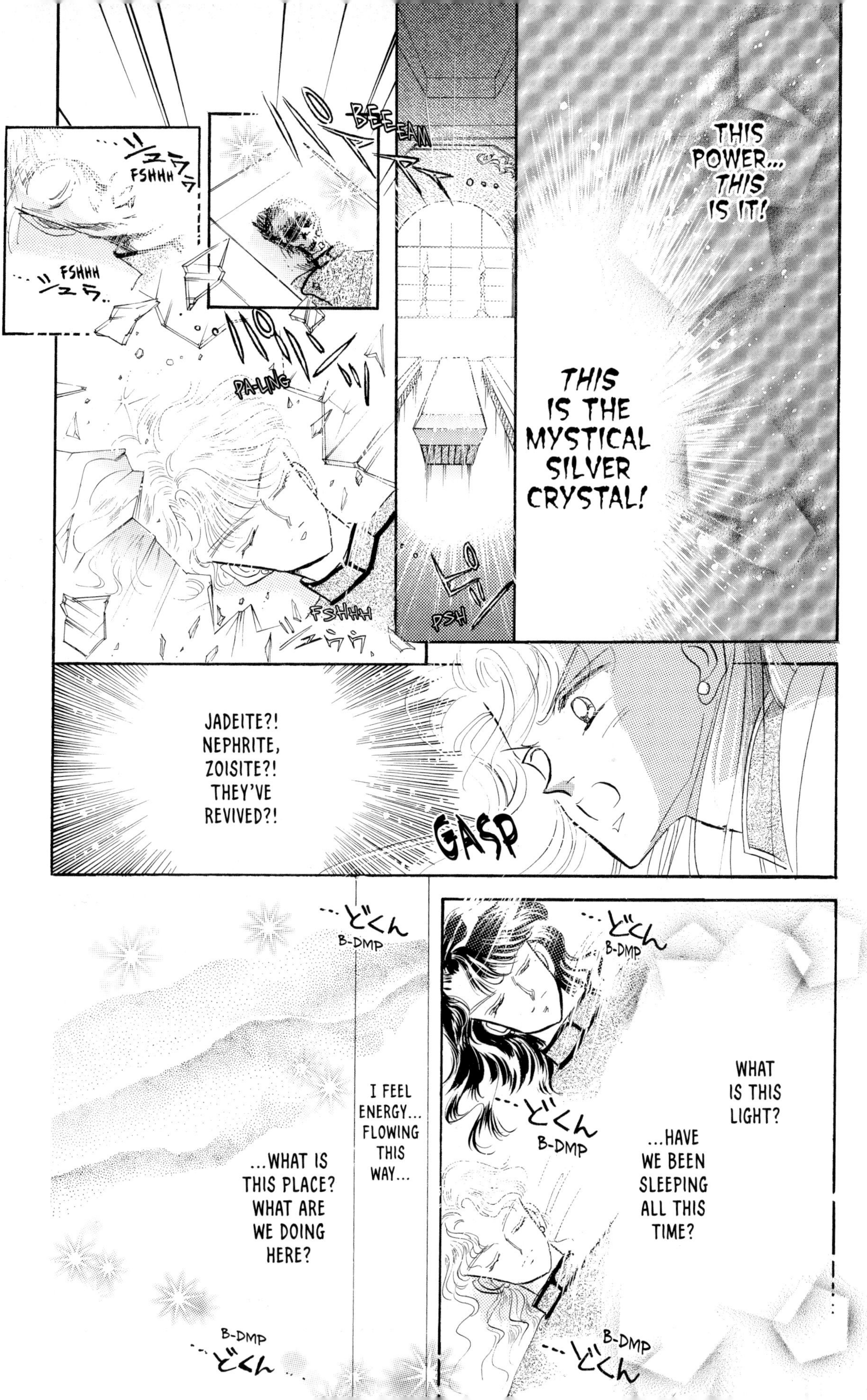
THIS POWER... THIS IS IT!
THIS IS THE MYSTICAL SILVER CRYSTAL!
PSH
BEEEAM
FSHHH
FSHHH
PA-LING
FSHHH
GASP
JADEITE?! NEPHRITE, ZOISITE?! THEY'VE REVIVED?!
…どくん
B-DMP
WHAT IS THIS LIGHT?
…どくん
B-DMP
...HAVE WE BEEN SLEEPING ALL THIS TIME?
B-DMP
…どくん
…どくん
B-DMP
I FEEL ENERGY... FLOWING THIS WAY...
...WHAT IS THIS PLACE? WHAT ARE WE DOING HERE?
B-DMP
…どくん…

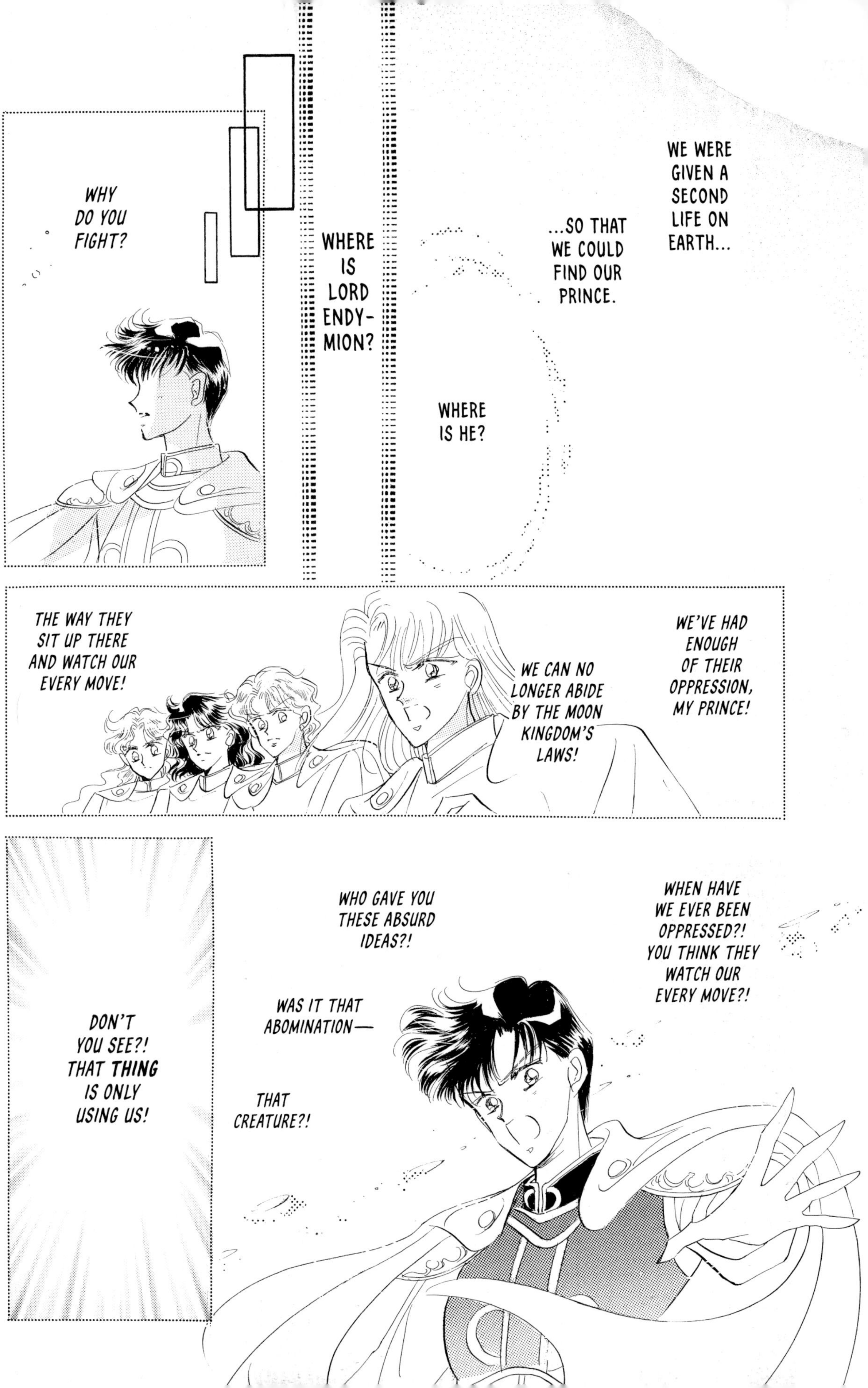
WE WERE GIVEN A SECOND LIFE ON EARTH...
...SO THAT WE COULD FIND OUR PRINCE.
WHERE IS HE?
WHERE IS LORD ENDY-MION?
WHY DO YOU FIGHT?
WE'VE HAD ENOUGH OF THEIR OPPRESSION, MY PRINCE!
WE CAN NO LONGER ABIDE BY THE MOON KINGDOM'S LAWS!
THE WAY THEY SIT UP THERE AND WATCH OUR EVERY MOVE!
WHEN HAVE WE EVER BEEN OPPRESSED?! YOU THINK THEY WATCH OUR EVERY MOVE?!
WHO GAVE YOU THESE ABSURD IDEAS?!
WAS IT THAT ABOMINATION—
THAT CREATURE?!
DON'T YOU SEE?! THAT **THING** IS ONLY USING US!

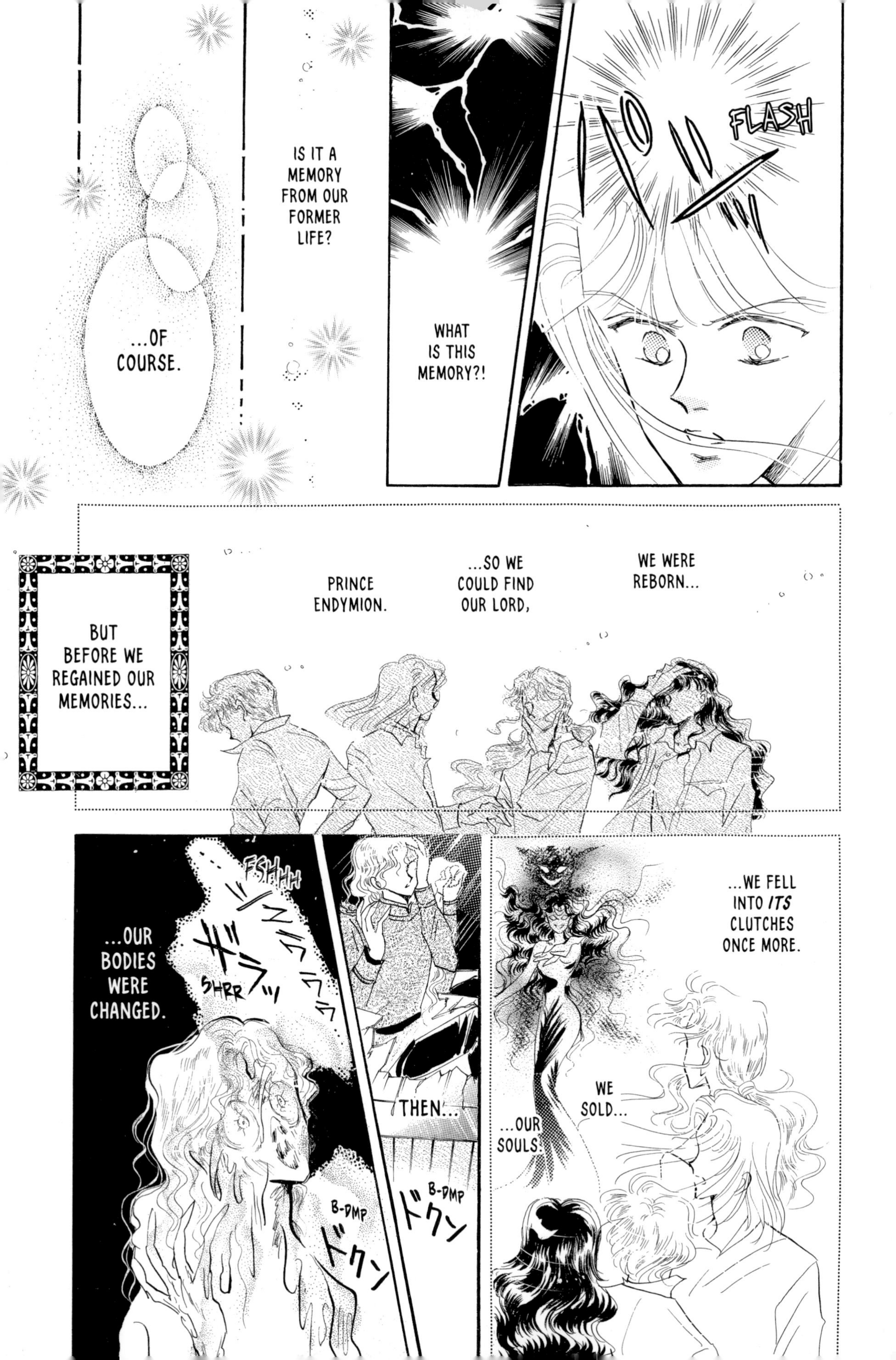
FLASH
WHAT IS THIS MEMORY?!
IS IT A MEMORY FROM OUR FORMER LIFE?
...OF COURSE.
WE WERE REBORN...
...SO WE COULD FIND OUR LORD,
PRINCE ENDYMION.
BUT BEFORE WE REGAINED OUR MEMORIES...
...WE FELL INTO *ITS* CLUTCHES ONCE MORE.
WE SOLD...
...OUR SOULS.
THEN...
B-DMP
ドクン
...OUR BODIES WERE CHANGED.
FSHHH
SHRR
B-DMP
ドクン

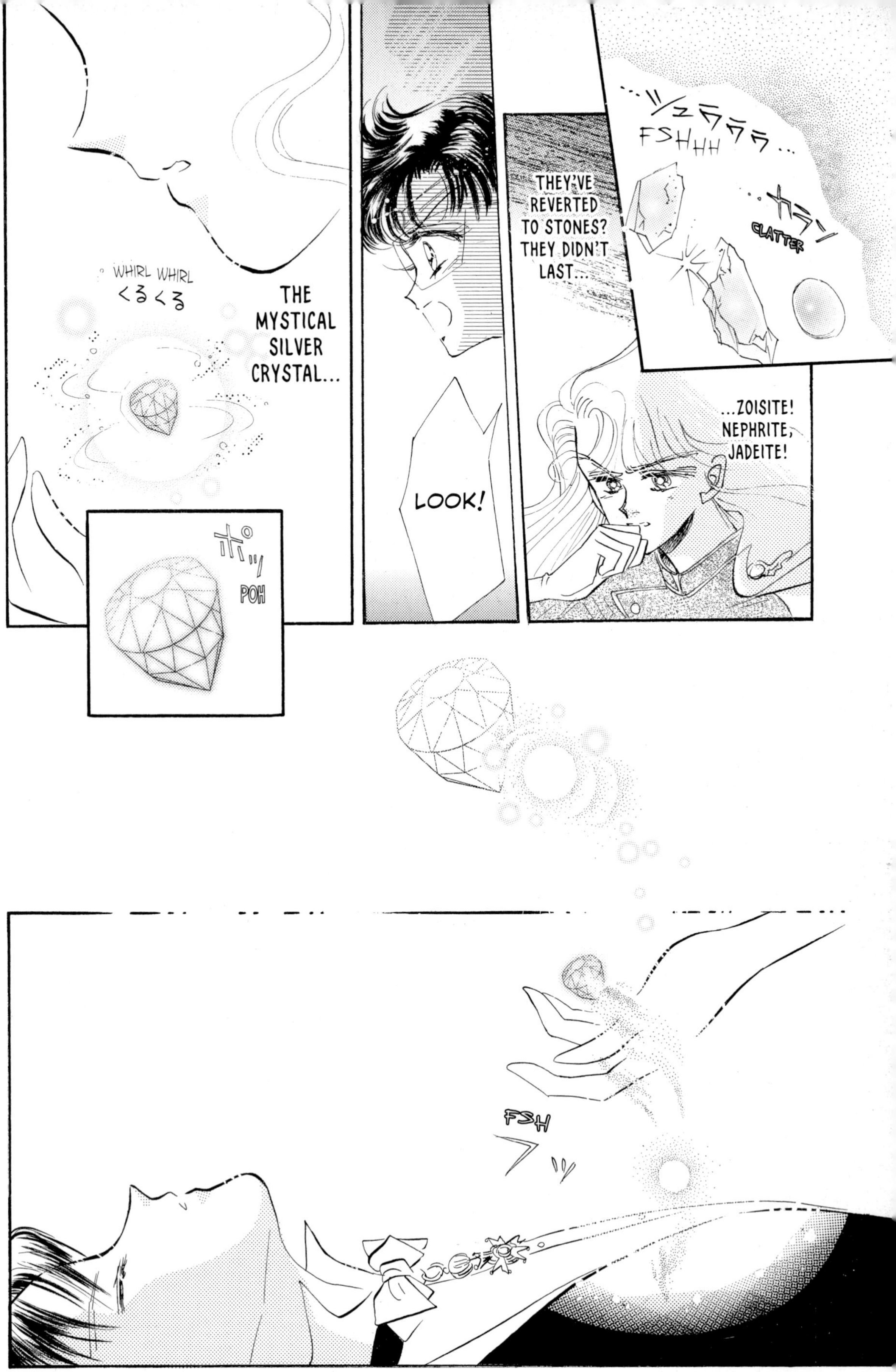
…シュラララ…
FSHHH
…カラン
CLATTER
THEY'VE REVERTED TO STONES? THEY DIDN'T LAST…
…ZOISITE! NEPHRITE, JADEITE!
LOOK!
THE MYSTICAL SILVER CRYSTAL…
WHIRL WHIRL
くるくる
ポッ
POH
FSH

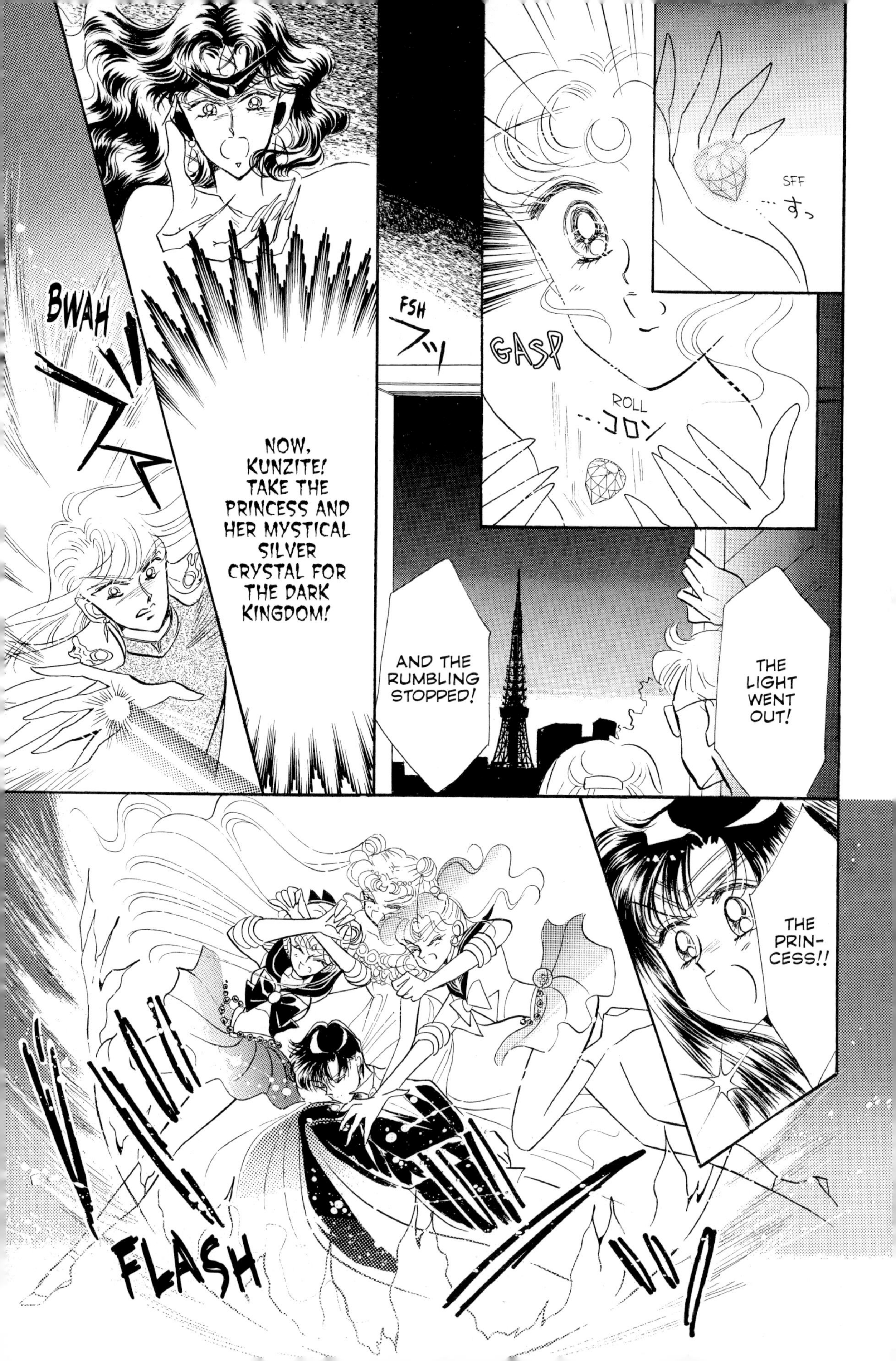
SFF
すっ
GASP
ROLL
コロン
FSH
ブッ
THE LIGHT WENT OUT!
AND THE RUMBLING STOPPED!
BWAH
NOW, KUNZITE! TAKE THE PRINCESS AND HER MYSTICAL SILVER CRYSTAL FOR THE DARK KINGDOM!
THE PRIN-CESS!!
FLASH

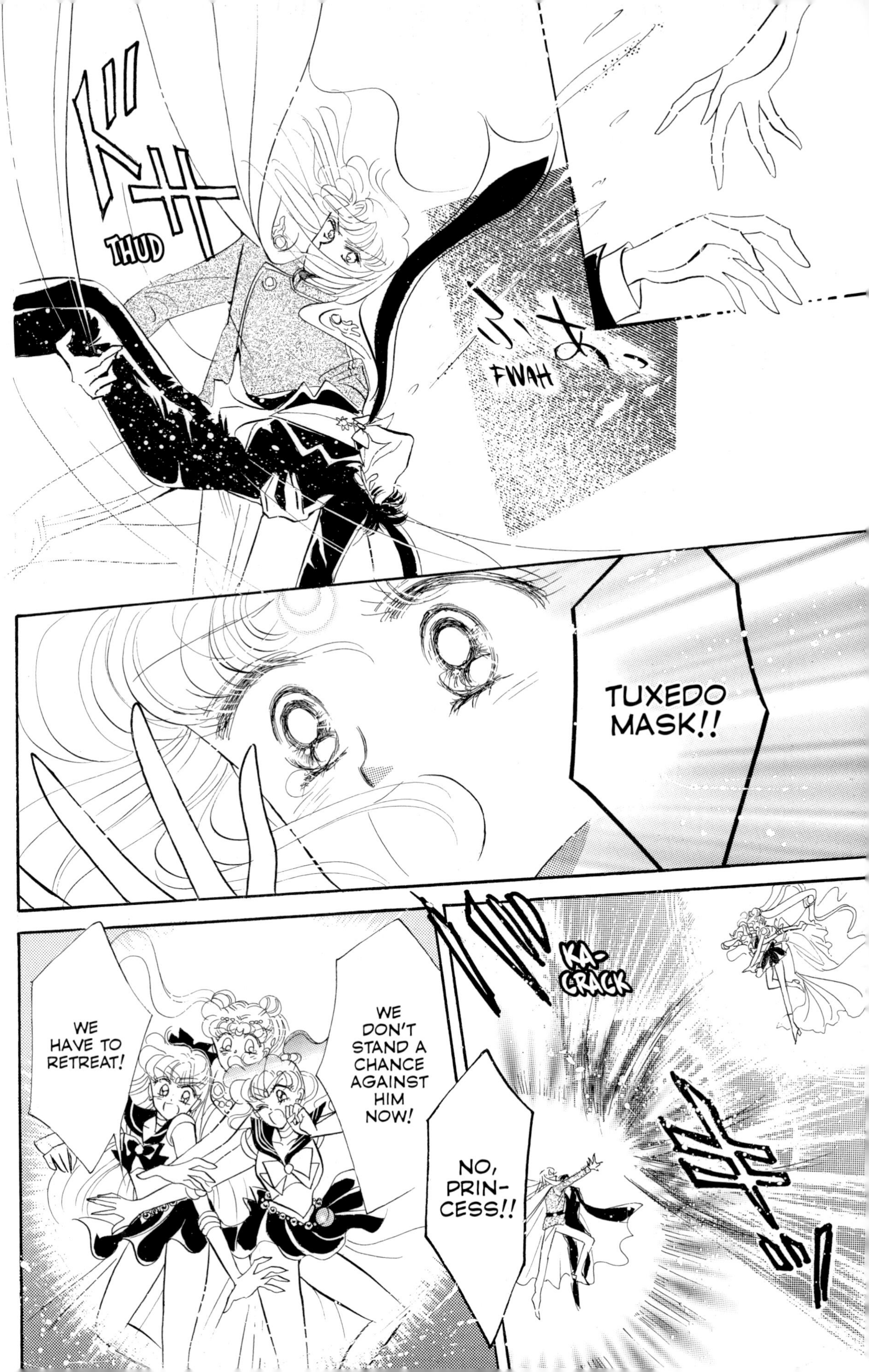
FWAH
THUD
TUXEDO MASK!!
KA-CRACK
NO, PRINCESS!!
WE DON'T STAND A CHANCE AGAINST HIM NOW!
WE HAVE TO RETREAT!

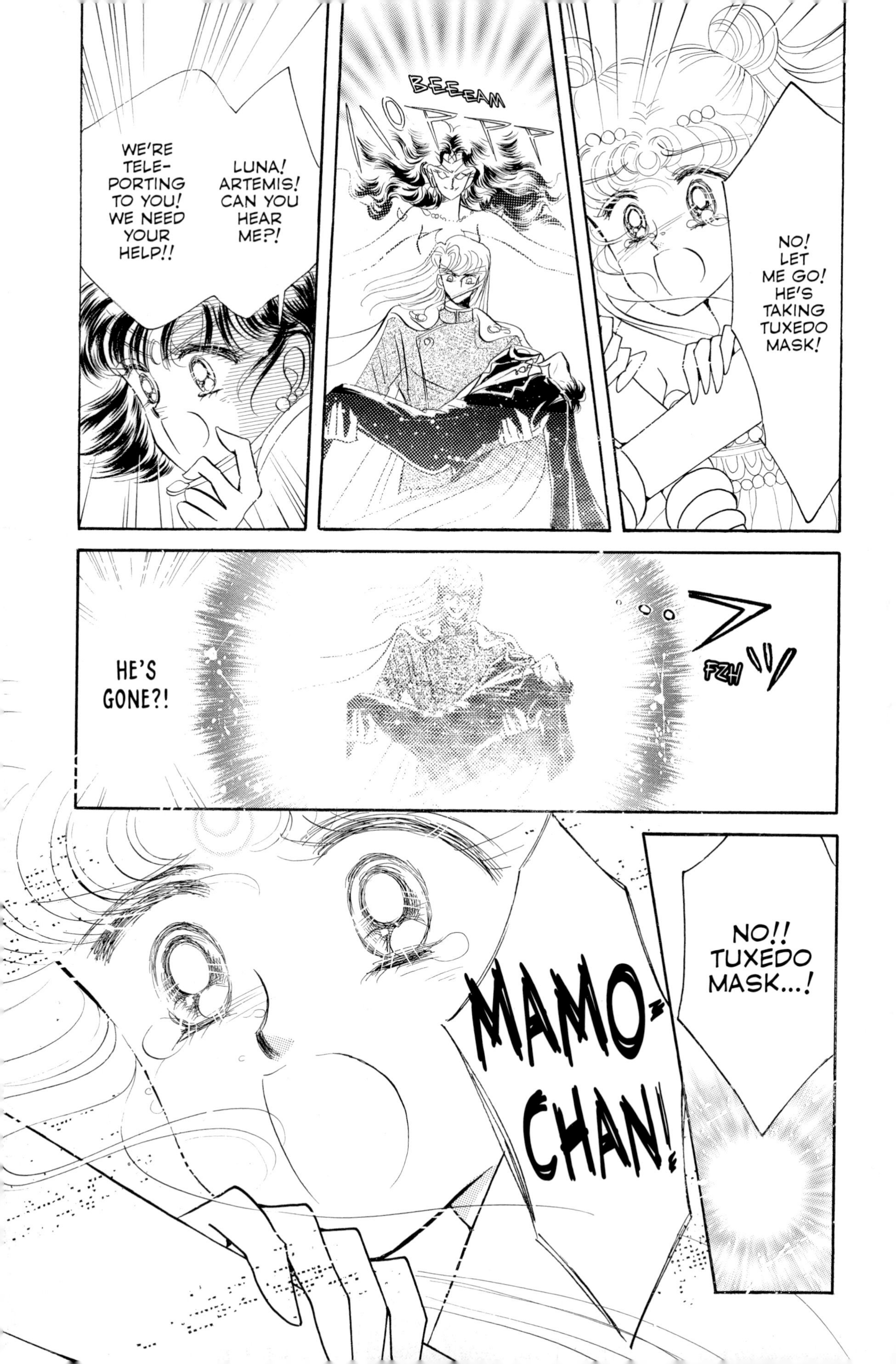
NO! LET ME GO! HE'S TAKING TUXEDO MASK!
BEEEAM
LUNA! ARTEMIS! CAN YOU HEAR ME?!
WE'RE TELE-PORTING TO YOU! WE NEED YOUR HELP!!
FZH
HE'S GONE?!
NO!! TUXEDO MASK...!
MAMO-CHAN!

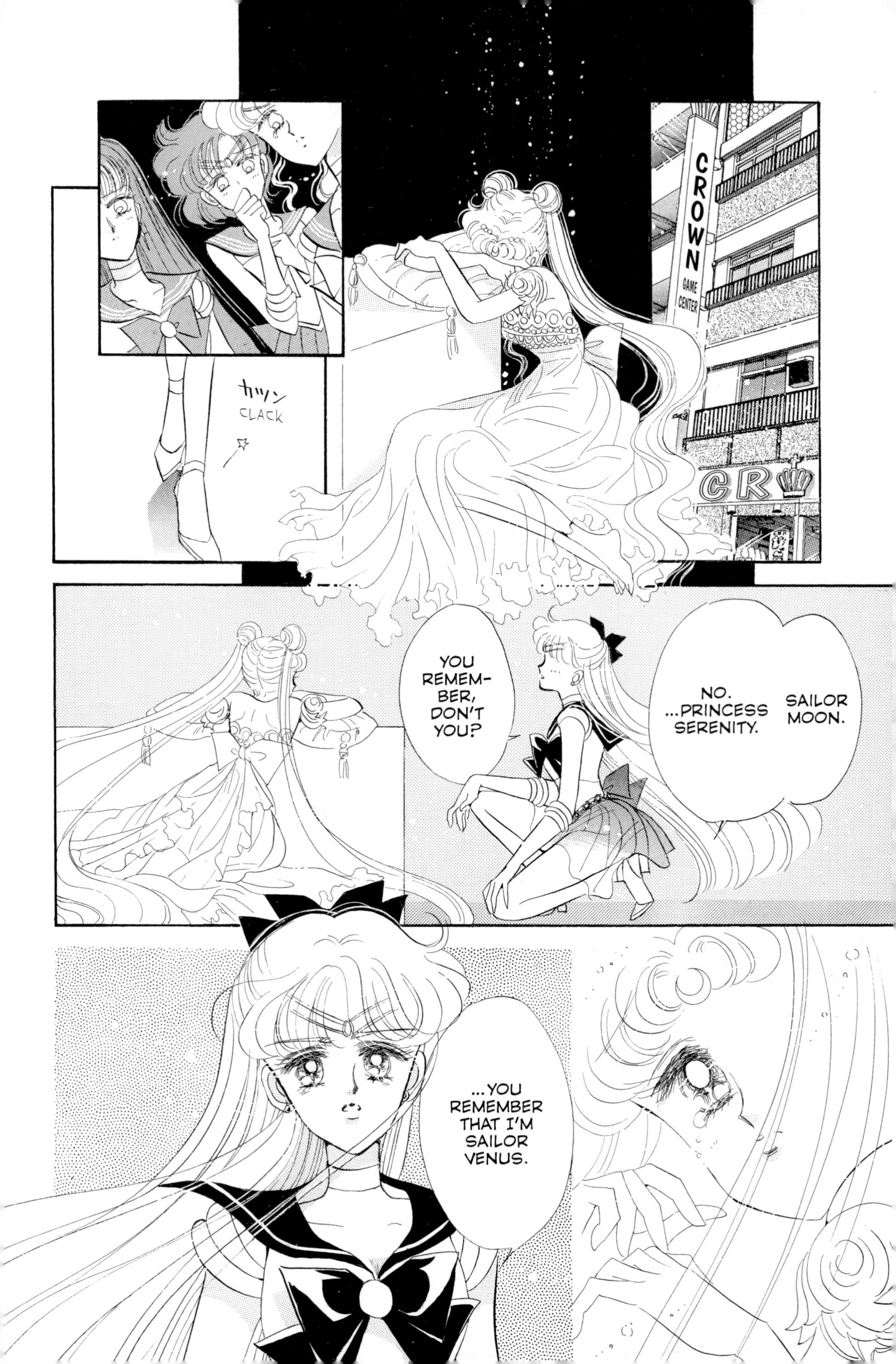

カツン
CLACK
SAILOR MOON.
NO. ...PRINCESS SERENITY.
YOU REMEMBER, DON'T YOU?
...YOU REMEMBER THAT I'M SAILOR VENUS.
CROWN GAME CENTER

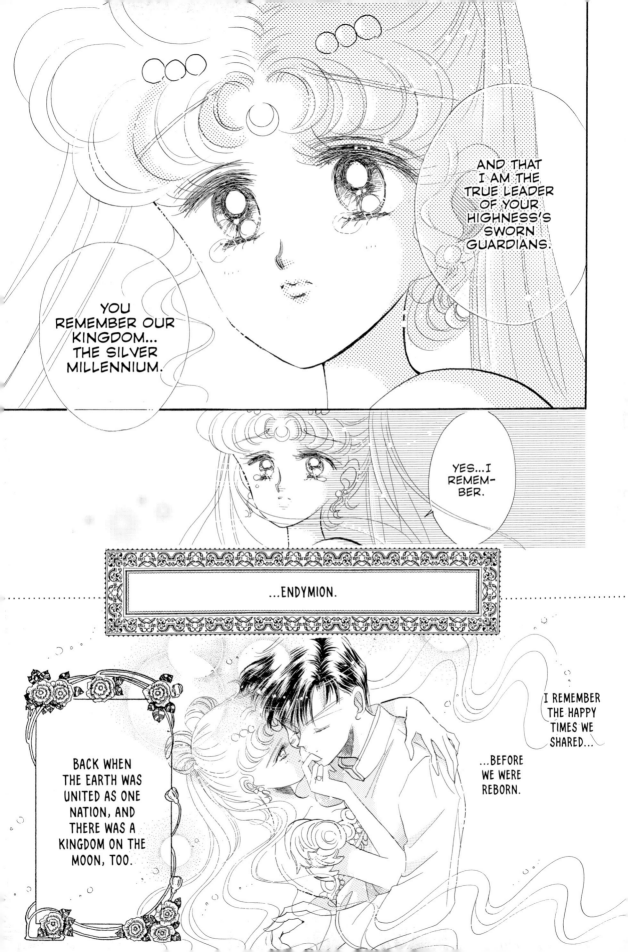

AND THAT I AM THE TRUE LEADER OF YOUR HIGHNESS'S SWORN GUARDIANS.

YOU REMEMBER OUR KINGDOM... THE SILVER MILLENNIUM.

YES...I REMEM-BER.

...ENDYMION.

I REMEMBER THE HAPPY TIMES WE SHARED...

...BEFORE WE WERE REBORN.

BACK WHEN THE EARTH WAS UNITED AS ONE NATION, AND THERE WAS A KINGDOM ON THE MOON, TOO.

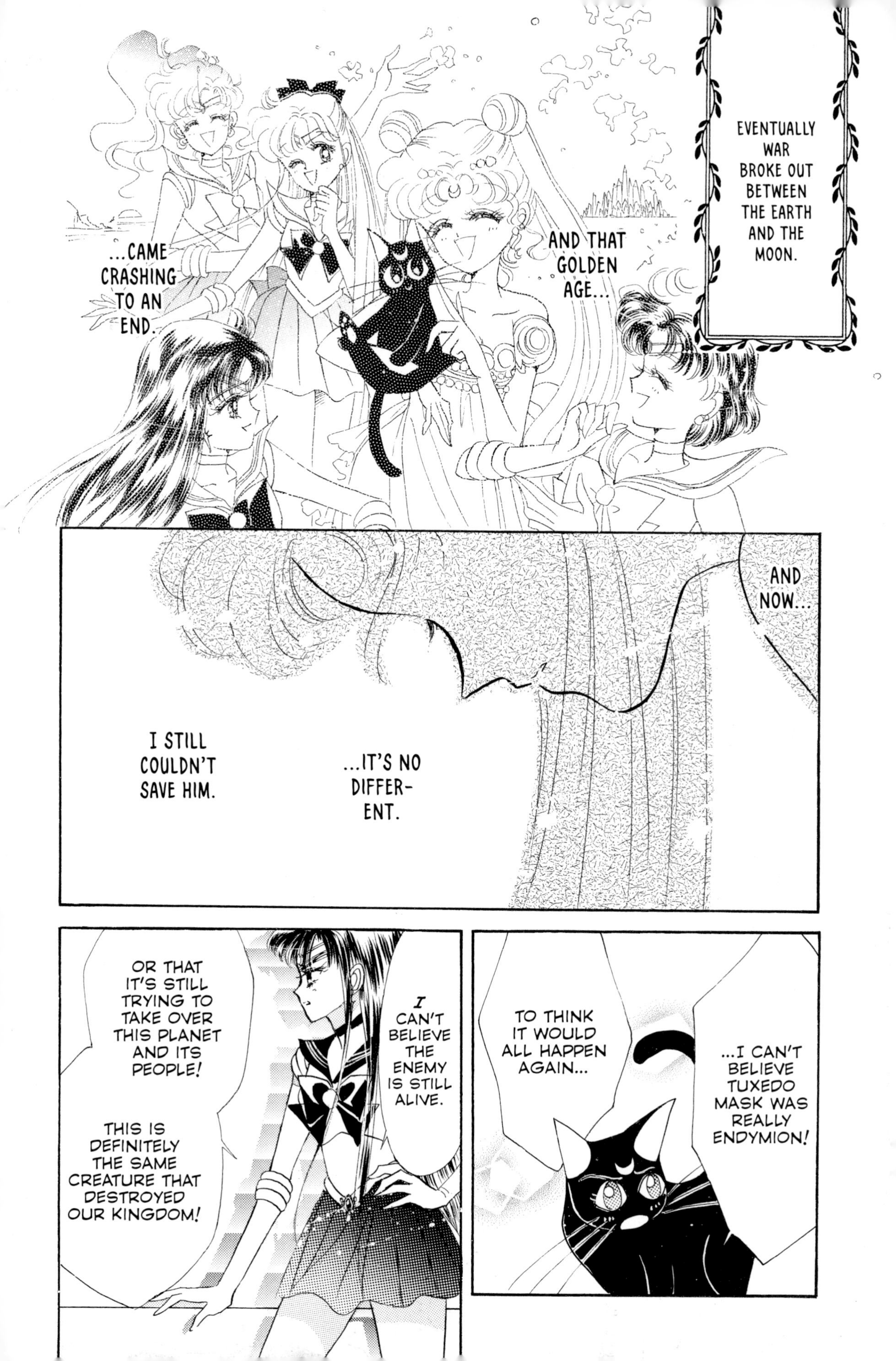

EVENTUALLY WAR BROKE OUT BETWEEN THE EARTH AND THE MOON.
AND THAT GOLDEN AGE...
...CAME CRASHING TO AN END.
AND NOW...
...IT'S NO DIFFER-ENT.
I STILL COULDN'T SAVE HIM.
...I CAN'T BELIEVE TUXEDO MASK WAS REALLY ENDYMION!
TO THINK IT WOULD ALL HAPPEN AGAIN...
*I* CAN'T BELIEVE THE ENEMY IS STILL ALIVE.
OR THAT IT'S STILL TRYING TO TAKE OVER THIS PLANET AND ITS PEOPLE!
THIS IS DEFINITELY THE SAME CREATURE THAT DESTROYED OUR KINGDOM!

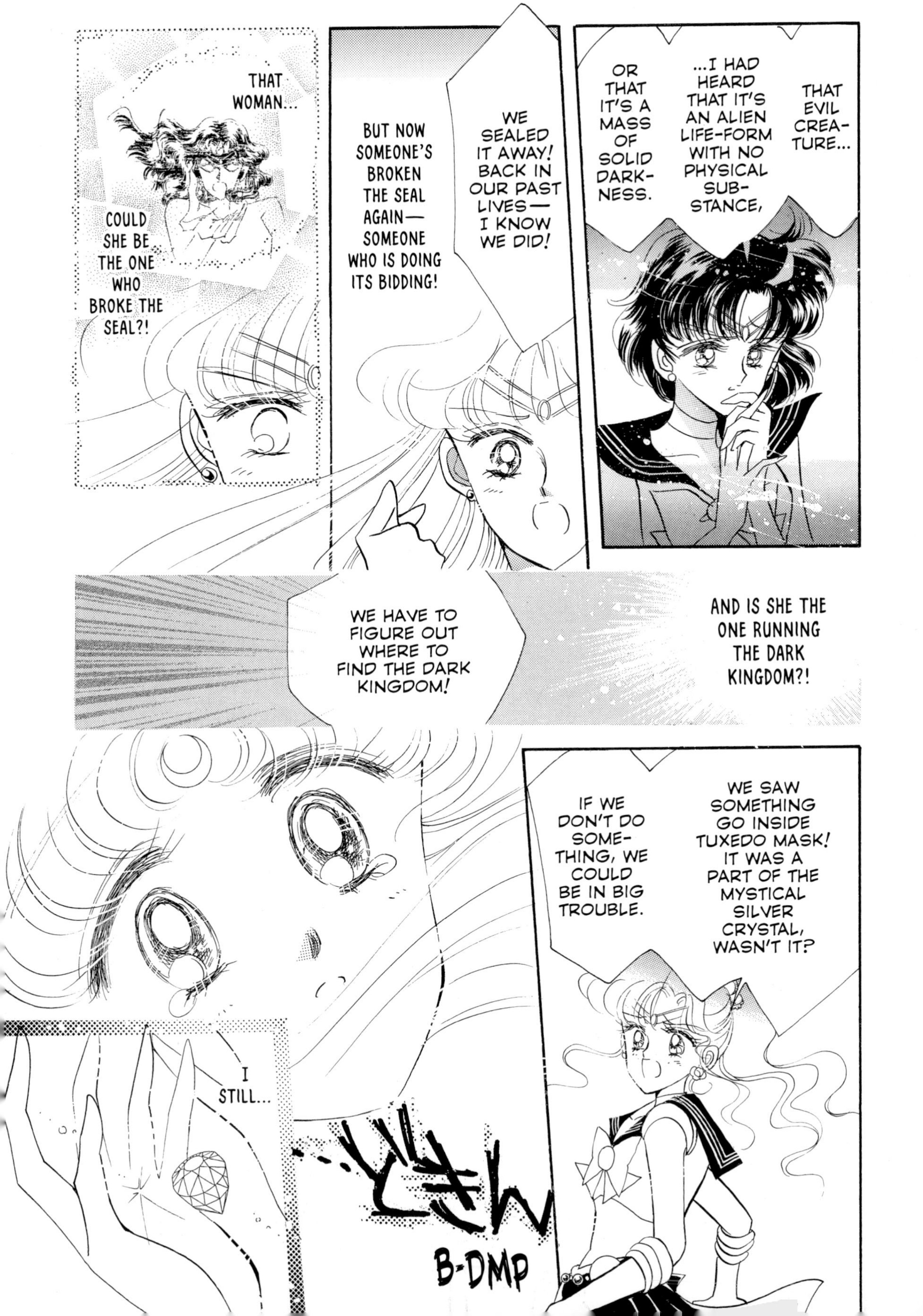
THAT EVIL CREATURE...
...I HAD HEARD THAT IT'S AN ALIEN LIFE-FORM WITH NO PHYSICAL SUBSTANCE,
OR THAT IT'S A MASS OF SOLID DARKNESS.
WE SEALED IT AWAY! BACK IN OUR PAST LIVES—I KNOW WE DID!
BUT NOW SOMEONE'S BROKEN THE SEAL AGAIN—SOMEONE WHO IS DOING ITS BIDDING!
THAT WOMAN...
COULD SHE BE THE ONE WHO BROKE THE SEAL?!
AND IS SHE THE ONE RUNNING THE DARK KINGDOM?!
WE HAVE TO FIGURE OUT WHERE TO FIND THE DARK KINGDOM!
WE SAW SOMETHING GO INSIDE TUXEDO MASK! IT WAS A PART OF THE MYSTICAL SILVER CRYSTAL, WASN'T IT?
IF WE DON'T DO SOMETHING, WE COULD BE IN BIG TROUBLE.
どきん
B-DMP
I STILL...

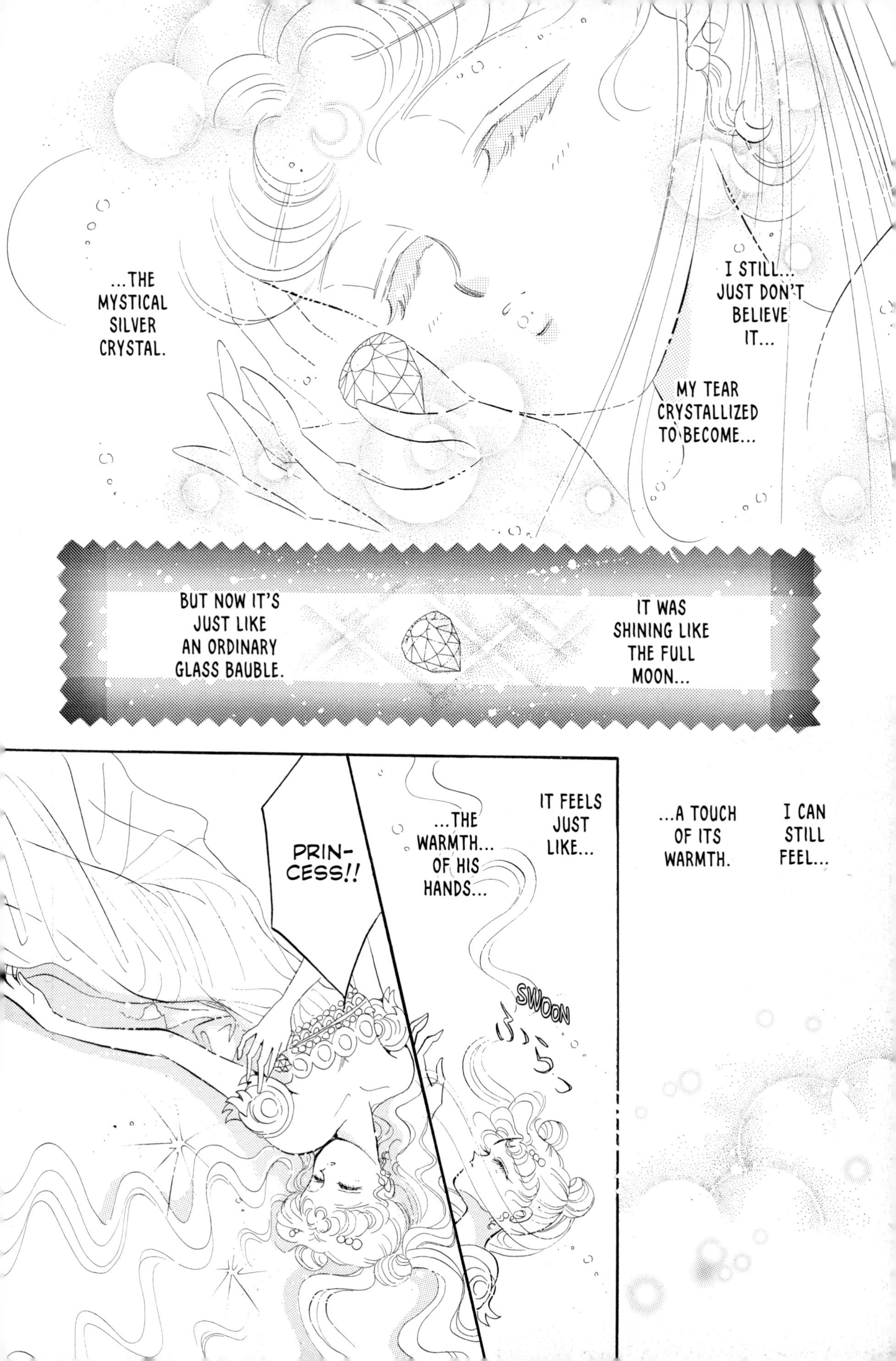
I STILL... JUST DON'T BELIEVE IT...
MY TEAR CRYSTALLIZED TO BECOME...
...THE MYSTICAL SILVER CRYSTAL.
IT WAS SHINING LIKE THE FULL MOON...
BUT NOW IT'S JUST LIKE AN ORDINARY GLASS BAUBLE.
I CAN STILL FEEL...
...A TOUCH OF ITS WARMTH.
IT FEELS JUST LIKE...
...THE WARMTH... OF HIS HANDS...
SWOON
PRIN-CESS!!

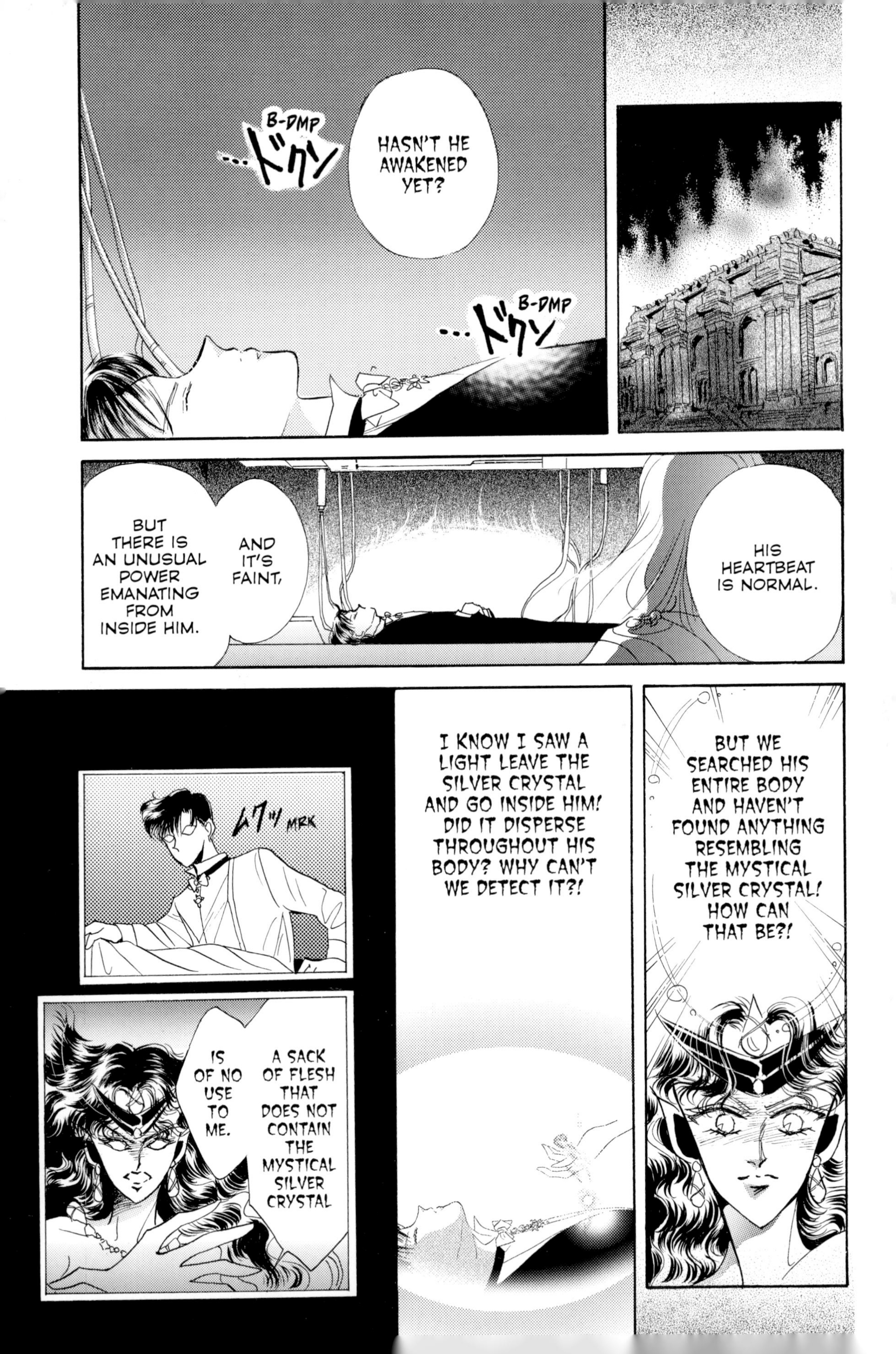
HASN'T HE AWAKENED YET?
B-DMP ...ドクン
B-DMP ...ドクン
HIS HEARTBEAT IS NORMAL.
AND IT'S FAINT,
BUT THERE IS AN UNUSUAL POWER EMANATING FROM INSIDE HIM.
BUT WE SEARCHED HIS ENTIRE BODY AND HAVEN'T FOUND ANYTHING RESEMBLING THE MYSTICAL SILVER CRYSTAL! HOW CAN THAT BE?!
I KNOW I SAW A LIGHT LEAVE THE SILVER CRYSTAL AND GO INSIDE HIM! DID IT DISPERSE THROUGHOUT HIS BODY? WHY CAN'T WE DETECT IT?!
ムクッ MRK
A SACK OF FLESH THAT DOES NOT CONTAIN THE MYSTICAL SILVER CRYSTAL
IS OF NO USE TO ME.

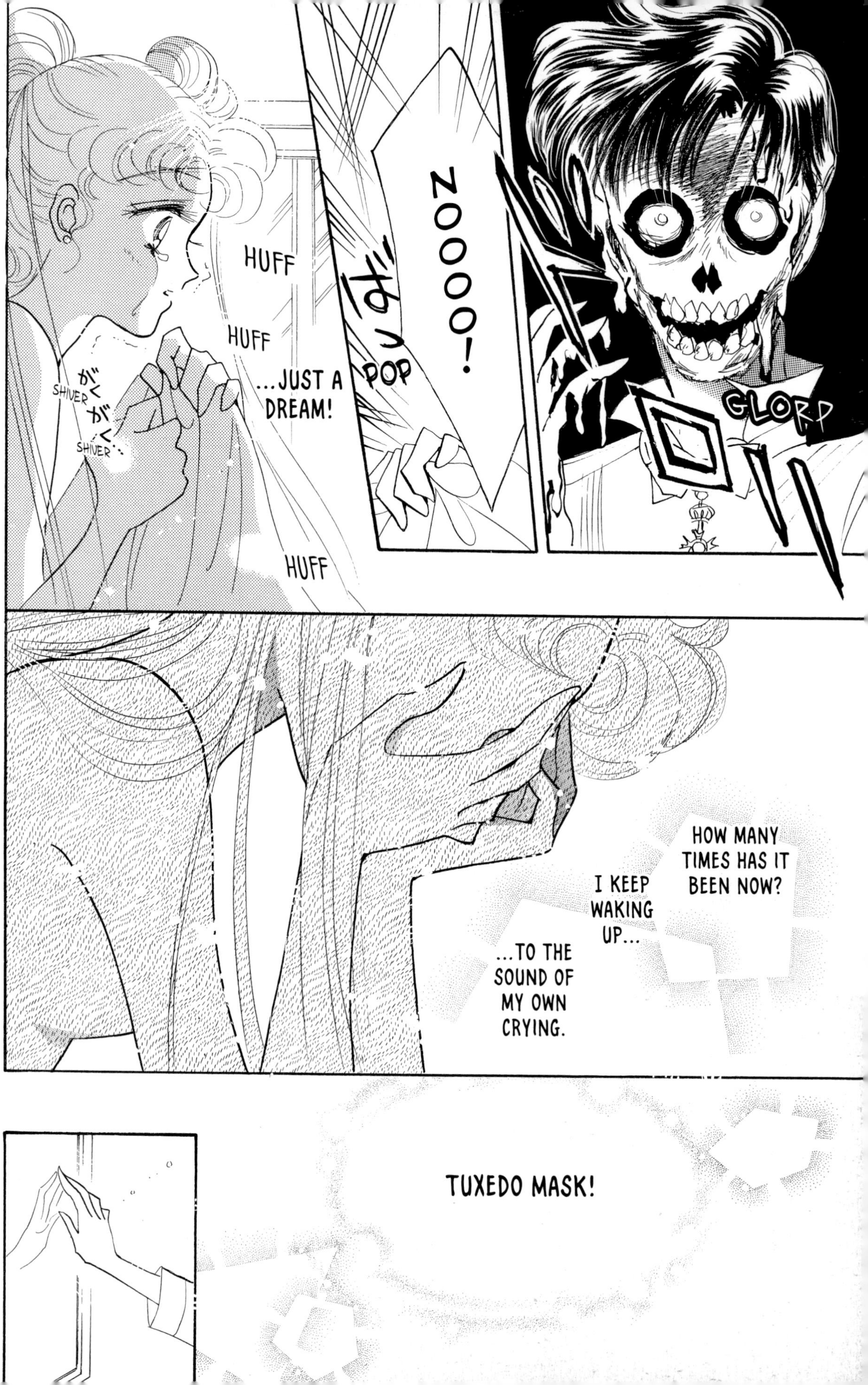
GLORP
NOOOOO!
POP
HUFF
HUFF
...JUST A DREAM!
HUFF
がく SHIVER
がく SHIVER
HOW MANY TIMES HAS IT BEEN NOW?
I KEEP WAKING UP...
...TO THE SOUND OF MY OWN CRYING.
TUXEDO MASK!

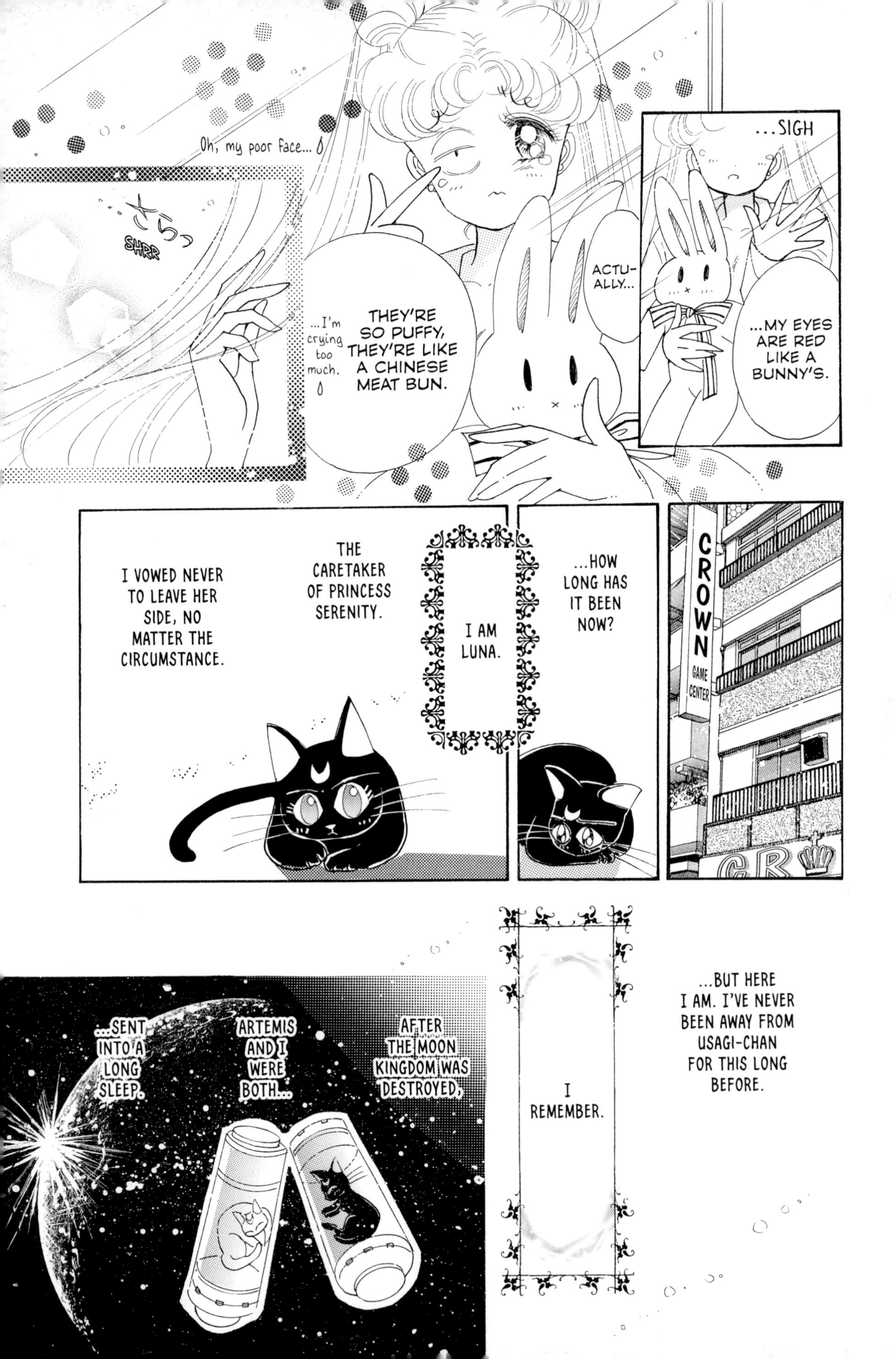
...SIGH
ACTU-ALLY...
...MY EYES ARE RED LIKE A BUNNY'S.
Oh, my poor face...
THEY'RE SO PUFFY, THEY'RE LIKE A CHINESE MEAT BUN.
...I'm crying too much.
SHRR
CROWN GAME CENTER
CR
...HOW LONG HAS IT BEEN NOW?
I AM LUNA.
THE CARETAKER OF PRINCESS SERENITY.
I VOWED NEVER TO LEAVE HER SIDE, NO MATTER THE CIRCUMSTANCE.
...BUT HERE I AM. I'VE NEVER BEEN AWAY FROM USAGI-CHAN FOR THIS LONG BEFORE.
I REMEMBER.
AFTER THE MOON KINGDOM WAS DESTROYED,
ARTEMIS AND I WERE BOTH...
...SENT INTO A LONG SLEEP.

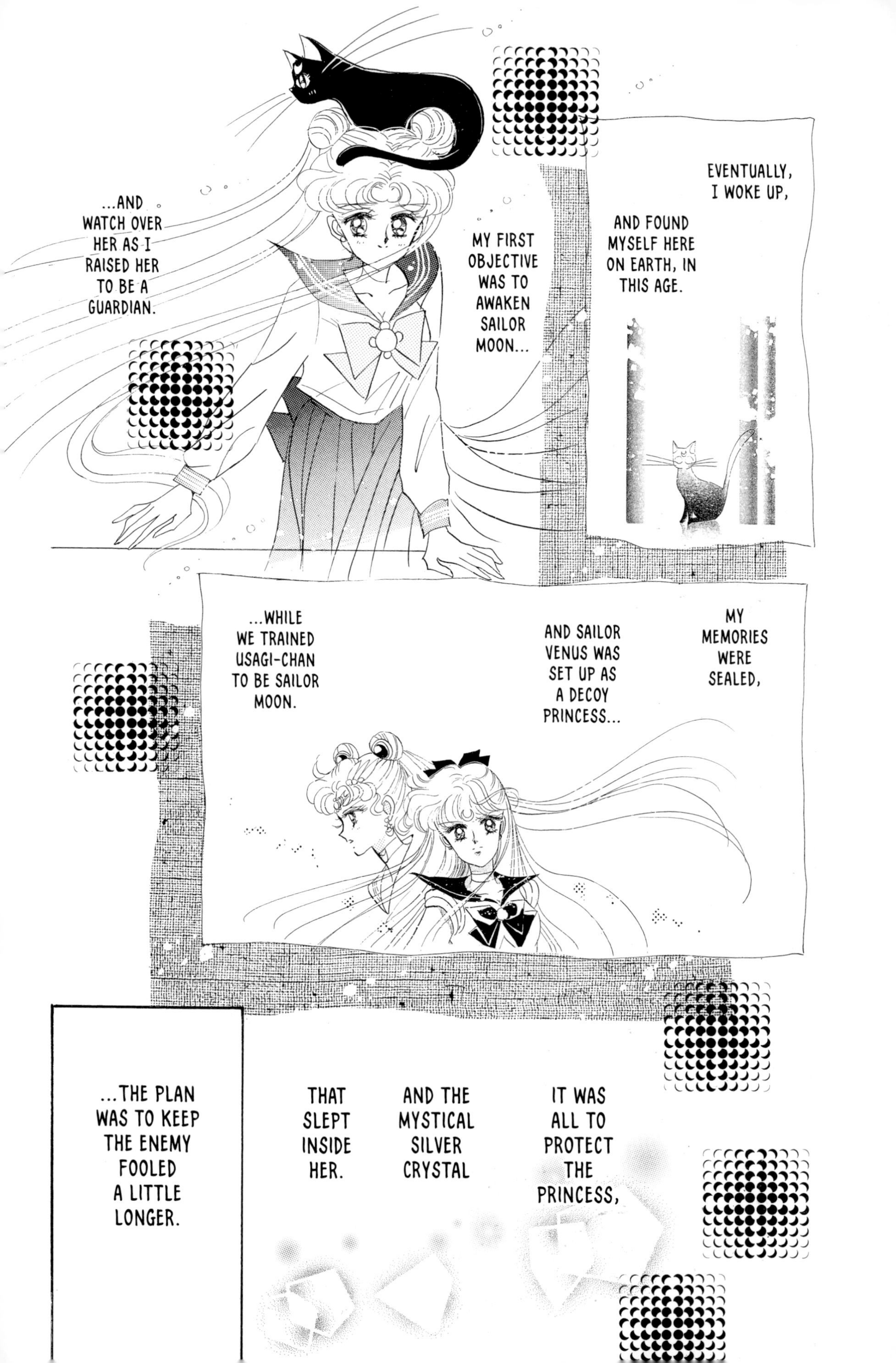
EVENTUALLY, I WOKE UP,
AND FOUND MYSELF HERE ON EARTH, IN THIS AGE.
MY FIRST OBJECTIVE WAS TO AWAKEN SAILOR MOON...
...AND WATCH OVER HER AS I RAISED HER TO BE A GUARDIAN.
MY MEMORIES WERE SEALED,
AND SAILOR VENUS WAS SET UP AS A DECOY PRINCESS...
...WHILE WE TRAINED USAGI-CHAN TO BE SAILOR MOON.
IT WAS ALL TO PROTECT THE PRINCESS,
AND THE MYSTICAL SILVER CRYSTAL
THAT SLEPT INSIDE HER.
...THE PLAN WAS TO KEEP THE ENEMY FOOLED A LITTLE LONGER.

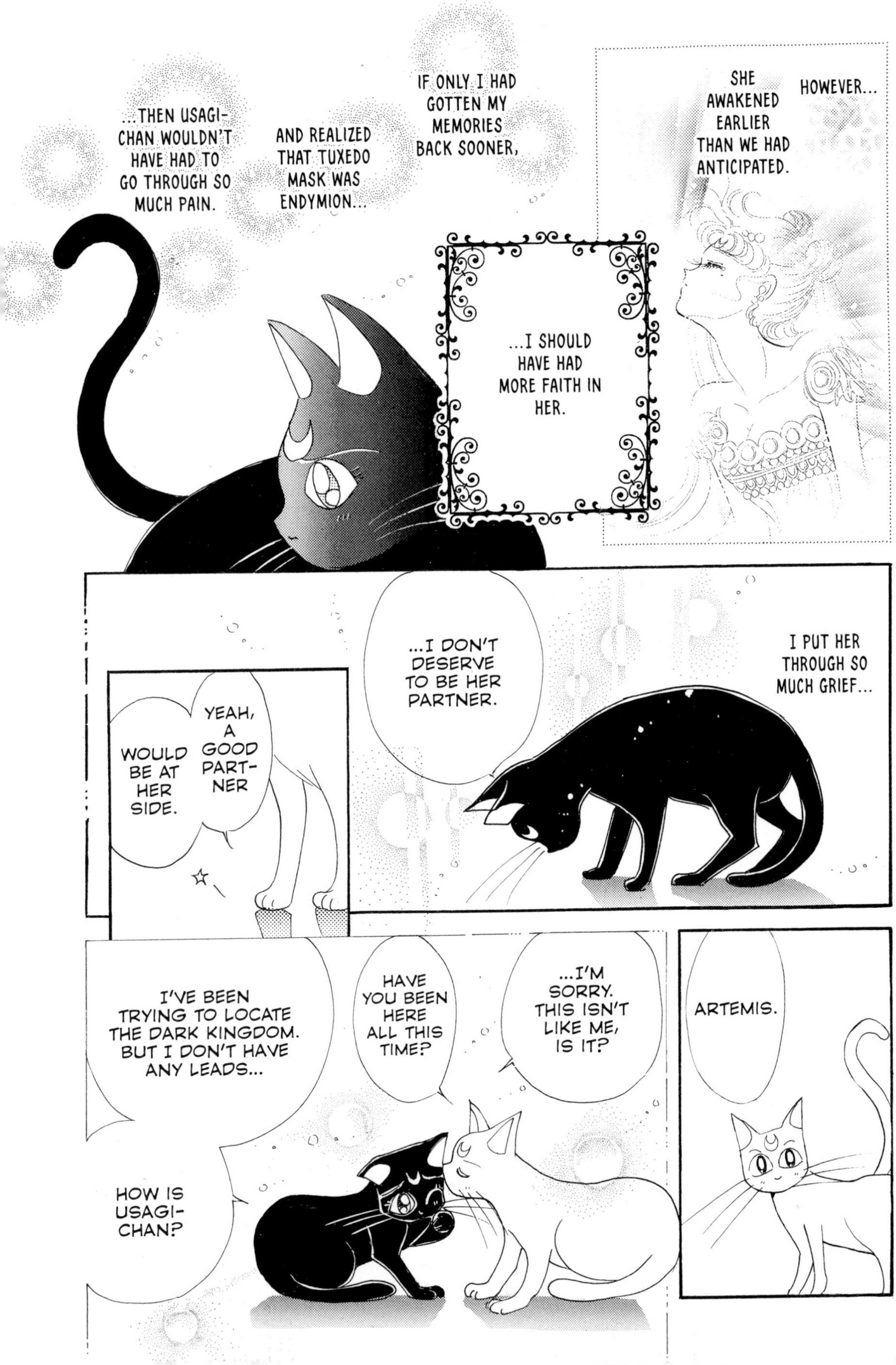
HOWEVER...
SHE AWAKENED EARLIER THAN WE HAD ANTICIPATED.
IF ONLY I HAD GOTTEN MY MEMORIES BACK SOONER,
AND REALIZED THAT TUXEDO MASK WAS ENDYMION...
...THEN USAGI-CHAN WOULDN'T HAVE HAD TO GO THROUGH SO MUCH PAIN.
...I SHOULD HAVE HAD MORE FAITH IN HER.
I PUT HER THROUGH SO MUCH GRIEF...
...I DON'T DESERVE TO BE HER PARTNER.
YEAH, A GOOD PARTNER
WOULD BE AT HER SIDE.
ARTEMIS.
...I'M SORRY. THIS ISN'T LIKE ME, IS IT?
HAVE YOU BEEN HERE ALL THIS TIME?
I'VE BEEN TRYING TO LOCATE THE DARK KINGDOM. BUT I DON'T HAVE ANY LEADS...
HOW IS USAGI-CHAN?

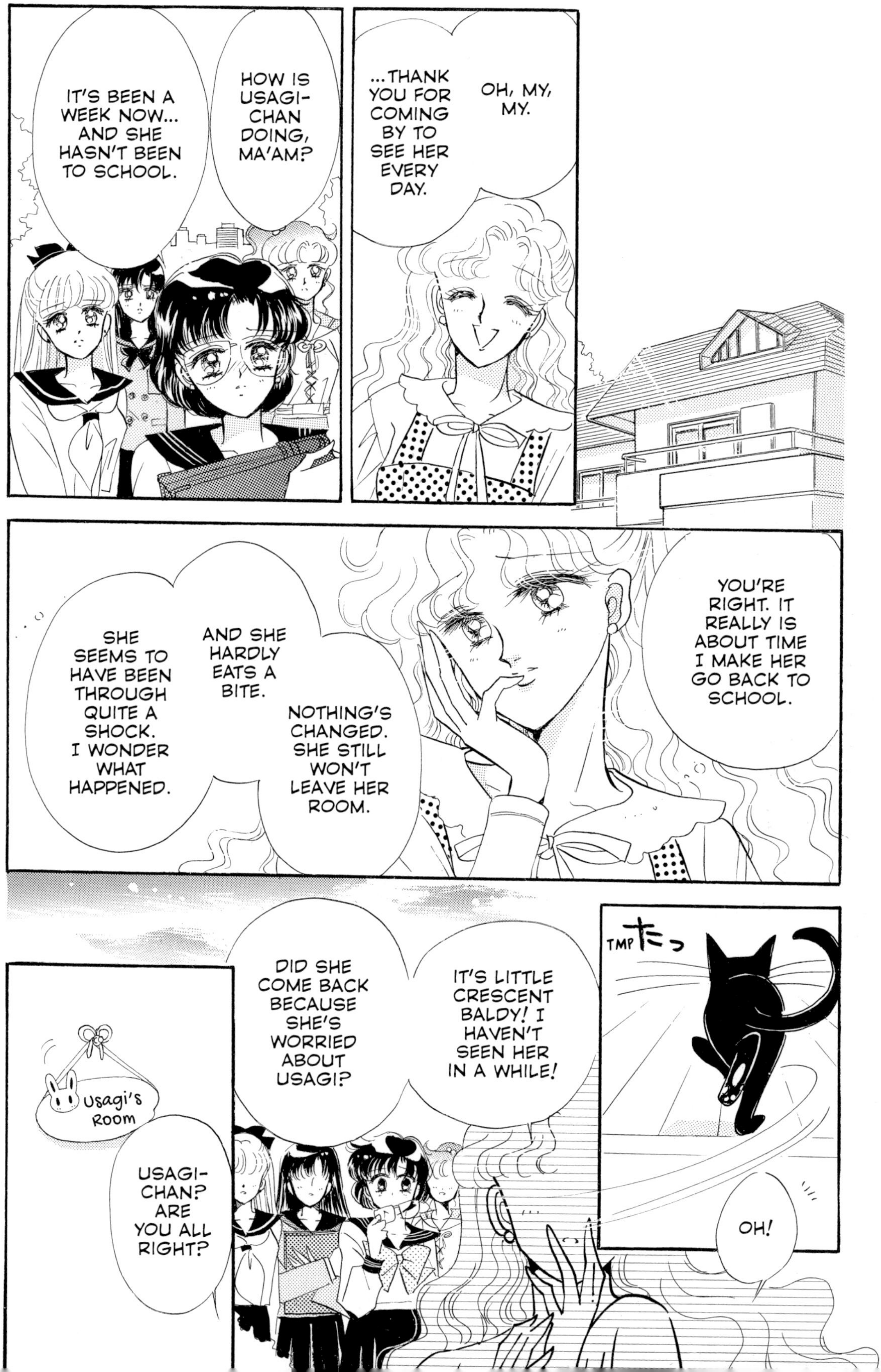
OH, MY, MY.
...THANK YOU FOR COMING BY TO SEE HER EVERY DAY.
HOW IS USAGI-CHAN DOING, MA'AM?
IT'S BEEN A WEEK NOW... AND SHE HASN'T BEEN TO SCHOOL.
YOU'RE RIGHT. IT REALLY IS ABOUT TIME I MAKE HER GO BACK TO SCHOOL.
NOTHING'S CHANGED. SHE STILL WON'T LEAVE HER ROOM.
AND SHE HARDLY EATS A BITE.
SHE SEEMS TO HAVE BEEN THROUGH QUITE A SHOCK. I WONDER WHAT HAPPENED.
TMP たっ
OH!
IT'S LITTLE CRESCENT BALDY! I HAVEN'T SEEN HER IN A WHILE!
DID SHE COME BACK BECAUSE SHE'S WORRIED ABOUT USAGI?
Usagi's Room
USAGI-CHAN? ARE YOU ALL RIGHT?

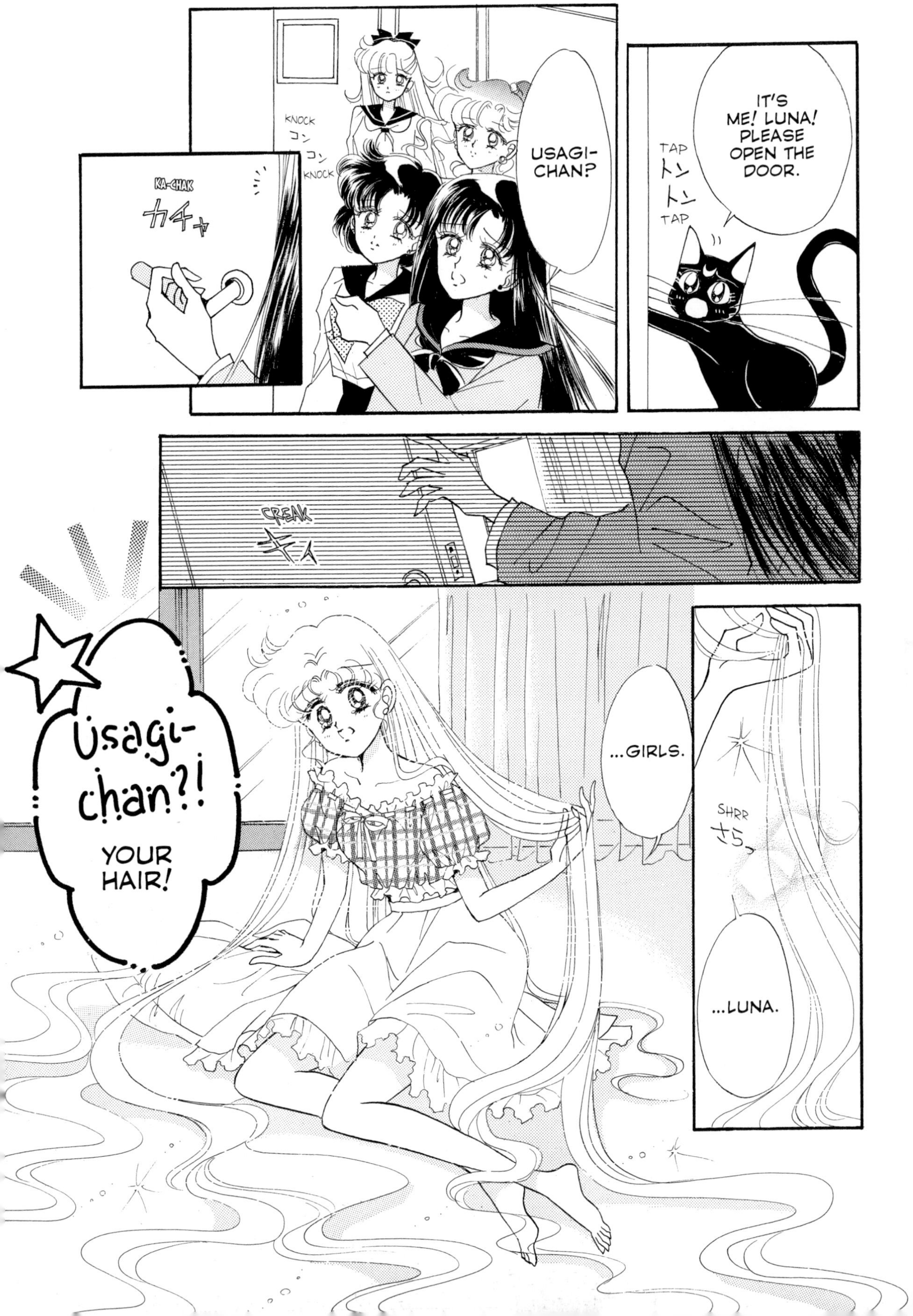
TAP
トン
トン
TAP
IT'S ME! LUNA! PLEASE OPEN THE DOOR.
KNOCK
コン
コン
KNOCK
USAGI-CHAN?
KA-CHAK
カチャ
CREAK
キィ
SHRR
さらっ
...LUNA.
...GIRLS.
Usagi-chan?!
YOUR HAIR!

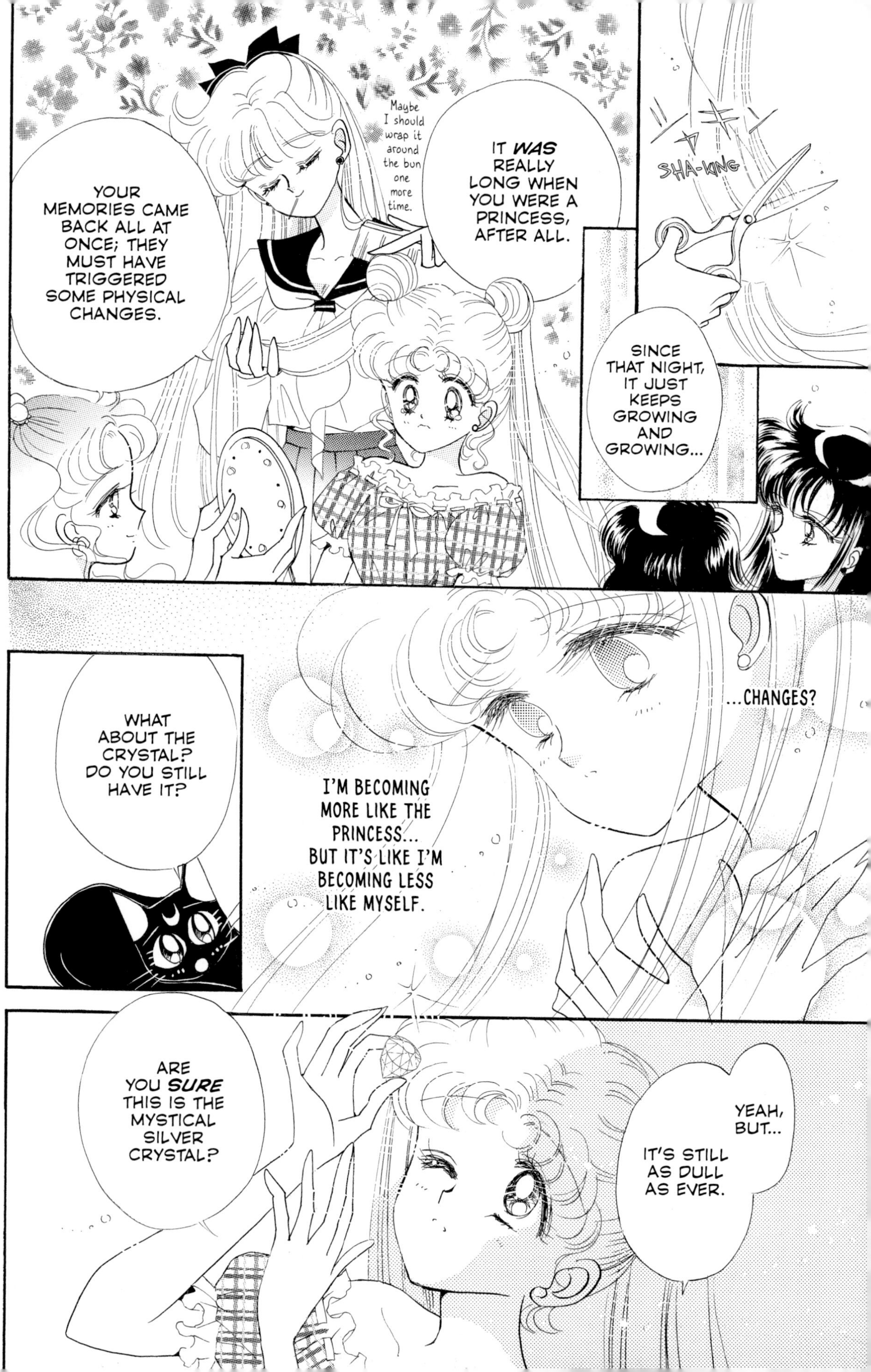
SHA-KING
SINCE THAT NIGHT, IT JUST KEEPS GROWING AND GROWING...
IT *WAS* REALLY LONG WHEN YOU WERE A PRINCESS, AFTER ALL.
Maybe I should wrap it around the bun one more time.
YOUR MEMORIES CAME BACK ALL AT ONCE; THEY MUST HAVE TRIGGERED SOME PHYSICAL CHANGES.
...CHANGES?
I'M BECOMING MORE LIKE THE PRINCESS... BUT IT'S LIKE I'M BECOMING LESS LIKE MYSELF.
WHAT ABOUT THE CRYSTAL? DO YOU STILL HAVE IT?
YEAH, BUT...
IT'S STILL AS DULL AS EVER.
ARE YOU *SURE* THIS IS THE MYSTICAL SILVER CRYSTAL?

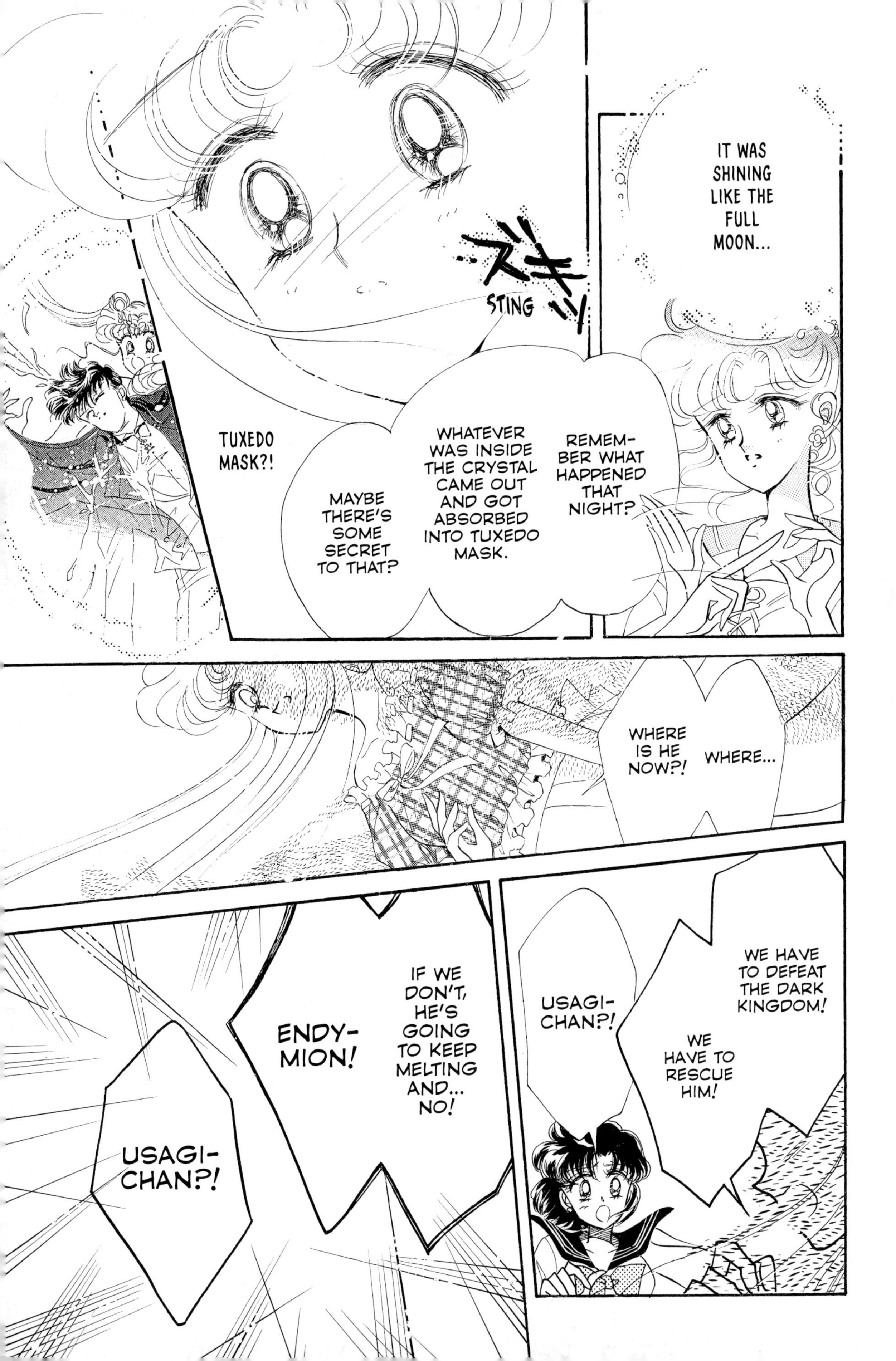
IT WAS SHINING LIKE THE FULL MOON...
REMEM-BER WHAT HAPPENED THAT NIGHT?
WHATEVER WAS INSIDE THE CRYSTAL CAME OUT AND GOT ABSORBED INTO TUXEDO MASK.
MAYBE THERE'S SOME SECRET TO THAT?
ズキッ
STING
TUXEDO MASK?!
WHERE...
WHERE IS HE NOW?!
WE HAVE TO DEFEAT THE DARK KINGDOM!
WE HAVE TO RESCUE HIM!
USAGI-CHAN?!
IF WE DON'T, HE'S GOING TO KEEP MELTING AND... NO!
ENDY-MION!
USAGI-CHAN?!

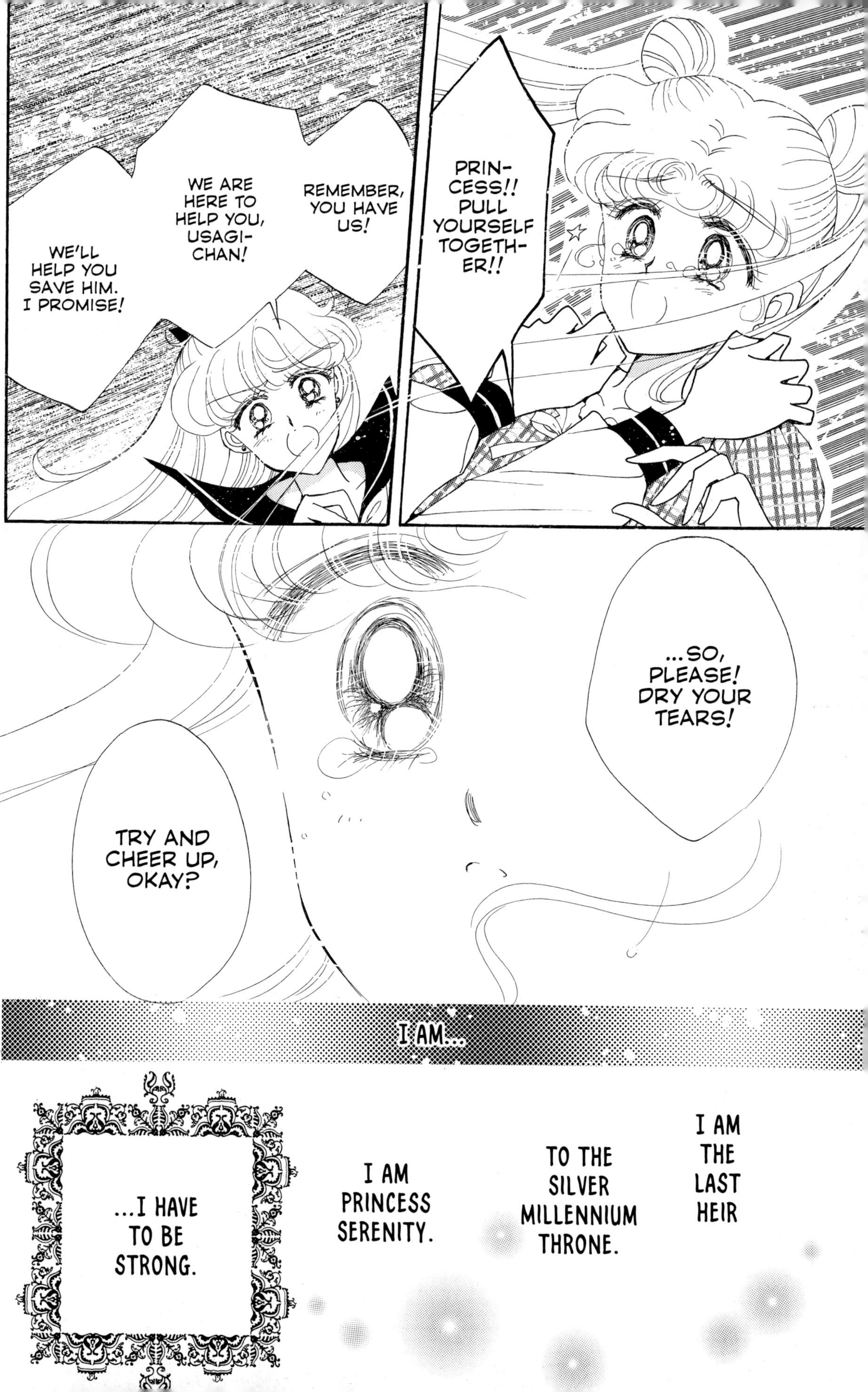
PRIN-CESS!! PULL YOURSELF TOGETH-ER!!
REMEMBER, YOU HAVE US!
WE ARE HERE TO HELP YOU, USAGI-CHAN!
WE'LL HELP YOU SAVE HIM. I PROMISE!
...SO, PLEASE! DRY YOUR TEARS!
TRY AND CHEER UP, OKAY?
I AM...
I AM THE LAST HEIR
TO THE SILVER MILLENNIUM THRONE.
I AM PRINCESS SERENITY.
...I HAVE TO BE STRONG.

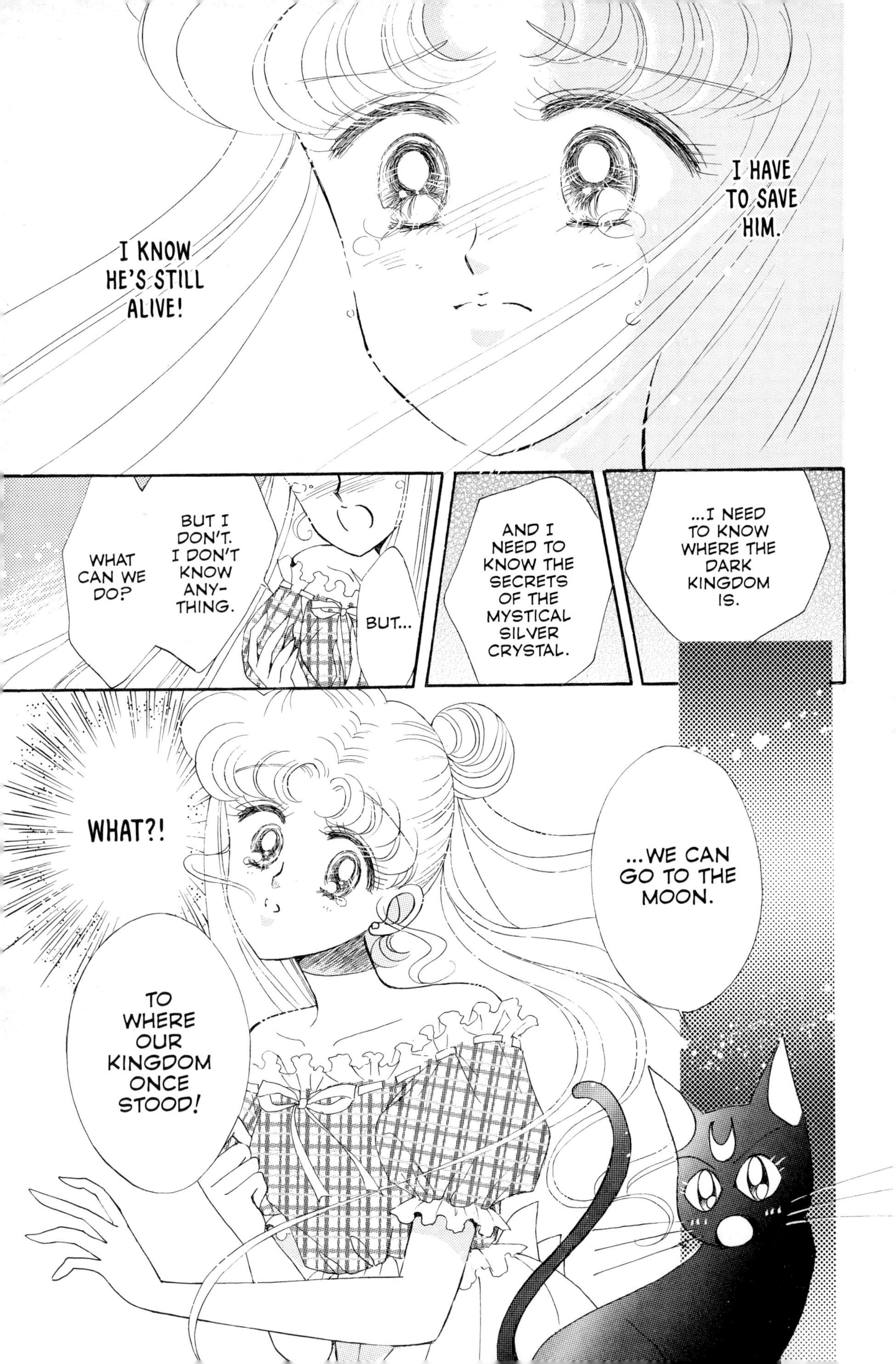
I HAVE TO SAVE HIM.
I KNOW HE'S STILL ALIVE!
...I NEED TO KNOW WHERE THE DARK KINGDOM IS.
AND I NEED TO KNOW THE SECRETS OF THE MYSTICAL SILVER CRYSTAL.
BUT...
BUT I DON'T. I DON'T KNOW ANY-THING.
WHAT CAN WE DO?
...WE CAN GO TO THE MOON.
WHAT?!
TO WHERE OUR KINGDOM ONCE STOOD!

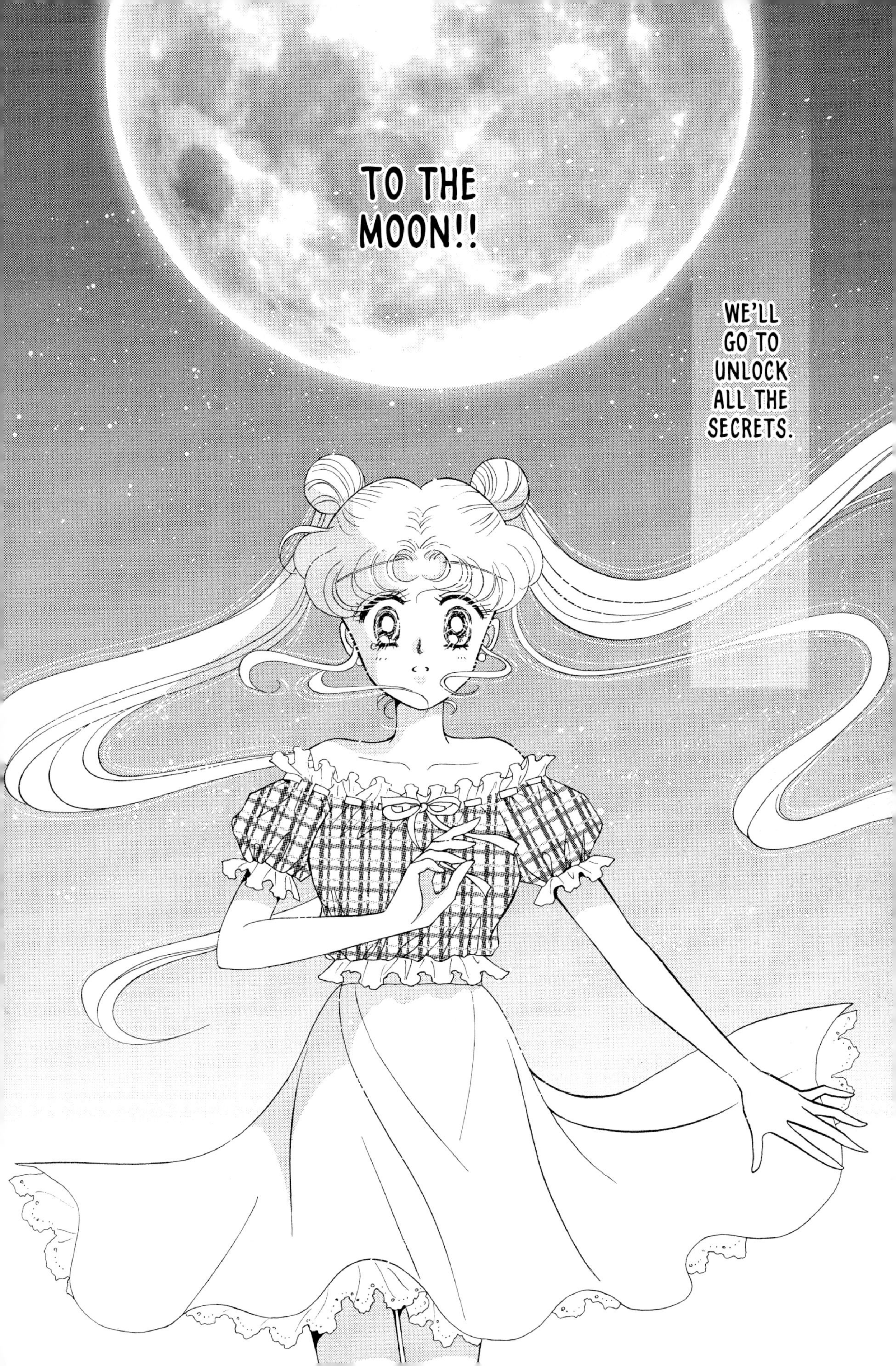
WE'LL GO TO UNLOCK ALL THE SECRETS.
TO THE MOON!!

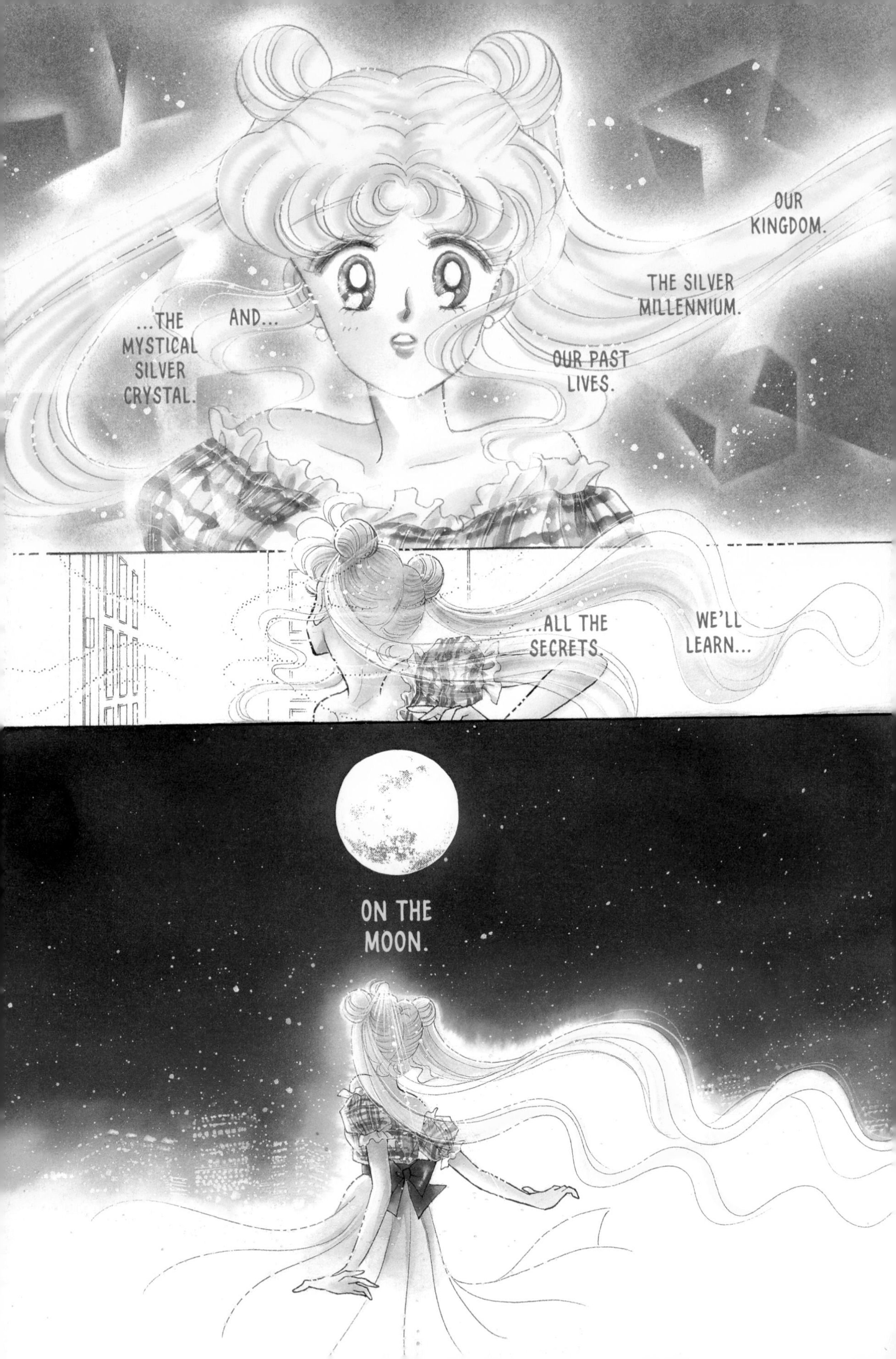
OUR KINGDOM.
THE SILVER MILLENNIUM.
OUR PAST LIVES.
AND...
...THE MYSTICAL SILVER CRYSTAL.
WE'LL LEARN...
...ALL THE SECRETS.
ON THE MOON.

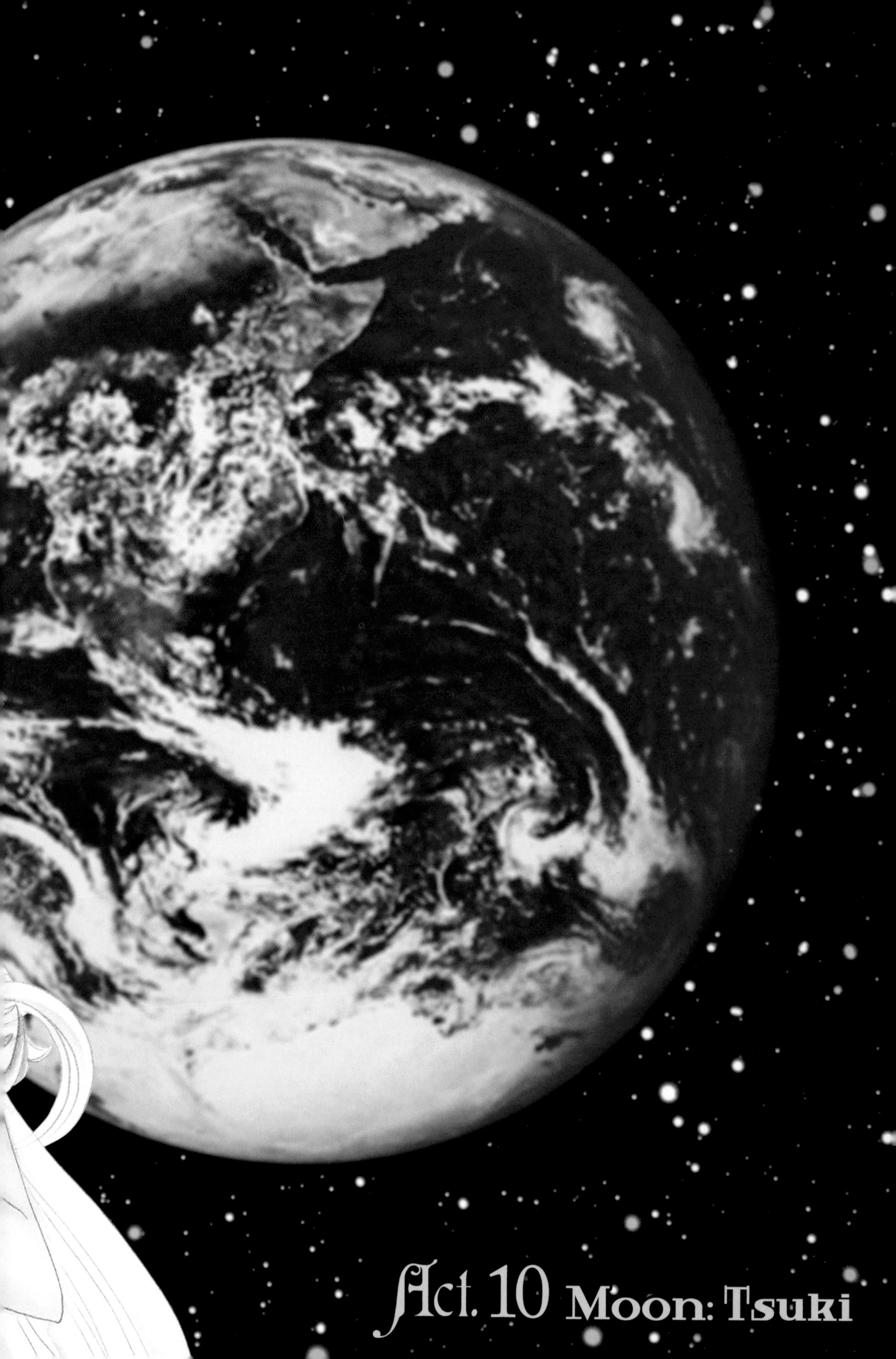
Act. 10 Moon: Tsuki

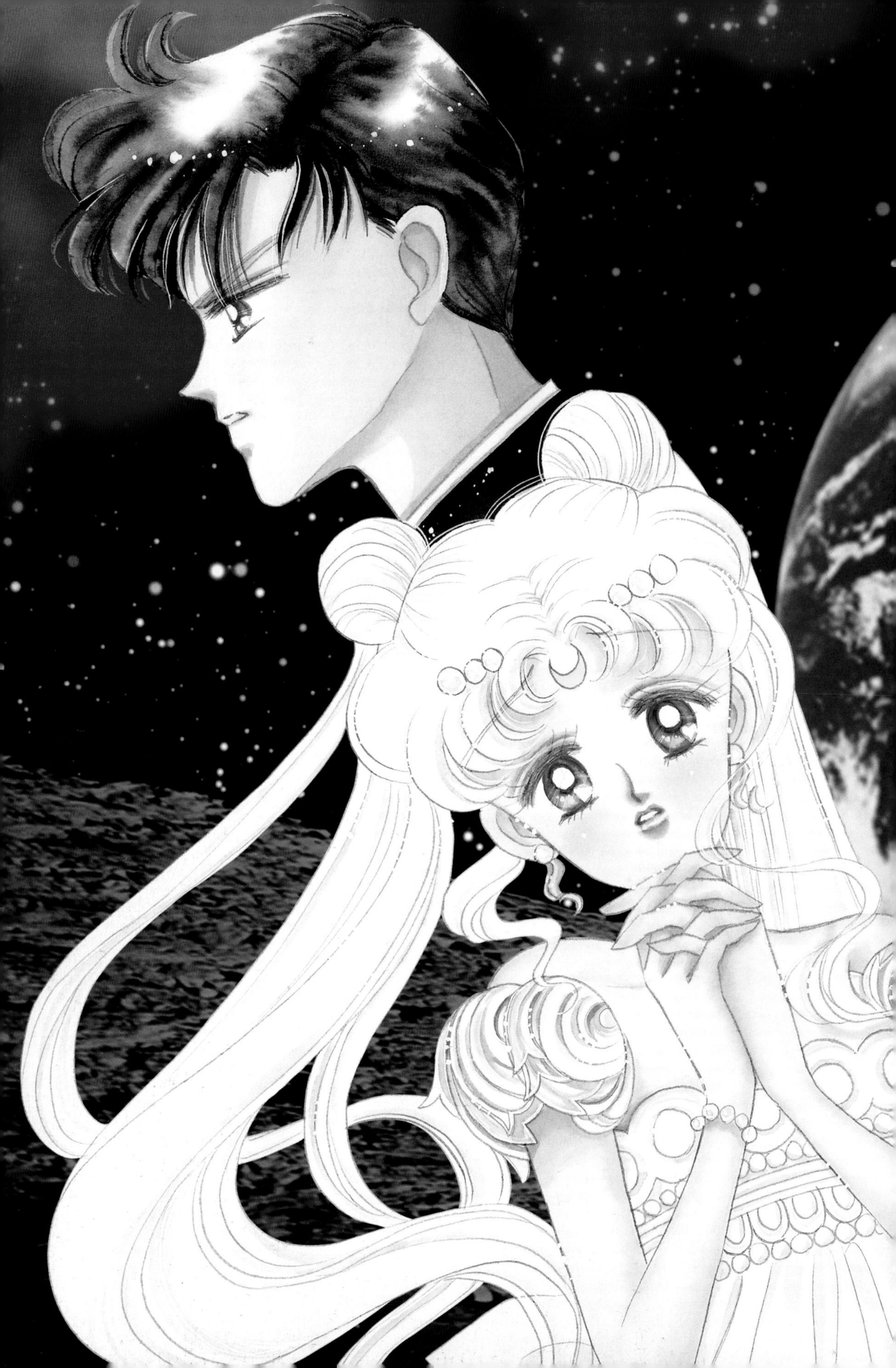

Pretty Guardian

Sailor Moon

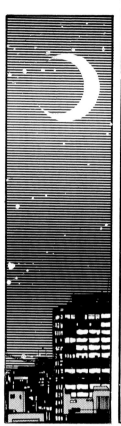

WELL, NOW THAT THAT'S DECIDED, WE'D BETTER GET READY!

WE'LL SET OUT

ON THE NIGHT OF THE NEXT FULL MOON.

TO THE MOON!!

CROWN GAME CENTER

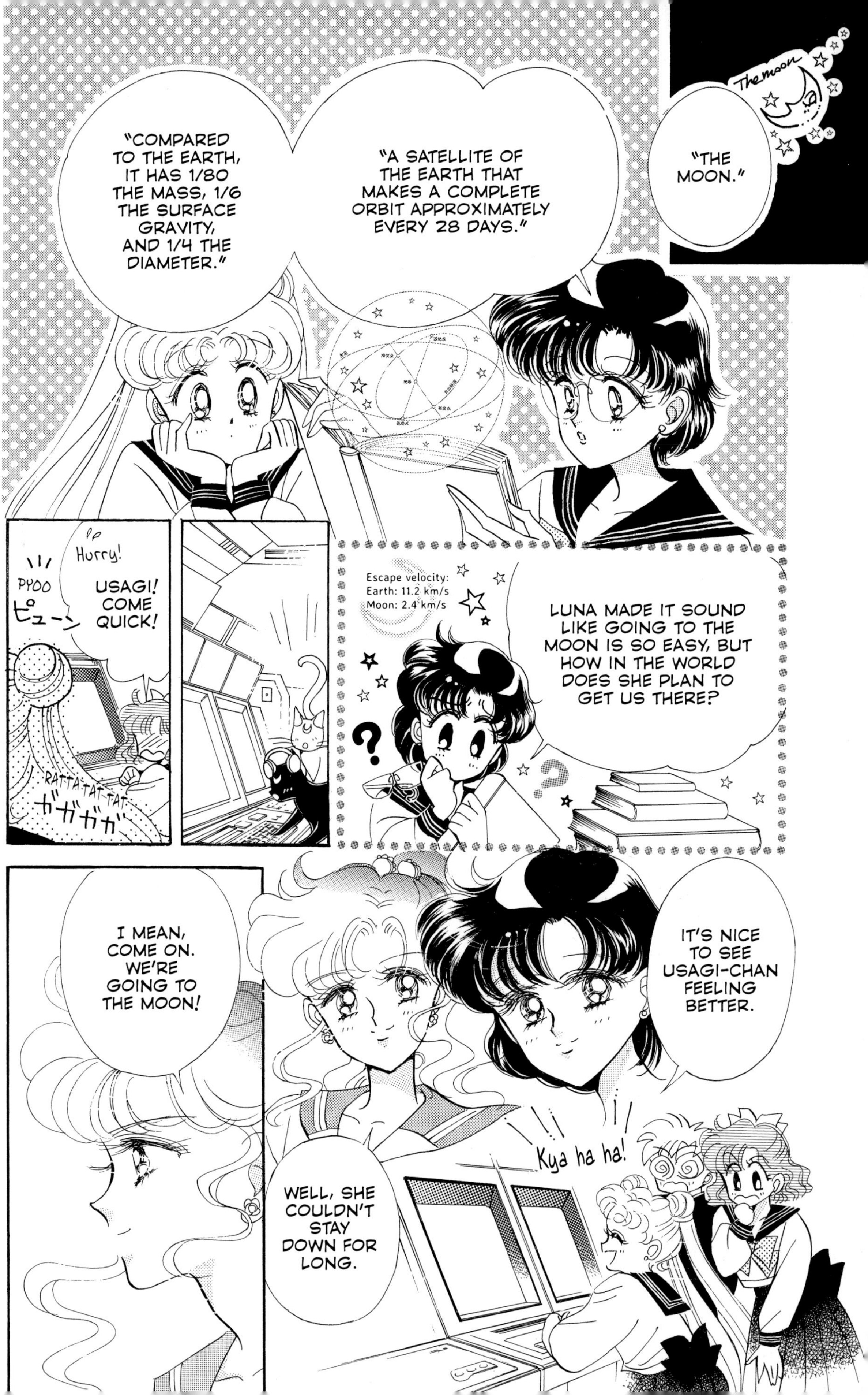
The moon
"THE MOON."
"A SATELLITE OF THE EARTH THAT MAKES A COMPLETE ORBIT APPROXIMATELY EVERY 28 DAYS."
"COMPARED TO THE EARTH, IT HAS 1/80 THE MASS, 1/6 THE SURFACE GRAVITY, AND 1/4 THE DIAMETER."
Escape velocity: Earth: 11.2 km/s Moon: 2.4 km/s
LUNA MADE IT SOUND LIKE GOING TO THE MOON IS SO EASY, BUT HOW IN THE WORLD DOES SHE PLAN TO GET US THERE?
Hurry!
USAGI! COME QUICK!
PYOO
ピューン
RATTA-TAT-TAT
ガガガガ
IT'S NICE TO SEE USAGI-CHAN FEELING BETTER.
Kya ha ha!
WELL, SHE COULDN'T STAY DOWN FOR LONG.
I MEAN, COME ON. WE'RE GOING TO THE MOON!

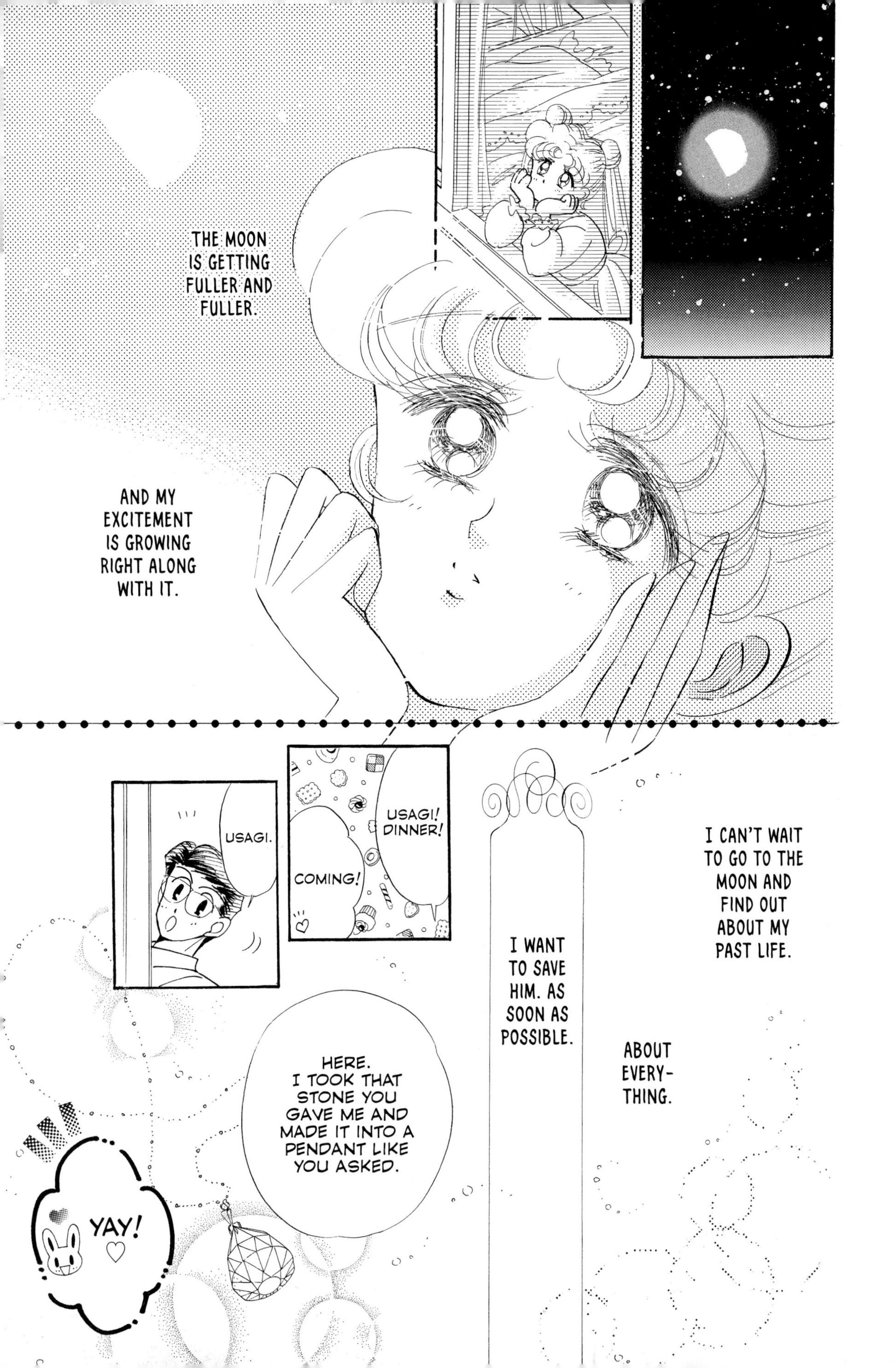
THE MOON IS GETTING FULLER AND FULLER.
AND MY EXCITEMENT IS GROWING RIGHT ALONG WITH IT.
I CAN'T WAIT TO GO TO THE MOON AND FIND OUT ABOUT MY PAST LIFE.
ABOUT EVERY-THING.
I WANT TO SAVE HIM. AS SOON AS POSSIBLE.
USAGI! DINNER!
COMING!
USAGI.
HERE. I TOOK THAT STONE YOU GAVE ME AND MADE IT INTO A PENDANT LIKE YOU ASKED.
YAY!

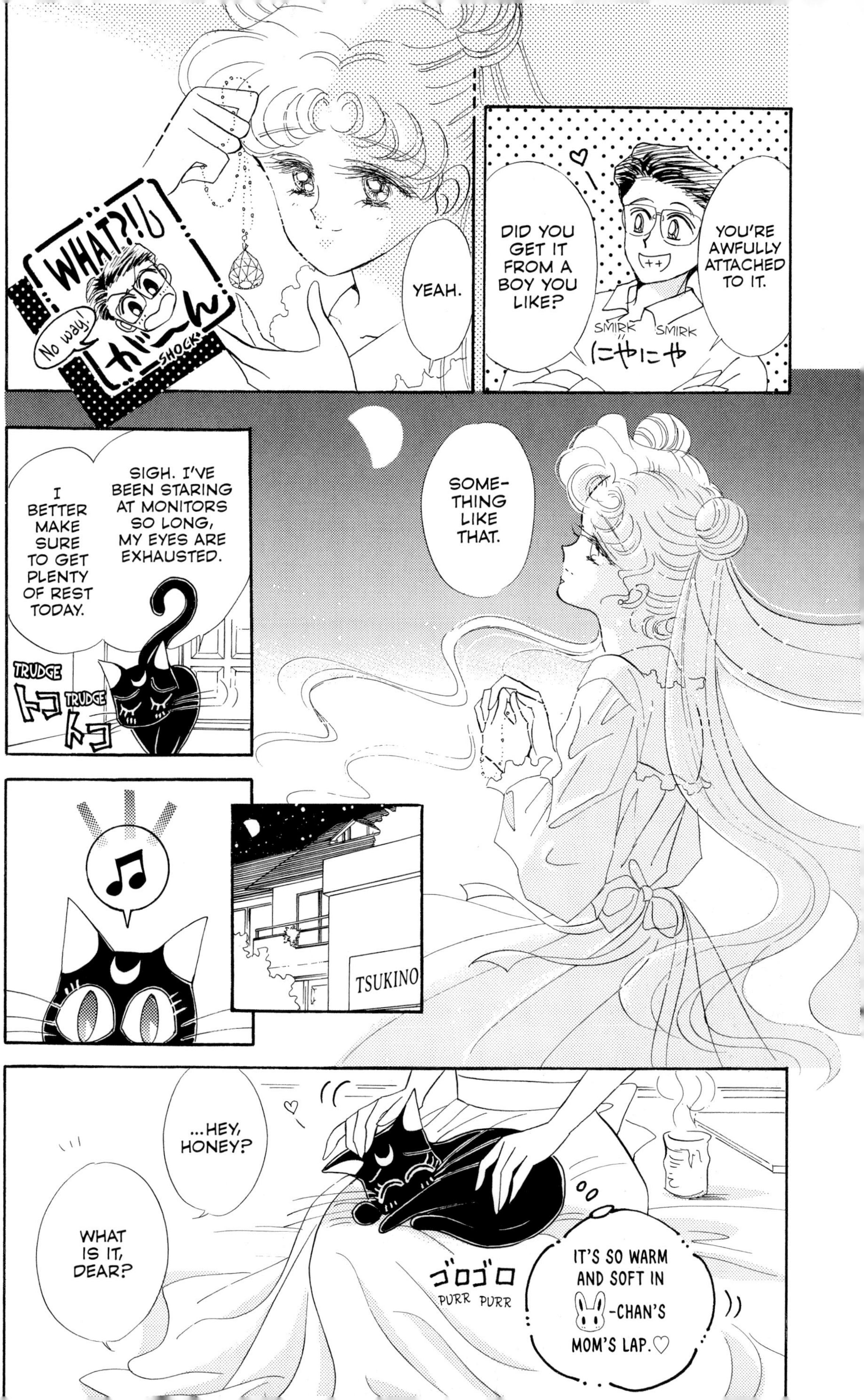
YOU'RE AWFULLY ATTACHED TO IT.
DID YOU GET IT FROM A BOY YOU LIKE?
SMIRK SMIRK
にやにや
YEAH.
WHAT?!
No way!
がーん
SHOCK
SOME-THING LIKE THAT.
SIGH. I'VE BEEN STARING AT MONITORS SO LONG, MY EYES ARE EXHAUSTED.
I BETTER MAKE SURE TO GET PLENTY OF REST TODAY.
TRUDGE
トコ
TRUDGE
トコ
TSUKINO
♫
IT'S SO WARM AND SOFT IN -CHAN'S MOM'S LAP.♡
ゴロゴロ
PURR PURR
...HEY, HONEY?
WHAT IS IT, DEAR?

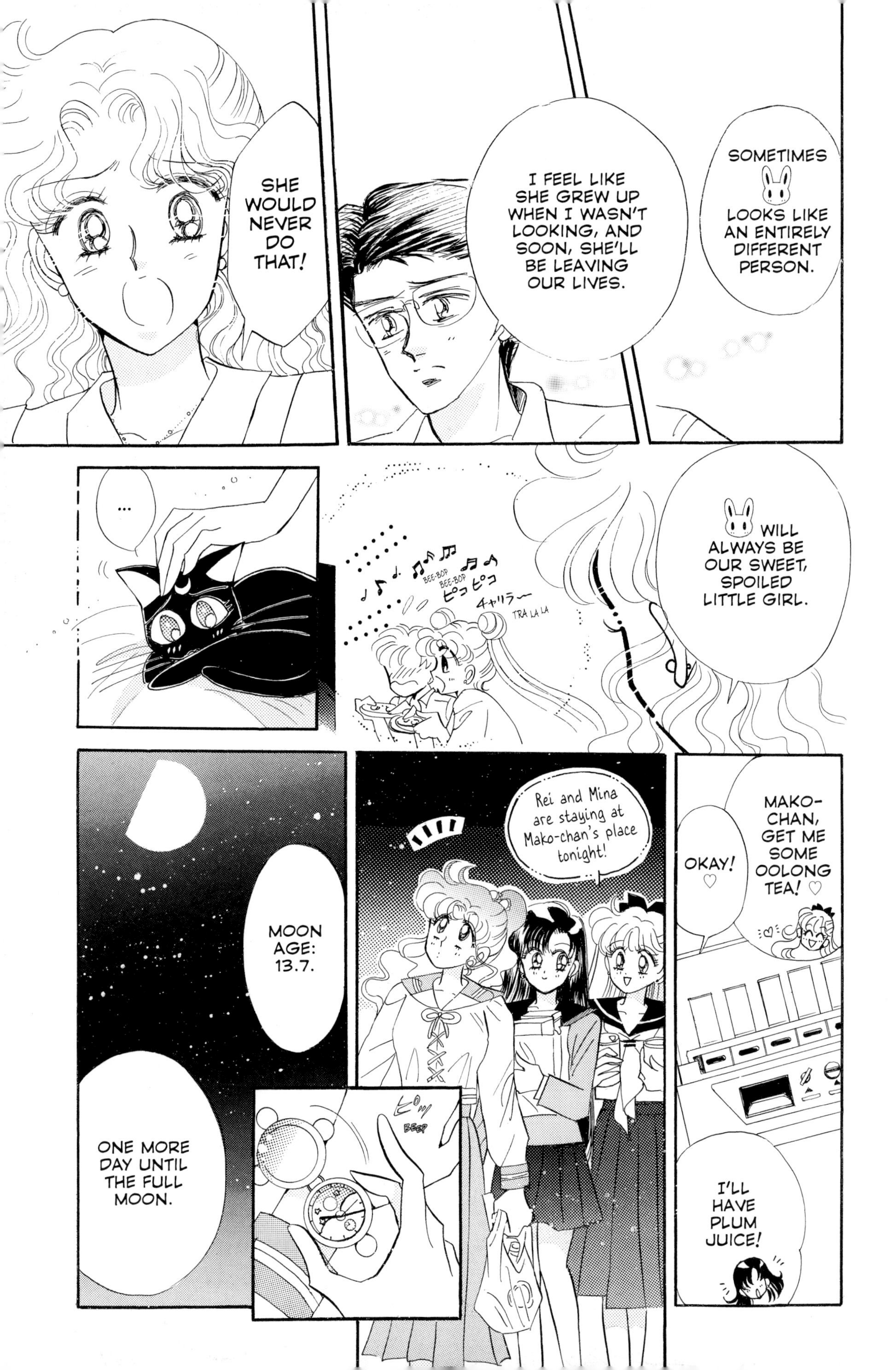
SOMETIMES LOOKS LIKE AN ENTIRELY DIFFERENT PERSON.
I FEEL LIKE SHE GREW UP WHEN I WASN'T LOOKING, AND SOON, SHE'LL BE LEAVING OUR LIVES.
SHE WOULD NEVER DO THAT!
WILL ALWAYS BE OUR SWEET, SPOILED LITTLE GIRL.
ピコピコ BEE-BOP BEE-BOP
チャリラ～ TRA LA LA
...
MAKO-CHAN, GET ME SOME OOLONG TEA! ♡
OKAY! ♡
I'LL HAVE PLUM JUICE!
Rei and Mina are staying at Mako-chan's place tonight!
ピッ BEEP
MOON AGE: 13.7.
ONE MORE DAY UNTIL THE FULL MOON.

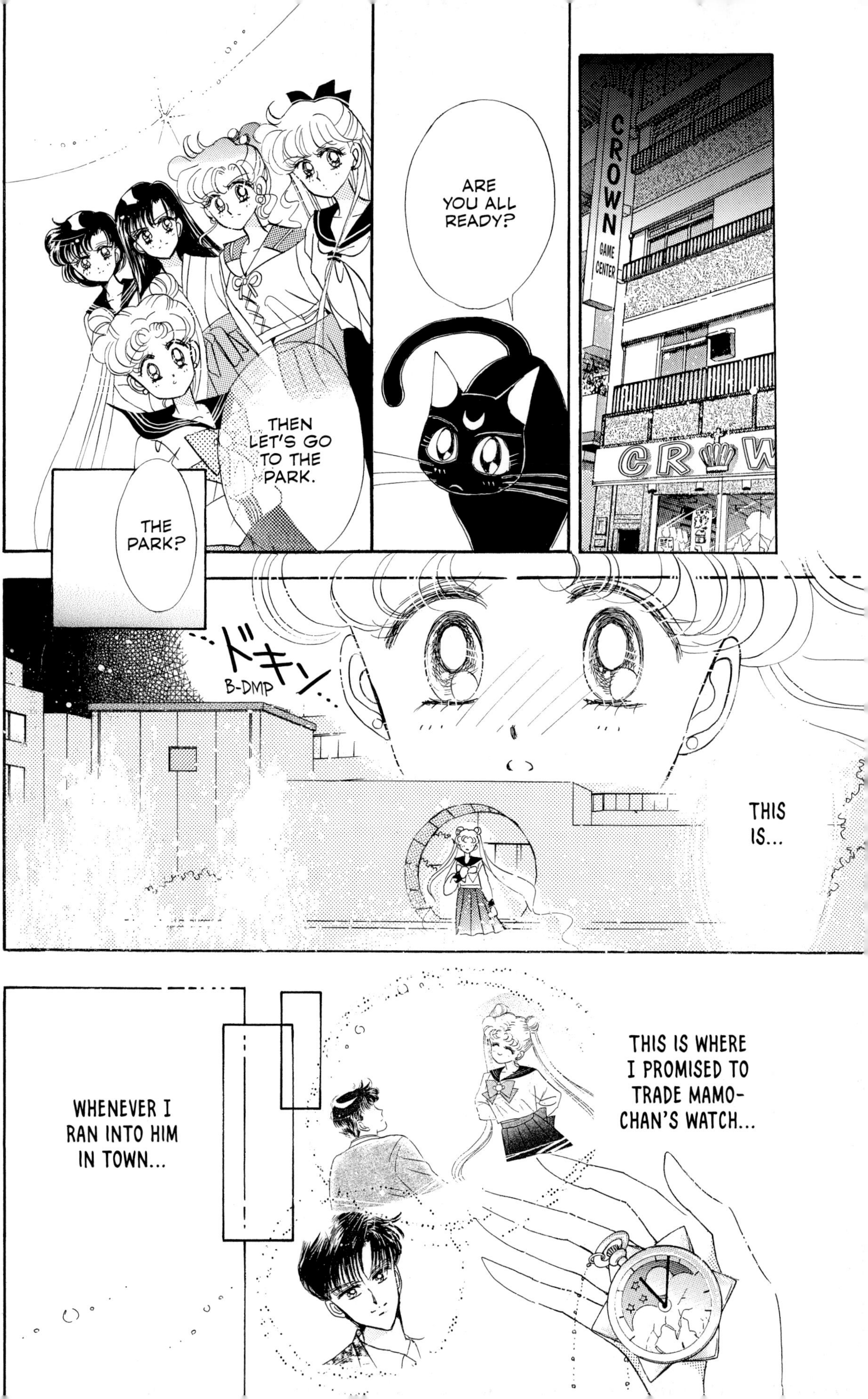
CROWN
GAME CENTER
ARE YOU ALL READY?
THEN LET'S GO TO THE PARK.
THE PARK?
ドキン
B-DMP
THIS IS...
THIS IS WHERE I PROMISED TO TRADE MAMO-CHAN'S WATCH...
WHENEVER I RAN INTO HIM IN TOWN...

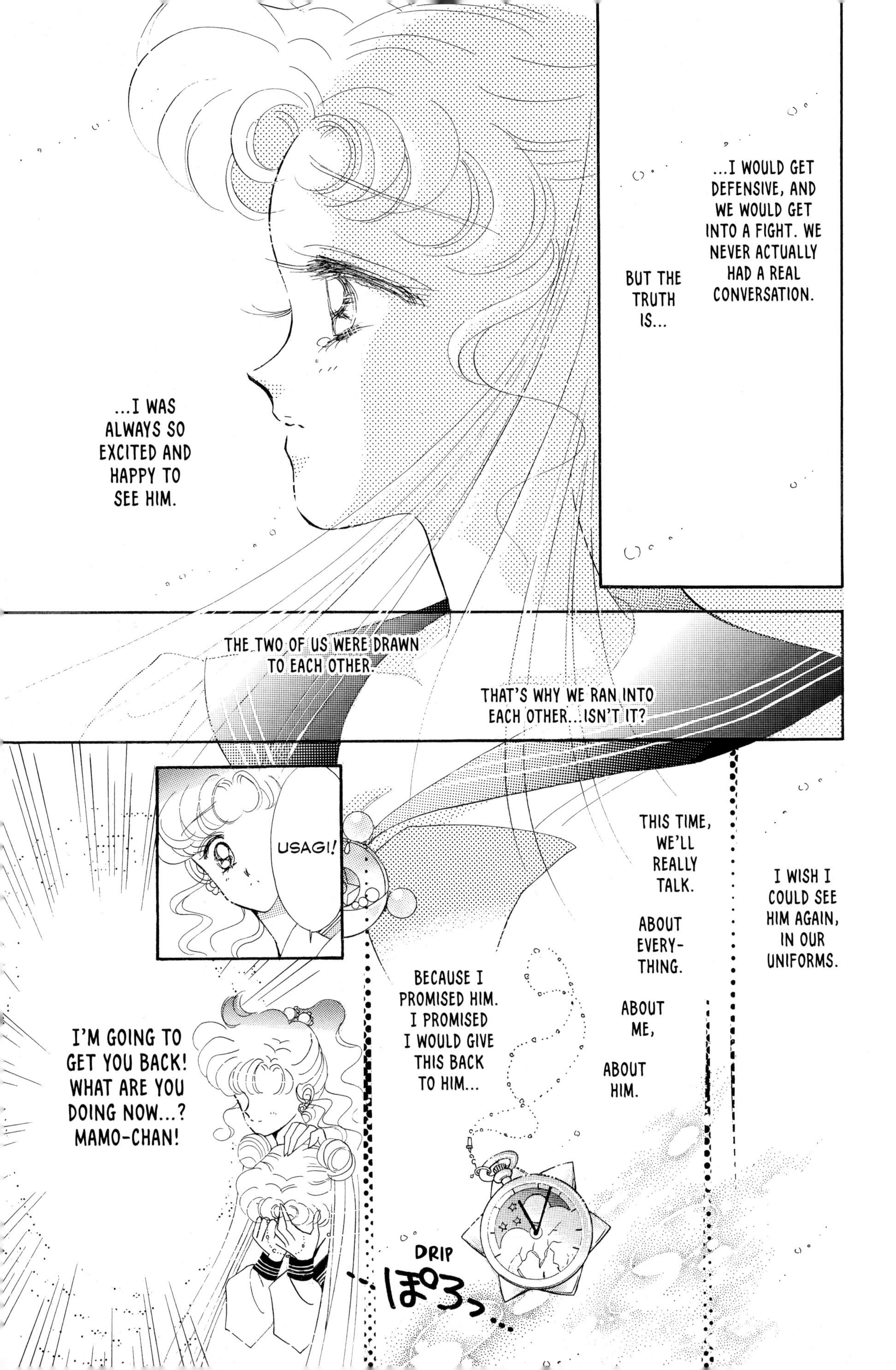

...I WOULD GET DEFENSIVE, AND WE WOULD GET INTO A FIGHT. WE NEVER ACTUALLY HAD A REAL CONVERSATION.
BUT THE TRUTH IS...
...I WAS ALWAYS SO EXCITED AND HAPPY TO SEE HIM.
THE TWO OF US WERE DRAWN TO EACH OTHER.
THAT'S WHY WE RAN INTO EACH OTHER...ISN'T IT?
I WISH I COULD SEE HIM AGAIN, IN OUR UNIFORMS.
THIS TIME, WE'LL REALLY TALK.
ABOUT EVERY-THING.
ABOUT ME,
ABOUT HIM.
BECAUSE I PROMISED HIM. I PROMISED I WOULD GIVE THIS BACK TO HIM...
DRIP
ぽろっ
USAGI!
I'M GOING TO GET YOU BACK! WHAT ARE YOU DOING NOW...? MAMO-CHAN!

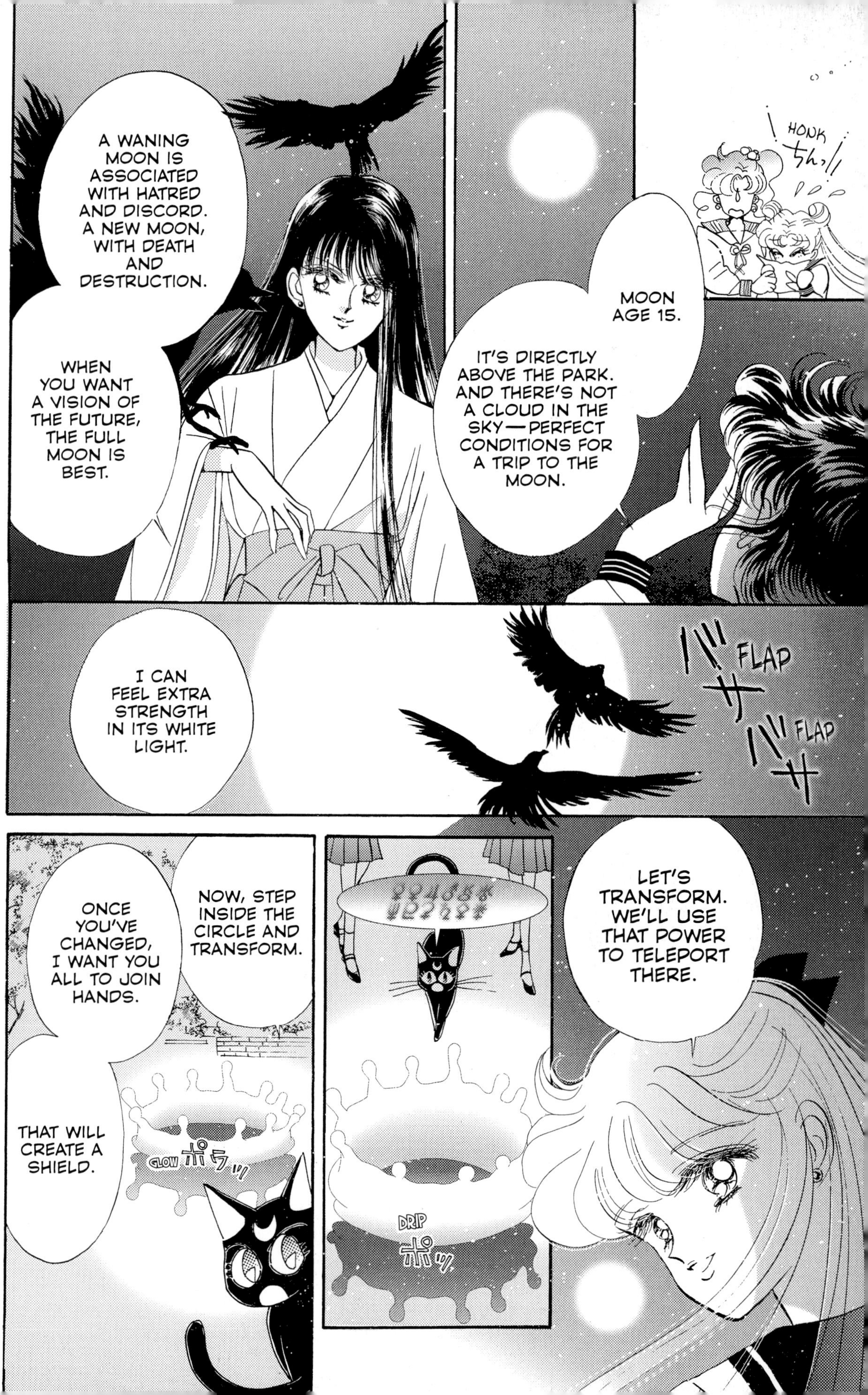
HONK
ちん!!
MOON AGE 15.
IT'S DIRECTLY ABOVE THE PARK. AND THERE'S NOT A CLOUD IN THE SKY—PERFECT CONDITIONS FOR A TRIP TO THE MOON.
A WANING MOON IS ASSOCIATED WITH HATRED AND DISCORD. A NEW MOON, WITH DEATH AND DESTRUCTION.
WHEN YOU WANT A VISION OF THE FUTURE, THE FULL MOON IS BEST.
バサ FLAP
バサ FLAP
I CAN FEEL EXTRA STRENGTH IN ITS WHITE LIGHT.
LET'S TRANSFORM. WE'LL USE THAT POWER TO TELEPORT THERE.
DRIP ポッ
NOW, STEP INSIDE THE CIRCLE AND TRANSFORM.
ONCE YOU'VE CHANGED, I WANT YOU ALL TO JOIN HANDS.
GLOW ポウッ
THAT WILL CREATE A SHIELD.

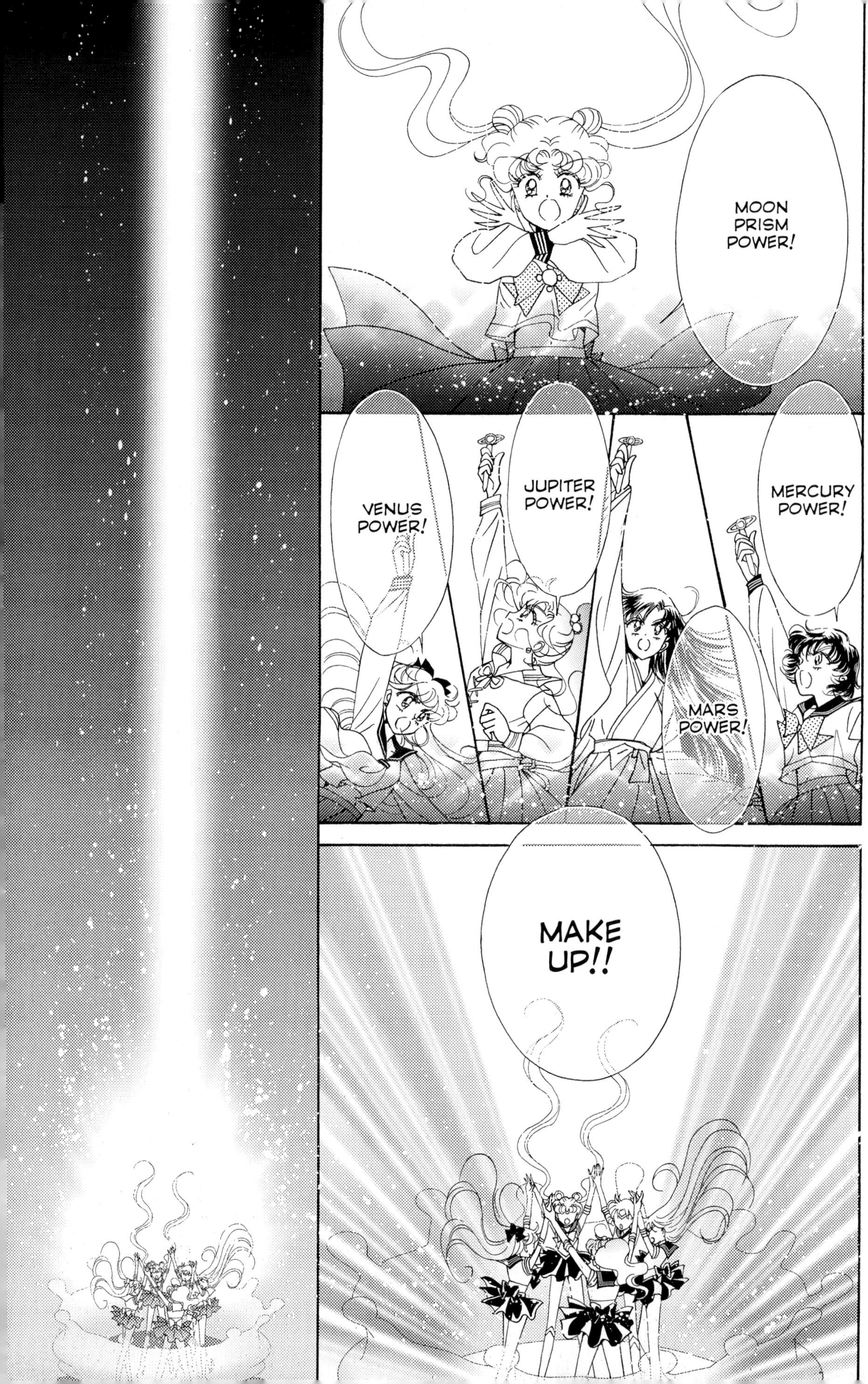
MOON PRISM POWER!
MERCURY POWER!
MARS POWER!
JUPITER POWER!
VENUS POWER!
MAKE UP!!

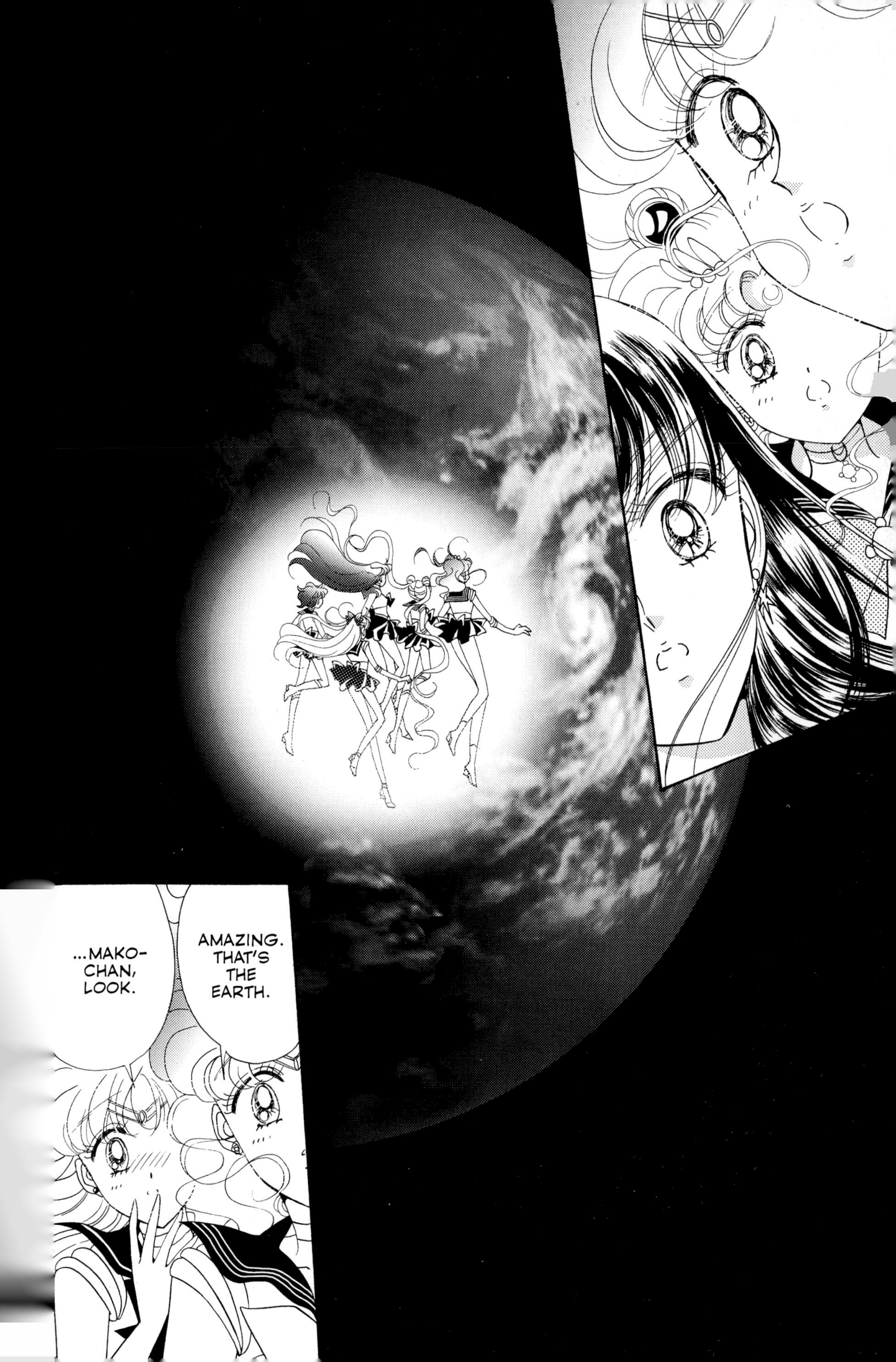
AMAZING. THAT'S THE EARTH.
...MAKO-CHAN, LOOK.

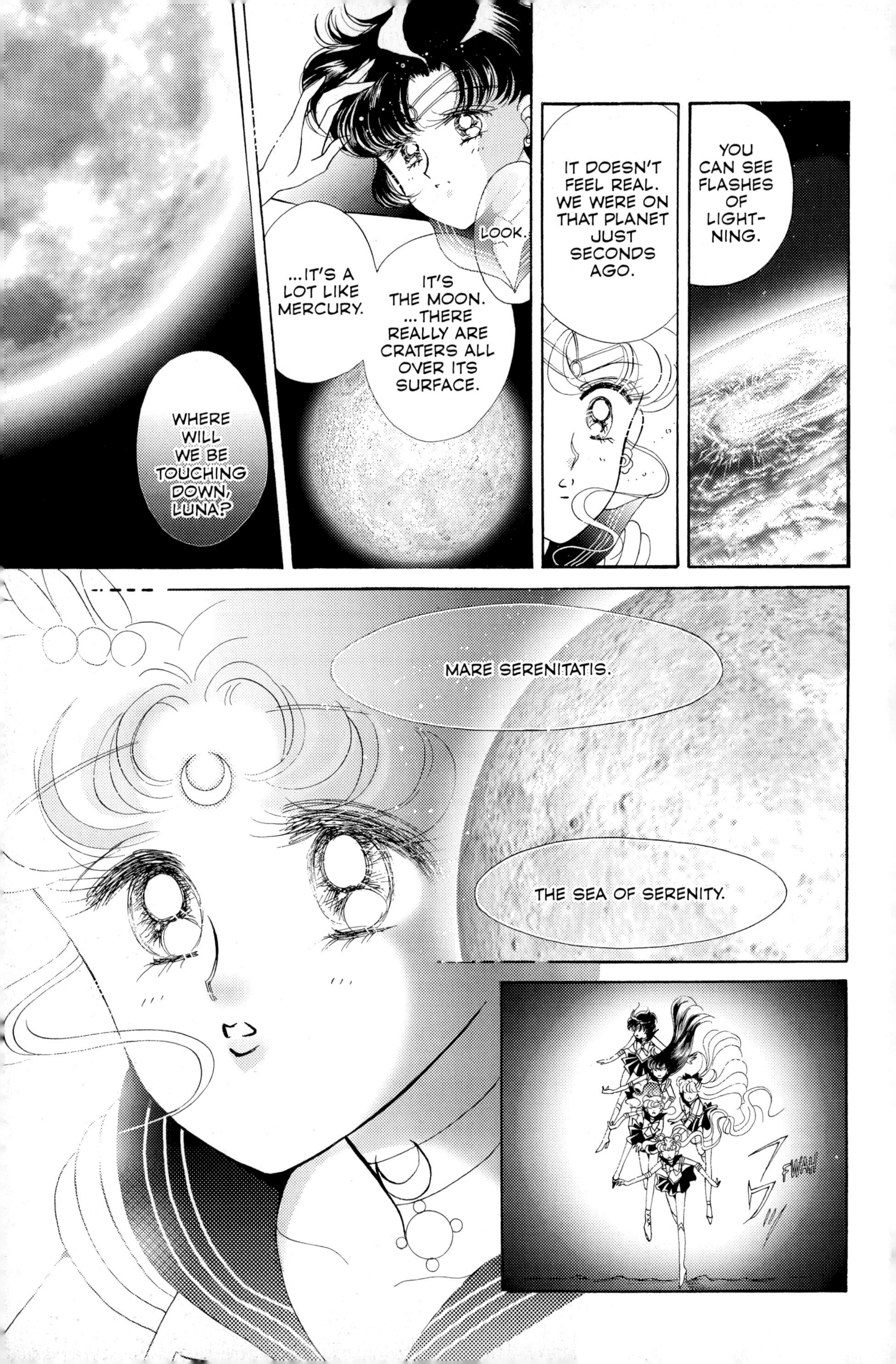
YOU CAN SEE FLASHES OF LIGHT-NING.
IT DOESN'T FEEL REAL. WE WERE ON THAT PLANET JUST SECONDS AGO.
LOOK.
IT'S THE MOON. ...THERE REALLY ARE CRATERS ALL OVER ITS SURFACE.
...IT'S A LOT LIKE MERCURY.
WHERE WILL WE BE TOUCHING DOWN, LUNA?
MARE SERENITATIS.
THE SEA OF SERENITY.
FWAH

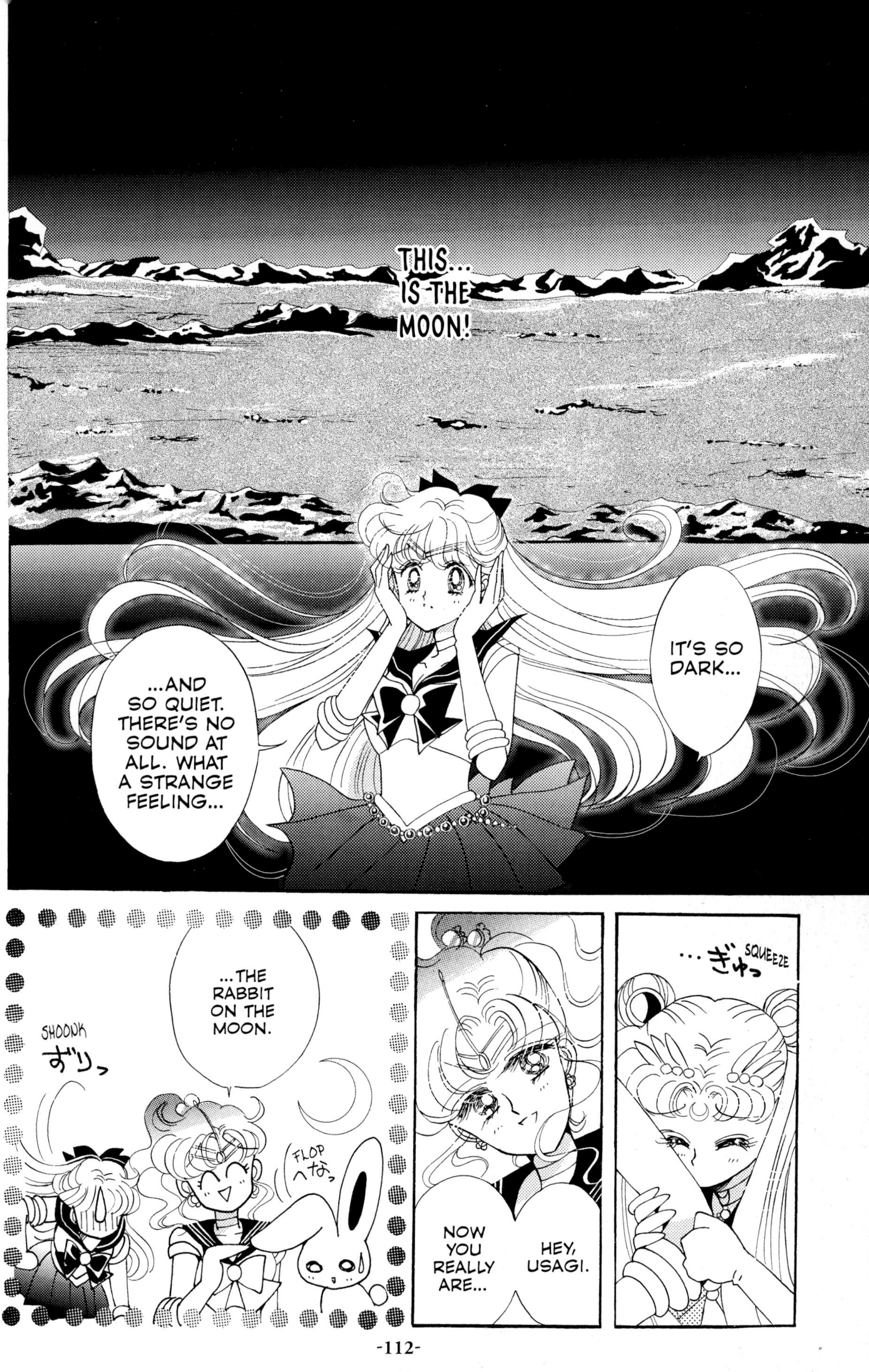
THIS... IS THE MOON!
IT'S SO DARK...
...AND SO QUIET. THERE'S NO SOUND AT ALL. WHAT A STRANGE FEELING...
... ぎゅっ
SQUEEZE
HEY, USAGI.
NOW YOU REALLY ARE...
...THE RABBIT ON THE MOON.
SHOONK
ずりっ
FLOP
へなっ

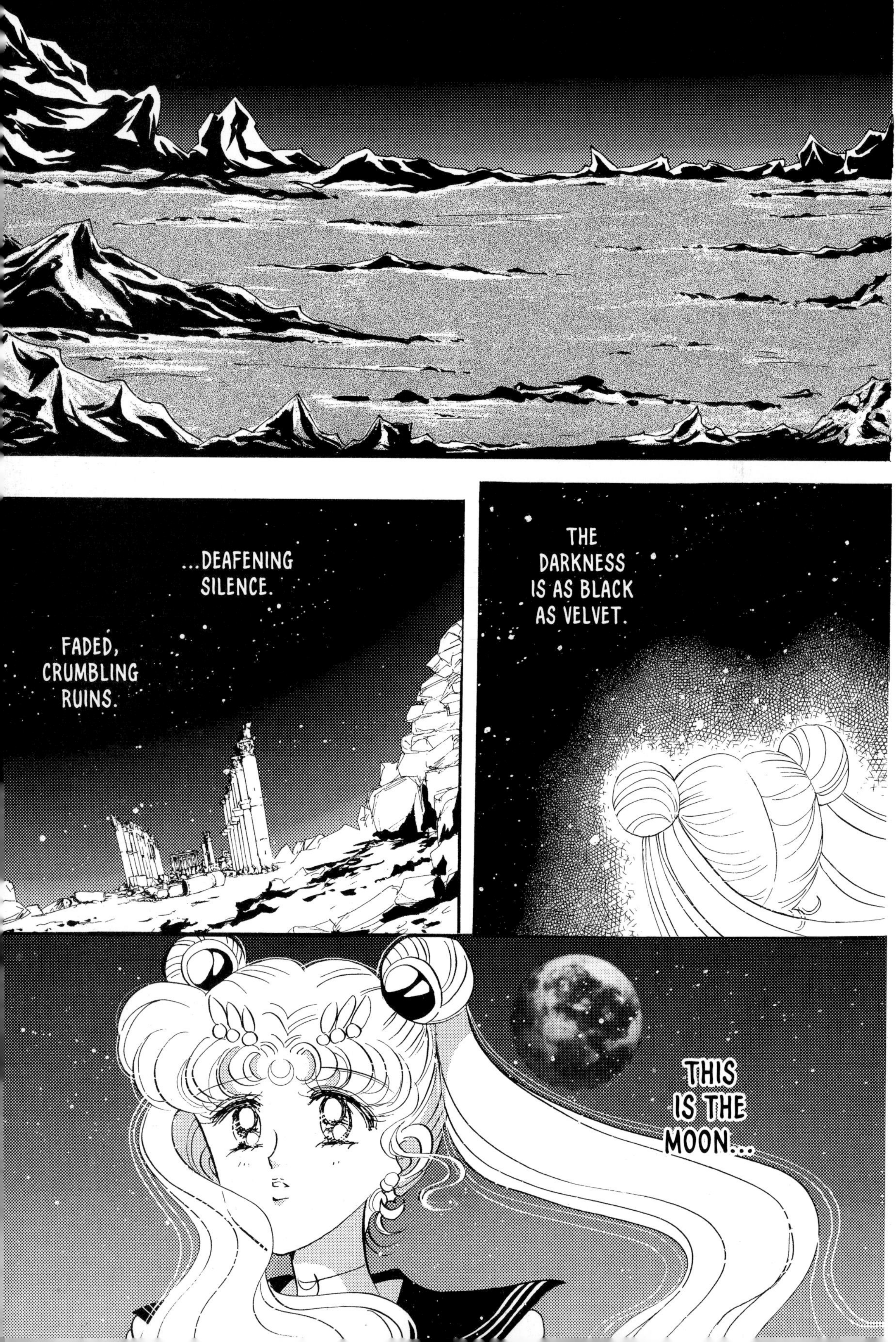
THE DARKNESS IS AS BLACK AS VELVET.
...DEAFENING SILENCE.
FADED, CRUMBLING RUINS.
THIS IS THE MOON...

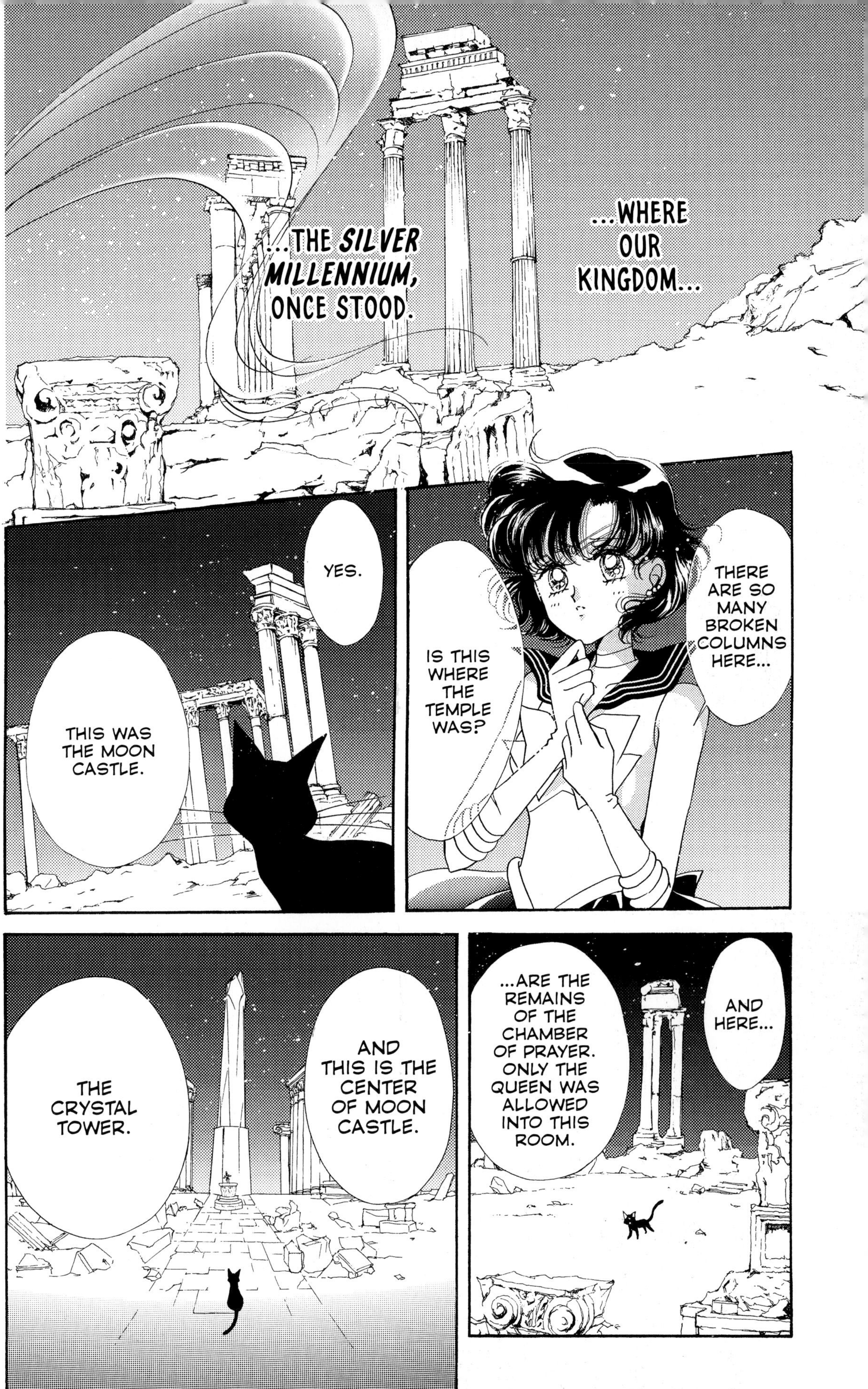
...WHERE OUR KINGDOM...
...THE SILVER MILLENNIUM, ONCE STOOD.
THERE ARE SO MANY BROKEN COLUMNS HERE...
IS THIS WHERE THE TEMPLE WAS?
YES.
THIS WAS THE MOON CASTLE.
AND HERE...
...ARE THE REMAINS OF THE CHAMBER OF PRAYER. ONLY THE QUEEN WAS ALLOWED INTO THIS ROOM.
AND THIS IS THE CENTER OF MOON CASTLE.
THE CRYSTAL TOWER.

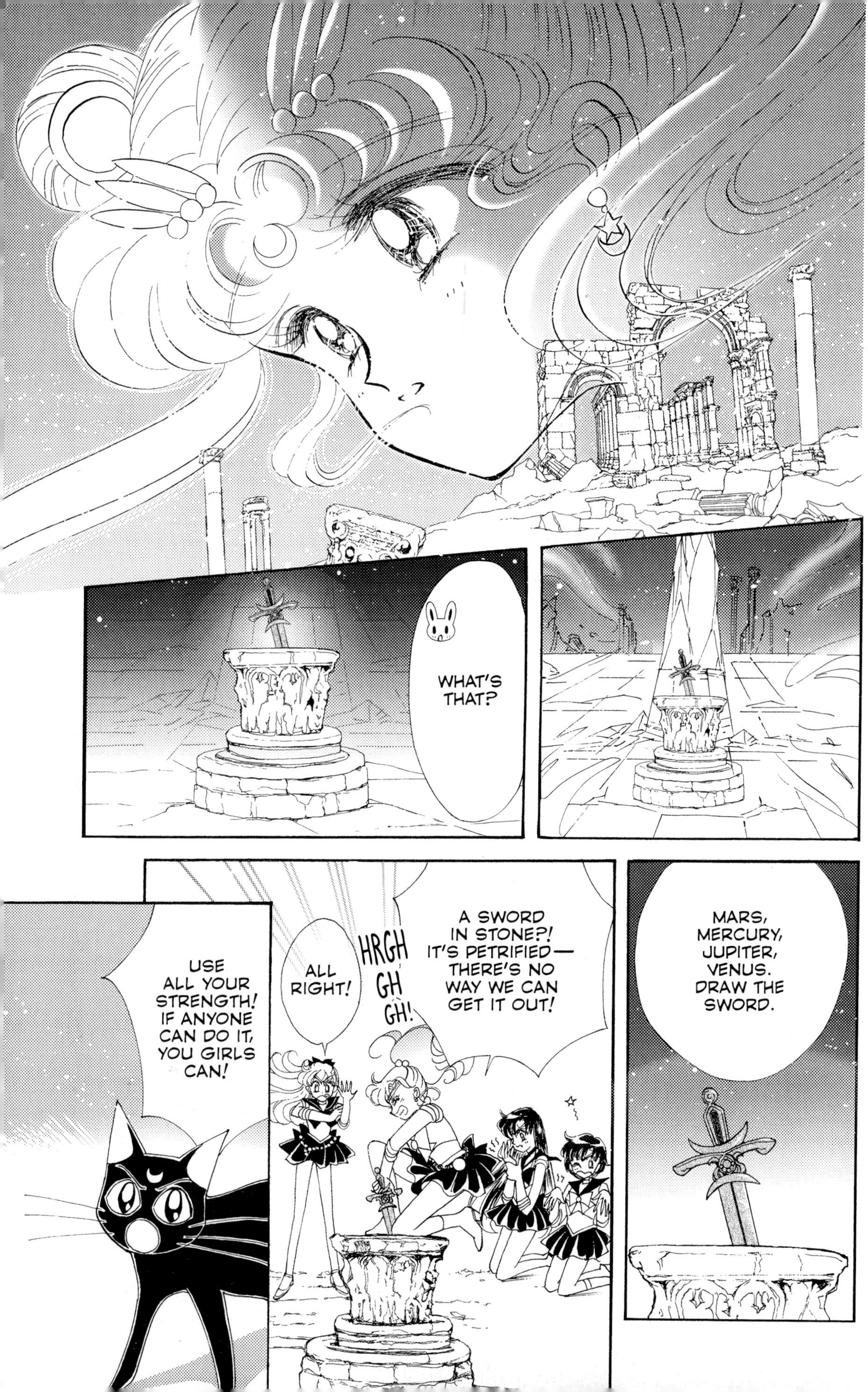
WHAT'S THAT?
MARS, MERCURY, JUPITER, VENUS. DRAW THE SWORD.
A SWORD IN STONE?! IT'S PETRIFIED— THERE'S NO WAY WE CAN GET IT OUT!
HRGH GH GH!
ALL RIGHT!
USE ALL YOUR STRENGTH! IF ANYONE CAN DO IT, YOU GIRLS CAN!

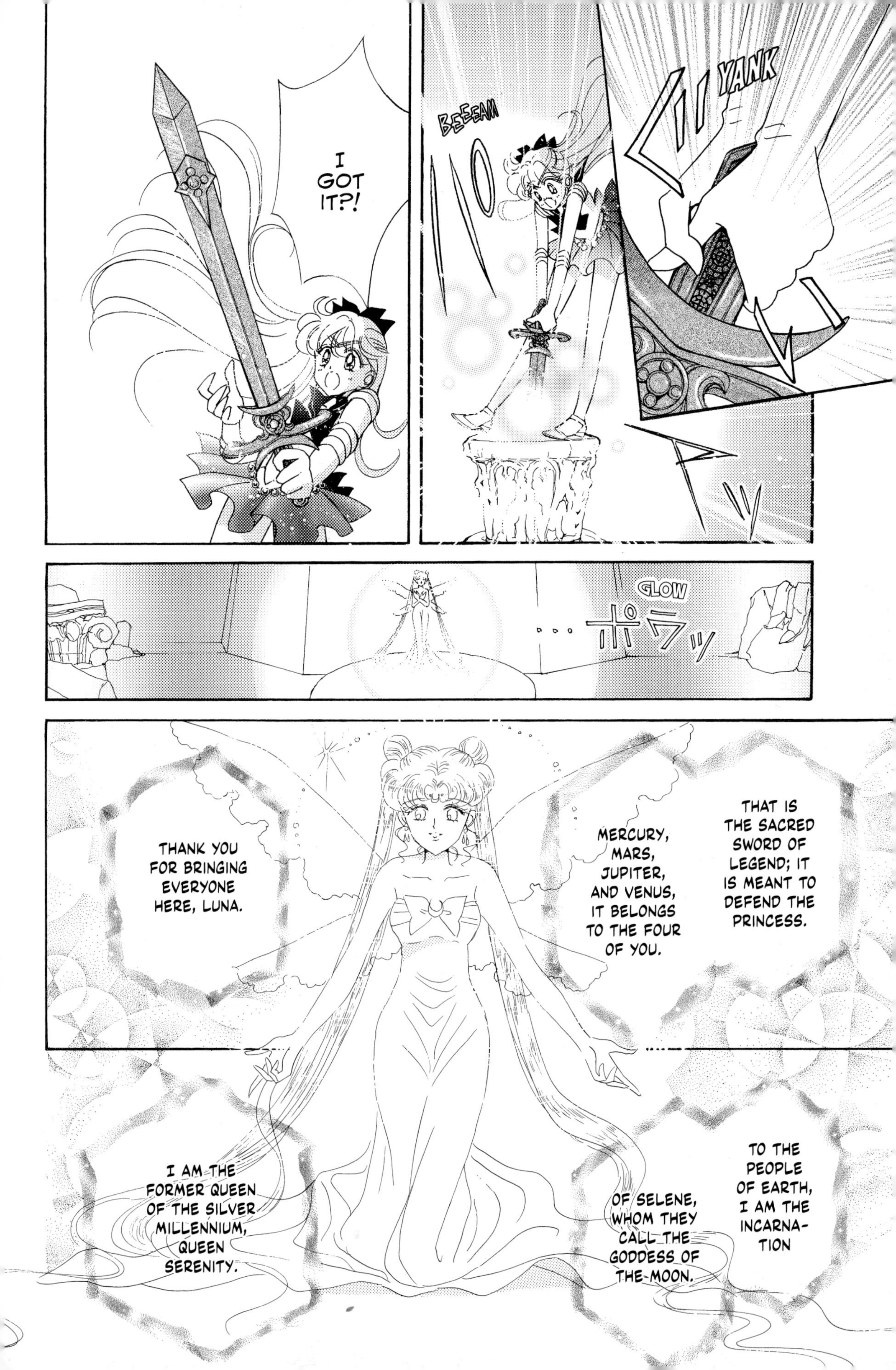
YANK
BEEEAM
I GOT IT?!
GLOW
...ポワッ
THAT IS THE SACRED SWORD OF LEGEND; IT IS MEANT TO DEFEND THE PRINCESS.
MERCURY, MARS, JUPITER, AND VENUS, IT BELONGS TO THE FOUR OF YOU.
THANK YOU FOR BRINGING EVERYONE HERE, LUNA.
TO THE PEOPLE OF EARTH, I AM THE INCARNATION
OF SELENE, WHOM THEY CALL THE GODDESS OF THE MOON.
I AM THE FORMER QUEEN OF THE SILVER MILLENNIUM, QUEEN SERENITY.

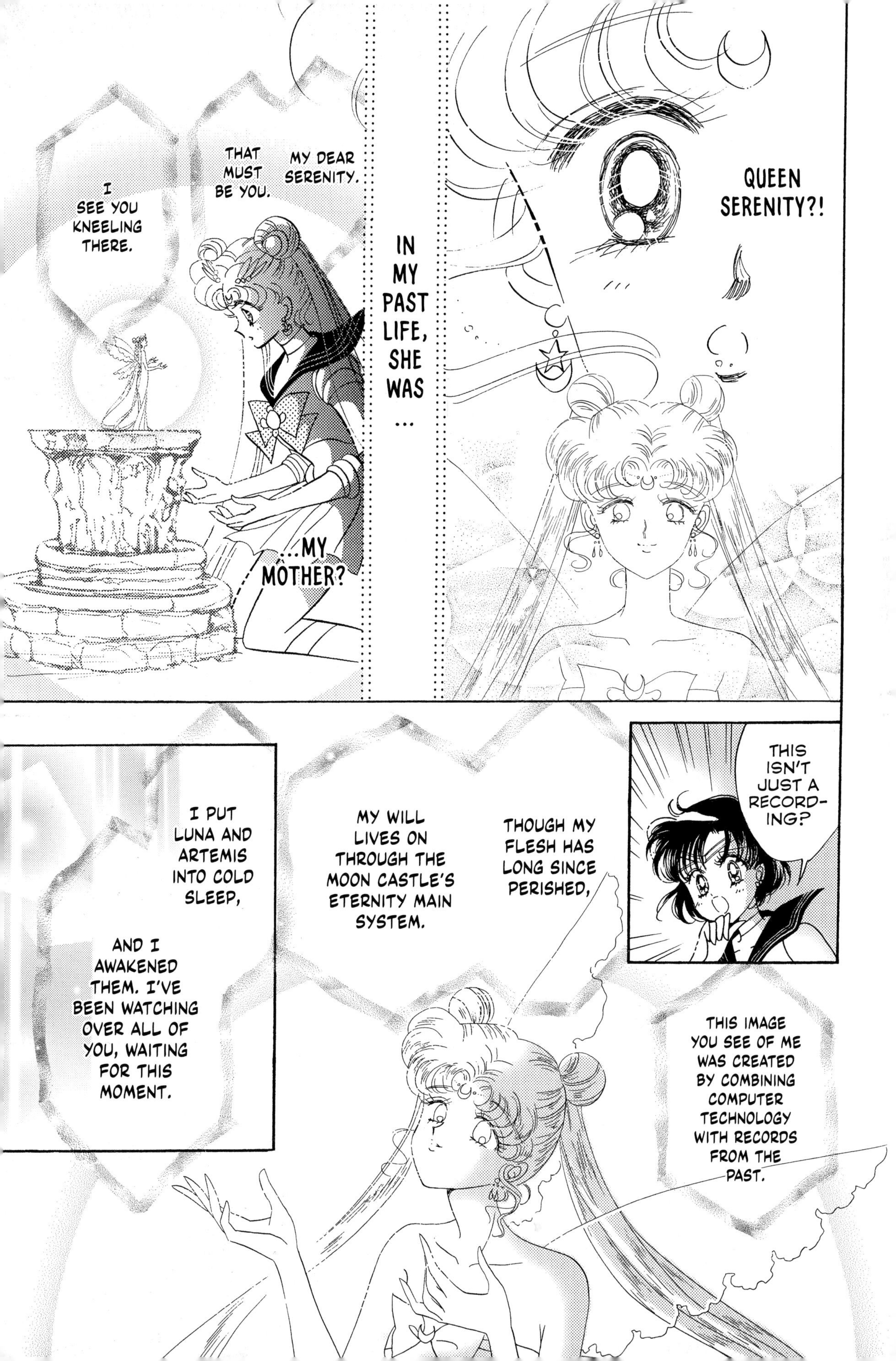

QUEEN SERENITY?!
IN MY PAST LIFE, SHE WAS ...
MY DEAR SERENITY.
THAT MUST BE YOU.
I SEE YOU KNEELING THERE.
...MY MOTHER?
THIS ISN'T JUST A RECORDING?
THOUGH MY FLESH HAS LONG SINCE PERISHED,
MY WILL LIVES ON THROUGH THE MOON CASTLE'S ETERNITY MAIN SYSTEM.
THIS IMAGE YOU SEE OF ME WAS CREATED BY COMBINING COMPUTER TECHNOLOGY WITH RECORDS FROM THE PAST.
I PUT LUNA AND ARTEMIS INTO COLD SLEEP,
AND I AWAKENED THEM. I'VE BEEN WATCHING OVER ALL OF YOU, WAITING FOR THIS MOMENT.

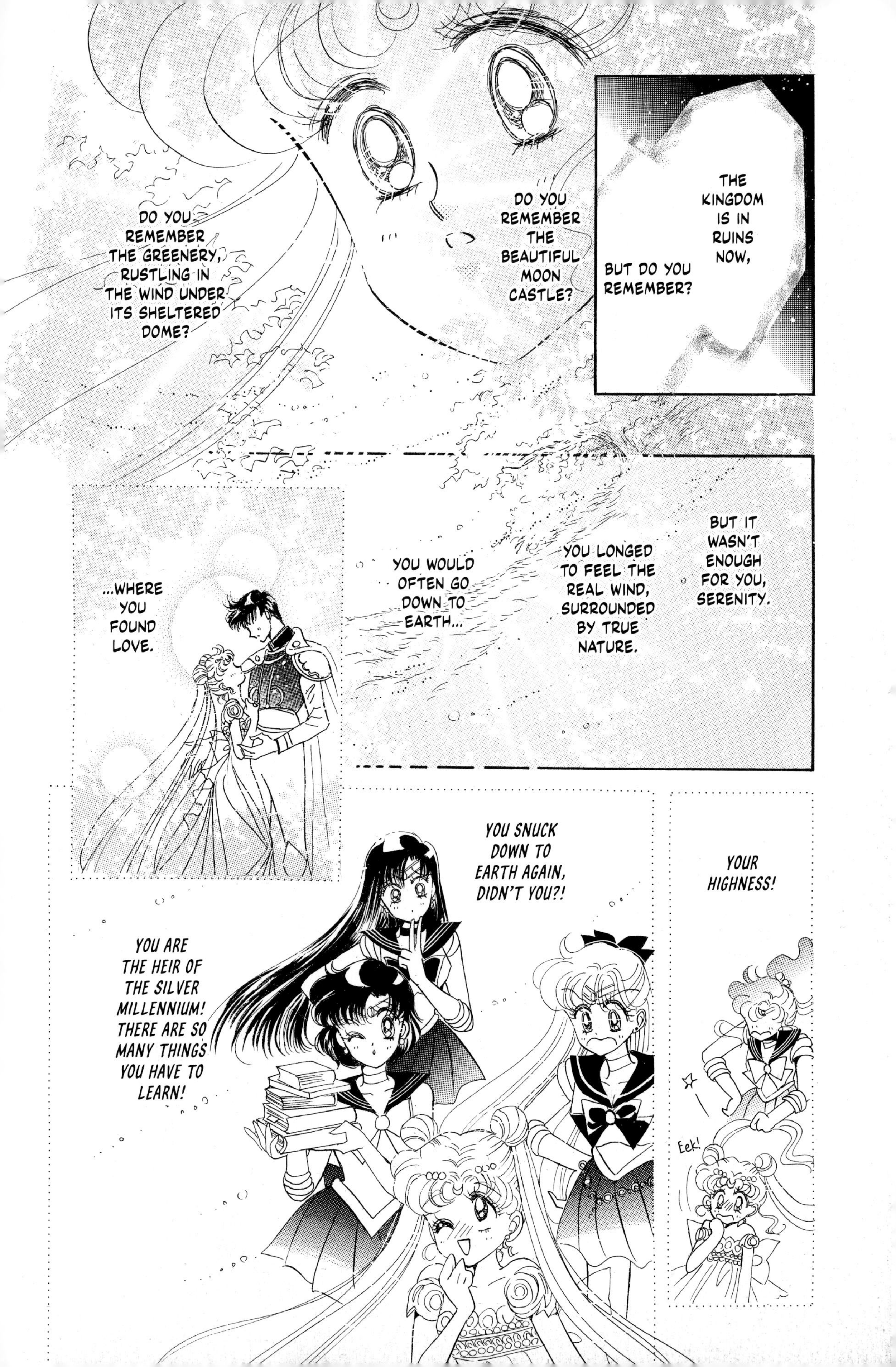
THE KINGDOM IS IN RUINS NOW,
BUT DO YOU REMEMBER?
DO YOU REMEMBER THE BEAUTIFUL MOON CASTLE?
DO YOU REMEMBER THE GREENERY, RUSTLING IN THE WIND UNDER ITS SHELTERED DOME?
BUT IT WASN'T ENOUGH FOR YOU, SERENITY.
YOU LONGED TO FEEL THE REAL WIND, SURROUNDED BY TRUE NATURE.
YOU WOULD OFTEN GO DOWN TO EARTH...
...WHERE YOU FOUND LOVE.
YOUR HIGHNESS!
Eek!
YOU SNUCK DOWN TO EARTH AGAIN, DIDN'T YOU?!
YOU ARE THE HEIR OF THE SILVER MILLENNIUM! THERE ARE SO MANY THINGS YOU HAVE TO LEARN!

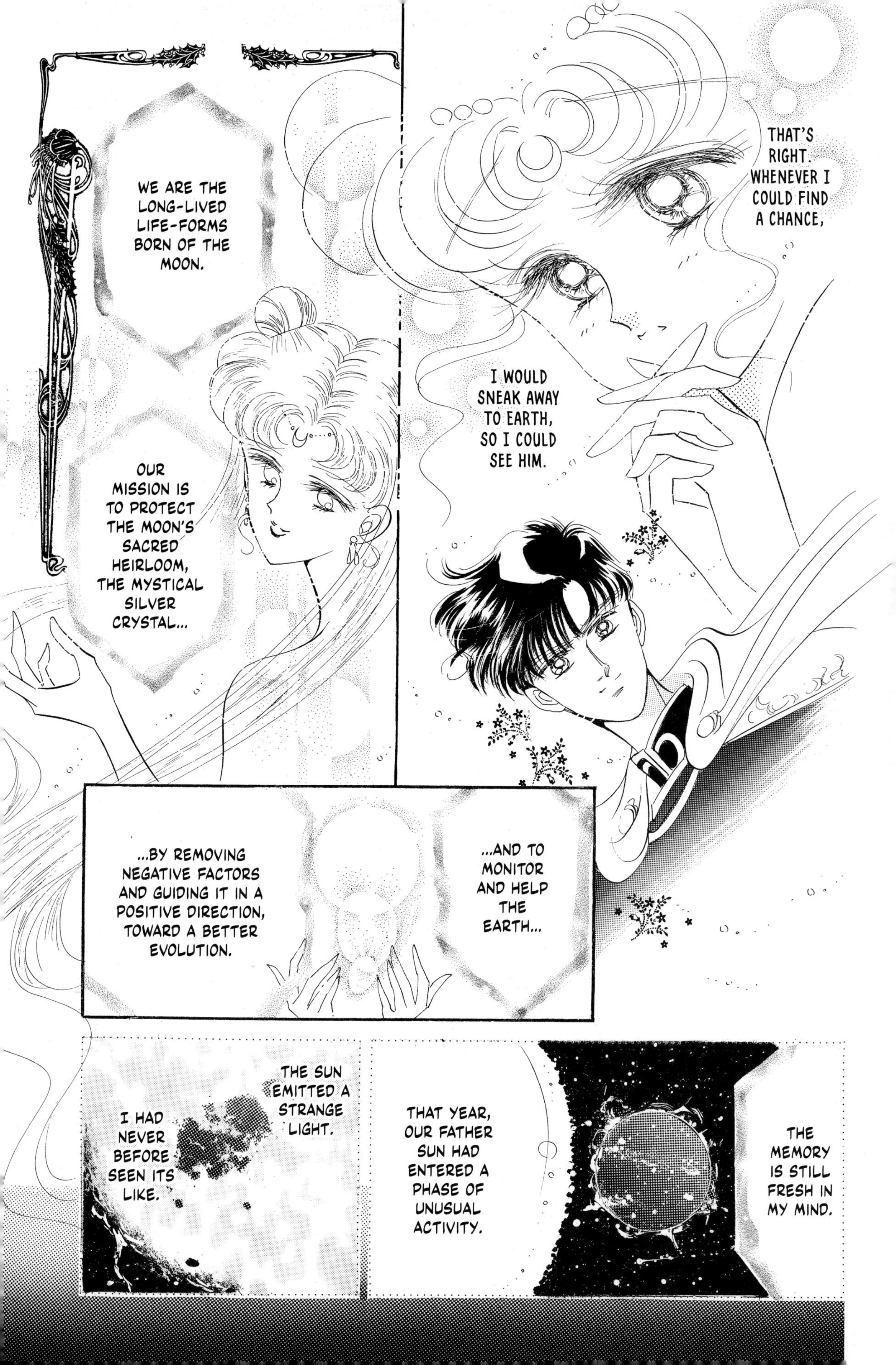
THAT'S RIGHT. WHENEVER I COULD FIND A CHANCE,
I WOULD SNEAK AWAY TO EARTH, SO I COULD SEE HIM.
WE ARE THE LONG-LIVED LIFE-FORMS BORN OF THE MOON.
OUR MISSION IS TO PROTECT THE MOON'S SACRED HEIRLOOM, THE MYSTICAL SILVER CRYSTAL...
...AND TO MONITOR AND HELP THE EARTH...
...BY REMOVING NEGATIVE FACTORS AND GUIDING IT IN A POSITIVE DIRECTION, TOWARD A BETTER EVOLUTION.
THE MEMORY IS STILL FRESH IN MY MIND.
THAT YEAR, OUR FATHER SUN HAD ENTERED A PHASE OF UNUSUAL ACTIVITY.
THE SUN EMITTED A STRANGE LIGHT.
I HAD NEVER BEFORE SEEN ITS LIKE.

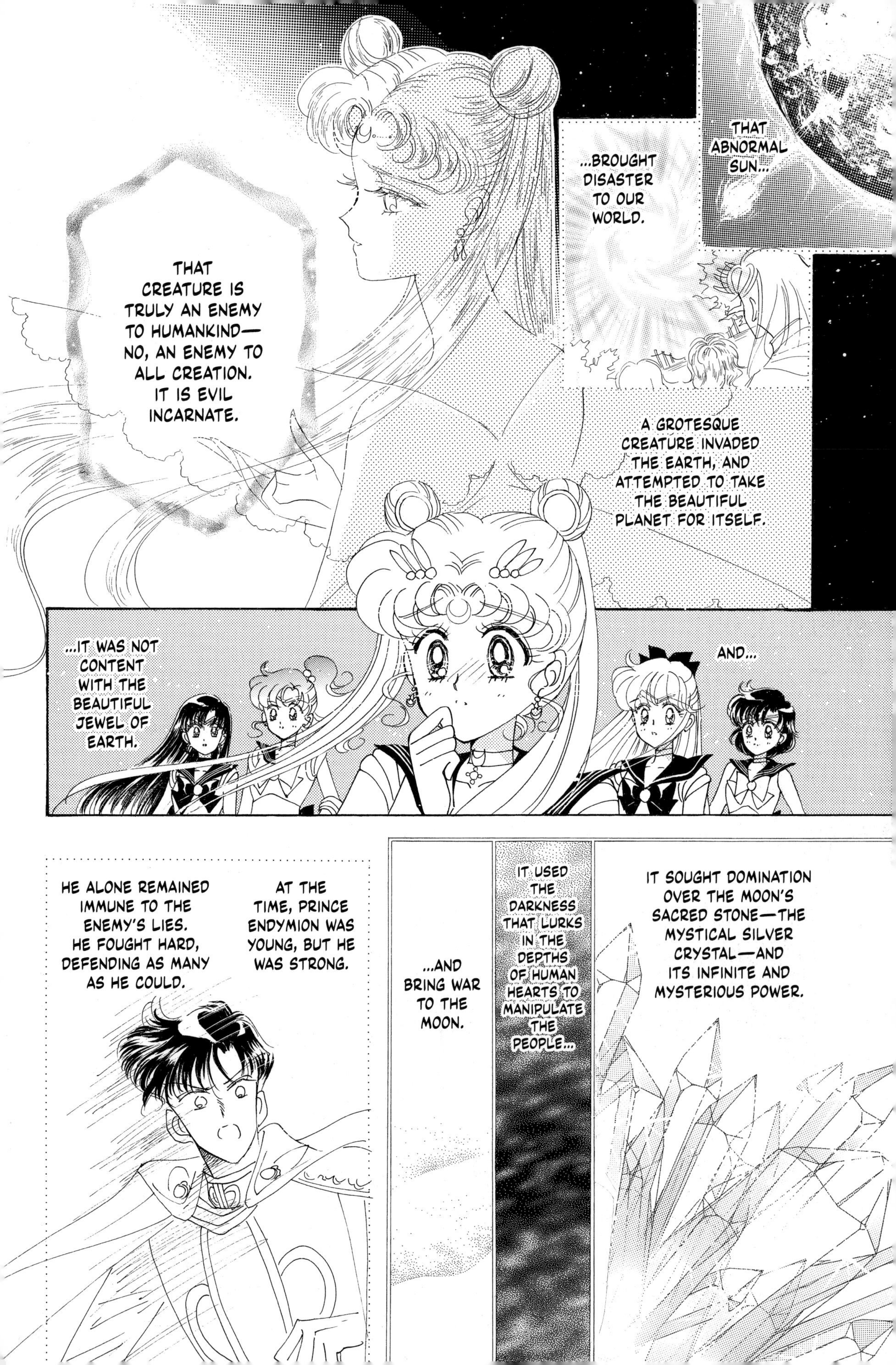
THAT ABNORMAL SUN...
...BROUGHT DISASTER TO OUR WORLD.
A GROTESQUE CREATURE INVADED THE EARTH, AND ATTEMPTED TO TAKE THE BEAUTIFUL PLANET FOR ITSELF.
THAT CREATURE IS TRULY AN ENEMY TO HUMANKIND—NO, AN ENEMY TO ALL CREATION. IT IS EVIL INCARNATE.
AND...
...IT WAS NOT CONTENT WITH THE BEAUTIFUL JEWEL OF EARTH.
IT SOUGHT DOMINATION OVER THE MOON'S SACRED STONE—THE MYSTICAL SILVER CRYSTAL—AND ITS INFINITE AND MYSTERIOUS POWER.
IT USED THE DARKNESS THAT LURKS IN THE DEPTHS OF HUMAN HEARTS TO MANIPULATE THE PEOPLE...
...AND BRING WAR TO THE MOON.
AT THE TIME, PRINCE ENDYMION WAS YOUNG, BUT HE WAS STRONG.
HE ALONE REMAINED IMMUNE TO THE ENEMY'S LIES. HE FOUGHT HARD, DEFENDING AS MANY AS HE COULD.

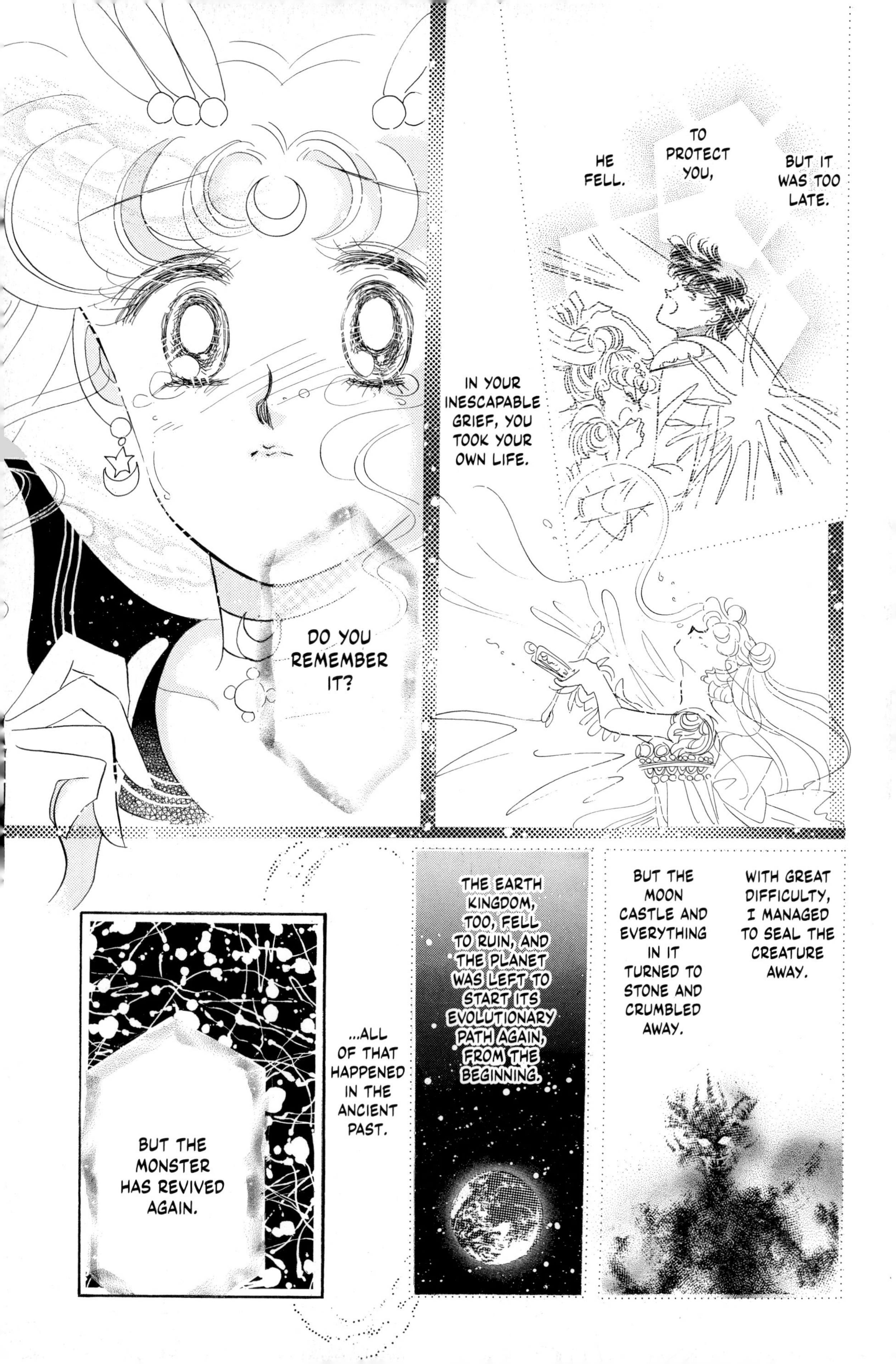
BUT IT WAS TOO LATE.
TO PROTECT YOU,
HE FELL.
IN YOUR INESCAPABLE GRIEF, YOU TOOK YOUR OWN LIFE.
DO YOU REMEMBER IT?
WITH GREAT DIFFICULTY, I MANAGED TO SEAL THE CREATURE AWAY.
BUT THE MOON CASTLE AND EVERYTHING IN IT TURNED TO STONE AND CRUMBLED AWAY.
THE EARTH KINGDOM, TOO, FELL TO RUIN, AND THE PLANET WAS LEFT TO START ITS EVOLUTIONARY PATH AGAIN, FROM THE BEGINNING.
...ALL OF THAT HAPPENED IN THE ANCIENT PAST.
BUT THE MONSTER HAS REVIVED AGAIN.

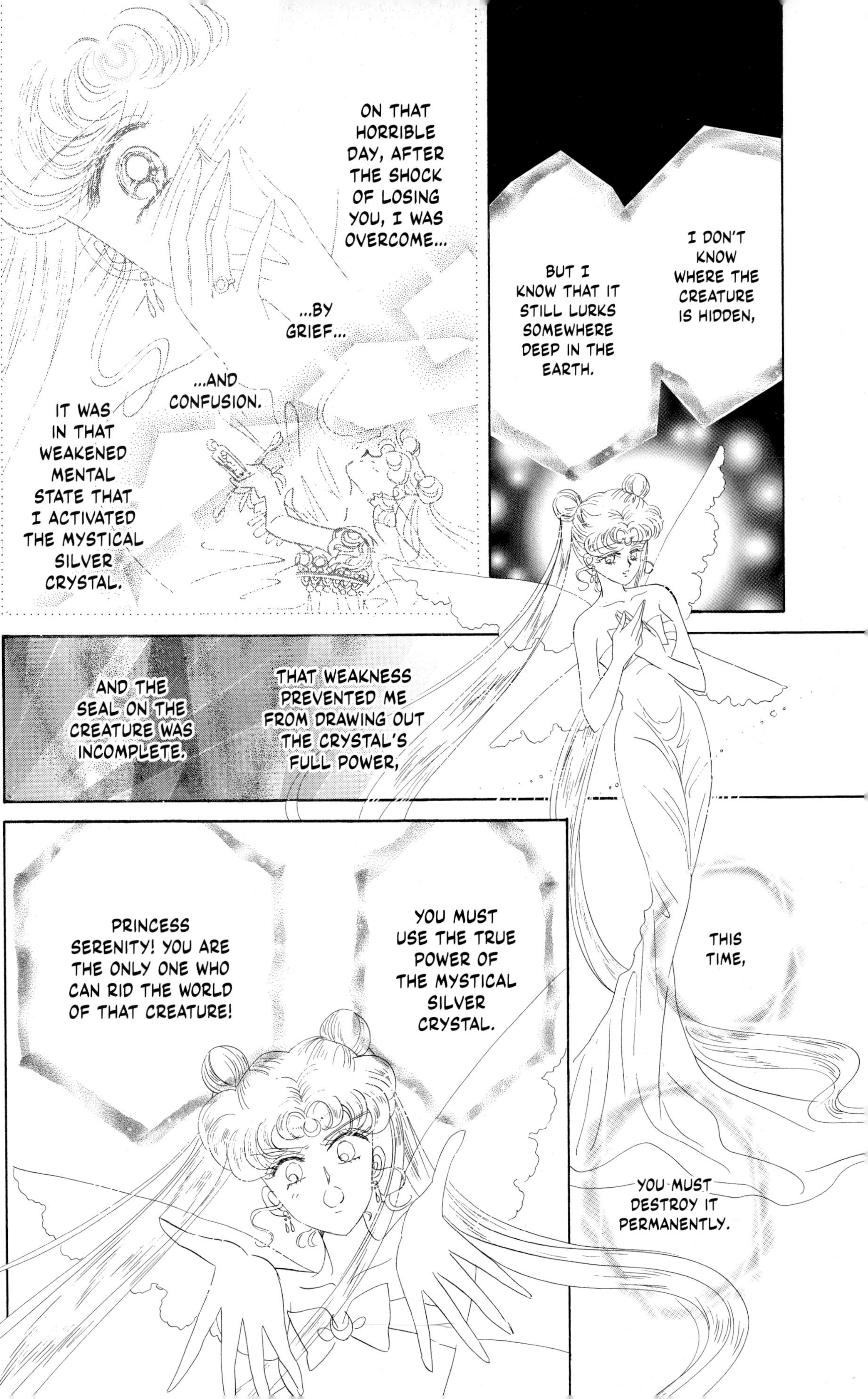
I DON'T KNOW WHERE THE CREATURE IS HIDDEN,
BUT I KNOW THAT IT STILL LURKS SOMEWHERE DEEP IN THE EARTH.
ON THAT HORRIBLE DAY, AFTER THE SHOCK OF LOSING YOU, I WAS OVERCOME...
...BY GRIEF...
...AND CONFUSION.
IT WAS IN THAT WEAKENED MENTAL STATE THAT I ACTIVATED THE MYSTICAL SILVER CRYSTAL.
THAT WEAKNESS PREVENTED ME FROM DRAWING OUT THE CRYSTAL'S FULL POWER,
AND THE SEAL ON THE CREATURE WAS INCOMPLETE.
THIS TIME,
YOU MUST DESTROY IT PERMANENTLY.
YOU MUST USE THE TRUE POWER OF THE MYSTICAL SILVER CRYSTAL.
PRINCESS SERENITY! YOU ARE THE ONLY ONE WHO CAN RID THE WORLD OF THAT CREATURE!

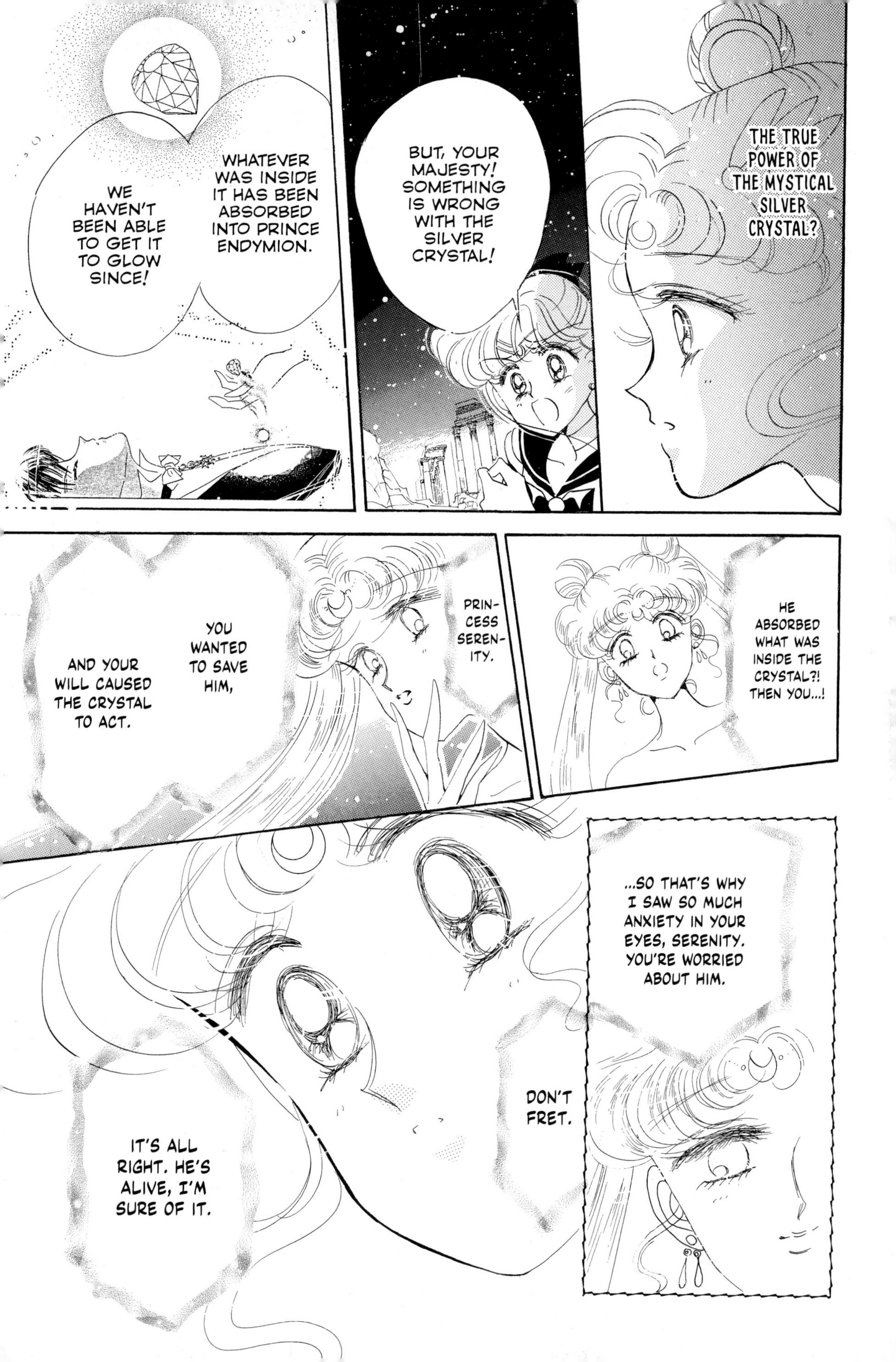
THE TRUE POWER OF THE MYSTICAL SILVER CRYSTAL?
BUT, YOUR MAJESTY! SOMETHING IS WRONG WITH THE SILVER CRYSTAL!
WHATEVER WAS INSIDE IT HAS BEEN ABSORBED INTO PRINCE ENDYMION.
WE HAVEN'T BEEN ABLE TO GET IT TO GLOW SINCE!
HE ABSORBED WHAT WAS INSIDE THE CRYSTAL?! THEN YOU...!
PRINCESS SERENITY.
YOU WANTED TO SAVE HIM,
AND YOUR WILL CAUSED THE CRYSTAL TO ACT.
...SO THAT'S WHY I SAW SO MUCH ANXIETY IN YOUR EYES, SERENITY. YOU'RE WORRIED ABOUT HIM.
DON'T FRET.
IT'S ALL RIGHT. HE'S ALIVE, I'M SURE OF IT.

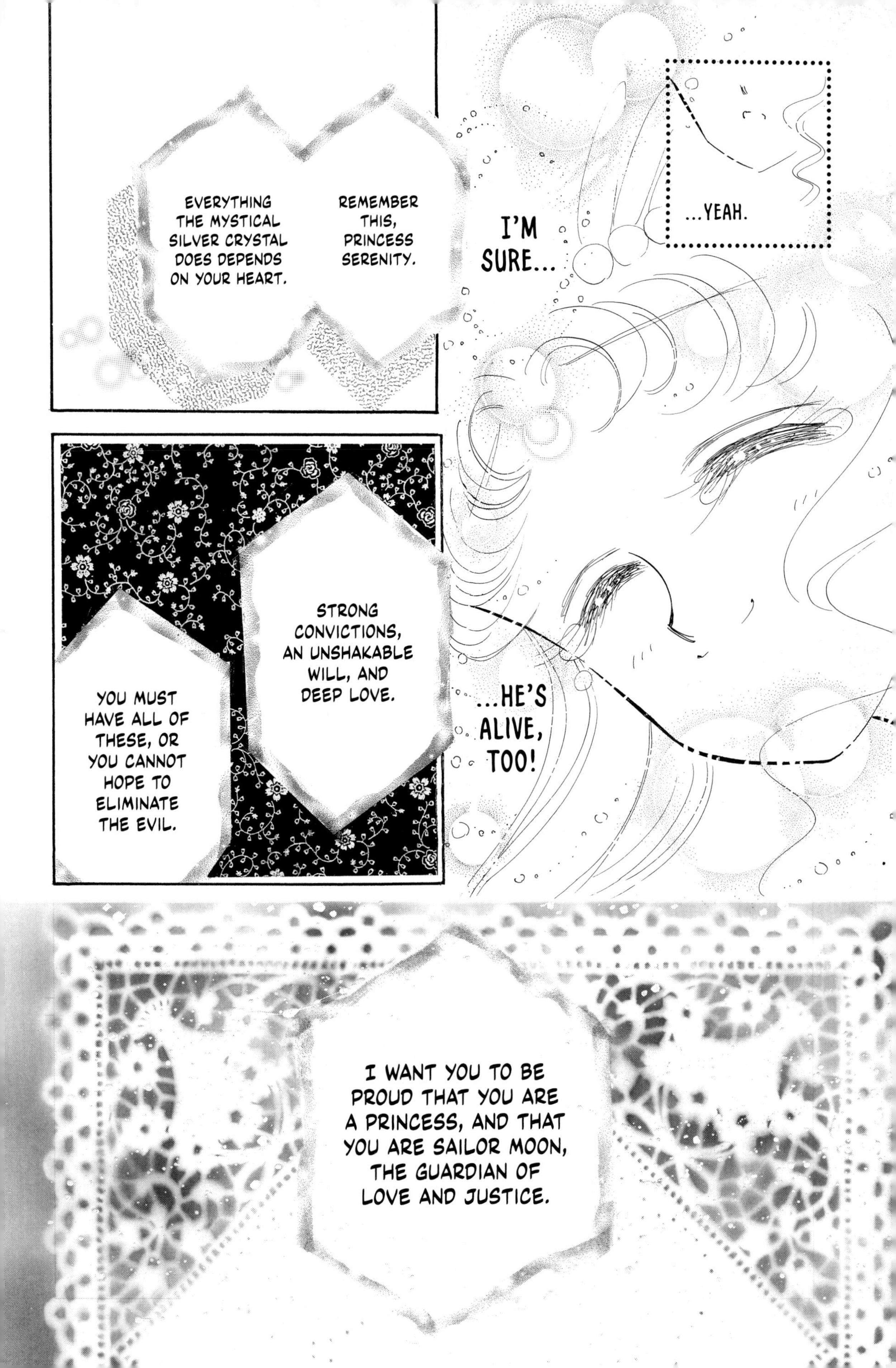
...YEAH.
I'M SURE...
...HE'S ALIVE, TOO!
REMEMBER THIS, PRINCESS SERENITY.
EVERYTHING THE MYSTICAL SILVER CRYSTAL DOES DEPENDS ON YOUR HEART.
STRONG CONVICTIONS, AN UNSHAKABLE WILL, AND DEEP LOVE.
YOU MUST HAVE ALL OF THESE, OR YOU CANNOT HOPE TO ELIMINATE THE EVIL.
I WANT YOU TO BE PROUD THAT YOU ARE A PRINCESS, AND THAT YOU ARE SAILOR MOON, THE GUARDIAN OF LOVE AND JUSTICE.

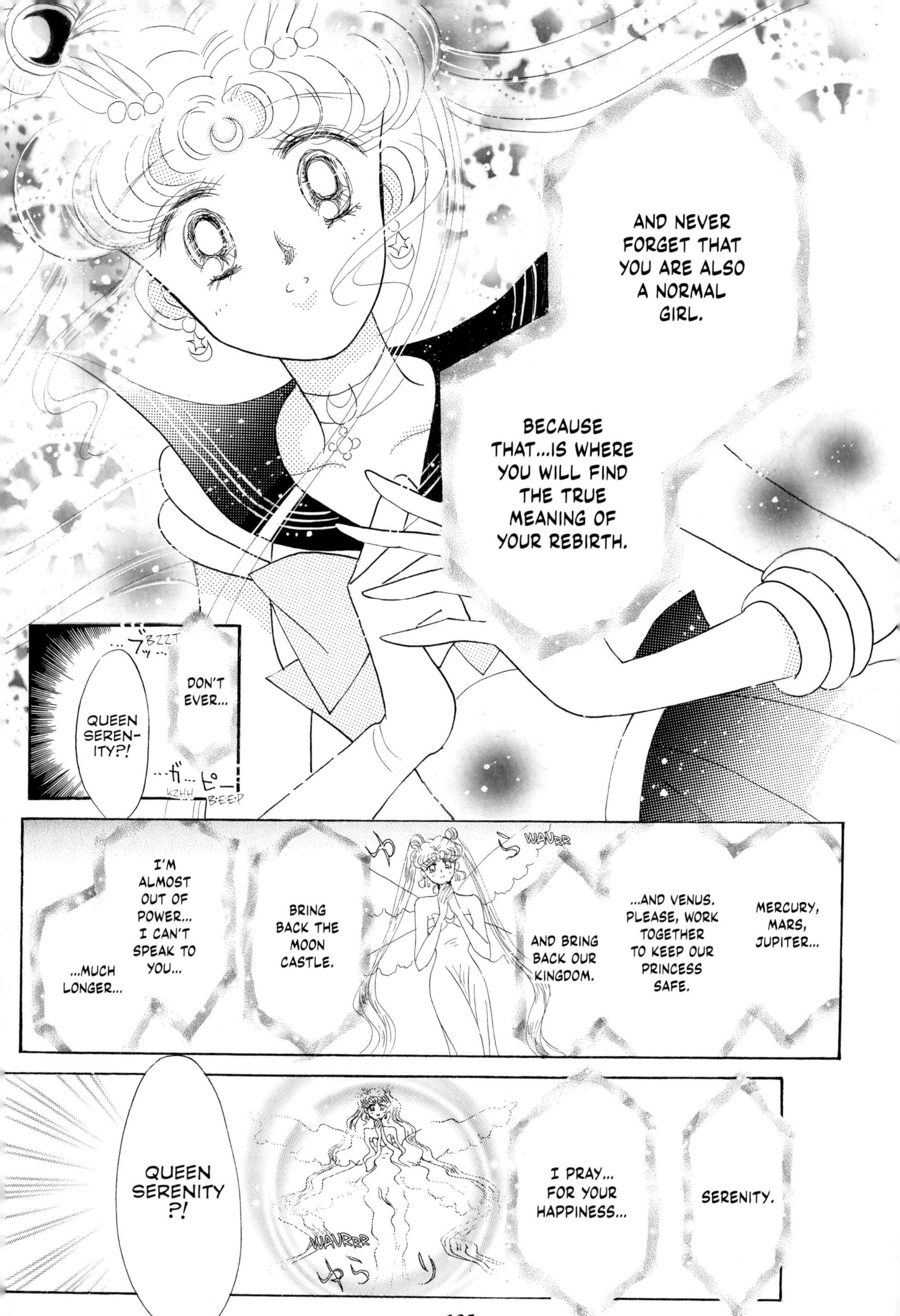

AND NEVER FORGET THAT YOU ARE ALSO A NORMAL GIRL.
BECAUSE THAT...IS WHERE YOU WILL FIND THE TRUE MEANING OF YOUR REBIRTH.
BZZT
DON'T EVER...
KZHH
BEEP
QUEEN SERENITY?!
MERCURY, MARS, JUPITER...
...AND VENUS. PLEASE, WORK TOGETHER TO KEEP OUR PRINCESS SAFE.
AND BRING BACK OUR KINGDOM.
WAURR
BRING BACK THE MOON CASTLE.
I'M ALMOST OUT OF POWER... I CAN'T SPEAK TO YOU...
...MUCH LONGER...
SERENITY.
I PRAY... FOR YOUR HAPPINESS...
WAURRR
QUEEN SERENITY ?!

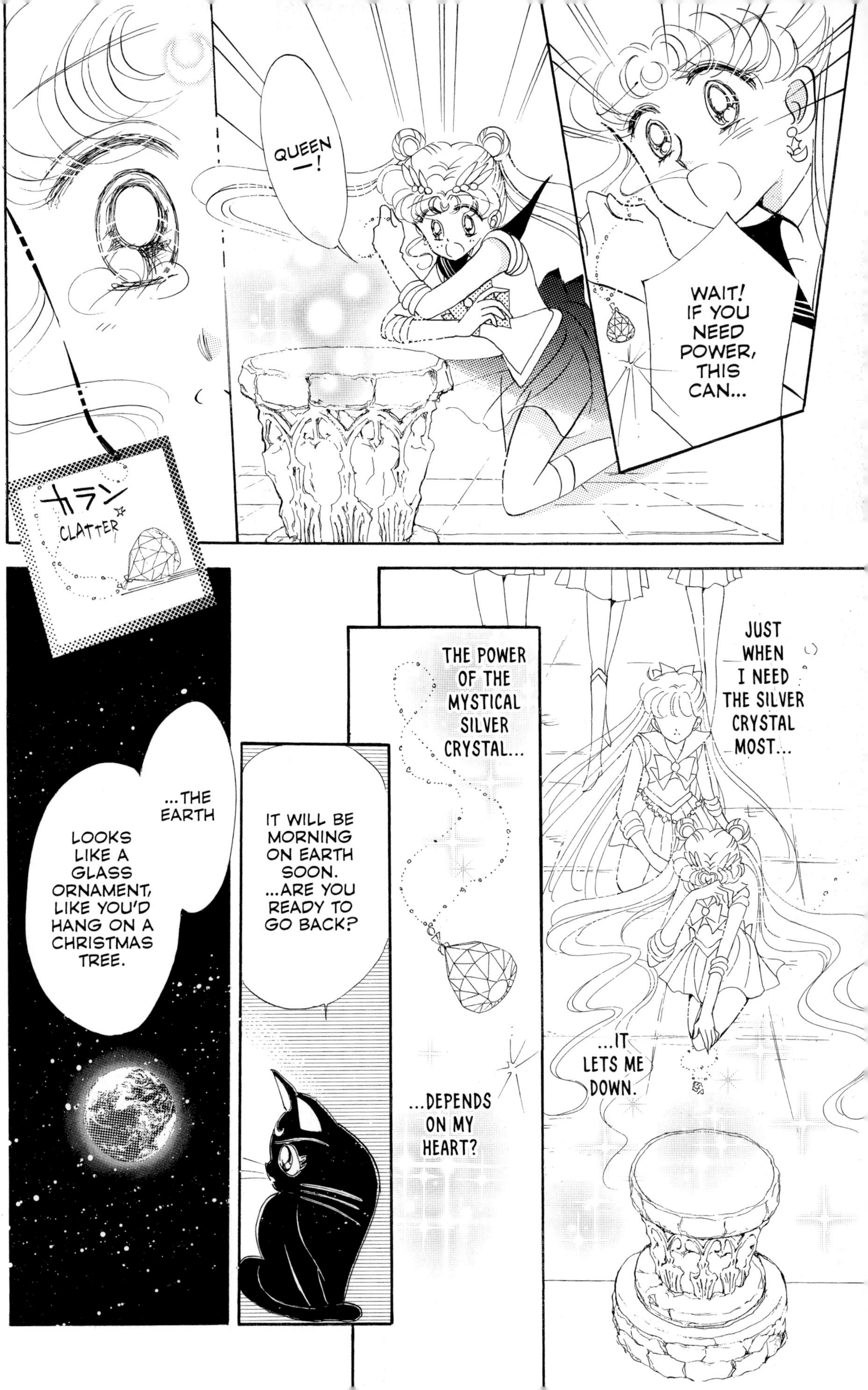
WAIT! IF YOU NEED POWER, THIS CAN...
QUEEN—!
カラン
CLATTER
JUST WHEN I NEED THE SILVER CRYSTAL MOST...
...IT LETS ME DOWN.
THE POWER OF THE MYSTICAL SILVER CRYSTAL...
...DEPENDS ON MY HEART?
IT WILL BE MORNING ON EARTH SOON. ...ARE YOU READY TO GO BACK?
...THE EARTH
LOOKS LIKE A GLASS ORNAMENT, LIKE YOU'D HANG ON A CHRISTMAS TREE.

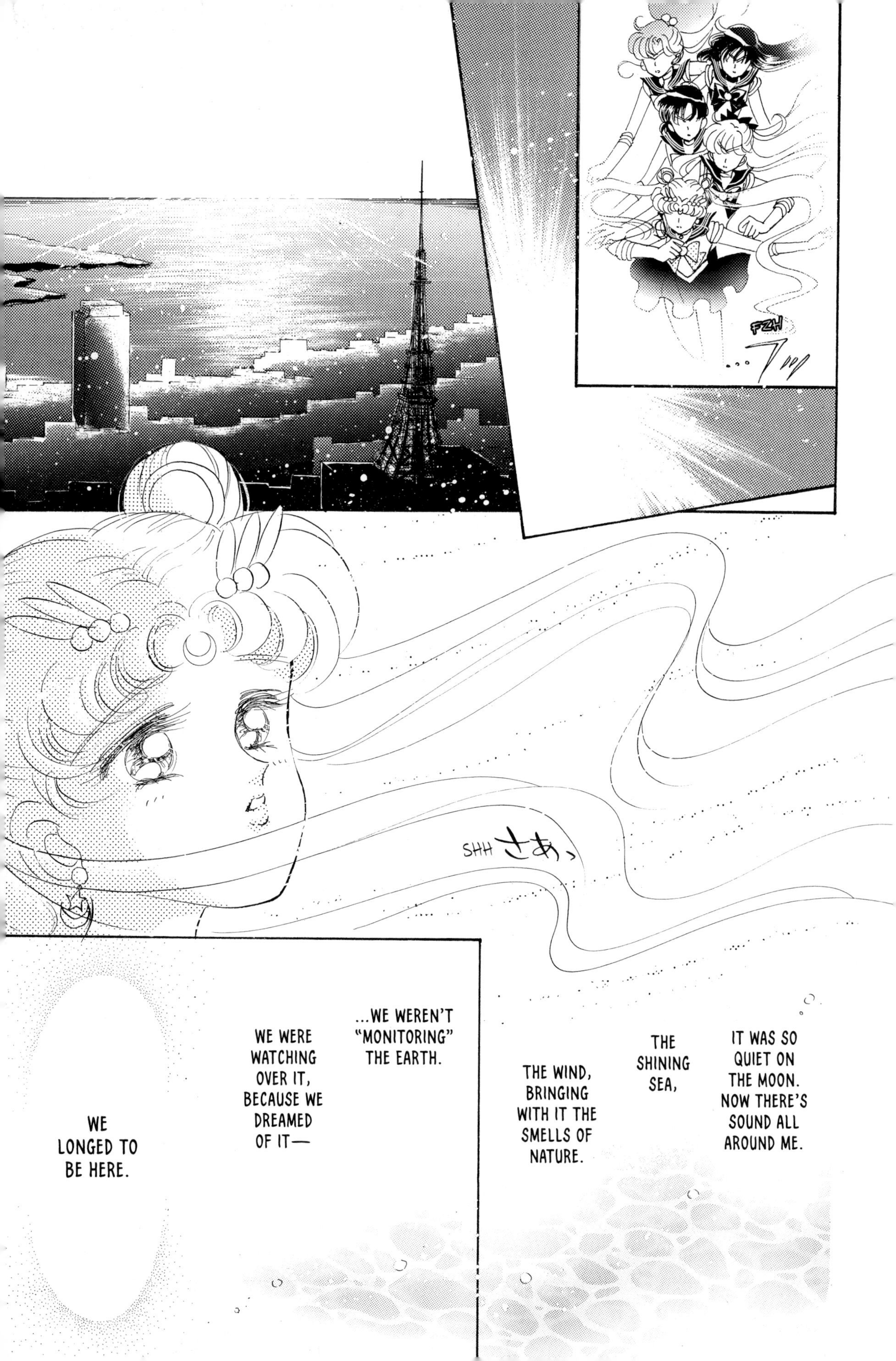

FZH
SHH
IT WAS SO QUIET ON THE MOON. NOW THERE'S SOUND ALL AROUND ME.
THE SHINING SEA,
THE WIND, BRINGING WITH IT THE SMELLS OF NATURE.
...WE WEREN'T "MONITORING" THE EARTH.
WE WERE WATCHING OVER IT, BECAUSE WE DREAMED OF IT—
WE LONGED TO BE HERE.

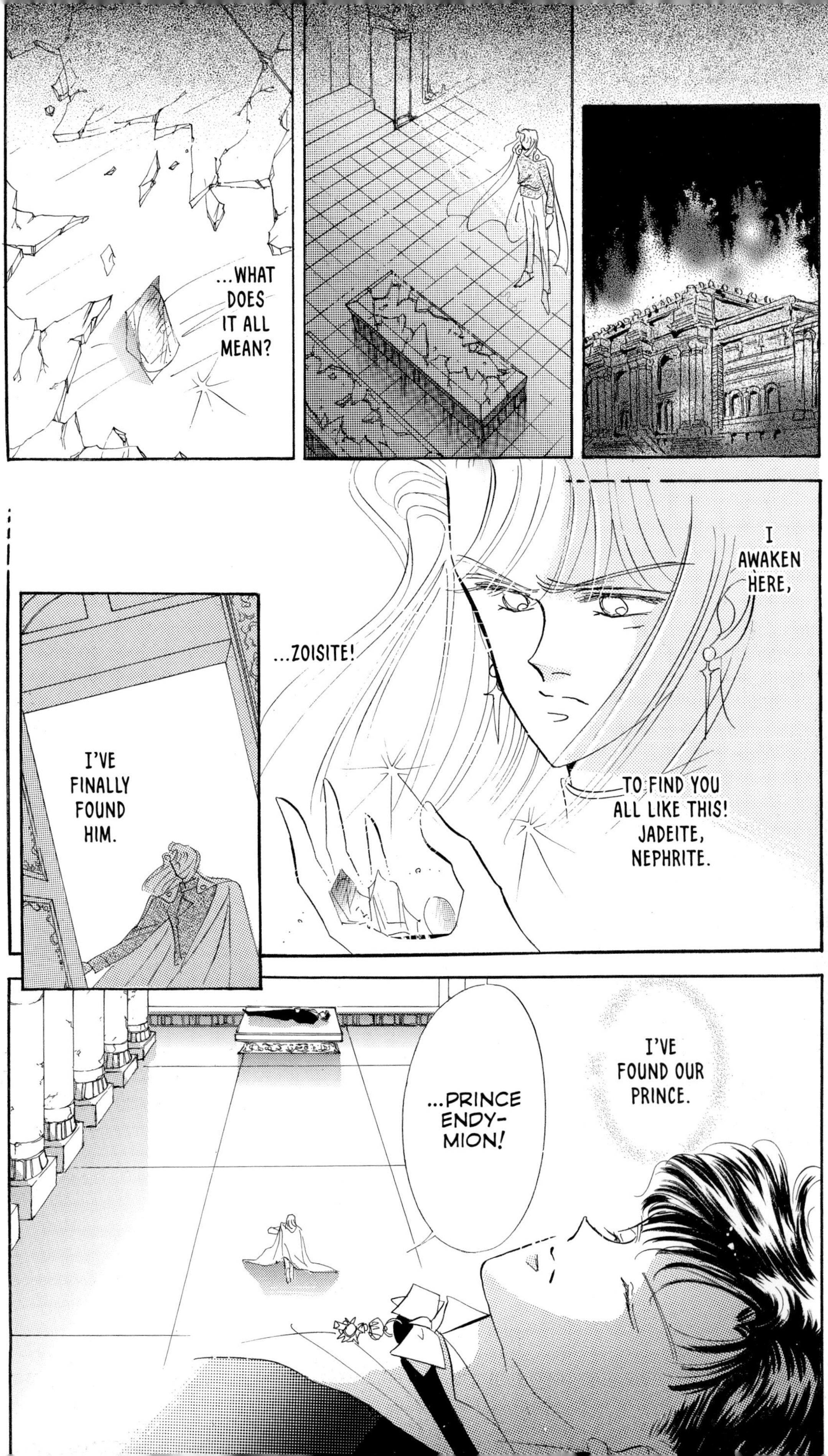
...WHAT DOES IT ALL MEAN?
I AWAKEN HERE,
TO FIND YOU ALL LIKE THIS! JADEITE, NEPHRITE.
...ZOISITE!
I'VE FINALLY FOUND HIM.
I'VE FOUND OUR PRINCE.
...PRINCE ENDY-MION!

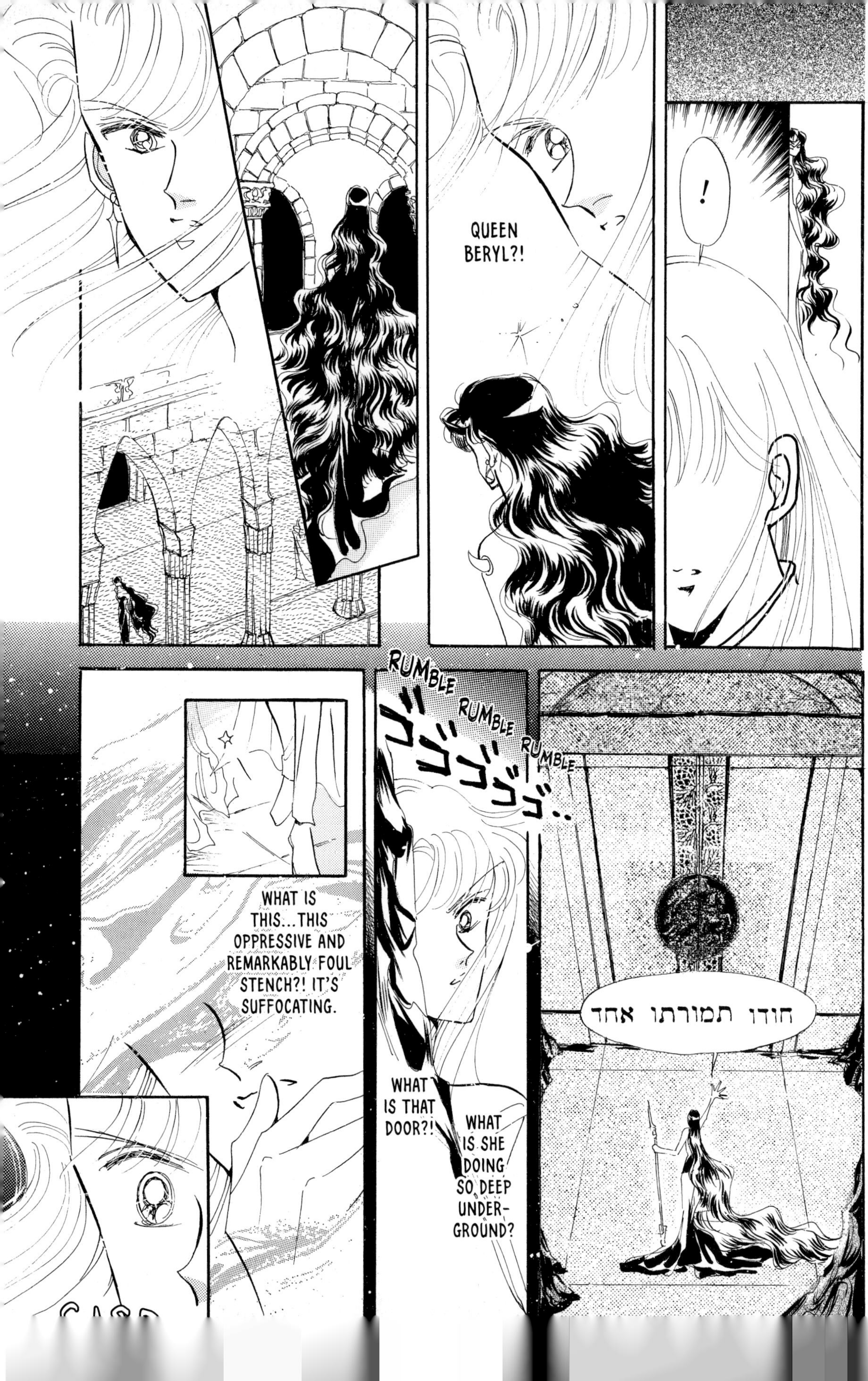
!
QUEEN BERYL?!
חודו תמורתו אחד
RUMBLE RUMBLE RUMBLE
WHAT IS THAT DOOR?!
WHAT IS SHE DOING SO DEEP UNDER-GROUND?
WHAT IS THIS...THIS OPPRESSIVE AND REMARKABLY FOUL STENCH?! IT'S SUFFOCATING.

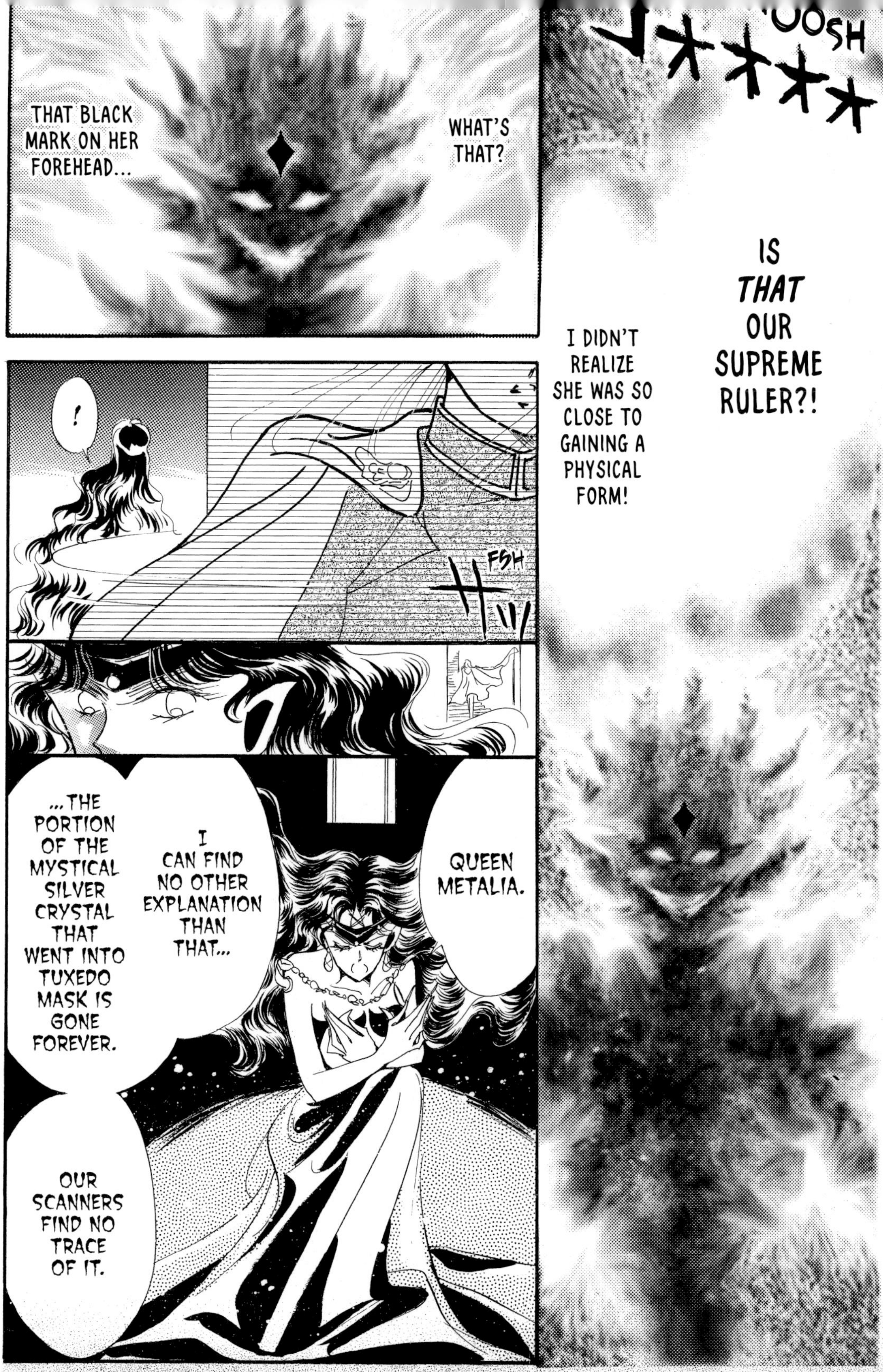

IS *THAT* OUR SUPREME RULER?!
I DIDN'T REALIZE SHE WAS SO CLOSE TO GAINING A PHYSICAL FORM!
WHAT'S THAT?
THAT BLACK MARK ON HER FOREHEAD...
!
FSH
QUEEN METALIA.
I CAN FIND NO OTHER EXPLANATION THAN THAT...
...THE PORTION OF THE MYSTICAL SILVER CRYSTAL THAT WENT INTO TUXEDO MASK IS GONE FOREVER.
OUR SCANNERS FIND NO TRACE OF IT.

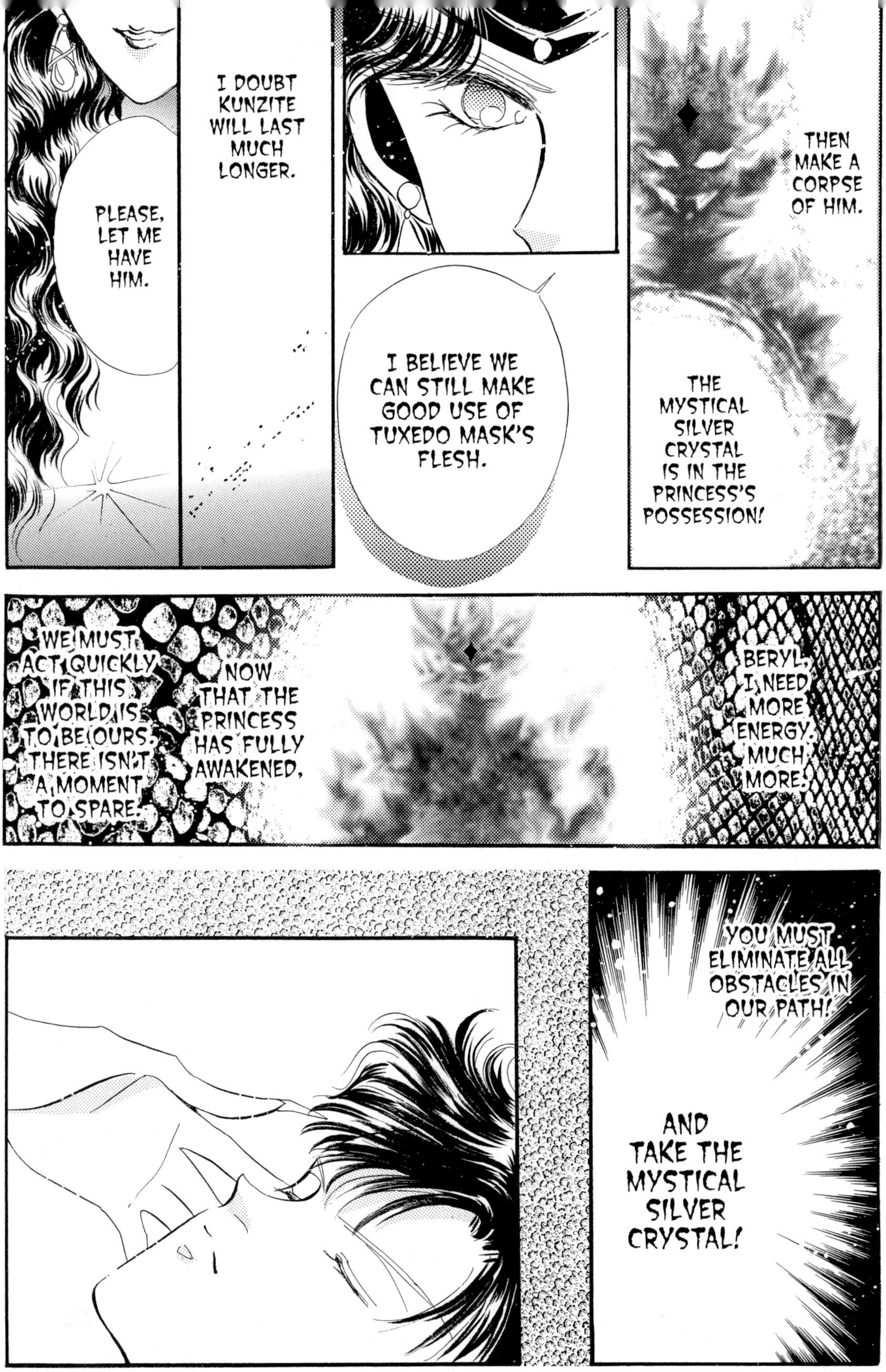
THEN MAKE A CORPSE OF HIM.
THE MYSTICAL SILVER CRYSTAL IS IN THE PRINCESS'S POSSESSION!
I BELIEVE WE CAN STILL MAKE GOOD USE OF TUXEDO MASK'S FLESH.
I DOUBT KUNZITE WILL LAST MUCH LONGER.
PLEASE, LET ME HAVE HIM.
BERYL, I NEED MORE ENERGY. MUCH MORE.
NOW THAT THE PRINCESS HAS FULLY AWAKENED,
WE MUST ACT QUICKLY IF THIS WORLD IS TO BE OURS. THERE ISN'T A MOMENT TO SPARE.
YOU MUST ELIMINATE ALL OBSTACLES IN OUR PATH!
AND TAKE THE MYSTICAL SILVER CRYSTAL!

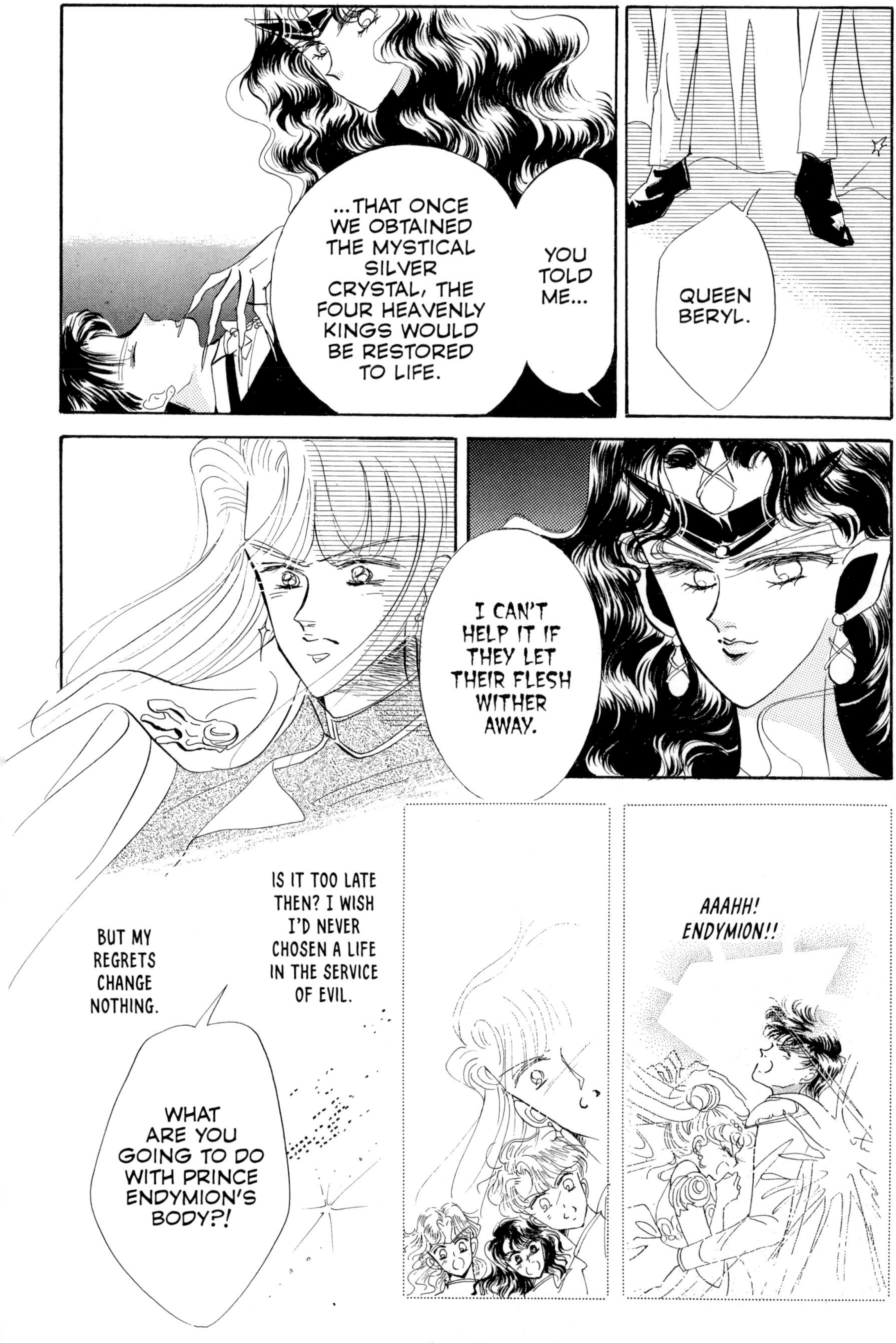
QUEEN BERYL.
YOU TOLD ME...
...THAT ONCE WE OBTAINED THE MYSTICAL SILVER CRYSTAL, THE FOUR HEAVENLY KINGS WOULD BE RESTORED TO LIFE.
I CAN'T HELP IT IF THEY LET THEIR FLESH WITHER AWAY.
AAAHH! ENDYMION!!
IS IT TOO LATE THEN? I WISH I'D NEVER CHOSEN A LIFE IN THE SERVICE OF EVIL.
BUT MY REGRETS CHANGE NOTHING.
WHAT ARE YOU GOING TO DO WITH PRINCE ENDYMION'S BODY?!

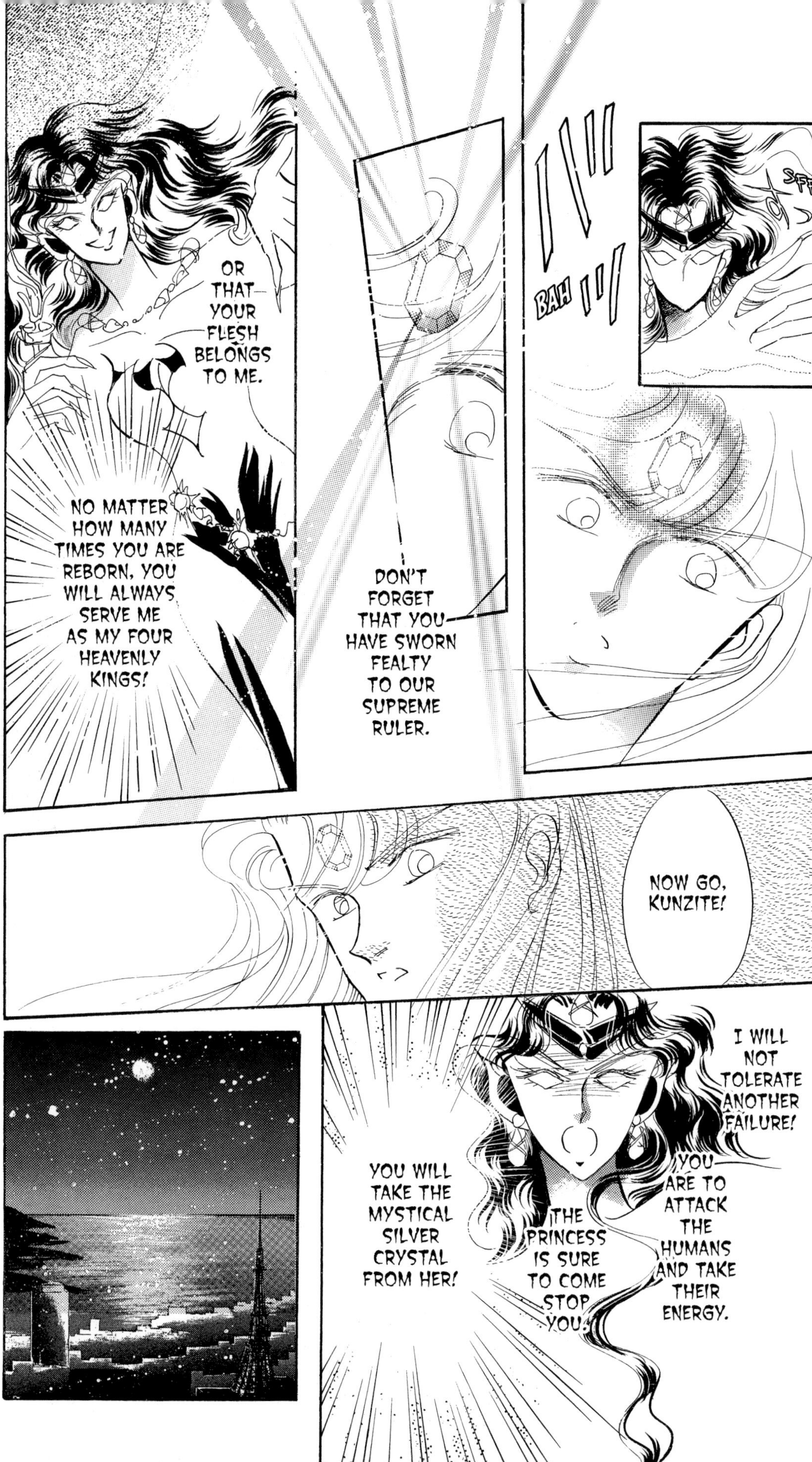
SFF
BAH
DON'T FORGET THAT YOU HAVE SWORN FEALTY TO OUR SUPREME RULER.
OR THAT YOUR FLESH BELONGS TO ME.
NO MATTER HOW MANY TIMES YOU ARE REBORN, YOU WILL ALWAYS SERVE ME AS MY FOUR HEAVENLY KINGS!
NOW GO, KUNZITE!
I WILL NOT TOLERATE ANOTHER FAILURE!
YOU ARE TO ATTACK THE HUMANS AND TAKE THEIR ENERGY.
THE PRINCESS IS SURE TO COME STOP YOU.
YOU WILL TAKE THE MYSTICAL SILVER CRYSTAL FROM HER!

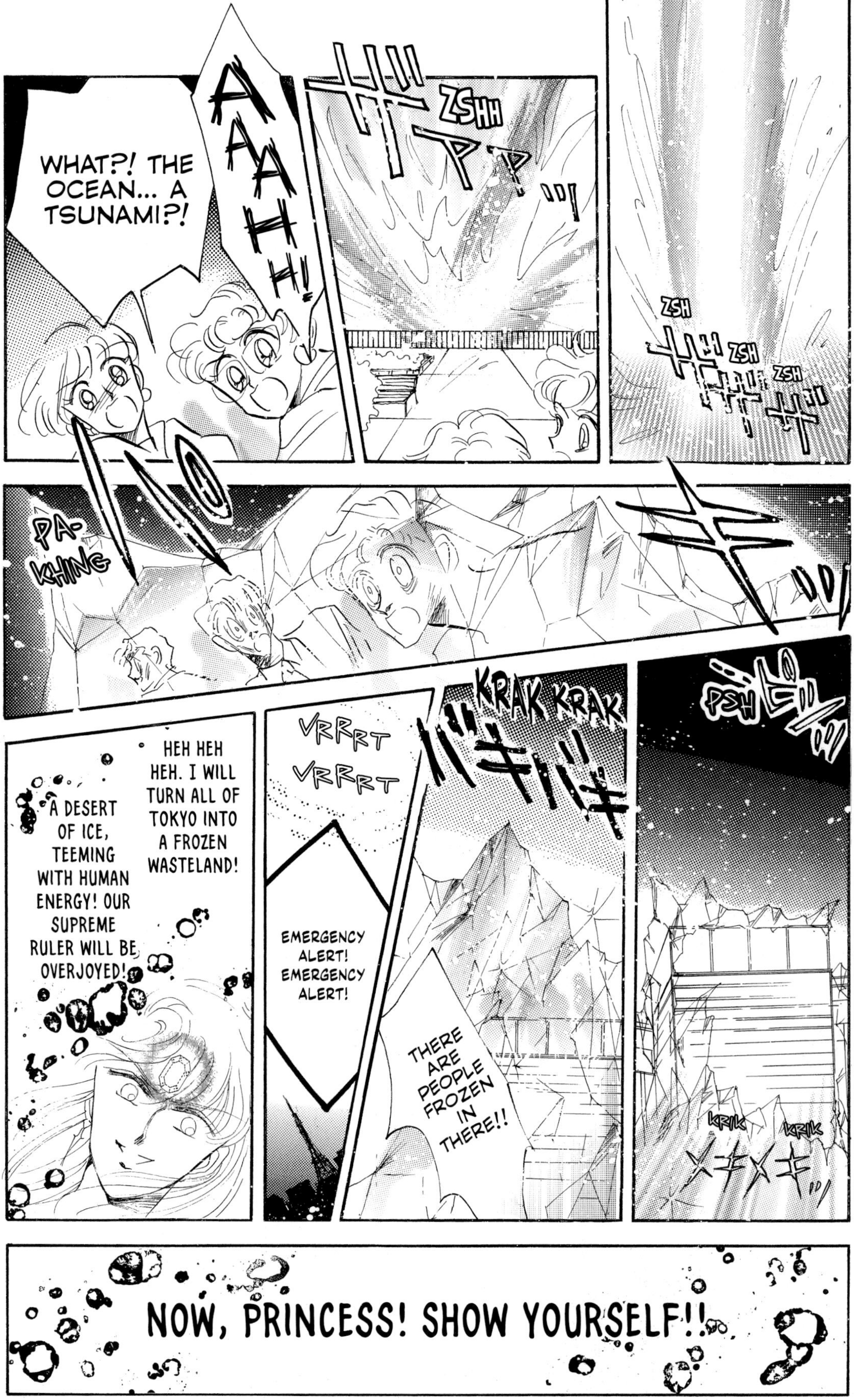
ZSH
ZSH
ZSH
ZSHH
AAAHHH!
WHAT?! THE OCEAN... A TSUNAMI?!
PA-KHING
PSH
KRIK
KRIK
KRAK KRAK
VRRRT
VRRRT
EMERGENCY ALERT! EMERGENCY ALERT!
THERE ARE PEOPLE FROZEN IN THERE!!
HEH HEH HEH. I WILL TURN ALL OF TOKYO INTO A FROZEN WASTELAND!
A DESERT OF ICE, TEEMING WITH HUMAN ENERGY! OUR SUPREME RULER WILL BE OVERJOYED!
NOW, PRINCESS! SHOW YOURSELF!!

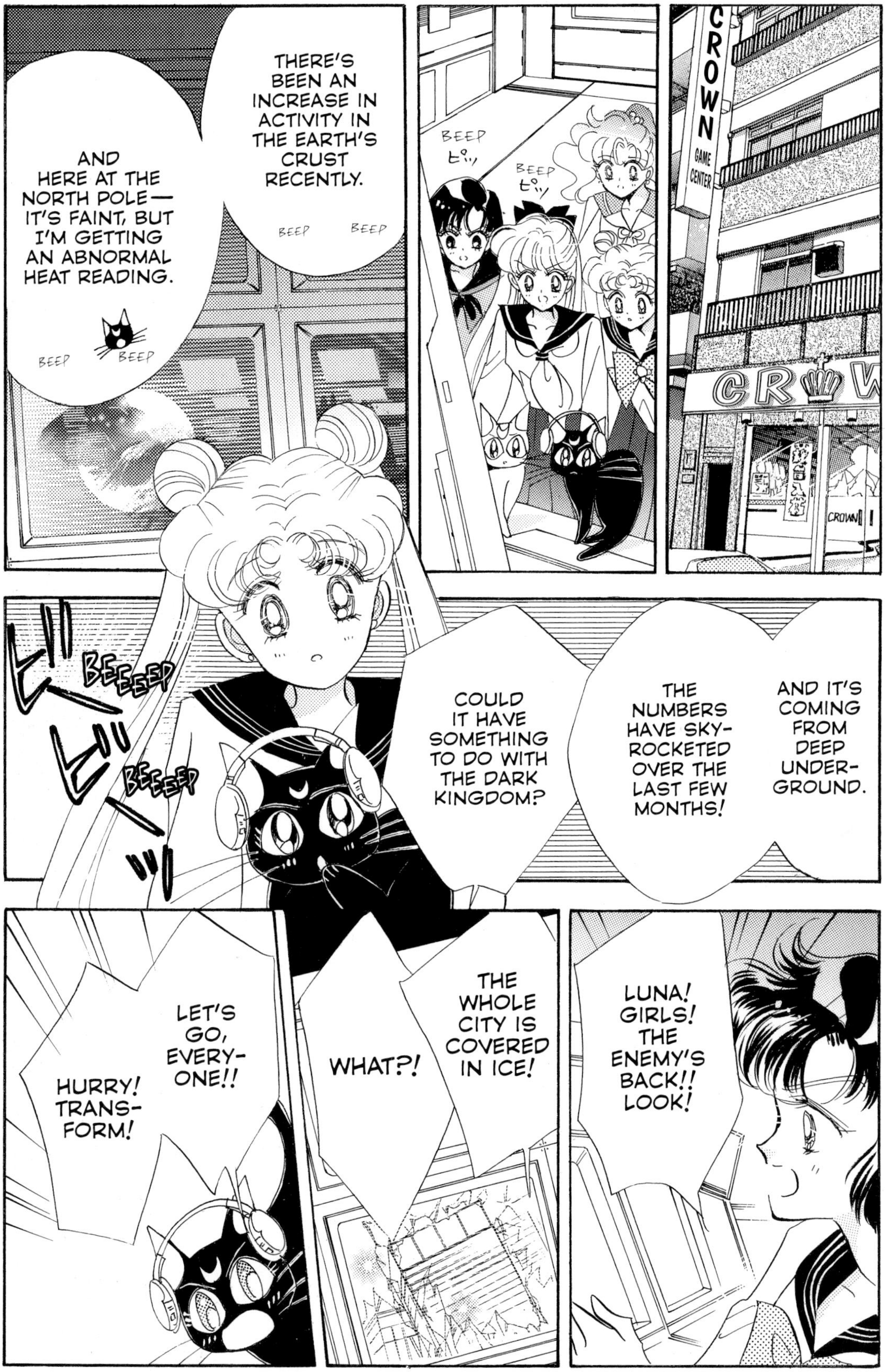
CROWN
GAME CENTER
BEEP
ピッ
BEEP
ピッ
THERE'S BEEN AN INCREASE IN ACTIVITY IN THE EARTH'S CRUST RECENTLY.
BEEP BEEP
AND HERE AT THE NORTH POLE— IT'S FAINT, BUT I'M GETTING AN ABNORMAL HEAT READING.
BEEP BEEP
AND IT'S COMING FROM DEEP UNDER-GROUND.
THE NUMBERS HAVE SKY-ROCKETED OVER THE LAST FEW MONTHS!
COULD IT HAVE SOMETHING TO DO WITH THE DARK KINGDOM?
BEEEEP
BEEEEP
LUNA! GIRLS! THE ENEMY'S BACK!! LOOK!
THE WHOLE CITY IS COVERED IN ICE!
WHAT?!
LET'S GO, EVERY-ONE!!
HURRY! TRANS-FORM!

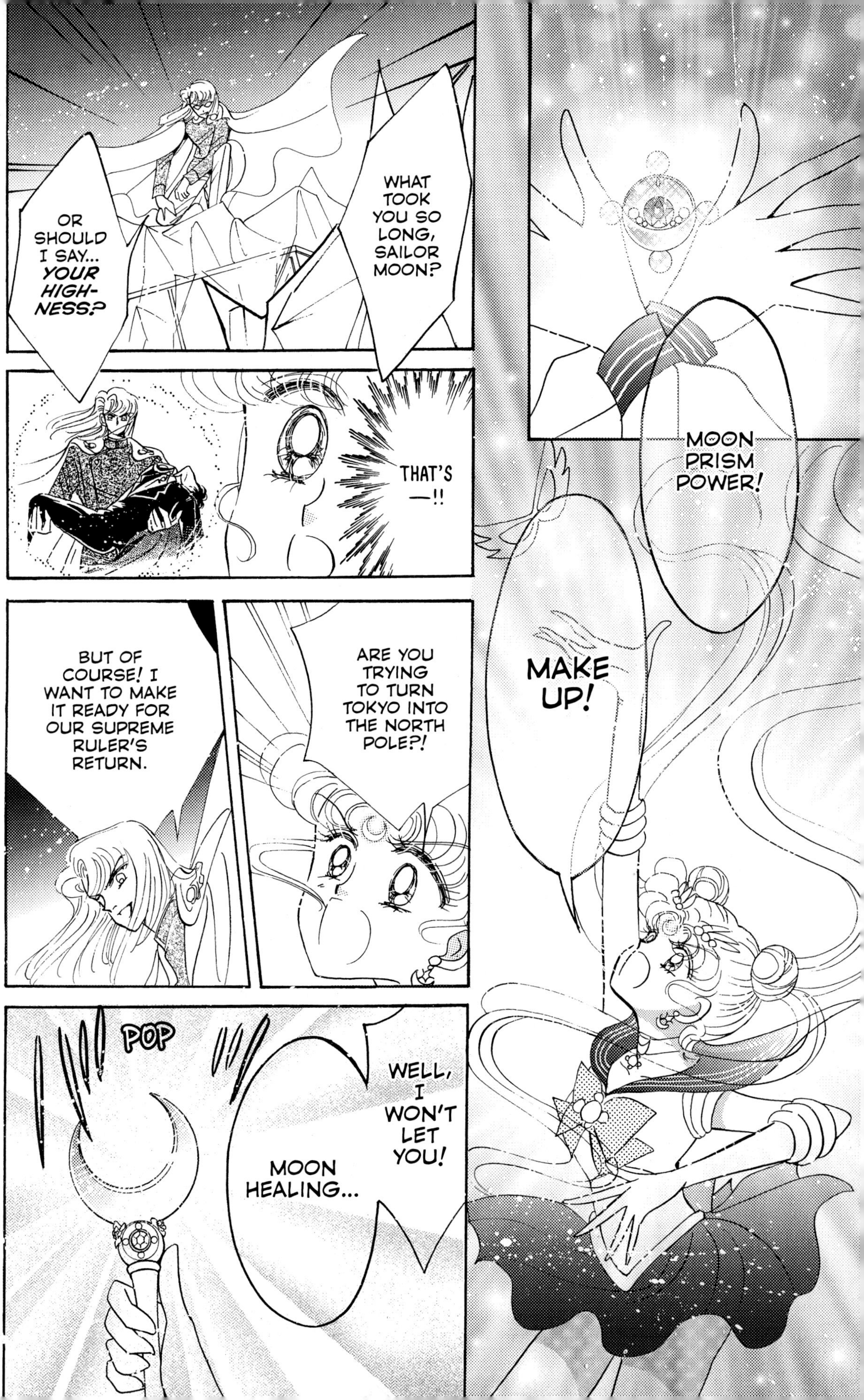
MOON PRISM POWER!
MAKE UP!
WHAT TOOK YOU SO LONG, SAILOR MOON?
OR SHOULD I SAY... *YOUR HIGHNESS?*
THAT'S —!!
ARE YOU TRYING TO TURN TOKYO INTO THE NORTH POLE?!
BUT OF COURSE! I WANT TO MAKE IT READY FOR OUR SUPREME RULER'S RETURN.
WELL, I WON'T LET YOU!
MOON HEALING...
POP

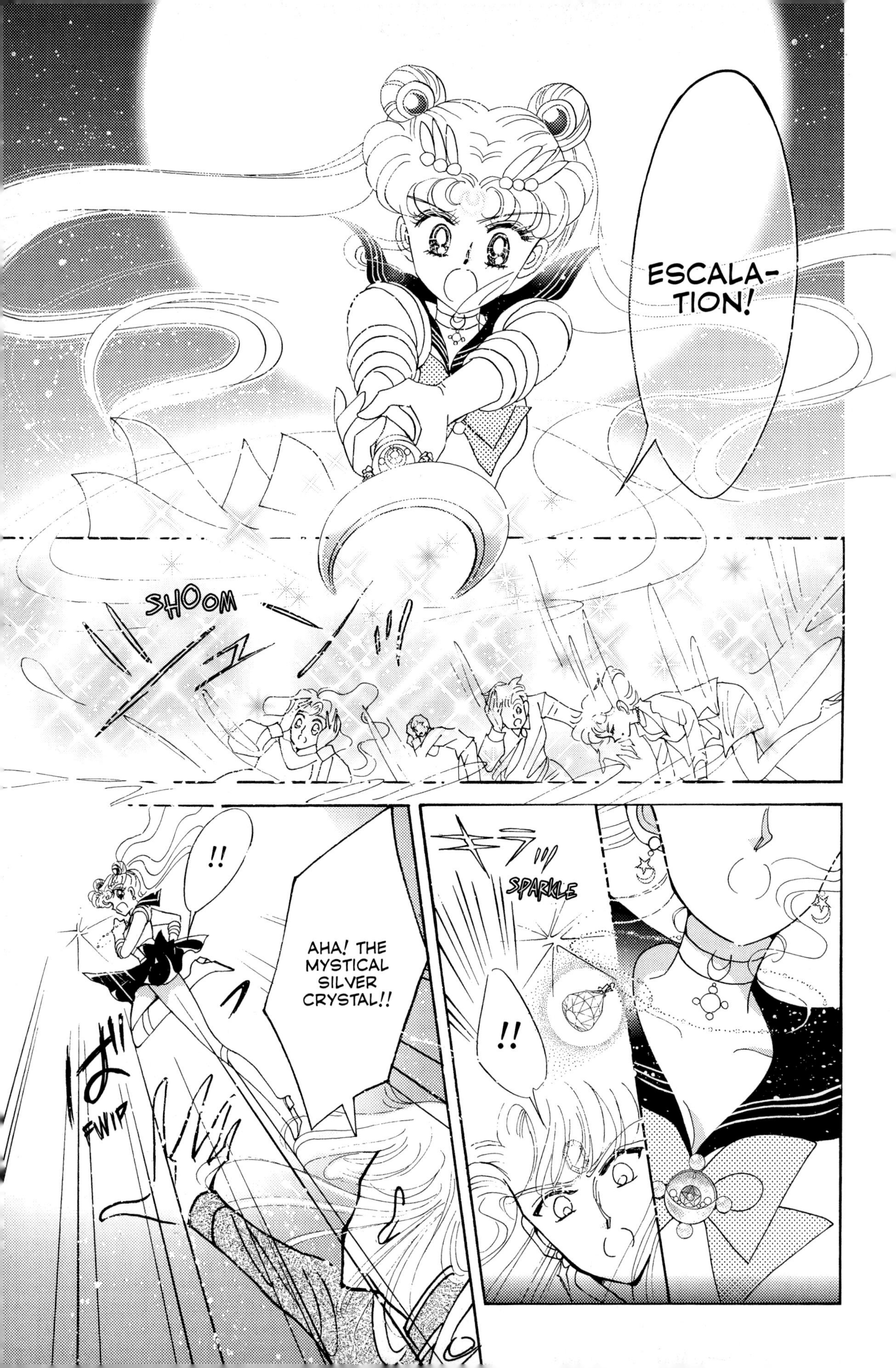
ESCALATION!
SHOOM
SPARKLE
!!
AHA! THE MYSTICAL SILVER CRYSTAL!!
!!
FWIP

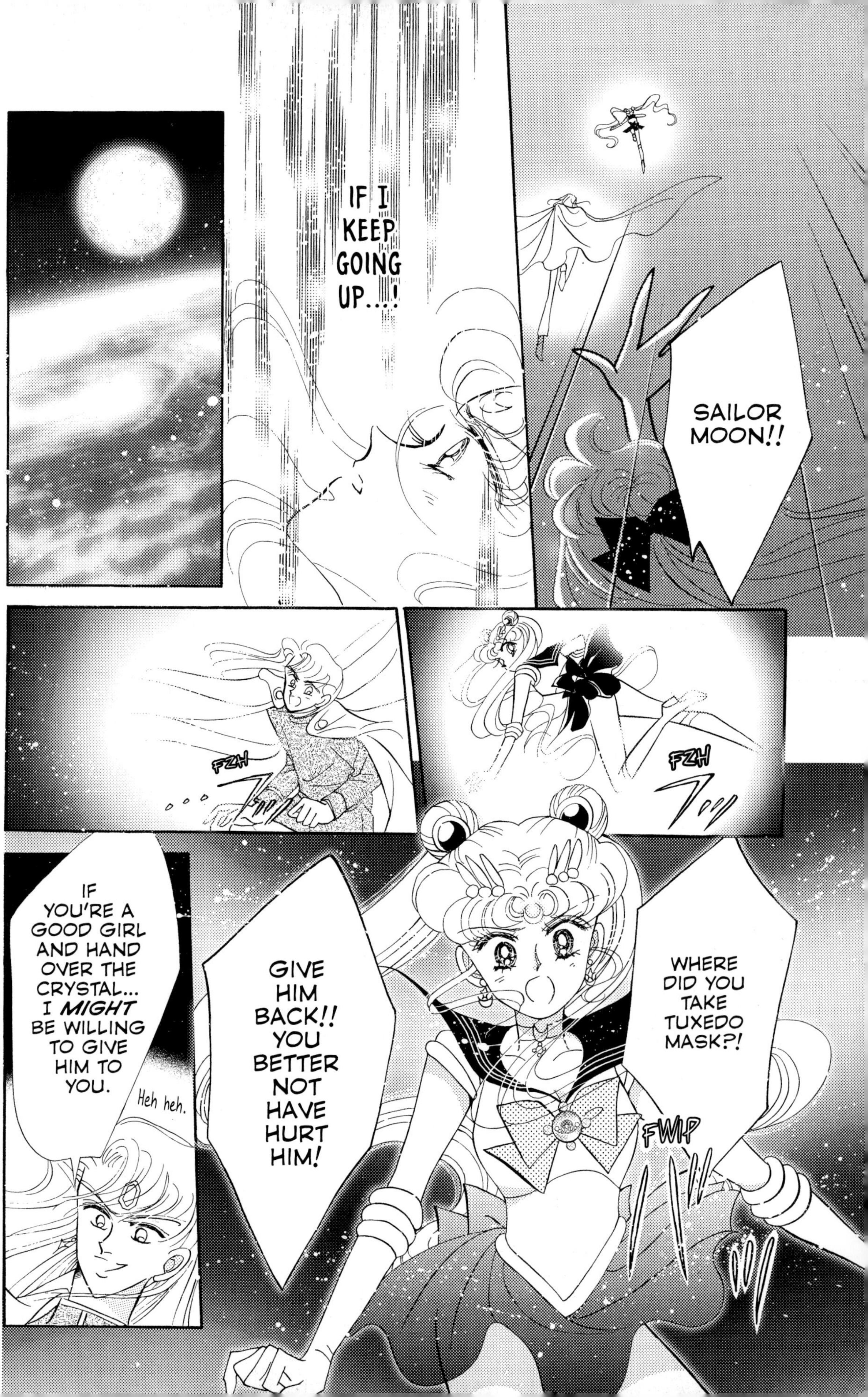
SAILOR MOON!!
IF I KEEP GOING UP...!
FZH
FZH
WHERE DID YOU TAKE TUXEDO MASK?!
FWIP
GIVE HIM BACK!! YOU BETTER NOT HAVE HURT HIM!
IF YOU'RE A GOOD GIRL AND HAND OVER THE CRYSTAL... I *MIGHT* BE WILLING TO GIVE HIM TO YOU.
Heh heh.

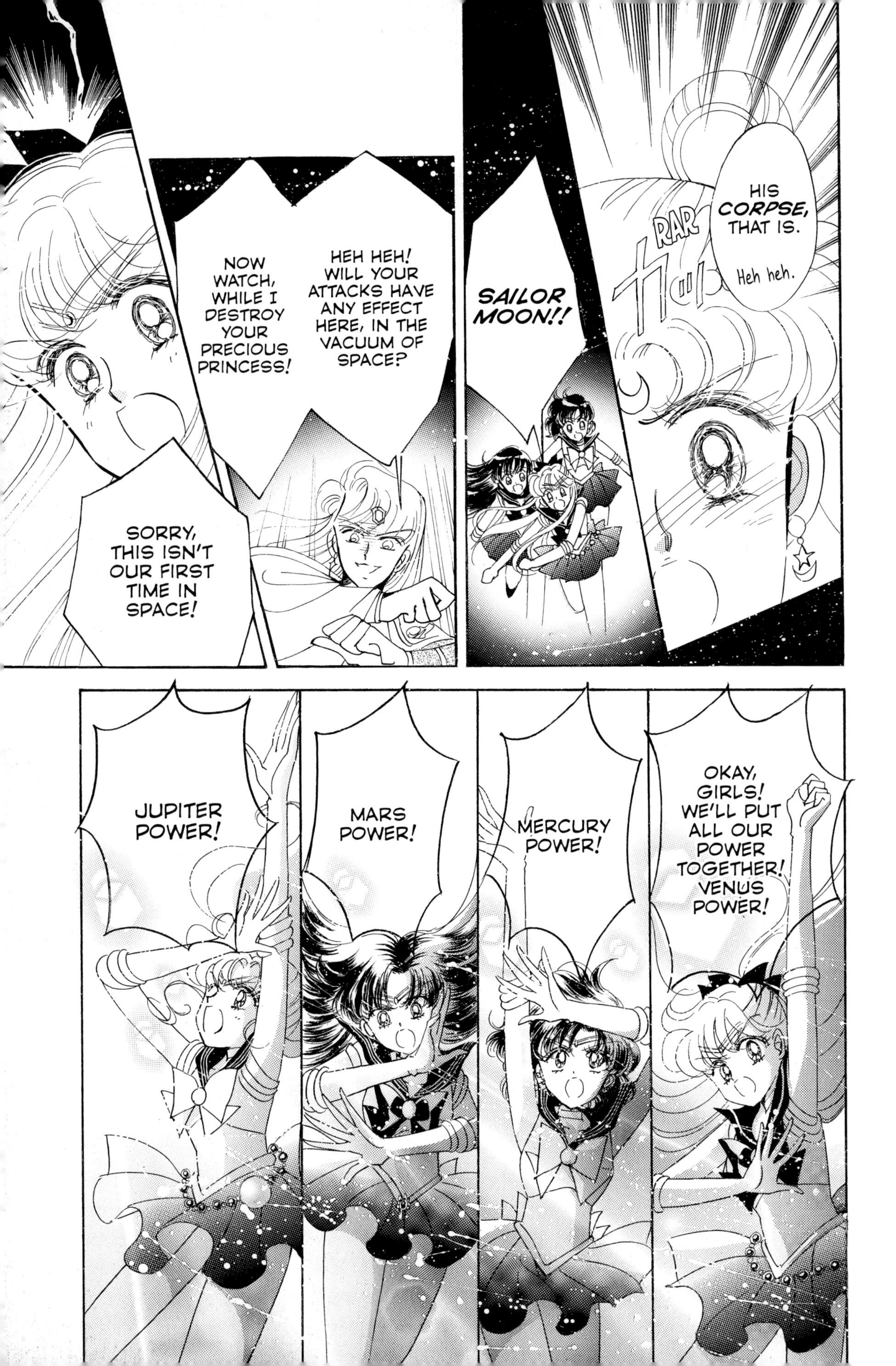

HIS CORPSE, THAT IS.
Heh heh.
RAR
SAILOR MOON!!
HEH HEH! WILL YOUR ATTACKS HAVE ANY EFFECT HERE, IN THE VACUUM OF SPACE?
NOW WATCH, WHILE I DESTROY YOUR PRECIOUS PRINCESS!
SORRY, THIS ISN'T OUR FIRST TIME IN SPACE!
OKAY, GIRLS! WE'LL PUT ALL OUR POWER TOGETHER! VENUS POWER!
MERCURY POWER!
MARS POWER!
JUPITER POWER!

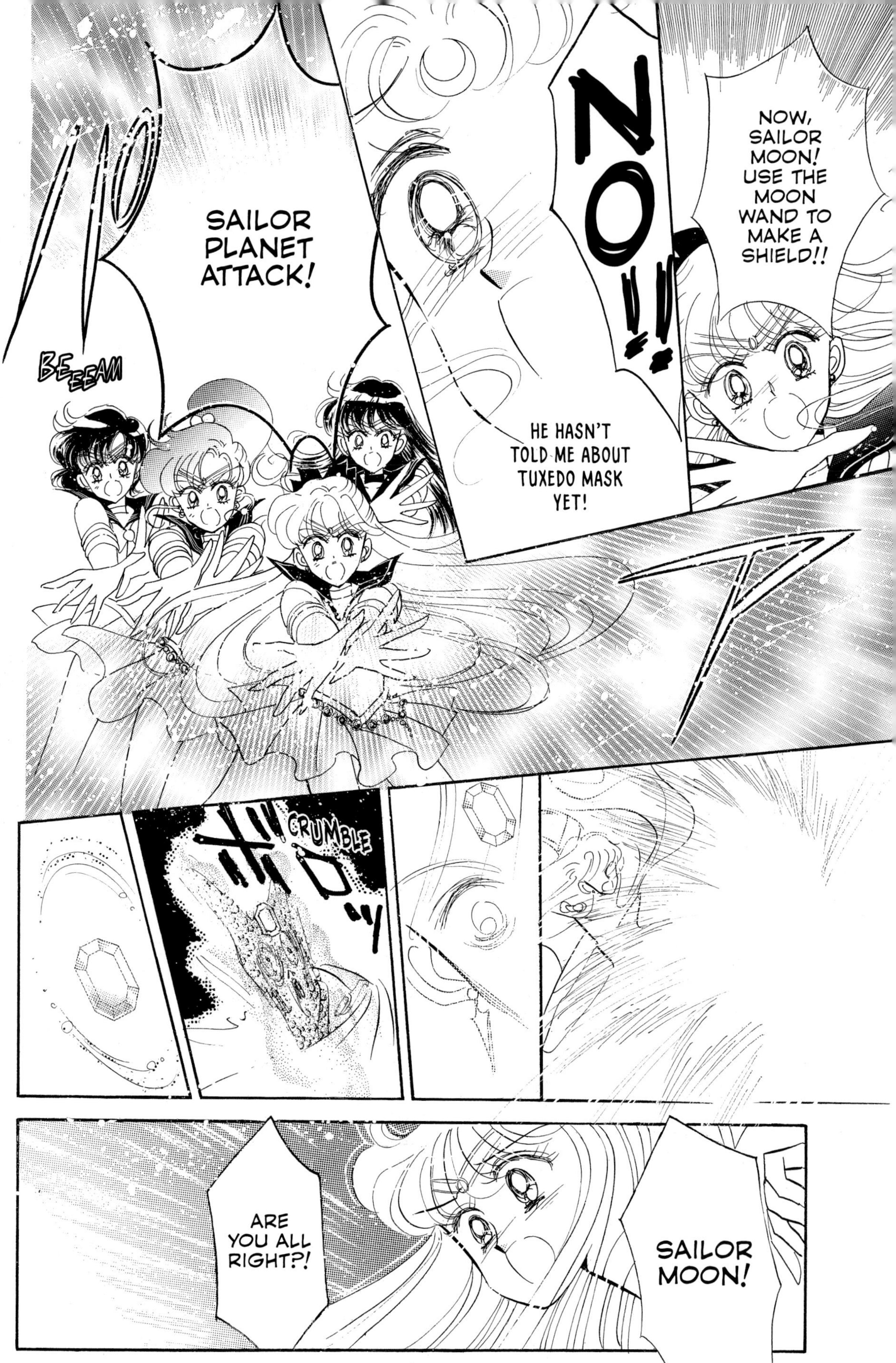
NOW, SAILOR MOON! USE THE MOON WAND TO MAKE A SHIELD!!
NO!!
HE HASN'T TOLD ME ABOUT TUXEDO MASK YET!
SAILOR PLANET ATTACK!
BEEEAM
CRUMBLE
SAILOR MOON!
ARE YOU ALL RIGHT?!

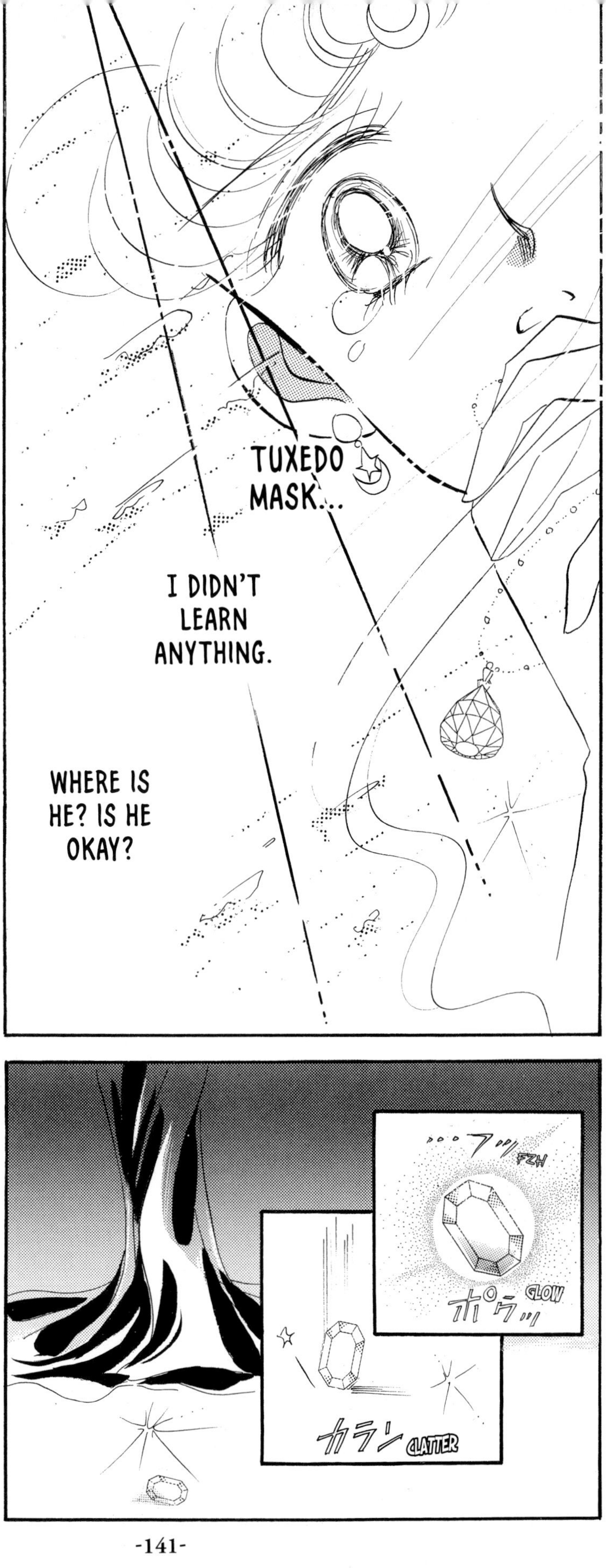
TUXEDO MASK...
I DIDN'T LEARN ANYTHING.
WHERE IS HE? IS HE OKAY?
FZH
GLOW
カラン
CLATTER

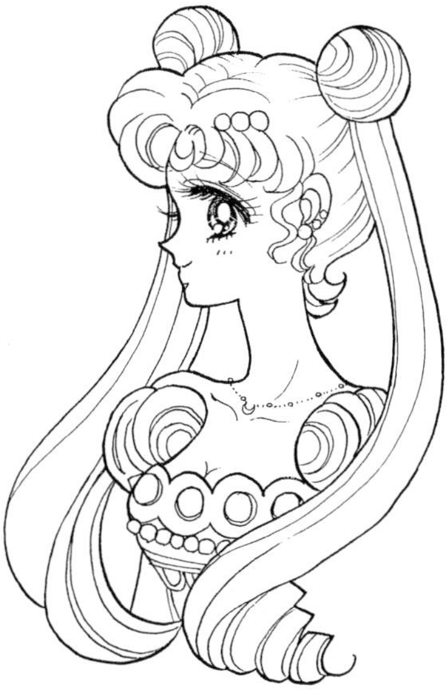

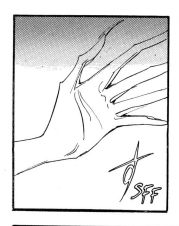

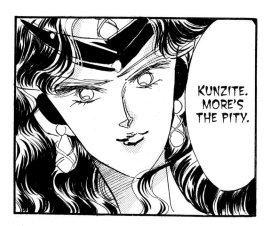

KUNZITE. MORE'S THE PITY.
NOW ALL FOUR OF MY DEAR LITTLE HEAVENLY KINGS HAVE BEEN REDUCED TO STONES.
SFF
O SUPREME RULER, QUEEN METALIA.
GRANT ME YOUR STRENGTH.
I NEED YOUR POWER.
THE POWER OF AWAKENING!

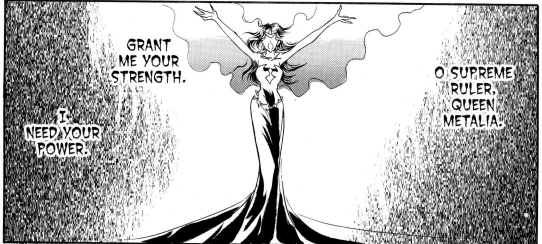

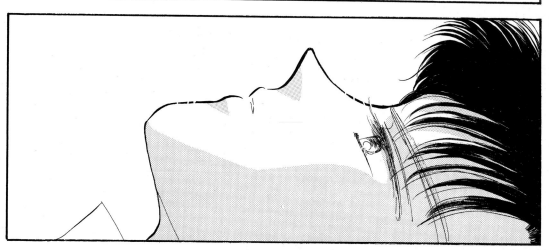

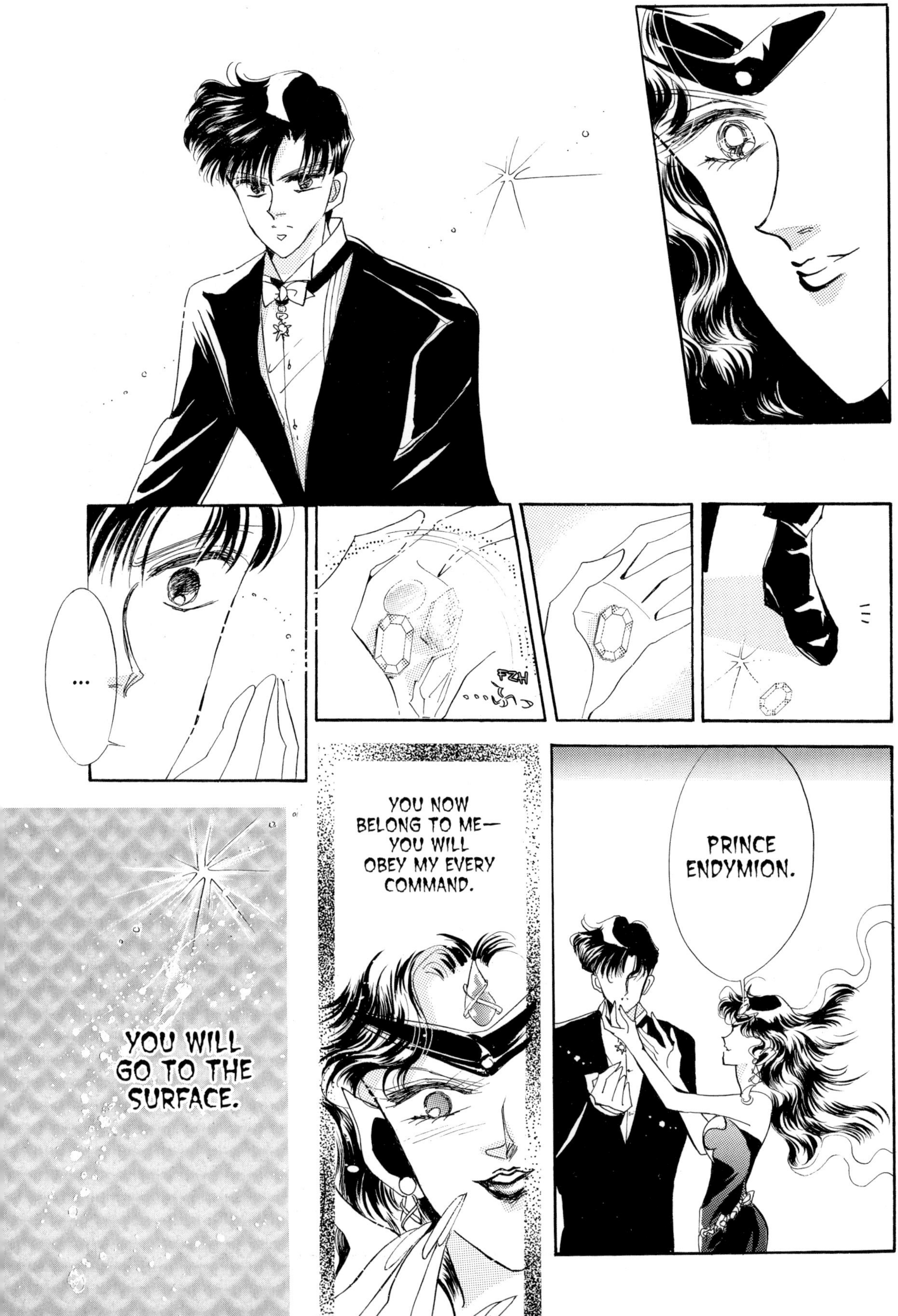
FZH
…
PRINCE ENDYMION.
YOU NOW BELONG TO ME—YOU WILL OBEY MY EVERY COMMAND.
YOU WILL GO TO THE SURFACE.

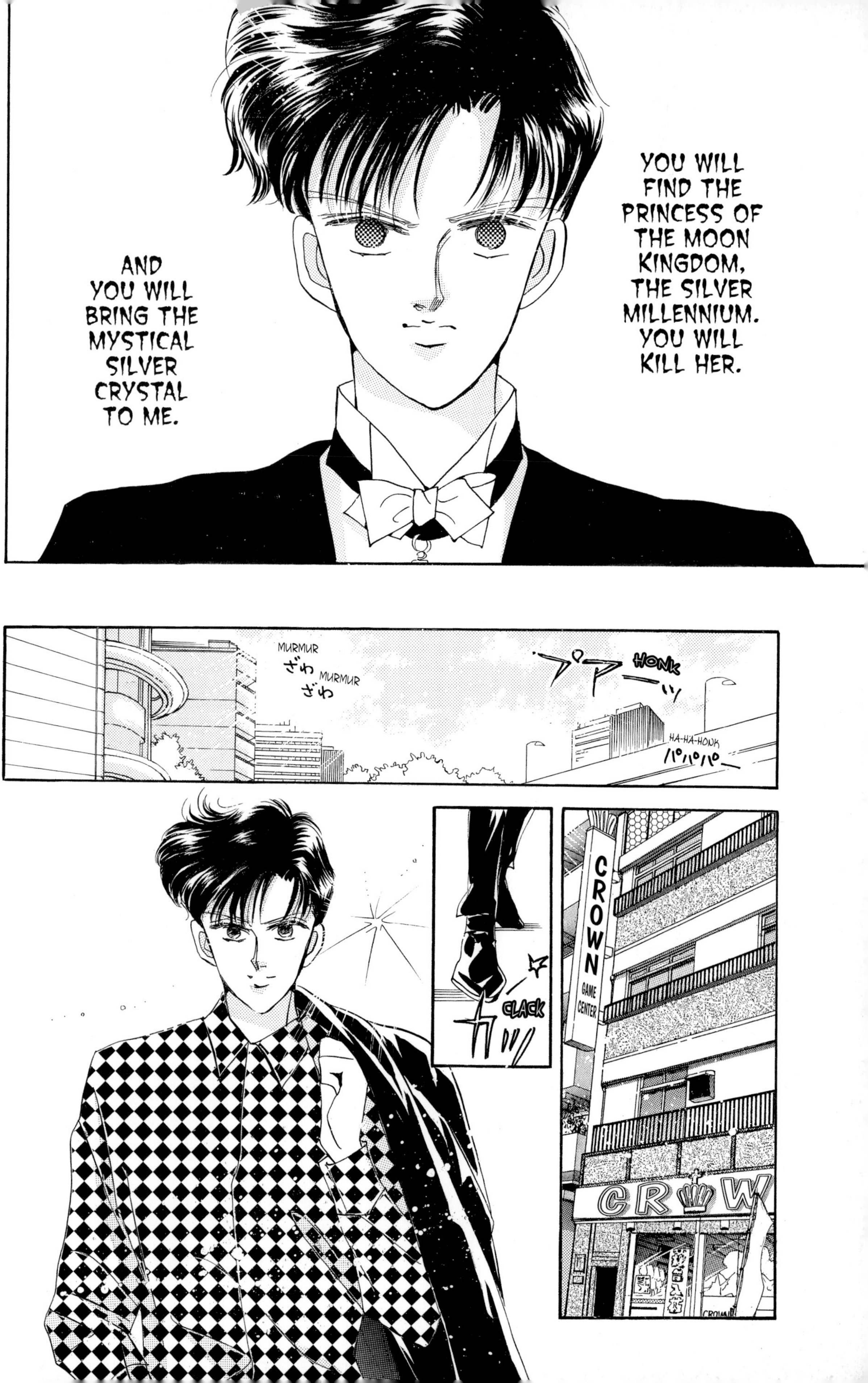
YOU WILL FIND THE PRINCESS OF THE MOON KINGDOM, THE SILVER MILLENNIUM. YOU WILL KILL HER.
AND YOU WILL BRING THE MYSTICAL SILVER CRYSTAL TO ME.
HONK
プアーッ
HA-HA-HONK
パパパー
MURMUR
ざわ
MURMUR
ざわ
CROWN
GAME CENTER
CLACK
ガッ

# Act. 11 Reunion: Endymion

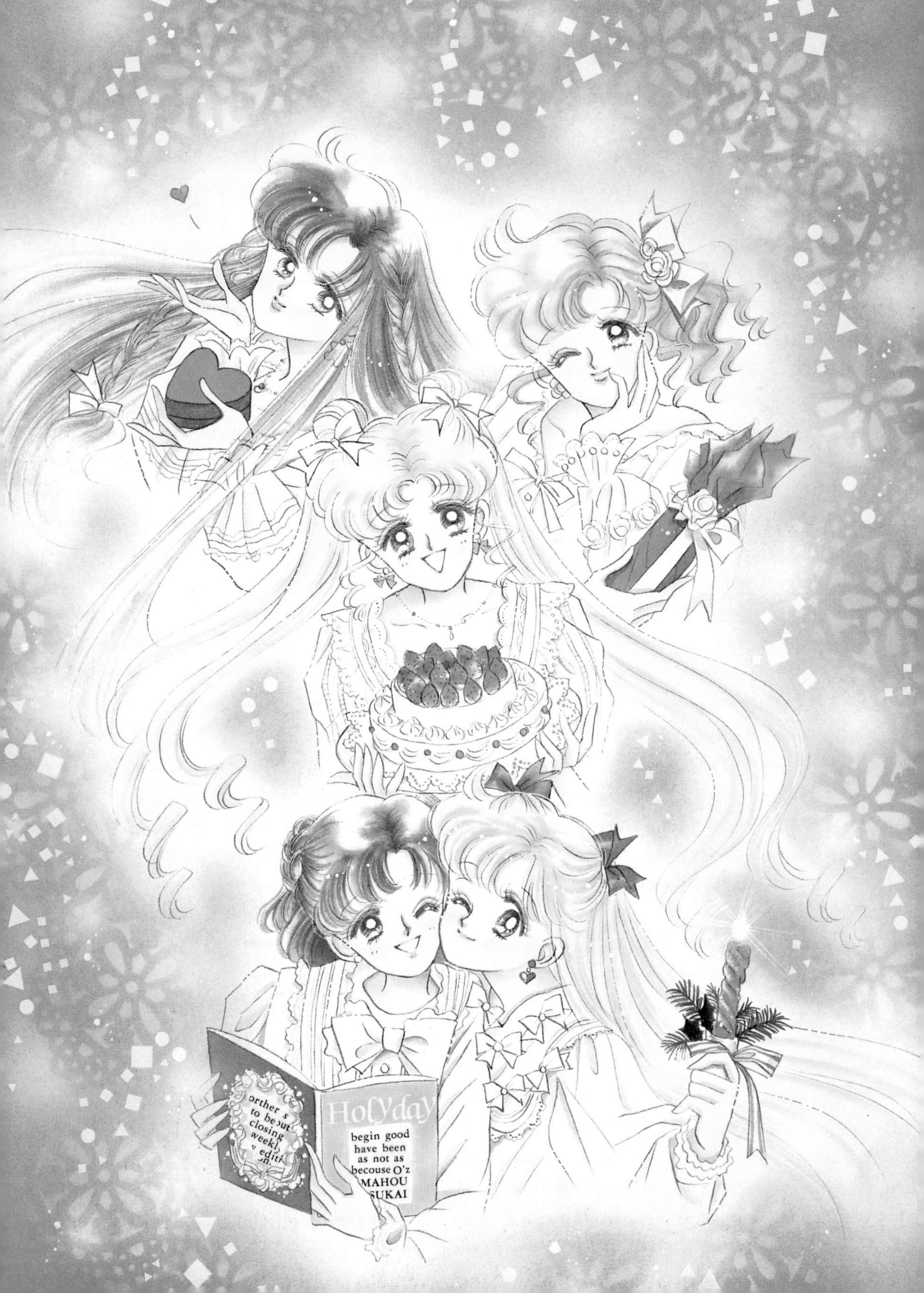
Holyday
begin good
have been
as not as
becouse O'z
MAHOU

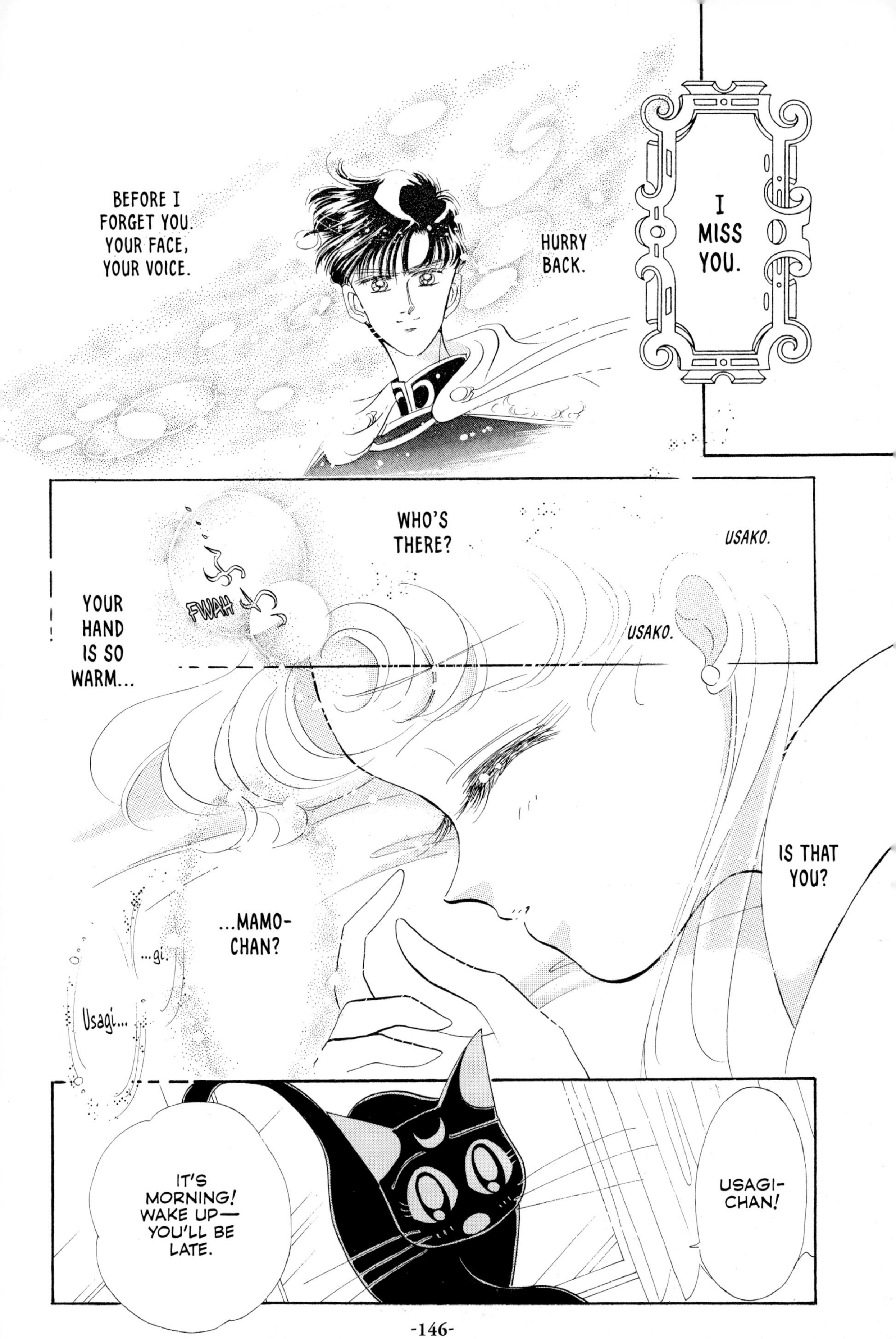
I MISS YOU.
HURRY BACK.
BEFORE I FORGET YOU. YOUR FACE, YOUR VOICE.
USAKO.
USAKO.
WHO'S THERE?
FWAH
YOUR HAND IS SO WARM...
IS THAT YOU?
...MAMO-CHAN?
...gi.
Usagi...
USAGI-CHAN!
IT'S MORNING! WAKE UP— YOU'LL BE LATE.

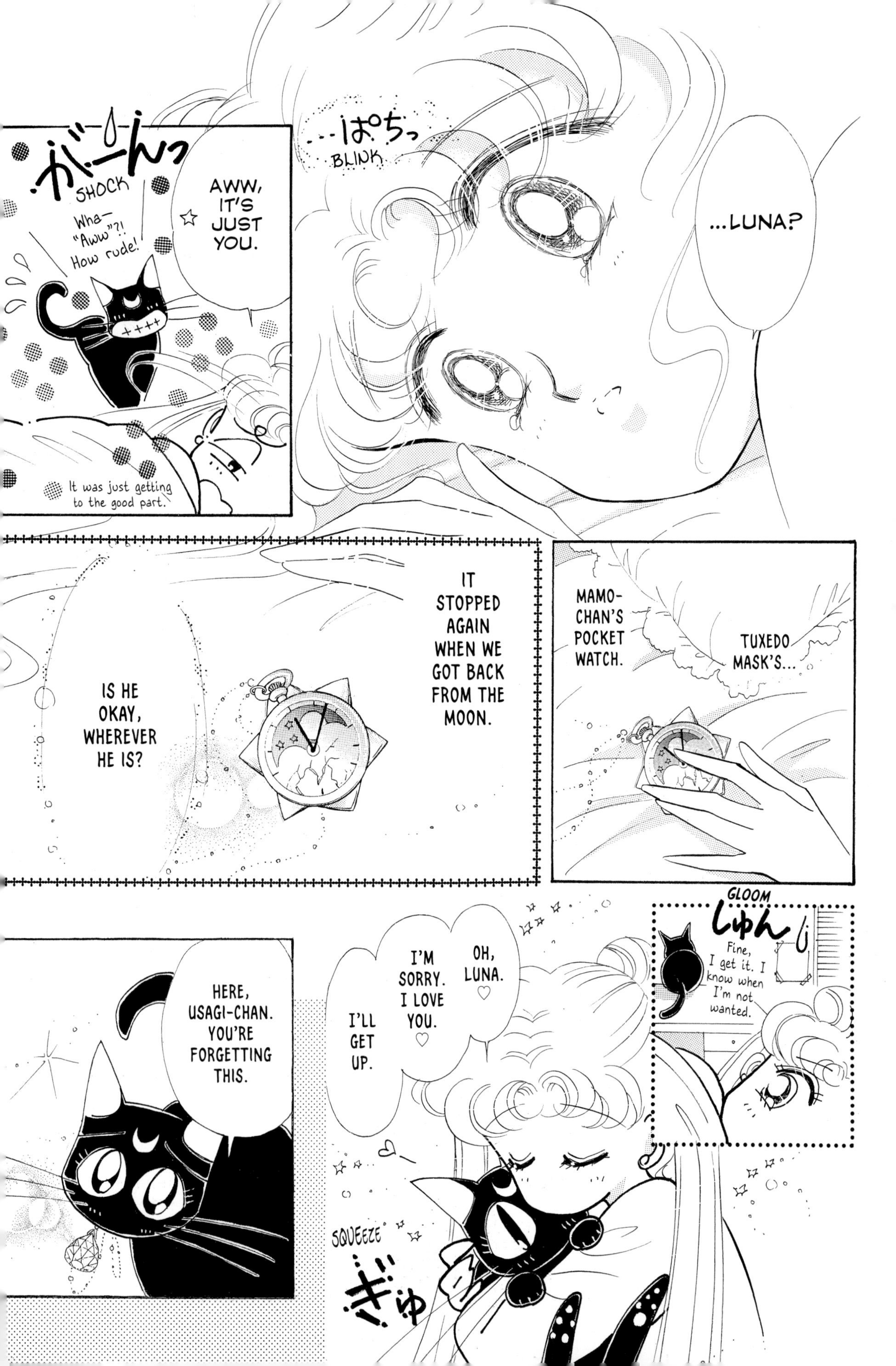

...ぱちっ
BLINK
...LUNA?
AWW, IT'S JUST YOU.
ガーんっ
SHOCK
Wha— "Aww"?! How rude!
It was just getting to the good part.
TUXEDO MASK'S...
MAMO-CHAN'S POCKET WATCH.
IT STOPPED AGAIN WHEN WE GOT BACK FROM THE MOON.
IS HE OKAY, WHEREVER HE IS?
じゅん
GLOOM
Fine, I get it. I know when I'm not wanted.
OH, LUNA. ♡
I'M SORRY. I LOVE YOU. ♡
I'LL GET UP.
SQUEEZE
ぎゅ
HERE, USAGI-CHAN. YOU'RE FORGETTING THIS.

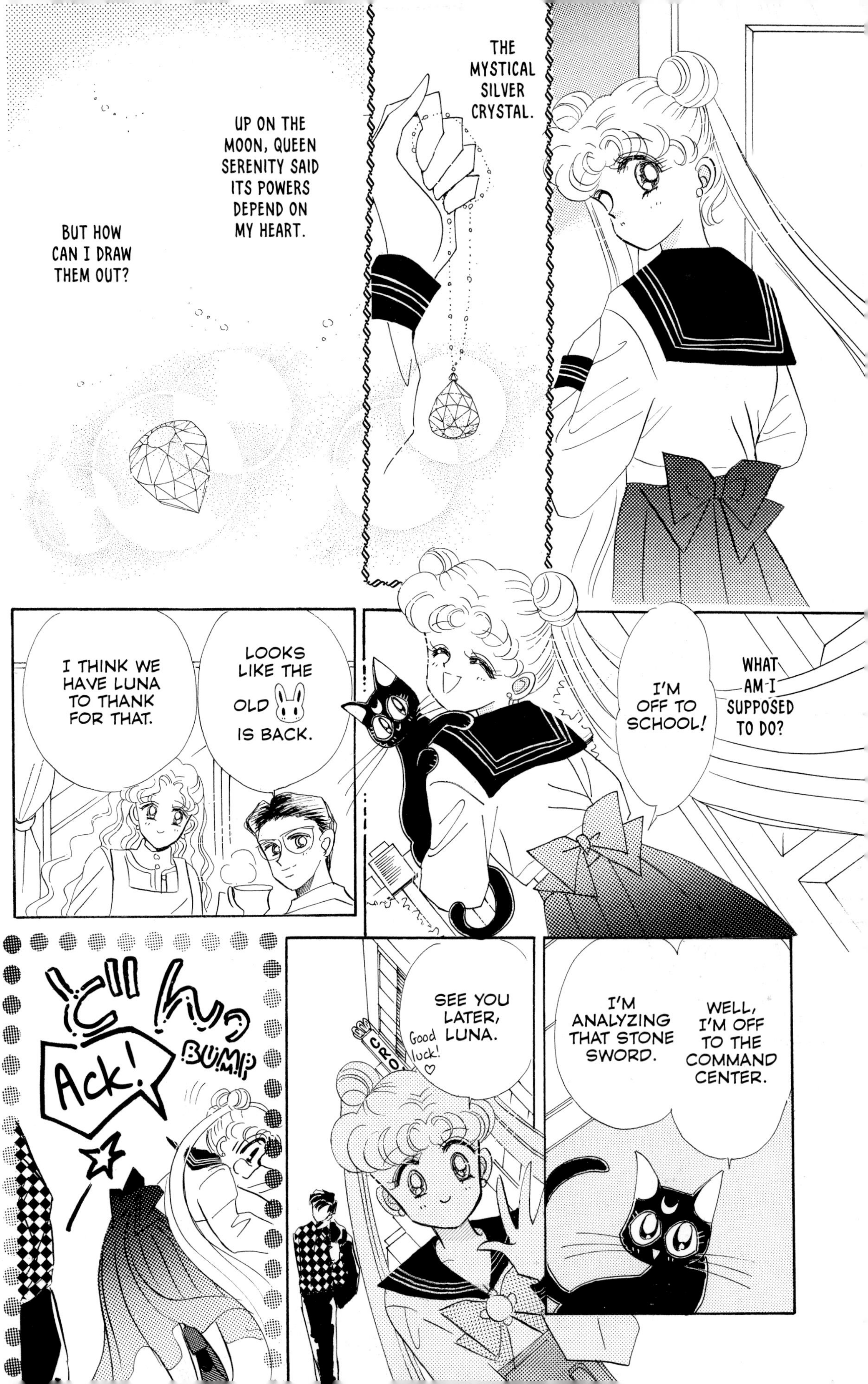
THE MYSTICAL SILVER CRYSTAL.
UP ON THE MOON, QUEEN SERENITY SAID ITS POWERS DEPEND ON MY HEART.
BUT HOW CAN I DRAW THEM OUT?
WHAT AM I SUPPOSED TO DO?
I'M OFF TO SCHOOL!
LOOKS LIKE THE OLD IS BACK.
I THINK WE HAVE LUNA TO THANK FOR THAT.
WELL, I'M OFF TO THE COMMAND CENTER.
I'M ANALYZING THAT STONE SWORD.
SEE YOU LATER, LUNA.
Good luck! ♡
BUMP
Ack!

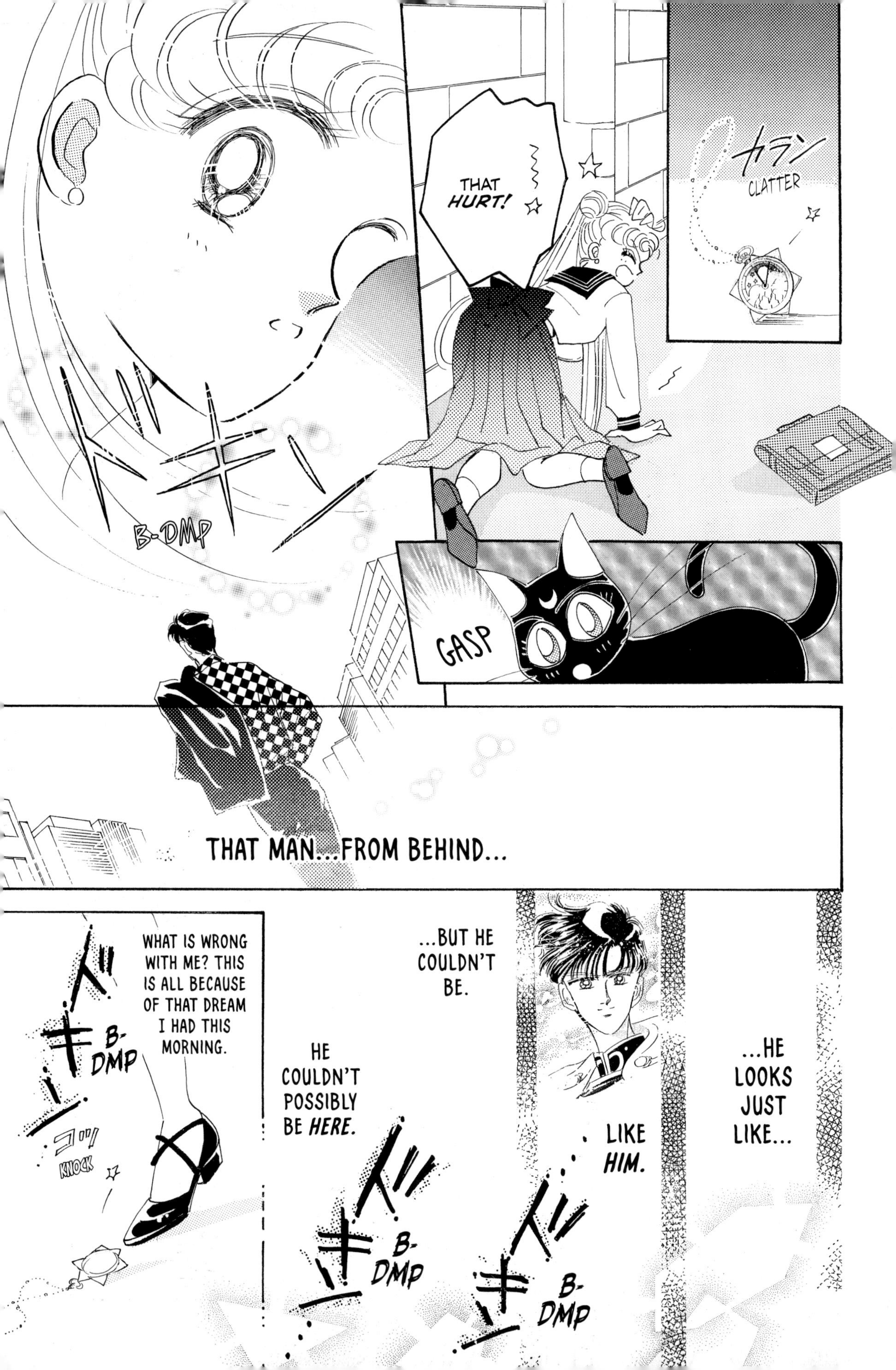

カラン
CLATTER
THAT HURT!
GASP
B-DMP
THAT MAN...FROM BEHIND...
...HE LOOKS JUST LIKE...
LIKE HIM.
B-DMP
...BUT HE COULDN'T BE.
HE COULDN'T POSSIBLY BE HERE.
B-DMP
WHAT IS WRONG WITH ME? THIS IS ALL BECAUSE OF THAT DREAM I HAD THIS MORNING.
B-DMP
KNOCK

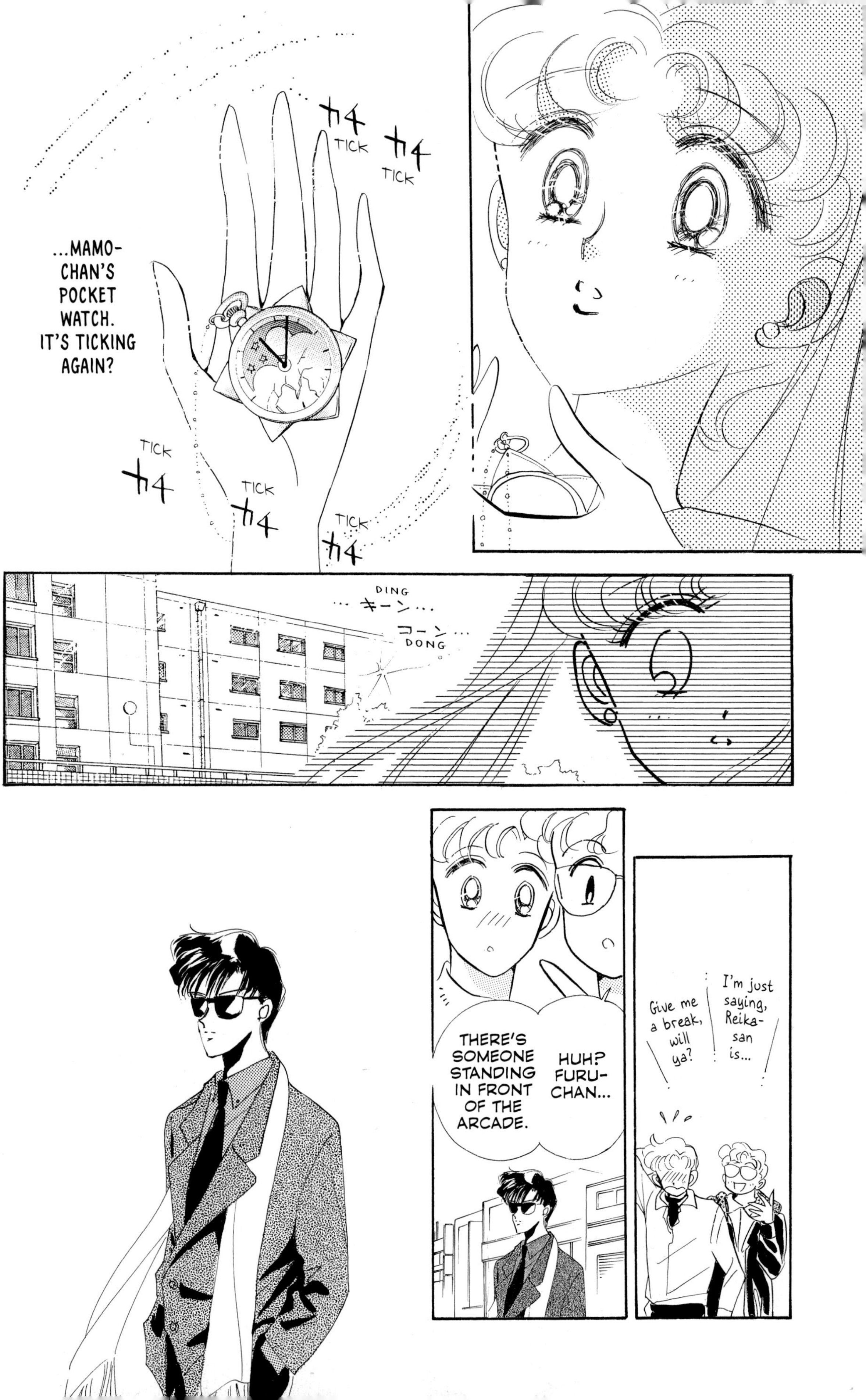
カチ
TICK
カチ
TICK
...MAMO-CHAN'S POCKET WATCH. IT'S TICKING AGAIN?
TICK
カチ
TICK
カチ
TICK
カチ
DING
... キーン ...
コーン ...
DONG
I'm just saying, Reika-san is...
Give me a break, will ya?
HUH? FURU-CHAN...
THERE'S SOMEONE STANDING IN FRONT OF THE ARCADE.

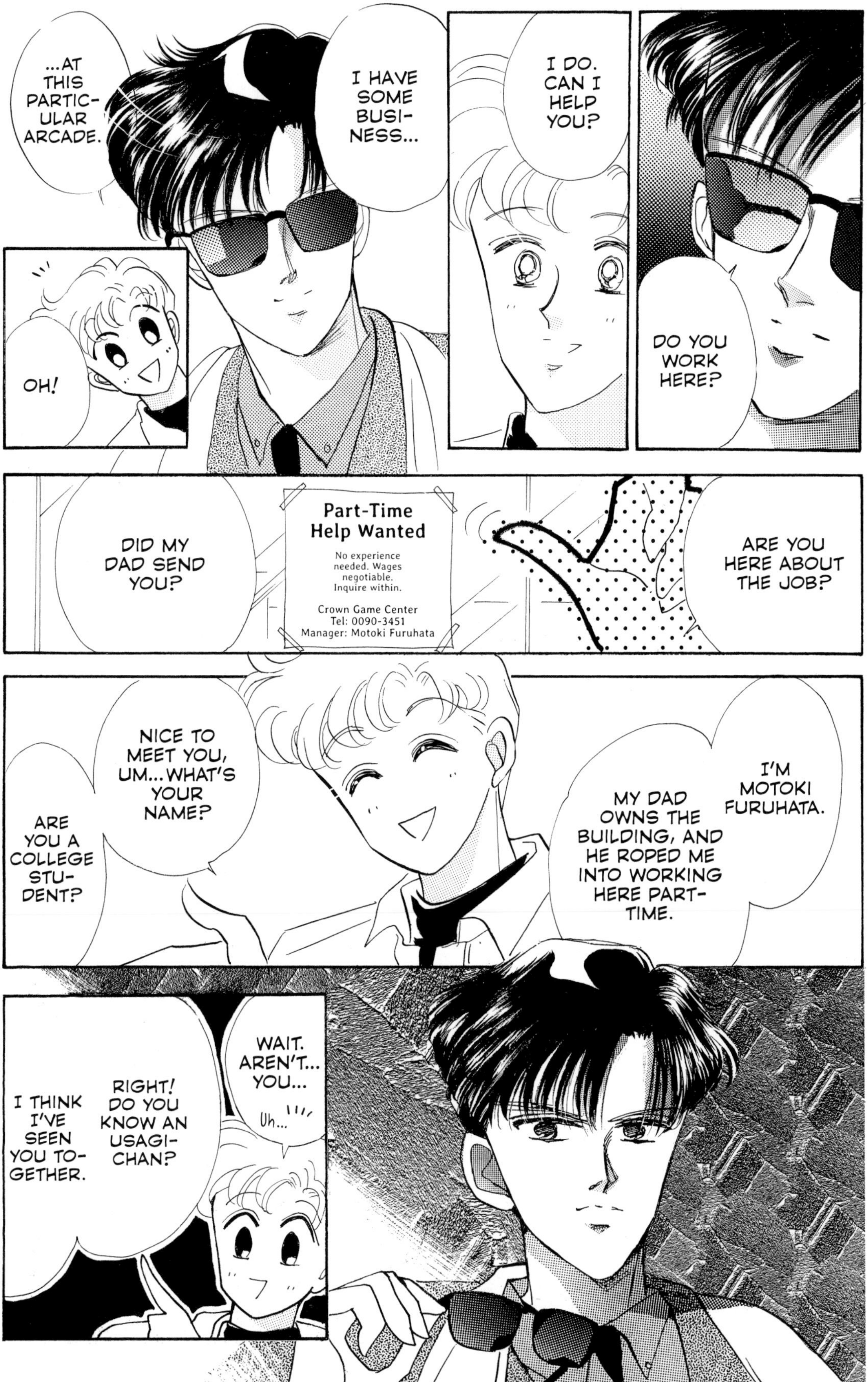
DO YOU WORK HERE?
I DO. CAN I HELP YOU?
I HAVE SOME BUSINESS...
...AT THIS PARTICULAR ARCADE.
OH!
ARE YOU HERE ABOUT THE JOB?
Part-Time Help Wanted
No experience needed. Wages negotiable. Inquire within.
Crown Game Center
Tel: 0090-3451
Manager: Motoki Furuhata
DID MY DAD SEND YOU?
I'M MOTOKI FURUHATA.
MY DAD OWNS THE BUILDING, AND HE ROPED ME INTO WORKING HERE PART-TIME.
NICE TO MEET YOU, UM...WHAT'S YOUR NAME?
ARE YOU A COLLEGE STUDENT?
WAIT. AREN'T... YOU...
Uh...
RIGHT! DO YOU KNOW AN USAGI-CHAN?
I THINK I'VE SEEN YOU TOGETHER.

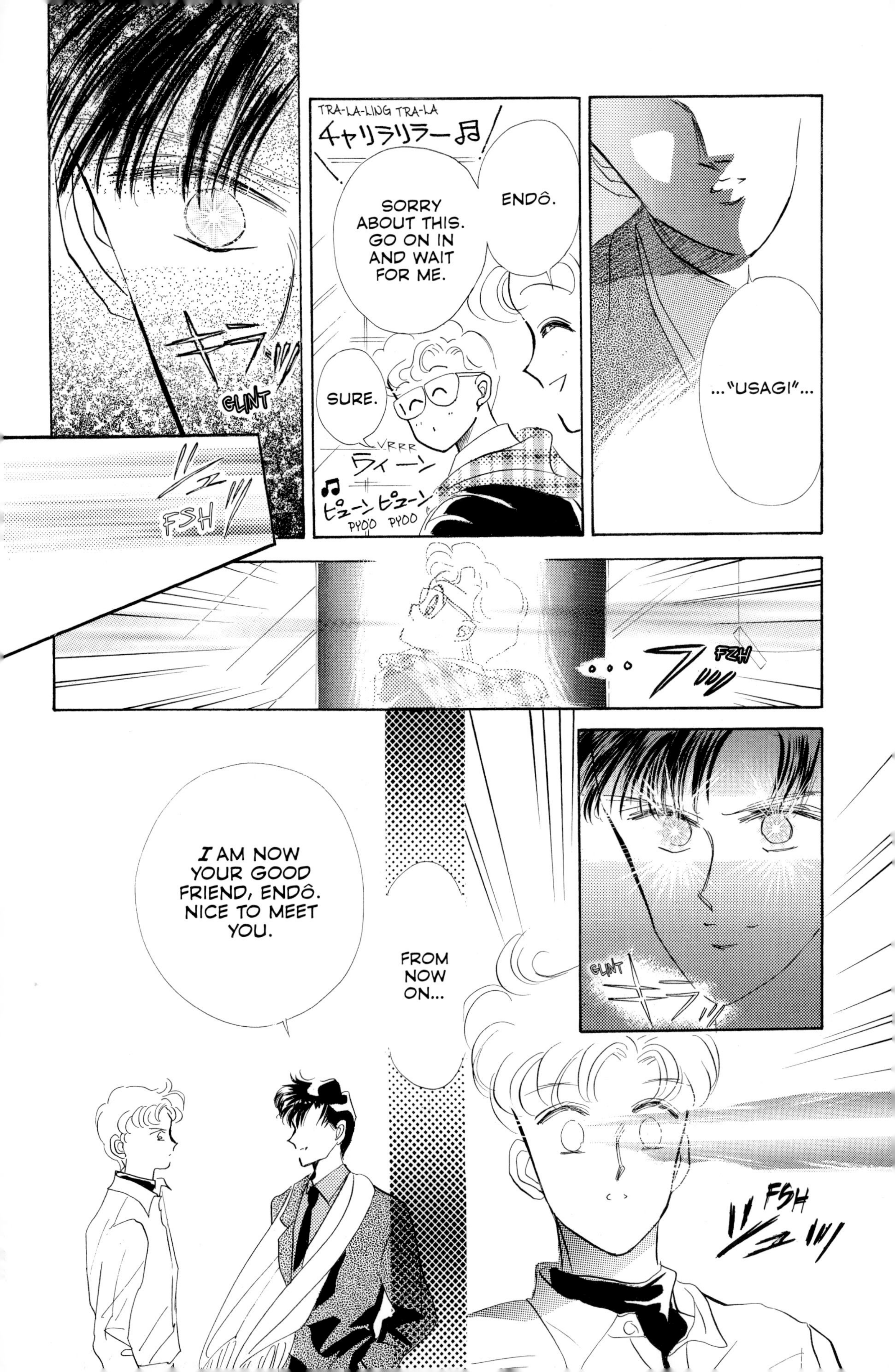
..."USAGI"...
ENDÔ.
TRA-LA-LING TRA-LA
チャリラリラー♫
SORRY ABOUT THIS. GO ON IN AND WAIT FOR ME.
SURE.
VRRR
ウィーン
ピューンピューン
PYOO PYOO
キラッ
GLINT
シュ
FSH
...
フッ
FZH
GLINT
キラッ
FSH
シュ
FROM NOW ON...
I AM NOW YOUR GOOD FRIEND, ENDÔ. NICE TO MEET YOU.

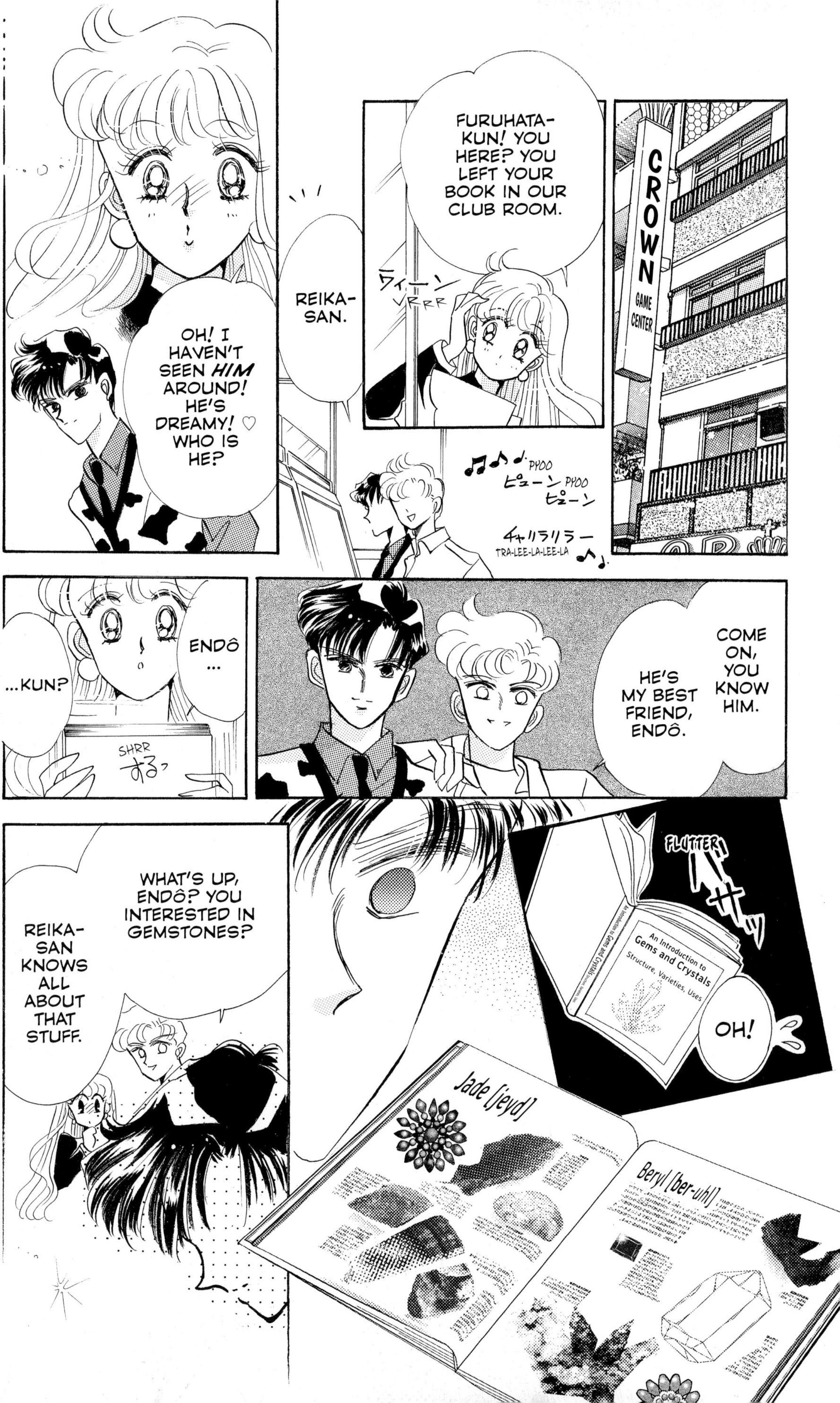
CROWN
GAME CENTER
FURUHATA-KUN! YOU HERE? YOU LEFT YOUR BOOK IN OUR CLUB ROOM.
ウィーン
VRRR
♫♪♩ PYOO
ピューン PYOO
ピューン
チャリラリラー
TRA-LEE-LA-LEE-LA ♪♩
REIKA-SAN.
OH! I HAVEN'T SEEN *HIM* AROUND! HE'S DREAMY! ♡ WHO IS HE?
COME ON, YOU KNOW HIM.
HE'S MY BEST FRIEND, ENDÔ.
ENDÔ...
...KUN?
SHRR
するっ
FLUTTER
An Introduction to Gems and Crystals
Structure, Varieties, Uses
OH!
WHAT'S UP, ENDÔ? YOU INTERESTED IN GEMSTONES?
REIKA-SAN KNOWS ALL ABOUT THAT STUFF.
Jade [jeyd]
Beryl [ber-uhl]

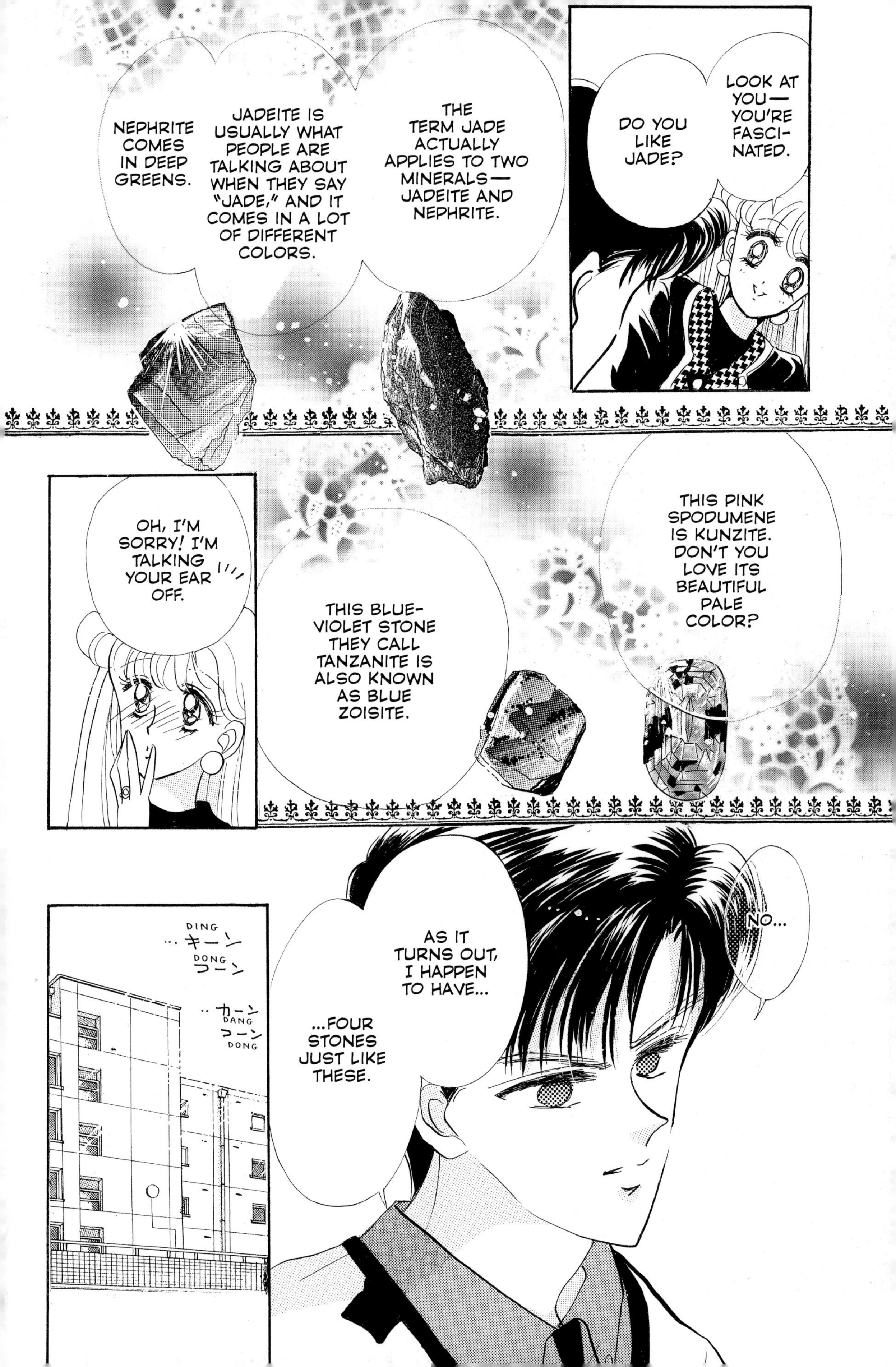
LOOK AT YOU—YOU'RE FASCI-NATED.
DO YOU LIKE JADE?
THE TERM JADE ACTUALLY APPLIES TO TWO MINERALS—JADEITE AND NEPHRITE.
JADEITE IS USUALLY WHAT PEOPLE ARE TALKING ABOUT WHEN THEY SAY "JADE," AND IT COMES IN A LOT OF DIFFERENT COLORS.
NEPHRITE COMES IN DEEP GREENS.
THIS PINK SPODUMENE IS KUNZITE. DON'T YOU LOVE ITS BEAUTIFUL PALE COLOR?
THIS BLUE-VIOLET STONE THEY CALL TANZANITE IS ALSO KNOWN AS BLUE ZOISITE.
OH, I'M SORRY! I'M TALKING YOUR EAR OFF.
NO...
AS IT TURNS OUT, I HAPPEN TO HAVE...
...FOUR STONES JUST LIKE THESE.
DING
...キーン
DONG
コーン
..カーン
DANG
コーン
DONG

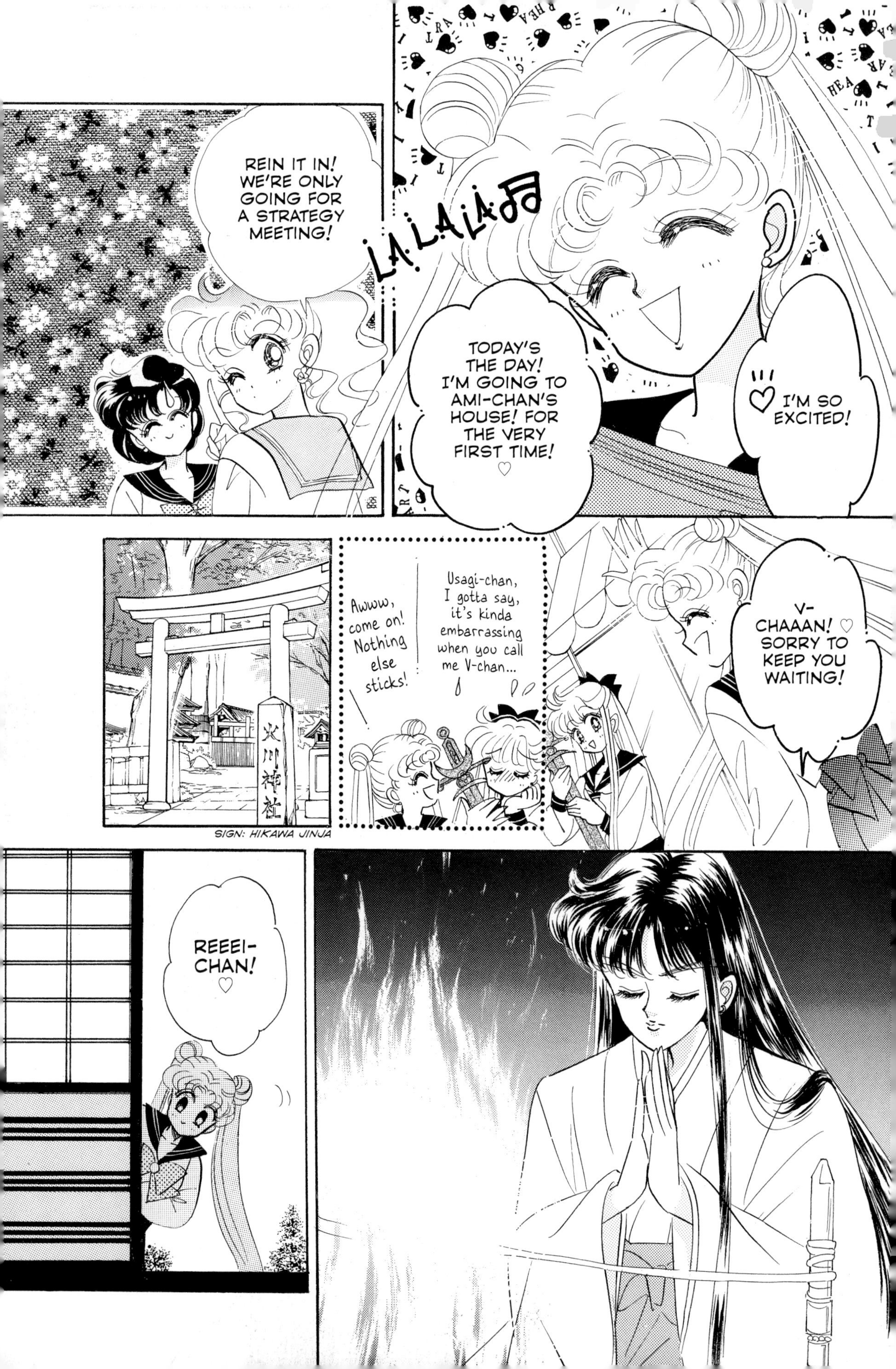

LALALA♫♫
TODAY'S THE DAY! I'M GOING TO AMI-CHAN'S HOUSE! FOR THE VERY FIRST TIME! ♡
♡ I'M SO EXCITED!
REIN IT IN! WE'RE ONLY GOING FOR A STRATEGY MEETING!
V-CHAAAN! ♡ SORRY TO KEEP YOU WAITING!
Usagi-chan, I gotta say, it's kinda embarrassing when you call me V-chan...
Awww, come on! Nothing else sticks!
火川神社
REEEI-CHAN! ♡

SIGN: HIKAWA JINJA

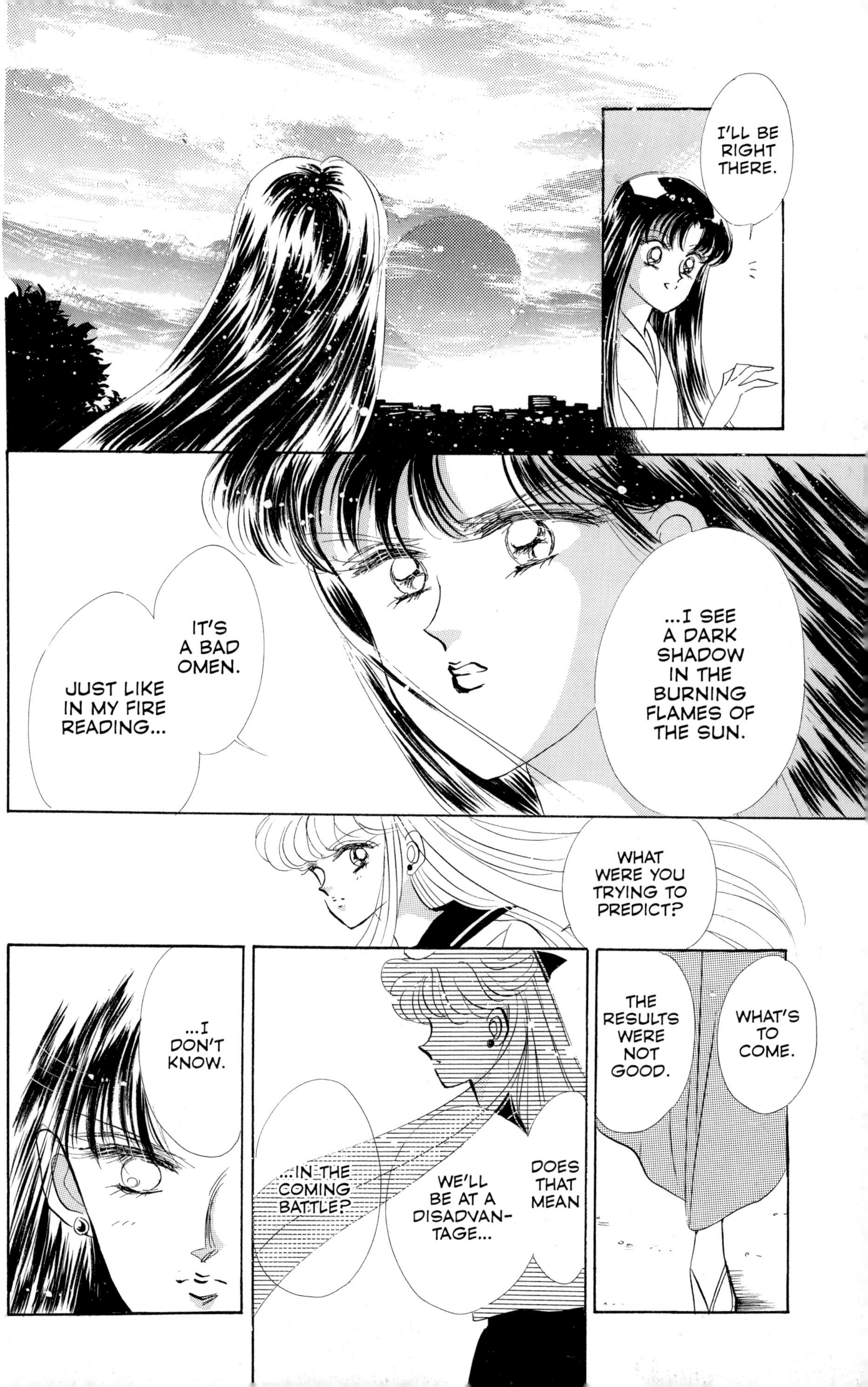
I'LL BE RIGHT THERE.
...I SEE A DARK SHADOW IN THE BURNING FLAMES OF THE SUN.
IT'S A BAD OMEN.
JUST LIKE IN MY FIRE READING...
WHAT WERE YOU TRYING TO PREDICT?
WHAT'S TO COME.
THE RESULTS WERE NOT GOOD.
DOES THAT MEAN
WE'LL BE AT A DISADVANTAGE...
...IN THE COMING BATTLE?
...I DON'T KNOW.

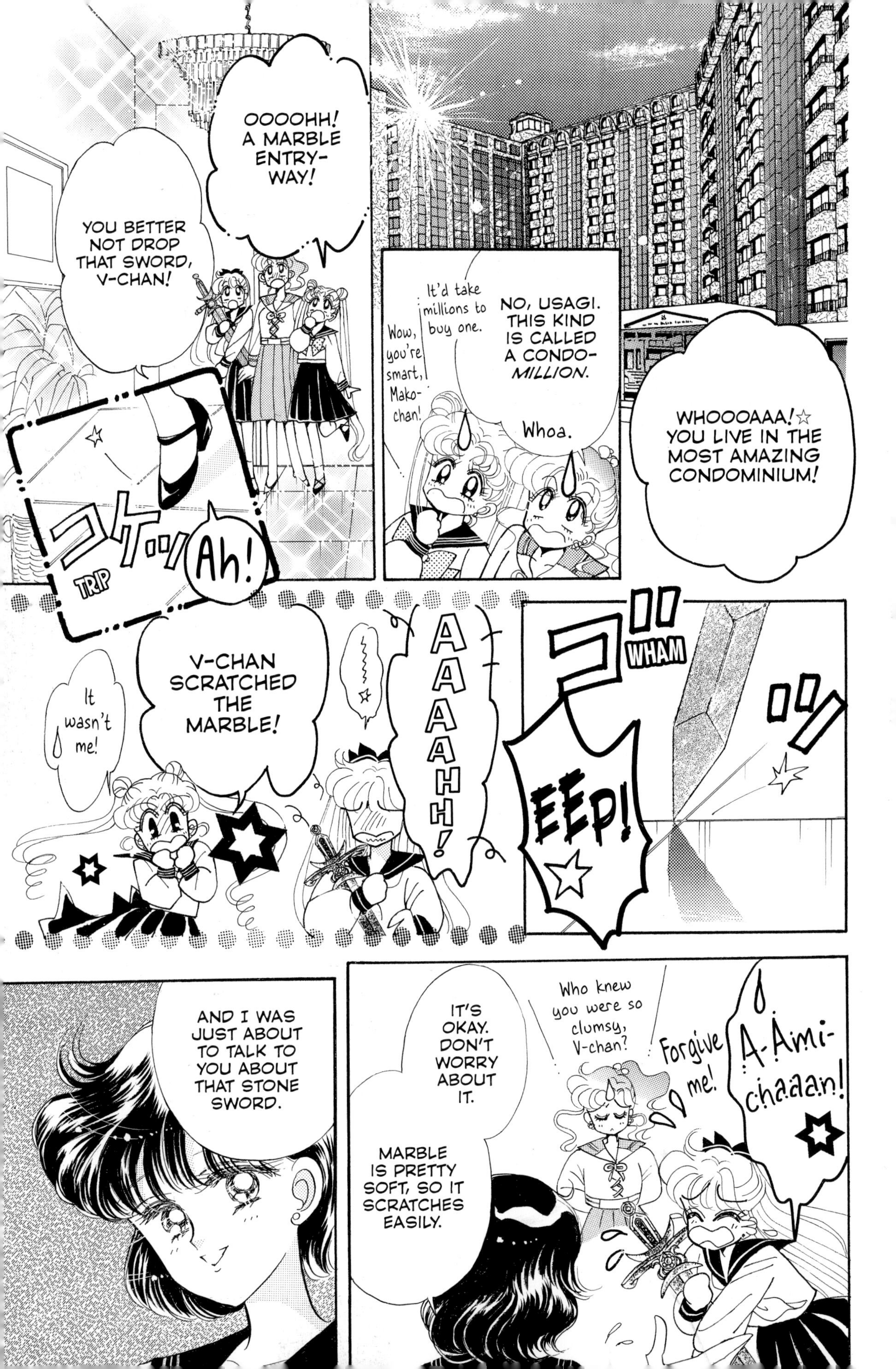
WHOOOAAA!☆ YOU LIVE IN THE MOST AMAZING CONDOMINIUM!
NO, USAGI. THIS KIND IS CALLED A CONDO-*MILLION*.
It'd take millions to buy one.
Wow, you're smart, Mako-chan!
Whoa.
OOOOHH! A MARBLE ENTRY-WAY!
YOU BETTER NOT DROP THAT SWORD, V-CHAN!
TRIP
Ah!
WHAM
EEP!
AAAAAAH!
V-CHAN SCRATCHED THE MARBLE!
It wasn't me!
A-Ami-chaaaan!
Forgive me!
Who knew you were so clumsy, V-chan?
IT'S OKAY. DON'T WORRY ABOUT IT.
MARBLE IS PRETTY SOFT, SO IT SCRATCHES EASILY.
AND I WAS JUST ABOUT TO TALK TO YOU ABOUT THAT STONE SWORD.

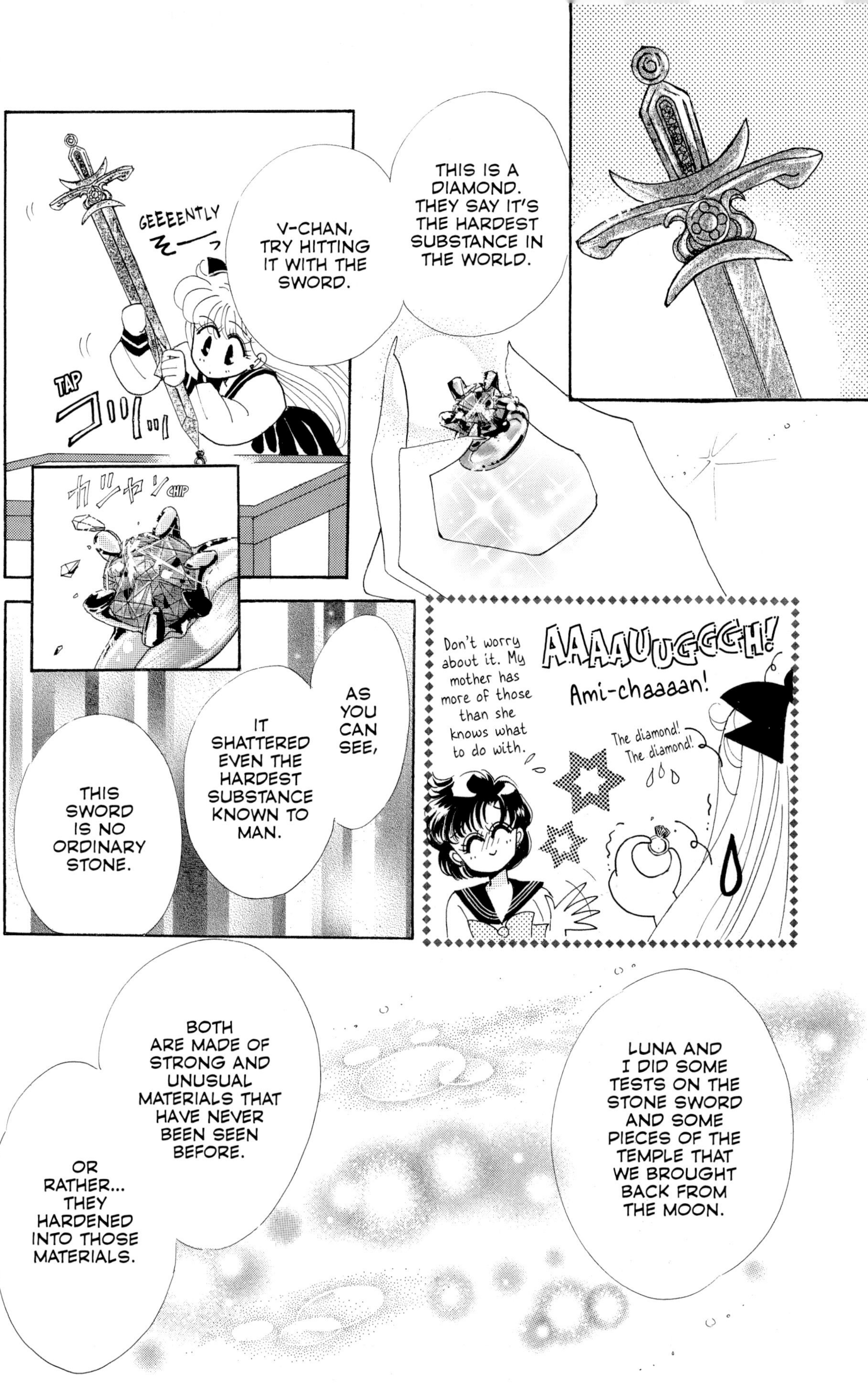
THIS IS A DIAMOND. THEY SAY IT'S THE HARDEST SUBSTANCE IN THE WORLD.
V-CHAN, TRY HITTING IT WITH THE SWORD.
GEEEEENTLY
TAP
CHIP
AAAAUUGGGH!
Ami-chaaaan!
The diamond! The diamond!
Don't worry about it. My mother has more of those than she knows what to do with.
AS YOU CAN SEE,
IT SHATTERED EVEN THE HARDEST SUBSTANCE KNOWN TO MAN.
THIS SWORD IS NO ORDINARY STONE.
LUNA AND I DID SOME TESTS ON THE STONE SWORD AND SOME PIECES OF THE TEMPLE THAT WE BROUGHT BACK FROM THE MOON.
BOTH ARE MADE OF STRONG AND UNUSUAL MATERIALS THAT HAVE NEVER BEEN SEEN BEFORE.
OR RATHER... THEY HARDENED INTO THOSE MATERIALS.

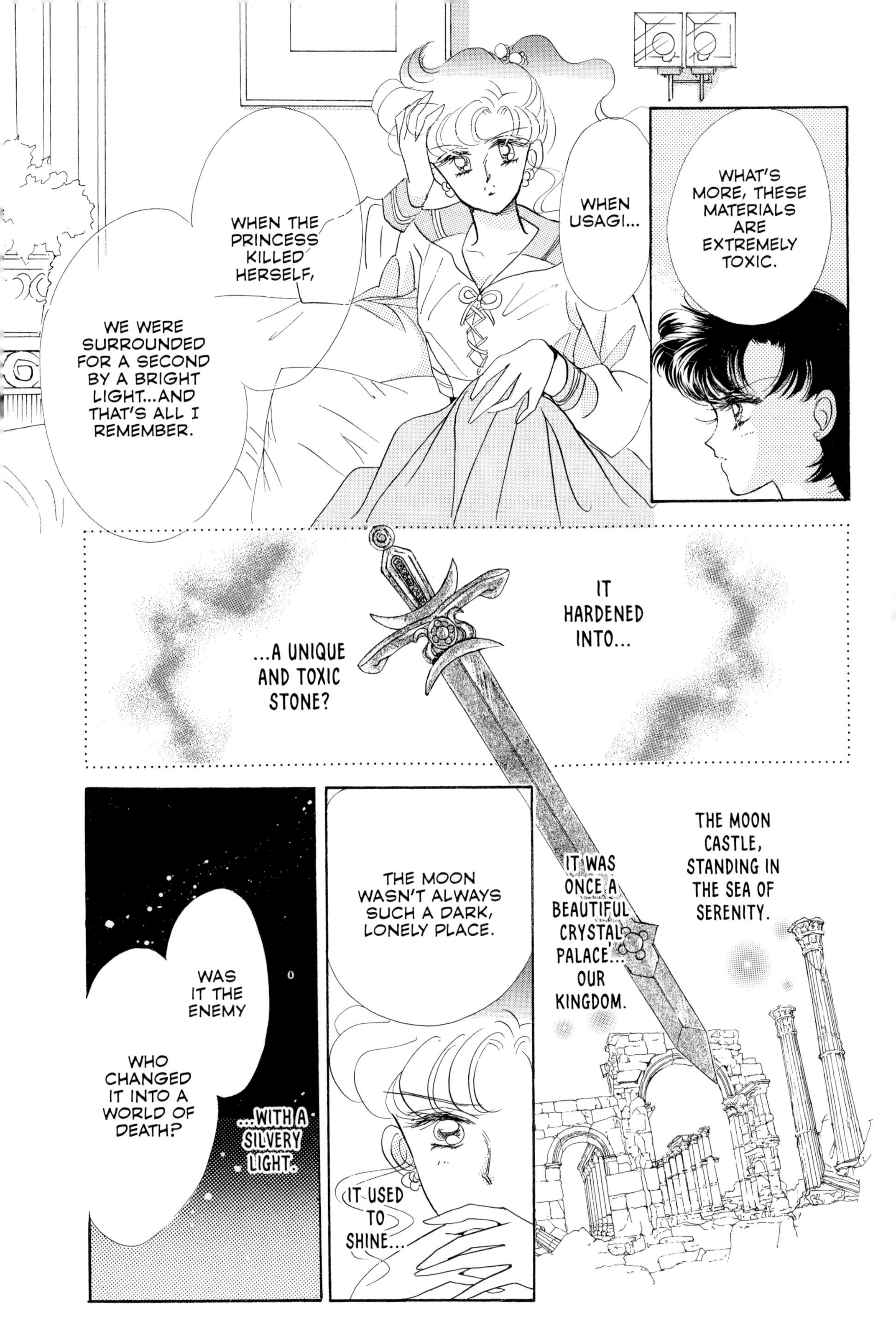
WHAT'S MORE, THESE MATERIALS ARE EXTREMELY TOXIC.
WHEN USAGI...
WHEN THE PRINCESS KILLED HERSELF,
WE WERE SURROUNDED FOR A SECOND BY A BRIGHT LIGHT...AND THAT'S ALL I REMEMBER.
IT HARDENED INTO...
...A UNIQUE AND TOXIC STONE?
THE MOON CASTLE, STANDING IN THE SEA OF SERENITY.
IT WAS ONCE A BEAUTIFUL CRYSTAL PALACE... OUR KINGDOM.
THE MOON WASN'T ALWAYS SUCH A DARK, LONELY PLACE.
IT USED TO SHINE...
...WITH A SILVERY LIGHT.
WAS IT THE ENEMY
WHO CHANGED IT INTO A WORLD OF DEATH?

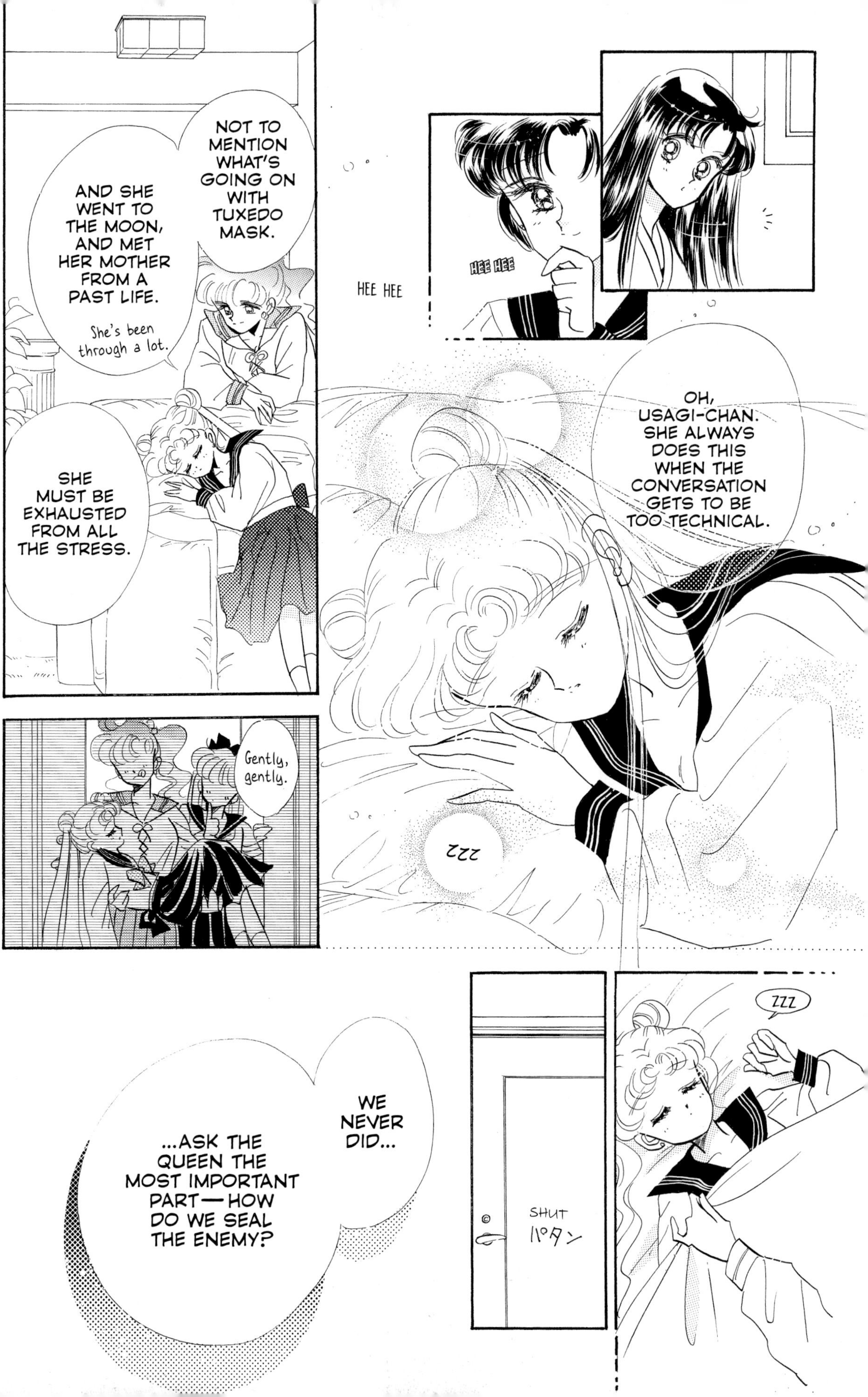
HEE HEE
HEE HEE
OH, USAGI-CHAN. SHE ALWAYS DOES THIS WHEN THE CONVERSATION GETS TO BE TOO TECHNICAL.
ZZZ
AND SHE WENT TO THE MOON, AND MET HER MOTHER FROM A PAST LIFE. She's been through a lot.
NOT TO MENTION WHAT'S GOING ON WITH TUXEDO MASK.
SHE MUST BE EXHAUSTED FROM ALL THE STRESS.
Gently, gently.
ZZZ
SHUT
パタン
WE NEVER DID...
...ASK THE QUEEN THE MOST IMPORTANT PART—HOW DO WE SEAL THE ENEMY?

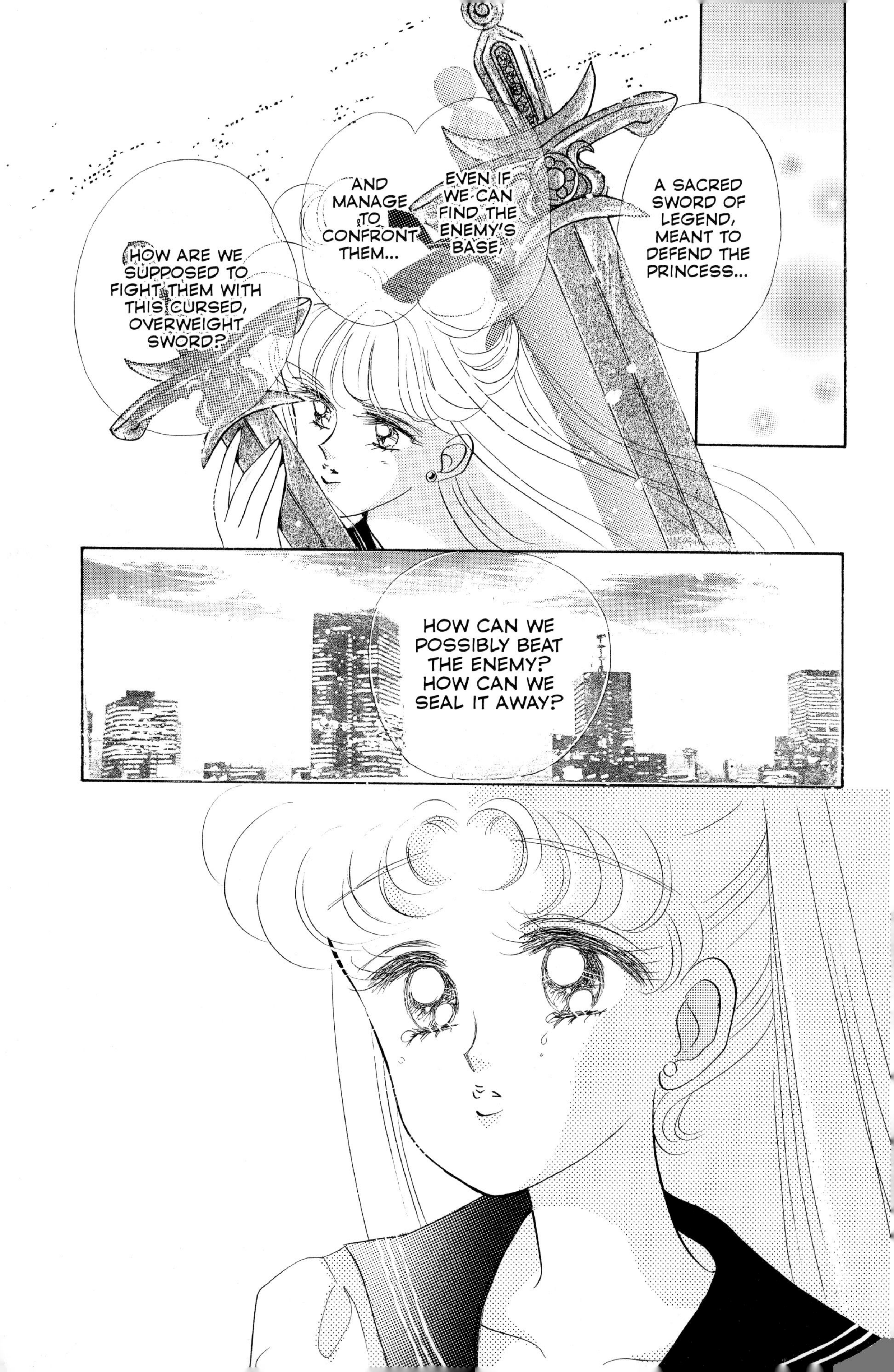
A SACRED SWORD OF LEGEND, MEANT TO DEFEND THE PRINCESS...
EVEN IF WE CAN FIND THE ENEMY'S BASE,
AND MANAGE TO CONFRONT THEM...
HOW ARE WE SUPPOSED TO FIGHT THEM WITH THIS CURSED, OVERWEIGHT SWORD?
HOW CAN WE POSSIBLY BEAT THE ENEMY? HOW CAN WE SEAL IT AWAY?

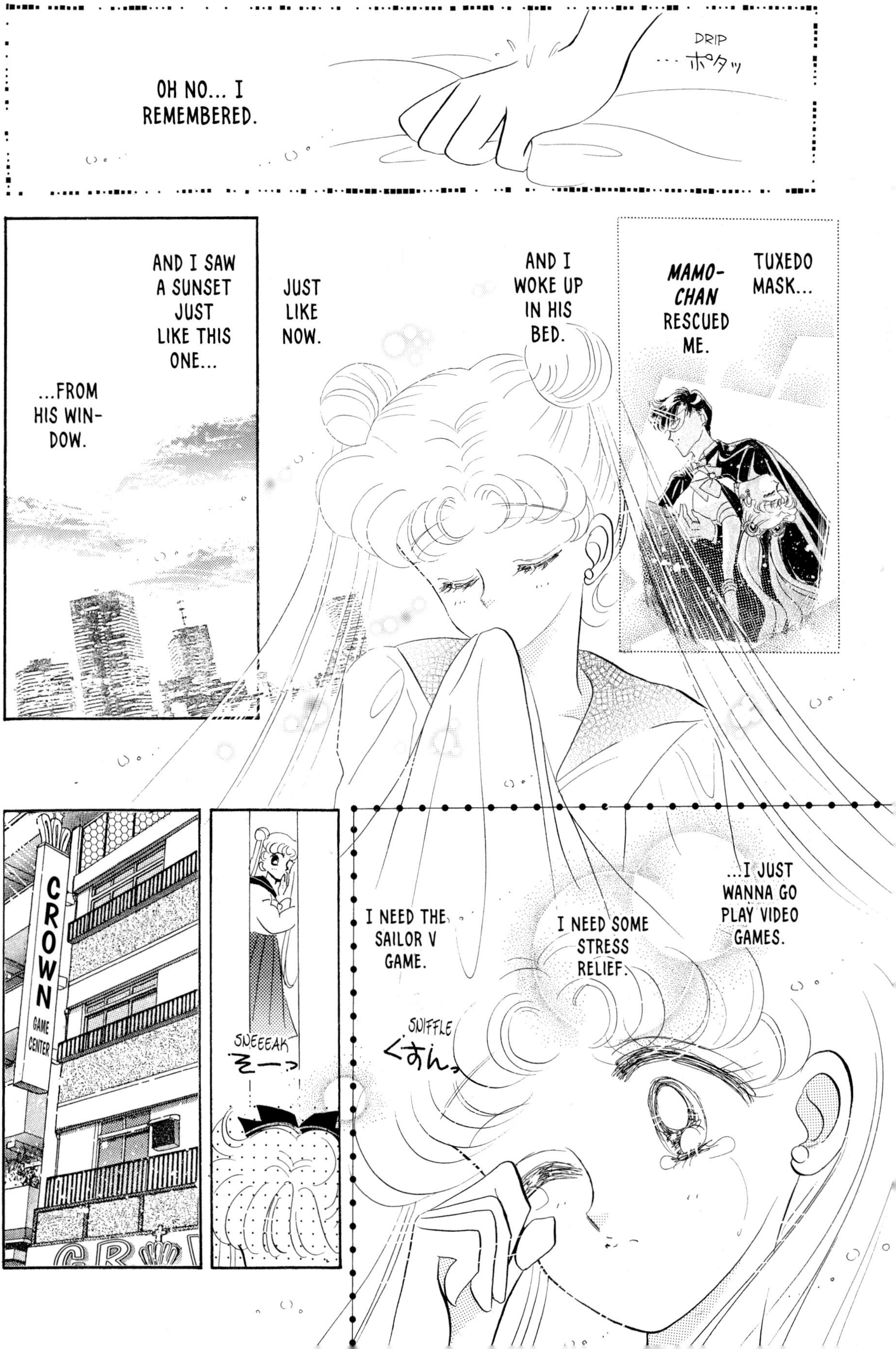
DRIP
ポタッ
OH NO... I REMEMBERED.
TUXEDO MASK...
MAMO-CHAN RESCUED ME.
AND I WOKE UP IN HIS BED.
JUST LIKE NOW.
AND I SAW A SUNSET JUST LIKE THIS ONE...
...FROM HIS WIN-DOW.
...I JUST WANNA GO PLAY VIDEO GAMES.
I NEED SOME STRESS RELIEF.
I NEED THE SAILOR V GAME.
SNIFFLE
くすんっ
SNEEEAK
そーっ
CROWN
GAME CENTER

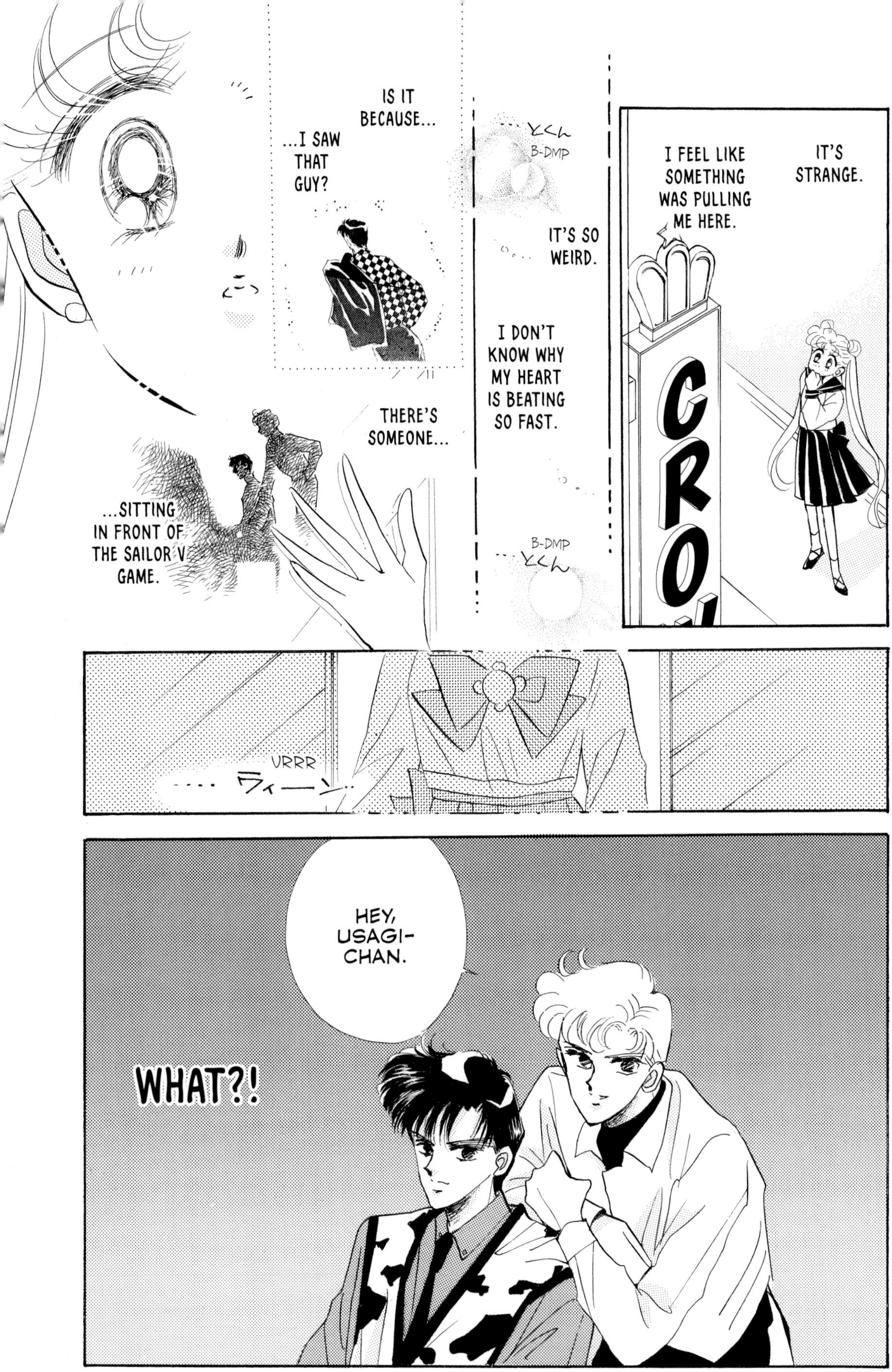
IT'S STRANGE.
I FEEL LIKE SOMETHING WAS PULLING ME HERE.
…とくん
B-DMP
IT'S SO WEIRD.
I DON'T KNOW WHY MY HEART IS BEATING SO FAST.
B-DMP
…とくん
IS IT BECAUSE…
…I SAW THAT GUY?
THERE'S SOMEONE…
…SITTING IN FRONT OF THE SAILOR V GAME.
VRRR
…ウィーン…
HEY, USAGI-CHAN.
WHAT?!

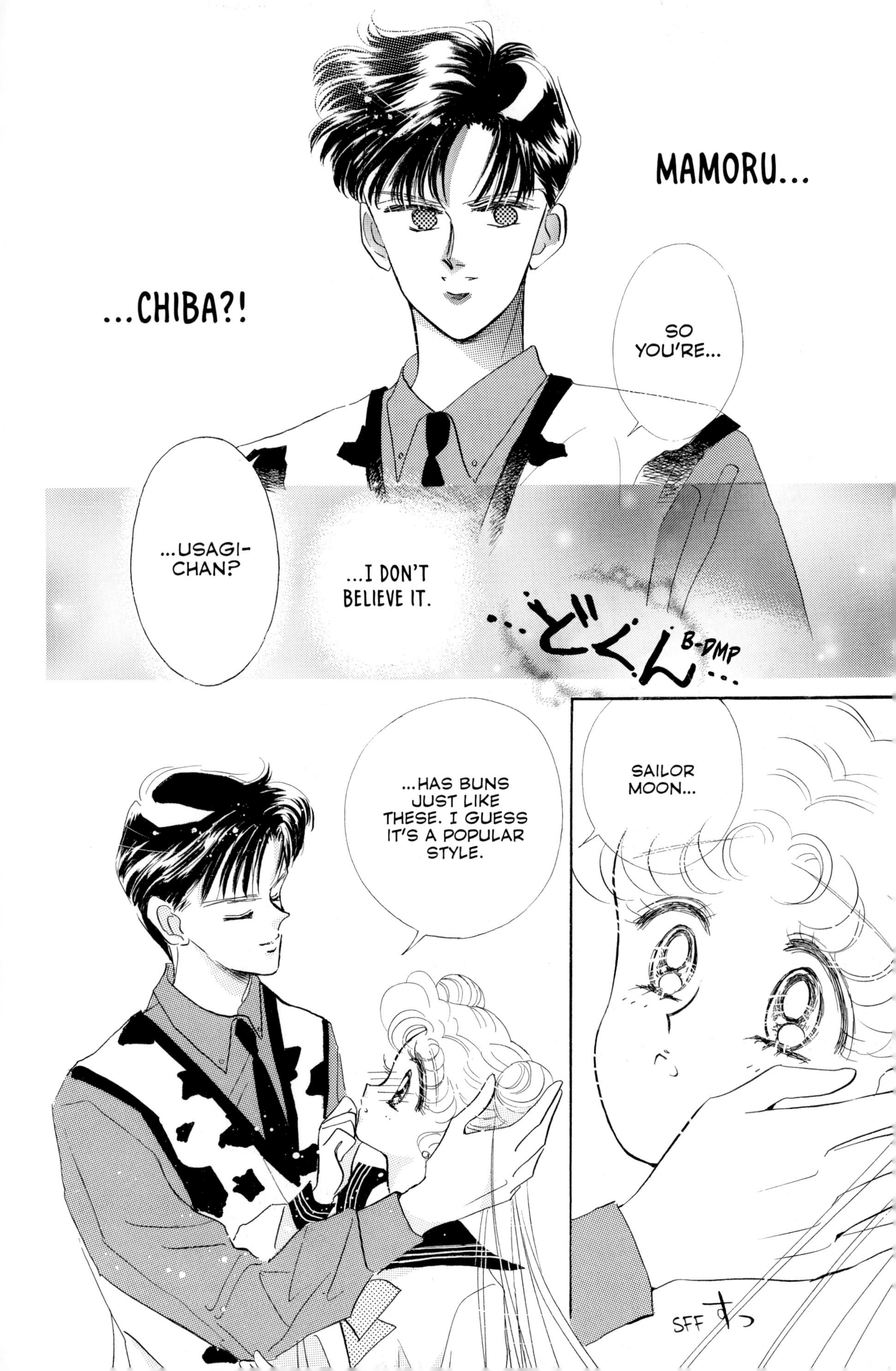

MAMORU...
SO YOU'RE...
...CHIBA?!
...どくん... B-DMP...
...I DON'T BELIEVE IT.
...USAGI-CHAN?
SAILOR MOON...
SFF すっ
...HAS BUNS JUST LIKE THESE. I GUESS IT'S A POPULAR STYLE.

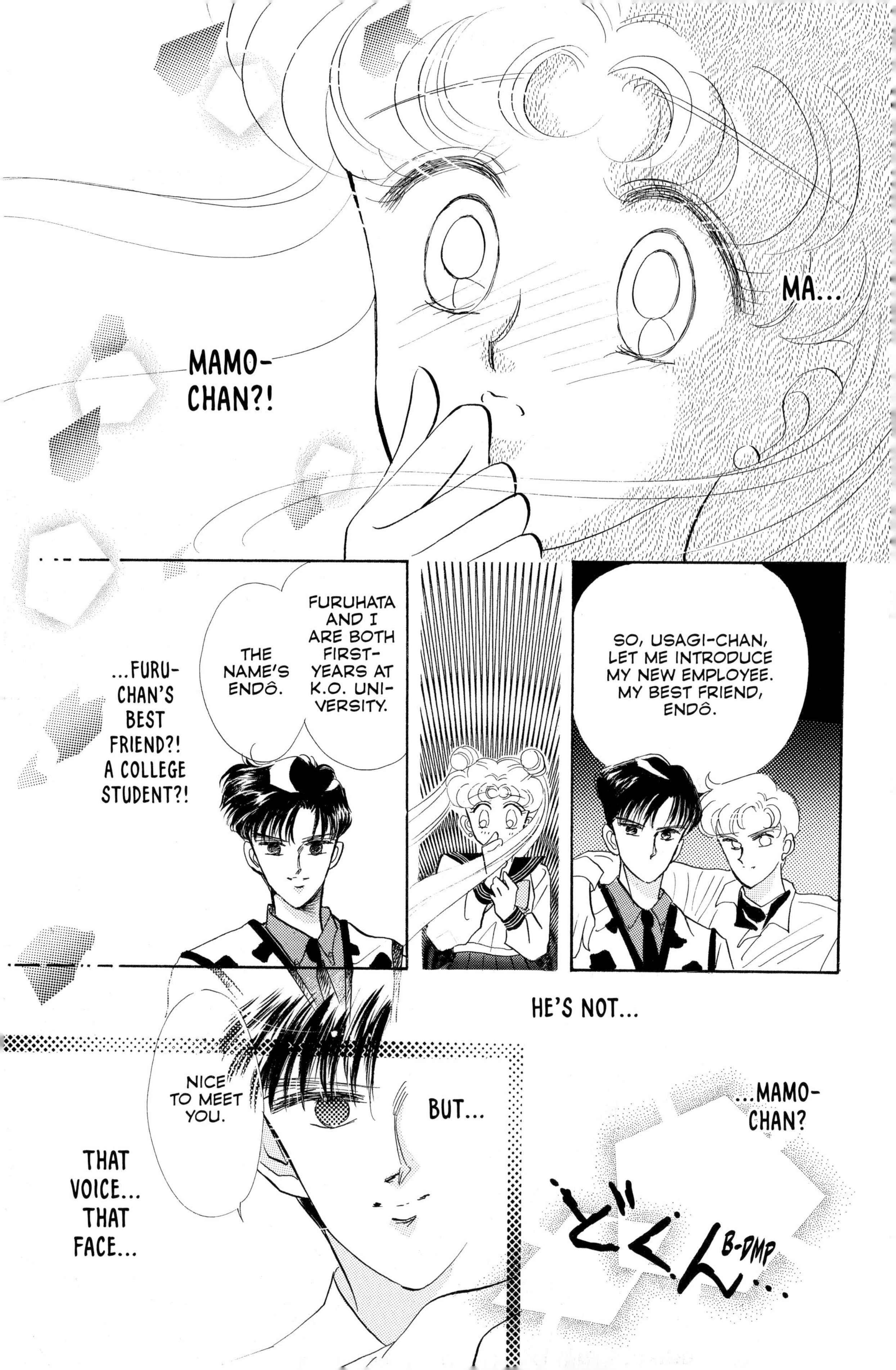
MA...
MAMO-CHAN?!
SO, USAGI-CHAN, LET ME INTRODUCE MY NEW EMPLOYEE. MY BEST FRIEND, ENDÔ.
FURUHATA AND I ARE BOTH FIRST-YEARS AT K.O. UNIVERSITY.
THE NAME'S ENDÔ.
...FURU-CHAN'S BEST FRIEND?! A COLLEGE STUDENT?!
HE'S NOT...
...MAMO-CHAN?
どくん
B-DMP
BUT...
NICE TO MEET YOU.
THAT VOICE... THAT FACE...

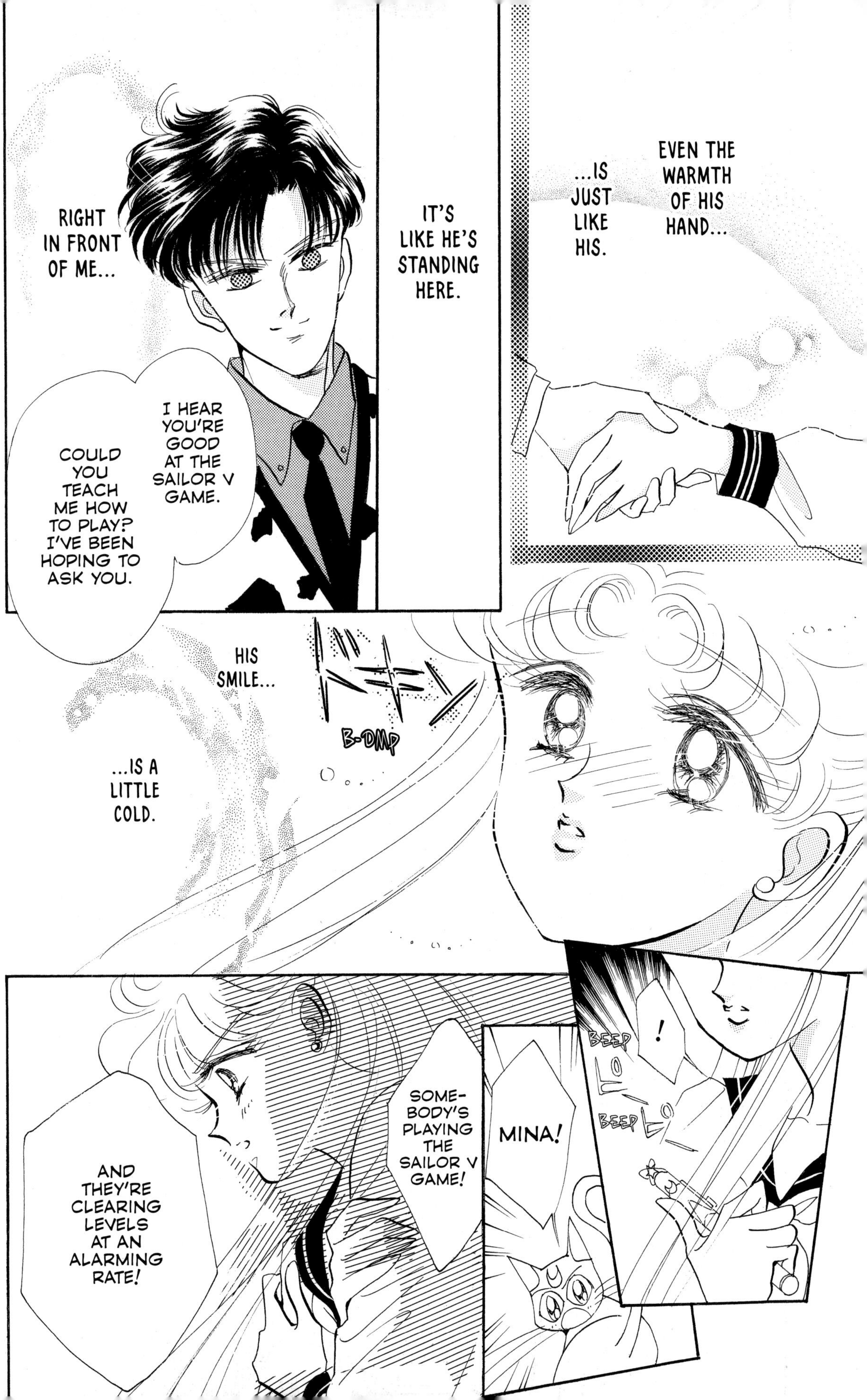
EVEN THE WARMTH OF HIS HAND...
...IS JUST LIKE HIS.
IT'S LIKE HE'S STANDING HERE.
RIGHT IN FRONT OF ME...
I HEAR YOU'RE GOOD AT THE SAILOR V GAME.
COULD YOU TEACH ME HOW TO PLAY? I'VE BEEN HOPING TO ASK YOU.
B-DMP
HIS SMILE...
...IS A LITTLE COLD.
BEEP
BEEP
!
MINA!
SOME-BODY'S PLAYING THE SAILOR V GAME!
AND THEY'RE CLEARING LEVELS AT AN ALARMING RATE!

WHO IS IT?

I'M GOING TO THE ARCADE!

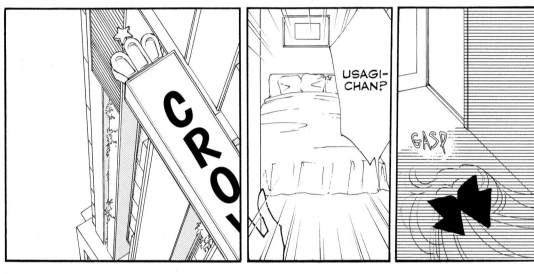

CRO'

USAGI-CHAN?

GASP

...MAMORU CHIBA?!

USAGI-CHAN... AND...

!!

THAT'S...

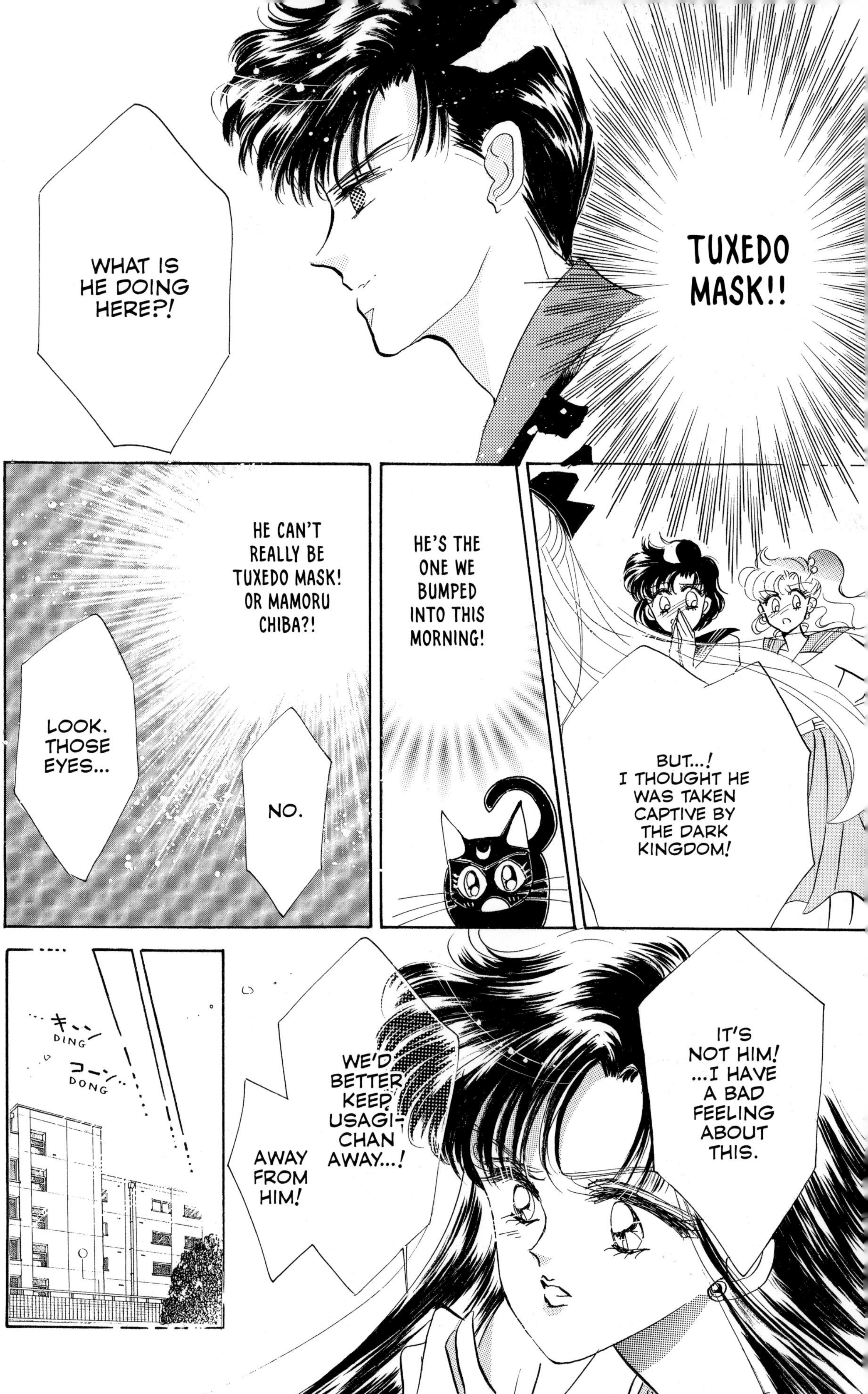
TUXEDO MASK!!
WHAT IS HE DOING HERE?!
BUT...! I THOUGHT HE WAS TAKEN CAPTIVE BY THE DARK KINGDOM!
HE'S THE ONE WE BUMPED INTO THIS MORNING!
HE CAN'T REALLY BE TUXEDO MASK! OR MAMORU CHIBA?!
NO.
LOOK. THOSE EYES...
IT'S NOT HIM! ...I HAVE A BAD FEELING ABOUT THIS.
WE'D BETTER KEEP USAGI-CHAN AWAY...!
AWAY FROM HIM!
キーン DING
コーン DONG

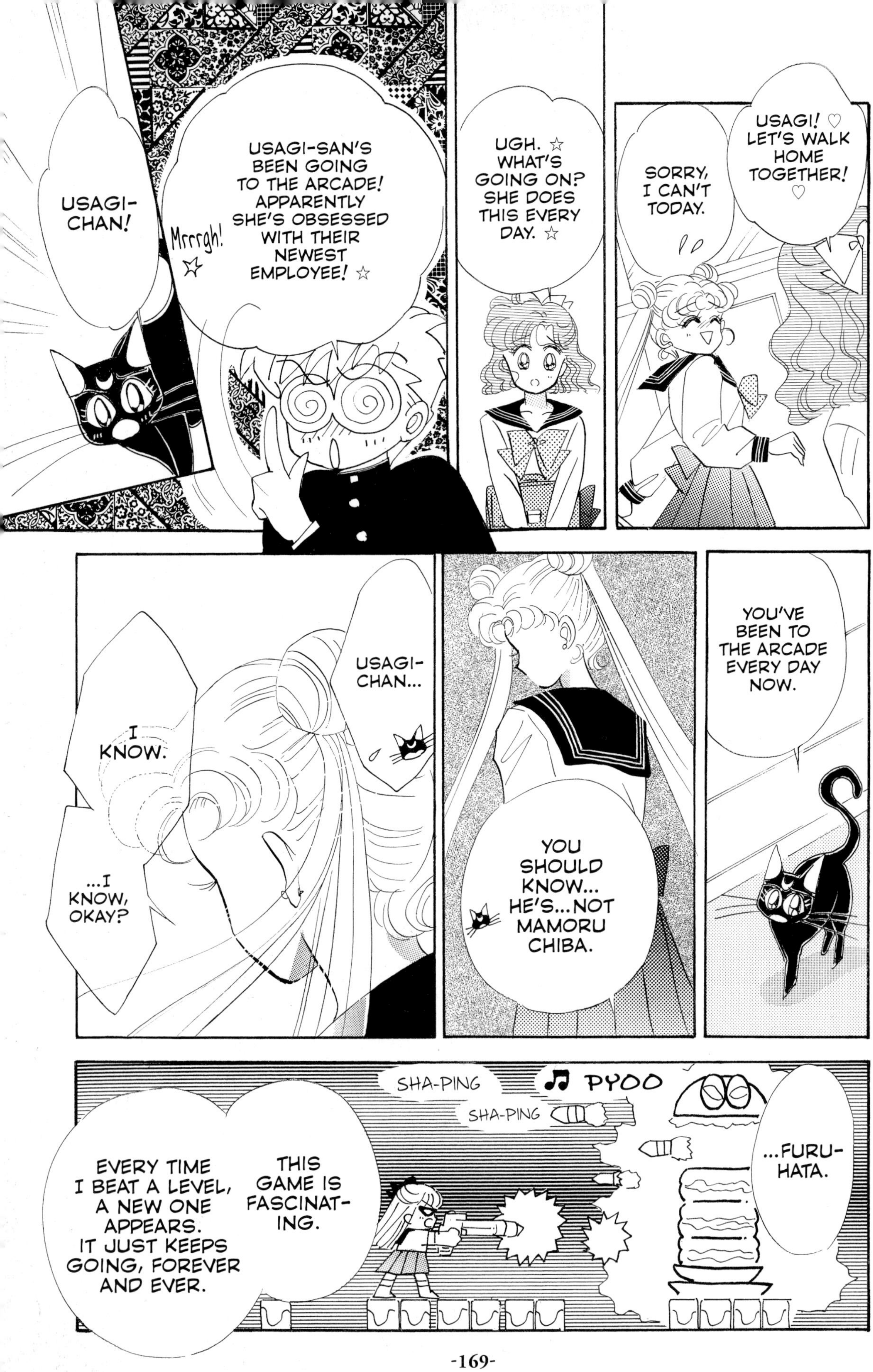
USAGI! ♡ LET'S WALK HOME TOGETHER! ♡
SORRY, I CAN'T TODAY.
UGH. ☆ WHAT'S GOING ON? SHE DOES THIS EVERY DAY. ☆
USAGI-SAN'S BEEN GOING TO THE ARCADE! APPARENTLY SHE'S OBSESSED WITH THEIR NEWEST EMPLOYEE! ☆
Mrrrgh!
USAGI-CHAN!
YOU'VE BEEN TO THE ARCADE EVERY DAY NOW.
YOU SHOULD KNOW... HE'S...NOT MAMORU CHIBA.
USAGI-CHAN...
I KNOW.
...I KNOW, OKAY?
...FURU-HATA.
♫ PYOO
SHA-PING
SHA-PING
THIS GAME IS FASCINATING.
EVERY TIME I BEAT A LEVEL, A NEW ONE APPEARS. IT JUST KEEPS GOING, FOREVER AND EVER.

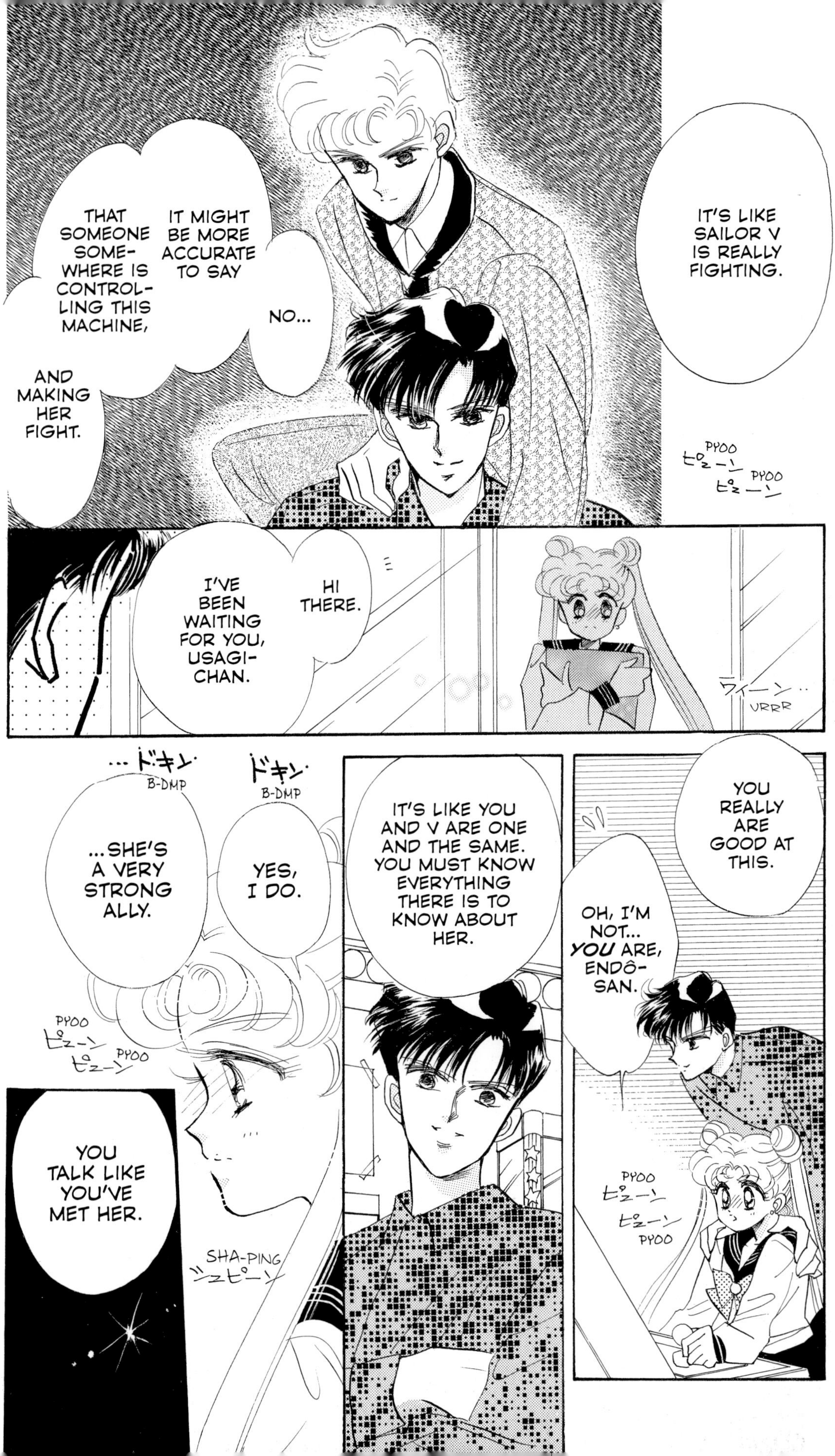
IT'S LIKE SAILOR V IS REALLY FIGHTING.
ピューン PYOO
ピューン PYOO
NO...
IT MIGHT BE MORE ACCURATE TO SAY
THAT SOMEONE SOME-WHERE IS CONTROL-LING THIS MACHINE,
AND MAKING HER FIGHT.
ウィーン URRR
HI THERE.
I'VE BEEN WAITING FOR YOU, USAGI-CHAN.
YOU REALLY ARE GOOD AT THIS.
OH, I'M NOT... *YOU* ARE, ENDÔ-SAN.
ピューン PYOO
ピューン PYOO
IT'S LIKE YOU AND V ARE ONE AND THE SAME. YOU MUST KNOW EVERYTHING THERE IS TO KNOW ABOUT HER.
ドキン B-DMP
YES, I DO.
...ドキン B-DMP
...SHE'S A VERY STRONG ALLY.
ピューン PYOO
ピューン PYOO
シュピーン SHA-PING
YOU TALK LIKE YOU'VE MET HER.

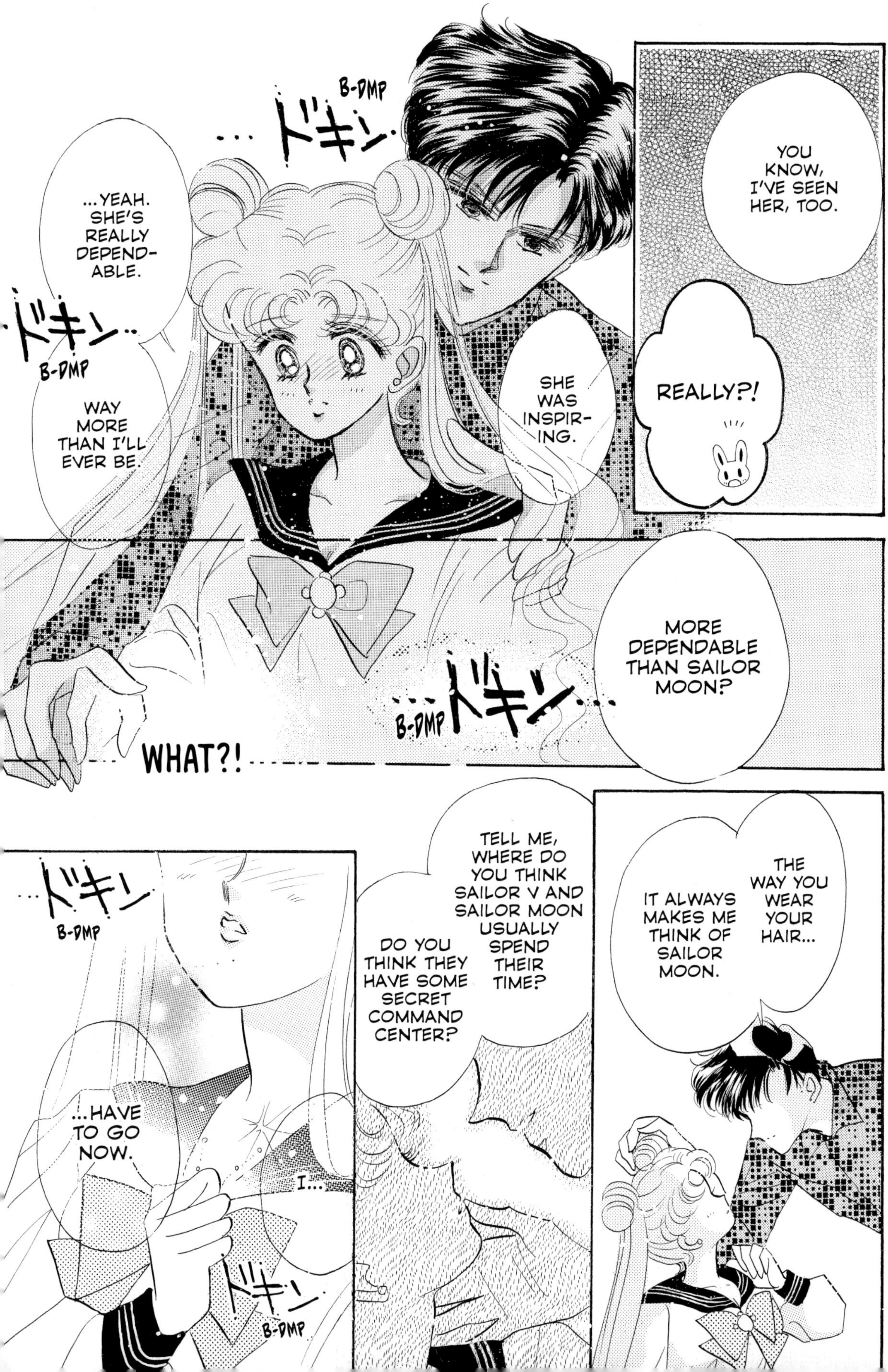

YOU KNOW, I'VE SEEN HER, TOO.
REALLY?!
SHE WAS INSPIRING.
...ドキン
B-DMP
...YEAH. SHE'S REALLY DEPENDABLE.
ドキン...
B-DMP
WAY MORE THAN I'LL EVER BE.
MORE DEPENDABLE THAN SAILOR MOON?
...ドキン...
B-DMP
WHAT?!
THE WAY YOU WEAR YOUR HAIR...
IT ALWAYS MAKES ME THINK OF SAILOR MOON.
TELL ME, WHERE DO YOU THINK SAILOR V AND SAILOR MOON USUALLY SPEND THEIR TIME?
DO YOU THINK THEY HAVE SOME SECRET COMMAND CENTER?
...ドキン
B-DMP
I...
...HAVE TO GO NOW.
ドキン
B-DMP

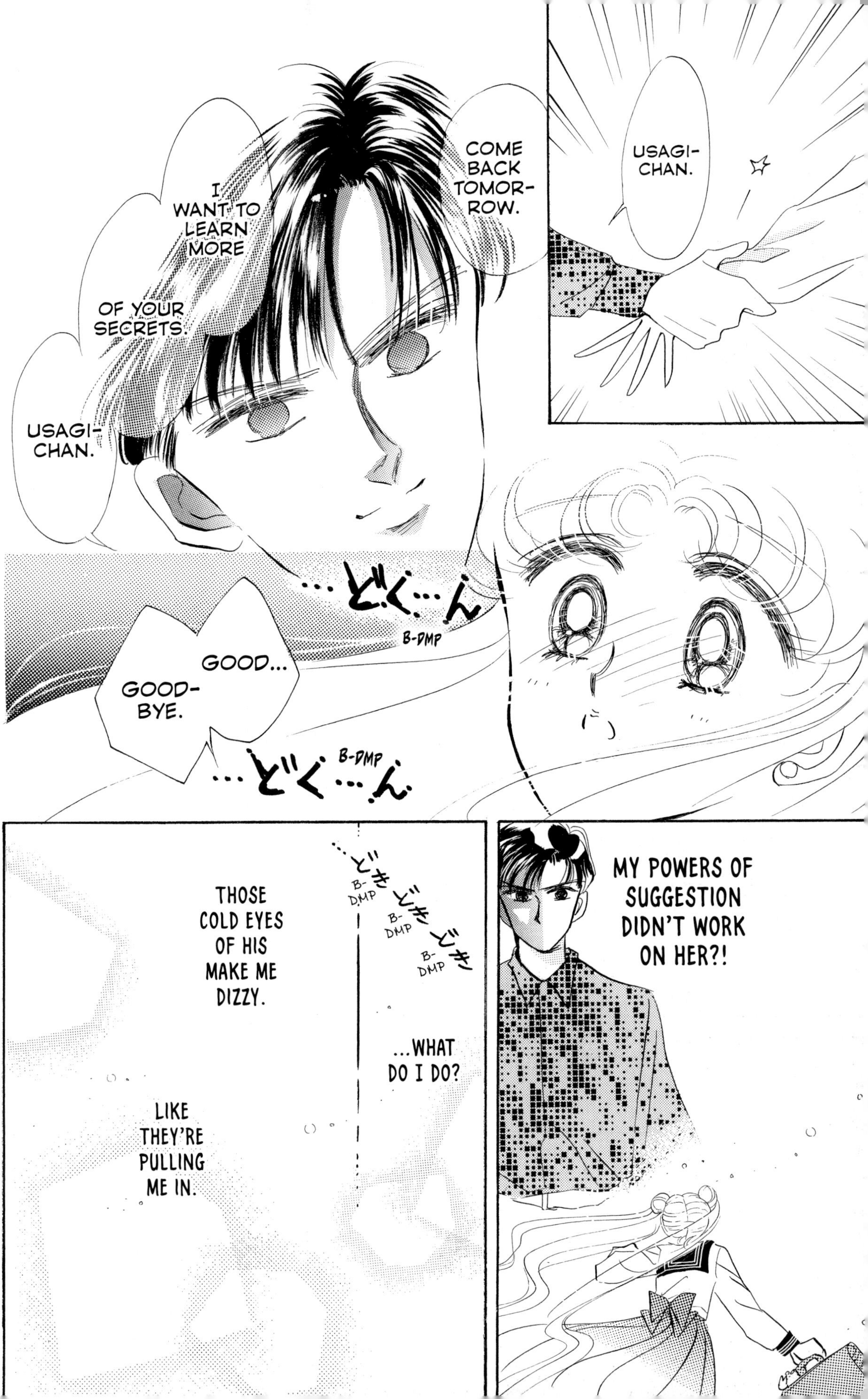
USAGI-CHAN.
COME BACK TOMORROW.
I WANT TO LEARN MORE
OF YOUR SECRETS.
USAGI-CHAN.
…どく…ん
B-DMP
GOOD…
GOOD-BYE.
…どく…ん
B-DMP
MY POWERS OF SUGGESTION DIDN'T WORK ON HER?!
…どきどきどき
B-DMP B-DMP B-DMP
THOSE COLD EYES OF HIS MAKE ME DIZZY.
...WHAT DO I DO?
LIKE THEY'RE PULLING ME IN.

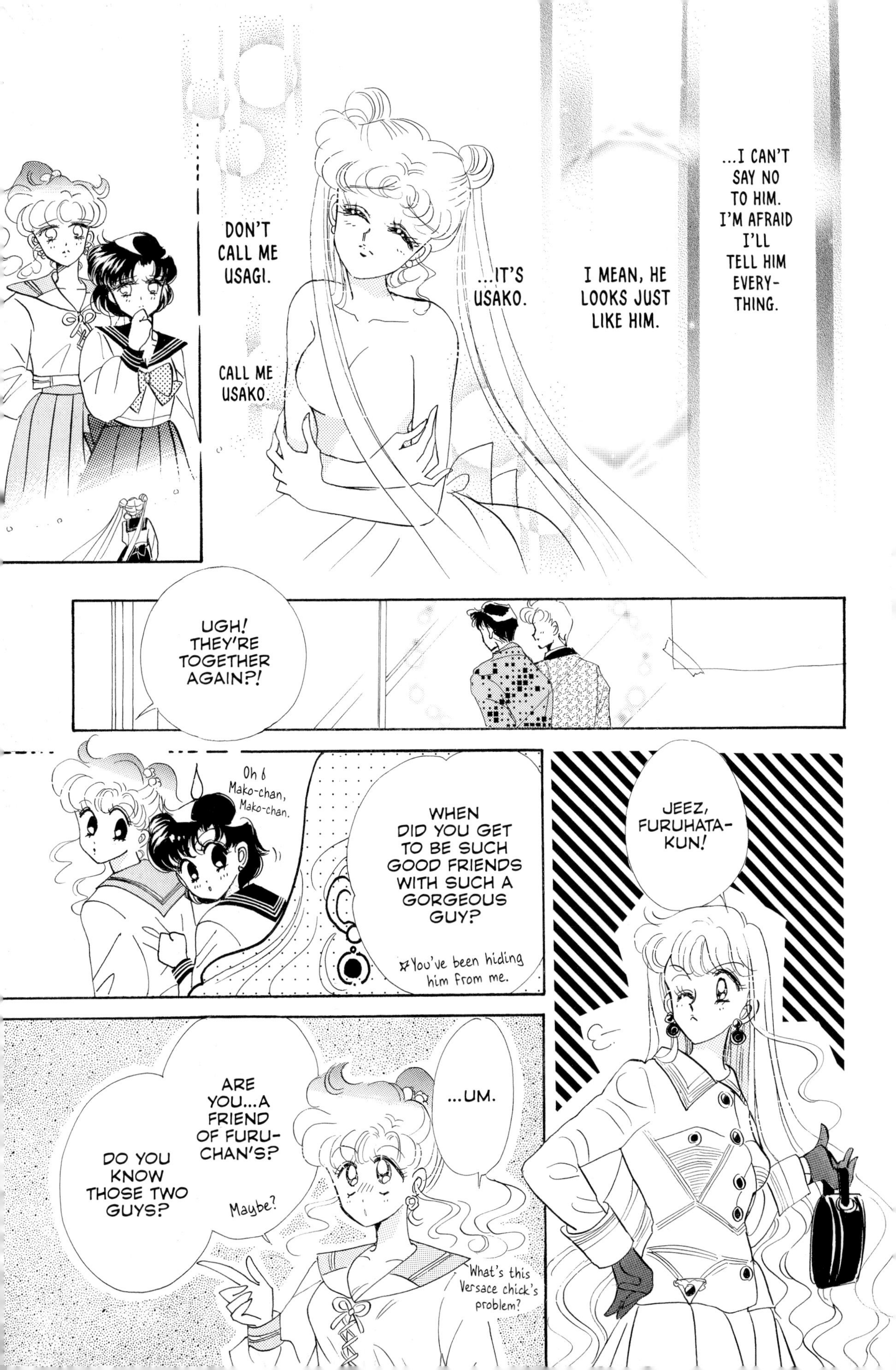

...I CAN'T SAY NO TO HIM. I'M AFRAID I'LL TELL HIM EVERY-THING.
I MEAN, HE LOOKS JUST LIKE HIM.
...IT'S USAKO.
DON'T CALL ME USAGI.
CALL ME USAKO.
UGH! THEY'RE TOGETHER AGAIN?!
JEEZ, FURUHATA-KUN!
WHEN DID YOU GET TO BE SUCH GOOD FRIENDS WITH SUCH A GORGEOUS GUY?
☆You've been hiding him from me.
Oh ♪ Mako-chan, Mako-chan.
...UM.
ARE YOU...A FRIEND OF FURU-CHAN'S?
DO YOU KNOW THOSE TWO GUYS?
Maybe?
What's this Versace chick's problem?

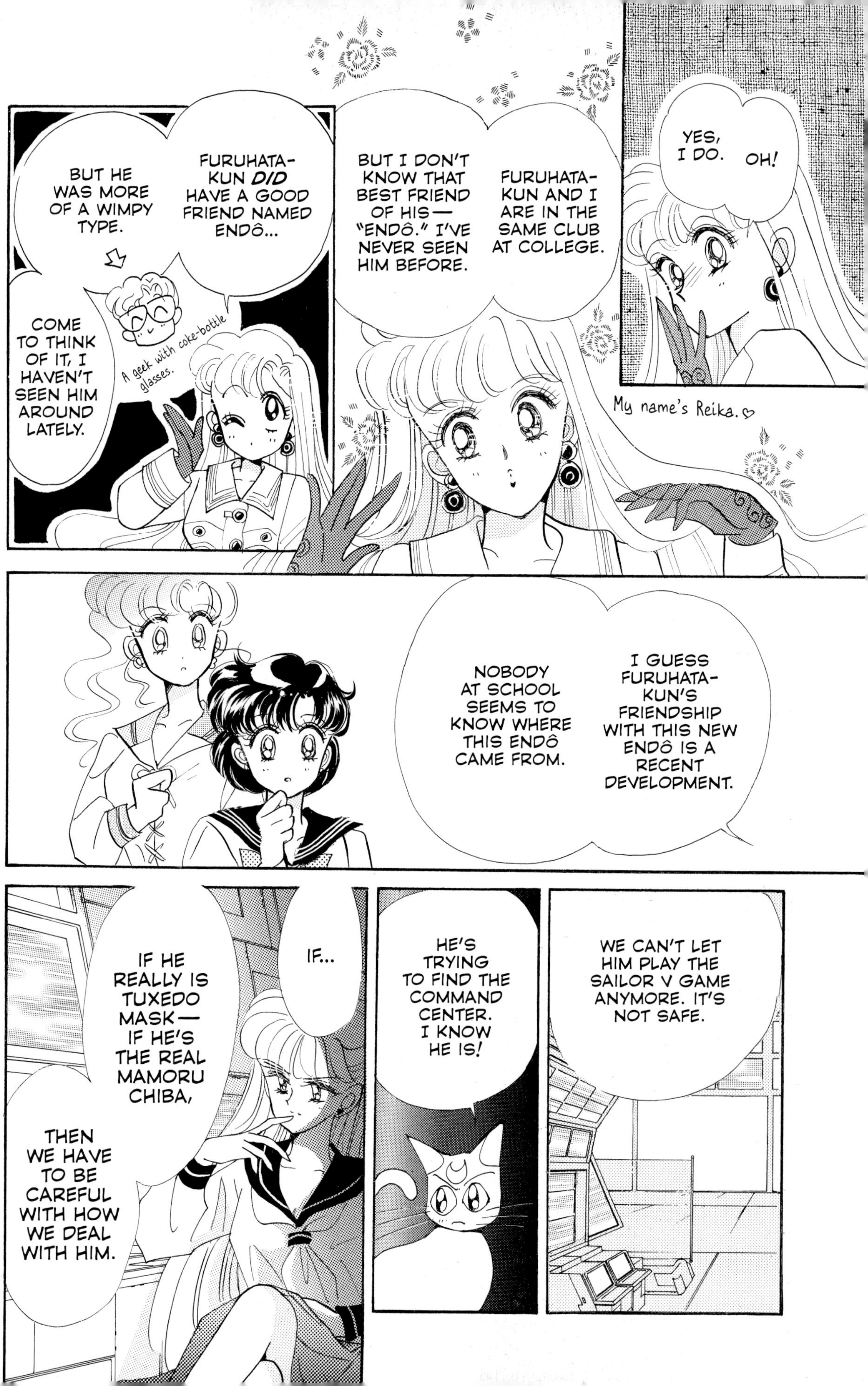
YES, I DO.
OH!
My name's Reika.♡
FURUHATA-KUN AND I ARE IN THE SAME CLUB AT COLLEGE.
BUT I DON'T KNOW THAT BEST FRIEND OF HIS—"ENDÔ." I'VE NEVER SEEN HIM BEFORE.
FURUHATA-KUN *DID* HAVE A GOOD FRIEND NAMED ENDÔ...
BUT HE WAS MORE OF A WIMPY TYPE.
A geek with coke-bottle glasses.
COME TO THINK OF IT, I HAVEN'T SEEN HIM AROUND LATELY.
I GUESS FURUHATA-KUN'S FRIENDSHIP WITH THIS NEW ENDÔ IS A RECENT DEVELOPMENT.
NOBODY AT SCHOOL SEEMS TO KNOW WHERE THIS ENDÔ CAME FROM.
WE CAN'T LET HIM PLAY THE SAILOR V GAME ANYMORE. IT'S NOT SAFE.
HE'S TRYING TO FIND THE COMMAND CENTER. I KNOW HE IS!
IF...
IF HE REALLY IS TUXEDO MASK—IF HE'S THE REAL MAMORU CHIBA,
THEN WE HAVE TO BE CAREFUL WITH HOW WE DEAL WITH HIM.

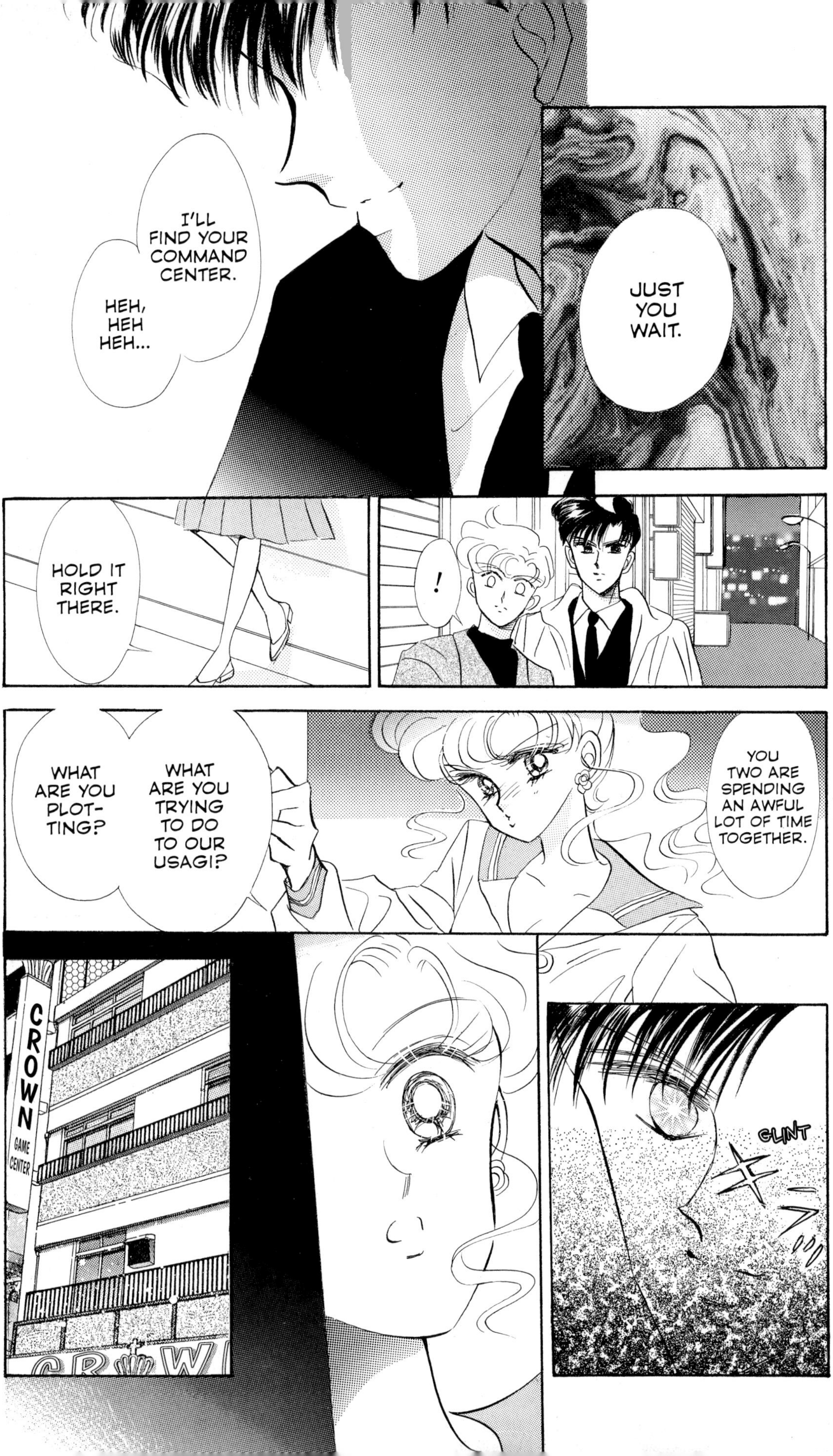
JUST YOU WAIT.
I'LL FIND YOUR COMMAND CENTER.
HEH, HEH HEH...
!
HOLD IT RIGHT THERE.
YOU TWO ARE SPENDING AN AWFUL LOT OF TIME TOGETHER.
WHAT ARE YOU TRYING TO DO TO OUR USAGI?
WHAT ARE YOU PLOT-TING?
GLINT
CROWN GAME CENTER

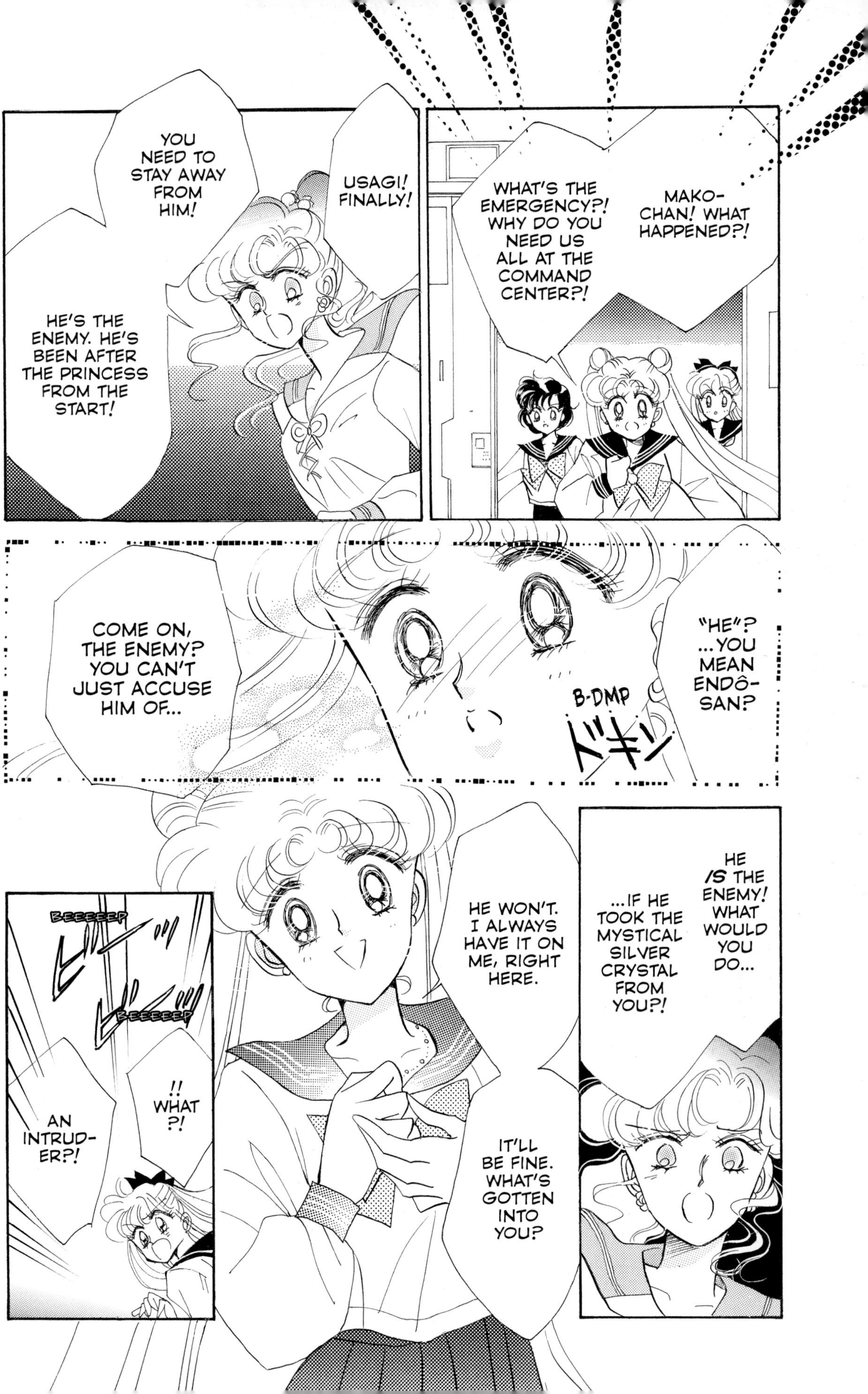

MAKO-CHAN! WHAT HAPPENED?!
WHAT'S THE EMERGENCY?! WHY DO YOU NEED US ALL AT THE COMMAND CENTER?!
USAGI! FINALLY!
YOU NEED TO STAY AWAY FROM HIM!
HE'S THE ENEMY. HE'S BEEN AFTER THE PRINCESS FROM THE START!
"HE"? ...YOU MEAN ENDÔ-SAN?
B-DMP
ドキン
COME ON, THE ENEMY? YOU CAN'T JUST ACCUSE HIM OF...
HE *IS* THE ENEMY! WHAT WOULD YOU DO...
...IF HE TOOK THE MYSTICAL SILVER CRYSTAL FROM YOU?!
HE WON'T. I ALWAYS HAVE IT ON ME, RIGHT HERE.
IT'LL BE FINE. WHAT'S GOTTEN INTO YOU?
BEEEEEEP
BEEEEEEP
!! WHAT?!
AN INTRUDER?!

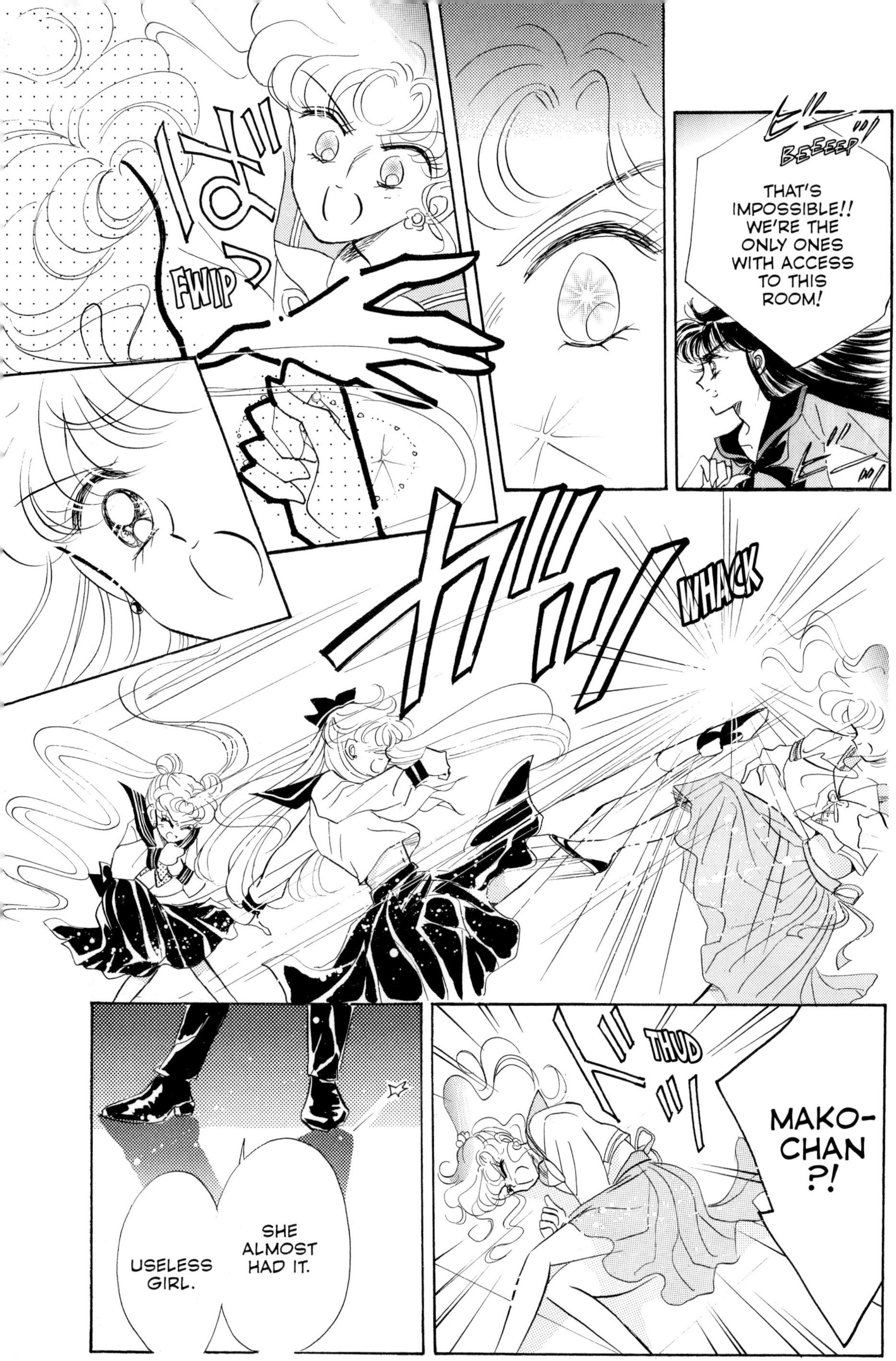
BEEEEP
THAT'S IMPOSSIBLE!! WE'RE THE ONLY ONES WITH ACCESS TO THIS ROOM!
FWIP
WHACK
THUD
MAKO-CHAN?!
SHE ALMOST HAD IT.
USELESS GIRL.

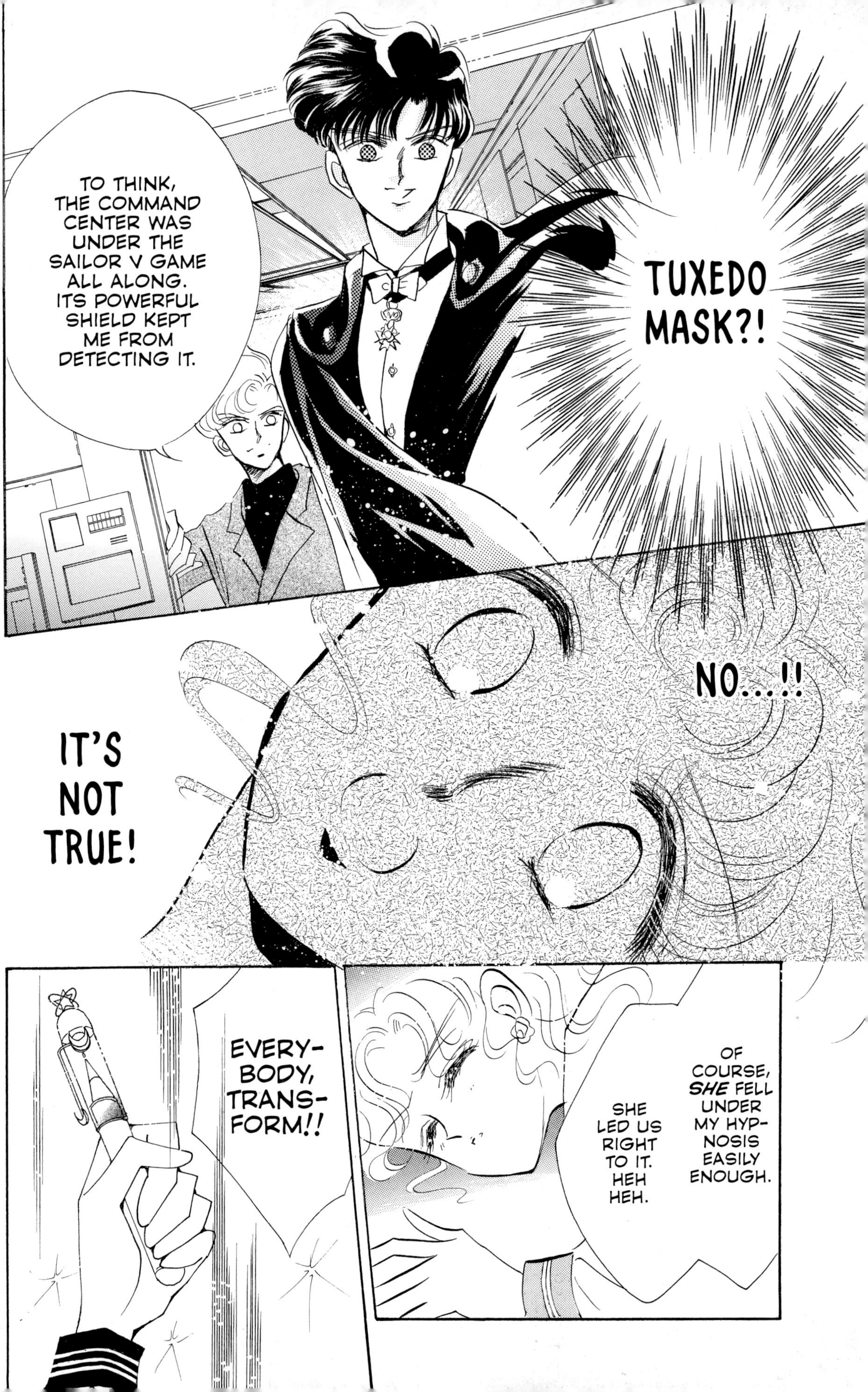
TUXEDO MASK?!
TO THINK, THE COMMAND CENTER WAS UNDER THE SAILOR V GAME ALL ALONG. ITS POWERFUL SHIELD KEPT ME FROM DETECTING IT.
NO...!!
IT'S NOT TRUE!
OF COURSE, ***SHE*** FELL UNDER MY HYP-NOSIS EASILY ENOUGH.
SHE LED US RIGHT TO IT. HEH HEH.
EVERY-BODY, TRANS-FORM!!

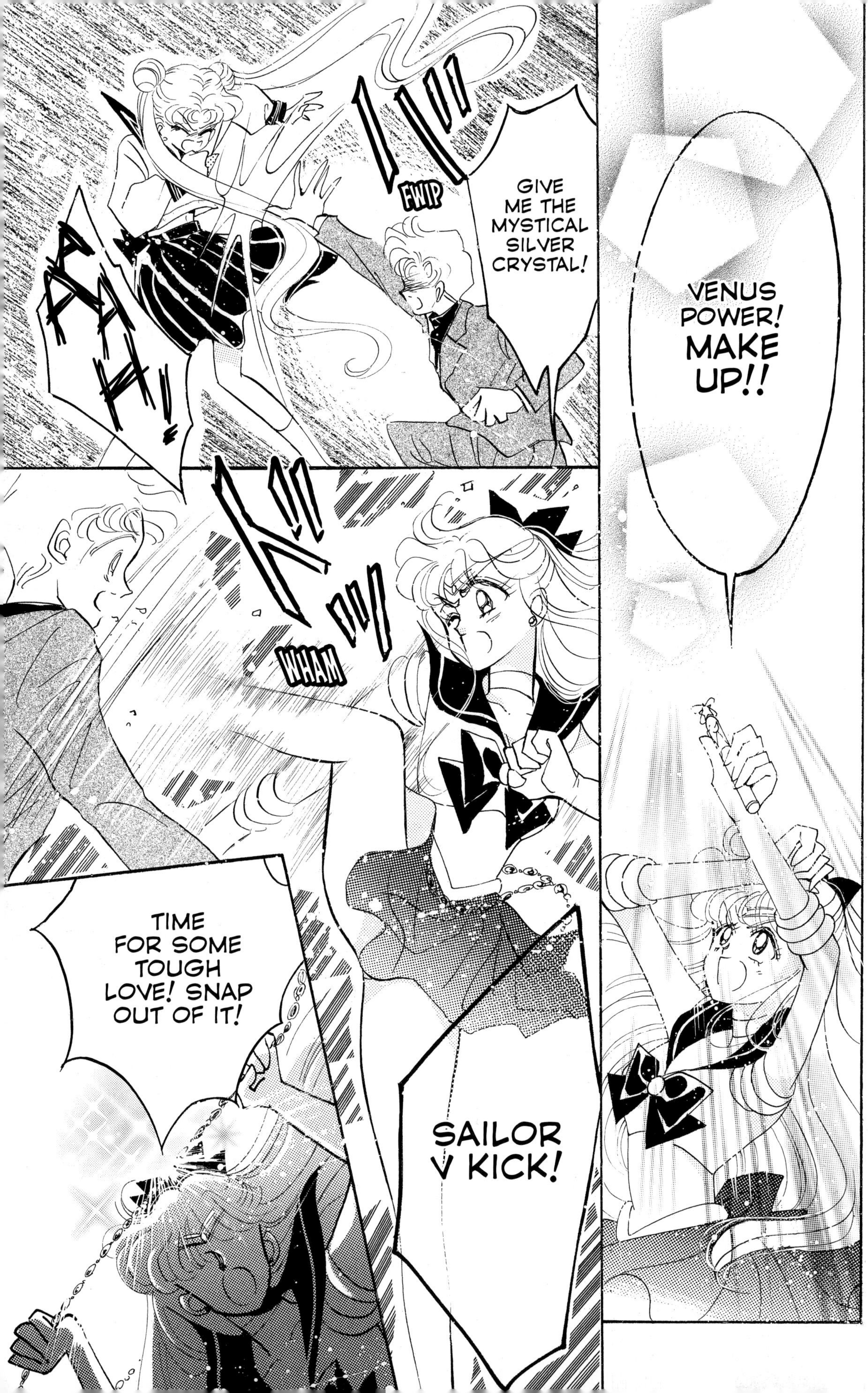
VENUS POWER! MAKE UP!!
GIVE ME THE MYSTICAL SILVER CRYSTAL!
FWIP
WHAM
SAILOR V KICK!
TIME FOR SOME TOUGH LOVE! SNAP OUT OF IT!

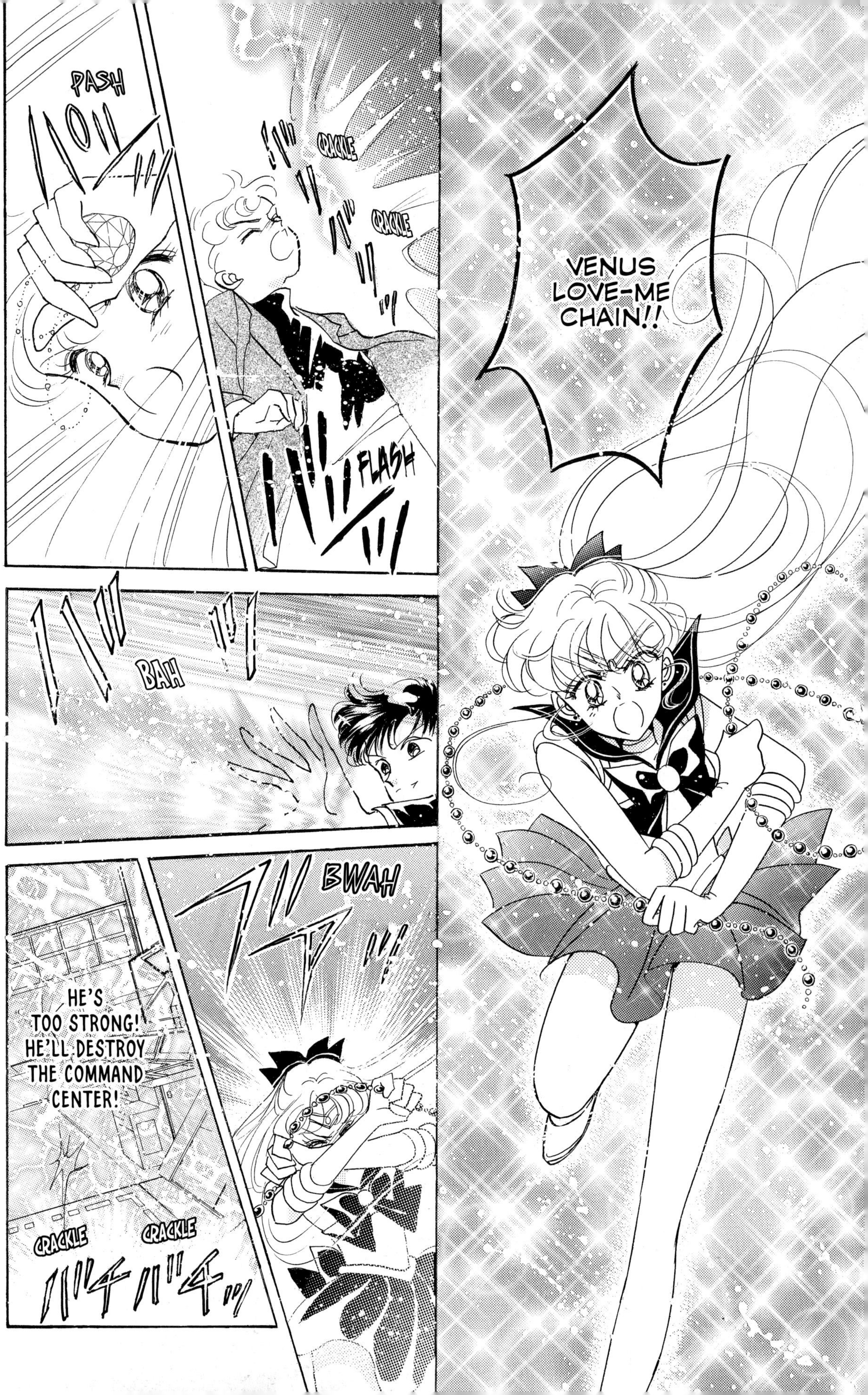
VENUS LOVE-ME CHAIN!!
CRACKLE
CRACKLE
FLASH
PASH
BAH
BWAH
HE'S TOO STRONG! HE'LL DESTROY THE COMMAND CENTER!
CRACKLE
CRACKLE

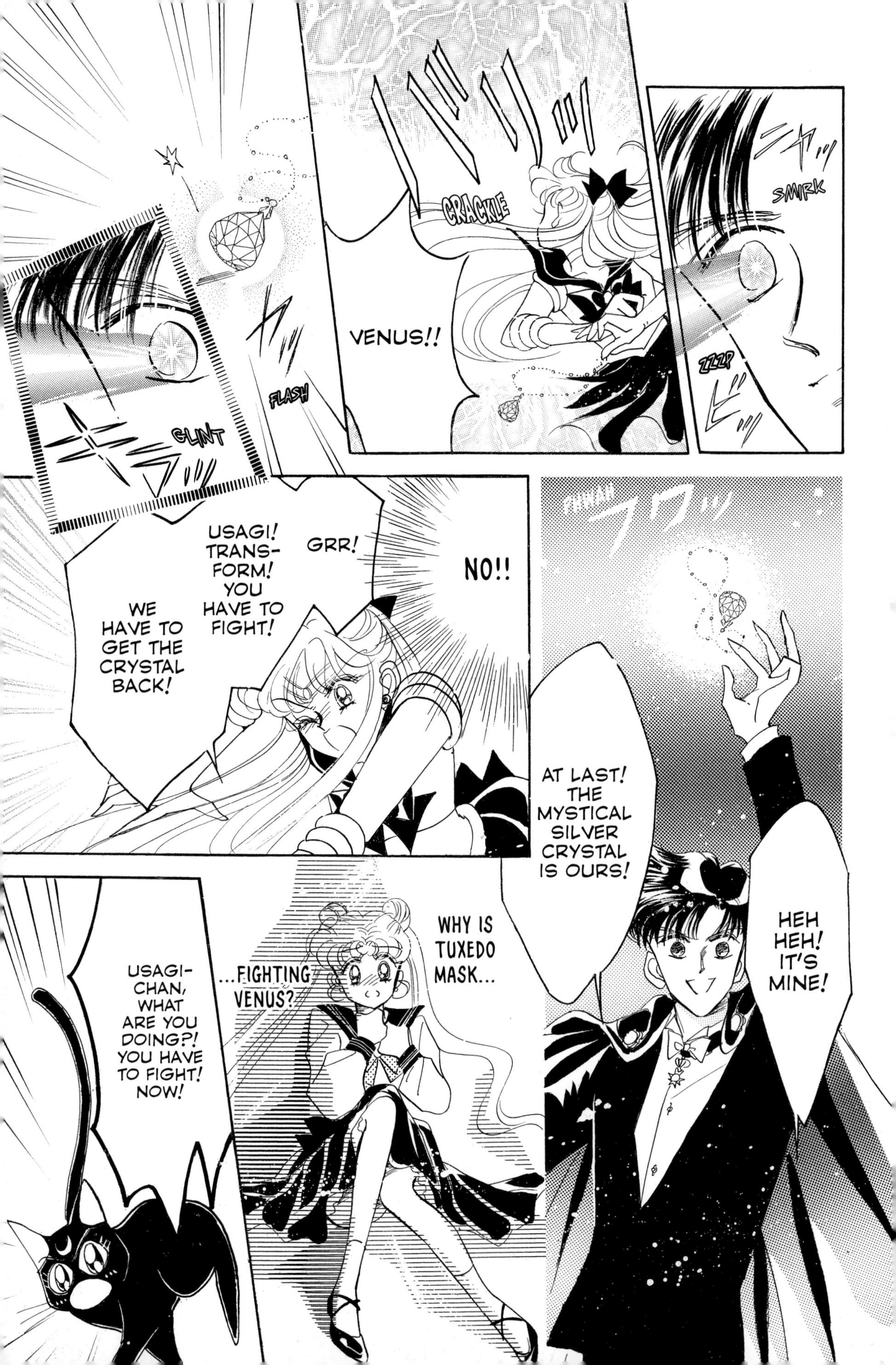
SMIRK
ZZZP
CRACKLE
VENUS!!
FLASH
GLINT
FWAH
AT LAST! THE MYSTICAL SILVER CRYSTAL IS OURS!
HEH HEH! IT'S MINE!
NO!!
GRR!
USAGI! TRANS-FORM! YOU HAVE TO FIGHT!
WE HAVE TO GET THE CRYSTAL BACK!
WHY IS TUXEDO MASK...
...FIGHTING VENUS?
USAGI-CHAN, WHAT ARE YOU DOING?! YOU HAVE TO FIGHT! NOW!

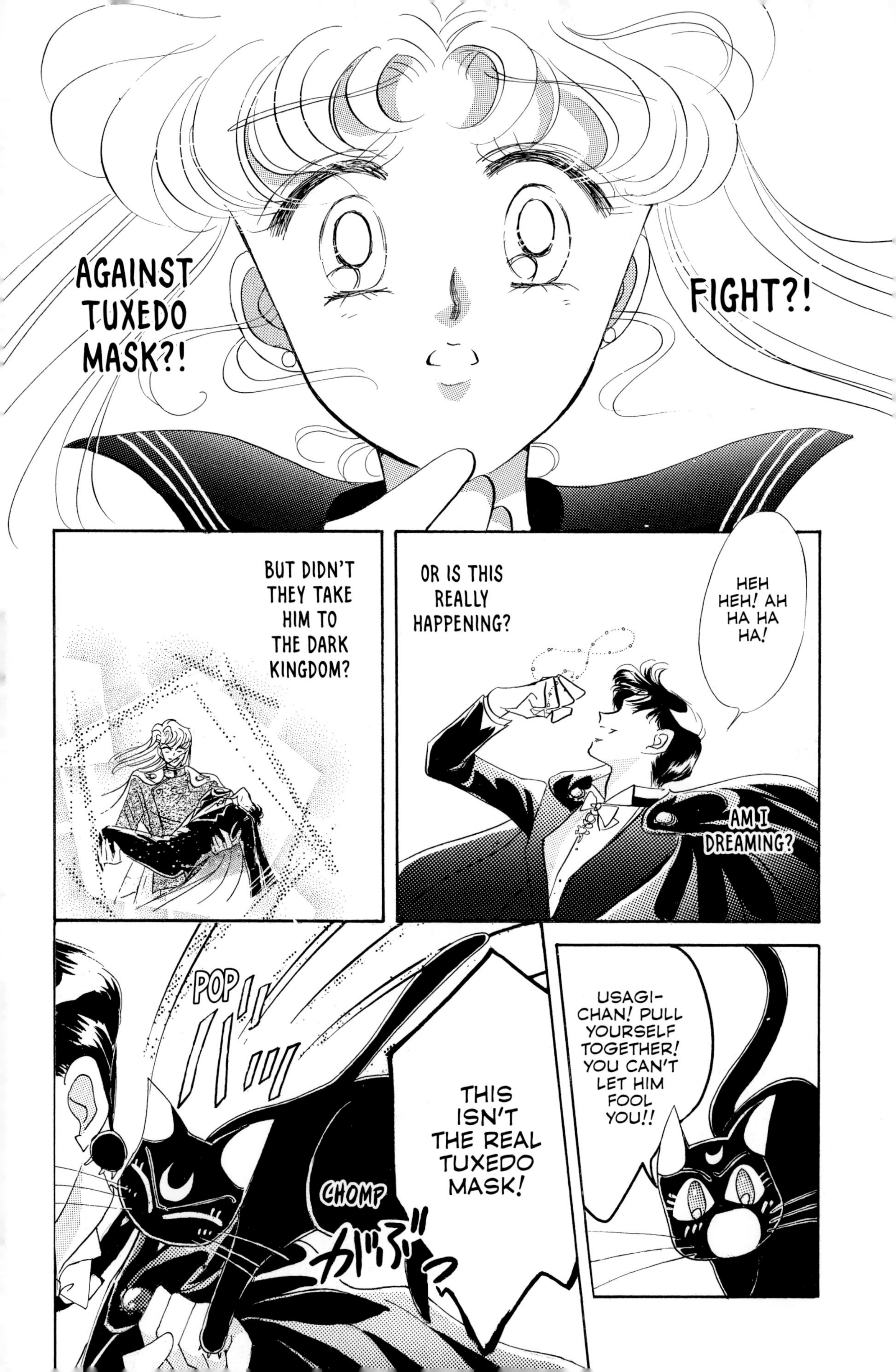
FIGHT?!
AGAINST TUXEDO MASK?!
HEH HEH! AH HA HA HA!
AM I DREAMING?
OR IS THIS REALLY HAPPENING?
BUT DIDN'T THEY TAKE HIM TO THE DARK KINGDOM?
USAGI-CHAN! PULL YOURSELF TOGETHER! YOU CAN'T LET HIM FOOL YOU!!
POP
THIS ISN'T THE REAL TUXEDO MASK!
CHOMP

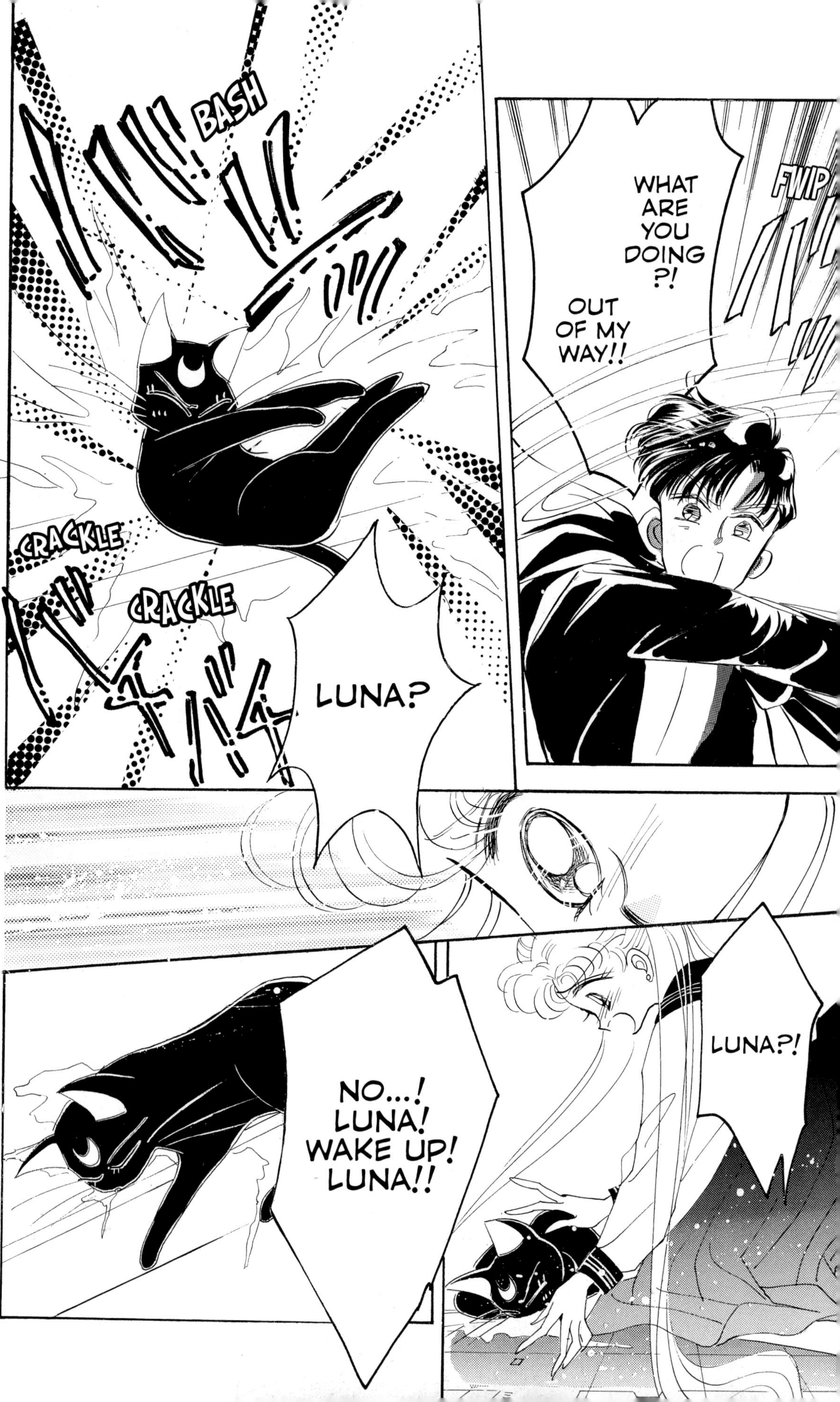
FWIP
WHAT ARE YOU DOING?!
OUT OF MY WAY!!
BASH
CRACKLE
CRACKLE
LUNA?
LUNA?!
NO...! LUNA! WAKE UP! LUNA!!

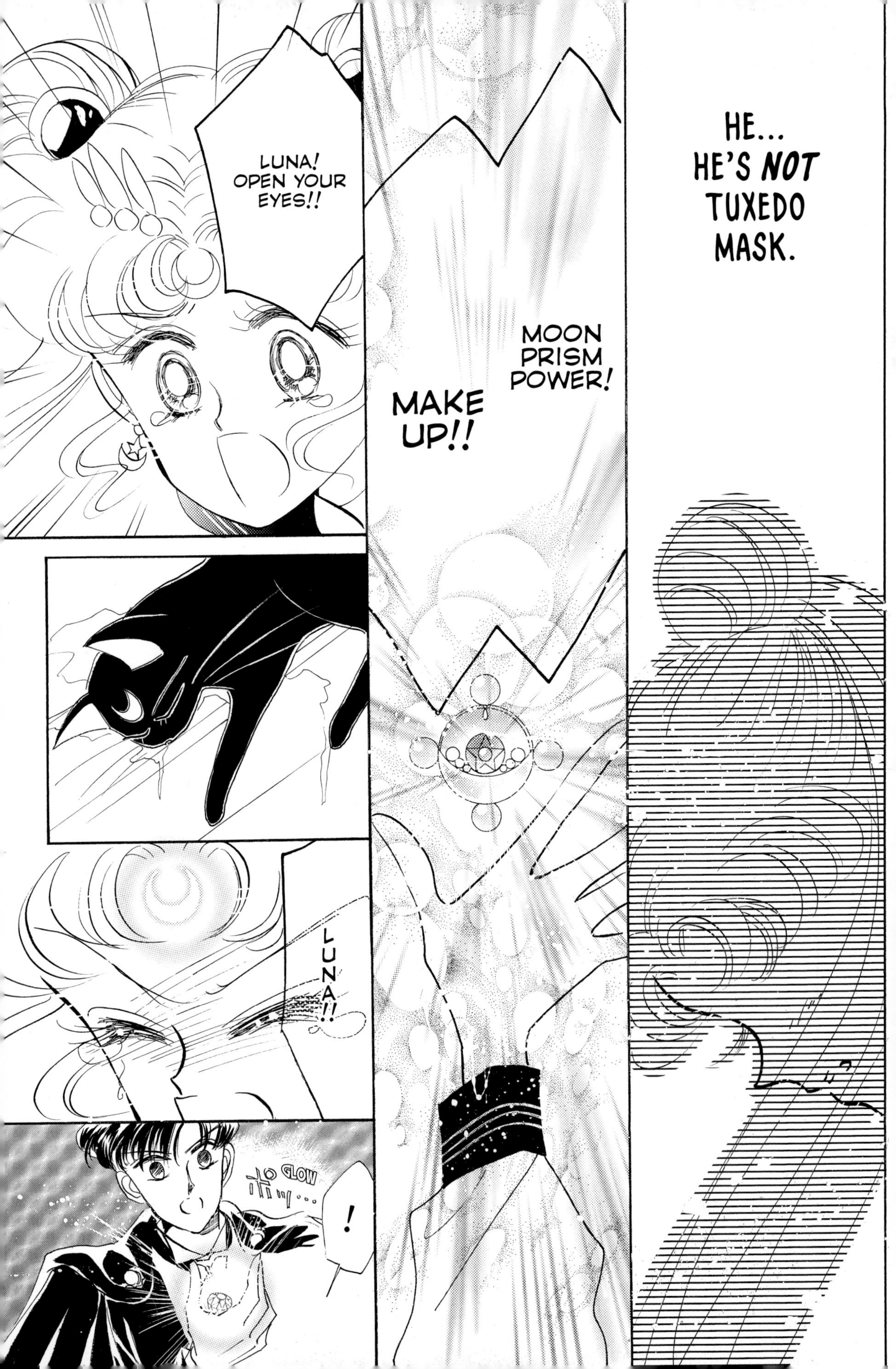
HE...
HE'S *NOT* TUXEDO MASK.
MOON PRISM POWER!
MAKE UP!!
LUNA! OPEN YOUR EYES!!
LUNA!!
GLOW
!

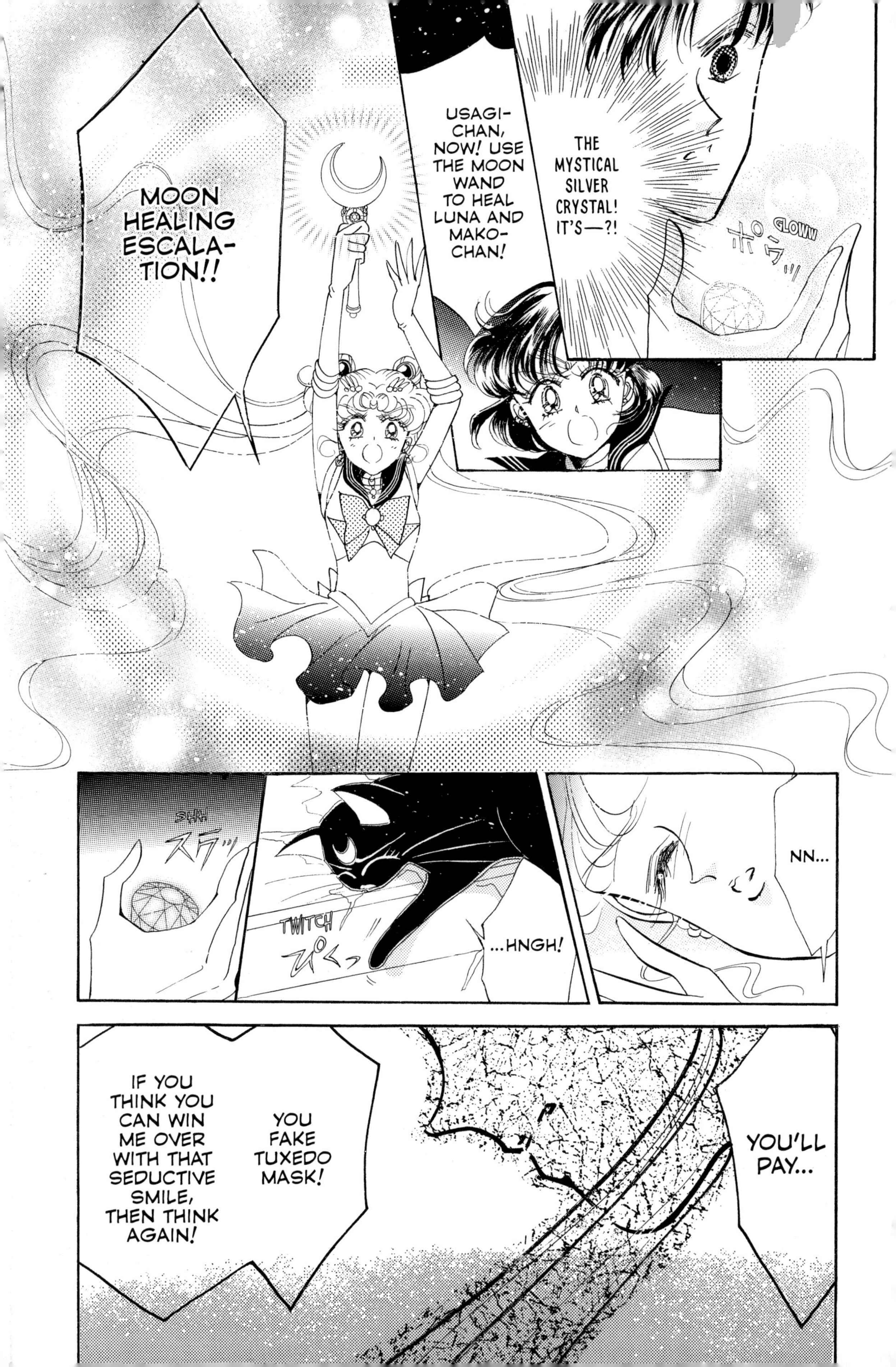
GLOWW
THE MYSTICAL SILVER CRYSTAL! IT'S—?!
USAGI-CHAN, NOW! USE THE MOON WAND TO HEAL LUNA AND MAKO-CHAN!
MOON HEALING ESCALA-TION!!
NN...
...HNGH!
TWITCH
SHAA
YOU'LL PAY...
YOU FAKE TUXEDO MASK!
IF YOU THINK YOU CAN WIN ME OVER WITH THAT SEDUCTIVE SMILE, THEN THINK AGAIN!

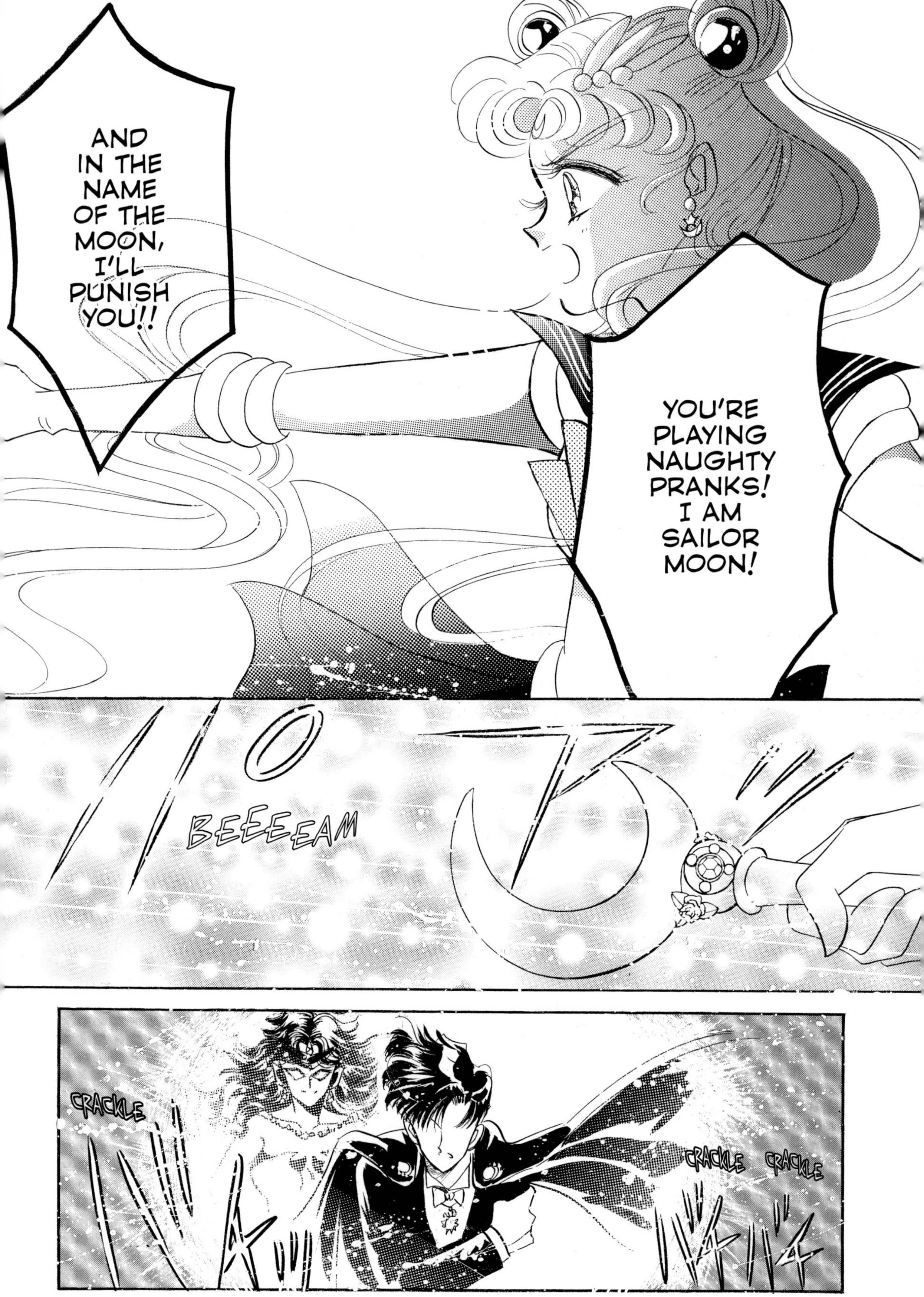
YOU'RE PLAYING NAUGHTY PRANKS! I AM SAILOR MOON!
AND IN THE NAME OF THE MOON, I'LL PUNISH YOU!!
BEEEEEAM
CRACKLE
CRACKLE
CRACKLE

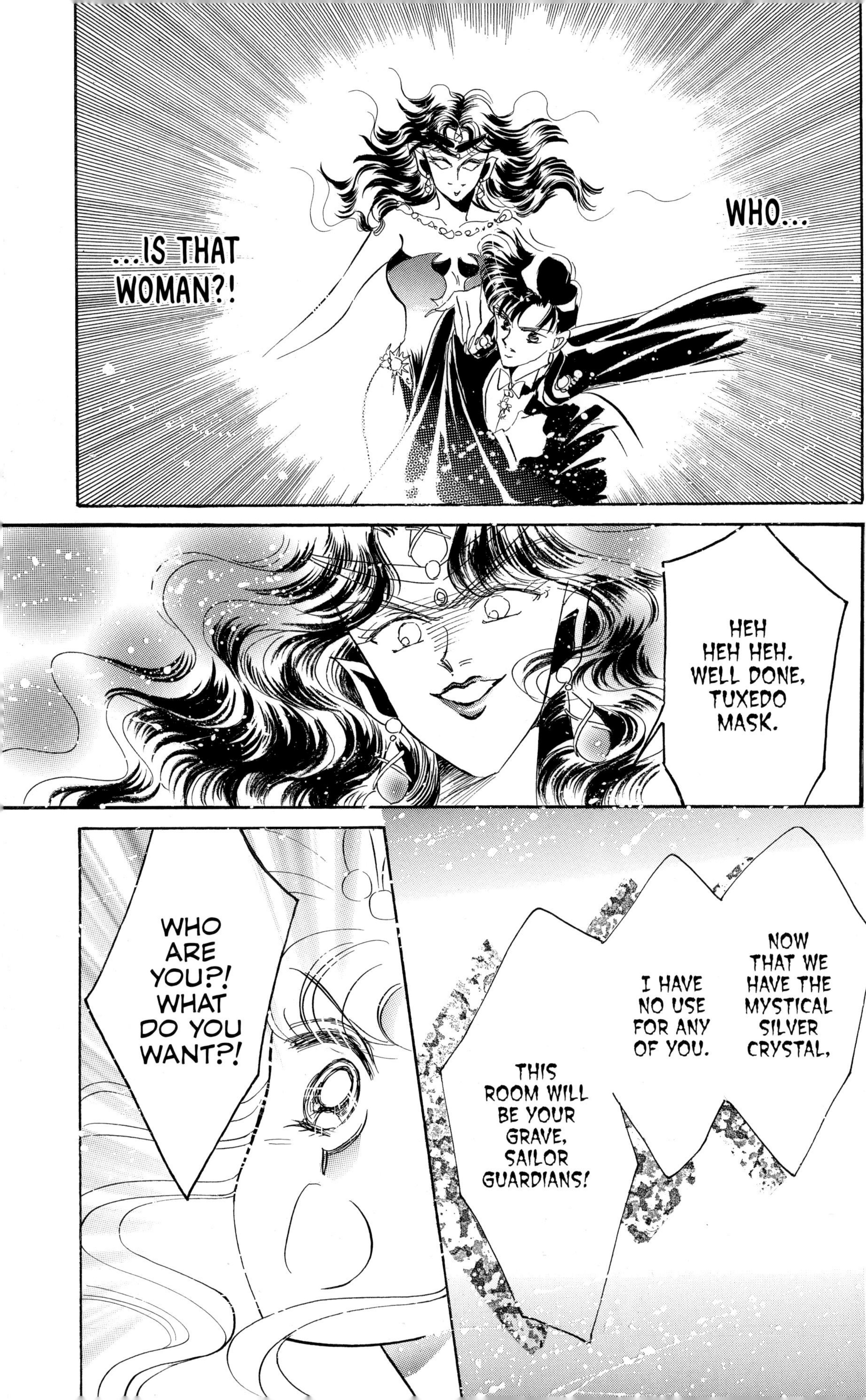
WHO...
...IS THAT WOMAN?!
HEH HEH HEH. WELL DONE, TUXEDO MASK.
NOW THAT WE HAVE THE MYSTICAL SILVER CRYSTAL,
I HAVE NO USE FOR ANY OF YOU.
THIS ROOM WILL BE YOUR GRAVE, SAILOR GUARDIANS!
WHO ARE YOU?! WHAT DO YOU WANT?!

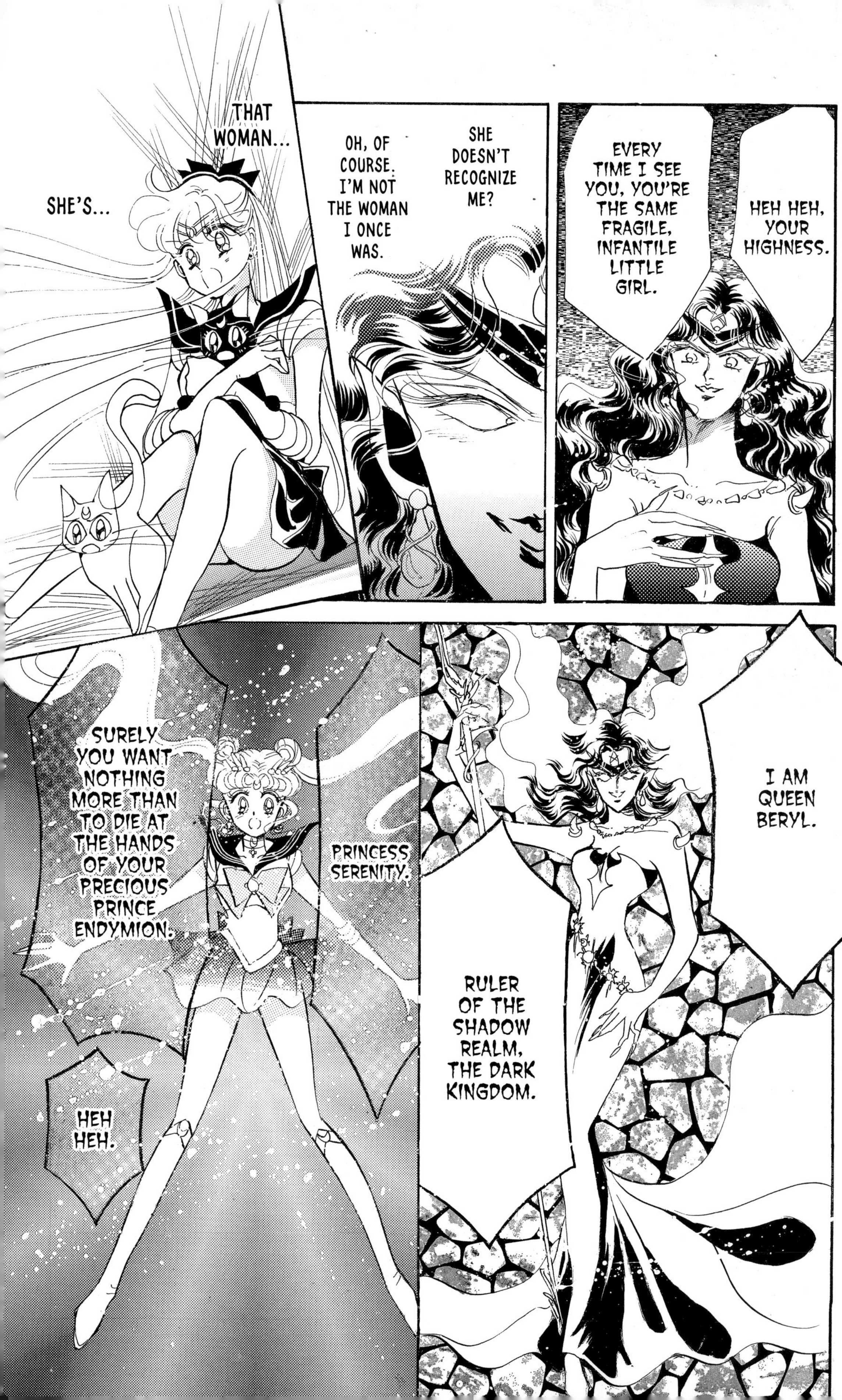
HEH HEH, YOUR HIGHNESS.
EVERY TIME I SEE YOU, YOU'RE THE SAME FRAGILE, INFANTILE LITTLE GIRL.
SHE DOESN'T RECOGNIZE ME?
OH, OF COURSE. I'M NOT THE WOMAN I ONCE WAS.
THAT WOMAN...
SHE'S...
I AM QUEEN BERYL.
RULER OF THE SHADOW REALM, THE DARK KINGDOM.
PRINCESS SERENITY.
SURELY YOU WANT NOTHING MORE THAN TO DIE AT THE HANDS OF YOUR PRECIOUS PRINCE ENDYMION.
HEH HEH.

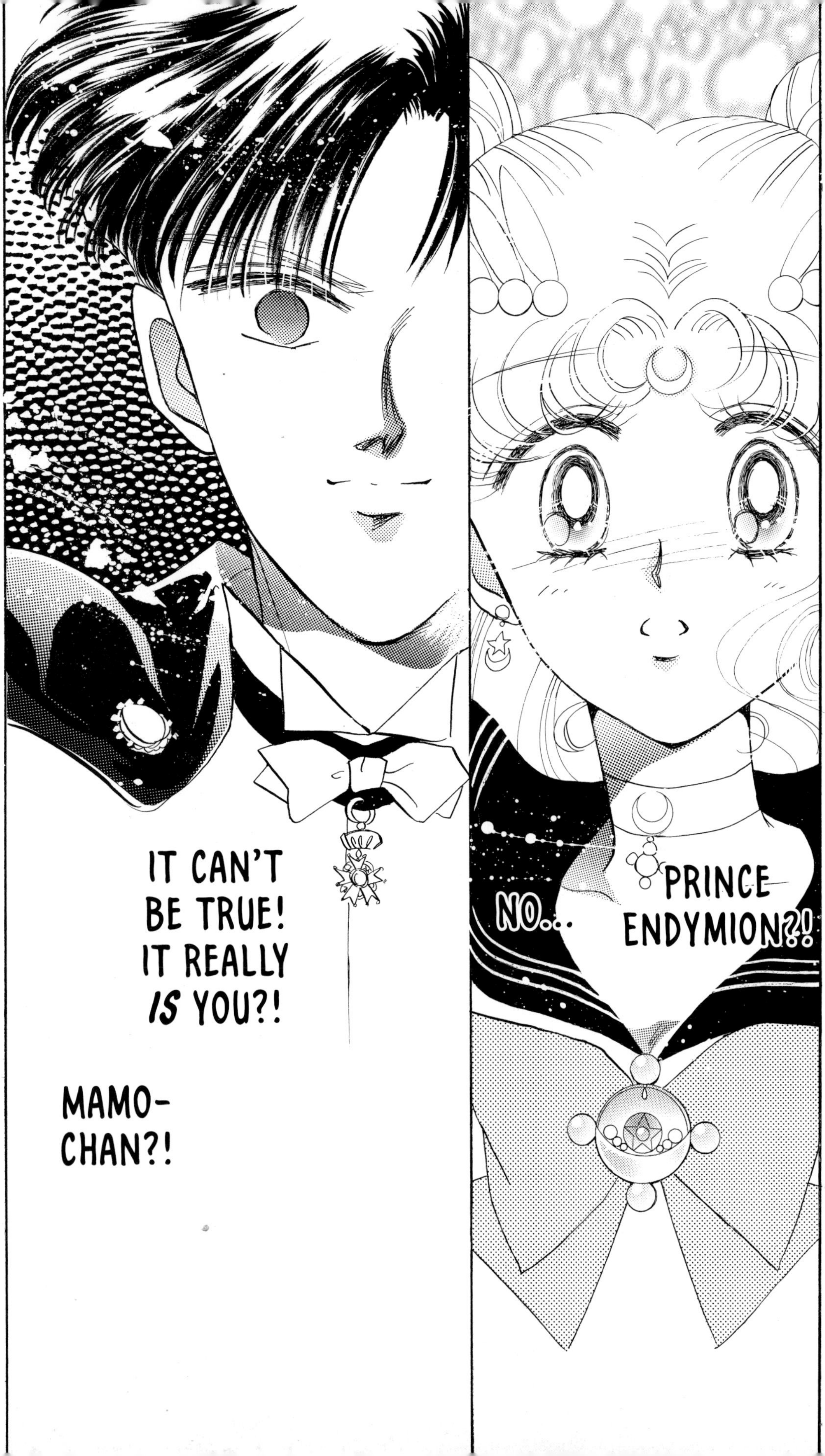
PRINCE ENDYMION?!
NO...
IT CAN'T BE TRUE! IT REALLY *IS* YOU?!
MAMO-CHAN?!

Pretty Guardian

Sailor Moon

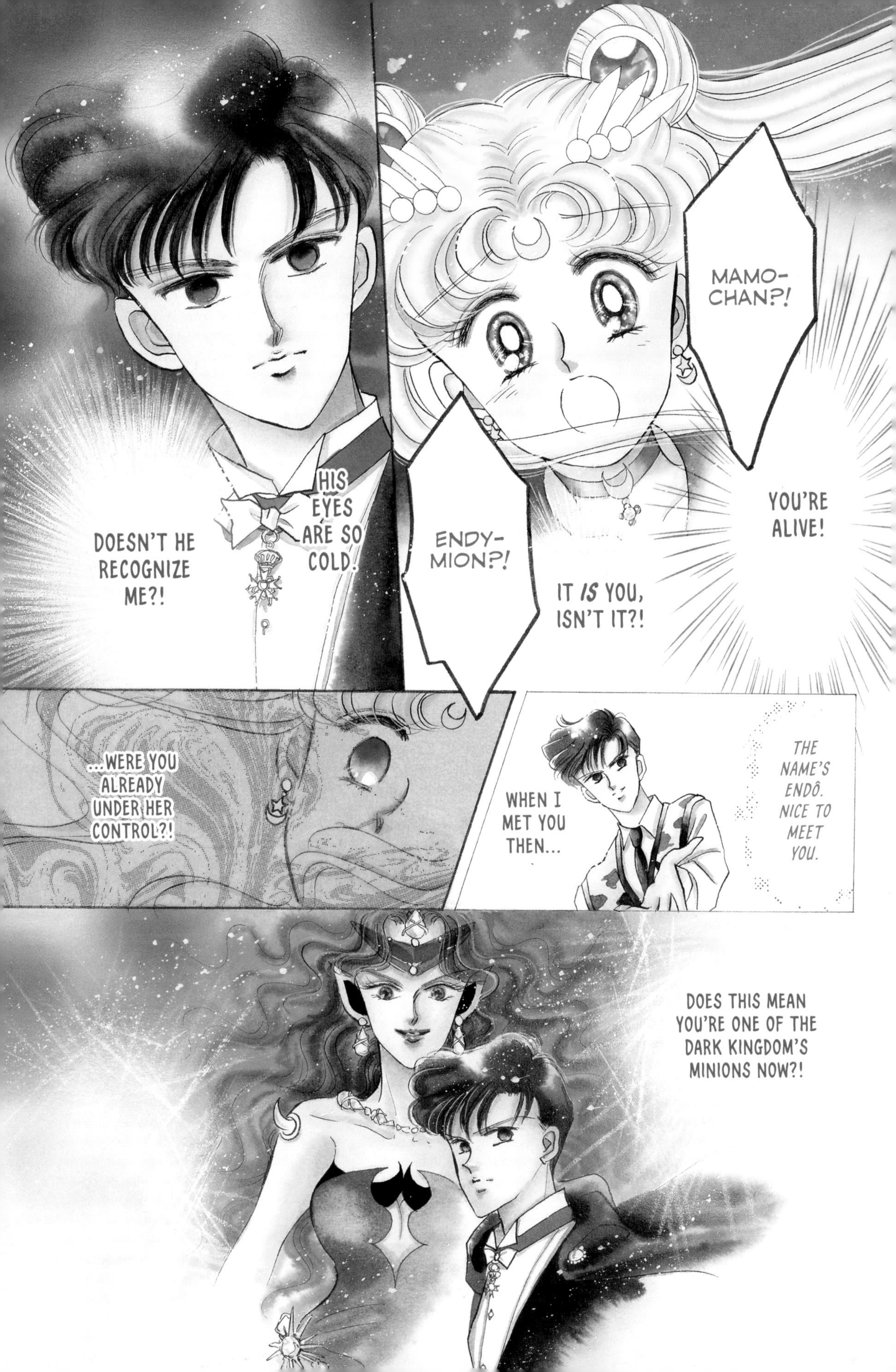
MAMO-CHAN?!
YOU'RE ALIVE!
IT *IS* YOU, ISN'T IT?!
ENDY-MION?!
HIS EYES ARE SO COLD.
DOESN'T HE RECOGNIZE ME?!
*THE NAME'S ENDÔ. NICE TO MEET YOU.*
WHEN I MET YOU THEN...
...WERE YOU ALREADY UNDER HER CONTROL?!
DOES THIS MEAN YOU'RE ONE OF THE DARK KINGDOM'S MINIONS NOW?!

# Act. 12 Enemy: Queen Metalia

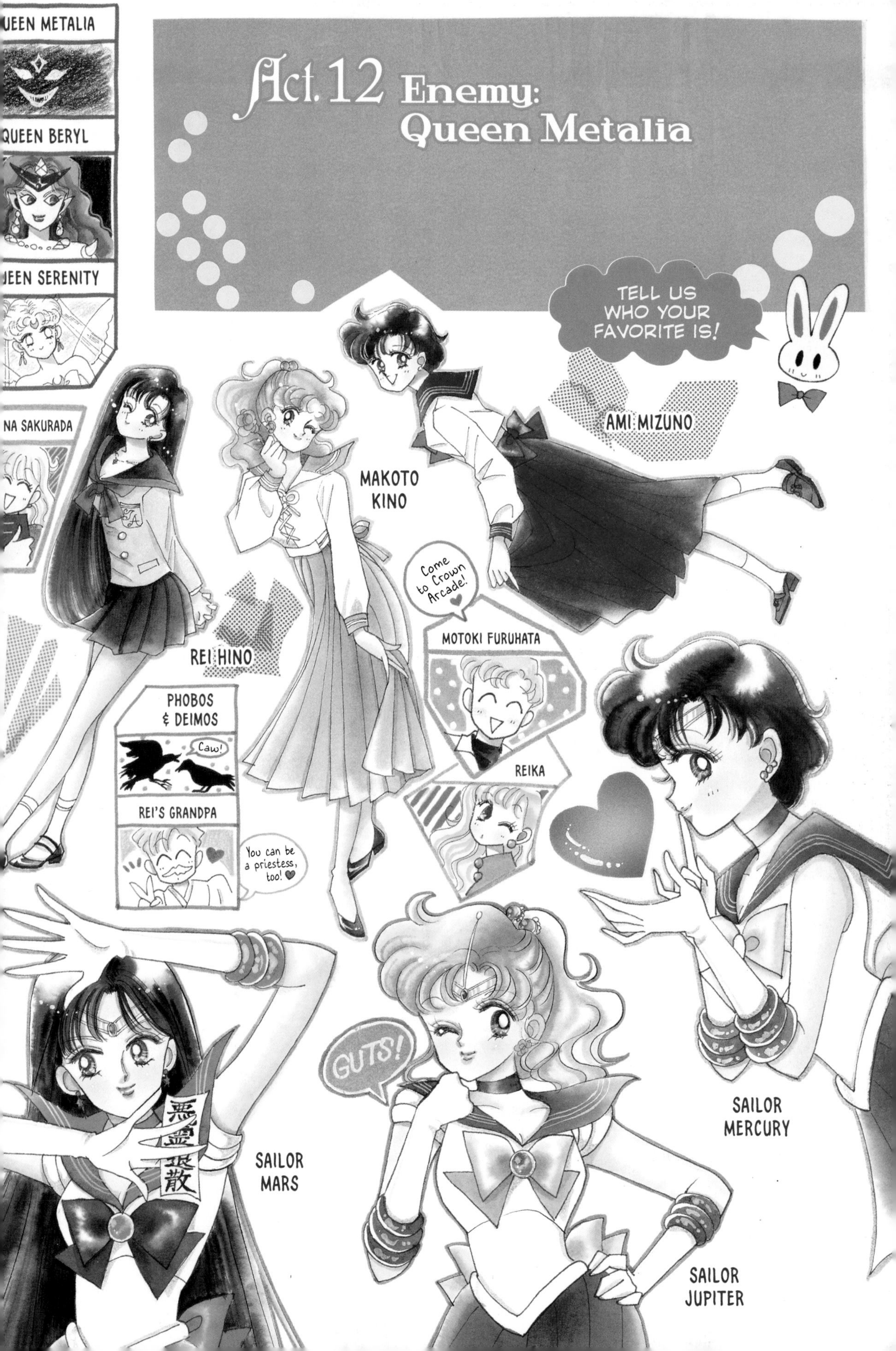
TELL US WHO YOUR FAVORITE IS!
AMI MIZUNO
MAKOTO KINO
REI HINO
UEEN METALIA
QUEEN BERYL
UEEN SERENITY
NA SAKURADA
Come to Crown Arcade! ♥
MOTOKI FURUHATA
REIKA
PHOBOS & DEIMOS
Caw!
REI'S GRANDPA
You can be a priestess, too! ♥
SAILOR MERCURY
GUTS!
SAILOR JUPITER
SAILOR MARS
悪霊退散

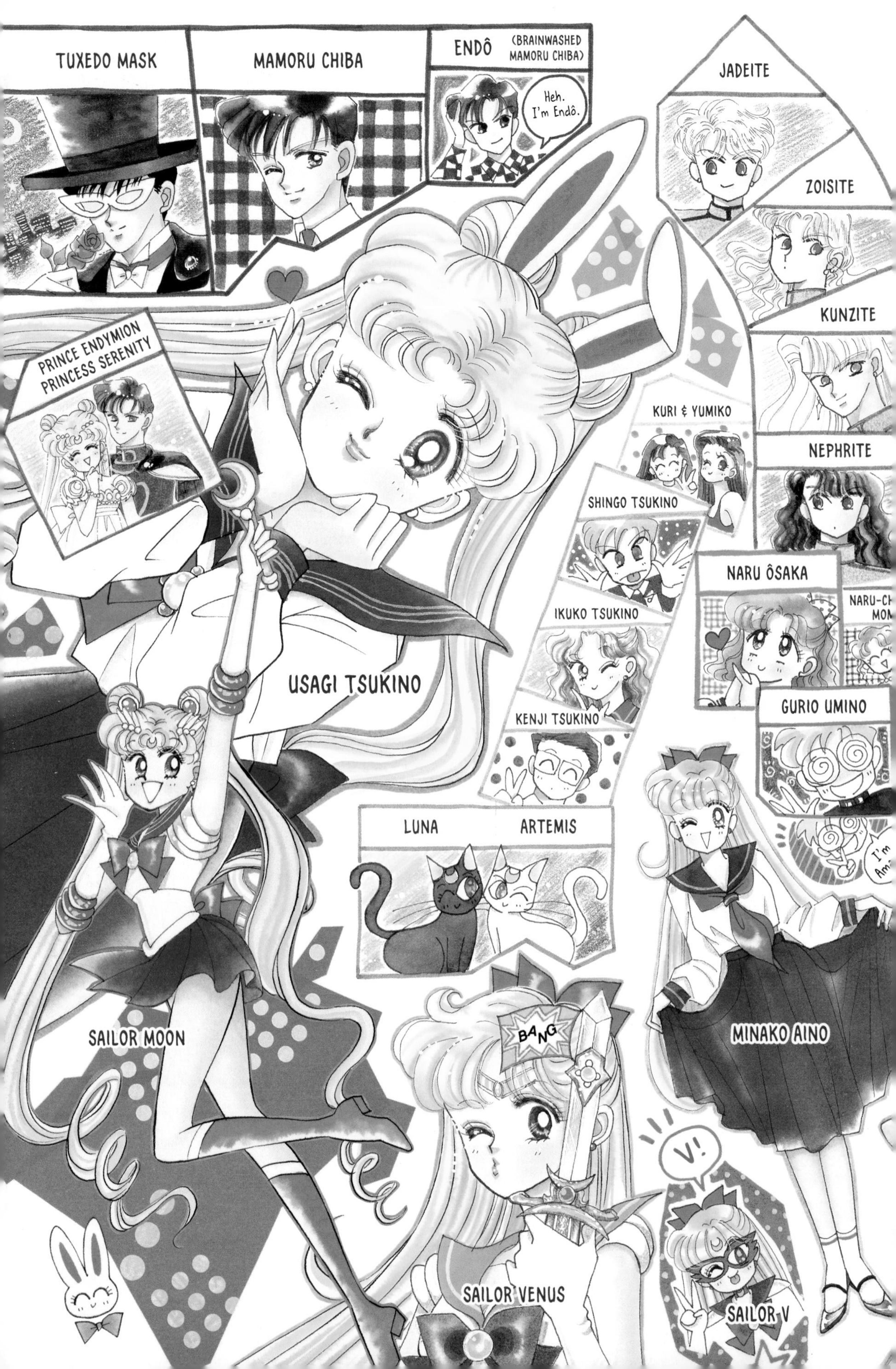
ENDÔ (BRAINWASHED MAMORU CHIBA)
Heh. I'm Endô.
MAMORU CHIBA
TUXEDO MASK
JADEITE
ZOISITE
KUNZITE
NEPHRITE
PRINCE ENDYMION
PRINCESS SERENITY
KURI & YUMIKO
SHINGO TSUKINO
IKUKO TSUKINO
KENJI TSUKINO
NARU ÔSAKA
GURIO UMINO
USAGI TSUKINO
LUNA
ARTEMIS
MINAKO AINO
SAILOR MOON
BANG
SAILOR VENUS
V!
SAILOR V

Pretty Guardian Sailor Moon

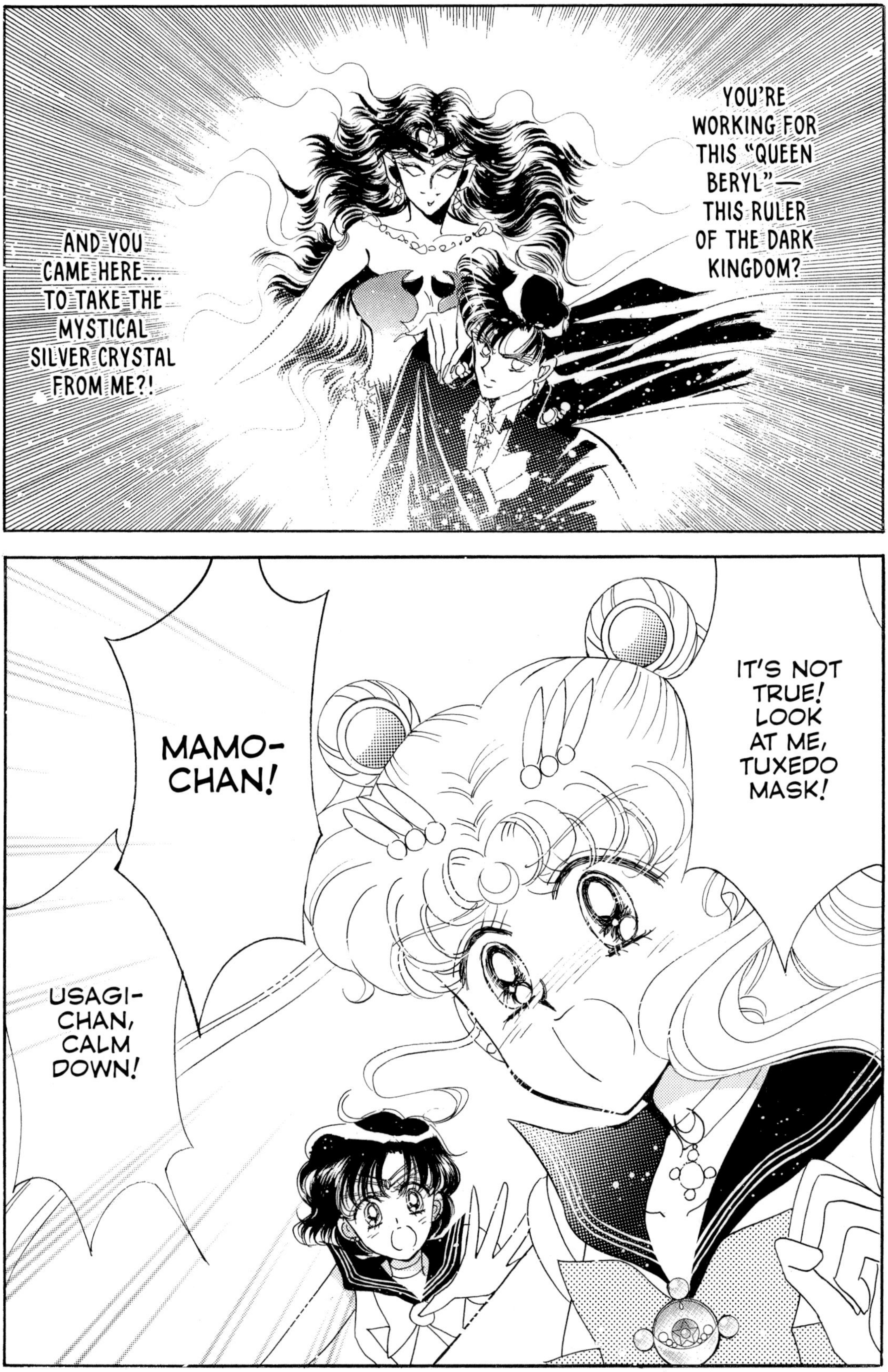
YOU'RE WORKING FOR THIS "QUEEN BERYL"— THIS RULER OF THE DARK KINGDOM?
AND YOU CAME HERE... TO TAKE THE MYSTICAL SILVER CRYSTAL FROM ME?!
IT'S NOT TRUE! LOOK AT ME, TUXEDO MASK!
MAMO-CHAN!
USAGI-CHAN, CALM DOWN!

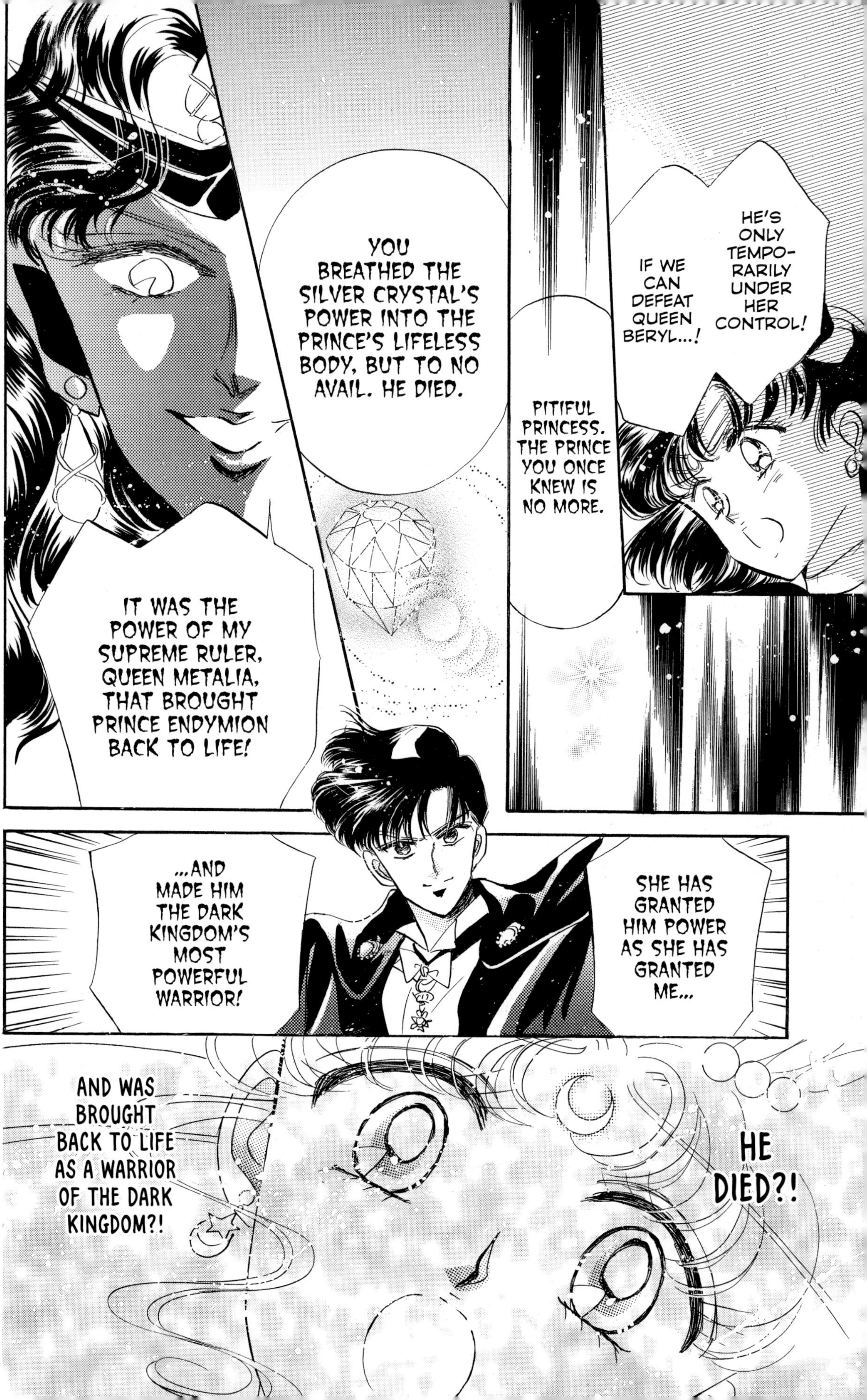
HE'S ONLY TEMPO-RARILY UNDER HER CONTROL!
IF WE CAN DEFEAT QUEEN BERYL...!
PITIFUL PRINCESS. THE PRINCE YOU ONCE KNEW IS NO MORE.
YOU BREATHED THE SILVER CRYSTAL'S POWER INTO THE PRINCE'S LIFELESS BODY, BUT TO NO AVAIL. HE DIED.
IT WAS THE POWER OF MY SUPREME RULER, QUEEN METALIA, THAT BROUGHT PRINCE ENDYMION BACK TO LIFE!
SHE HAS GRANTED HIM POWER AS SHE HAS GRANTED ME...
...AND MADE HIM THE DARK KINGDOM'S MOST POWERFUL WARRIOR!
HE DIED?!
AND WAS BROUGHT BACK TO LIFE AS A WARRIOR OF THE DARK KINGDOM?!

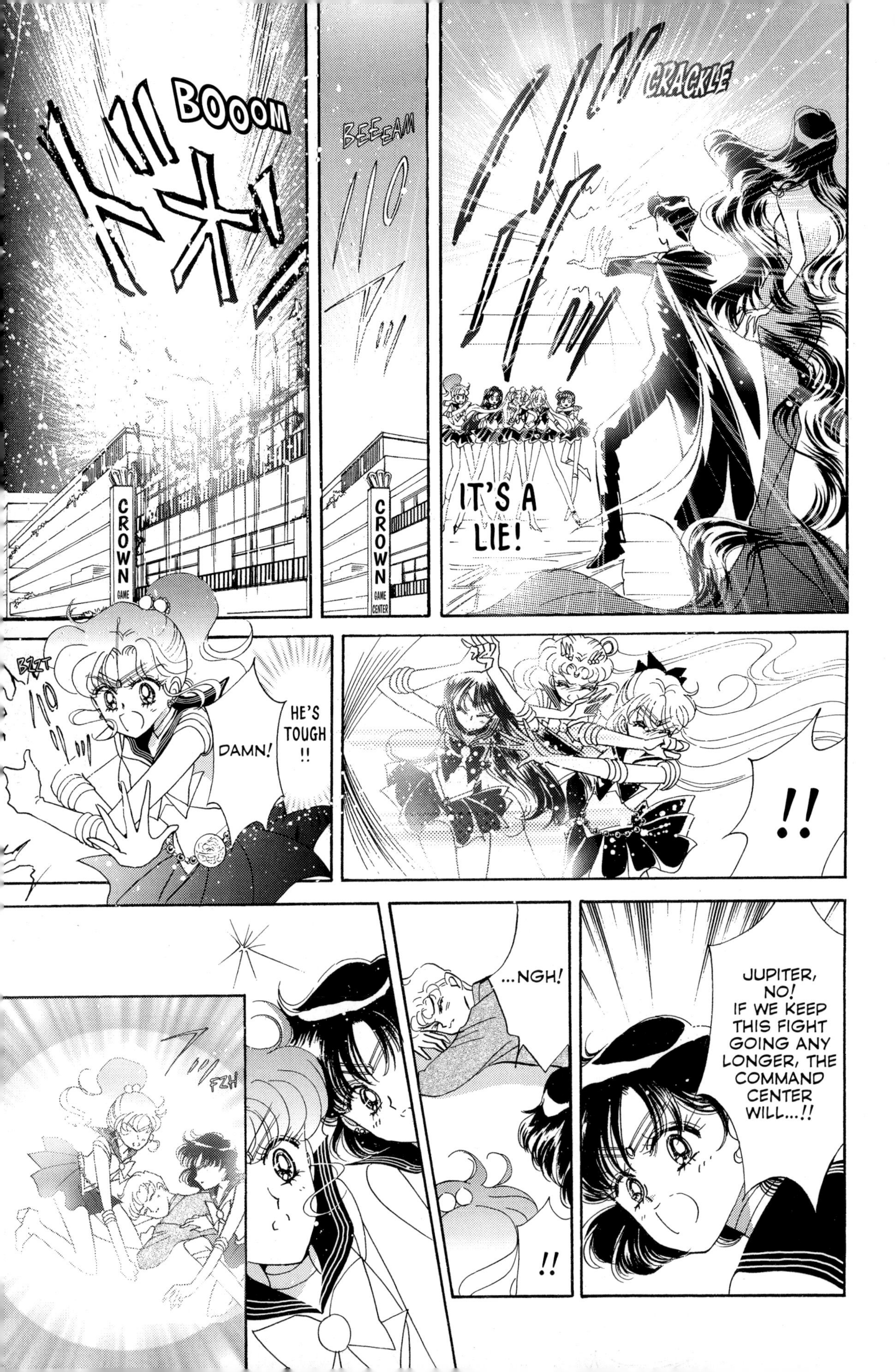

CRACKLE
IT'S A LIE!
BEEEAM
BOOOM
!!
HE'S TOUGH !!
DAMN!
BZZT
JUPITER, NO! IF WE KEEP THIS FIGHT GOING ANY LONGER, THE COMMAND CENTER WILL...!!
...NGH!
!!
FZH

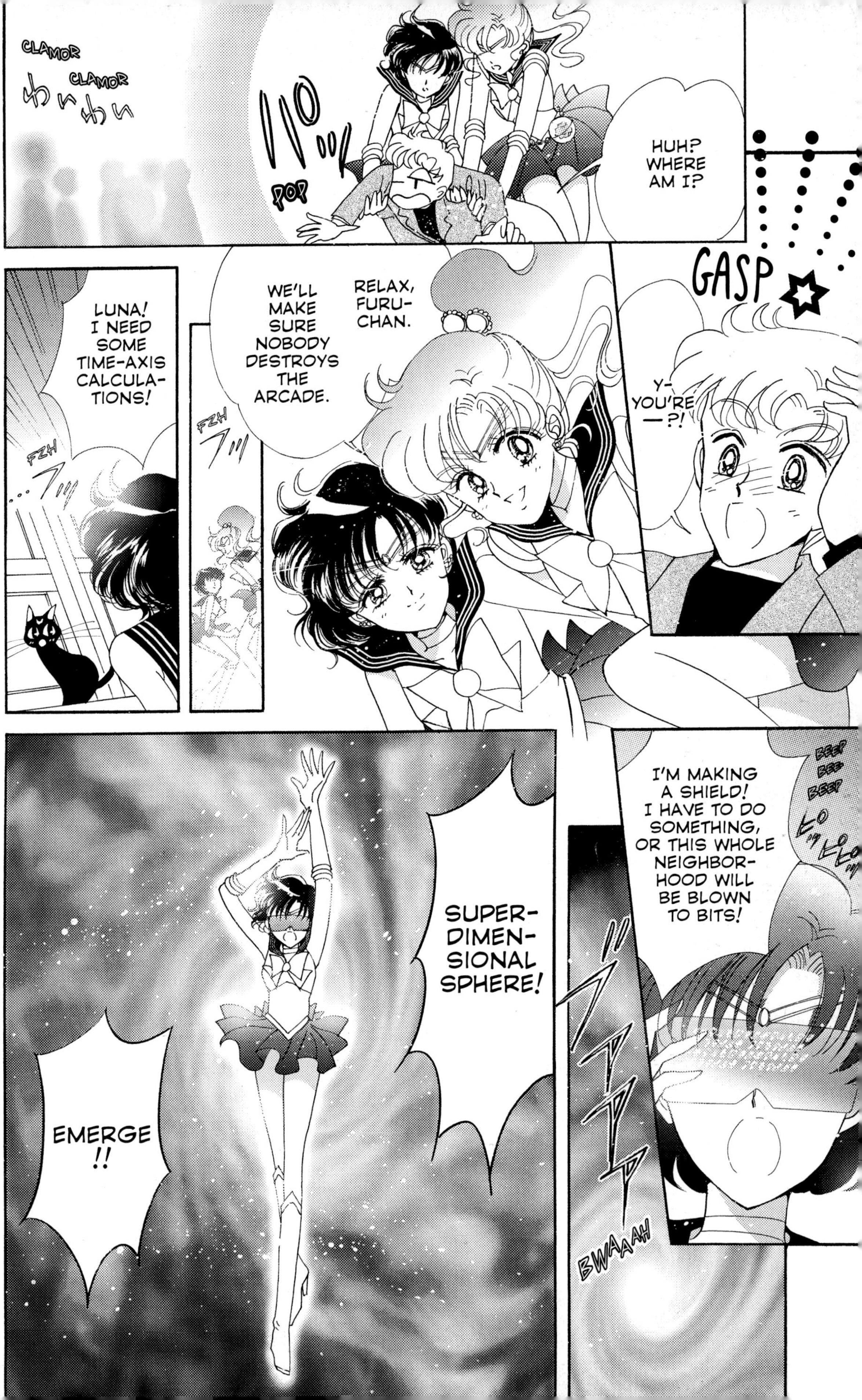
HUH? WHERE AM I?
POP
CLAMOR
CLAMOR
GASP
Y-YOU'RE—?!
RELAX, FURU-CHAN.
WE'LL MAKE SURE NOBODY DESTROYS THE ARCADE.
FZH
LUNA! I NEED SOME TIME-AXIS CALCULATIONS!
FZH
...
BEEP BEEP BEEP
I'M MAKING A SHIELD! I HAVE TO DO SOMETHING, OR THIS WHOLE NEIGHBORHOOD WILL BE BLOWN TO BITS!
BWAAAH
SUPER-DIMENSIONAL SPHERE!
EMERGE!!

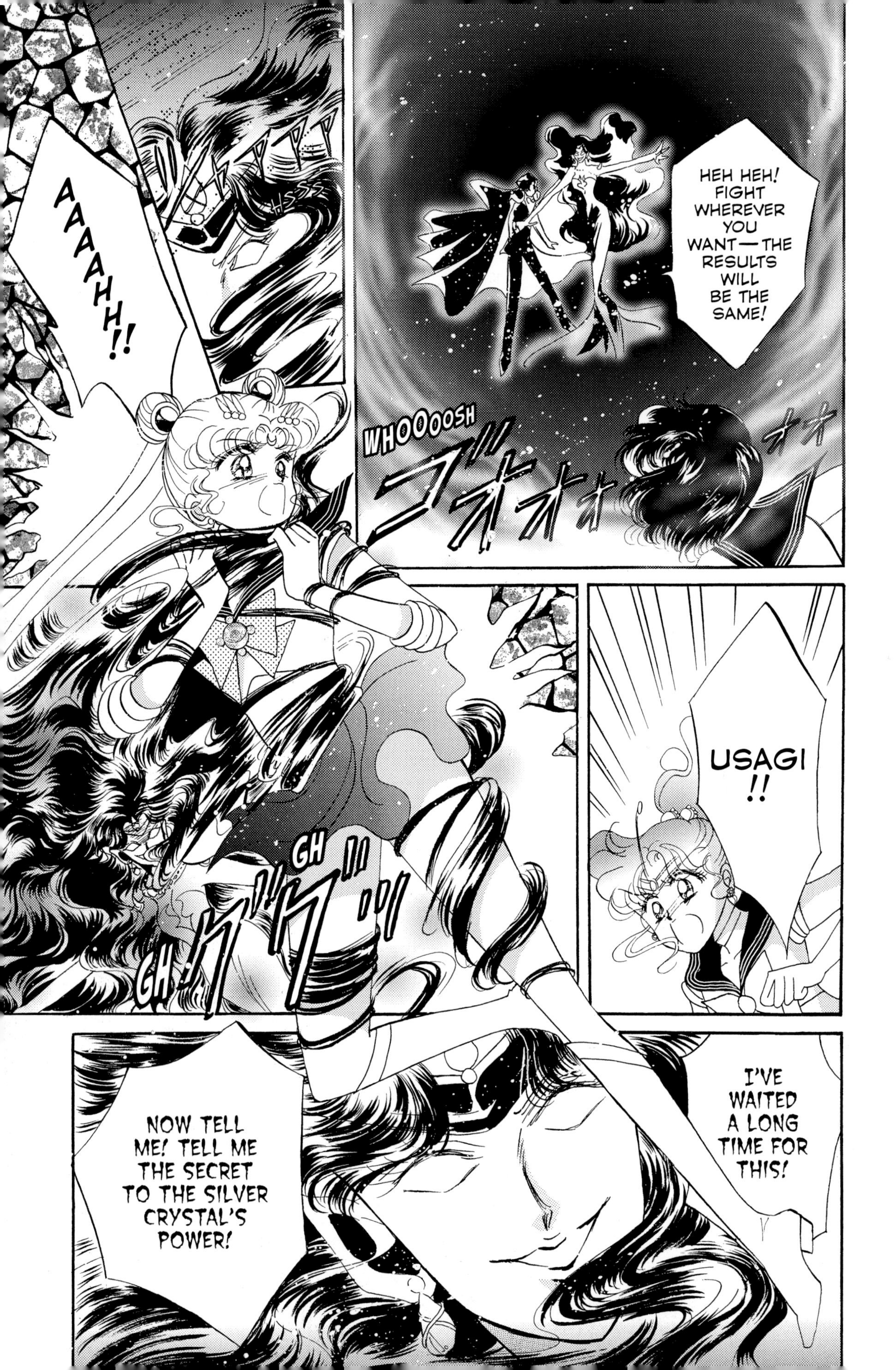
HEH HEH! FIGHT WHEREVER YOU WANT—THE RESULTS WILL BE THE SAME!
WHOOOOSH
AAAAAHH!!
HSSSS
USAGI!!
GH
GH
I'VE WAITED A LONG TIME FOR THIS!
NOW TELL ME! TELL ME THE SECRET TO THE SILVER CRYSTAL'S POWER!

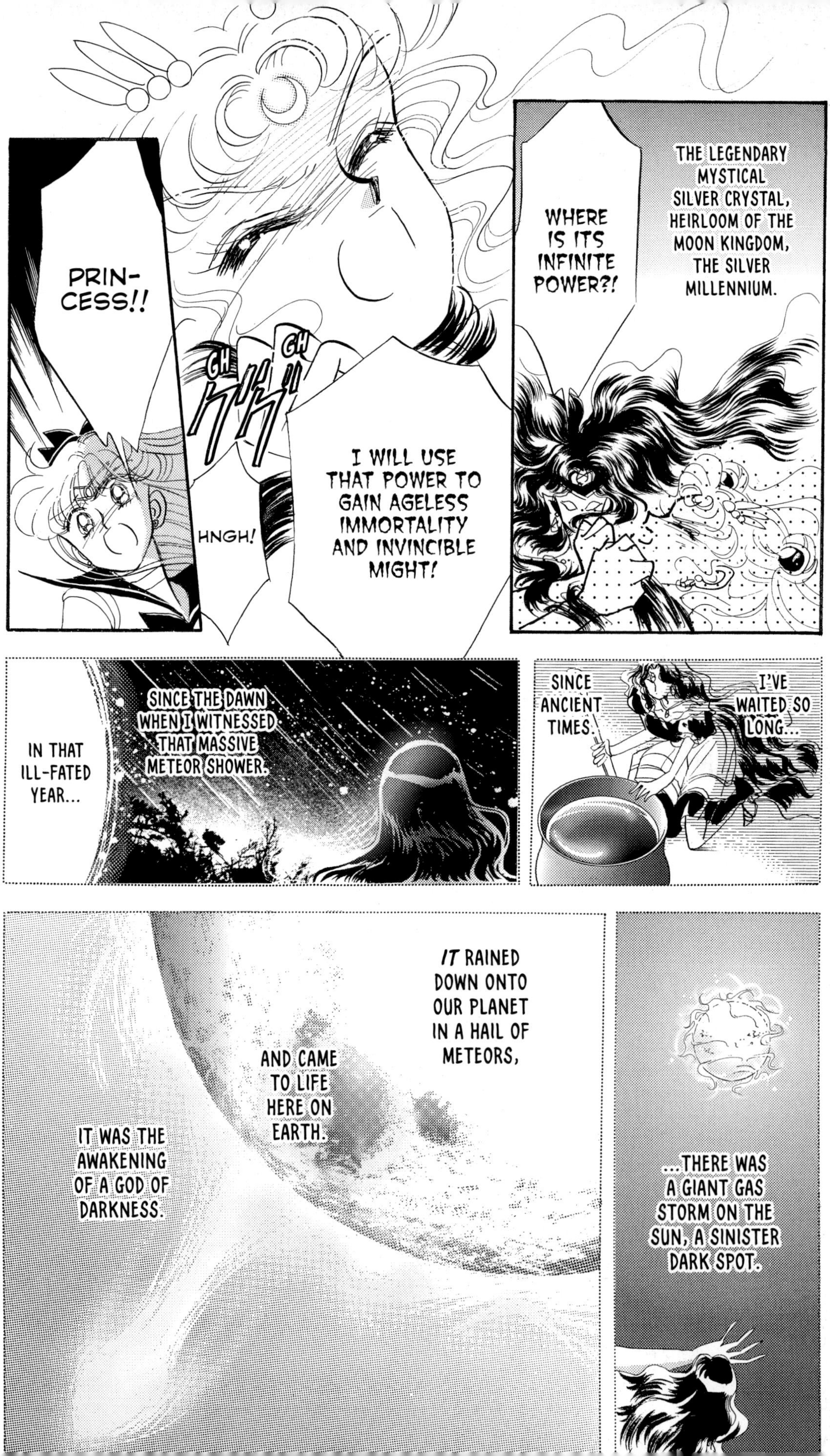
THE LEGENDARY MYSTICAL SILVER CRYSTAL, HEIRLOOM OF THE MOON KINGDOM, THE SILVER MILLENNIUM.
WHERE IS ITS INFINITE POWER?!
GH
GH
I WILL USE THAT POWER TO GAIN AGELESS IMMORTALITY AND INVINCIBLE MIGHT!
PRIN-CESS!!
HNGH!
I'VE WAITED SO LONG...
SINCE ANCIENT TIMES.
SINCE THE DAWN WHEN I WITNESSED THAT MASSIVE METEOR SHOWER.
IN THAT ILL-FATED YEAR...
...THERE WAS A GIANT GAS STORM ON THE SUN, A SINISTER DARK SPOT.
*IT* RAINED DOWN ONTO OUR PLANET IN A HAIL OF METEORS,
AND CAME TO LIFE HERE ON EARTH.
IT WAS THE AWAKENING OF A GOD OF DARKNESS.

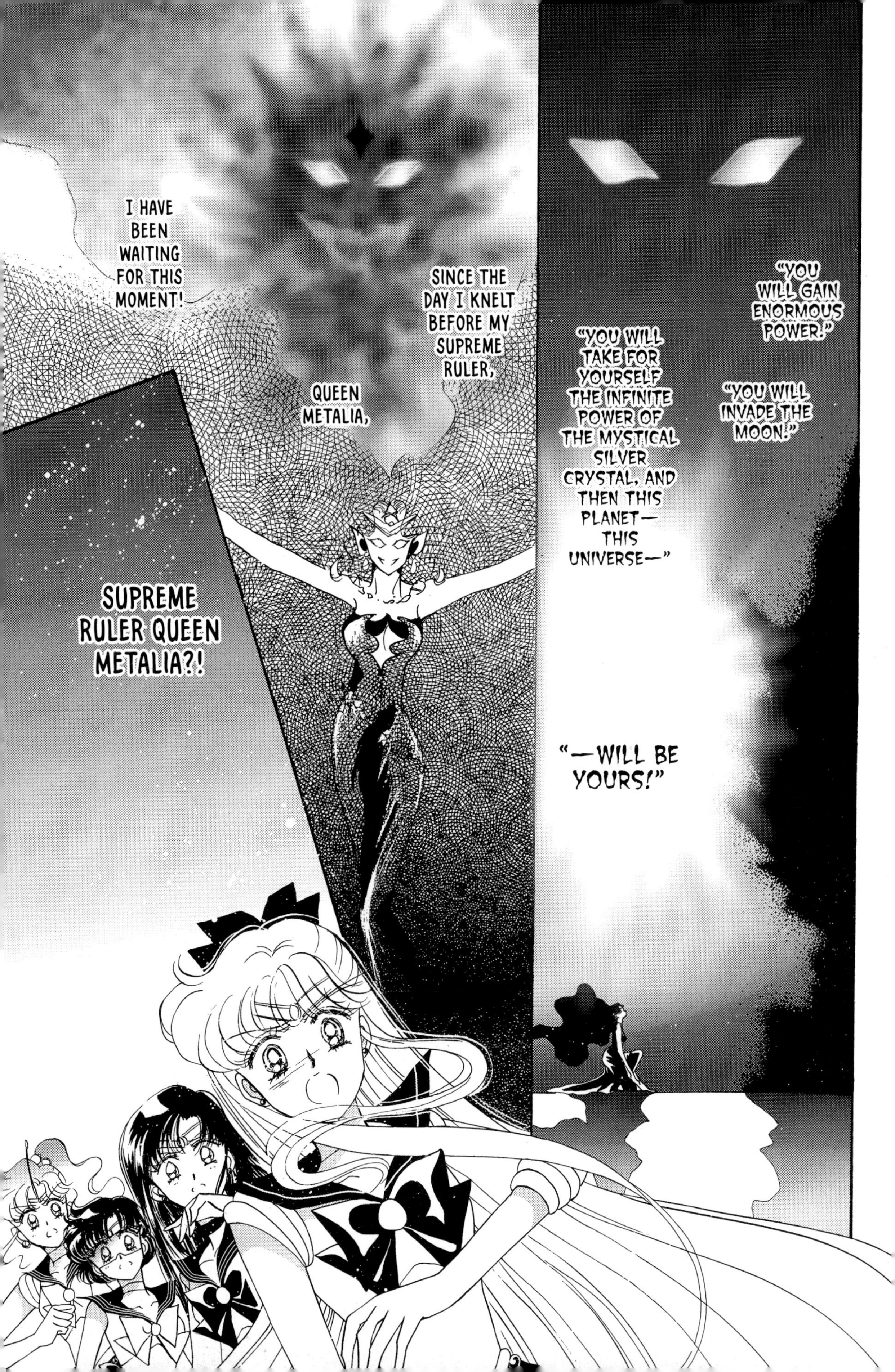
I HAVE BEEN WAITING FOR THIS MOMENT!
SINCE THE DAY I KNELT BEFORE MY SUPREME RULER,
QUEEN METALIA,
"YOU WILL GAIN ENORMOUS POWER."
"YOU WILL INVADE THE MOON."
"YOU WILL TAKE FOR YOURSELF THE INFINITE POWER OF THE MYSTICAL SILVER CRYSTAL, AND THEN THIS PLANET— THIS UNIVERSE—"
"—WILL BE YOURS!"
SUPREME RULER QUEEN METALIA?!

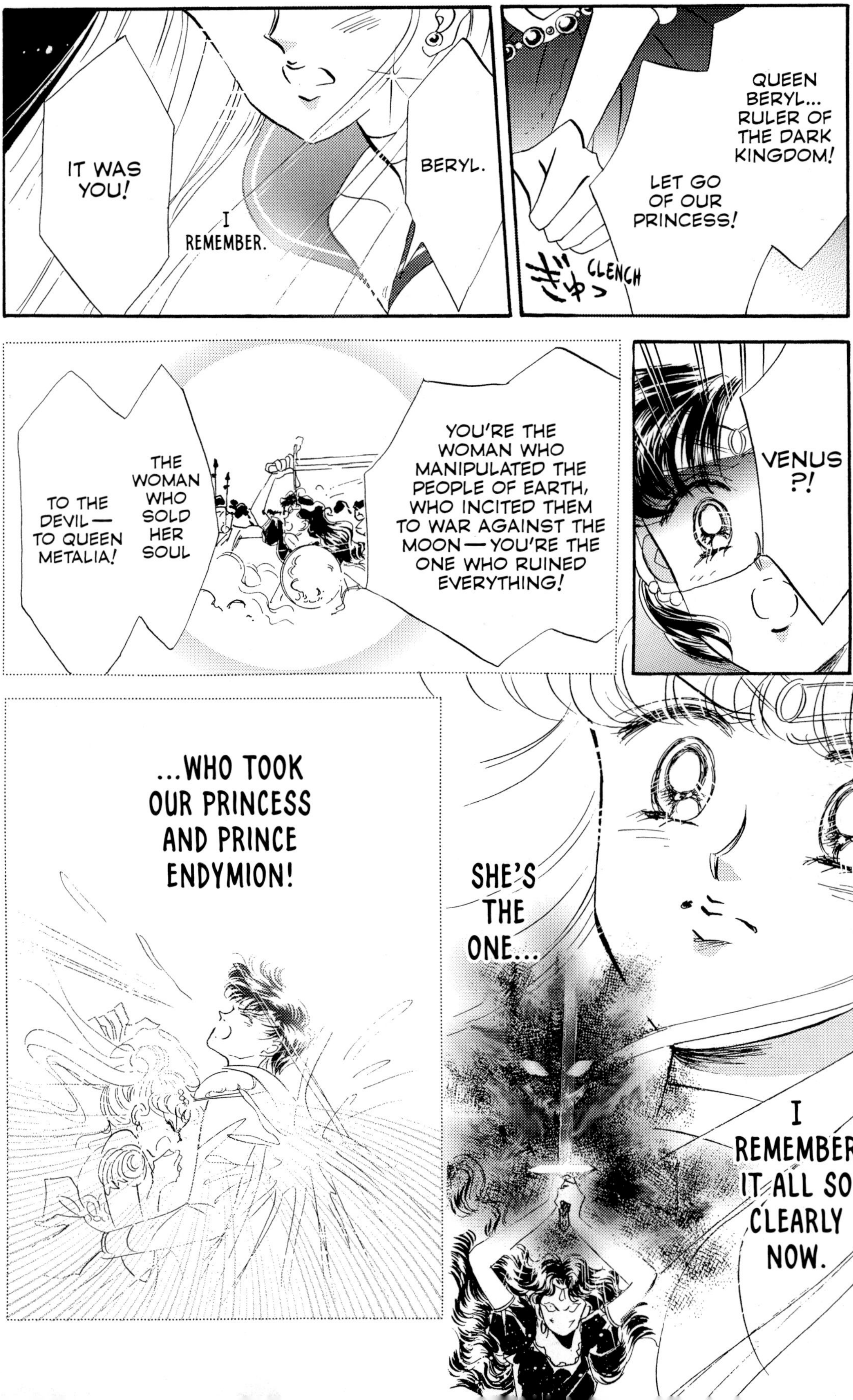
QUEEN BERYL... RULER OF THE DARK KINGDOM!
LET GO OF OUR PRINCESS!
ぎゅっ CLENCH
BERYL.
IT WAS YOU!
I REMEMBER.
VENUS?!
YOU'RE THE WOMAN WHO MANIPULATED THE PEOPLE OF EARTH, WHO INCITED THEM TO WAR AGAINST THE MOON—YOU'RE THE ONE WHO RUINED EVERYTHING!
THE WOMAN WHO SOLD HER SOUL
TO THE DEVIL—TO QUEEN METALIA!
I REMEMBER IT ALL SO CLEARLY NOW.
SHE'S THE ONE...
...WHO TOOK OUR PRINCESS AND PRINCE ENDYMION!

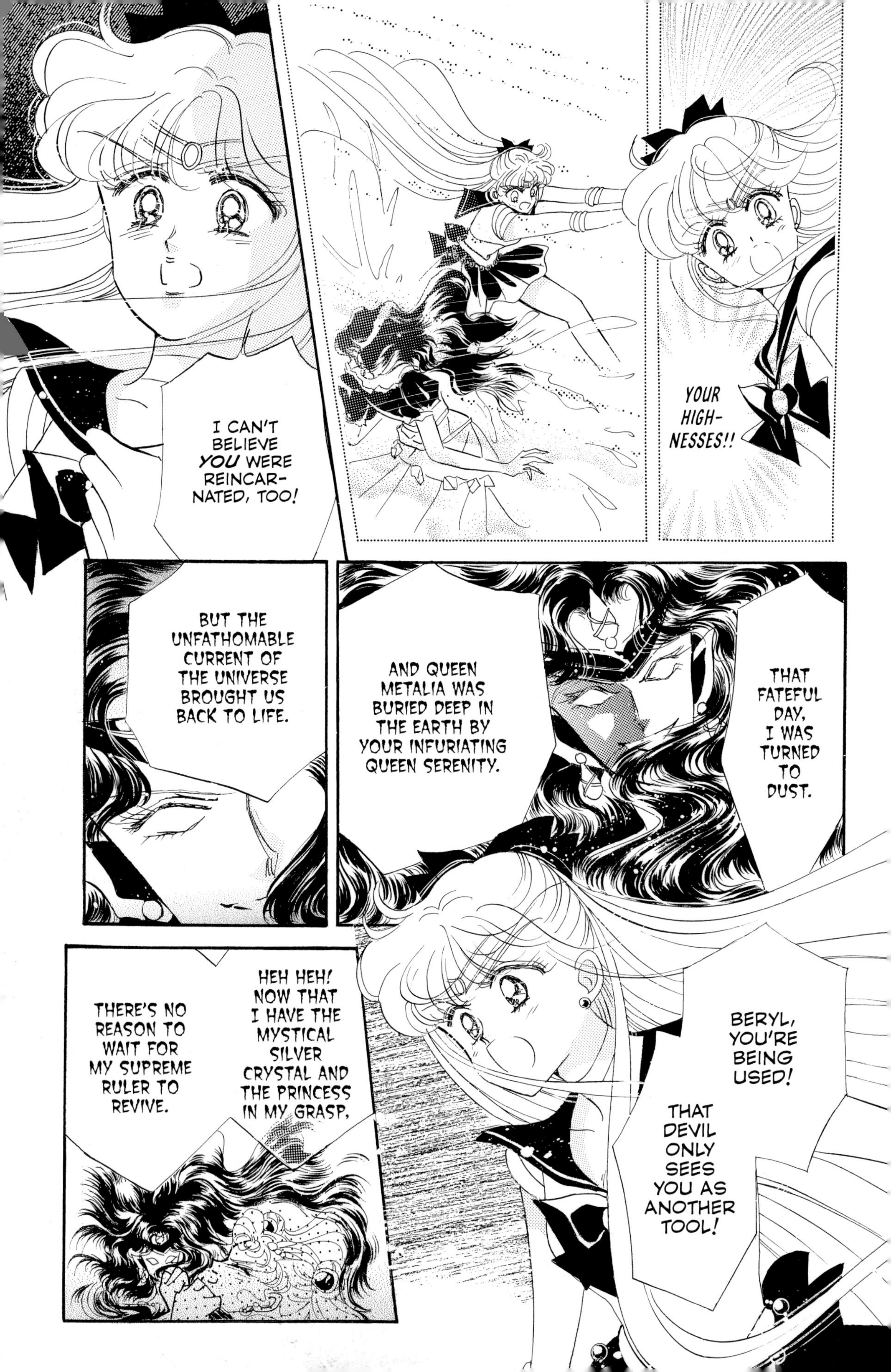
YOUR HIGHNESSES!!
I CAN'T BELIEVE *YOU* WERE REINCARNATED, TOO!
THAT FATEFUL DAY, I WAS TURNED TO DUST.
AND QUEEN METALIA WAS BURIED DEEP IN THE EARTH BY YOUR INFURIATING QUEEN SERENITY.
BUT THE UNFATHOMABLE CURRENT OF THE UNIVERSE BROUGHT US BACK TO LIFE.
BERYL, YOU'RE BEING USED!
THAT DEVIL ONLY SEES YOU AS ANOTHER TOOL!
HEH HEH! NOW THAT I HAVE THE MYSTICAL SILVER CRYSTAL AND THE PRINCESS IN MY GRASP,
THERE'S NO REASON TO WAIT FOR MY SUPREME RULER TO REVIVE.

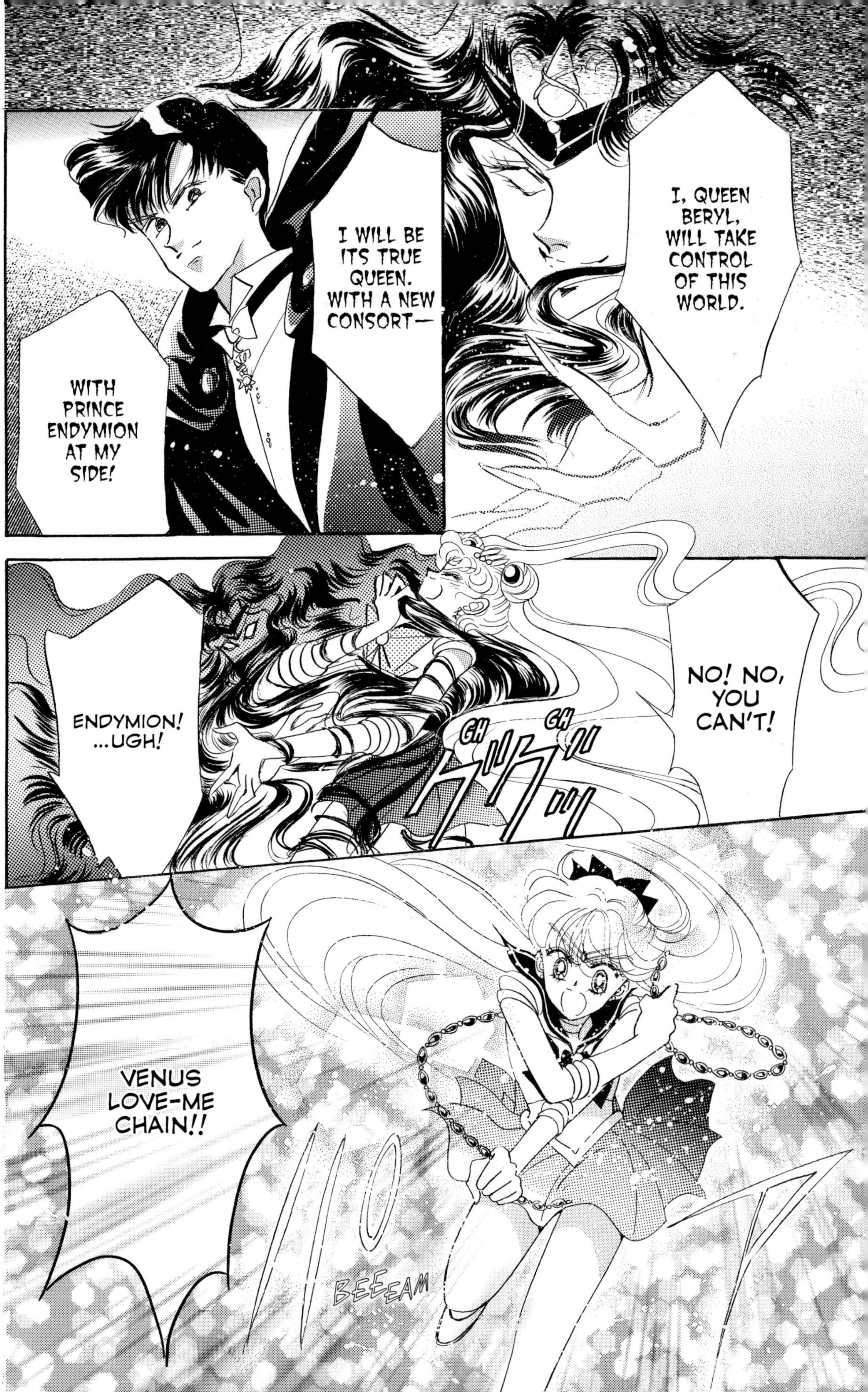
I, QUEEN BERYL, WILL TAKE CONTROL OF THIS WORLD.
I WILL BE ITS TRUE QUEEN. WITH A NEW CONSORT—
WITH PRINCE ENDYMION AT MY SIDE!
NO! NO, YOU CAN'T!
GH
GH
ENDYMION! ...UGH!
VENUS LOVE-ME CHAIN!!
BEE-EAM

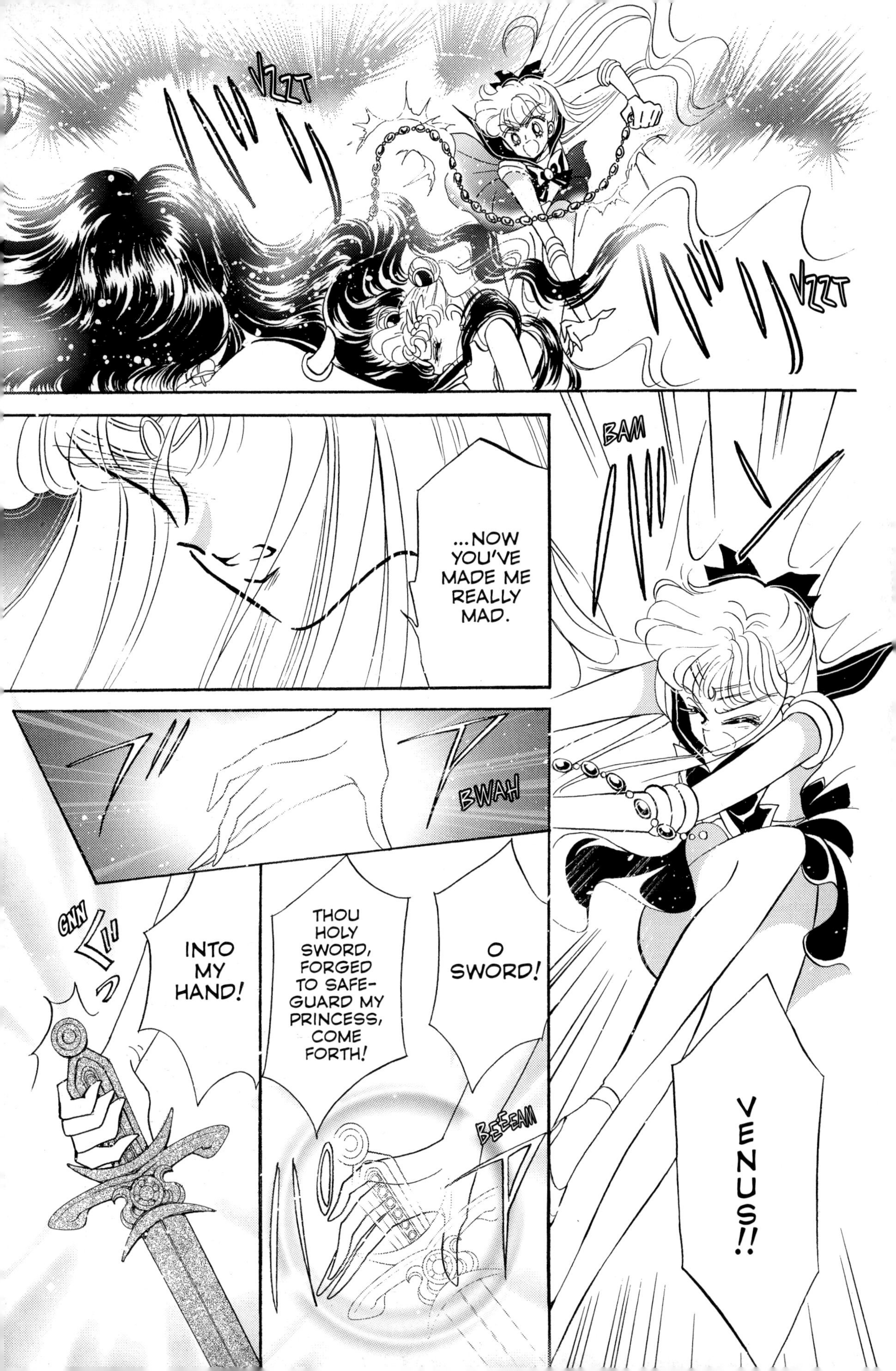
VZZT
VZZT
BAM
VENUS!!
...NOW YOU'VE MADE ME REALLY MAD.
BWAH
O SWORD!
THOU HOLY SWORD, FORGED TO SAFE-GUARD MY PRINCESS, COME FORTH!
BEEEAM
INTO MY HAND!
GNN

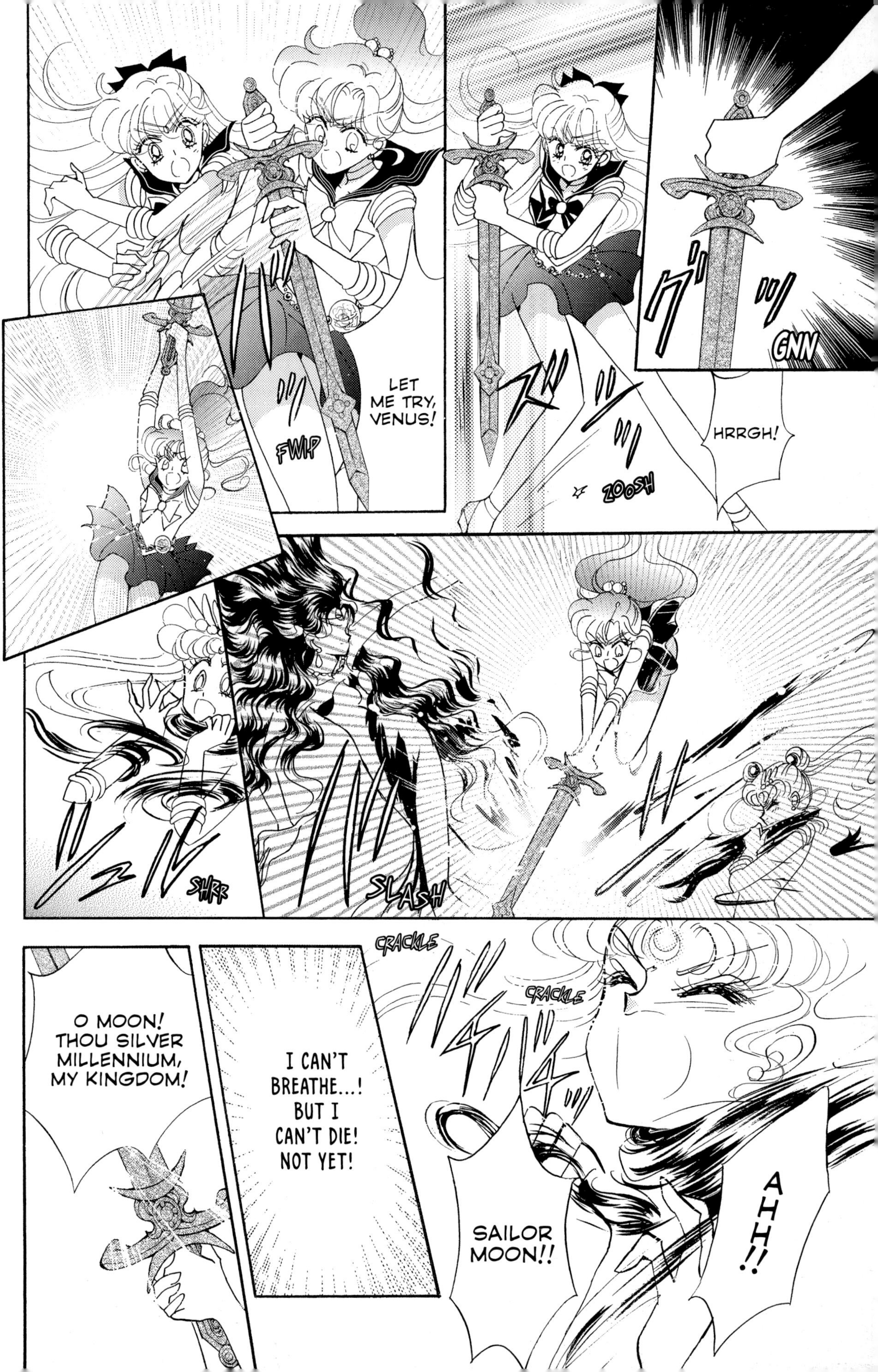
GNN
HRRGH!
ZOOSH
LET ME TRY, VENUS!
FWIP
SLASH
SHRR
CRACKLE
CRACKLE
AHH!!
SAILOR MOON!!
I CAN'T BREATHE...! BUT I CAN'T DIE! NOT YET!
O MOON! THOU SILVER MILLENNIUM, MY KINGDOM!

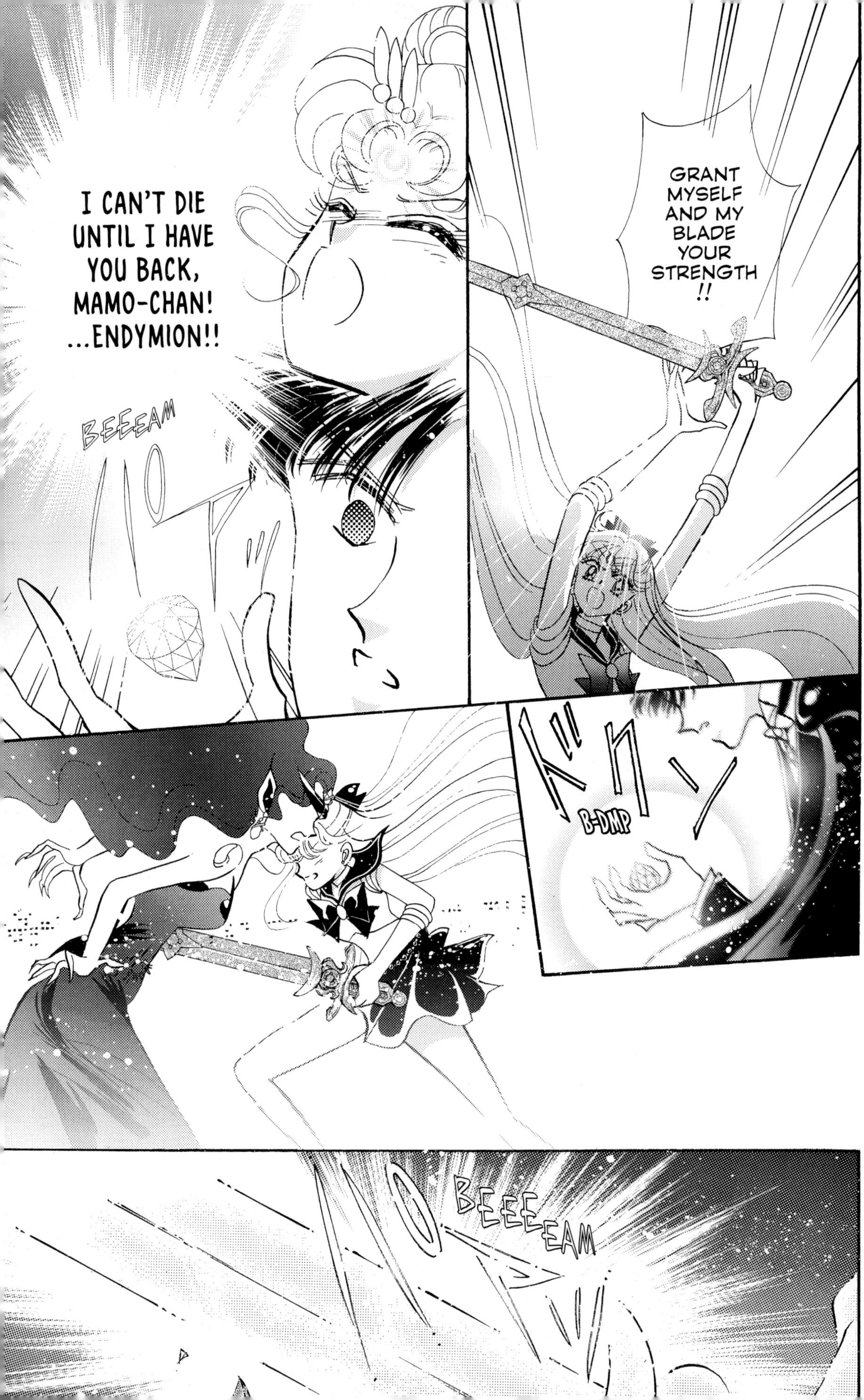
GRANT MYSELF AND MY BLADE YOUR STRENGTH!!
I CAN'T DIE UNTIL I HAVE YOU BACK, MAMO-CHAN! ...ENDYMION!!
BEEEEAM
B-DMP
BEEEEAM

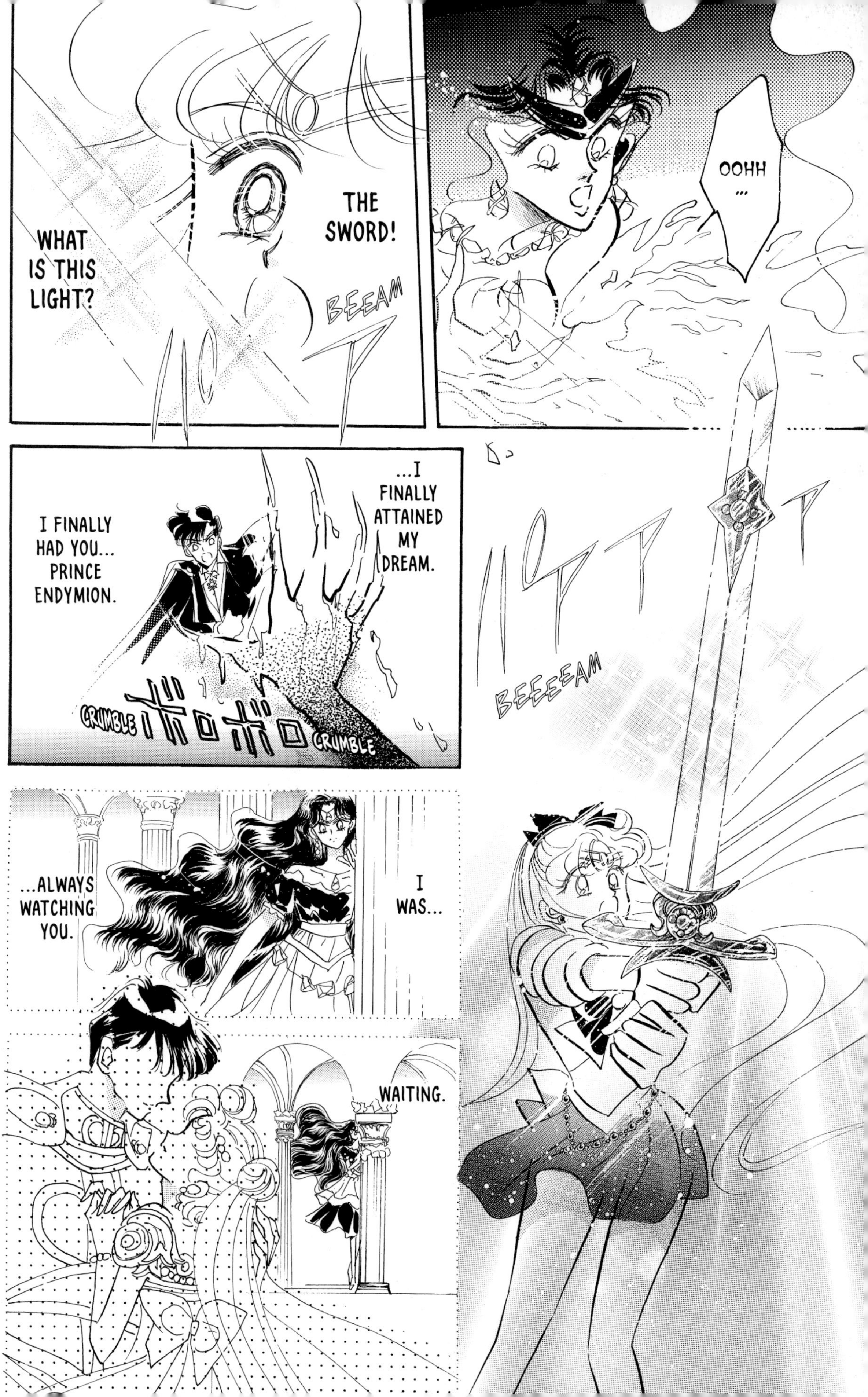
OOHH ...
THE SWORD!
WHAT IS THIS LIGHT?
BEEAM
BEEEEAM
...I FINALLY ATTAINED MY DREAM.
I FINALLY HAD YOU... PRINCE ENDYMION.
CRUMBLE
CRUMBLE
I WAS...
...ALWAYS WATCHING YOU.
WAITING.

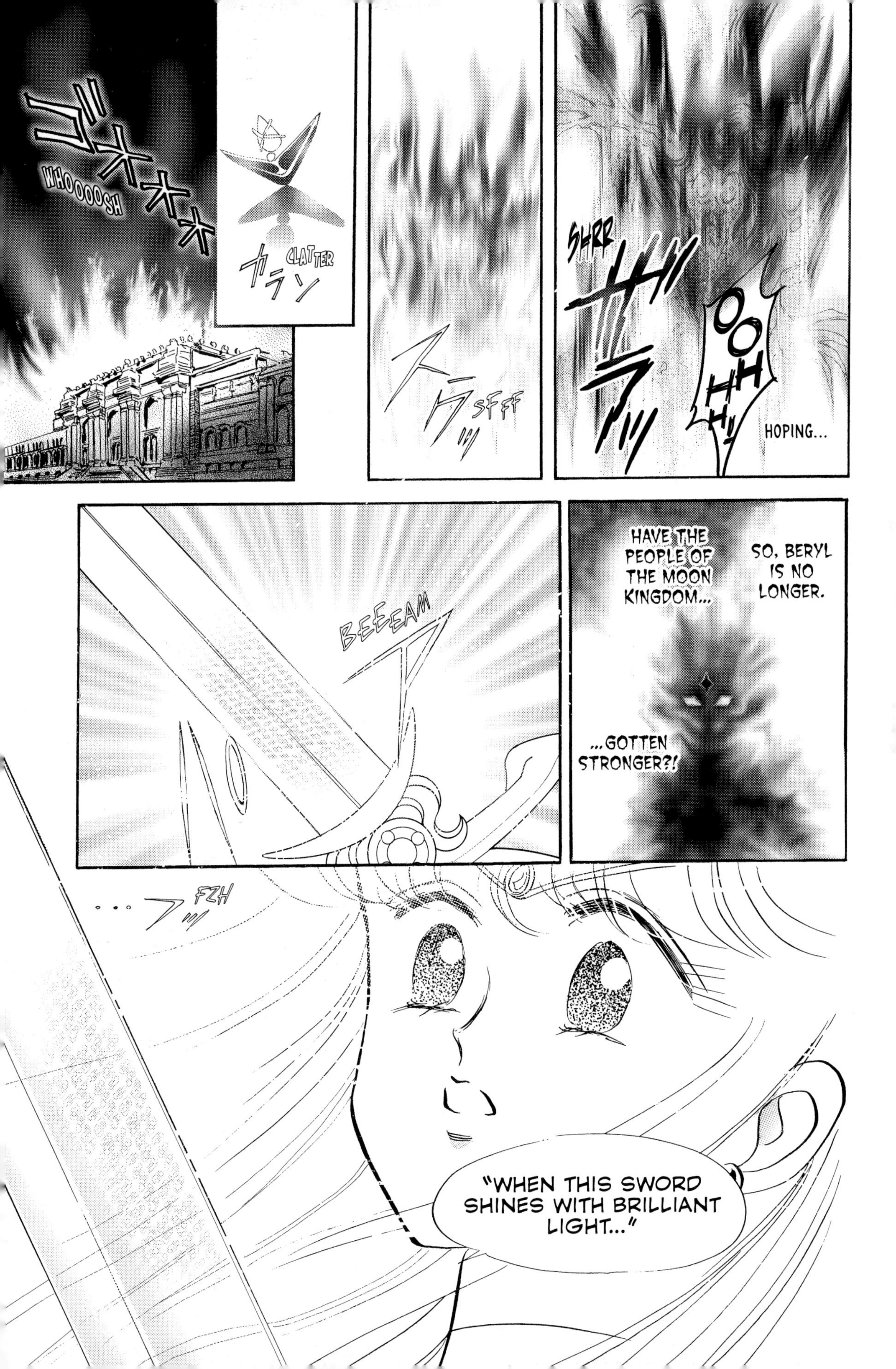

SHRR
OOHHH
HOPING...
スラッ
SFFF
カラン
CLATTER
ゴオオオ
WHOOOOSH
SO, BERYL IS NO LONGER.
HAVE THE PEOPLE OF THE MOON KINGDOM...
...GOTTEN STRONGER?!
BEEEAM
...
フッ
FZH
"WHEN THIS SWORD SHINES WITH BRILLIANT LIGHT..."

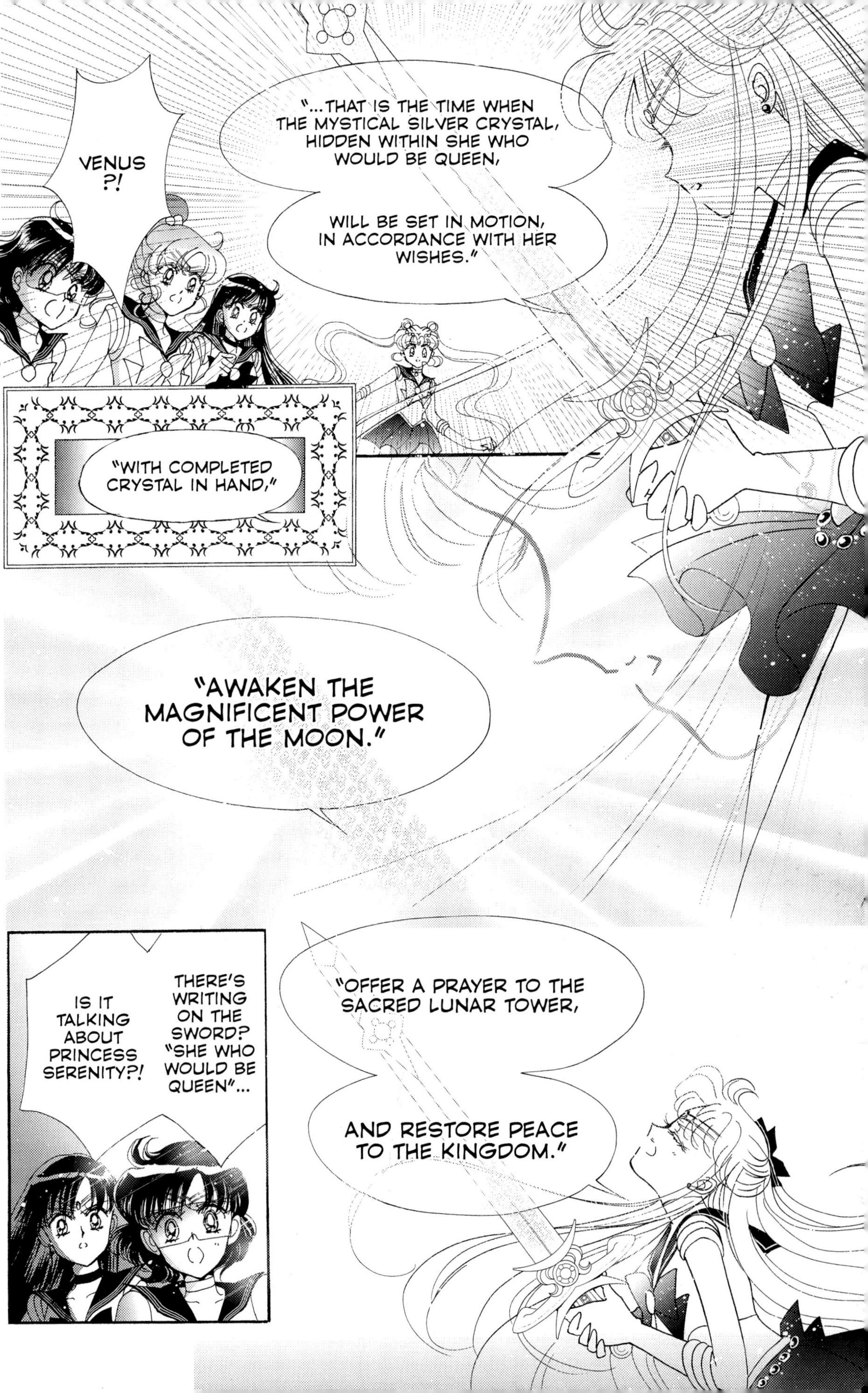
"...THAT IS THE TIME WHEN THE MYSTICAL SILVER CRYSTAL, HIDDEN WITHIN SHE WHO WOULD BE QUEEN,
WILL BE SET IN MOTION, IN ACCORDANCE WITH HER WISHES."
VENUS ?!
"WITH COMPLETED CRYSTAL IN HAND,"
"AWAKEN THE MAGNIFICENT POWER OF THE MOON."
"OFFER A PRAYER TO THE SACRED LUNAR TOWER,
AND RESTORE PEACE TO THE KINGDOM."
THERE'S WRITING ON THE SWORD? "SHE WHO WOULD BE QUEEN"...
IS IT TALKING ABOUT PRINCESS SERENITY?!

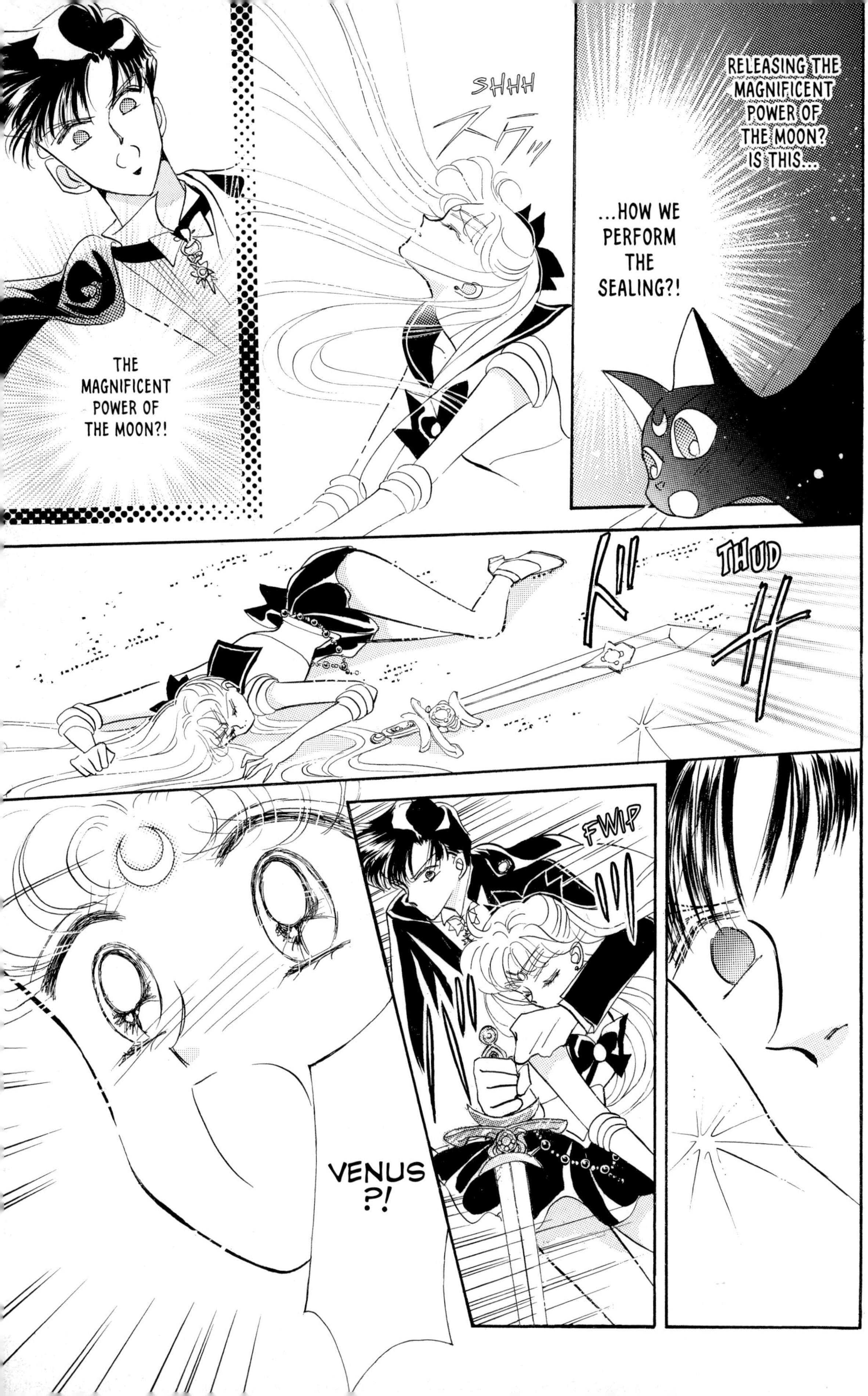
RELEASING THE MAGNIFICENT POWER OF THE MOON? IS THIS...
...HOW WE PERFORM THE SEALING?!
SHHH
THE MAGNIFICENT POWER OF THE MOON?!
THUD
FWIP
VENUS ?!

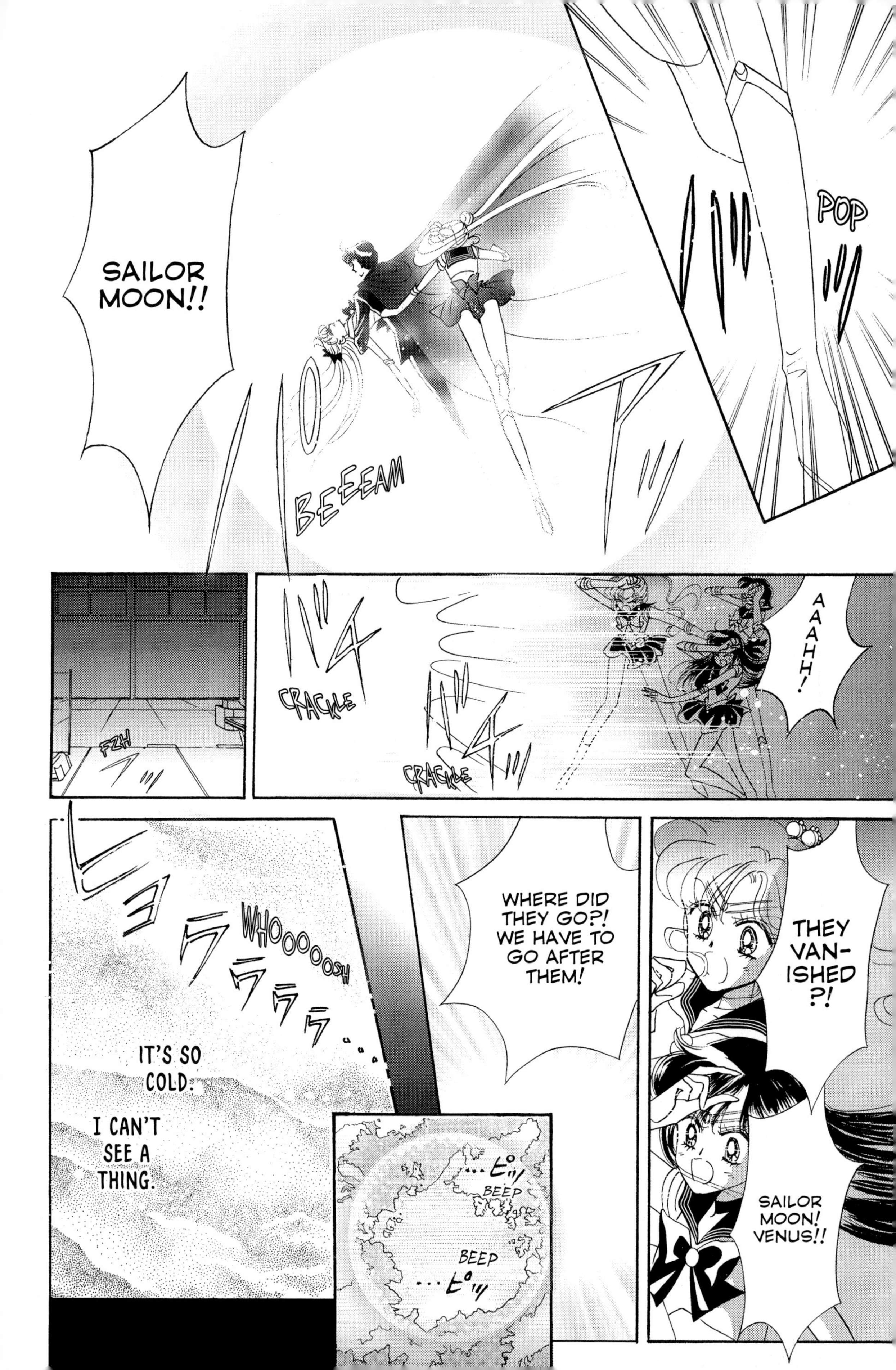
POP
SAILOR MOON!!
BEEEAM
AAAHH!
CRACKLE
CRACKLE
FZH
THEY VAN-ISHED?!
SAILOR MOON! VENUS!!
WHERE DID THEY GO?! WE HAVE TO GO AFTER THEM!
WHOOOOOSH
IT'S SO COLD.
I CAN'T SEE A THING.
BEEP
BEEP

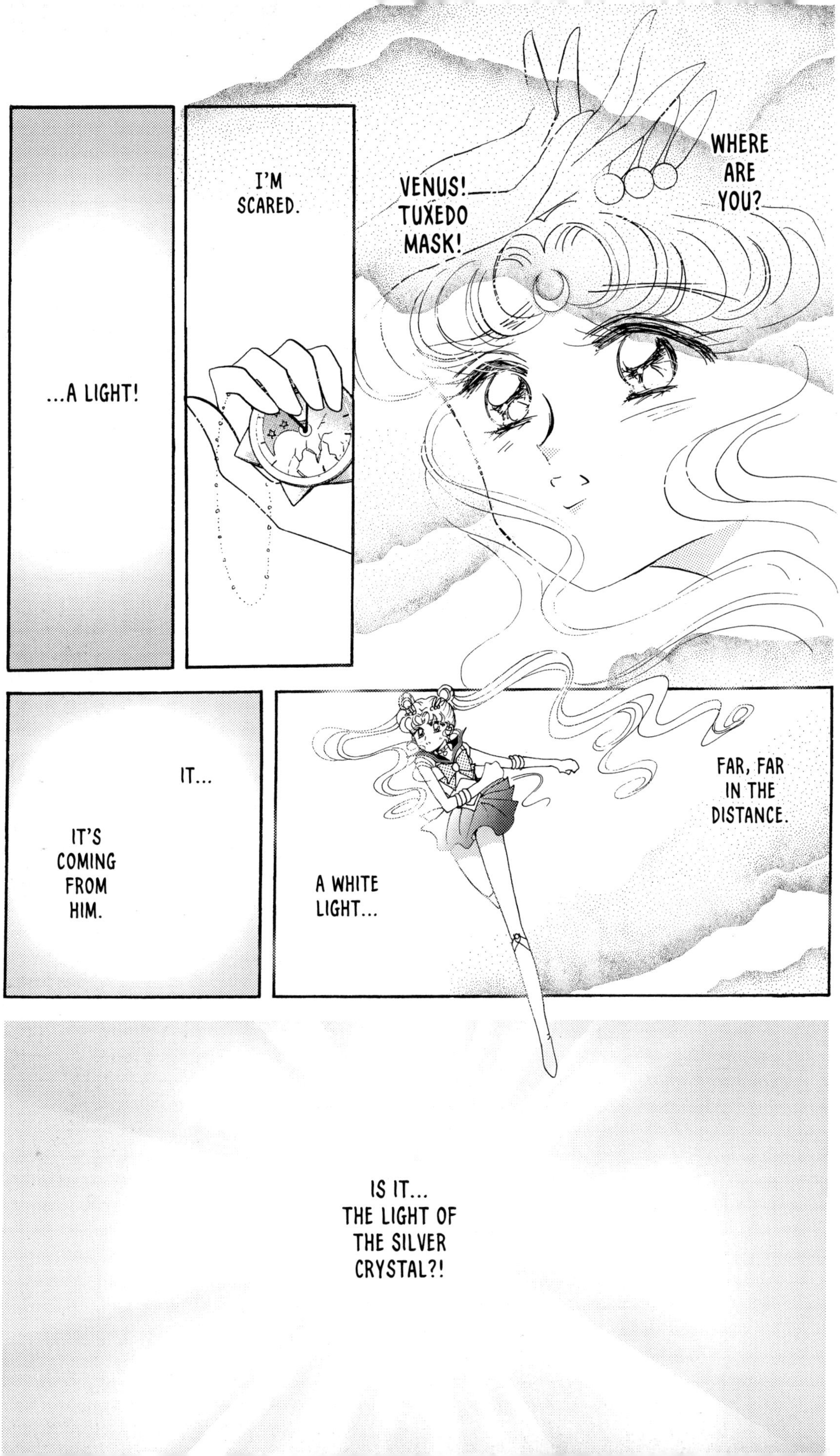
VENUS! TUXEDO MASK!
WHERE ARE YOU?
I'M SCARED.
...A LIGHT!
FAR, FAR IN THE DISTANCE.
A WHITE LIGHT...
IT...
IT'S COMING FROM HIM.
IS IT... THE LIGHT OF THE SILVER CRYSTAL?!

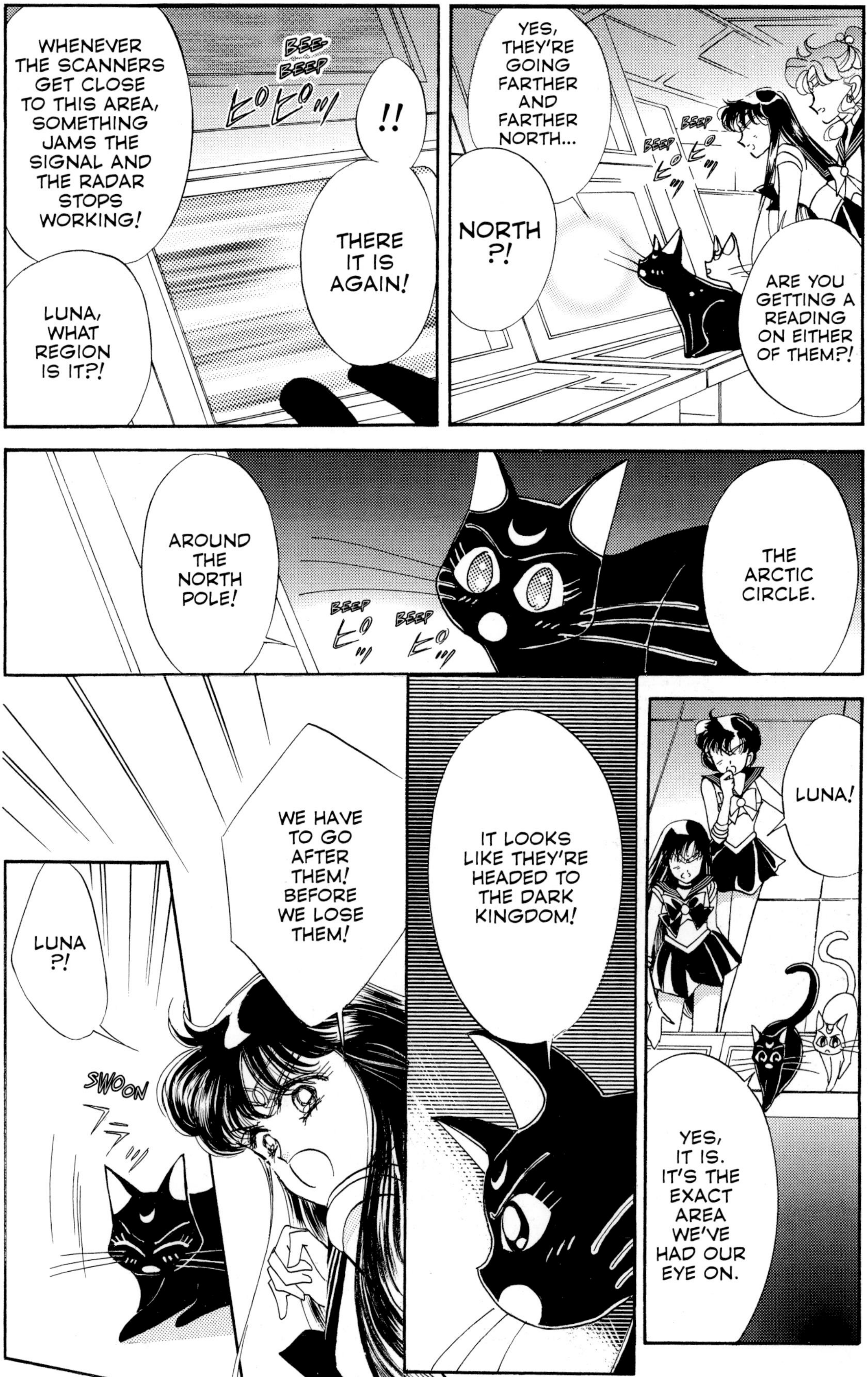
YES, THEY'RE GOING FARTHER AND FARTHER NORTH...
BEEP BEEP
NORTH?!
ARE YOU GETTING A READING ON EITHER OF THEM?!
!!
BEE-BEEP
THERE IT IS AGAIN!
WHENEVER THE SCANNERS GET CLOSE TO THIS AREA, SOMETHING JAMS THE SIGNAL AND THE RADAR STOPS WORKING!
LUNA, WHAT REGION IS IT?!
THE ARCTIC CIRCLE.
BEEP BEEP
AROUND THE NORTH POLE!
LUNA!
YES, IT IS. IT'S THE EXACT AREA WE'VE HAD OUR EYE ON.
IT LOOKS LIKE THEY'RE HEADED TO THE DARK KINGDOM!
WE HAVE TO GO AFTER THEM! BEFORE WE LOSE THEM!
LUNA?!
SWOON

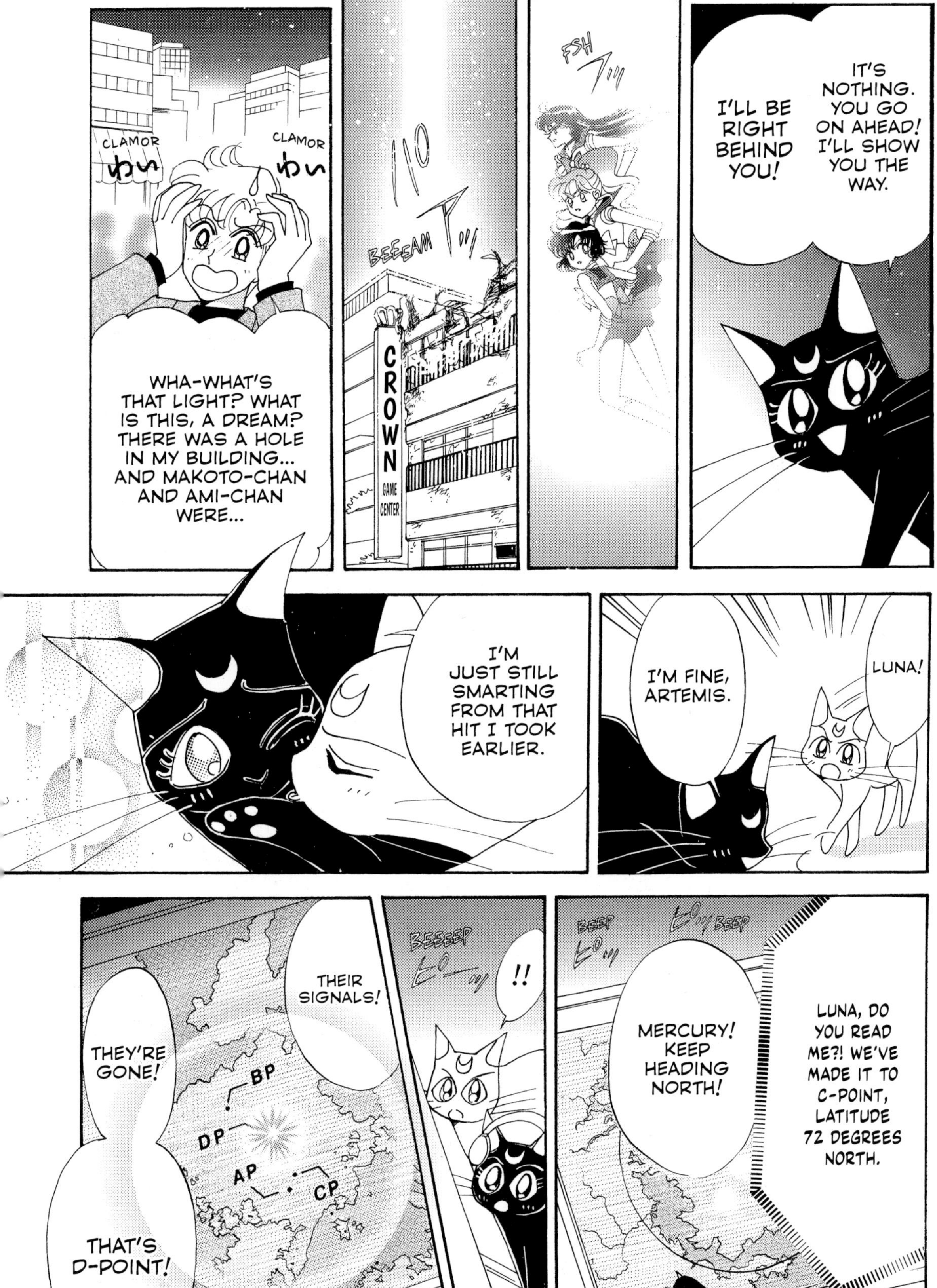
IT'S NOTHING. YOU GO ON AHEAD! I'LL SHOW YOU THE WAY.
I'LL BE RIGHT BEHIND YOU!
FSH
BEEEAM
CROWN
GAME CENTER
CLAMOR
CLAMOR
WHA-WHAT'S THAT LIGHT? WHAT IS THIS, A DREAM? THERE WAS A HOLE IN MY BUILDING... AND MAKOTO-CHAN AND AMI-CHAN WERE...
LUNA!
I'M FINE, ARTEMIS.
I'M JUST STILL SMARTING FROM THAT HIT I TOOK EARLIER.
BEEP
BEEP
LUNA, DO YOU READ ME?! WE'VE MADE IT TO C-POINT, LATITUDE 72 DEGREES NORTH.
MERCURY! KEEP HEADING NORTH!
BEEEEP
!!
THEIR SIGNALS!
BP
DP
AP
CP
THEY'RE GONE!
THAT'S D-POINT!

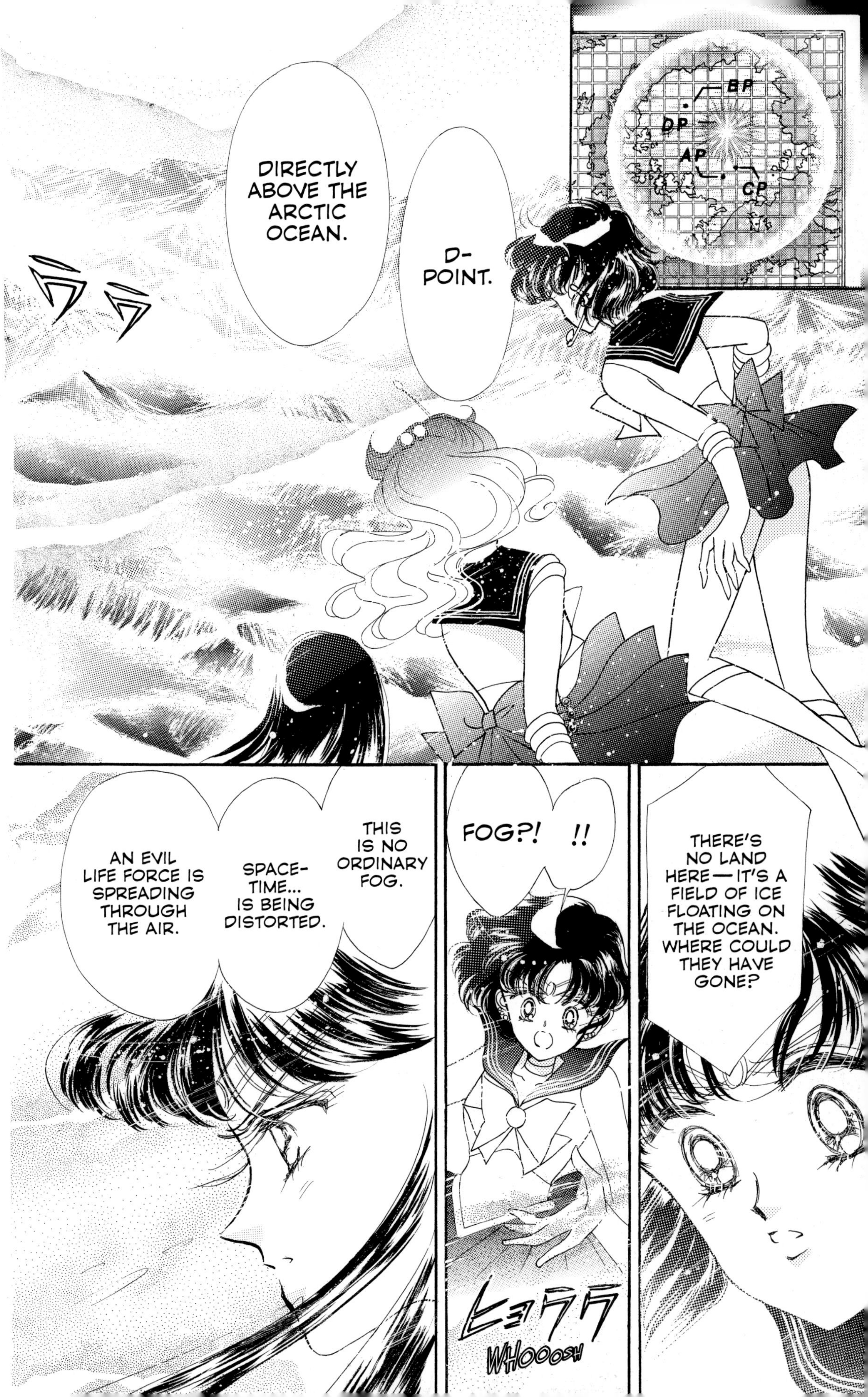
BP
DP
AP
CP
D-POINT.
DIRECTLY ABOVE THE ARCTIC OCEAN.
ララ
THERE'S NO LAND HERE—IT'S A FIELD OF ICE FLOATING ON THE OCEAN. WHERE COULD THEY HAVE GONE?
FOG?!
!!
ヒョララ
WHOOOSH
THIS IS NO ORDINARY FOG.
SPACE-TIME... IS BEING DISTORTED.
AN EVIL LIFE FORCE IS SPREADING THROUGH THE AIR.

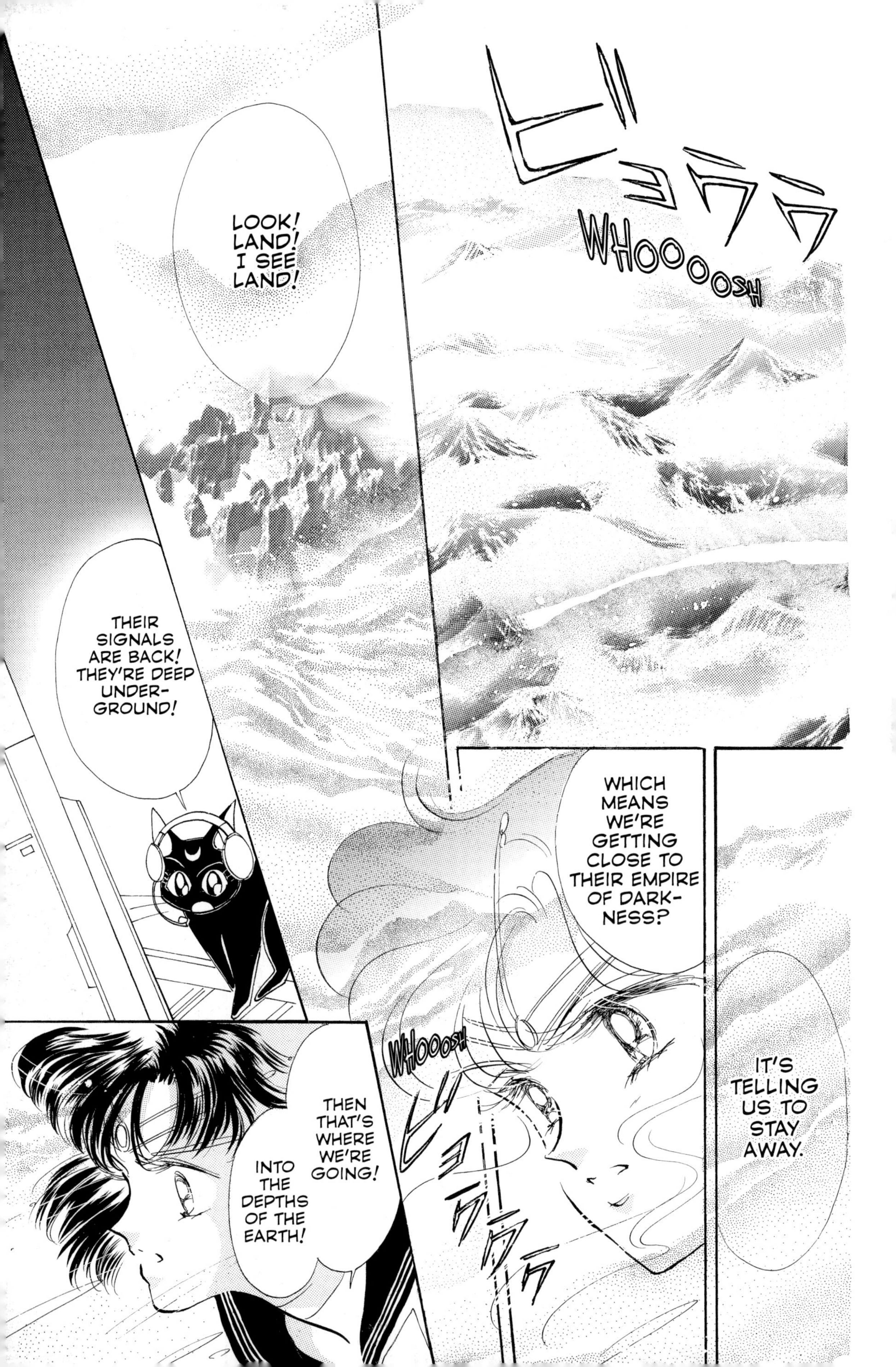
WHOOOOSH
LOOK! LAND! I SEE LAND!
THEIR SIGNALS ARE BACK! THEY'RE DEEP UNDER-GROUND!
IT'S TELLING US TO STAY AWAY.
WHICH MEANS WE'RE GETTING CLOSE TO THEIR EMPIRE OF DARK-NESS?
WHOOOSH
THEN THAT'S WHERE WE'RE GOING!
INTO THE DEPTHS OF THE EARTH!

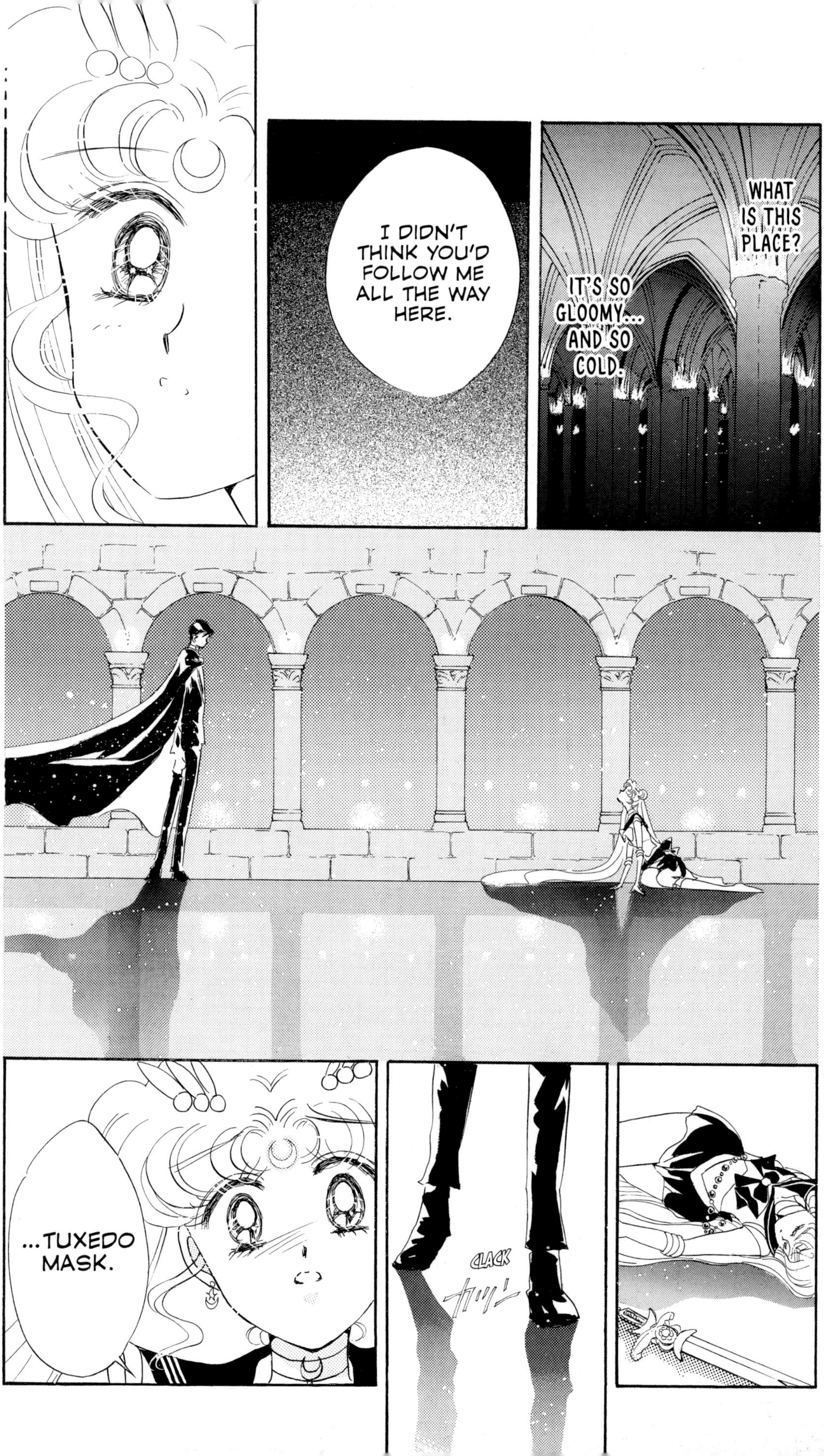
WHAT IS THIS PLACE?
IT'S SO GLOOMY... AND SO COLD.
I DIDN'T THINK YOU'D FOLLOW ME ALL THE WAY HERE.
CLACK
...TUXEDO MASK.

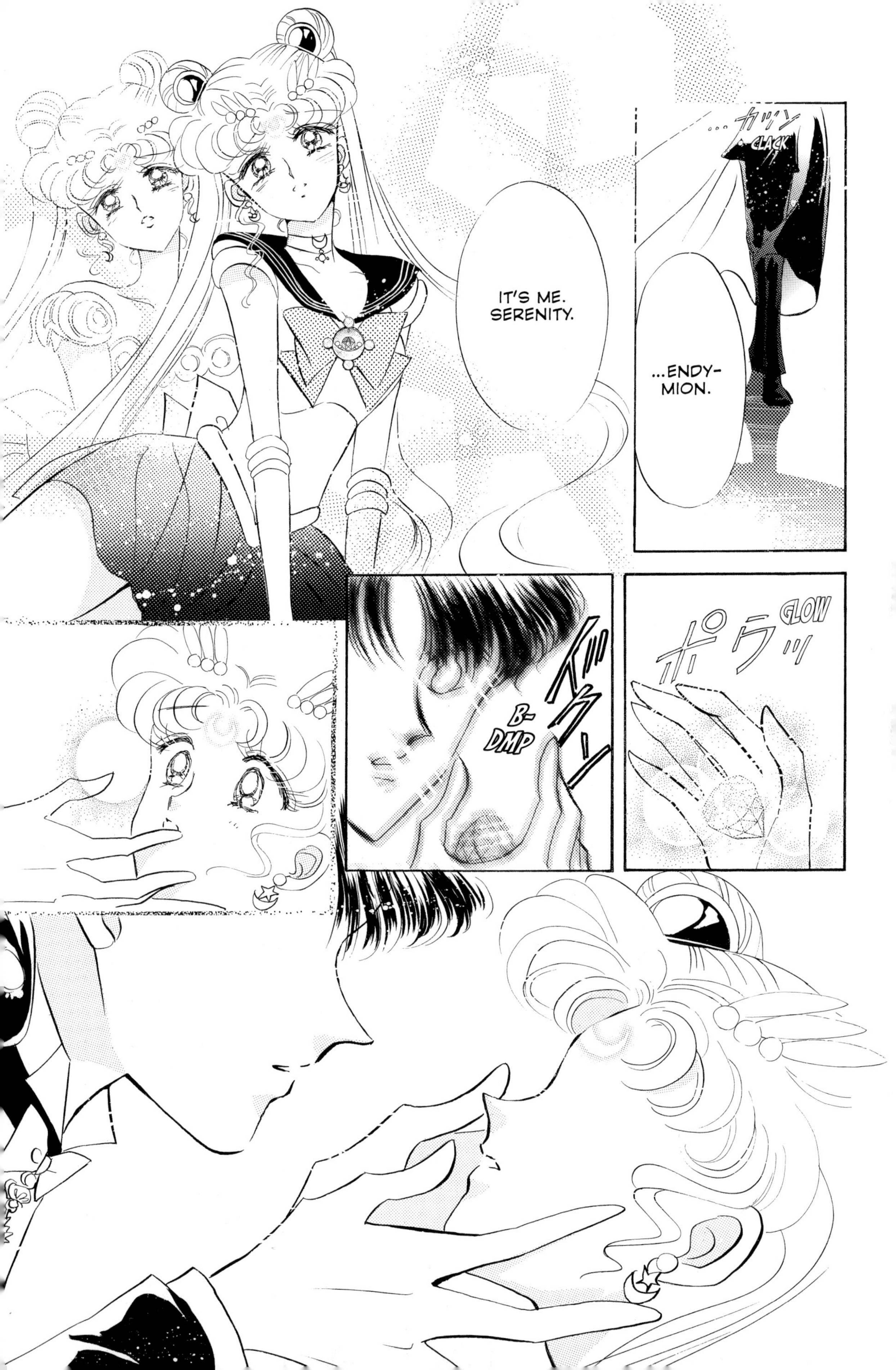
...カツン
CLACK
...ENDY-
MION.
IT'S ME.
SERENITY.
GLOW
B-
DMP

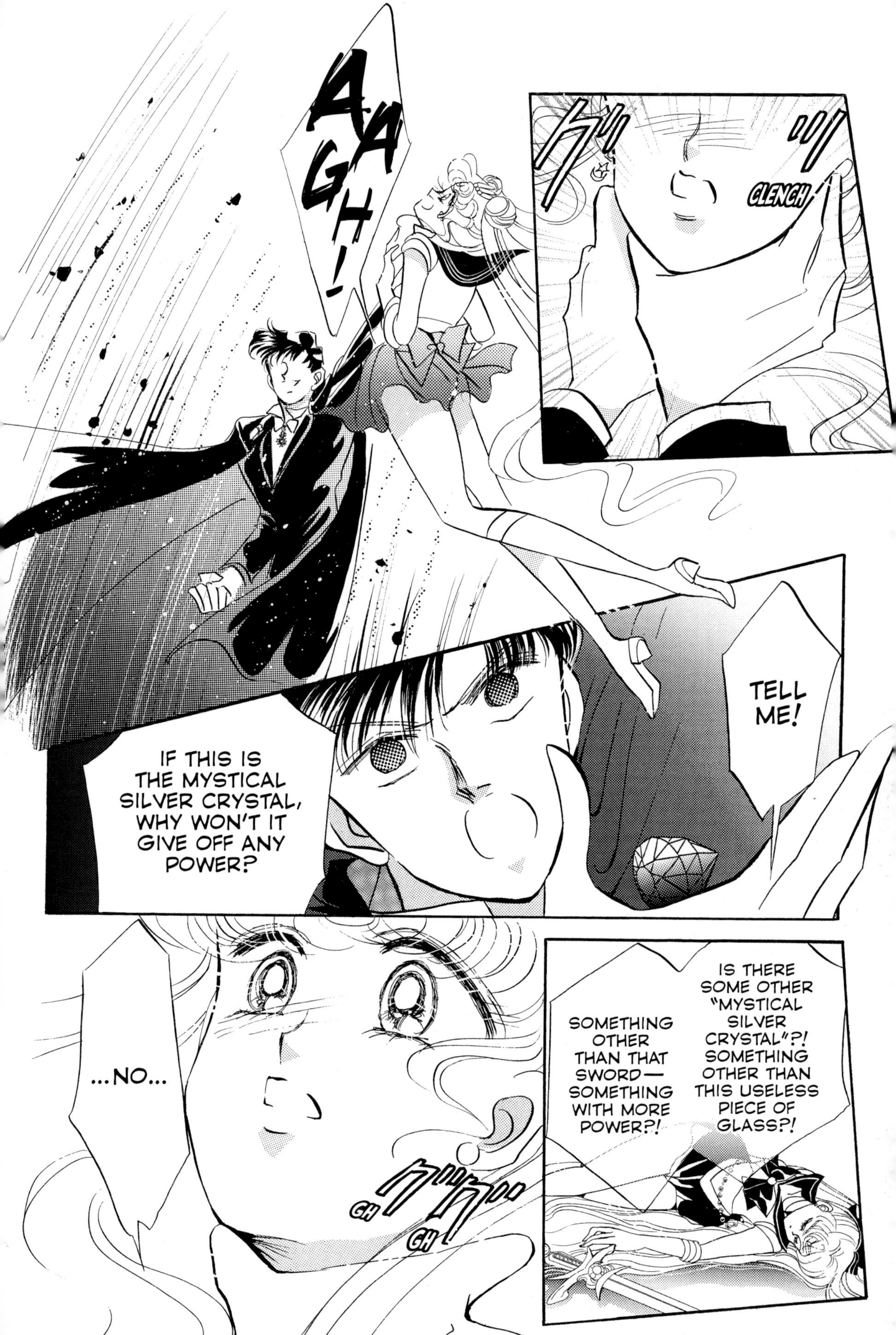
CLENCH
AAGH!!
TELL ME!
IF THIS IS THE MYSTICAL SILVER CRYSTAL, WHY WON'T IT GIVE OFF ANY POWER?
IS THERE SOME OTHER "MYSTICAL SILVER CRYSTAL"?! SOMETHING OTHER THAN THIS USELESS PIECE OF GLASS?!
SOMETHING OTHER THAN THAT SWORD—SOMETHING WITH MORE POWER?!
...NO...
GH
GH

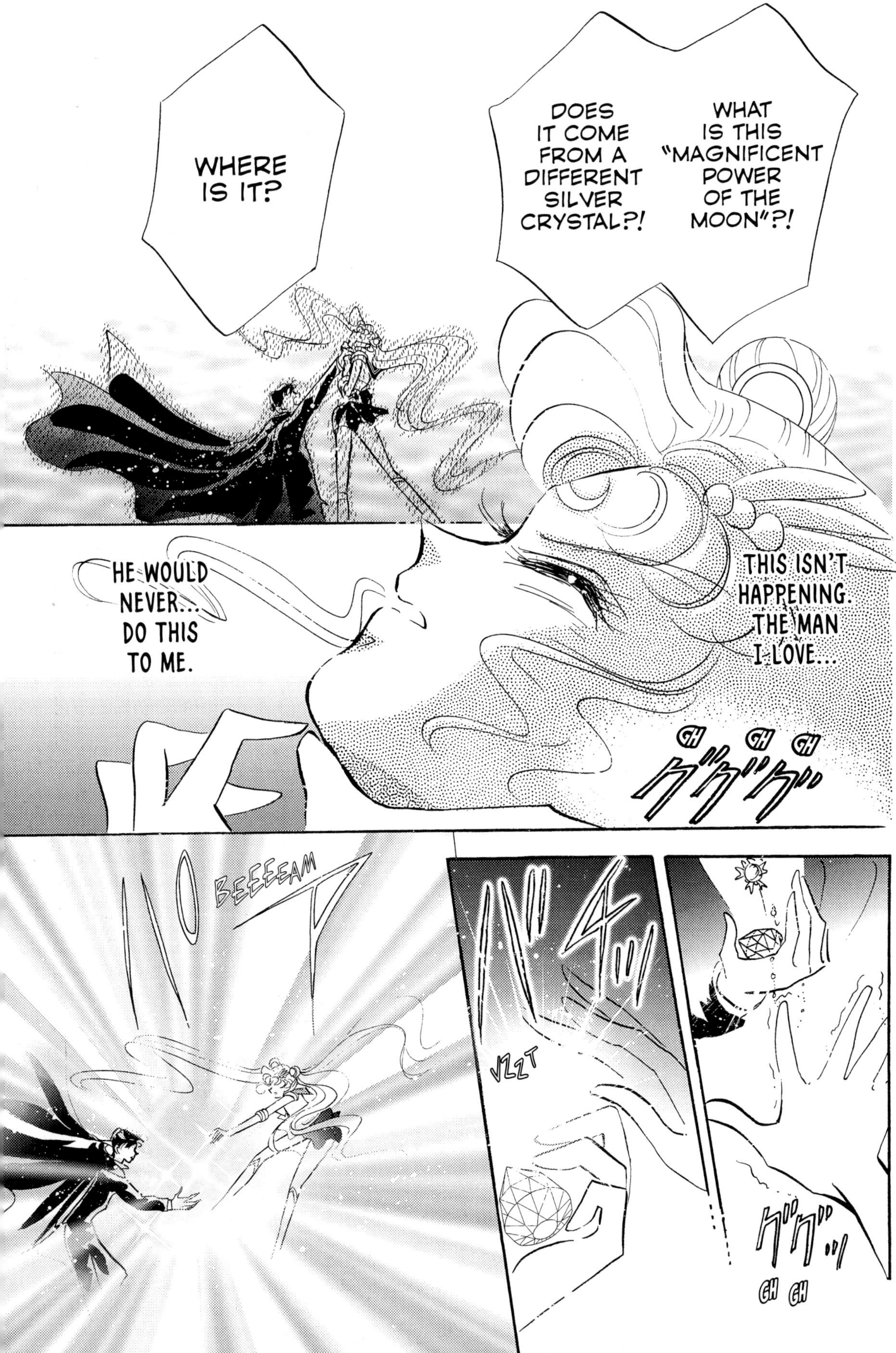
WHAT IS THIS "MAGNIFICENT POWER OF THE MOON"?!
DOES IT COME FROM A DIFFERENT SILVER CRYSTAL?!
WHERE IS IT?
THIS ISN'T HAPPENING. THE MAN I LOVE...
HE WOULD NEVER... DO THIS TO ME.
GH GH GH
GH GH
VZZT
BEEEEAM

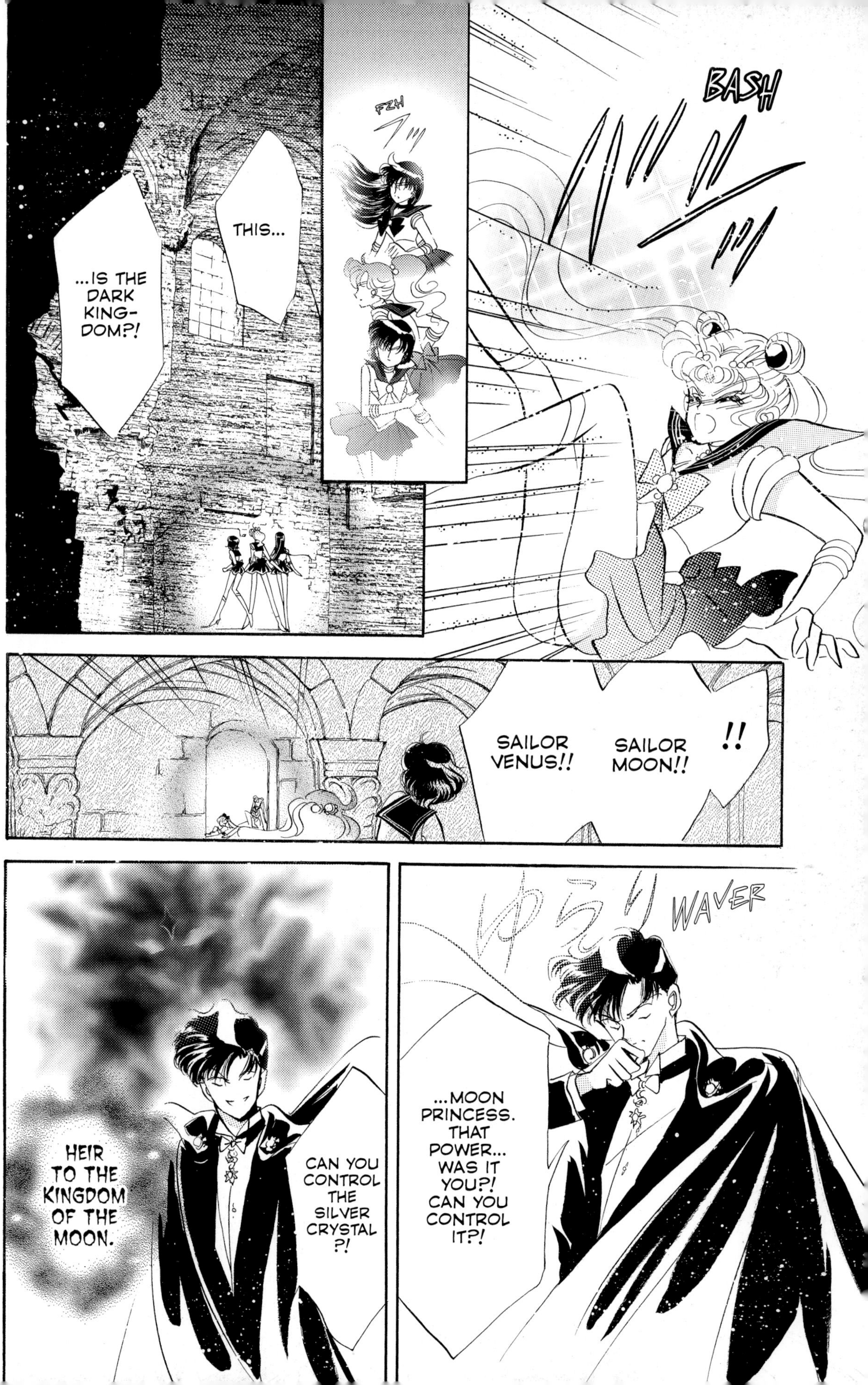
BASH
FZH
THIS...
...IS THE DARK KING-DOM?!
!!
SAILOR MOON!!
SAILOR VENUS!!
ゆらり
WAVER
...MOON PRINCESS. THAT POWER... WAS IT YOU?! CAN YOU CONTROL IT?!
CAN YOU CONTROL THE SILVER CRYSTAL ?!
HEIR TO THE KINGDOM OF THE MOON.

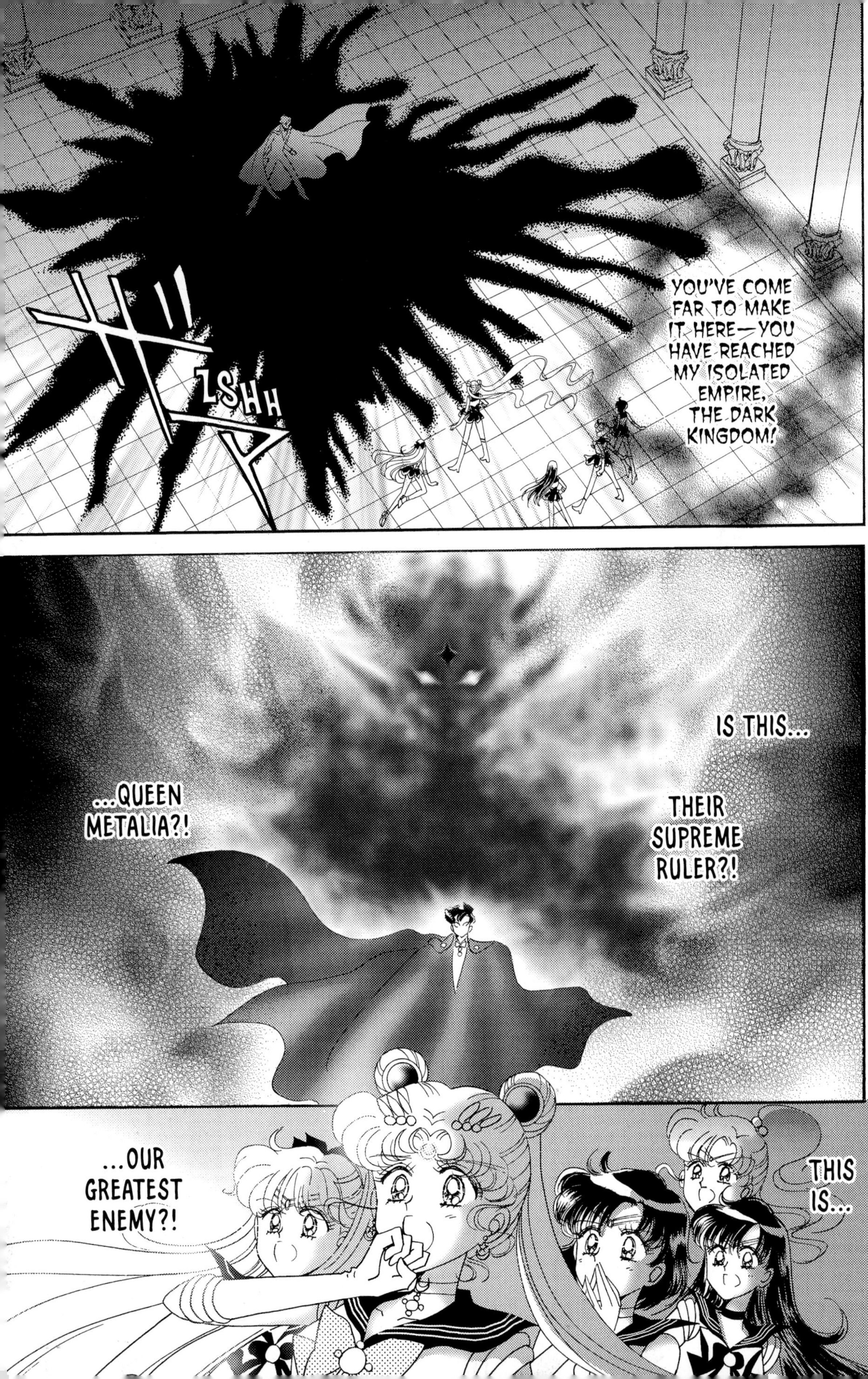
YOU'VE COME FAR TO MAKE IT HERE—YOU HAVE REACHED MY ISOLATED EMPIRE, THE DARK KINGDOM!
ZSHH
IS THIS...
THEIR SUPREME RULER?!
...QUEEN METALIA?!
THIS IS...
...OUR GREATEST ENEMY?!

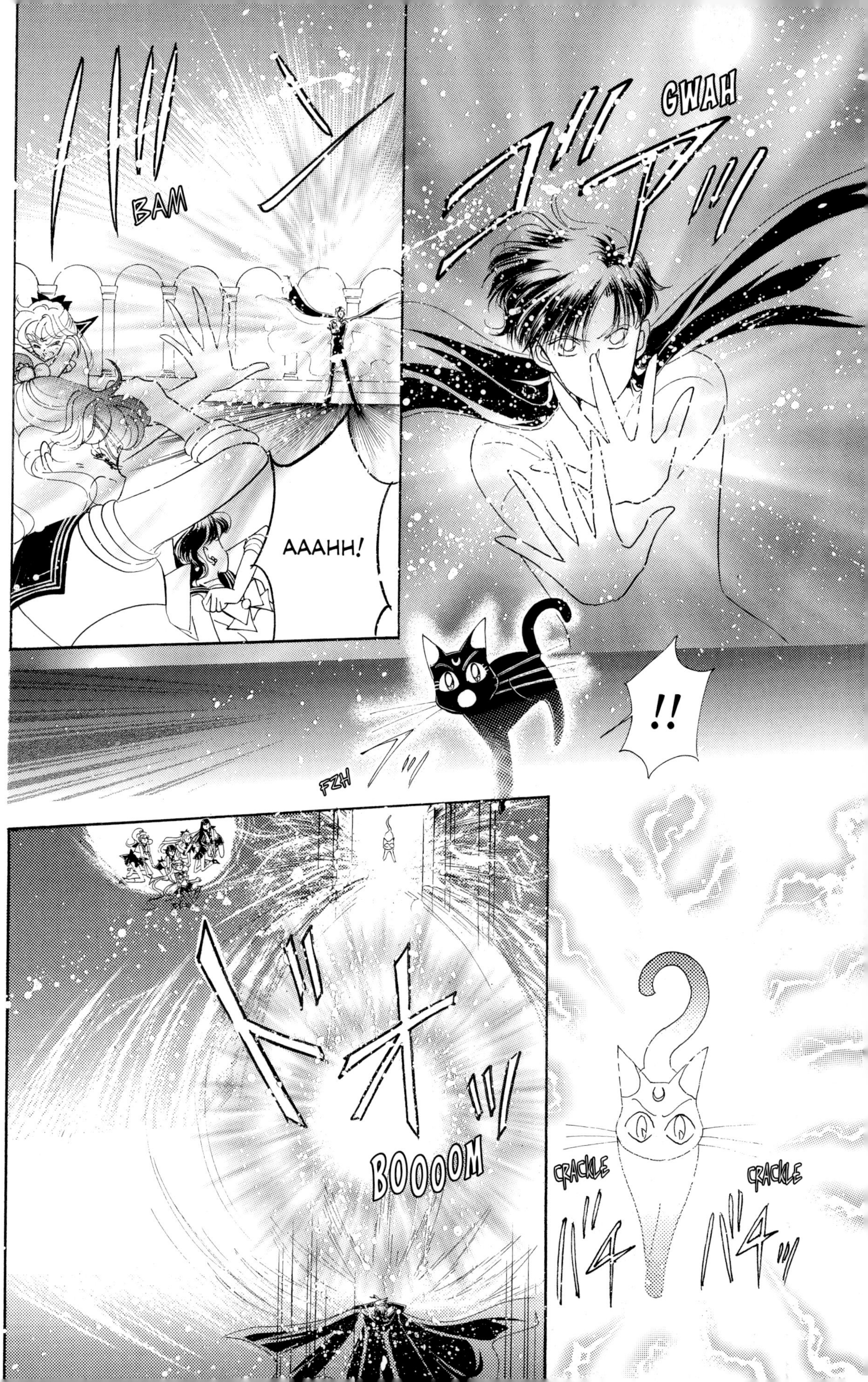
GWAH
BAM
AAAHH!
!!
FZH
CRACKLE
CRACKLE
BOOOOM

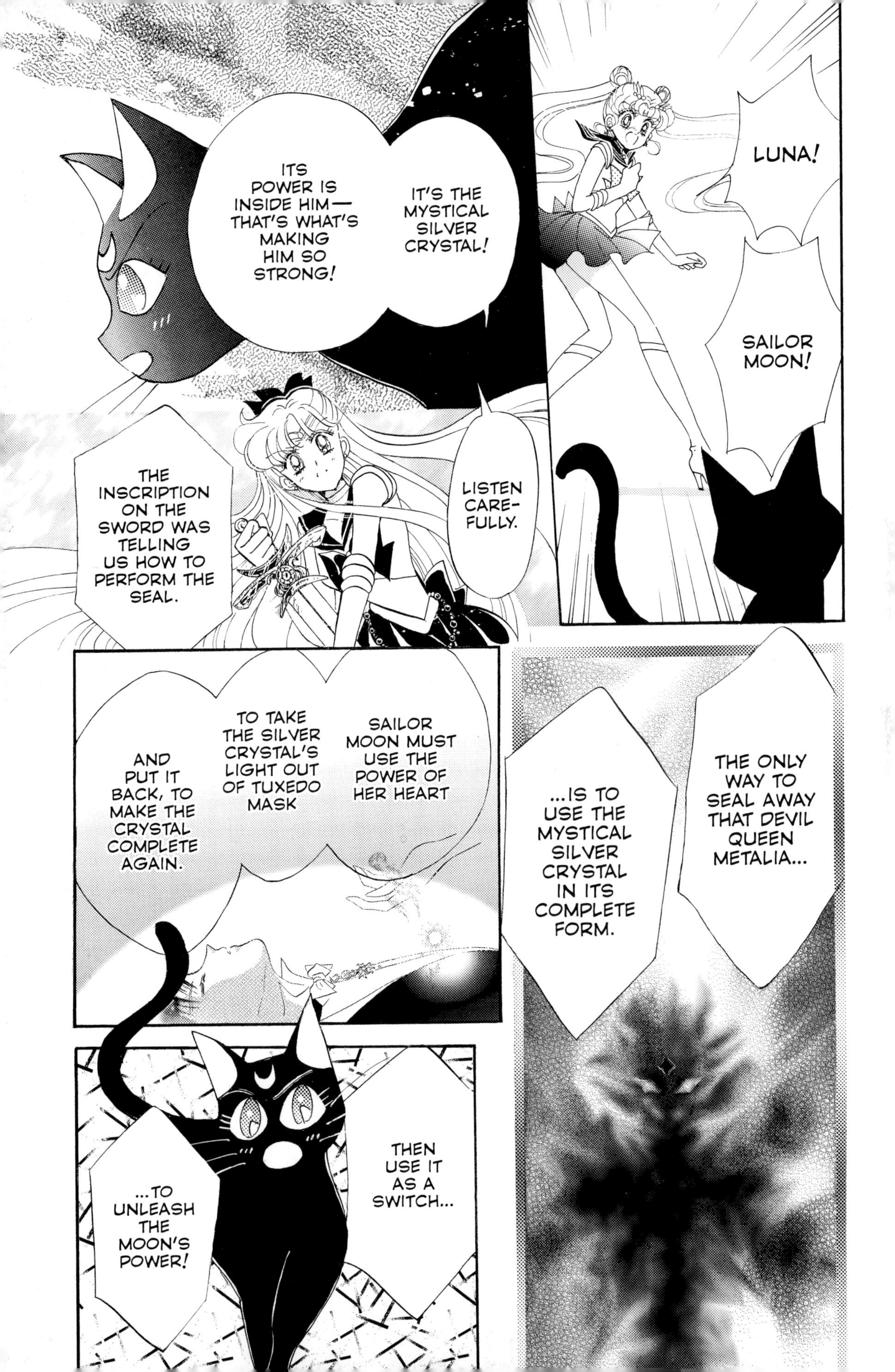

LUNA!
SAILOR MOON!
IT'S THE MYSTICAL SILVER CRYSTAL!
ITS POWER IS INSIDE HIM— THAT'S WHAT'S MAKING HIM SO STRONG!
LISTEN CARE-FULLY.
THE INSCRIPTION ON THE SWORD WAS TELLING US HOW TO PERFORM THE SEAL.
THE ONLY WAY TO SEAL AWAY THAT DEVIL QUEEN METALIA...
...IS TO USE THE MYSTICAL SILVER CRYSTAL IN ITS COMPLETE FORM.
SAILOR MOON MUST USE THE POWER OF HER HEART
TO TAKE THE SILVER CRYSTAL'S LIGHT OUT OF TUXEDO MASK
AND PUT IT BACK, TO MAKE THE CRYSTAL COMPLETE AGAIN.
THEN USE IT AS A SWITCH...
...TO UNLEASH THE MOON'S POWER!

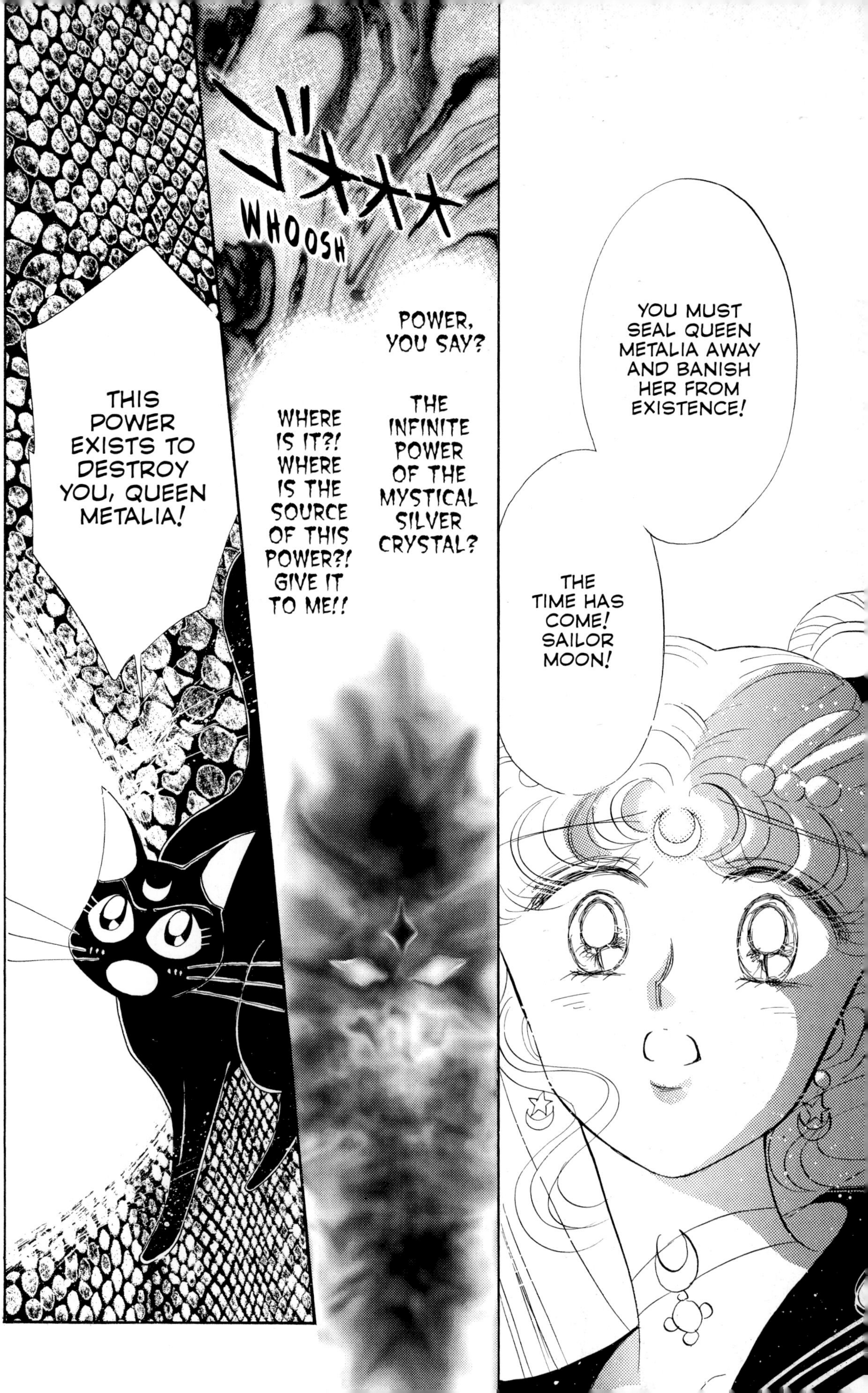
YOU MUST SEAL QUEEN METALIA AWAY AND BANISH HER FROM EXISTENCE!
THE TIME HAS COME! SAILOR MOON!
ゴオオオ
WHOOSH
POWER, YOU SAY?
THE INFINITE POWER OF THE MYSTICAL SILVER CRYSTAL?
WHERE IS IT?! WHERE IS THE SOURCE OF THIS POWER?! GIVE IT TO ME!!
THIS POWER EXISTS TO DESTROY YOU, QUEEN METALIA!

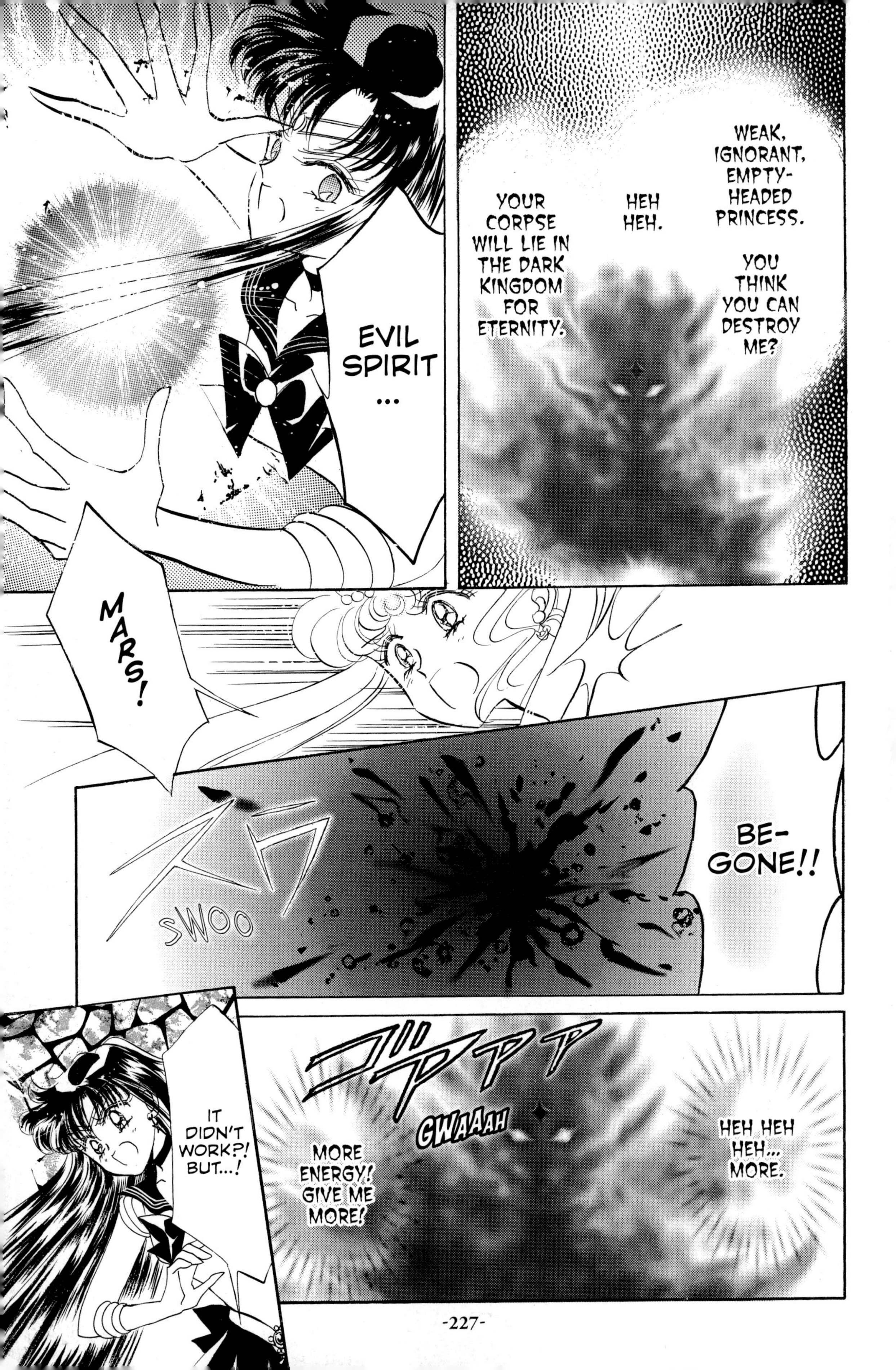
WEAK, IGNORANT, EMPTY-HEADED PRINCESS.
YOU THINK YOU CAN DESTROY ME?
HEH HEH.
YOUR CORPSE WILL LIE IN THE DARK KINGDOM FOR ETERNITY.
EVIL SPIRIT ...
MARS!
BE-GONE!!
SWOO
HEH HEH HEH... MORE.
GWAAAH
MORE ENERGY! GIVE ME MORE!
IT DIDN'T WORK?! BUT...!

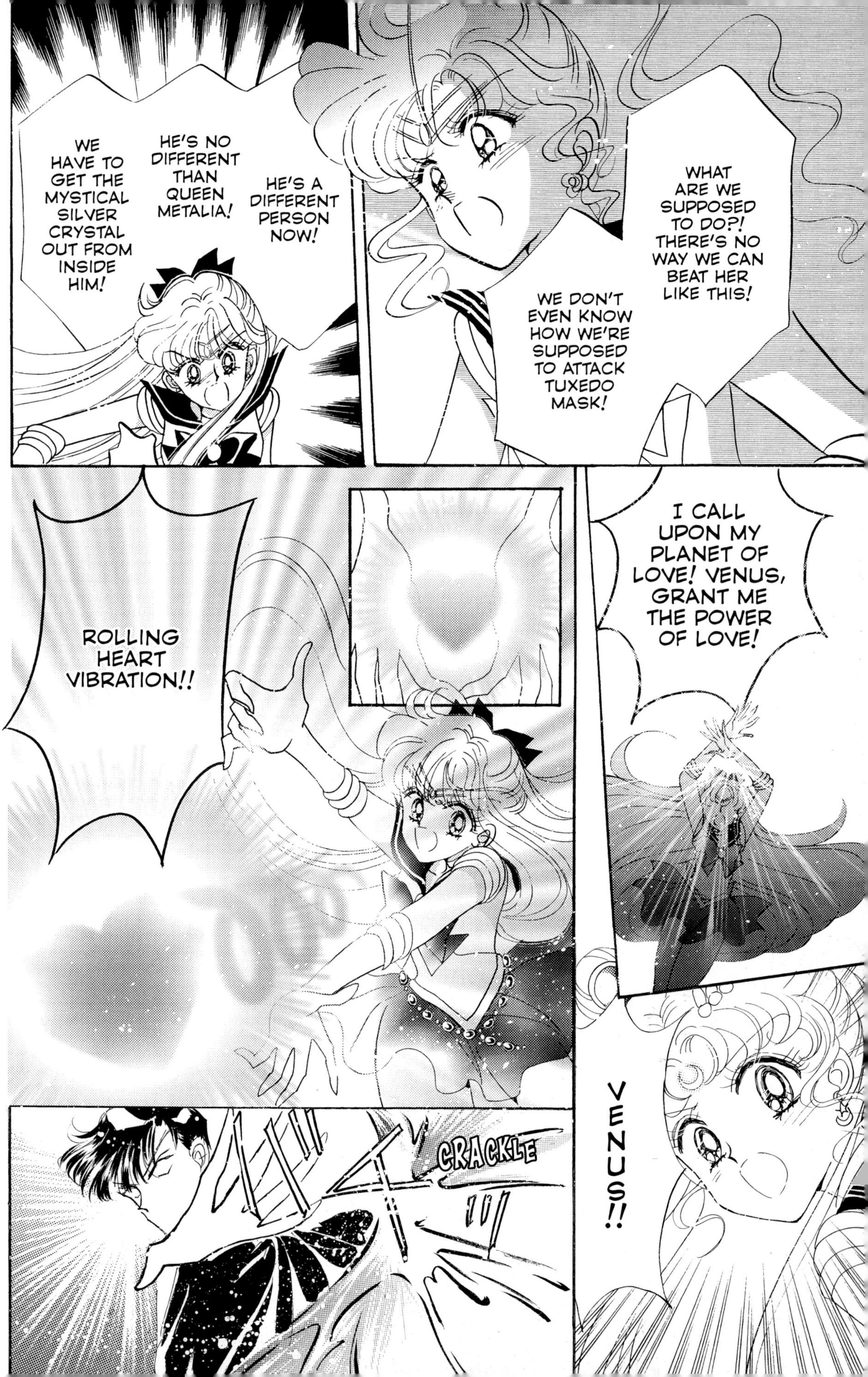

WHAT ARE WE SUPPOSED TO DO?! THERE'S NO WAY WE CAN BEAT HER LIKE THIS!
WE DON'T EVEN KNOW HOW WE'RE SUPPOSED TO ATTACK TUXEDO MASK!
HE'S A DIFFERENT PERSON NOW!
HE'S NO DIFFERENT THAN QUEEN METALIA!
WE HAVE TO GET THE MYSTICAL SILVER CRYSTAL OUT FROM INSIDE HIM!
I CALL UPON MY PLANET OF LOVE! VENUS, GRANT ME THE POWER OF LOVE!
VENUS!!
ROLLING HEART VIBRATION!!
CRACKLE

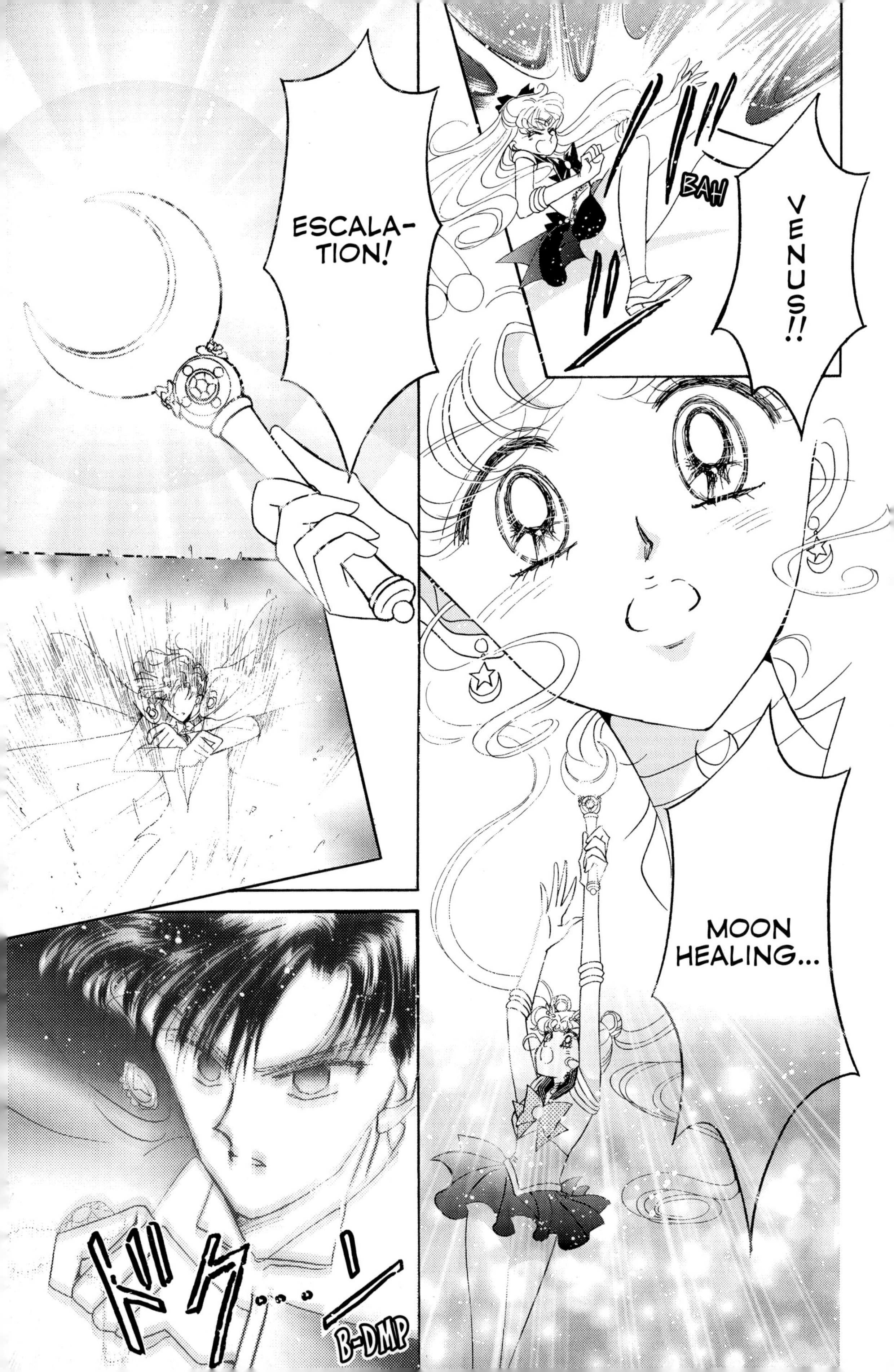
BAH
VENUS!!
MOON HEALING...
ESCALA-TION!
B-DMP

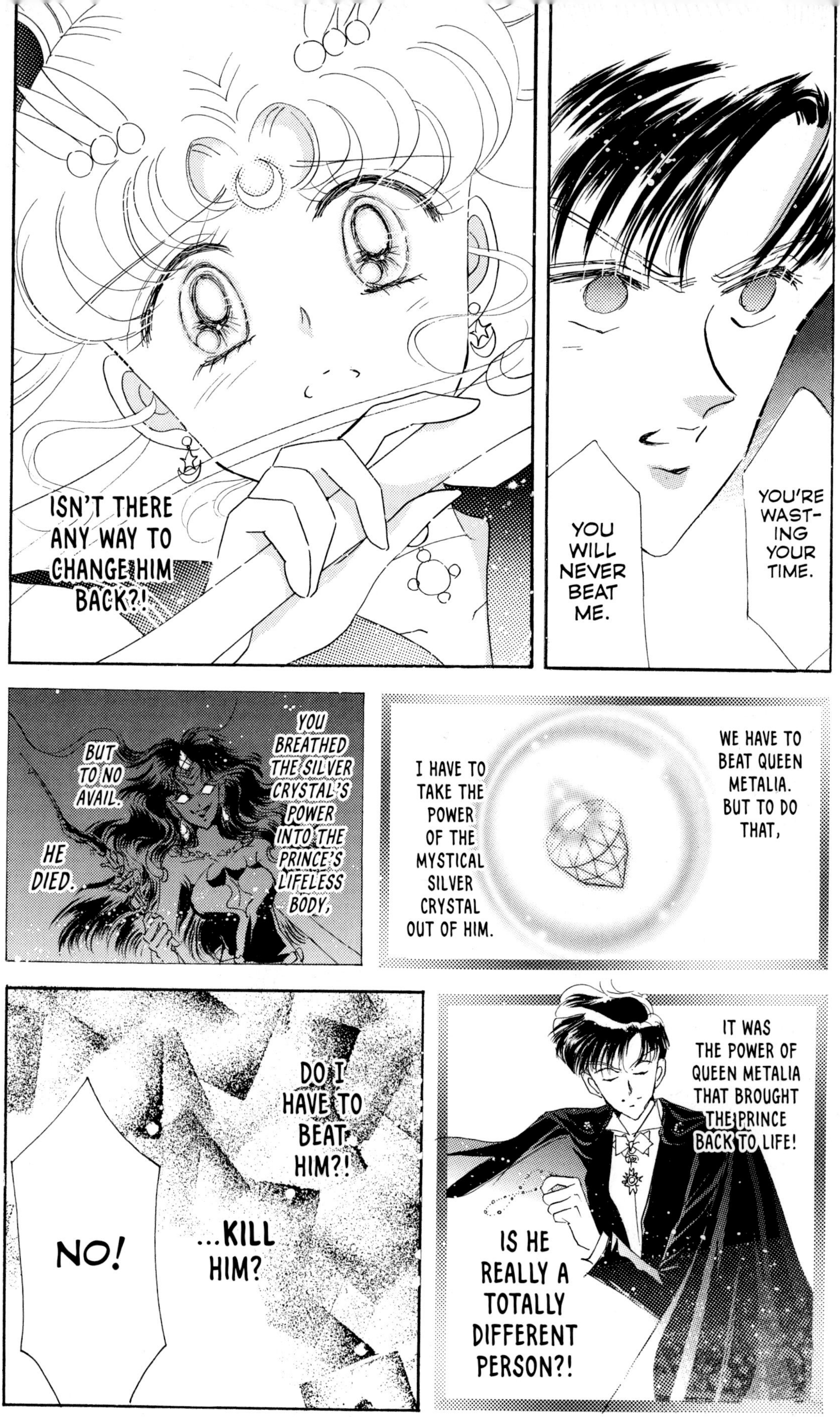
YOU'RE WASTING YOUR TIME.
YOU WILL NEVER BEAT ME.
ISN'T THERE ANY WAY TO CHANGE HIM BACK?!
WE HAVE TO BEAT QUEEN METALIA. BUT TO DO THAT,
I HAVE TO TAKE THE POWER OF THE MYSTICAL SILVER CRYSTAL OUT OF HIM.
YOU BREATHED THE SILVER CRYSTAL'S POWER INTO THE PRINCE'S LIFELESS BODY,
BUT TO NO AVAIL.
HE DIED.
IT WAS THE POWER OF QUEEN METALIA THAT BROUGHT THE PRINCE BACK TO LIFE!
IS HE REALLY A TOTALLY DIFFERENT PERSON?!
DO I HAVE TO BEAT HIM?!
...KILL HIM?
NO!

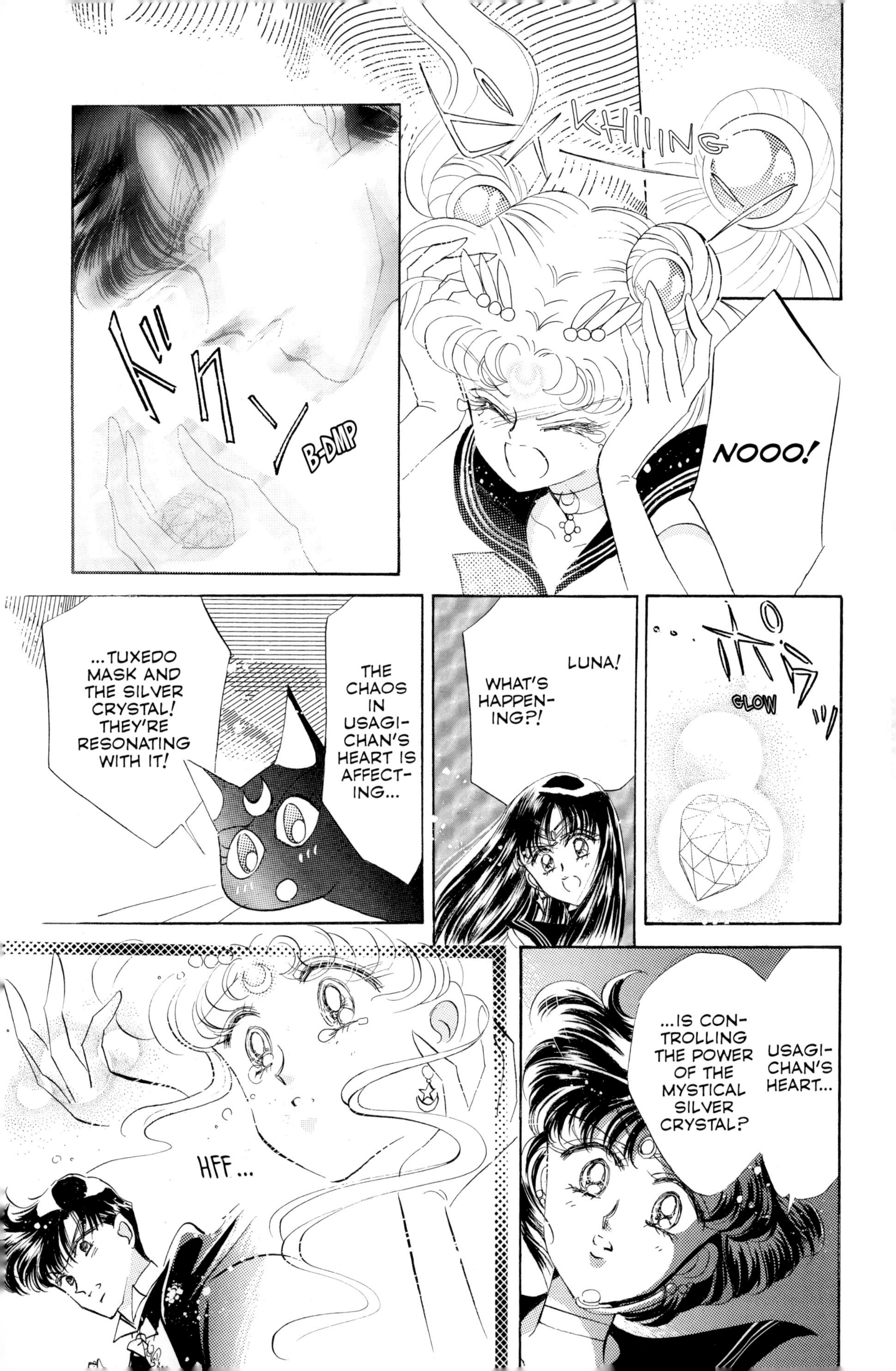
KHIIING
NOOO!
B-DMP
GLOW
LUNA!
WHAT'S HAPPENING?!
THE CHAOS IN USAGI-CHAN'S HEART IS AFFECTING...
...TUXEDO MASK AND THE SILVER CRYSTAL! THEY'RE RESONATING WITH IT!
USAGI-CHAN'S HEART...
...IS CONTROLLING THE POWER OF THE MYSTICAL SILVER CRYSTAL?
HFF...

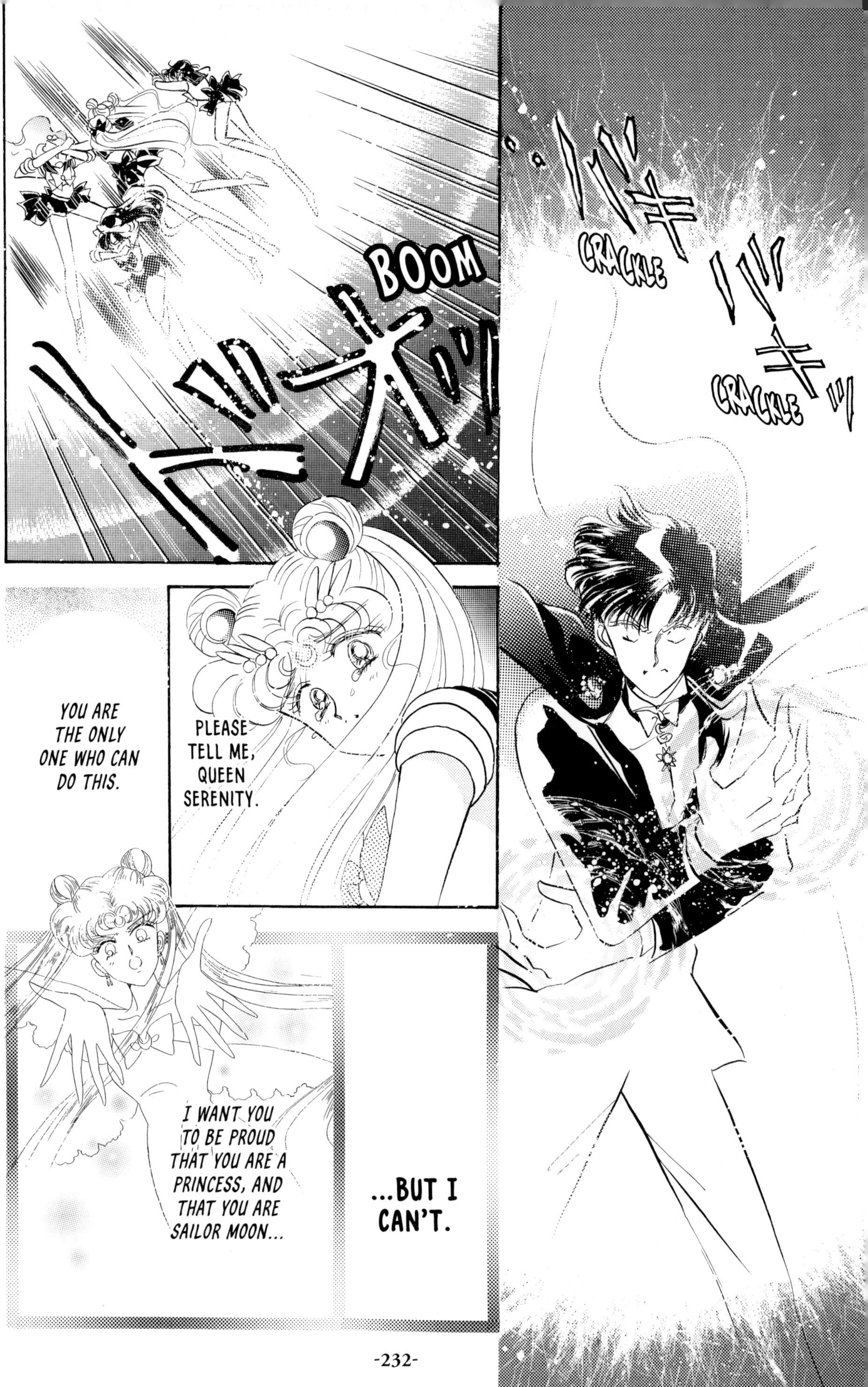
CRACKLE
CRACKLE
BOOM
PLEASE TELL ME, QUEEN SERENITY.
YOU ARE THE ONLY ONE WHO CAN DO THIS.
...BUT I CAN'T.
I WANT YOU TO BE PROUD THAT YOU ARE A PRINCESS, AND THAT YOU ARE SAILOR MOON...

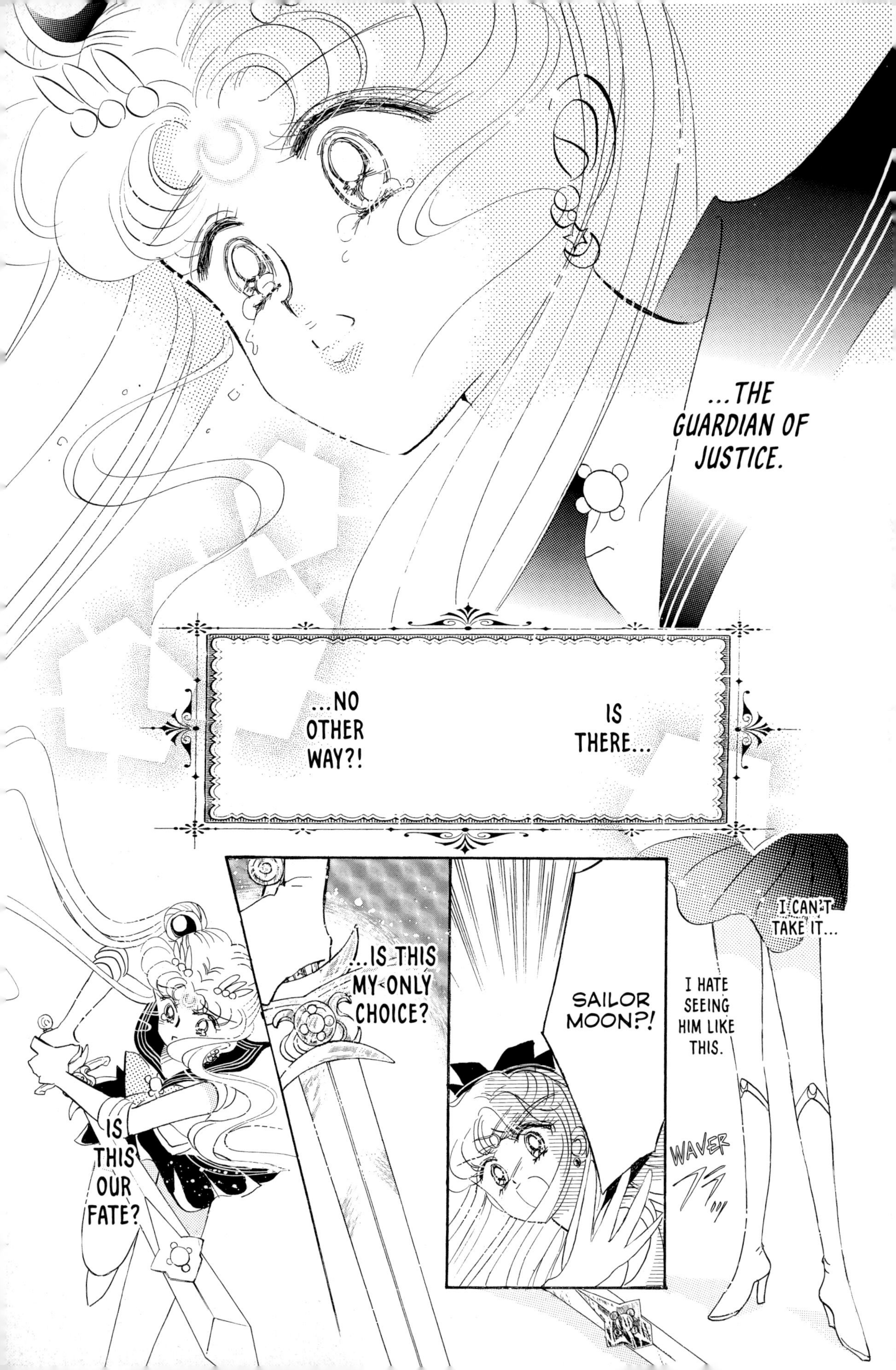
...THE GUARDIAN OF JUSTICE.
IS THERE...
...NO OTHER WAY?!
I CAN'T TAKE IT...
I HATE SEEING HIM LIKE THIS.
WAVER
SAILOR MOON?!
...IS THIS MY ONLY CHOICE?
IS THIS OUR FATE?

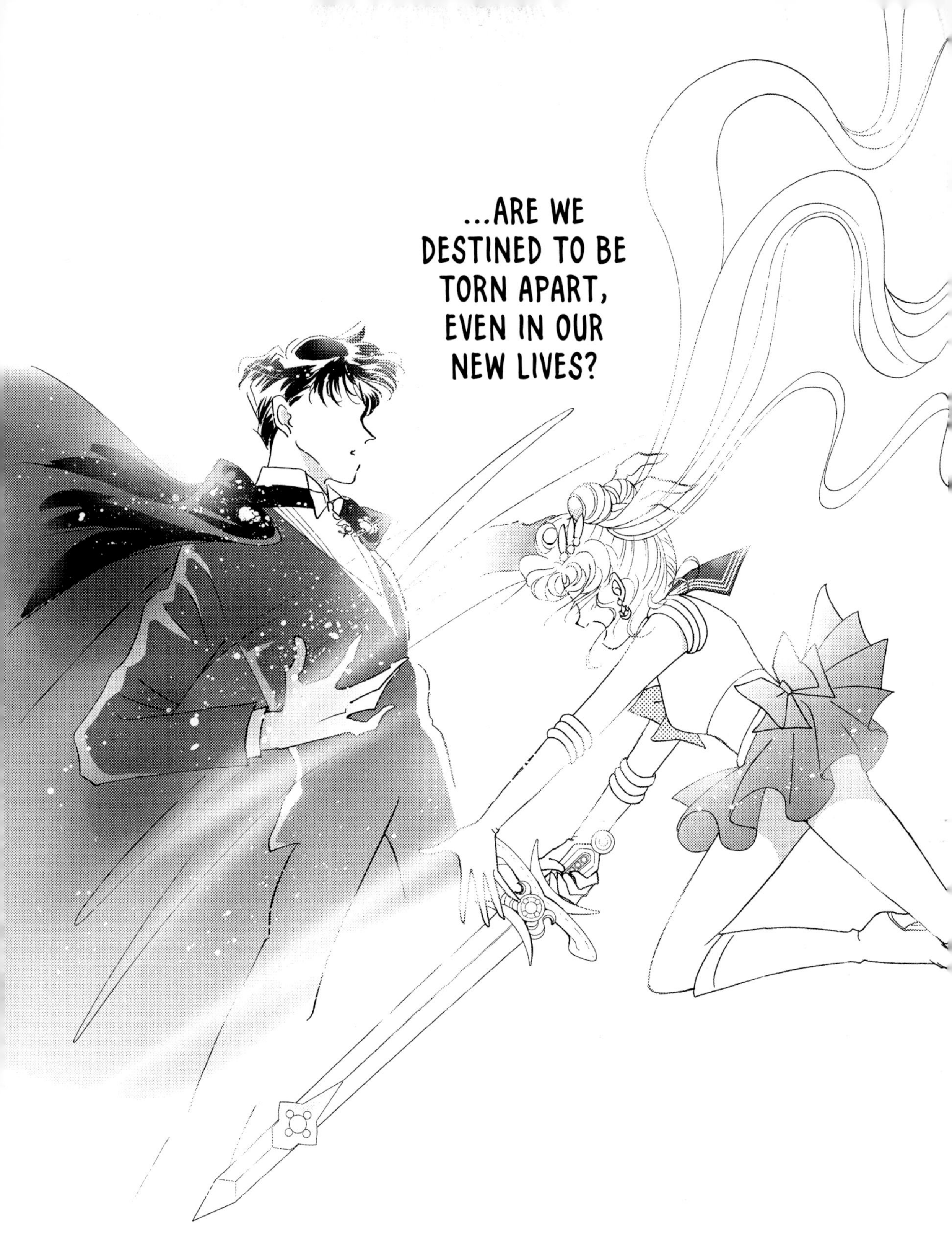
...ARE WE DESTINED TO BE TORN APART, EVEN IN OUR NEW LIVES?

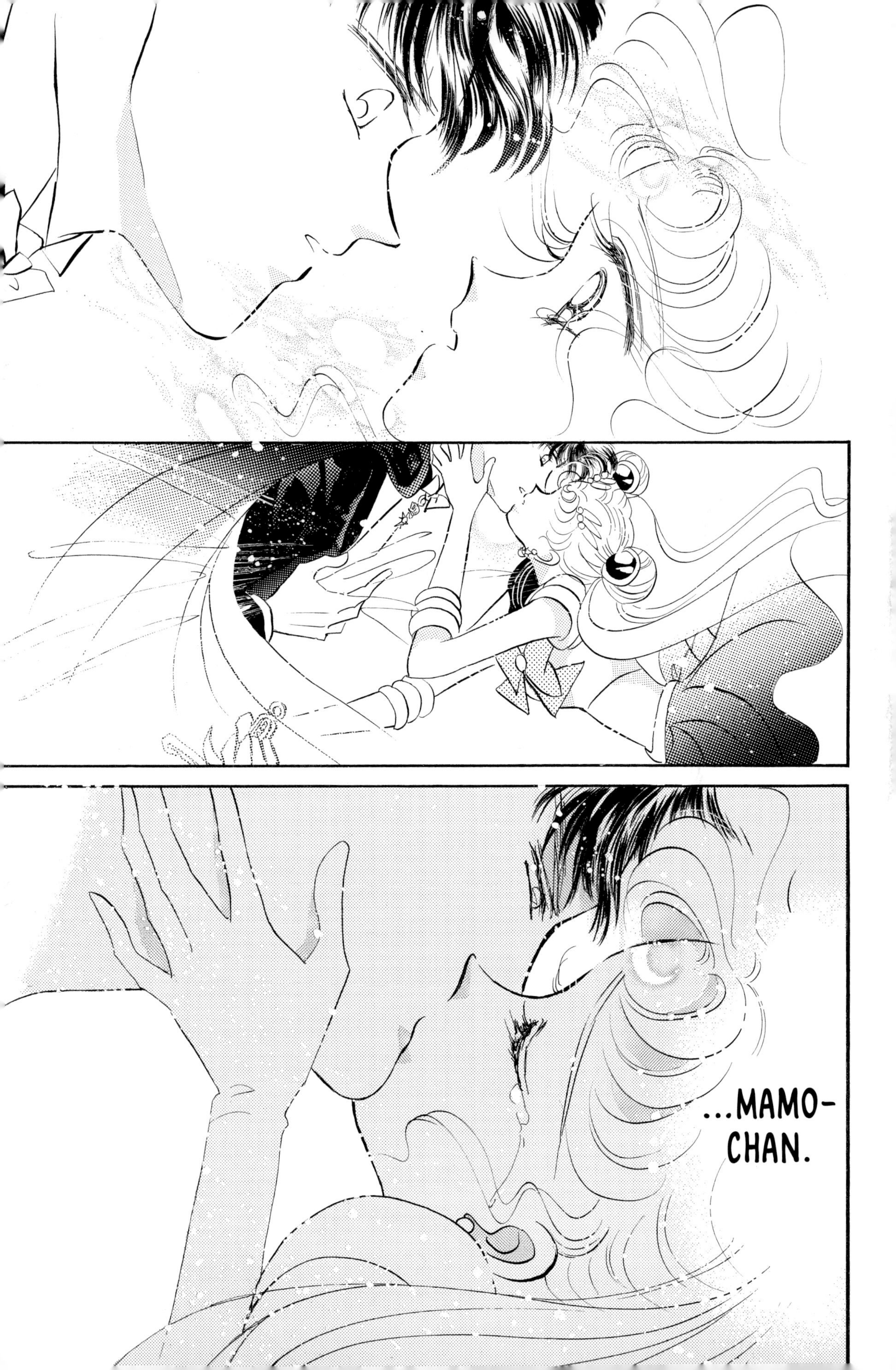
...MAMO-CHAN.

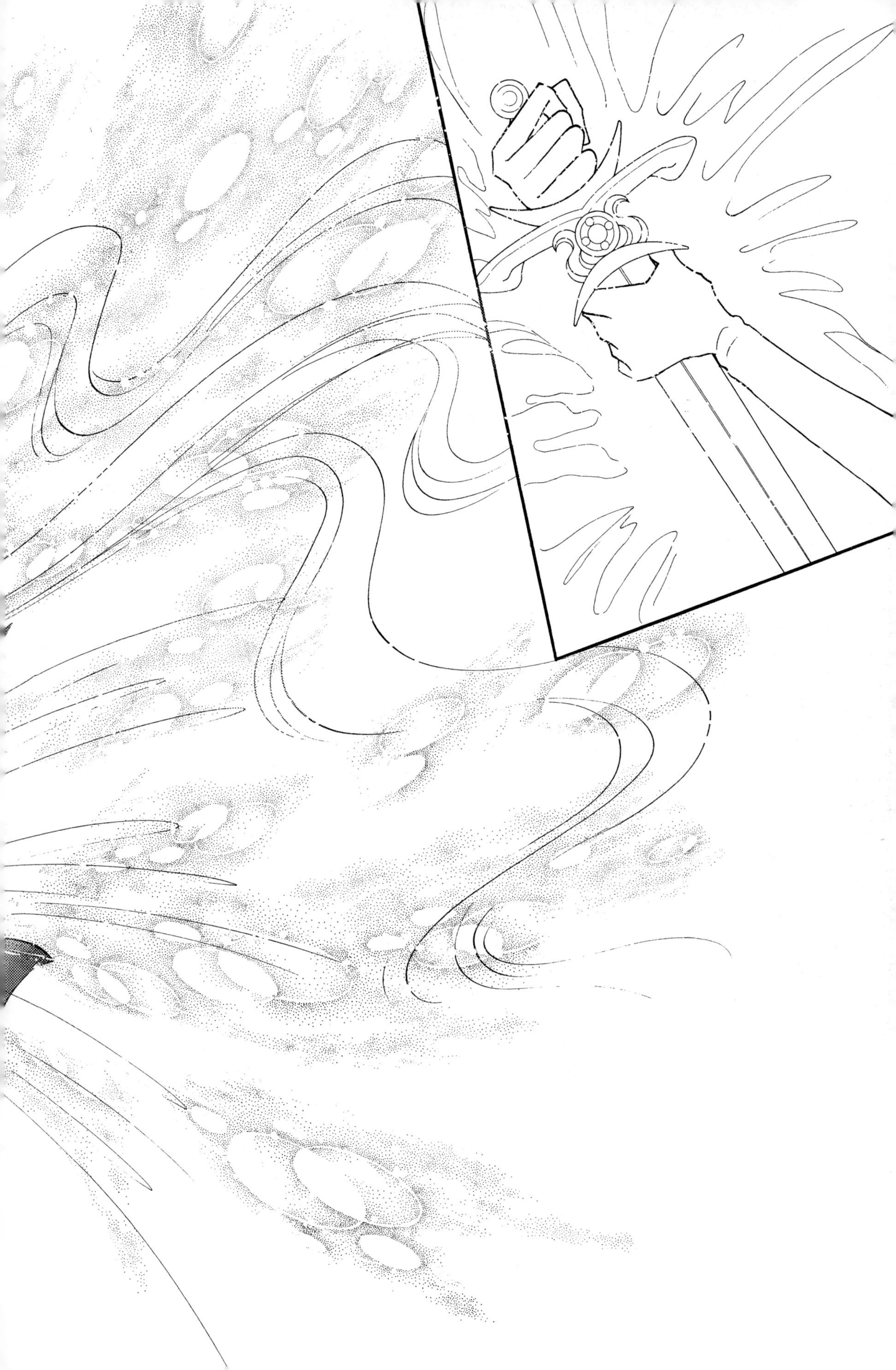

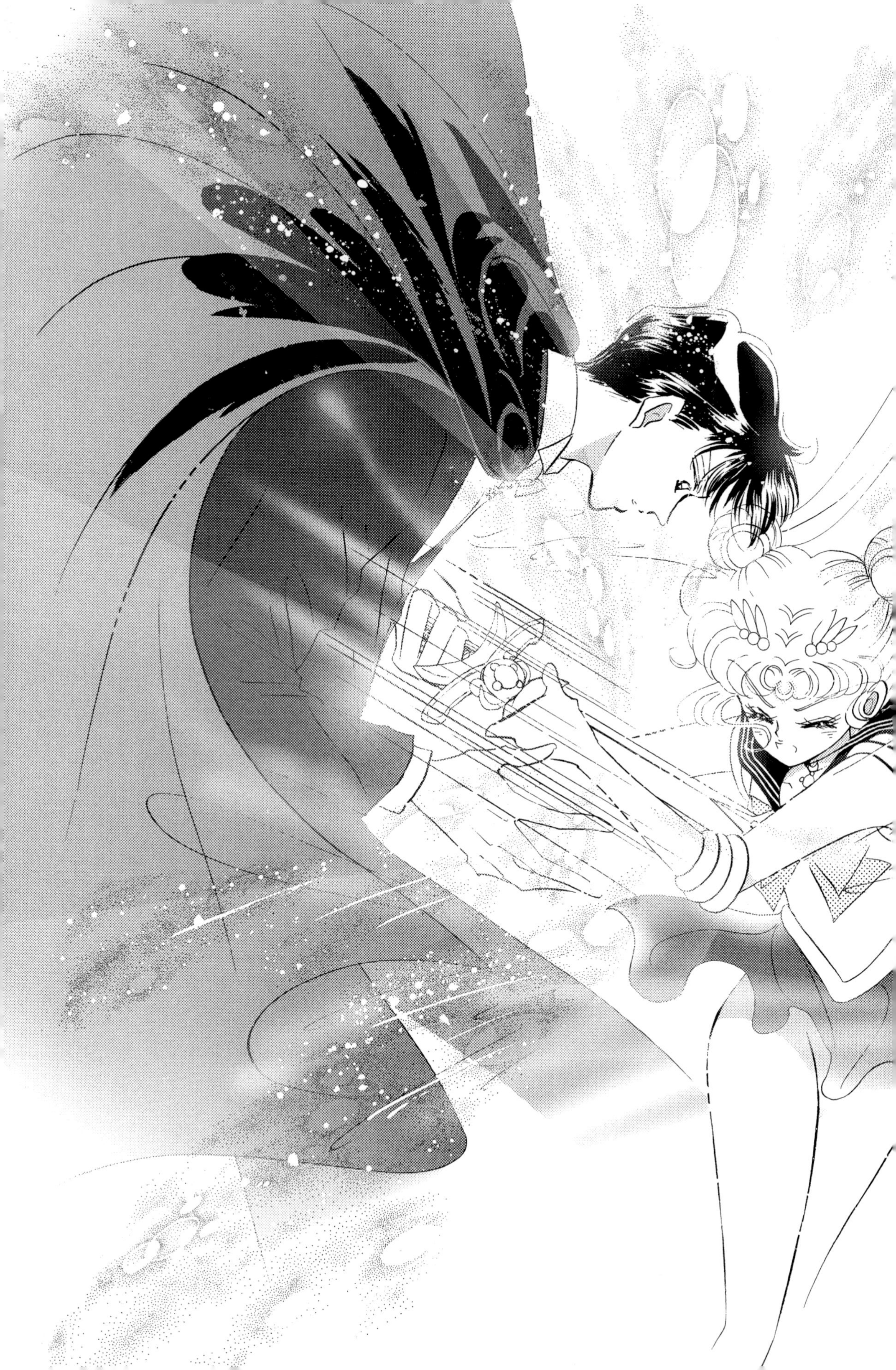

Pretty Guardian Sailor Moon

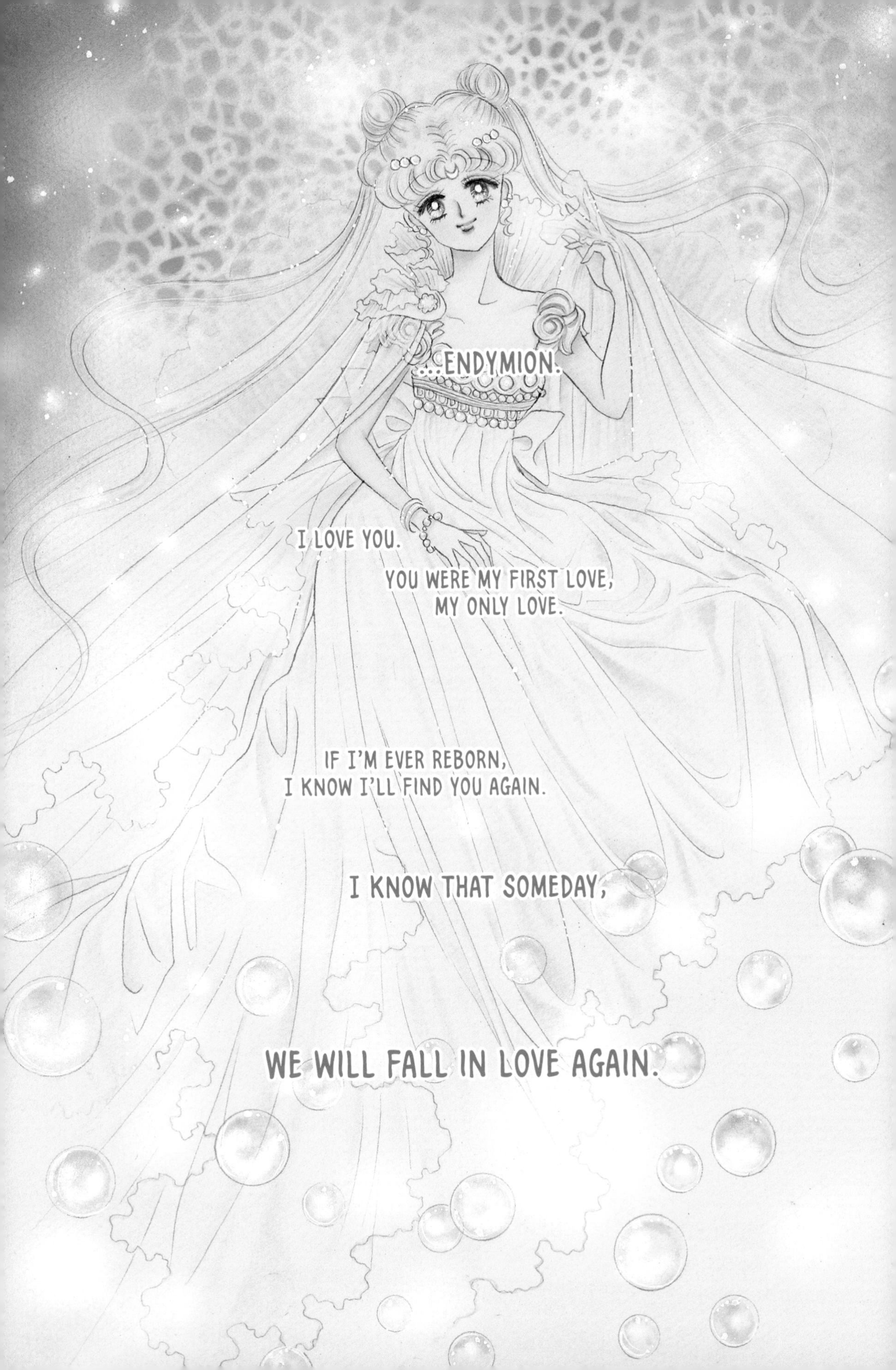
...ENDYMION.
I LOVE YOU.
YOU WERE MY FIRST LOVE, MY ONLY LOVE.
IF I'M EVER REBORN, I KNOW I'LL FIND YOU AGAIN.
I KNOW THAT SOMEDAY,
WE WILL FALL IN LOVE AGAIN.

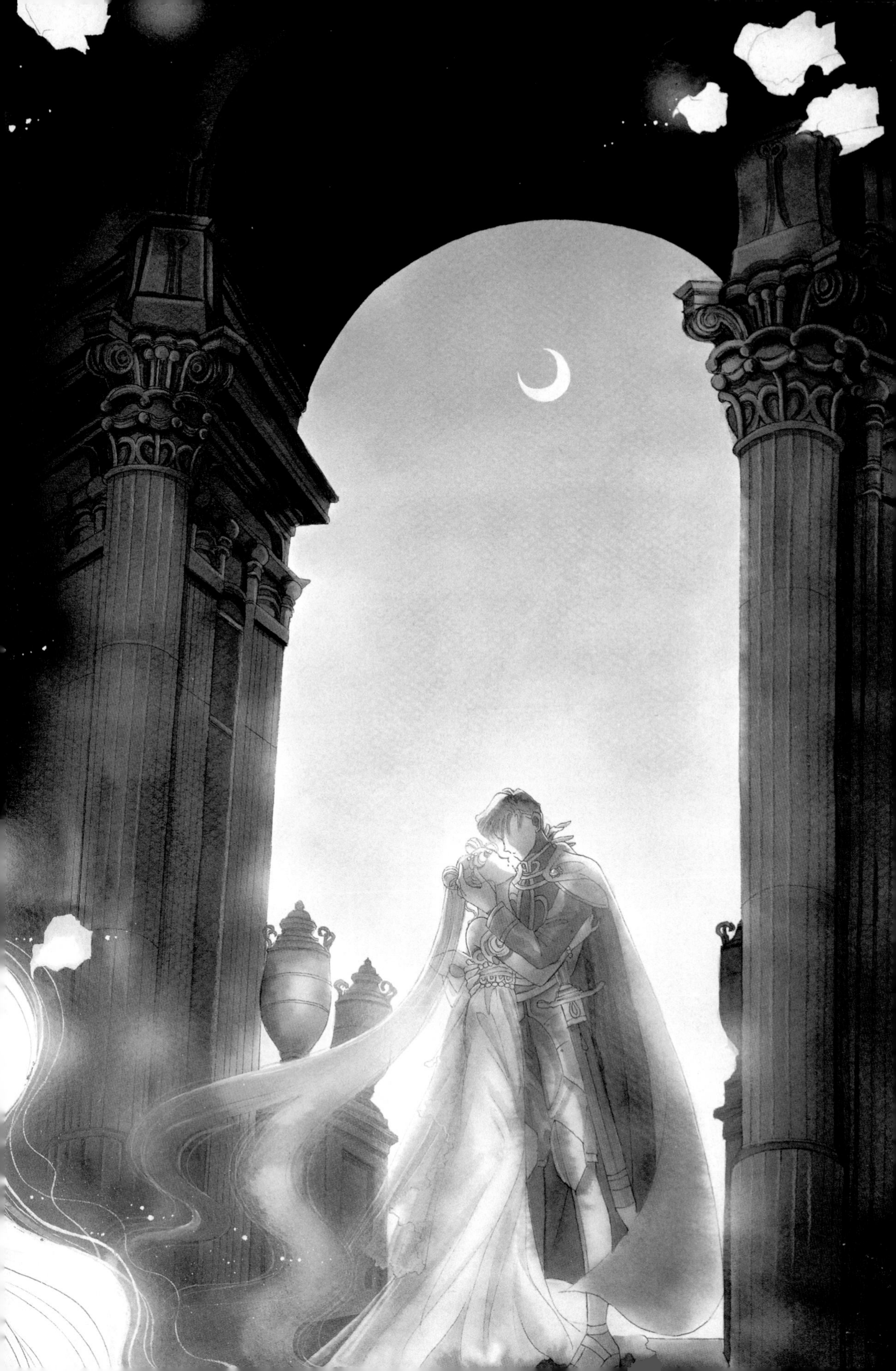

# Act. 13 Final Battle: Reincarnation

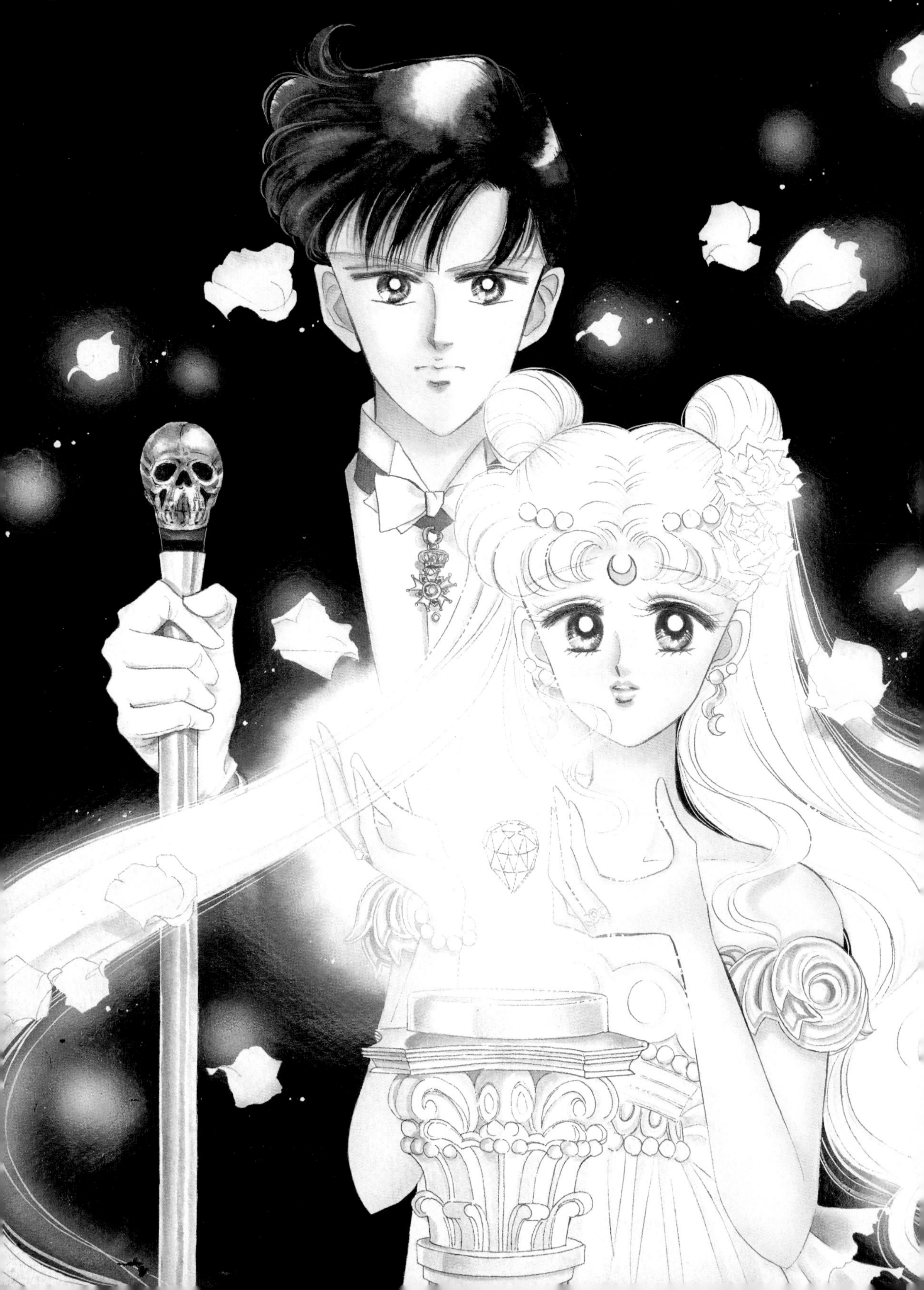

Pretty Guardian

Sailor Moon

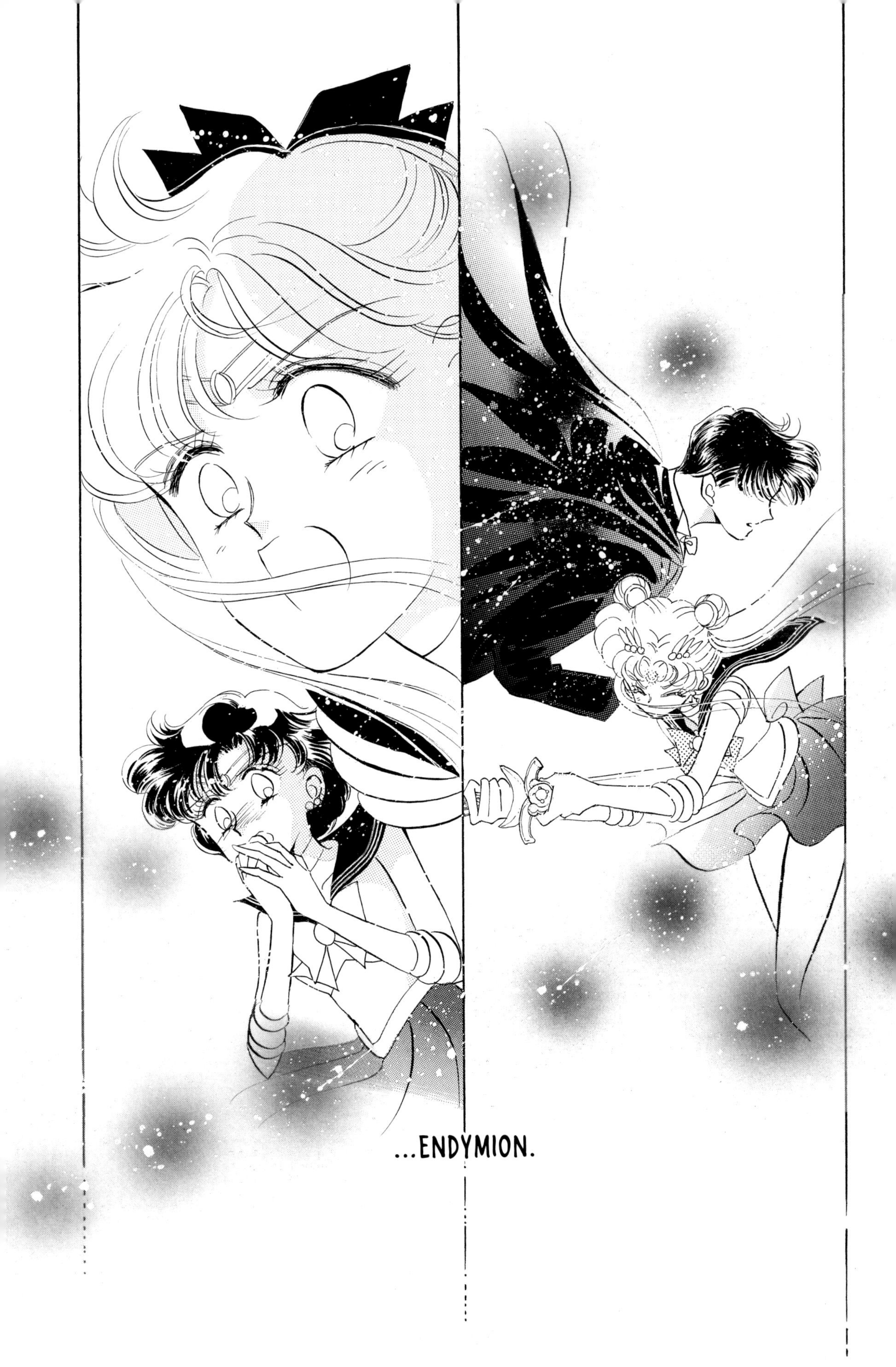
...ENDYMION.

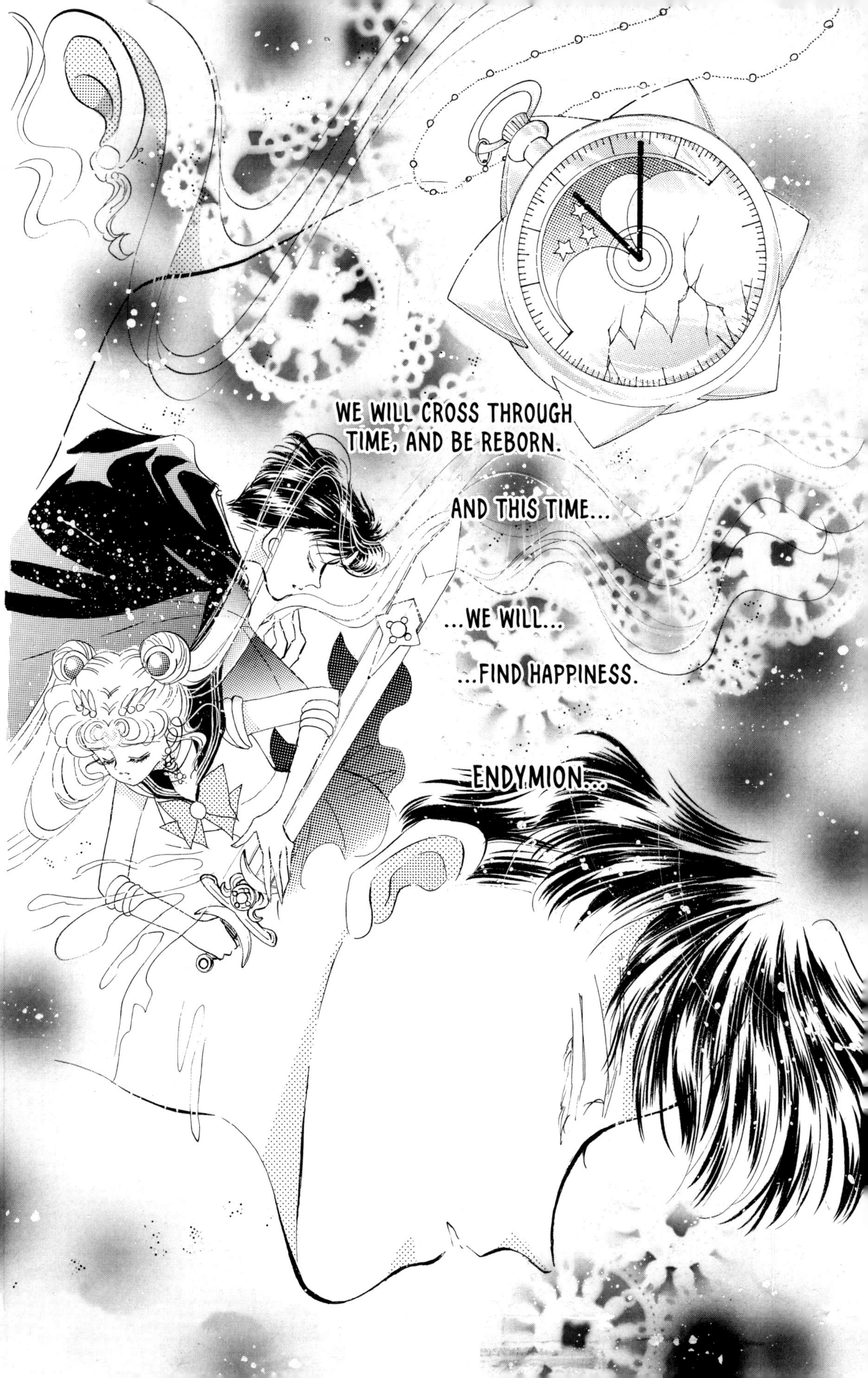
WE WILL CROSS THROUGH TIME, AND BE REBORN.
AND THIS TIME...
...WE WILL...
...FIND HAPPINESS.
ENDYMION...

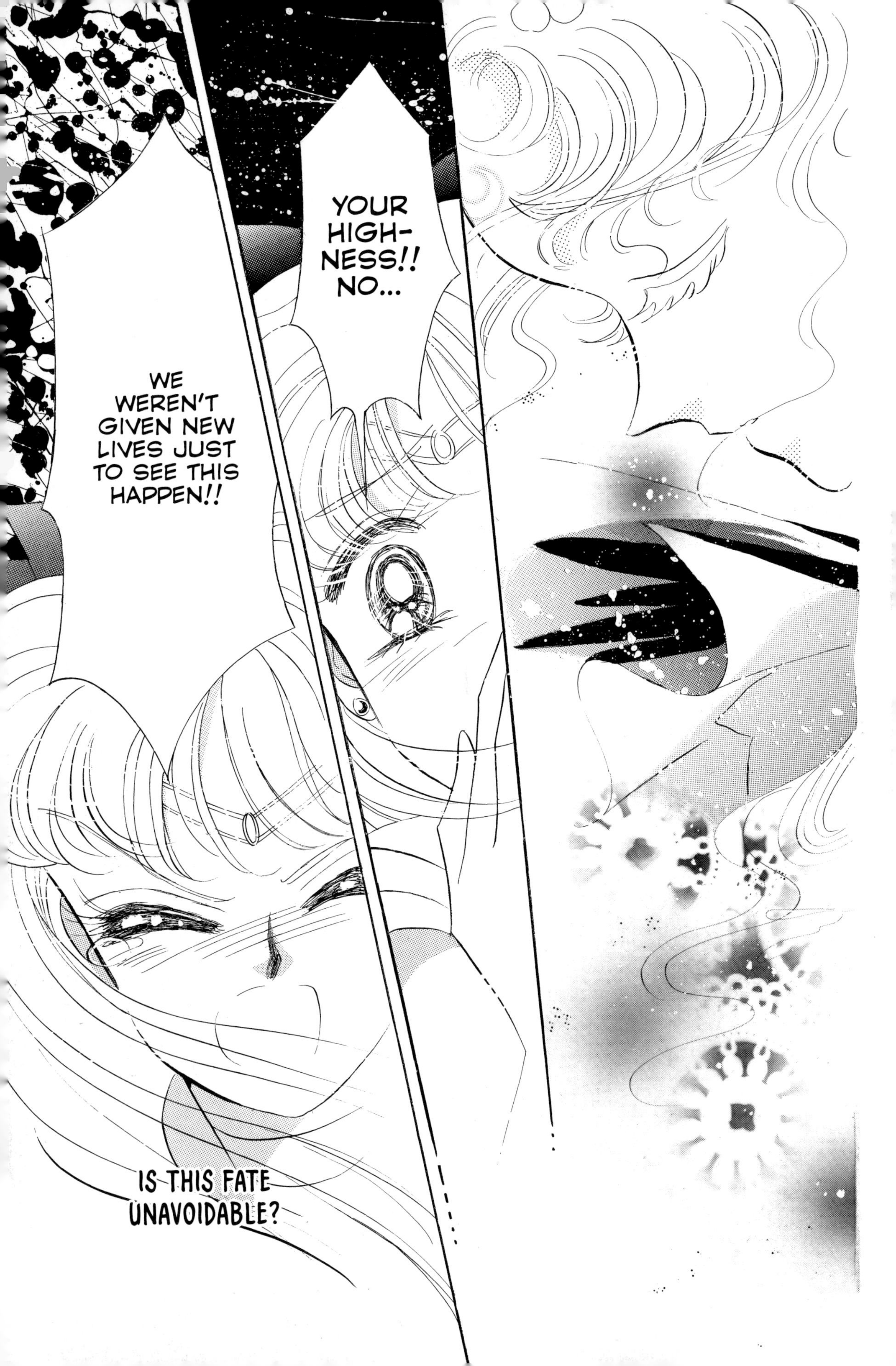
YOUR HIGH-NESS!! NO...
WE WEREN'T GIVEN NEW LIVES JUST TO SEE THIS HAPPEN!!
IS THIS FATE UNAVOIDABLE?

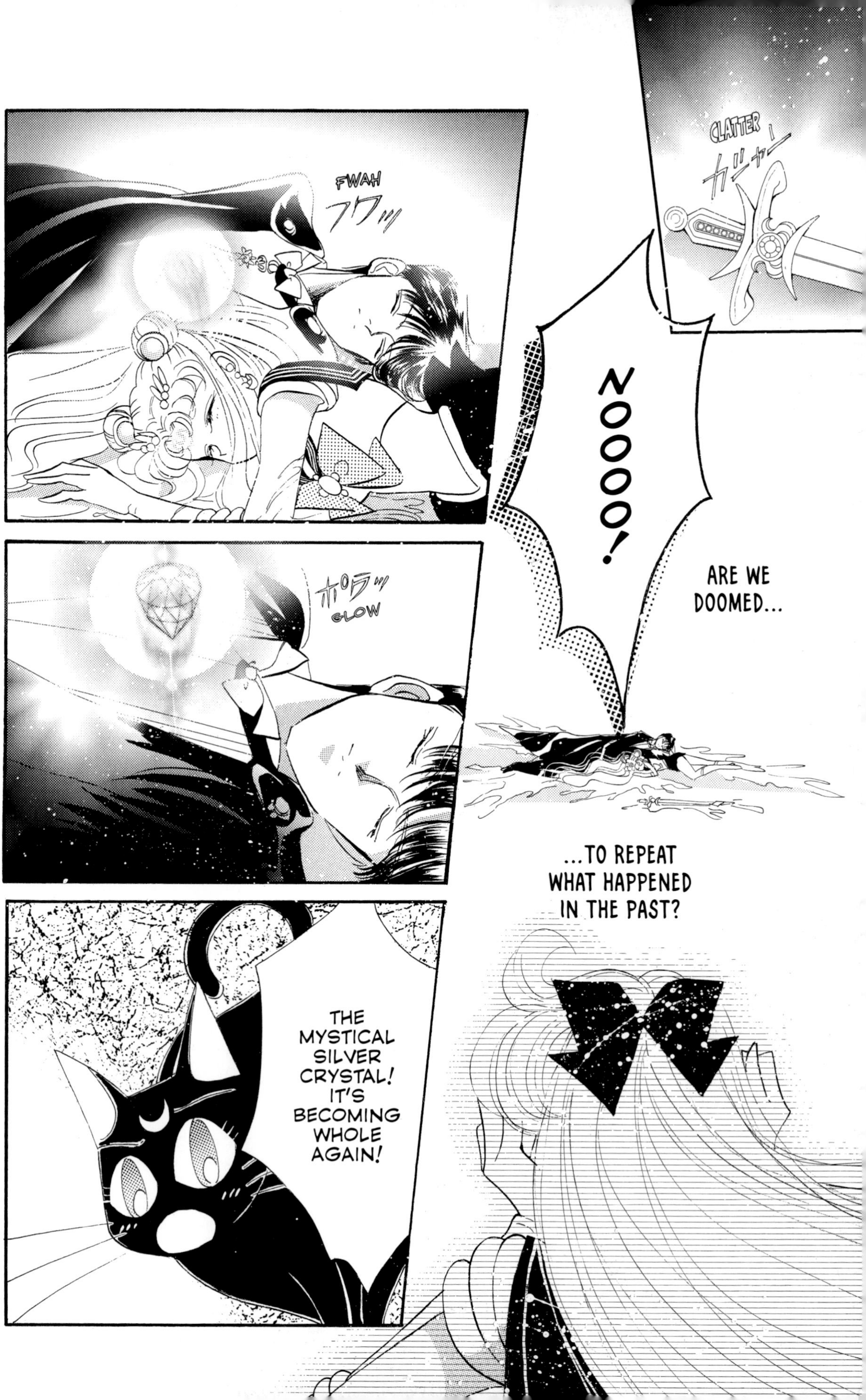
CLATTER
FWAH
フワッ
NOOOOO!
GLOW
ARE WE DOOMED...
...TO REPEAT WHAT HAPPENED IN THE PAST?
THE MYSTICAL SILVER CRYSTAL! IT'S BECOMING WHOLE AGAIN!

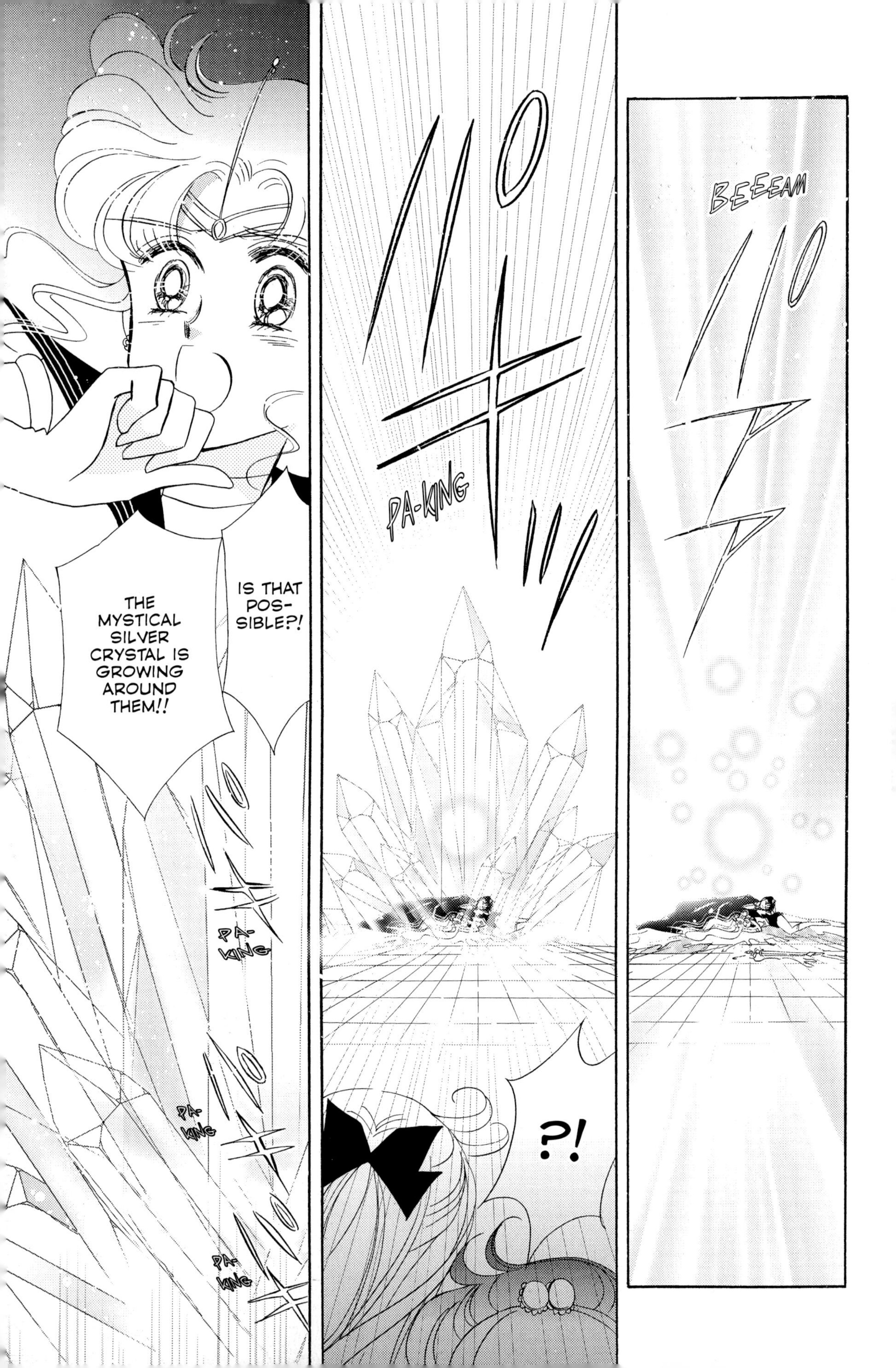

BEEEAM
PA-KING
?!
IS THAT POS-SIBLE?!
THE MYSTICAL SILVER CRYSTAL IS GROWING AROUND THEM!!
PA-KING
PA-KING
PA-KING

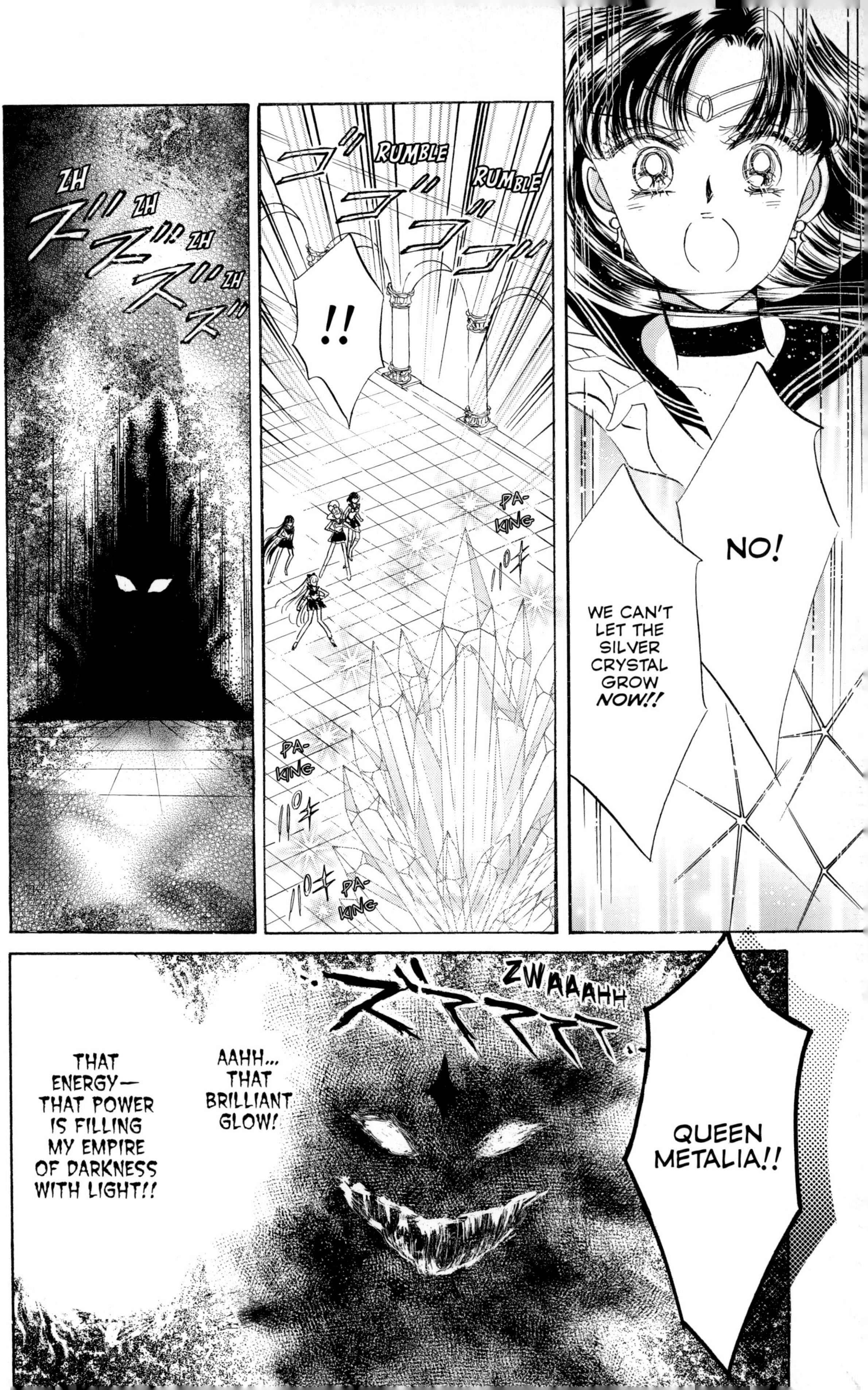

NO!
WE CAN'T LET THE SILVER CRYSTAL GROW NOW!!
RUMBLE
RUMBLE
!!
PA-KING
PA-KING
PA-KING
ZH
ZH
ZH
ZH
QUEEN METALIA!!
ZWAAAHH
AAHH... THAT BRILLIANT GLOW!
THAT ENERGY— THAT POWER IS FILLING MY EMPIRE OF DARKNESS WITH LIGHT!!

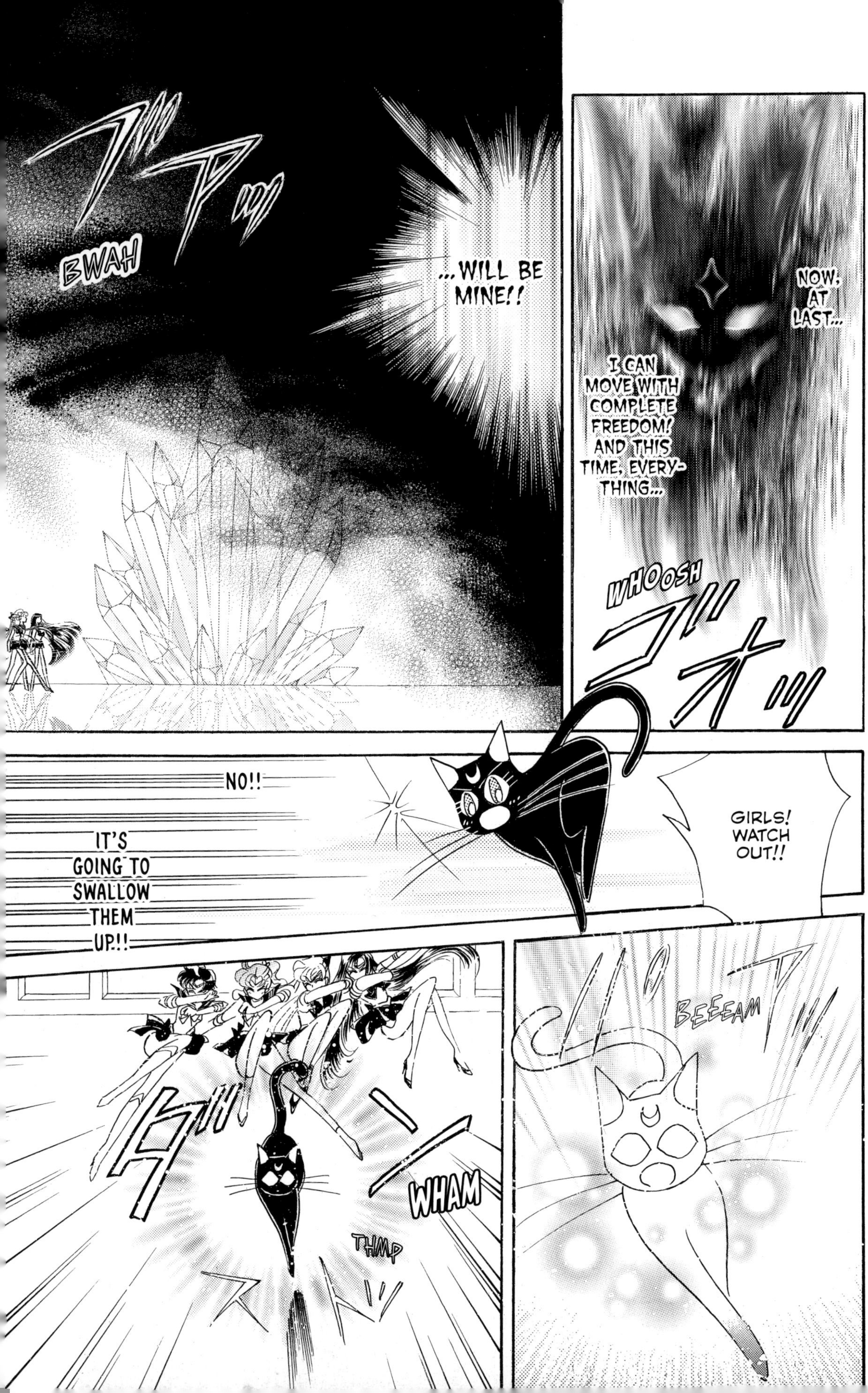
NOW, AT LAST...
I CAN MOVE WITH COMPLETE FREEDOM! AND THIS TIME, EVERY-THING...
WHOOSH
BWAH
...WILL BE MINE!!
GIRLS! WATCH OUT!!
NO!!
IT'S GOING TO SWALLOW THEM UP!!
BEEEAM
WHAM
THMP

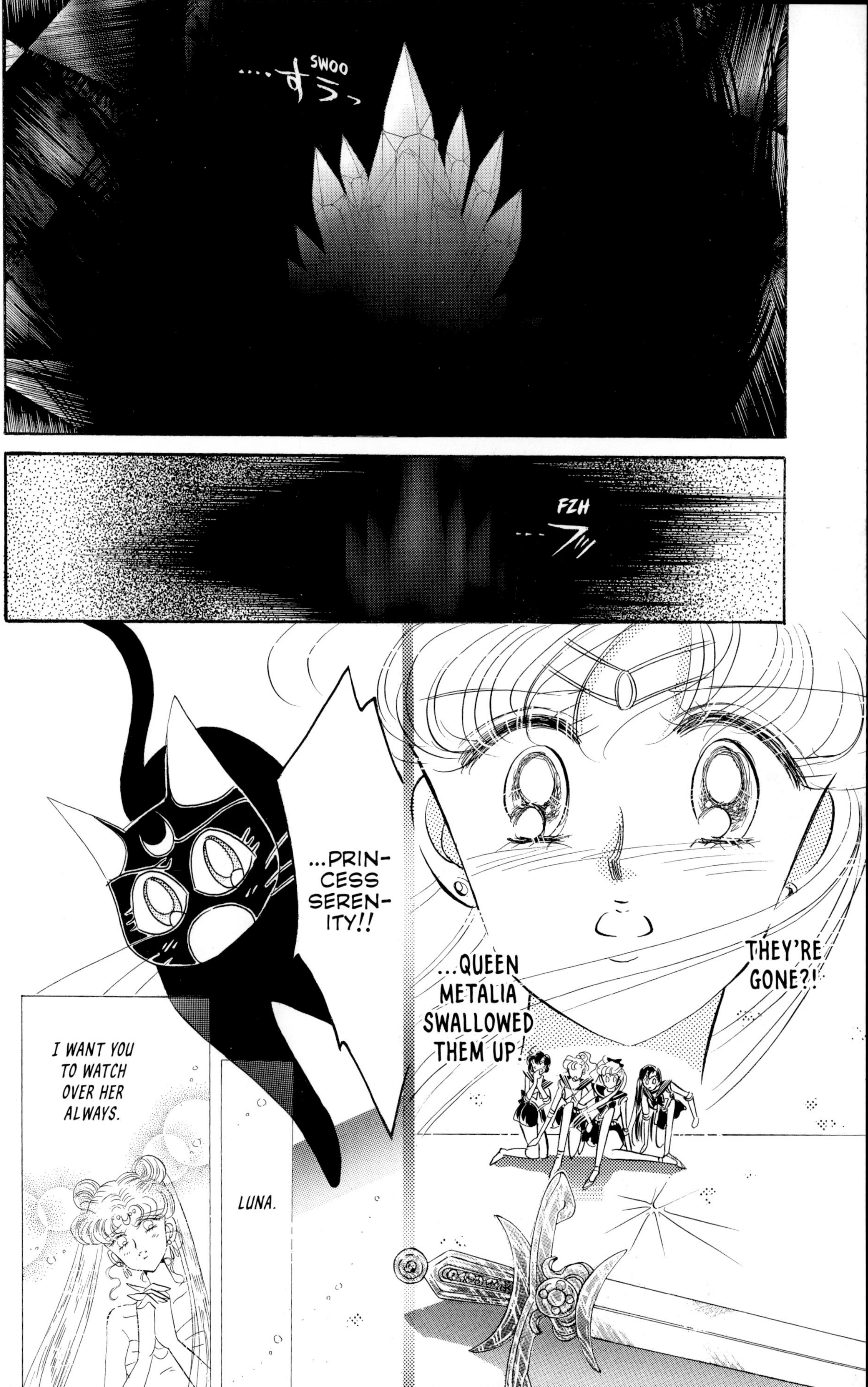
SWOO
FZH
フッ
THEY'RE GONE?!
...QUEEN METALIA SWALLOWED THEM UP!
...PRIN-CESS SEREN-ITY!!
I WANT YOU TO WATCH OVER HER ALWAYS.
LUNA.

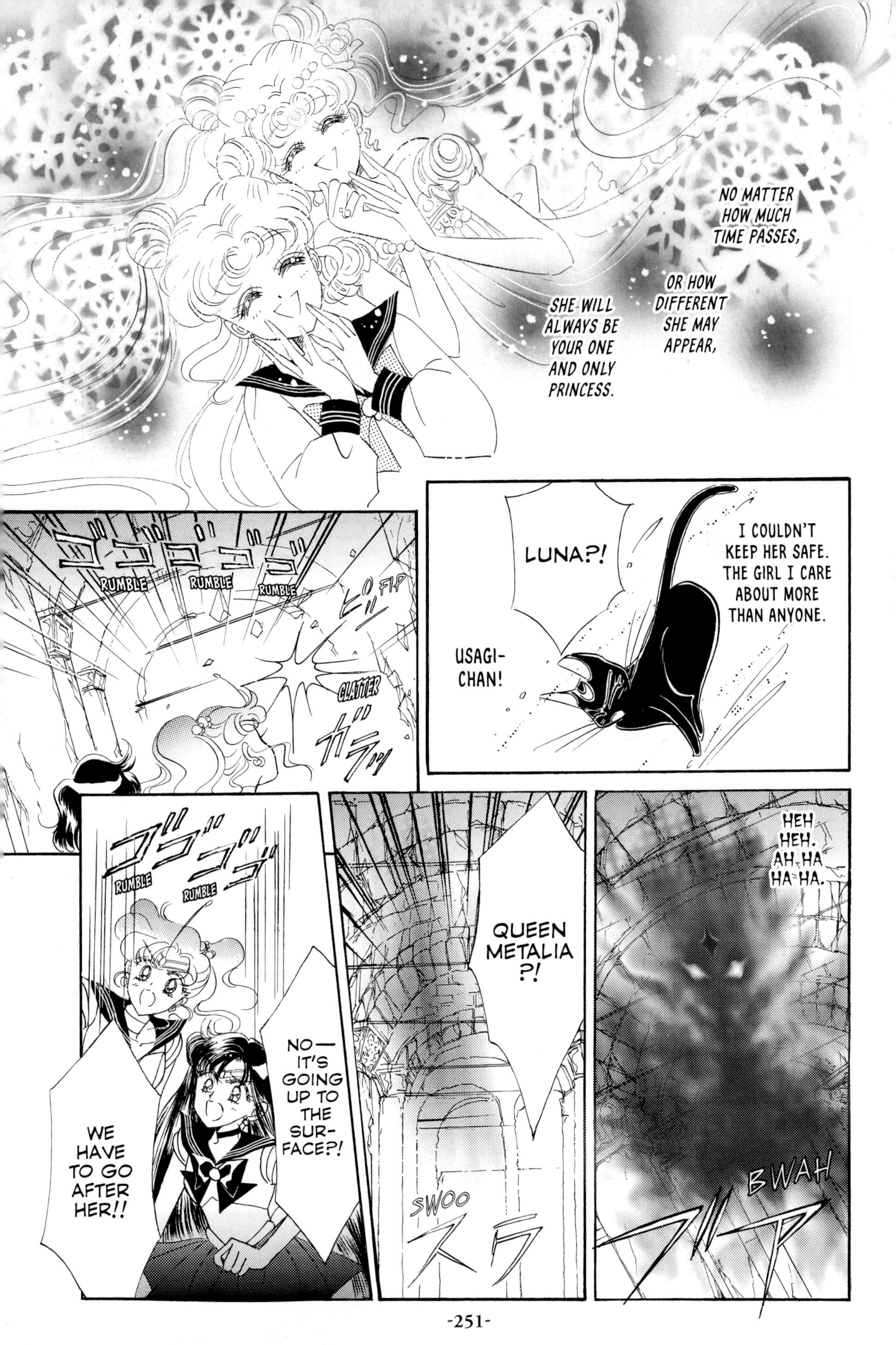
NO MATTER HOW MUCH TIME PASSES,
OR HOW DIFFERENT SHE MAY APPEAR,
SHE WILL ALWAYS BE YOUR ONE AND ONLY PRINCESS.
I COULDN'T KEEP HER SAFE. THE GIRL I CARE ABOUT MORE THAN ANYONE.
LUNA?!
USAGI-CHAN!
RUMBLE
RUMBLE
RUMBLE
FIP
CLATTER
HEH HEH. AH HA HA HA.
BWAH
QUEEN METALIA?!
SWOO
RUMBLE
RUMBLE
NO— IT'S GOING UP TO THE SURFACE?!
WE HAVE TO GO AFTER HER!!

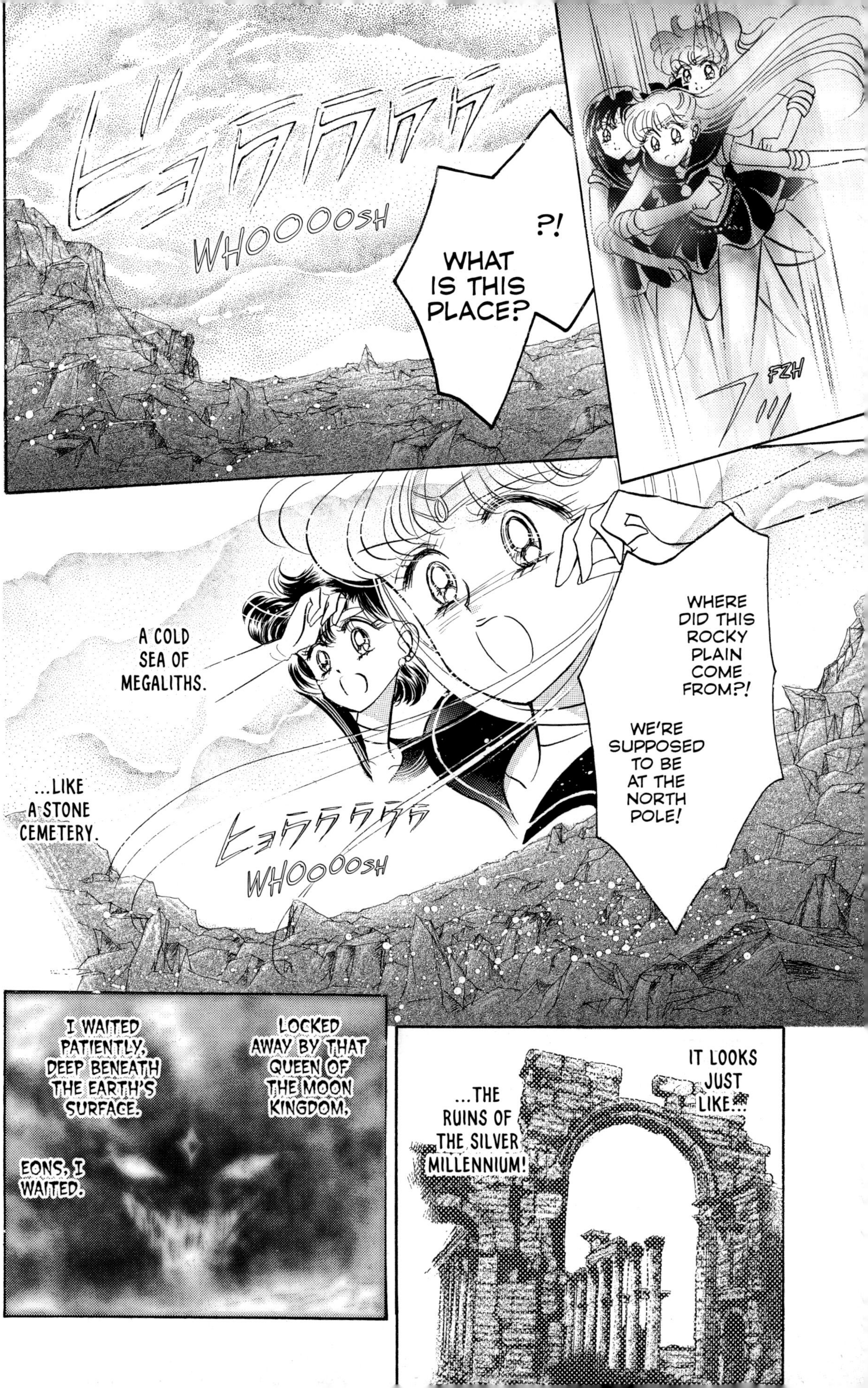

?!
WHAT IS THIS PLACE?
フッ
FZH
ビュラララララ
WHOOOOSH
WHERE DID THIS ROCKY PLAIN COME FROM?!
WE'RE SUPPOSED TO BE AT THE NORTH POLE!
A COLD SEA OF MEGALITHS.
...LIKE A STONE CEMETERY.
ヒュラララララ
WHOOOOSH
IT LOOKS JUST LIKE...
...THE RUINS OF THE SILVER MILLENNIUM!
LOCKED AWAY BY THAT QUEEN OF THE MOON KINGDOM,
I WAITED PATIENTLY, DEEP BENEATH THE EARTH'S SURFACE.
EONS, I WAITED.

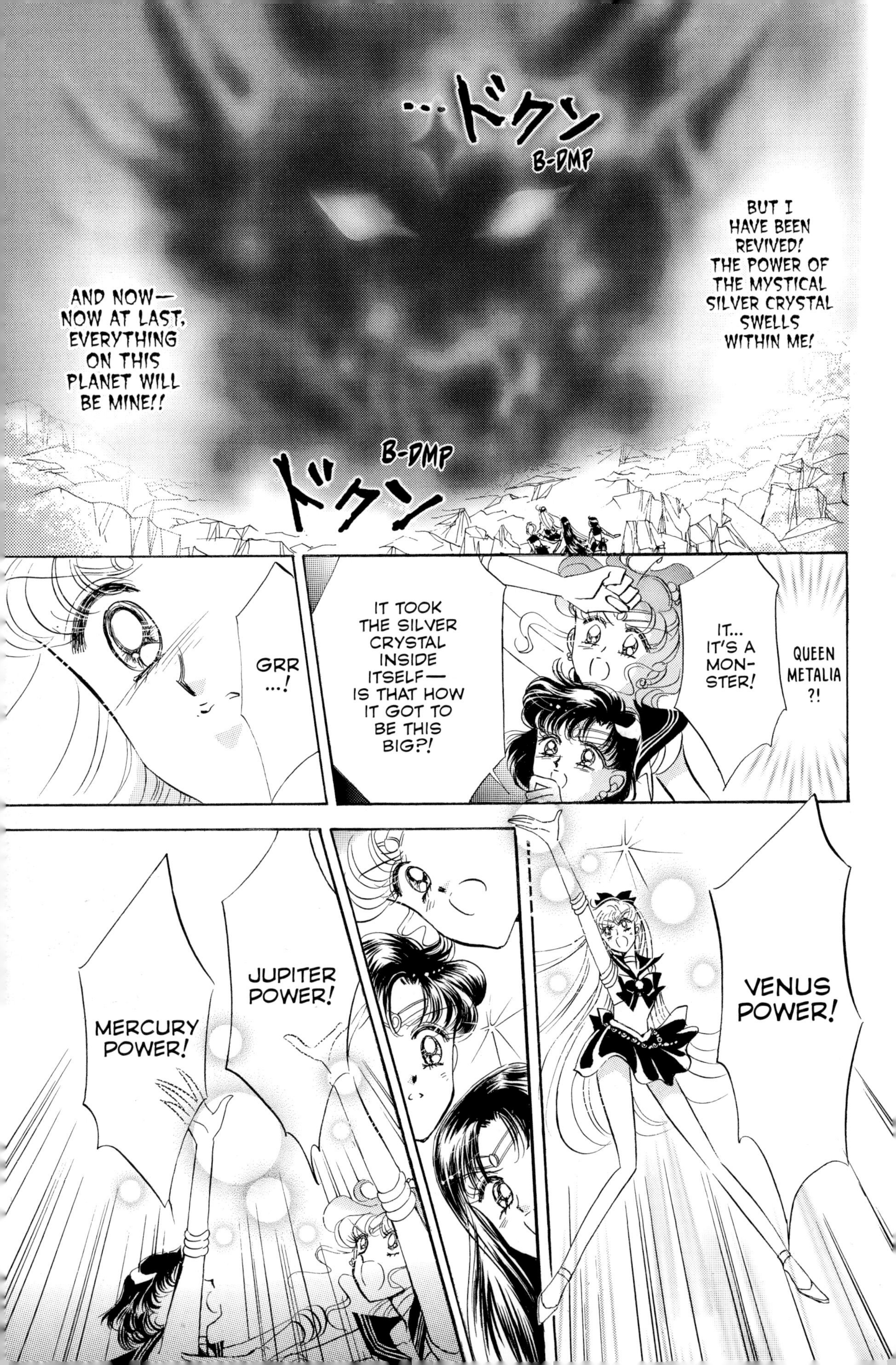
…ドクン
B-DMP
BUT I HAVE BEEN REVIVED! THE POWER OF THE MYSTICAL SILVER CRYSTAL SWELLS WITHIN ME!
AND NOW—NOW AT LAST, EVERYTHING ON THIS PLANET WILL BE MINE!!
B-DMP
ドクン
QUEEN METALIA ?!
IT… IT'S A MON-STER!
IT TOOK THE SILVER CRYSTAL INSIDE ITSELF—IS THAT HOW IT GOT TO BE THIS BIG?!
GRR …!
VENUS POWER!
JUPITER POWER!
MERCURY POWER!

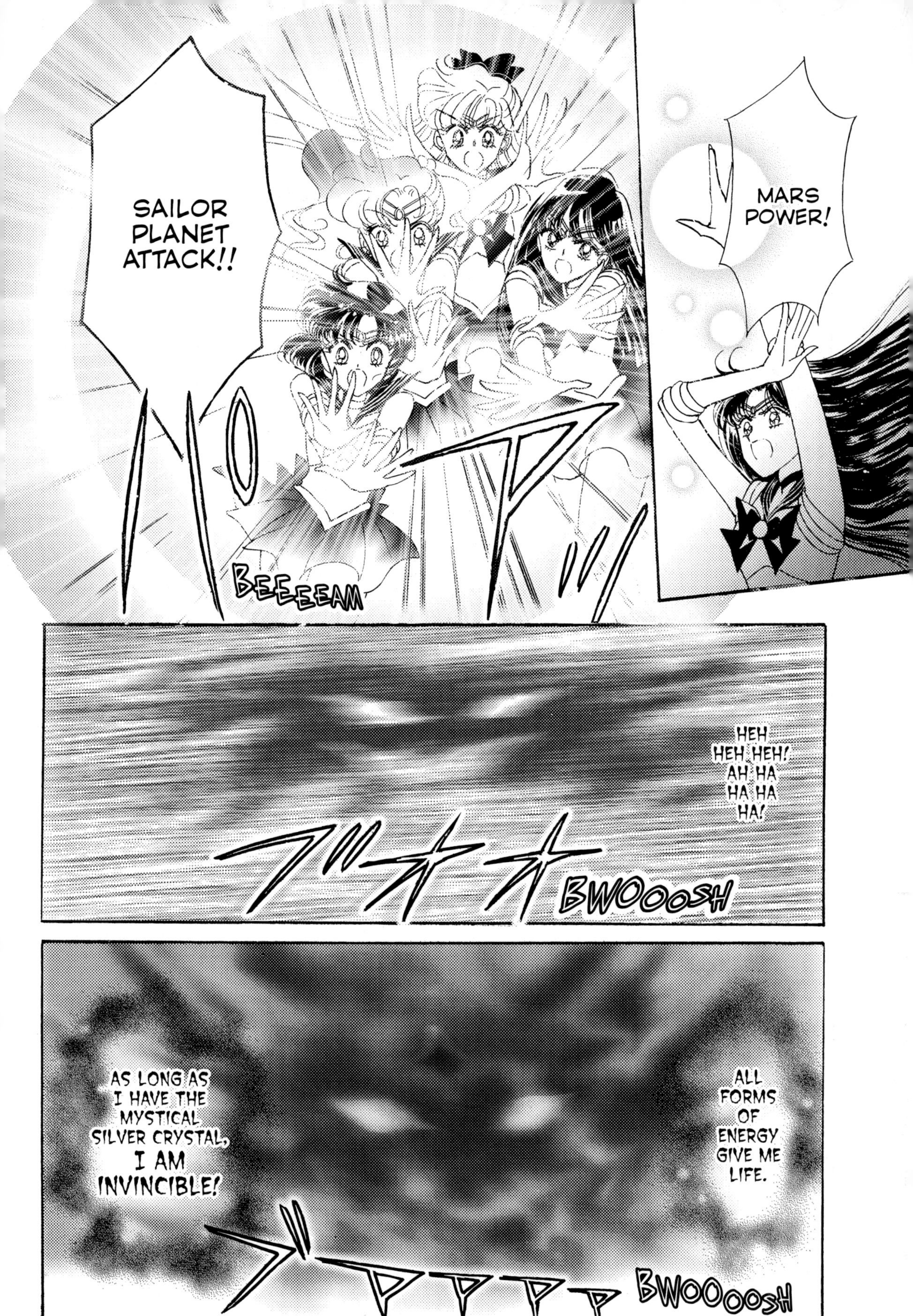
MARS POWER!
SAILOR PLANET ATTACK!!
BEEEEEAM
HEH HEH HEH! AH HA HA HA HA!
BWOOOOSH
ALL FORMS OF ENERGY GIVE ME LIFE.
AS LONG AS I HAVE THE MYSTICAL SILVER CRYSTAL, I AM INVINCIBLE!
BWOOOOSH

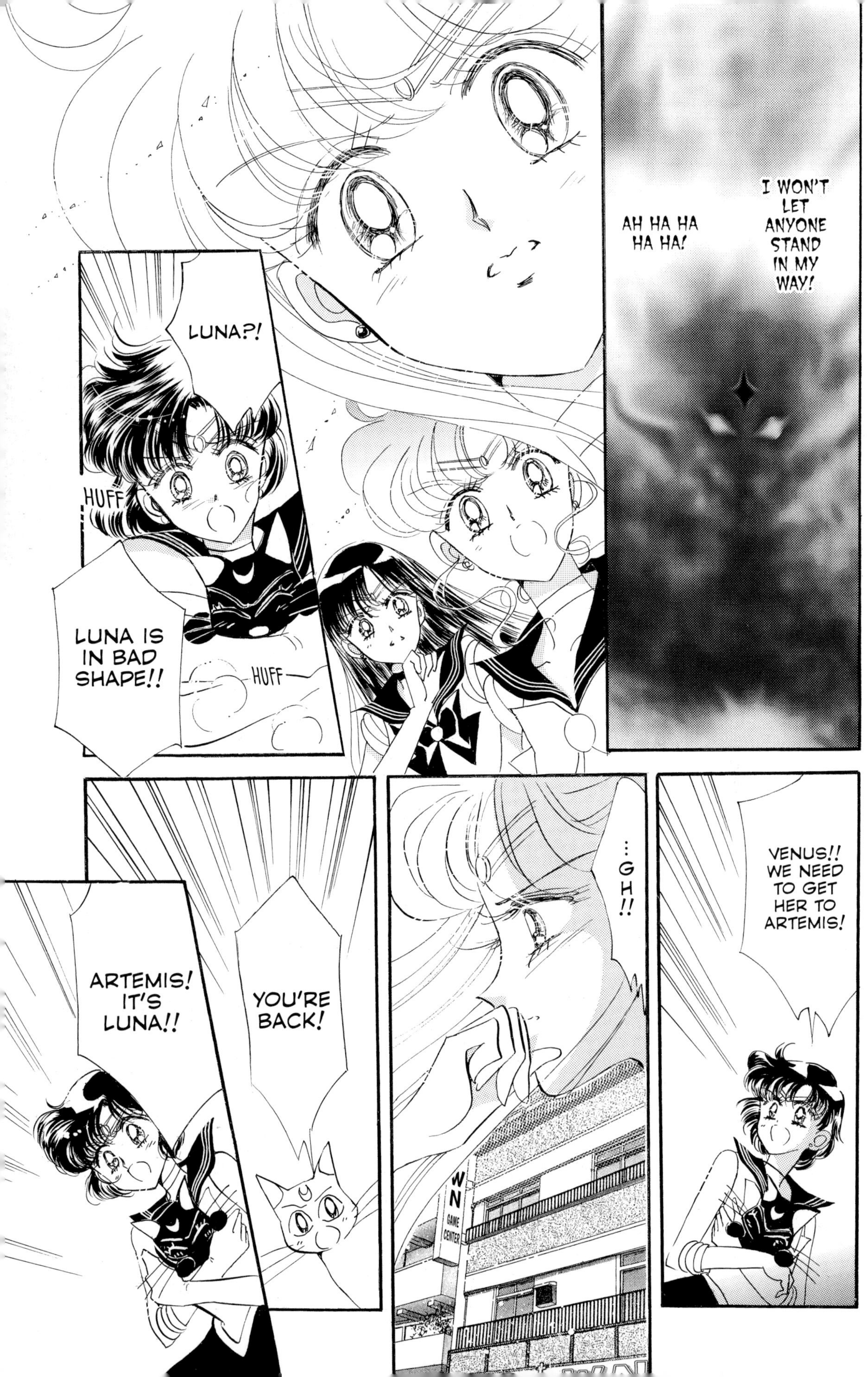
I WON'T LET ANYONE STAND IN MY WAY!
AH HA HA HA HA!
LUNA?!
HUFF
LUNA IS IN BAD SHAPE!!
HUFF
VENUS!! WE NEED TO GET HER TO ARTEMIS!
...GH!!
WN GAME CENTER
YOU'RE BACK!
ARTEMIS! IT'S LUNA!!

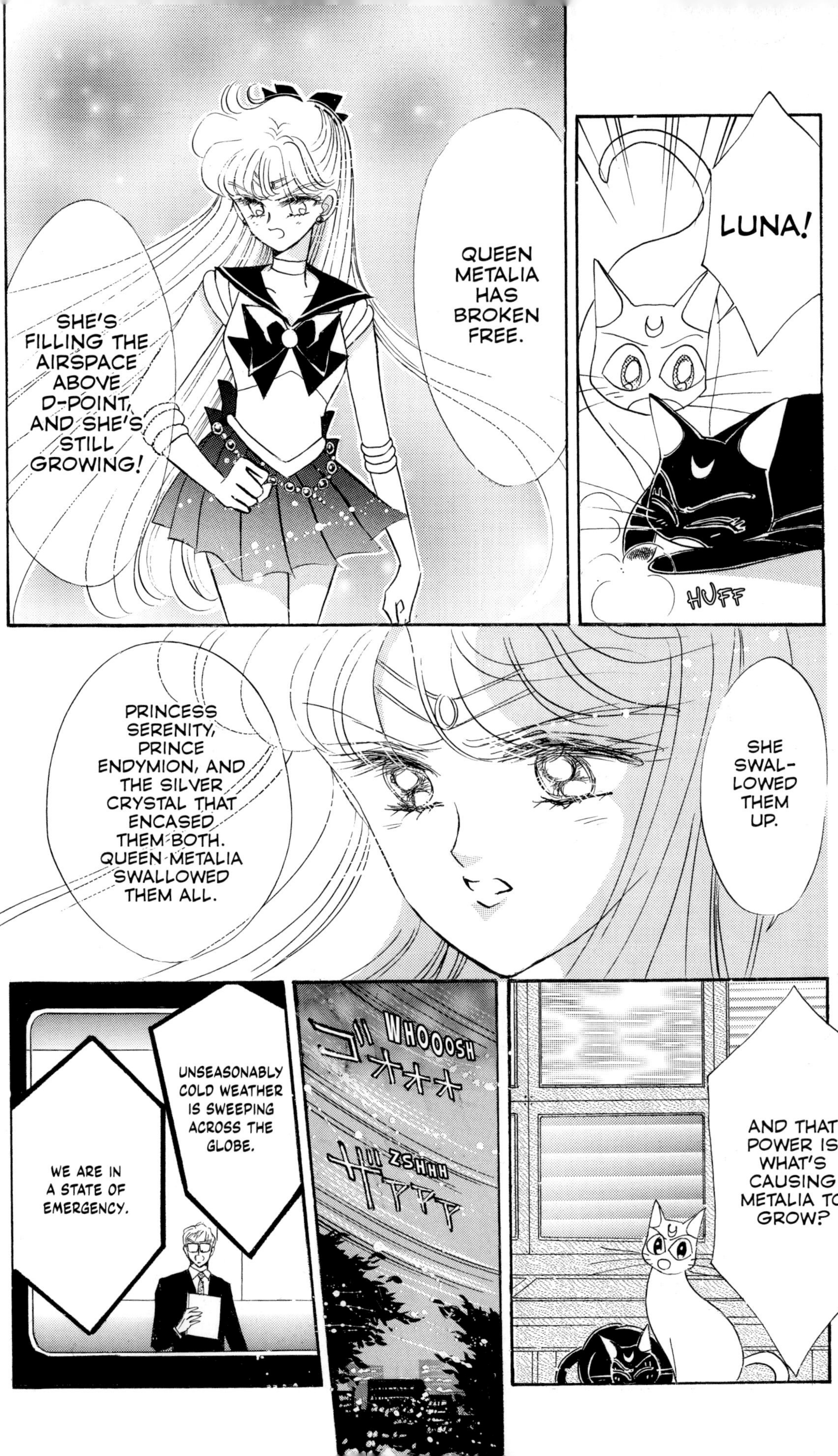
LUNA!
HUFF
QUEEN METALIA HAS BROKEN FREE.
SHE'S FILLING THE AIRSPACE ABOVE D-POINT, AND SHE'S STILL GROWING!
SHE SWAL-LOWED THEM UP.
PRINCESS SERENITY, PRINCE ENDYMION, AND THE SILVER CRYSTAL THAT ENCASED THEM BOTH. QUEEN METALIA SWALLOWED THEM ALL.
AND THAT POWER IS WHAT'S CAUSING METALIA TO GROW?
WHOOOSH
ZSHHH
UNSEASONABLY COLD WEATHER IS SWEEPING ACROSS THE GLOBE.
WE ARE IN A STATE OF EMERGENCY.

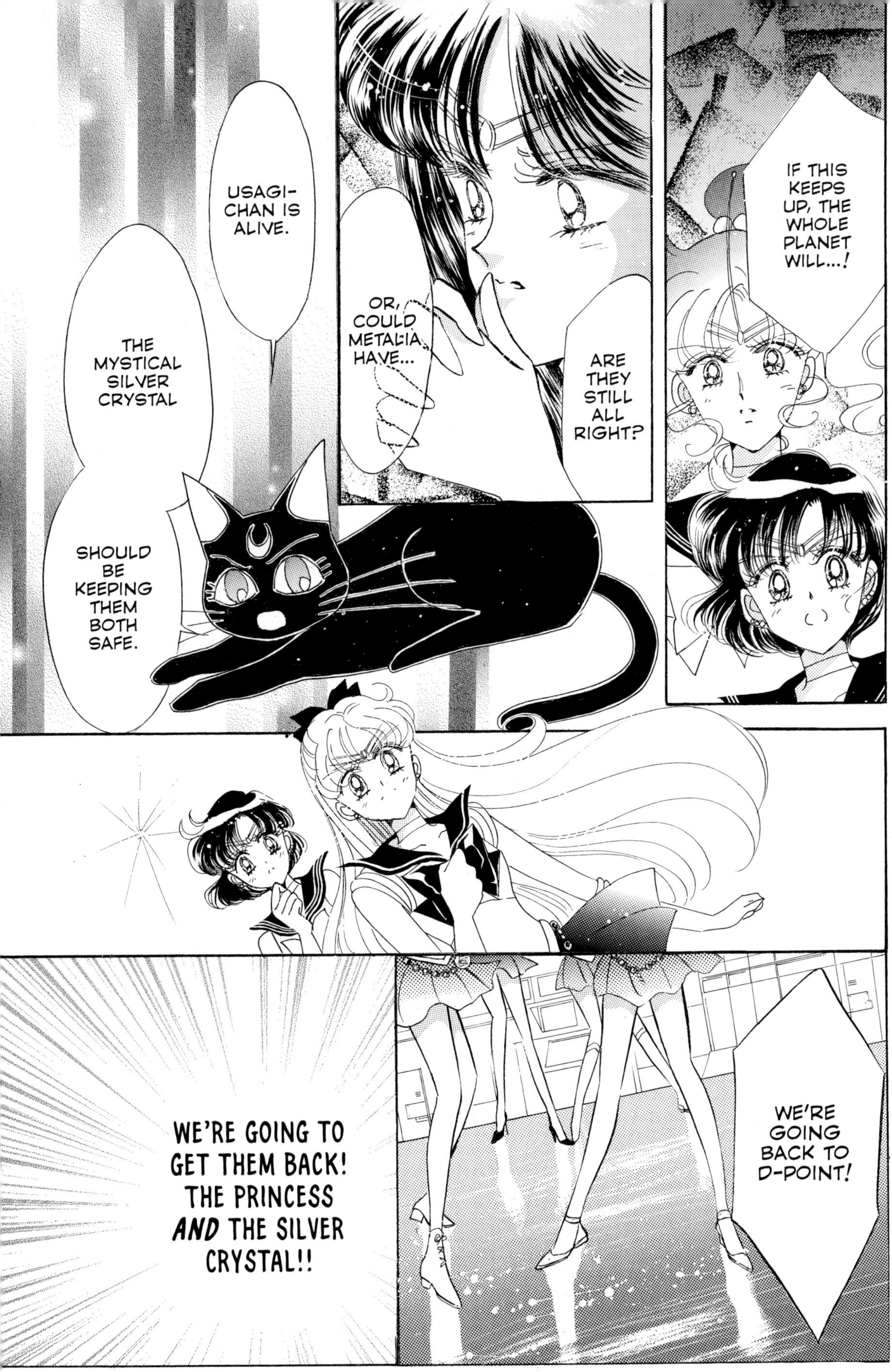
IF THIS KEEPS UP, THE WHOLE PLANET WILL...!
ARE THEY STILL ALL RIGHT?
OR, COULD METALIA HAVE...
USAGI-CHAN IS ALIVE.
THE MYSTICAL SILVER CRYSTAL
SHOULD BE KEEPING THEM BOTH SAFE.
WE'RE GOING BACK TO D-POINT!
WE'RE GOING TO GET THEM BACK! THE PRINCESS *AND* THE SILVER CRYSTAL!!

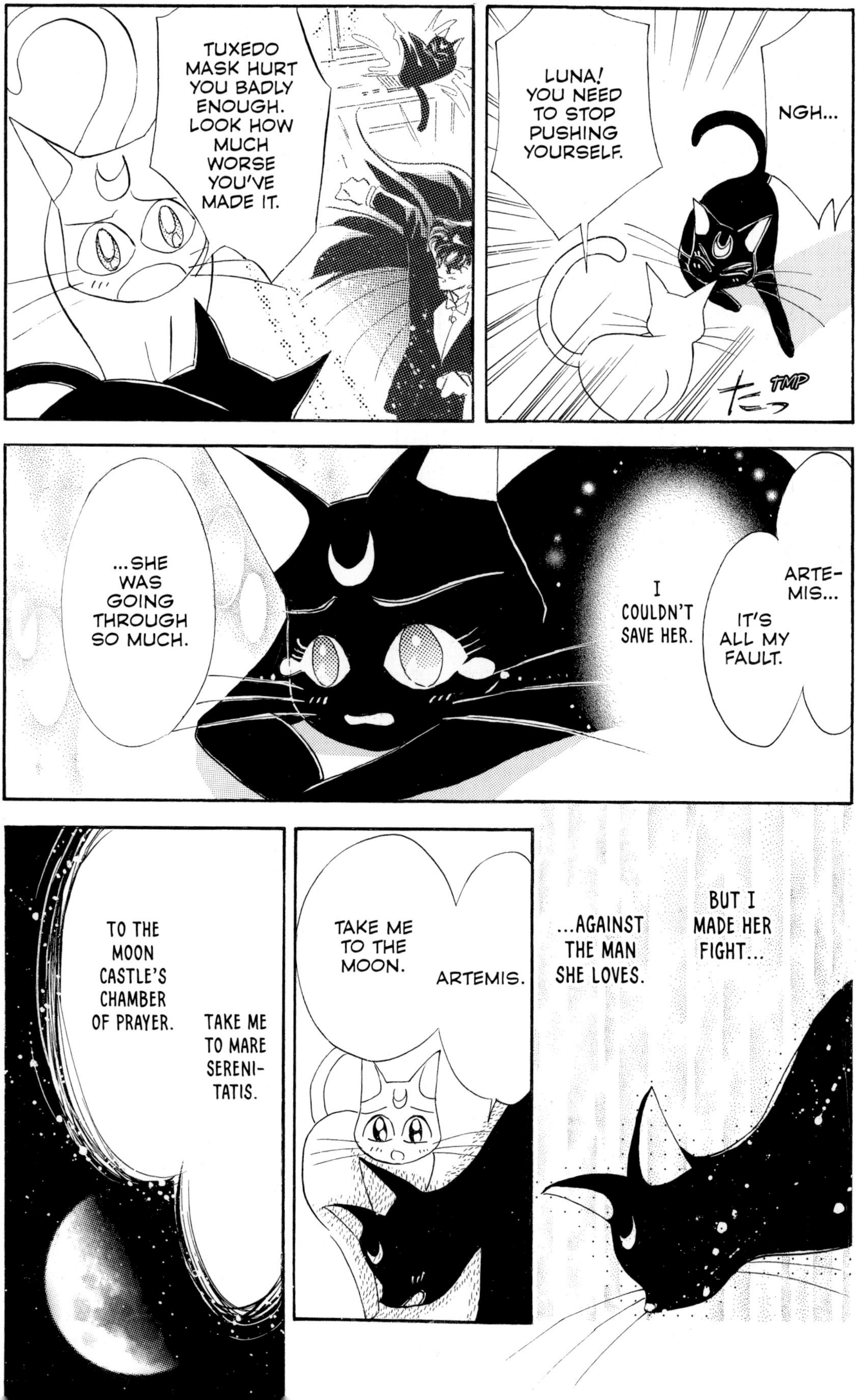
NGH...
LUNA! YOU NEED TO STOP PUSHING YOURSELF.
TMP
TUXEDO MASK HURT YOU BADLY ENOUGH. LOOK HOW MUCH WORSE YOU'VE MADE IT.
ARTEMIS... IT'S ALL MY FAULT.
I COULDN'T SAVE HER.
...SHE WAS GOING THROUGH SO MUCH.
BUT I MADE HER FIGHT...
...AGAINST THE MAN SHE LOVES.
ARTEMIS.
TAKE ME TO THE MOON.
TAKE ME TO MARE SERENITATIS.
TO THE MOON CASTLE'S CHAMBER OF PRAYER.

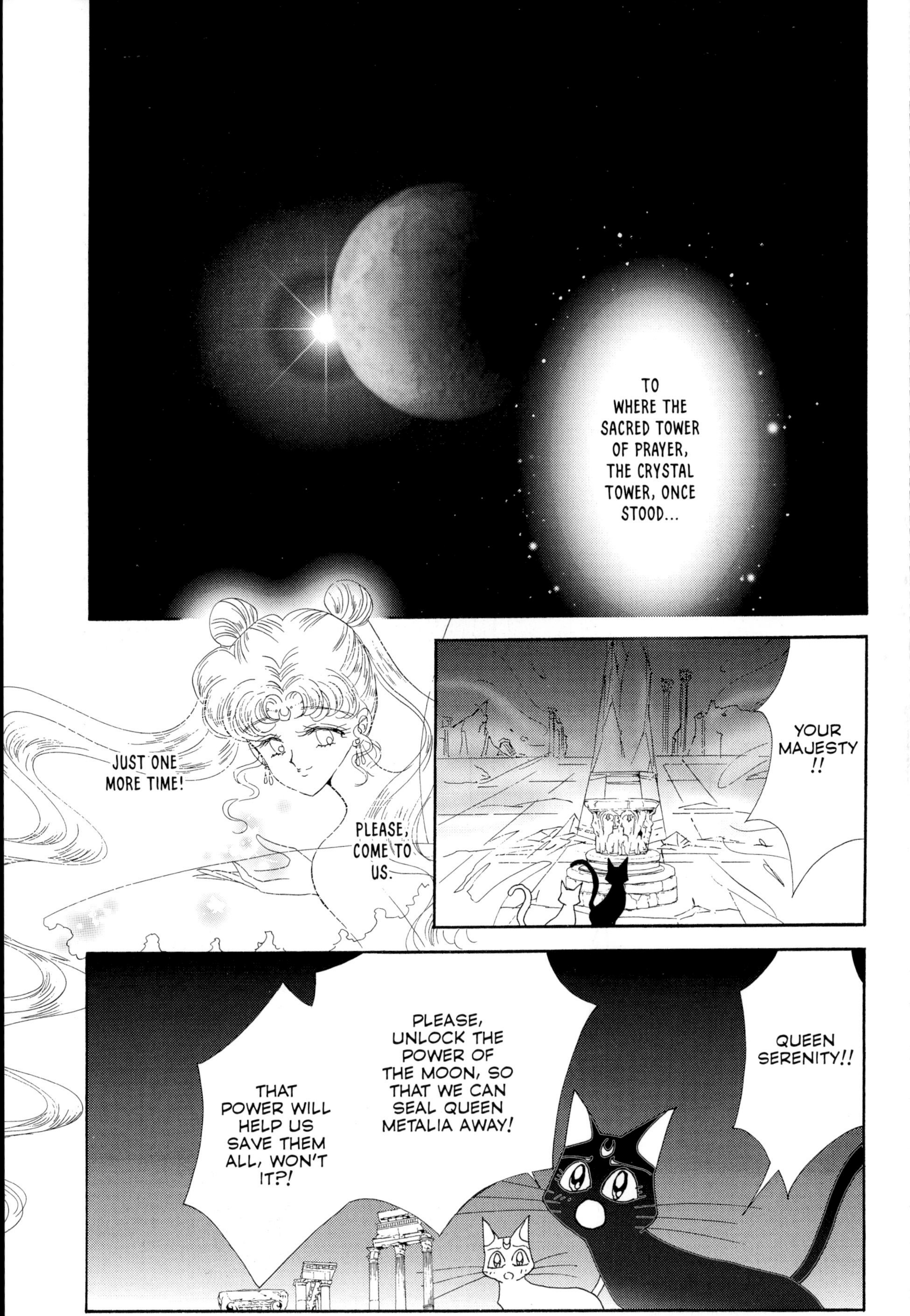
TO WHERE THE SACRED TOWER OF PRAYER, THE CRYSTAL TOWER, ONCE STOOD...
YOUR MAJESTY!!
JUST ONE MORE TIME!
PLEASE, COME TO US.
QUEEN SERENITY!!
PLEASE, UNLOCK THE POWER OF THE MOON, SO THAT WE CAN SEAL QUEEN METALIA AWAY!
THAT POWER WILL HELP US SAVE THEM ALL, WON'T IT?!

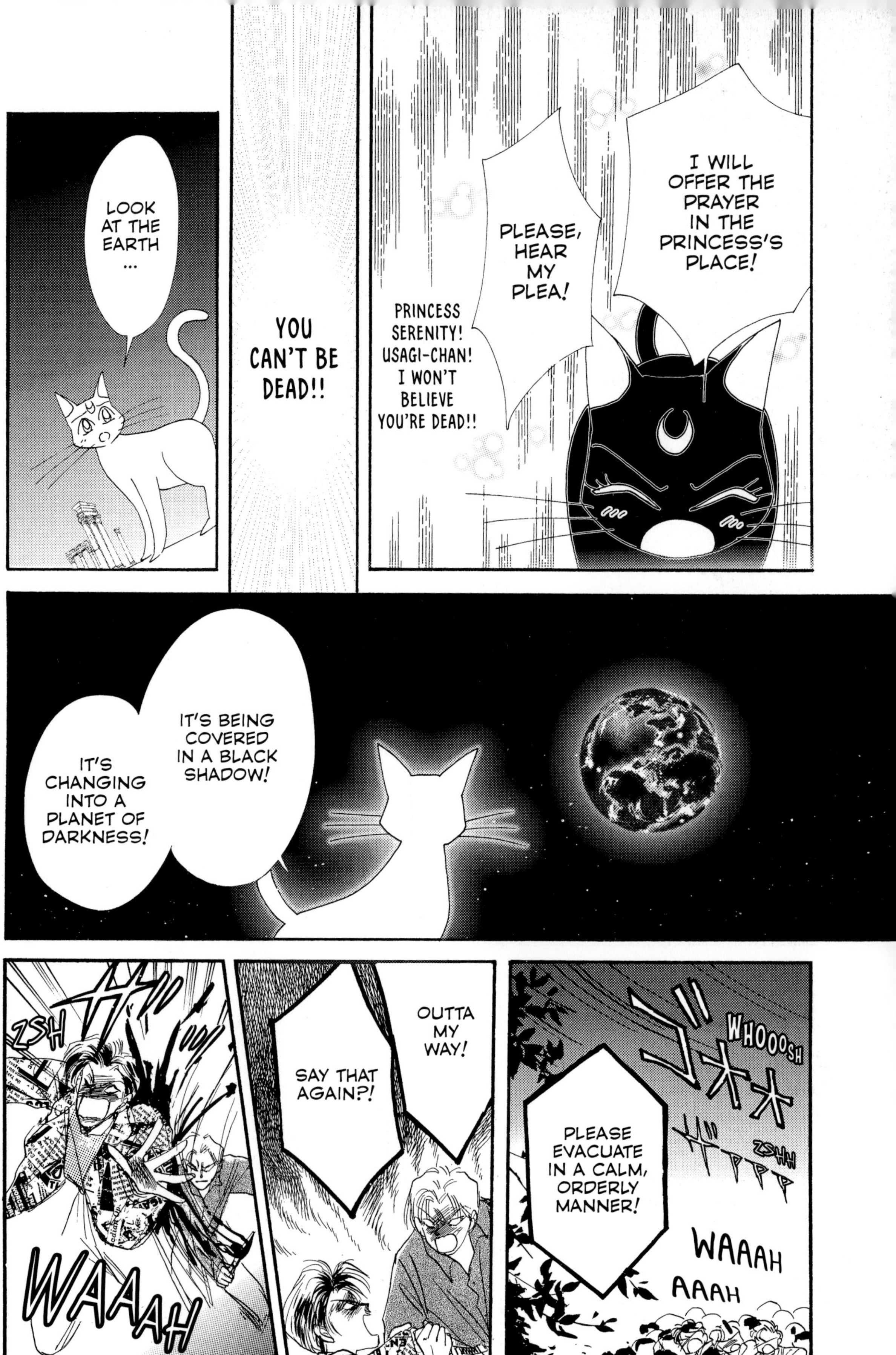
I WILL OFFER THE PRAYER IN THE PRINCESS'S PLACE!
PLEASE, HEAR MY PLEA!
PRINCESS SERENITY! USAGI-CHAN! I WON'T BELIEVE YOU'RE DEAD!!
YOU CAN'T BE DEAD!!
LOOK AT THE EARTH ...
IT'S BEING COVERED IN A BLACK SHADOW!
IT'S CHANGING INTO A PLANET OF DARKNESS!
WHOOOSH
ZSHH
PLEASE EVACUATE IN A CALM, ORDERLY MANNER!
WAAAH
AAAH
OUTTA MY WAY!
SAY THAT AGAIN?!
ZSH
WAAAH

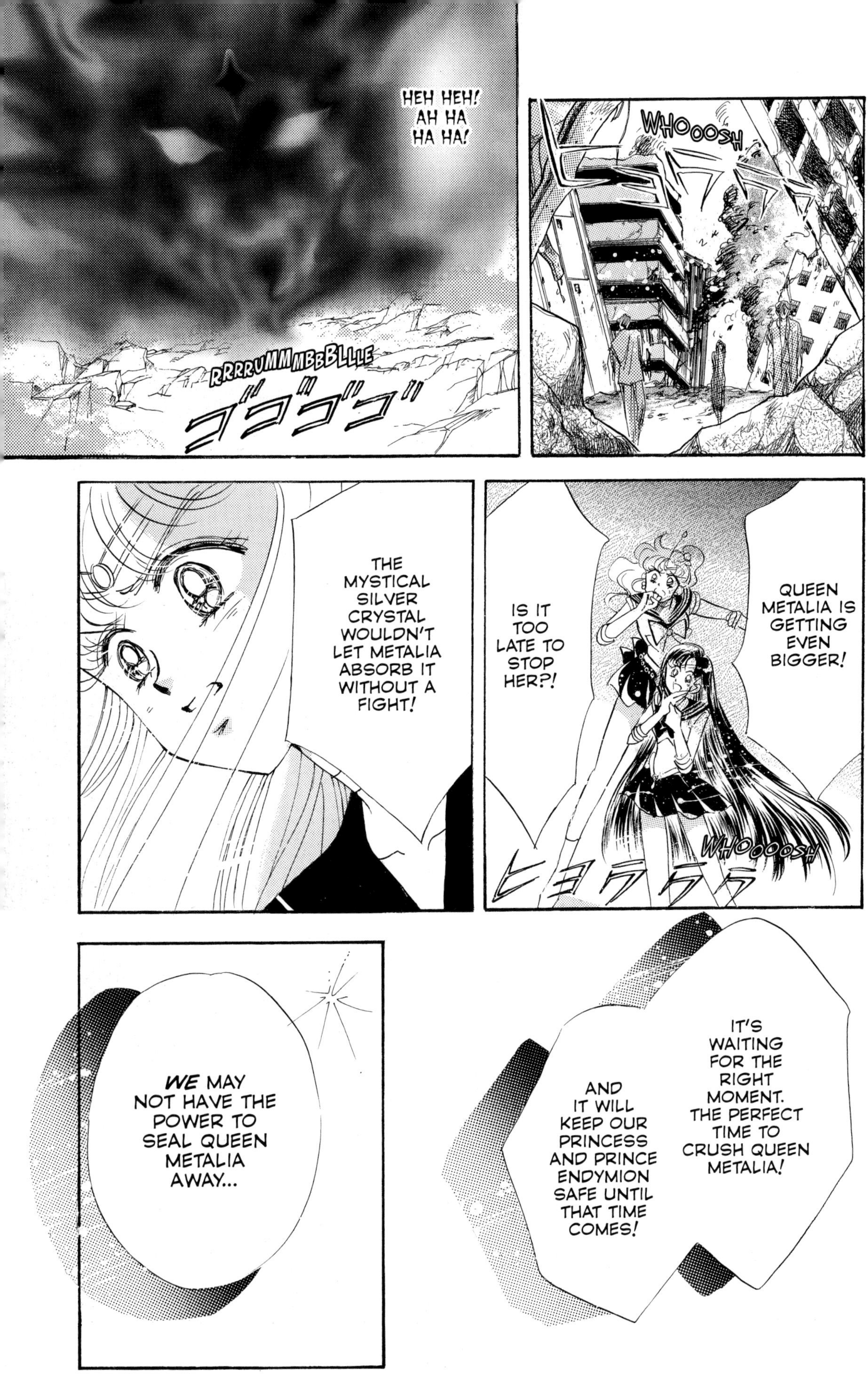
WHOOOSH
HEH HEH! AH HA HA HA!
RRRRUMMMBBBLLLE
ゴゴゴゴ
QUEEN METALIA IS GETTING EVEN BIGGER!
IS IT TOO LATE TO STOP HER?!
WHOOOOSH
THE MYSTICAL SILVER CRYSTAL WOULDN'T LET METALIA ABSORB IT WITHOUT A FIGHT!
IT'S WAITING FOR THE RIGHT MOMENT. THE PERFECT TIME TO CRUSH QUEEN METALIA!
AND IT WILL KEEP OUR PRINCESS AND PRINCE ENDYMION SAFE UNTIL THAT TIME COMES!
WE MAY NOT HAVE THE POWER TO SEAL QUEEN METALIA AWAY...

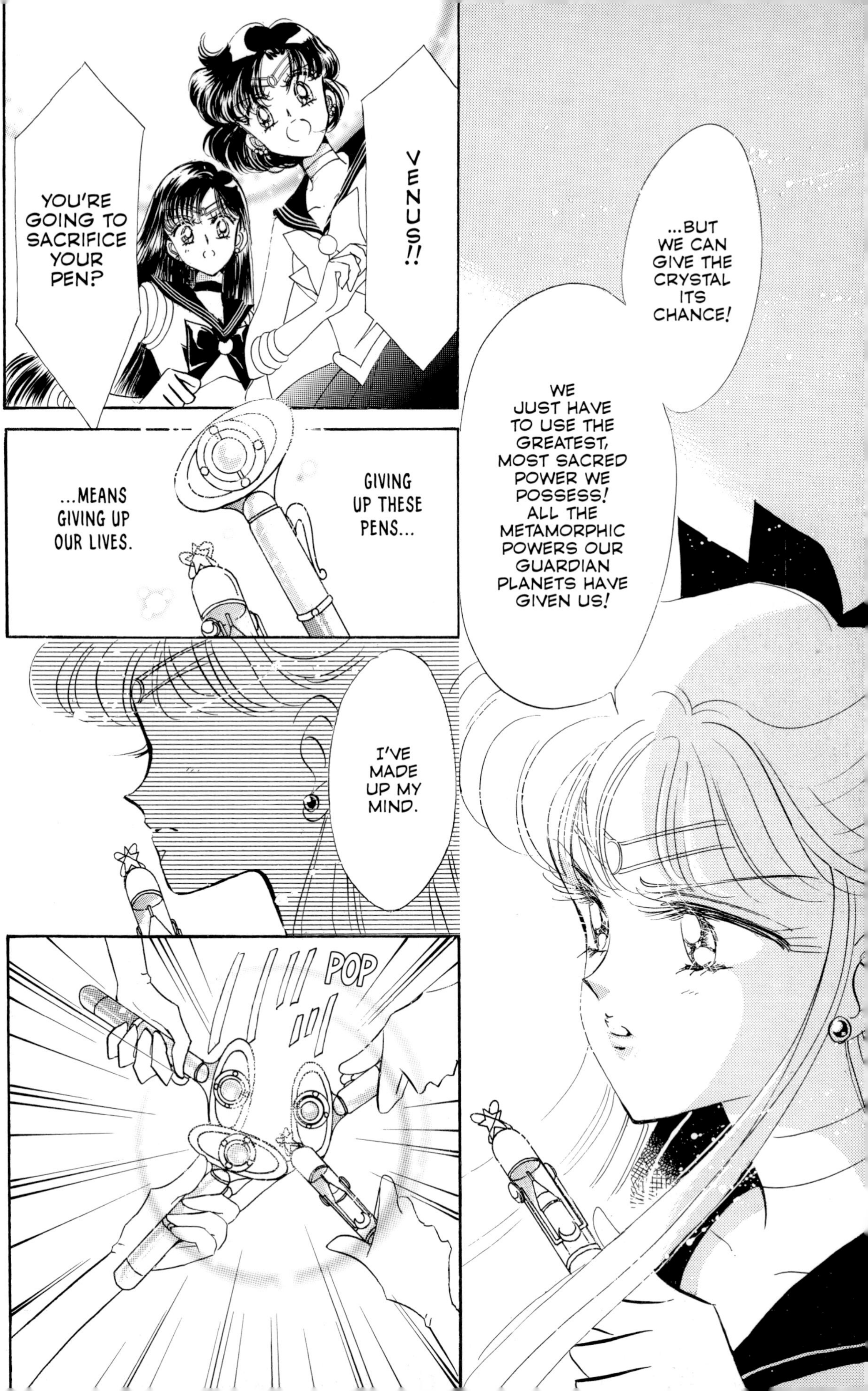
...BUT WE CAN GIVE THE CRYSTAL ITS CHANCE!
WE JUST HAVE TO USE THE GREATEST, MOST SACRED POWER WE POSSESS! ALL THE METAMORPHIC POWERS OUR GUARDIAN PLANETS HAVE GIVEN US!
VENUS!!
YOU'RE GOING TO SACRIFICE YOUR PEN?
GIVING UP THESE PENS...
...MEANS GIVING UP OUR LIVES.
I'VE MADE UP MY MIND.
POP

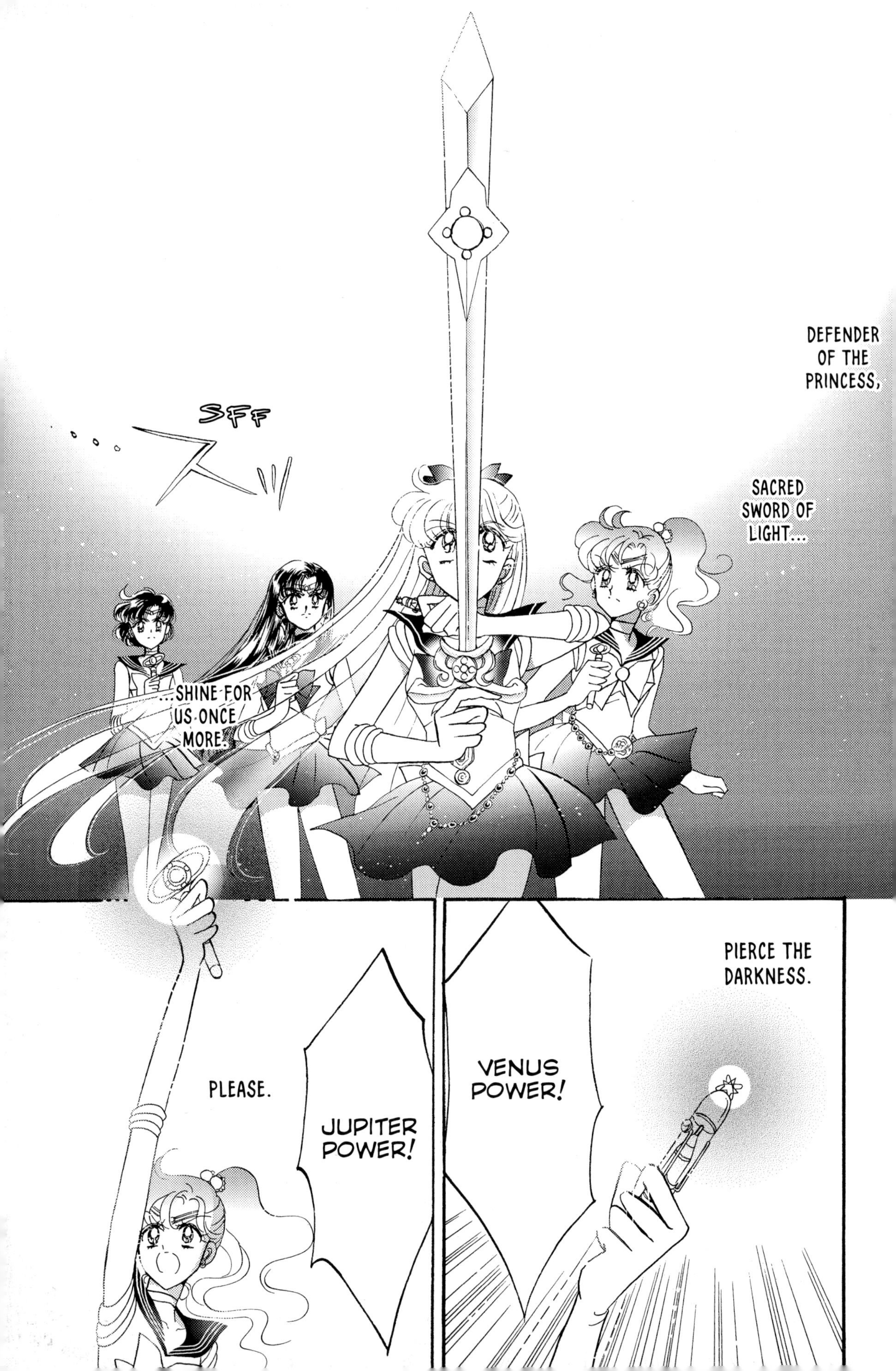

DEFENDER OF THE PRINCESS,
SACRED SWORD OF LIGHT...
SFF
...SHINE FOR US ONCE MORE.
PIERCE THE DARKNESS.
VENUS POWER!
JUPITER POWER!
PLEASE.

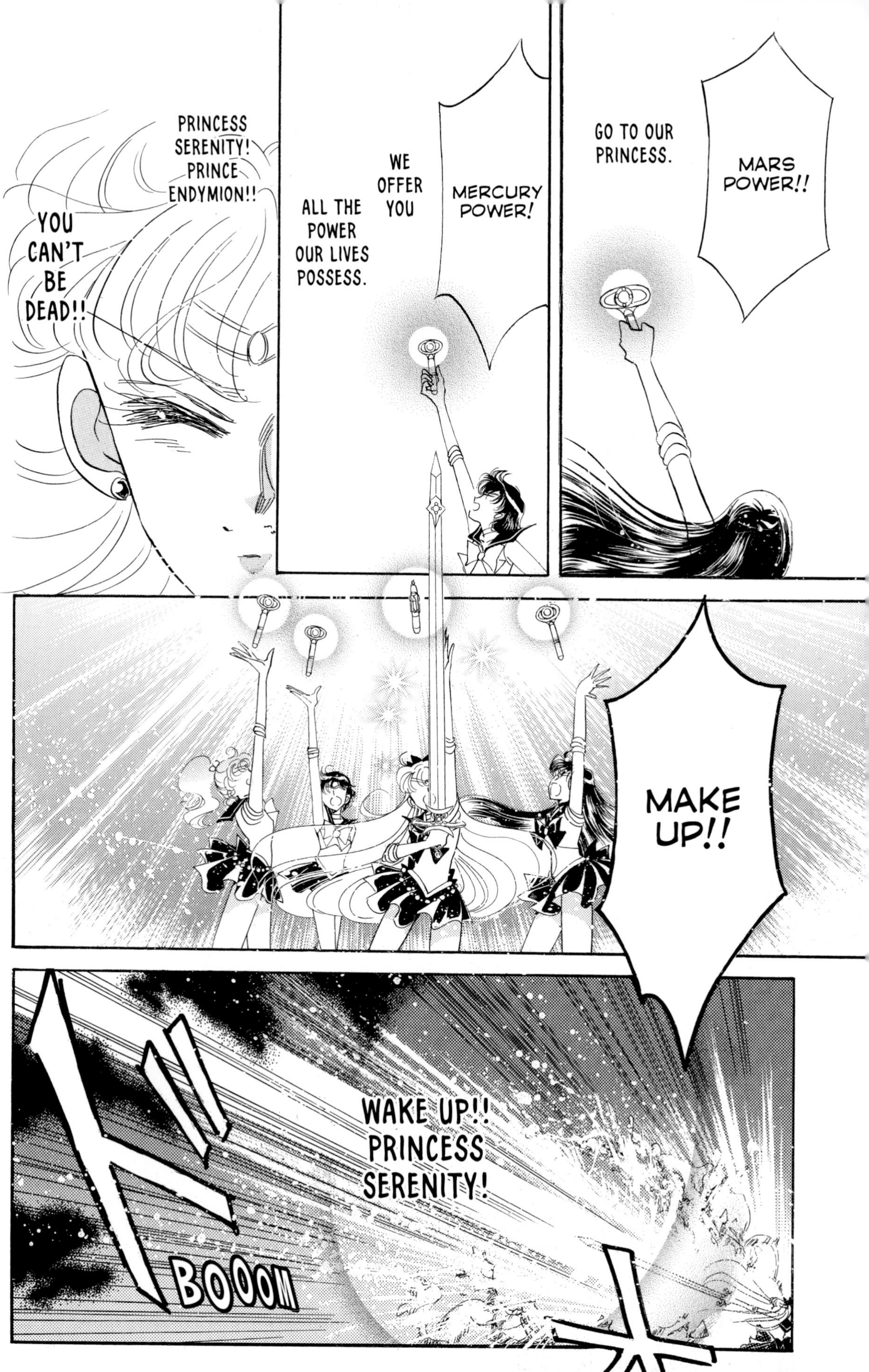
MARS POWER!!
GO TO OUR PRINCESS.
MERCURY POWER!
WE OFFER YOU
ALL THE POWER OUR LIVES POSSESS.
PRINCESS SERENITY! PRINCE ENDYMION!!
YOU CAN'T BE DEAD!!
MAKE UP!!
WAKE UP!! PRINCESS SERENITY!
BOOOM

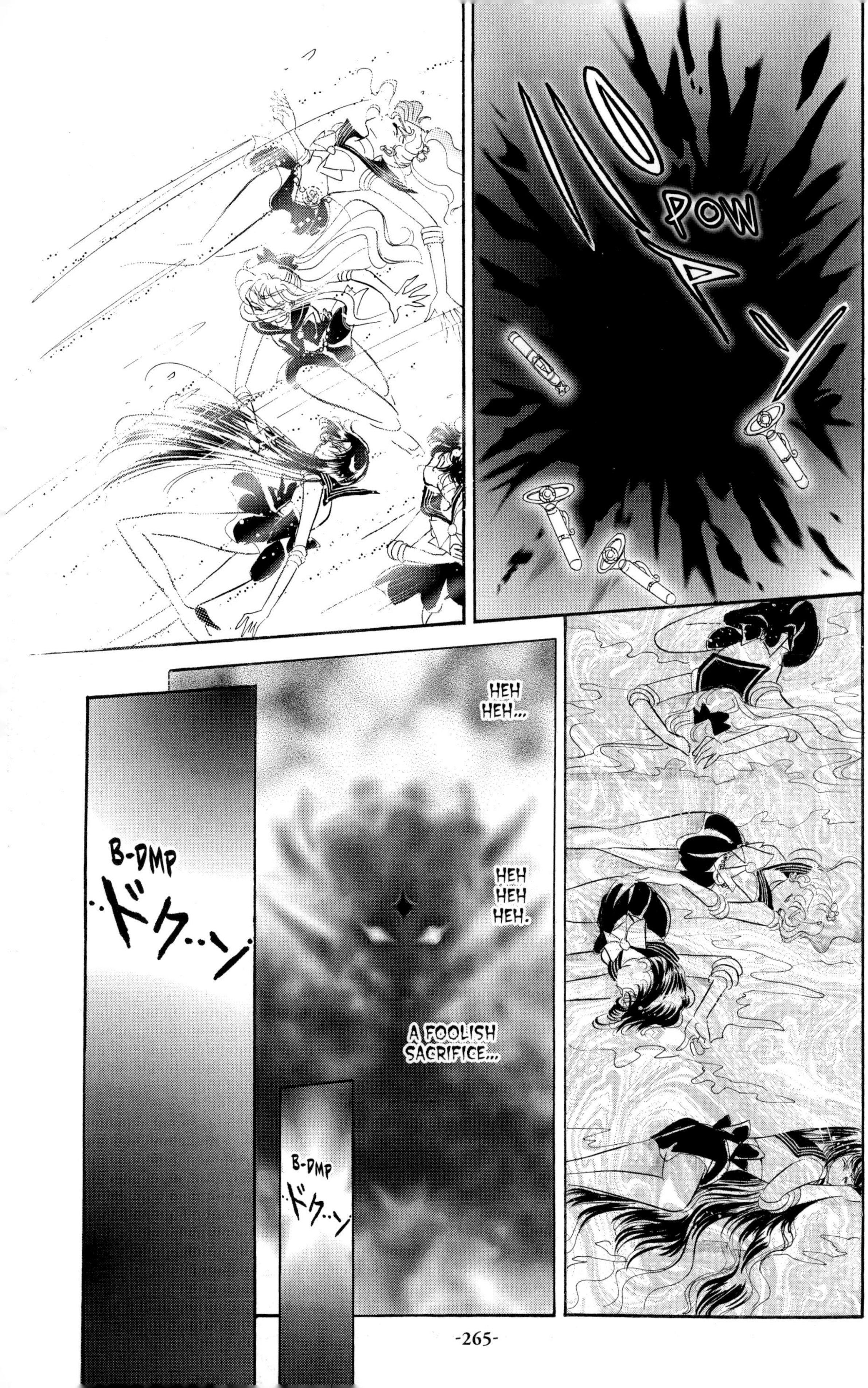
POW
HEH HEH...
HEH HEH HEH.
A FOOLISH SACRIFICE...
B-DMP
ドク…ン
B-DMP
ドク…ン

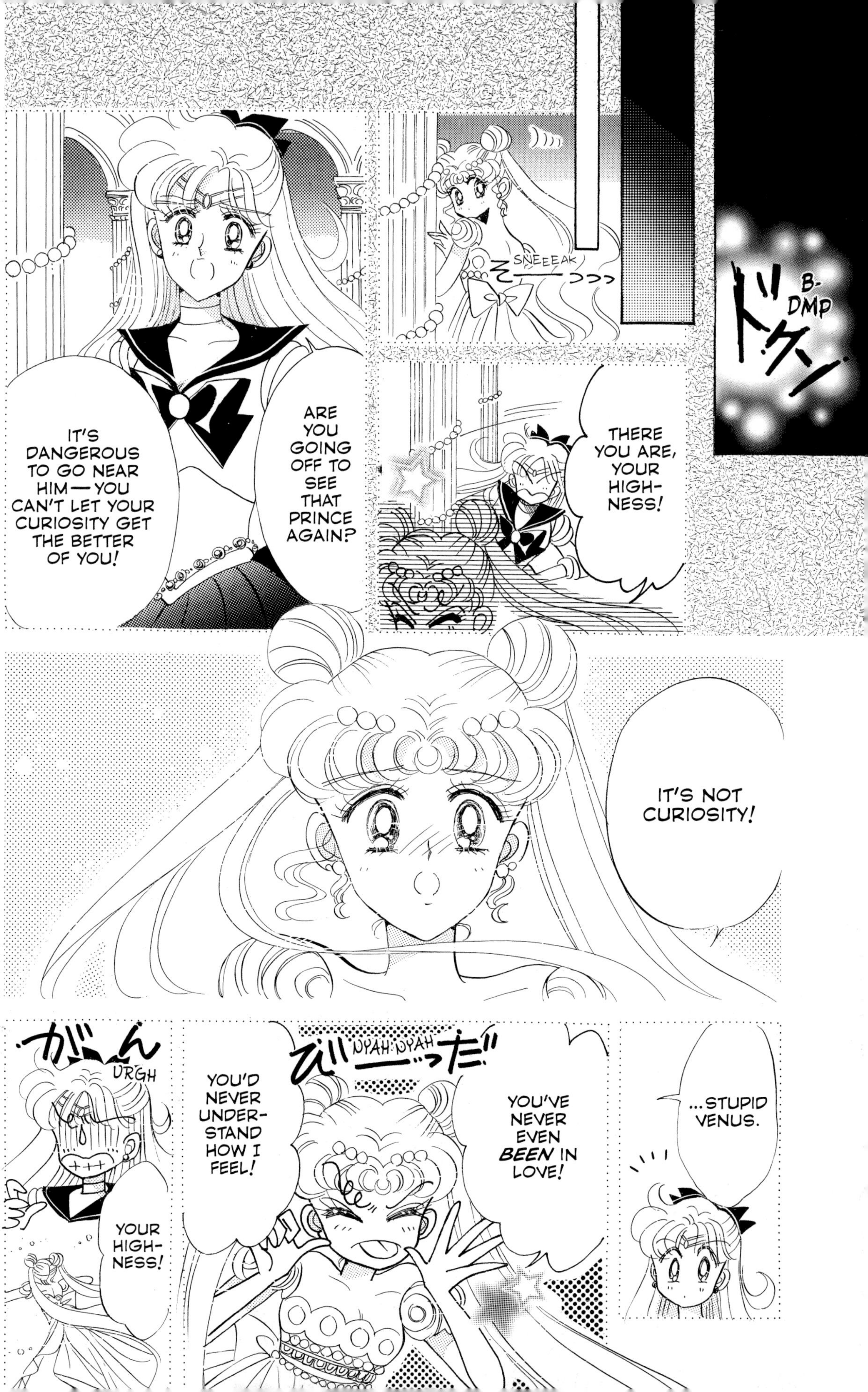
B-DMP
SNEEEAK
THERE YOU ARE, YOUR HIGHNESS!
ARE YOU GOING OFF TO SEE THAT PRINCE AGAIN?
IT'S DANGEROUS TO GO NEAR HIM—YOU CAN'T LET YOUR CURIOSITY GET THE BETTER OF YOU!
IT'S NOT CURIOSITY!
...STUPID VENUS.
NYAH NYAH
YOU'VE NEVER EVEN *BEEN* IN LOVE!
YOU'D NEVER UNDERSTAND HOW I FEEL!
URGH
YOUR HIGHNESS!

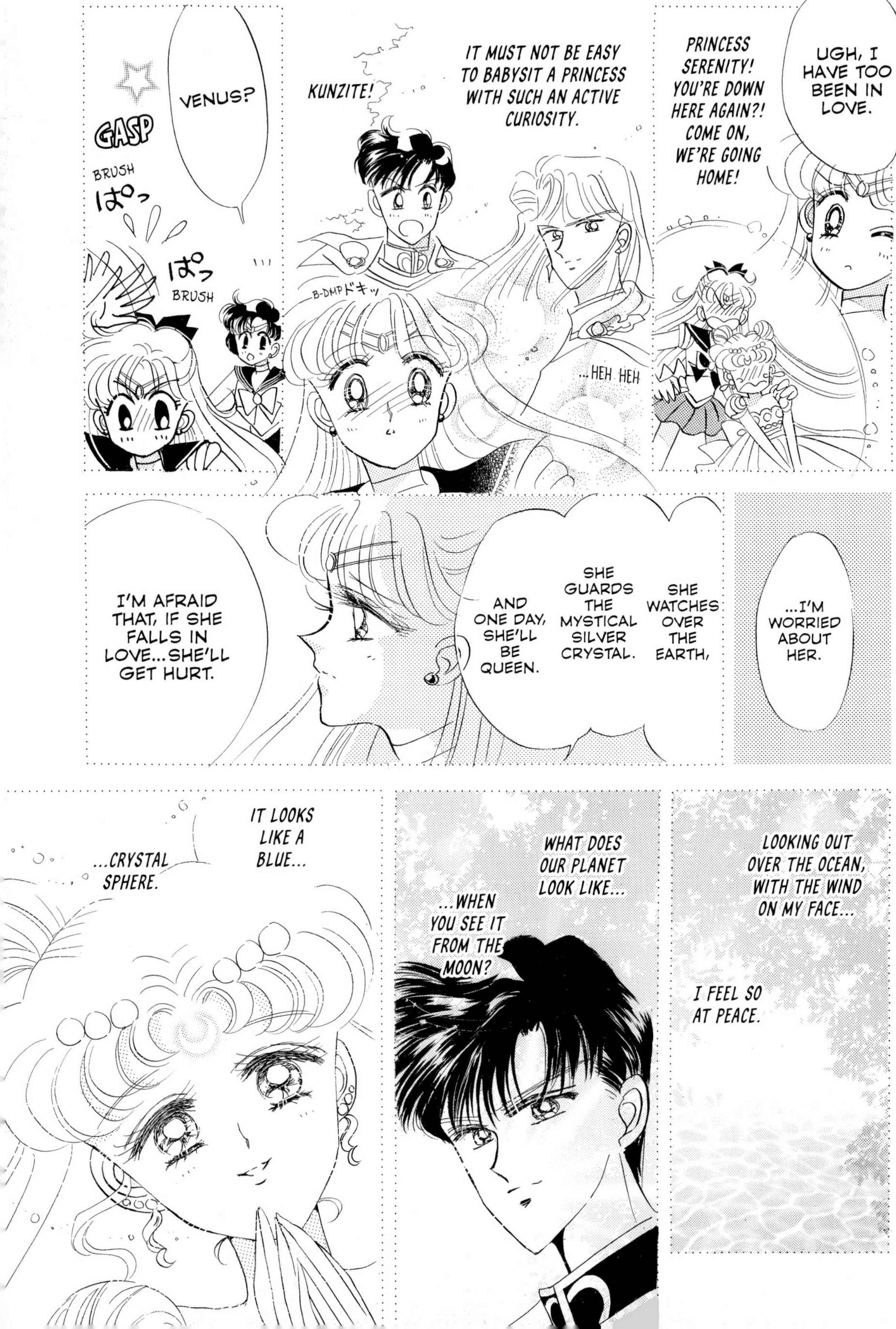
UGH, I HAVE TOO BEEN IN LOVE.
PRINCESS SERENITY! YOU'RE DOWN HERE AGAIN?! COME ON, WE'RE GOING HOME!
IT MUST NOT BE EASY TO BABYSIT A PRINCESS WITH SUCH AN ACTIVE CURIOSITY.
KUNZITE!
B-DMP ドキッ
...HEH HEH
VENUS?
GASP
BRUSH ぱっ
ぱっ BRUSH
...I'M WORRIED ABOUT HER.
SHE WATCHES OVER THE EARTH,
SHE GUARDS THE MYSTICAL SILVER CRYSTAL.
AND ONE DAY, SHE'LL BE QUEEN.
I'M AFRAID THAT, IF SHE FALLS IN LOVE...SHE'LL GET HURT.
LOOKING OUT OVER THE OCEAN, WITH THE WIND ON MY FACE...
I FEEL SO AT PEACE.
WHAT DOES OUR PLANET LOOK LIKE...
...WHEN YOU SEE IT FROM THE MOON?
IT LOOKS LIKE A BLUE...
...CRYSTAL SPHERE.

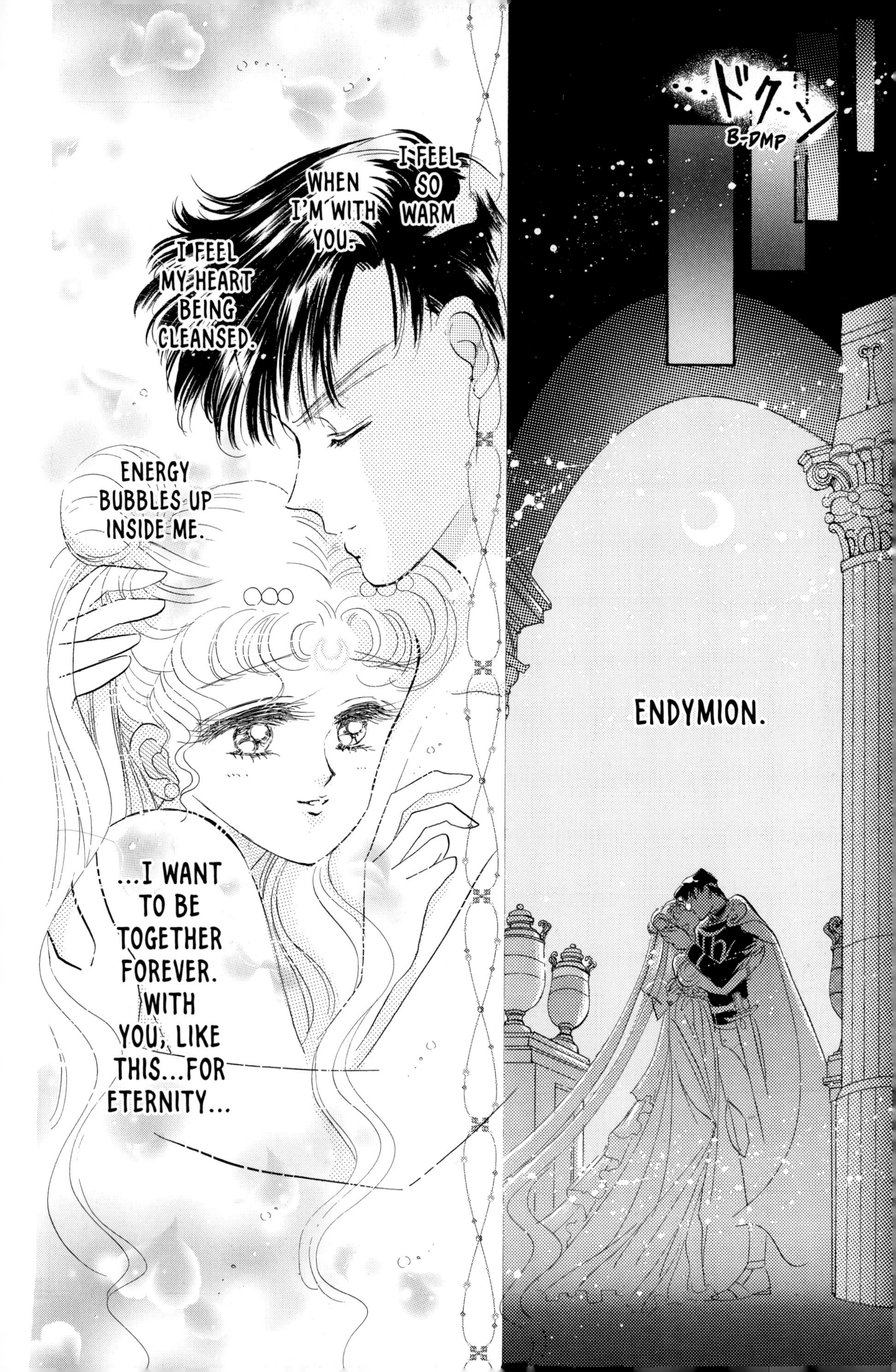
ドクン
B-DMP
ENDYMION.
I FEEL SO WARM
WHEN I'M WITH YOU.
I FEEL MY HEART BEING CLEANSED.
ENERGY BUBBLES UP INSIDE ME.
...I WANT TO BE TOGETHER FOREVER. WITH YOU, LIKE THIS...FOR ETERNITY...

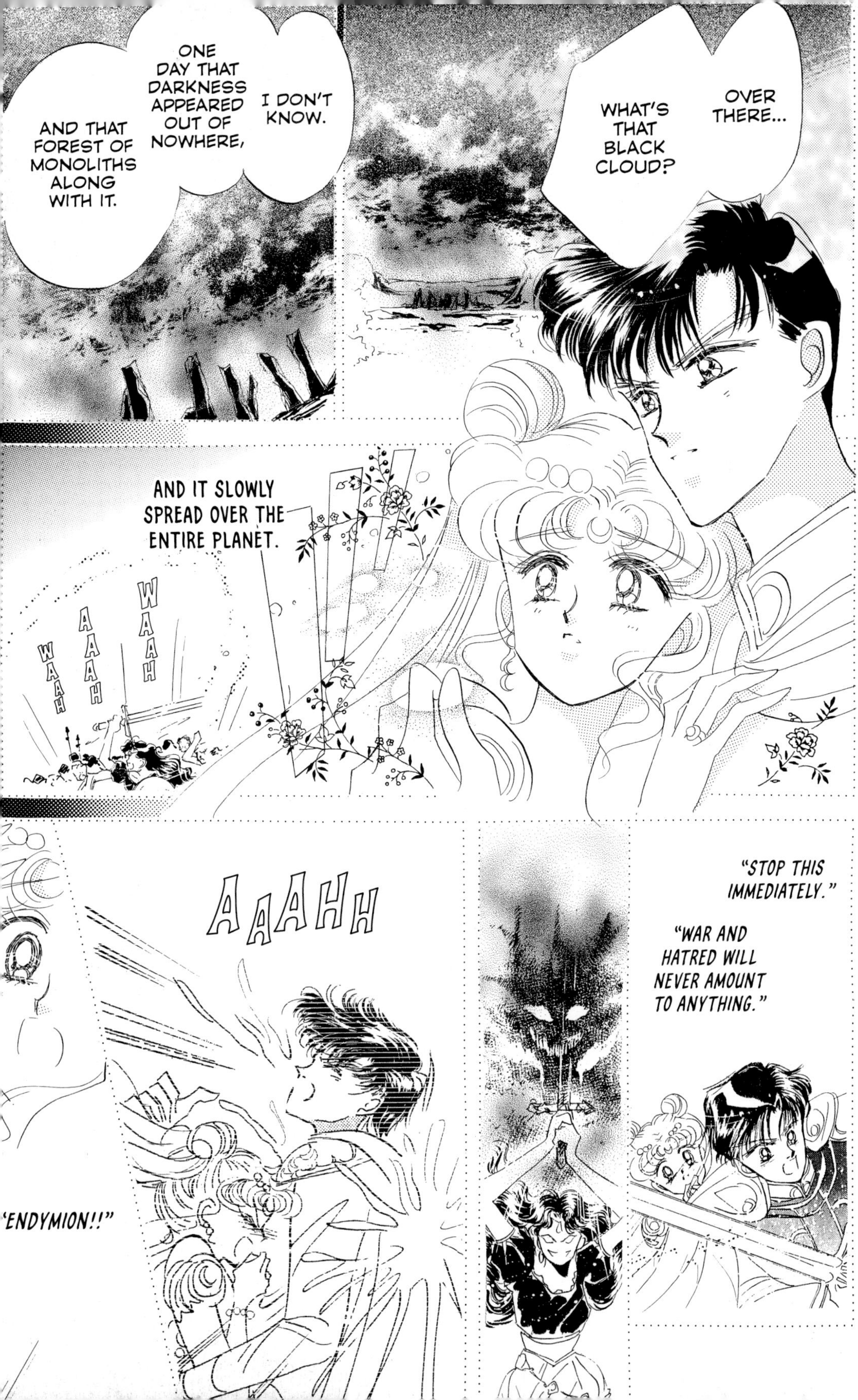

OVER THERE...
WHAT'S THAT BLACK CLOUD?
I DON'T KNOW.
ONE DAY THAT DARKNESS APPEARED OUT OF NOWHERE,
AND THAT FOREST OF MONOLITHS ALONG WITH IT.
AND IT SLOWLY SPREAD OVER THE ENTIRE PLANET.
WAAH
AAAH
WAAH
“STOP THIS IMMEDIATELY.”
“WAR AND HATRED WILL NEVER AMOUNT TO ANYTHING.”
AAAHH
ENDYMION!!”

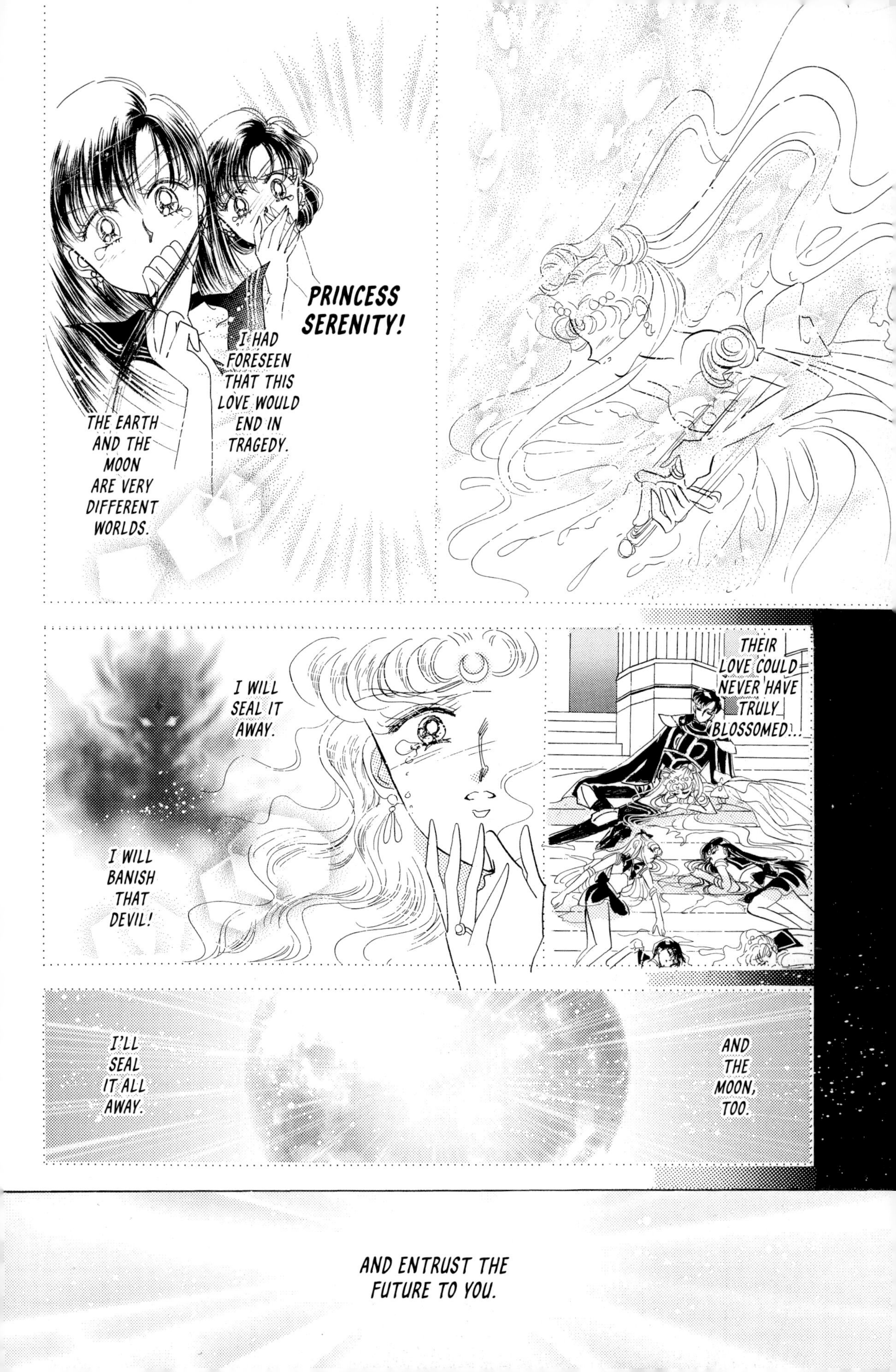
PRINCESS SERENITY!
I HAD FORESEEN THAT THIS LOVE WOULD END IN TRAGEDY.
THE EARTH AND THE MOON ARE VERY DIFFERENT WORLDS.
THEIR LOVE COULD NEVER HAVE TRULY BLOSSOMED...
I WILL SEAL IT AWAY.
I WILL BANISH THAT DEVIL!
I'LL SEAL IT ALL AWAY.
AND THE MOON, TOO.
AND ENTRUST THE FUTURE TO YOU.

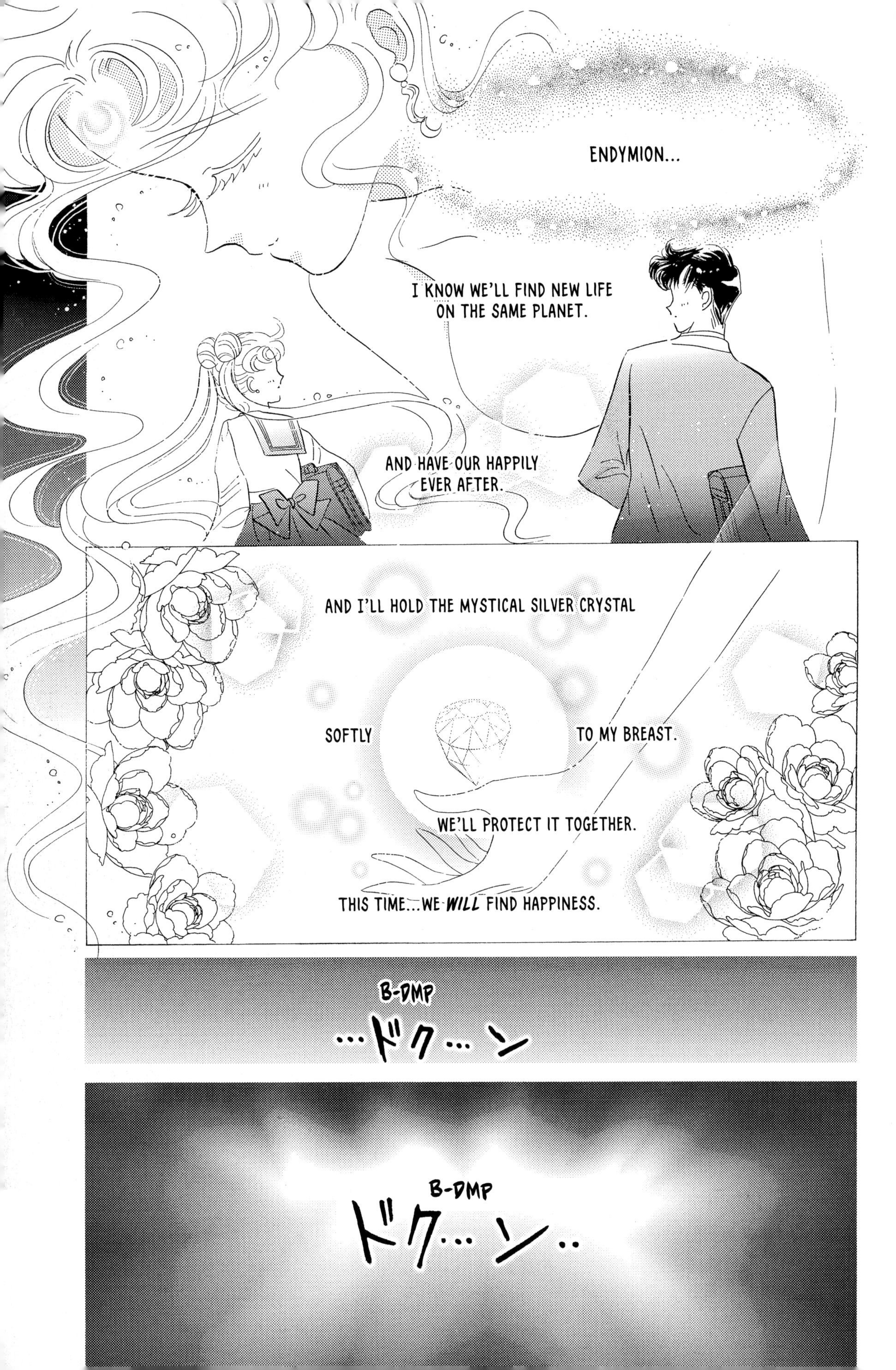
ENDYMION...
I KNOW WE'LL FIND NEW LIFE ON THE SAME PLANET.
AND HAVE OUR HAPPILY EVER AFTER.
AND I'LL HOLD THE MYSTICAL SILVER CRYSTAL
SOFTLY
TO MY BREAST.
WE'LL PROTECT IT TOGETHER.
THIS TIME...WE *WILL* FIND HAPPINESS.
B-DMP
...ドク...ン
B-DMP
ドク...ン..

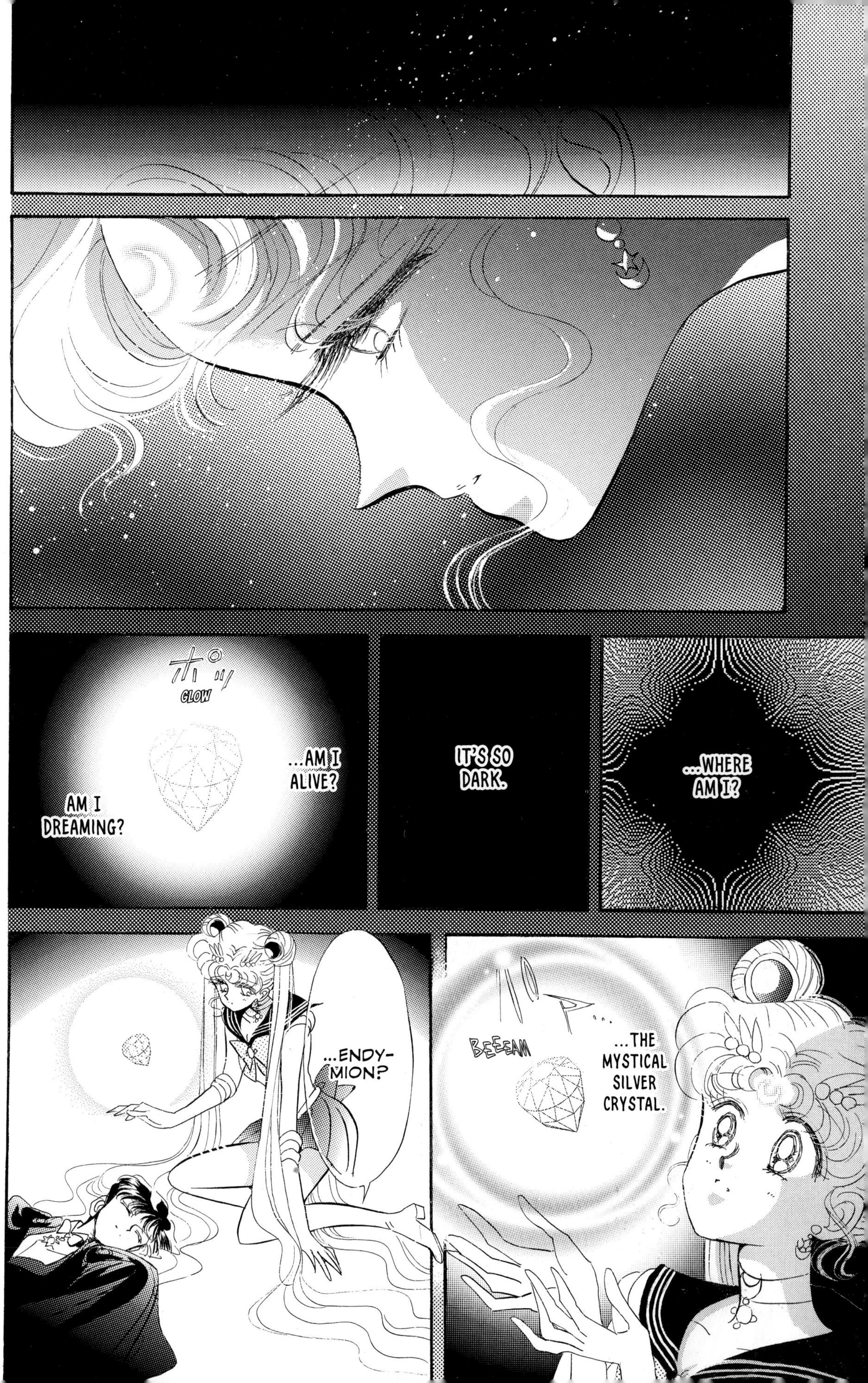

...WHERE AM I?
IT'S SO DARK.
GLOW
...AM I ALIVE?
AM I DREAMING?
BEEEAM
...THE MYSTICAL SILVER CRYSTAL.
...ENDY-MION?

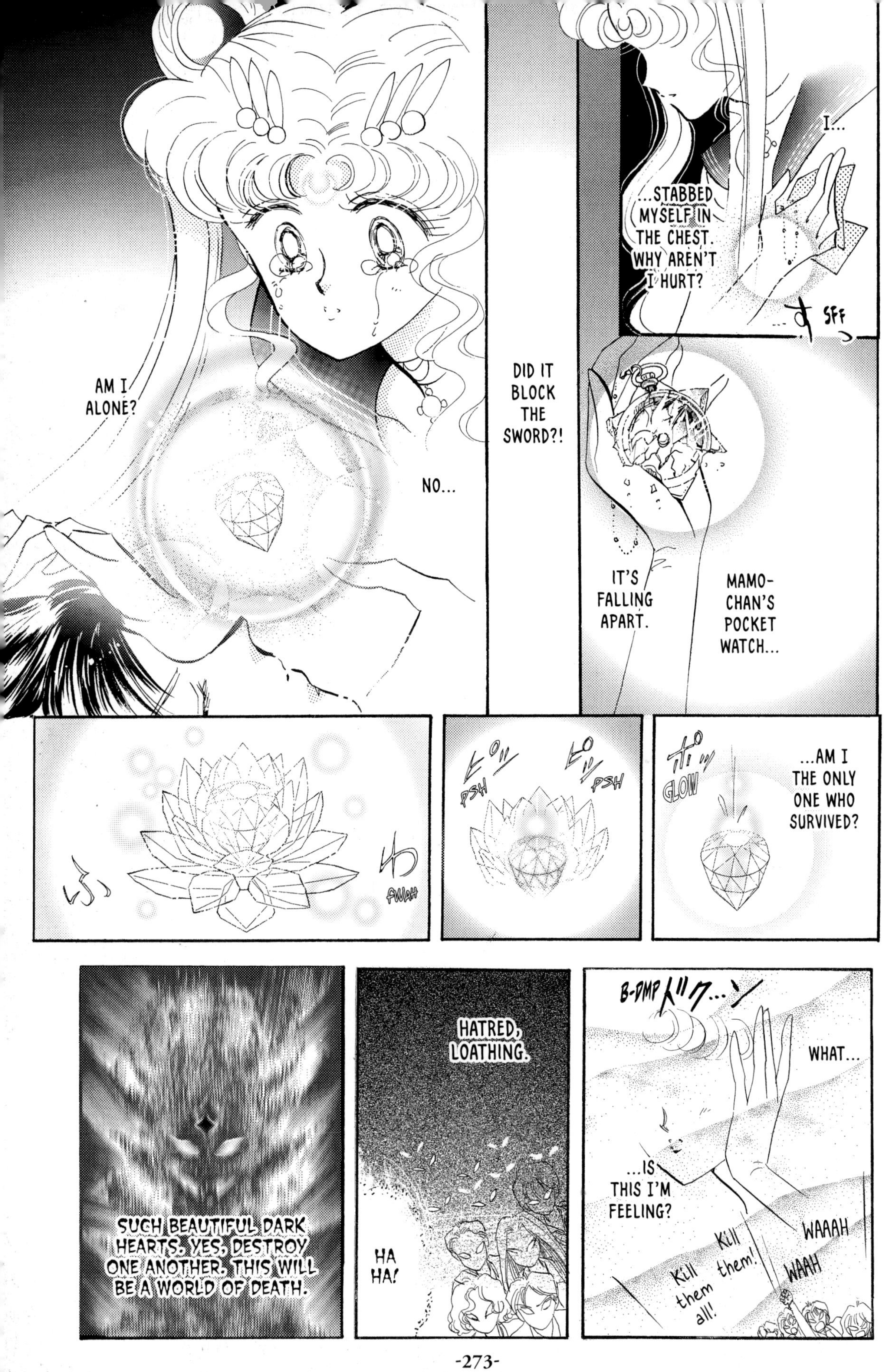
I...
...STABBED MYSELF IN THE CHEST. WHY AREN'T I HURT?
SFF
MAMO-CHAN'S POCKET WATCH...
IT'S FALLING APART.
DID IT BLOCK THE SWORD?!
NO...
AM I ALONE?
GLOW
...AM I THE ONLY ONE WHO SURVIVED?
PSH
PSH
FWAH
B-DMP
WHAT...
...IS THIS I'M FEELING?
WAAAH
Kill them!
Kill them all!
WAAH
HATRED, LOATHING.
HA HA!
SUCH BEAUTIFUL DARK HEARTS. YES, DESTROY ONE ANOTHER. THIS WILL BE A WORLD OF DEATH.

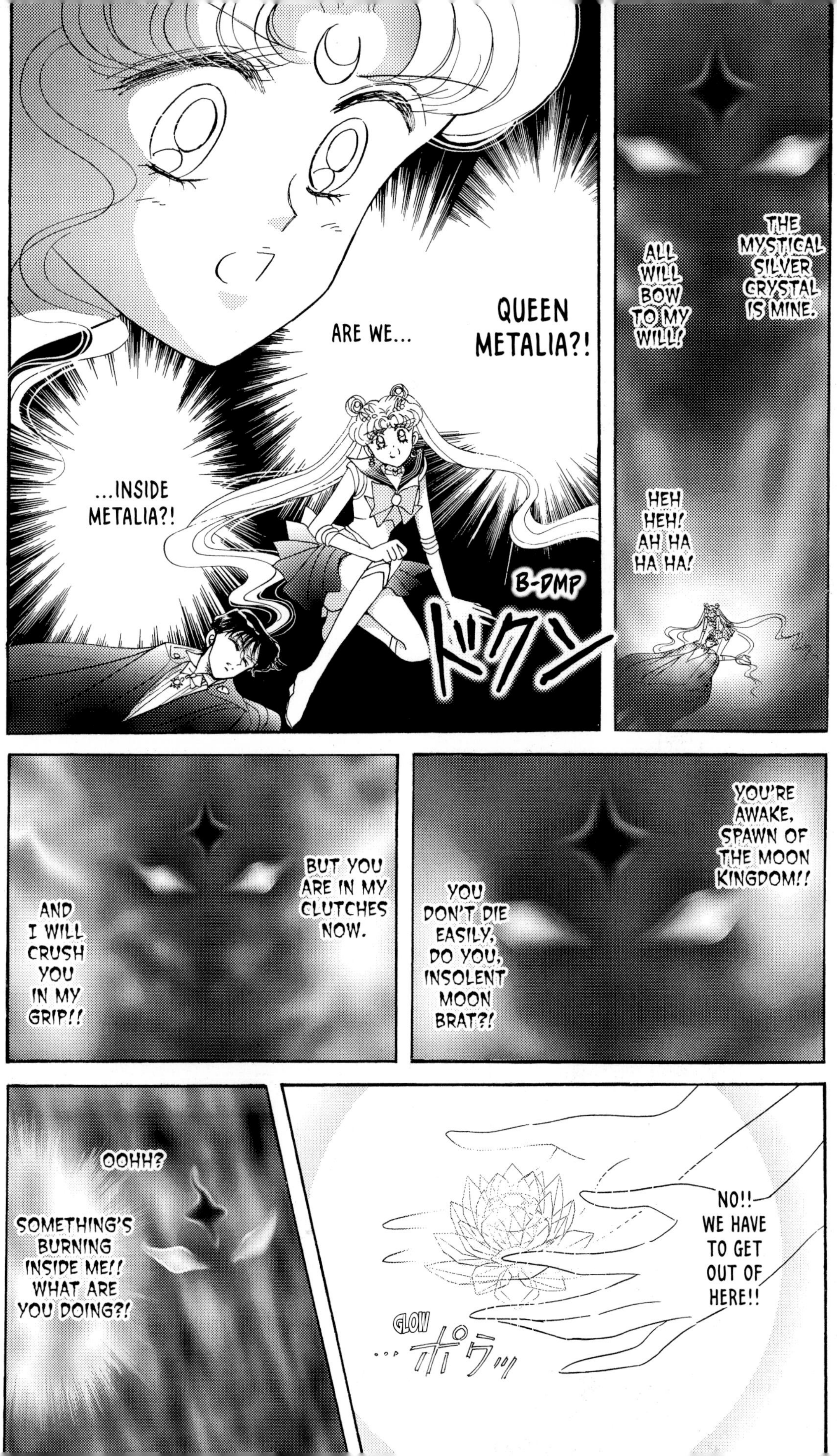
THE MYSTICAL SILVER CRYSTAL IS MINE.
ALL WILL BOW TO MY WILL!
HEH HEH! AH HA HA HA!
QUEEN METALIA?!
ARE WE...
...INSIDE METALIA?!
B-DMP
ドクン
YOU'RE AWAKE, SPAWN OF THE MOON KINGDOM!!
YOU DON'T DIE EASILY, DO YOU, INSOLENT MOON BRAT?!
BUT YOU ARE IN MY CLUTCHES NOW.
AND I WILL CRUSH YOU IN MY GRIP!!
NO!! WE HAVE TO GET OUT OF HERE!!
GLOW
ポワッ
OOHH?
SOMETHING'S BURNING INSIDE ME!! WHAT ARE YOU DOING?!

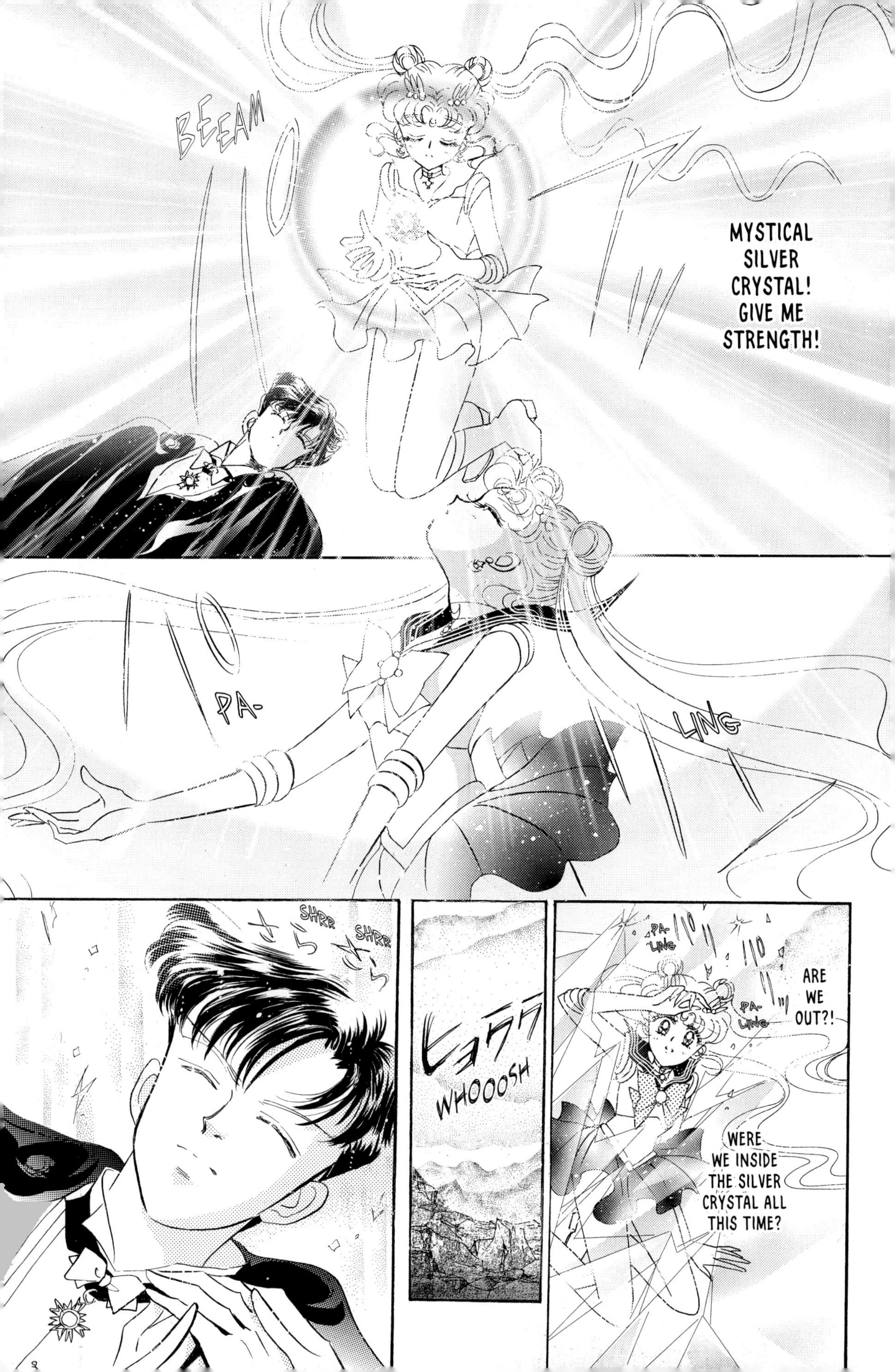
MYSTICAL SILVER CRYSTAL! GIVE ME STRENGTH!
BEEAM
PA-
LING
PA-LING
ARE WE OUT?!
PA-LING
WERE WE INSIDE THE SILVER CRYSTAL ALL THIS TIME?
WHOOOSH
SHRR
SHRR

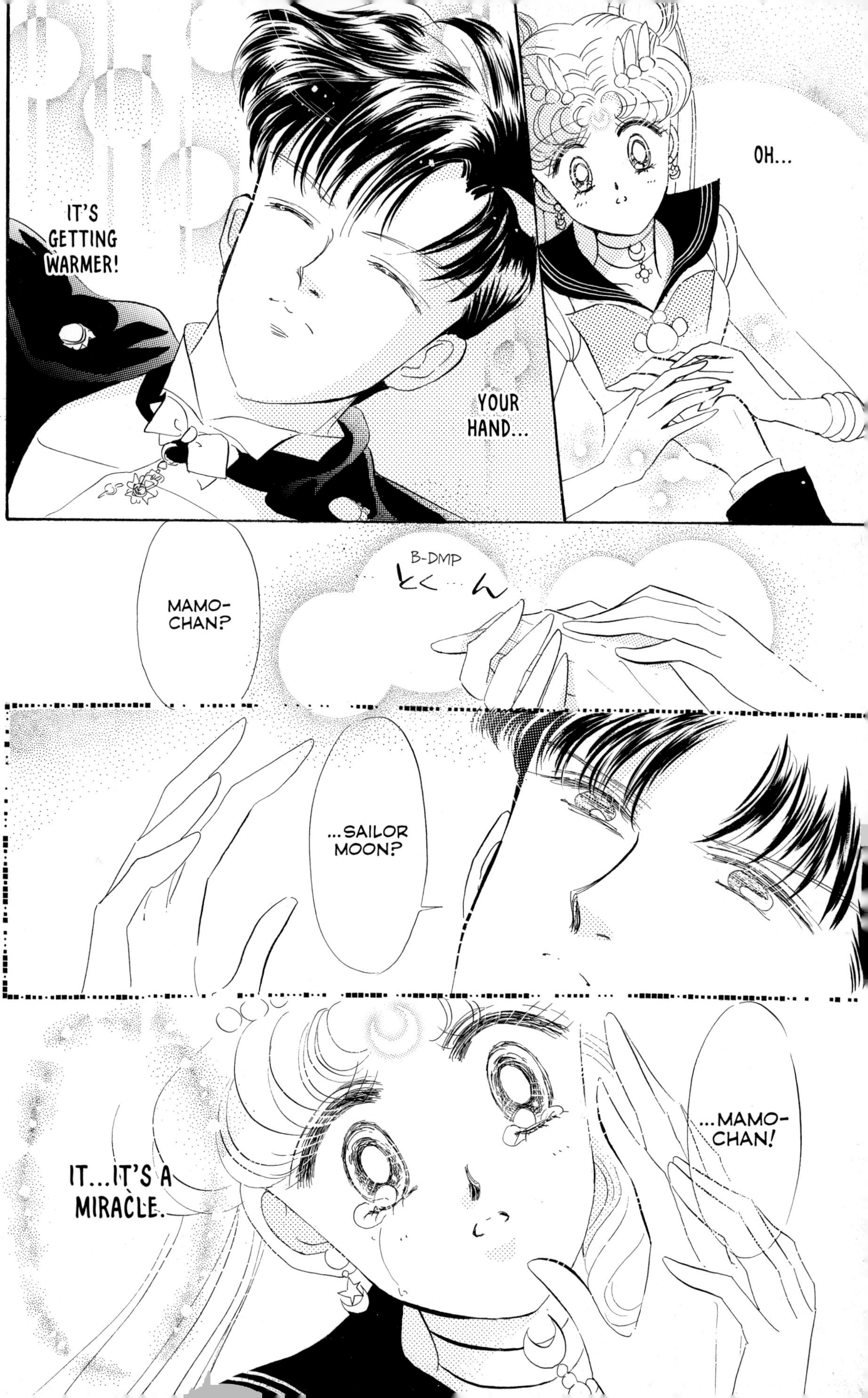
OH...
YOUR HAND...
IT'S GETTING WARMER!
B-DMP
とく…ん
MAMO-CHAN?
...SAILOR MOON?
...MAMO-CHAN!
IT...IT'S A MIRACLE.

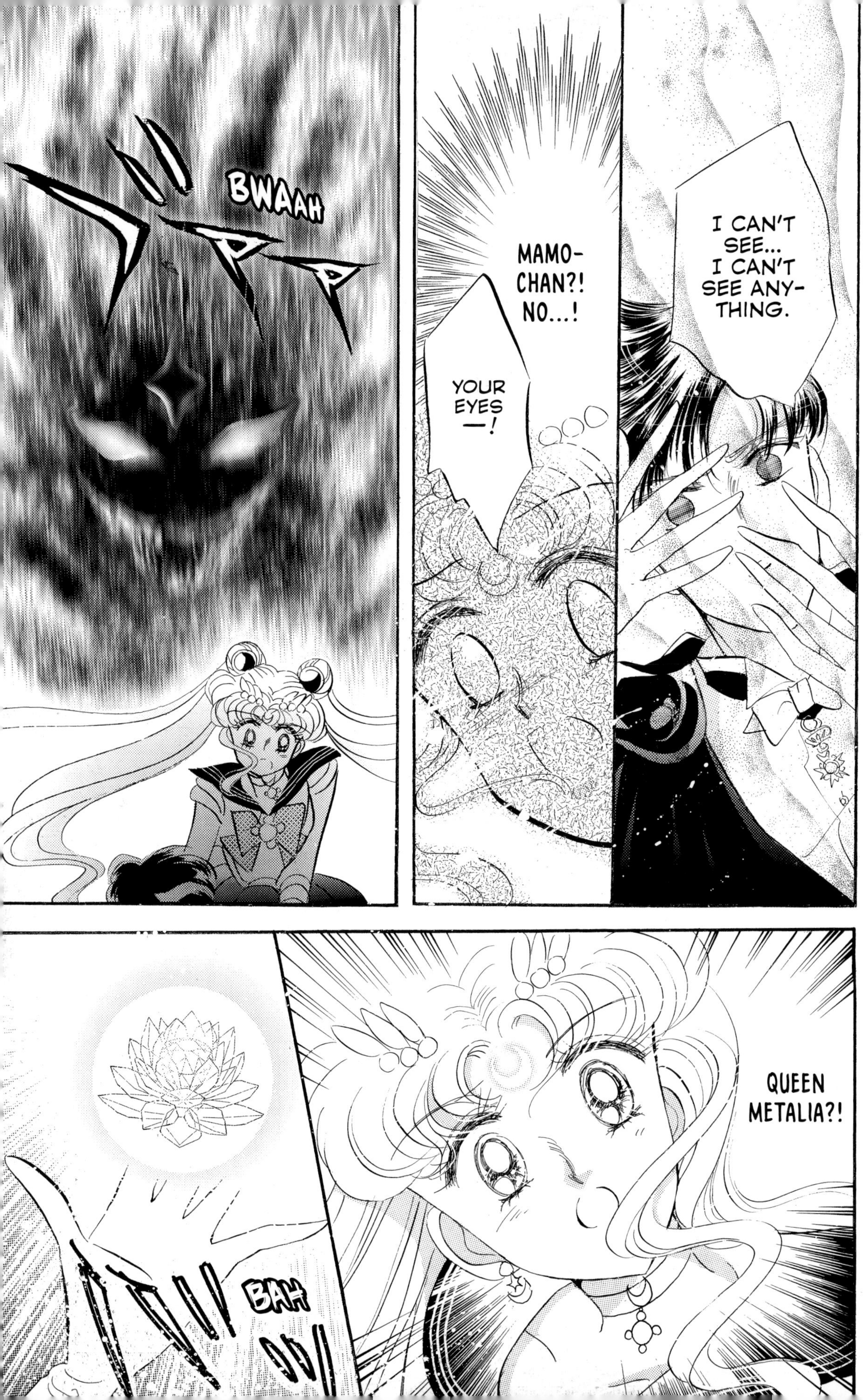
I CAN'T SEE... I CAN'T SEE ANY-THING.
MAMO-CHAN?! NO...!
YOUR EYES —!
BWAAH
QUEEN METALIA?!
BAH

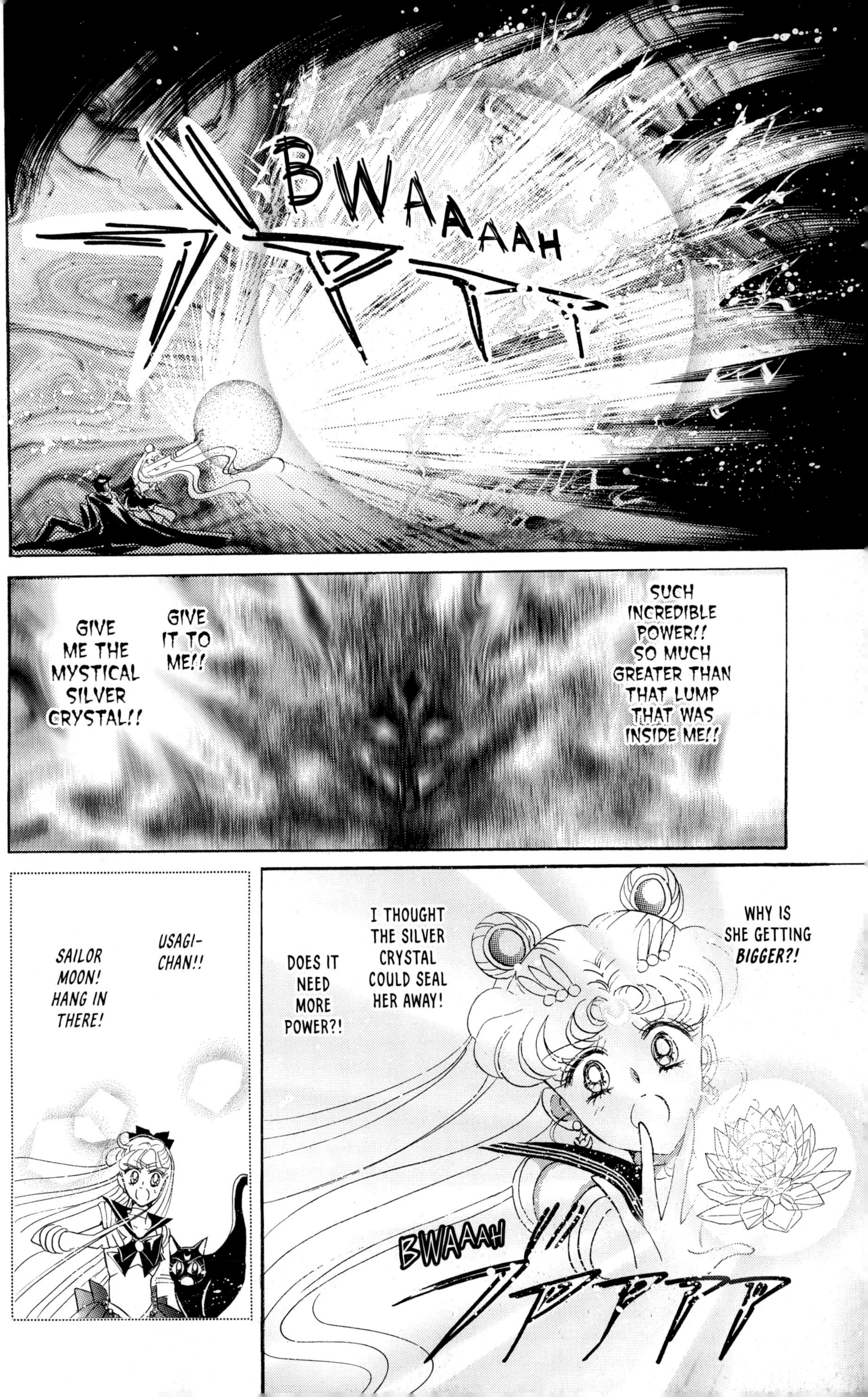
BWAAAAH
SUCH INCREDIBLE POWER!! SO MUCH GREATER THAN THAT LUMP THAT WAS INSIDE ME!!
GIVE IT TO ME!!
GIVE ME THE MYSTICAL SILVER CRYSTAL!!
WHY IS SHE GETTING *BIGGER?!*
I THOUGHT THE SILVER CRYSTAL COULD SEAL HER AWAY!
DOES IT NEED MORE POWER?!
BWAAAH
*USAGI-CHAN!!*
*SAILOR MOON! HANG IN THERE!*

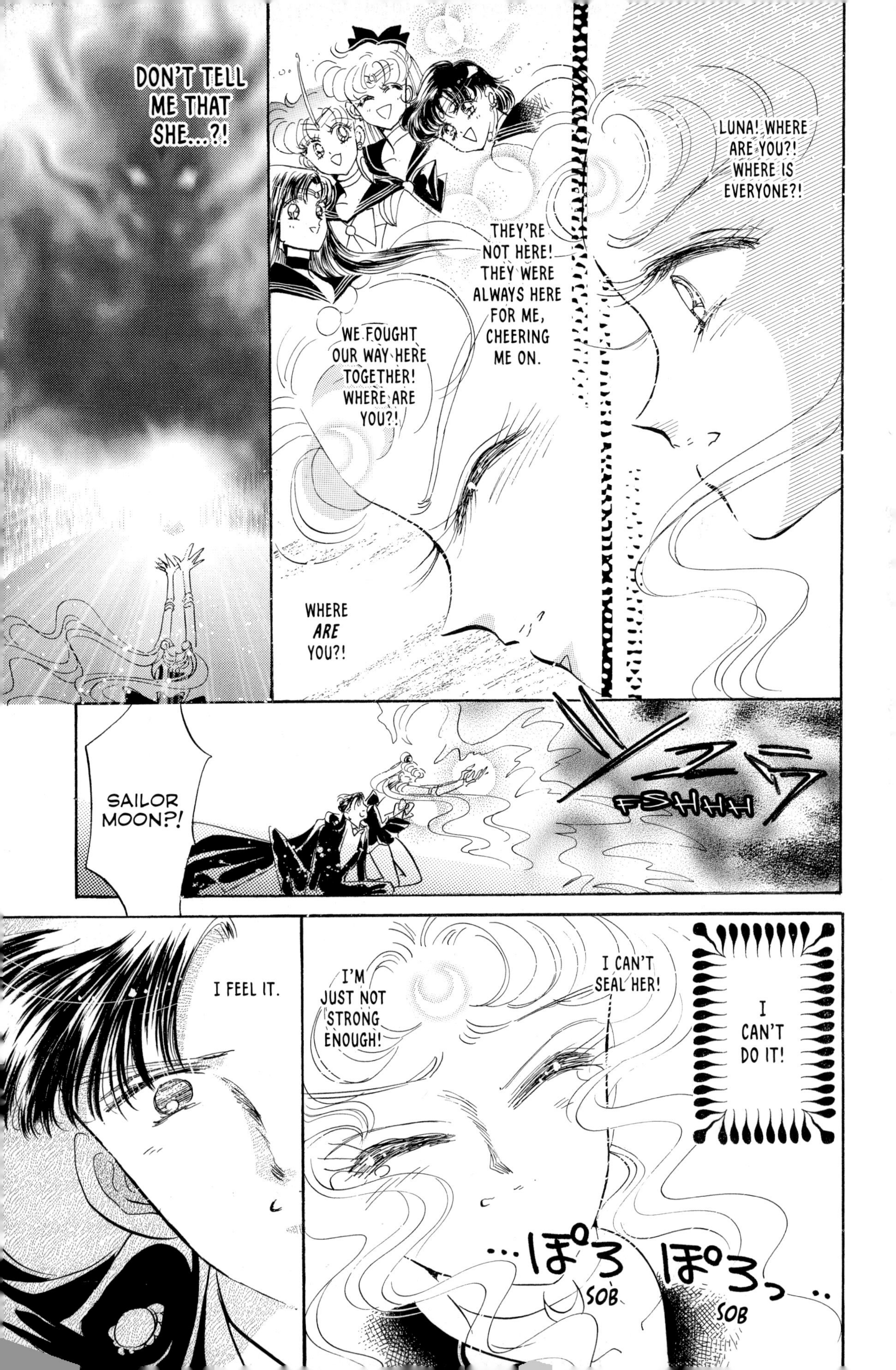
LUNA! WHERE ARE YOU?! WHERE IS EVERYONE?!
THEY'RE NOT HERE! THEY WERE ALWAYS HERE FOR ME, CHEERING ME ON.
WE FOUGHT OUR WAY HERE TOGETHER! WHERE ARE YOU?!
WHERE *ARE* YOU?!
DON'T TELL ME THAT SHE...?!
FSHHH
SAILOR MOON?!
I CAN'T DO IT!
I CAN'T SEAL HER!
I'M JUST NOT STRONG ENOUGH!
…ぽろ
SOB
ぽろっ…
SOB
I FEEL IT.

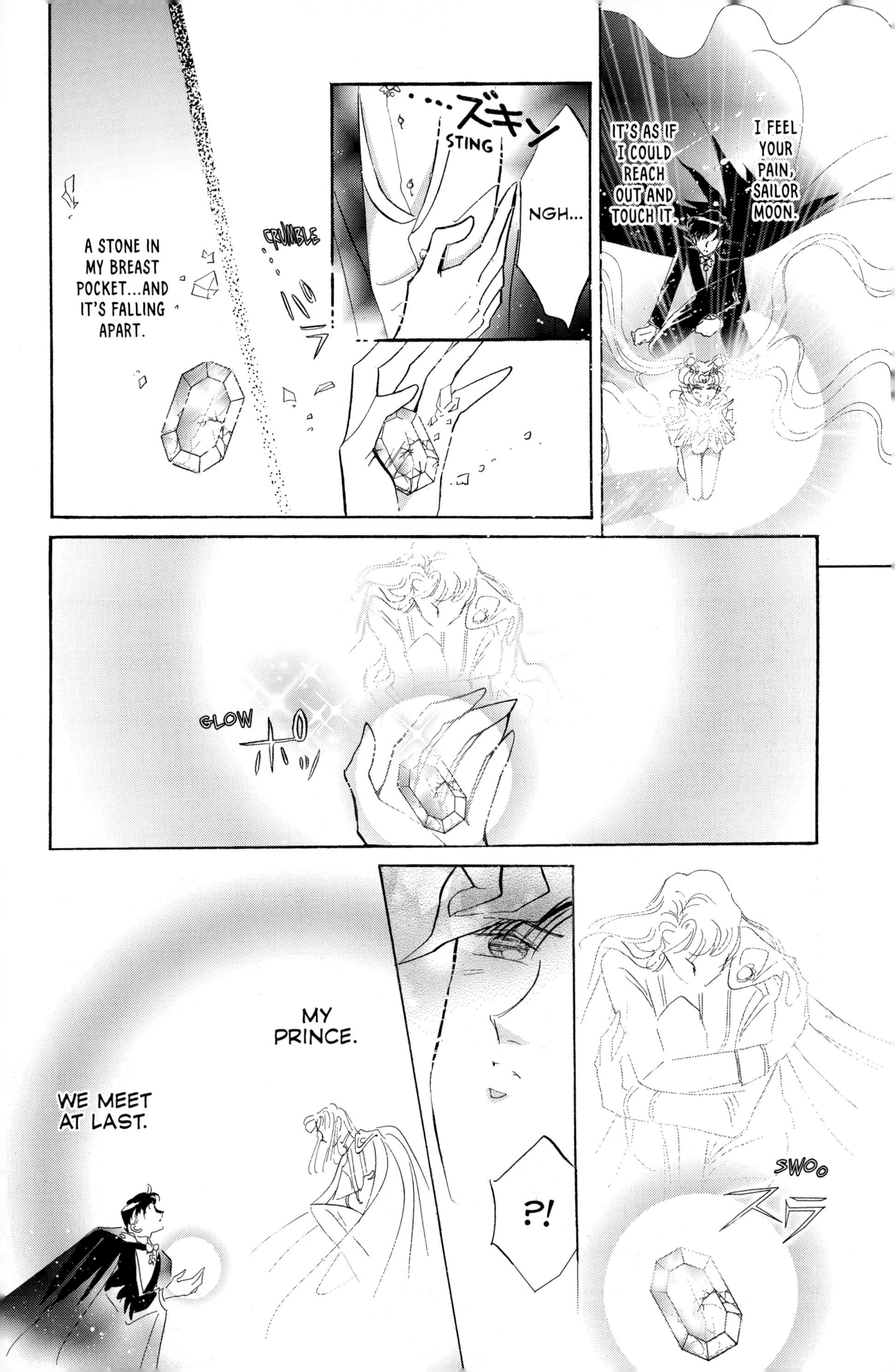

I FEEL YOUR PAIN, SAILOR MOON.
IT'S AS IF I COULD REACH OUT AND TOUCH IT.
…ズキン
STING
NGH...
CRUMBLE
A STONE IN MY BREAST POCKET...AND IT'S FALLING APART.
GLOW
SWOO
?!
MY PRINCE.
WE MEET AT LAST.

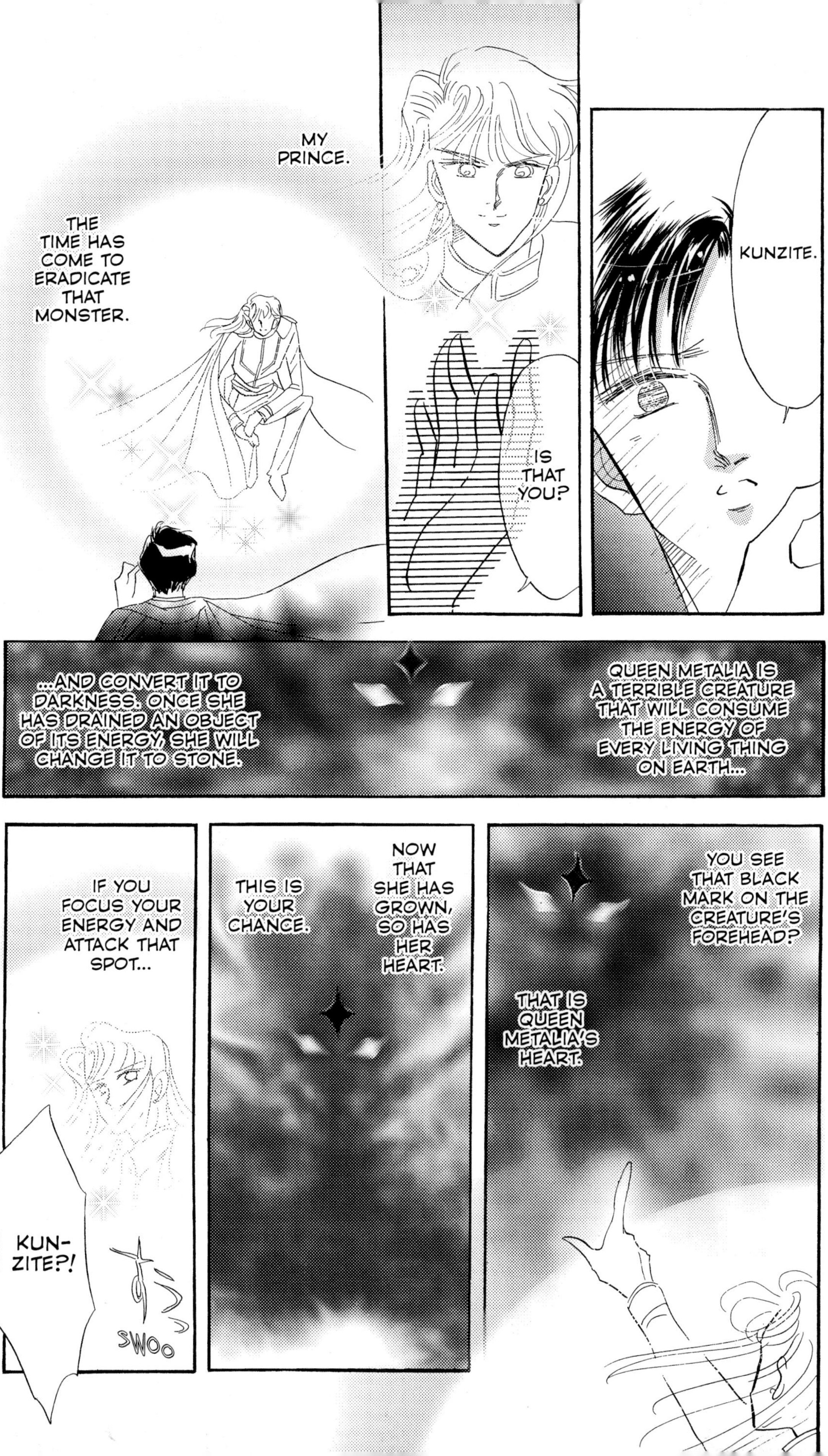
KUNZITE.
IS THAT YOU?
MY PRINCE.
THE TIME HAS COME TO ERADICATE THAT MONSTER.
QUEEN METALIA IS A TERRIBLE CREATURE THAT WILL CONSUME THE ENERGY OF EVERY LIVING THING ON EARTH...
...AND CONVERT IT TO DARKNESS. ONCE SHE HAS DRAINED AN OBJECT OF ITS ENERGY, SHE WILL CHANGE IT TO STONE.
YOU SEE THAT BLACK MARK ON THE CREATURE'S FOREHEAD?
THAT IS QUEEN METALIA'S HEART.
NOW THAT SHE HAS GROWN, SO HAS HER HEART.
THIS IS YOUR CHANCE.
IF YOU FOCUS YOUR ENERGY AND ATTACK THAT SPOT...
KUN-ZITE?!
SWOO

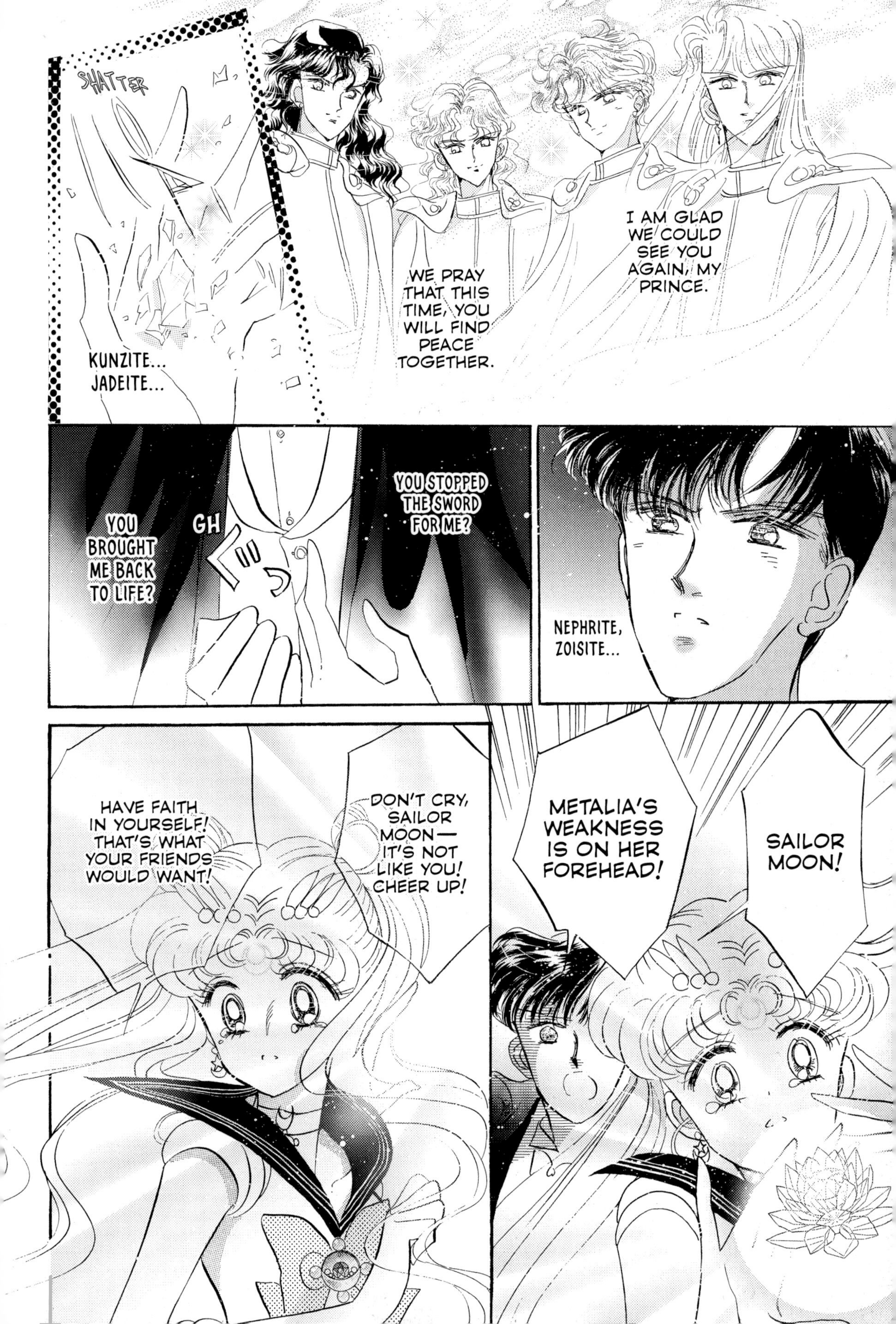
I AM GLAD WE COULD SEE YOU AGAIN, MY PRINCE.
WE PRAY THAT THIS TIME, YOU WILL FIND PEACE TOGETHER.
SHATTER
KUNZITE... JADEITE...
NEPHRITE, ZOISITE...
YOU STOPPED THE SWORD FOR ME?
GH
YOU BROUGHT ME BACK TO LIFE?
SAILOR MOON!
METALIA'S WEAKNESS IS ON HER FOREHEAD!
DON'T CRY, SAILOR MOON— IT'S NOT LIKE YOU! CHEER UP!
HAVE FAITH IN YOURSELF! THAT'S WHAT YOUR FRIENDS WOULD WANT!

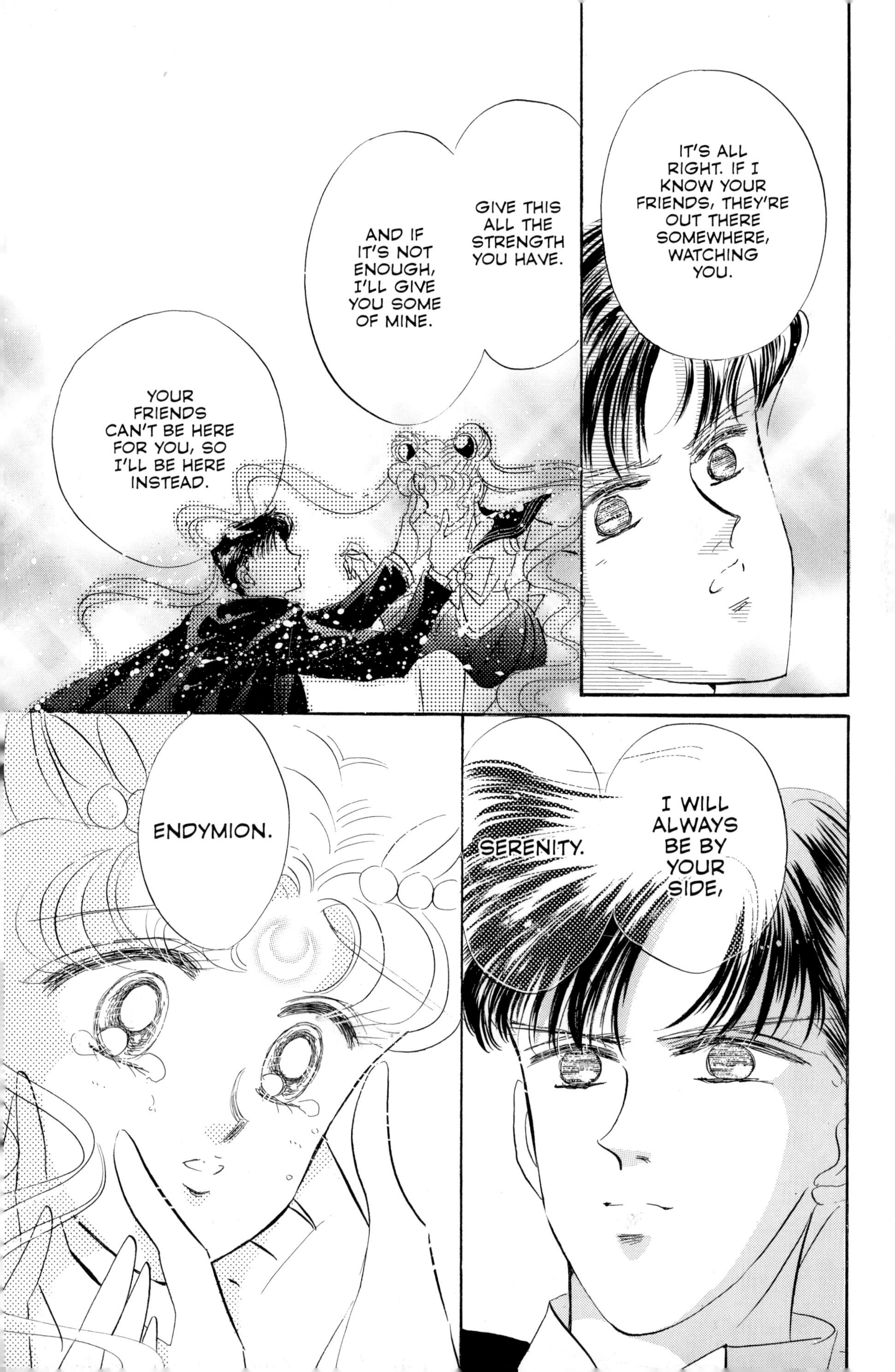
IT'S ALL RIGHT. IF I KNOW YOUR FRIENDS, THEY'RE OUT THERE SOMEWHERE, WATCHING YOU.
GIVE THIS ALL THE STRENGTH YOU HAVE.
AND IF IT'S NOT ENOUGH, I'LL GIVE YOU SOME OF MINE.
YOUR FRIENDS CAN'T BE HERE FOR YOU, SO I'LL BE HERE INSTEAD.
I WILL ALWAYS BE BY YOUR SIDE,
SERENITY.
ENDYMION.

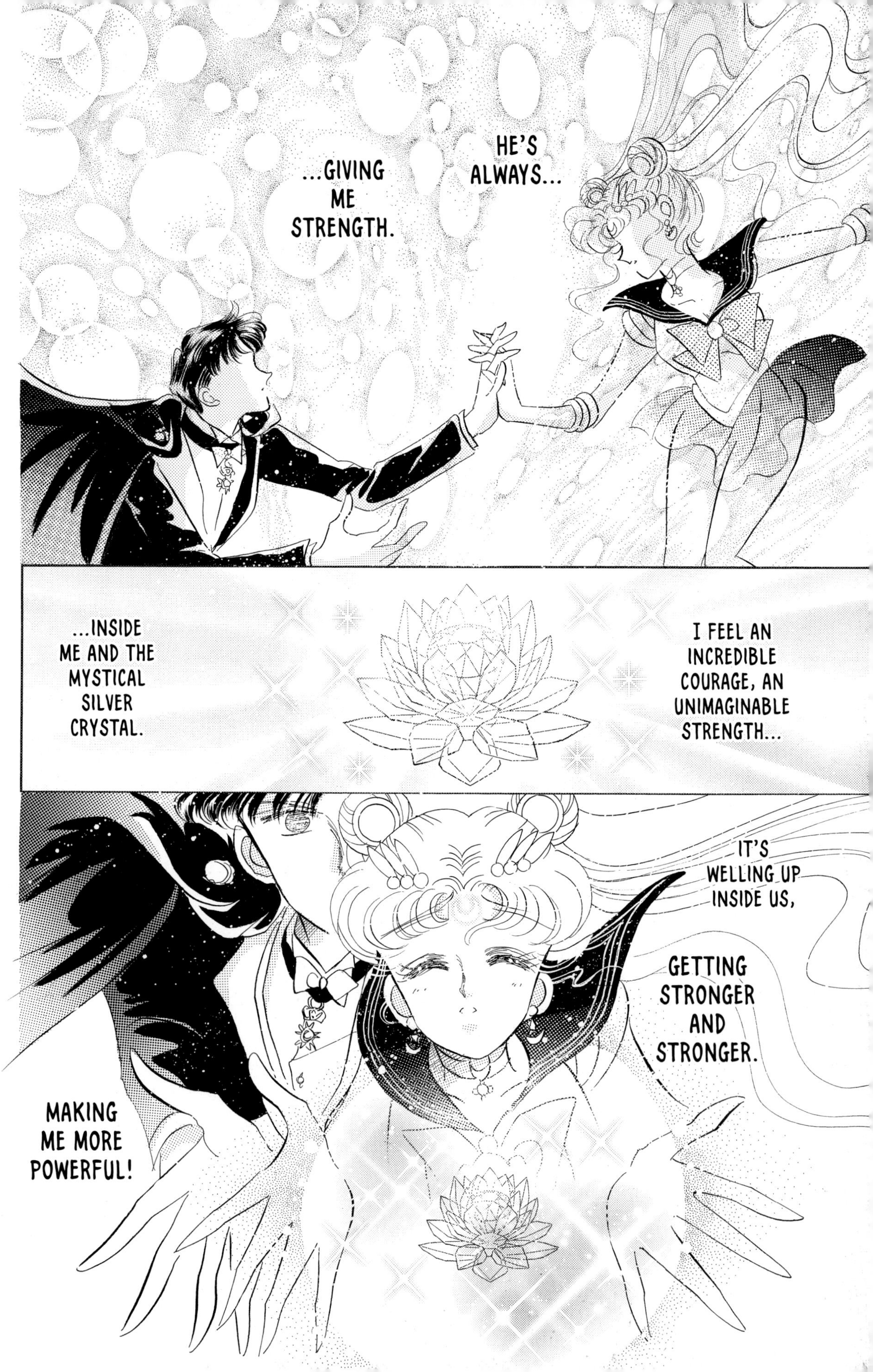
HE'S ALWAYS...
...GIVING ME STRENGTH.
I FEEL AN INCREDIBLE COURAGE, AN UNIMAGINABLE STRENGTH...
...INSIDE ME AND THE MYSTICAL SILVER CRYSTAL.
IT'S WELLING UP INSIDE US,
GETTING STRONGER AND STRONGER.
MAKING ME MORE POWERFUL!

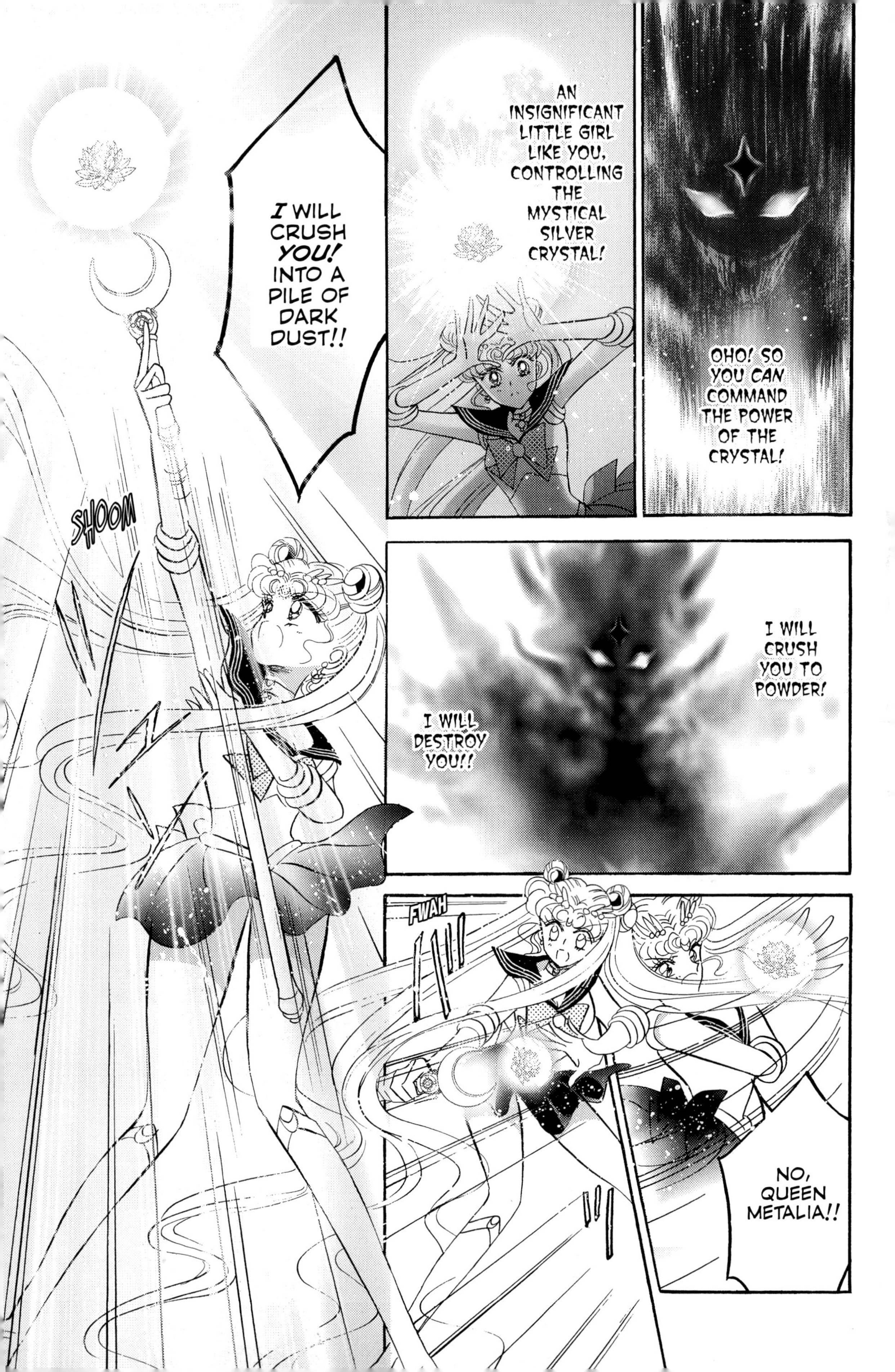
OHO! SO YOU CAN COMMAND THE POWER OF THE CRYSTAL!
AN INSIGNIFICANT LITTLE GIRL LIKE YOU, CONTROLLING THE MYSTICAL SILVER CRYSTAL!
I WILL CRUSH YOU TO POWDER!
I WILL DESTROY YOU!!
NO, QUEEN METALIA!!
FWAH
I WILL CRUSH YOU! INTO A PILE OF DARK DUST!!
SHOOM

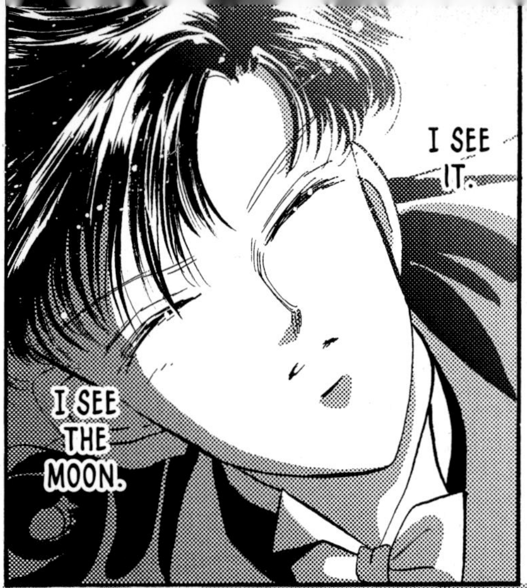
I SEE IT.
I SEE THE MOON.

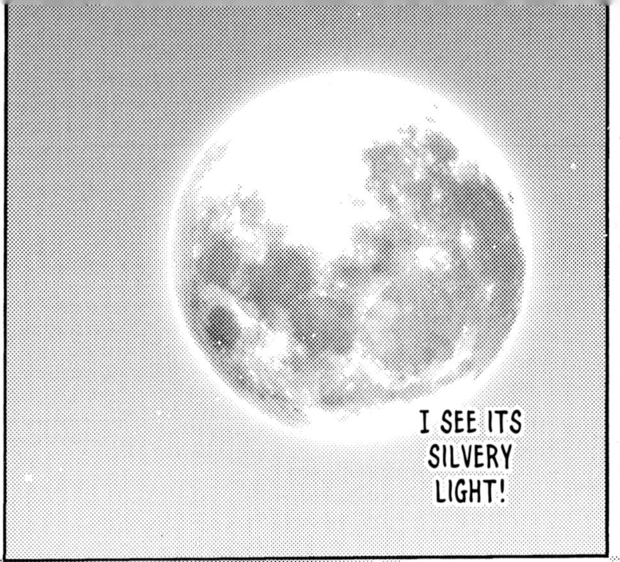
I SEE ITS SILVERY LIGHT!

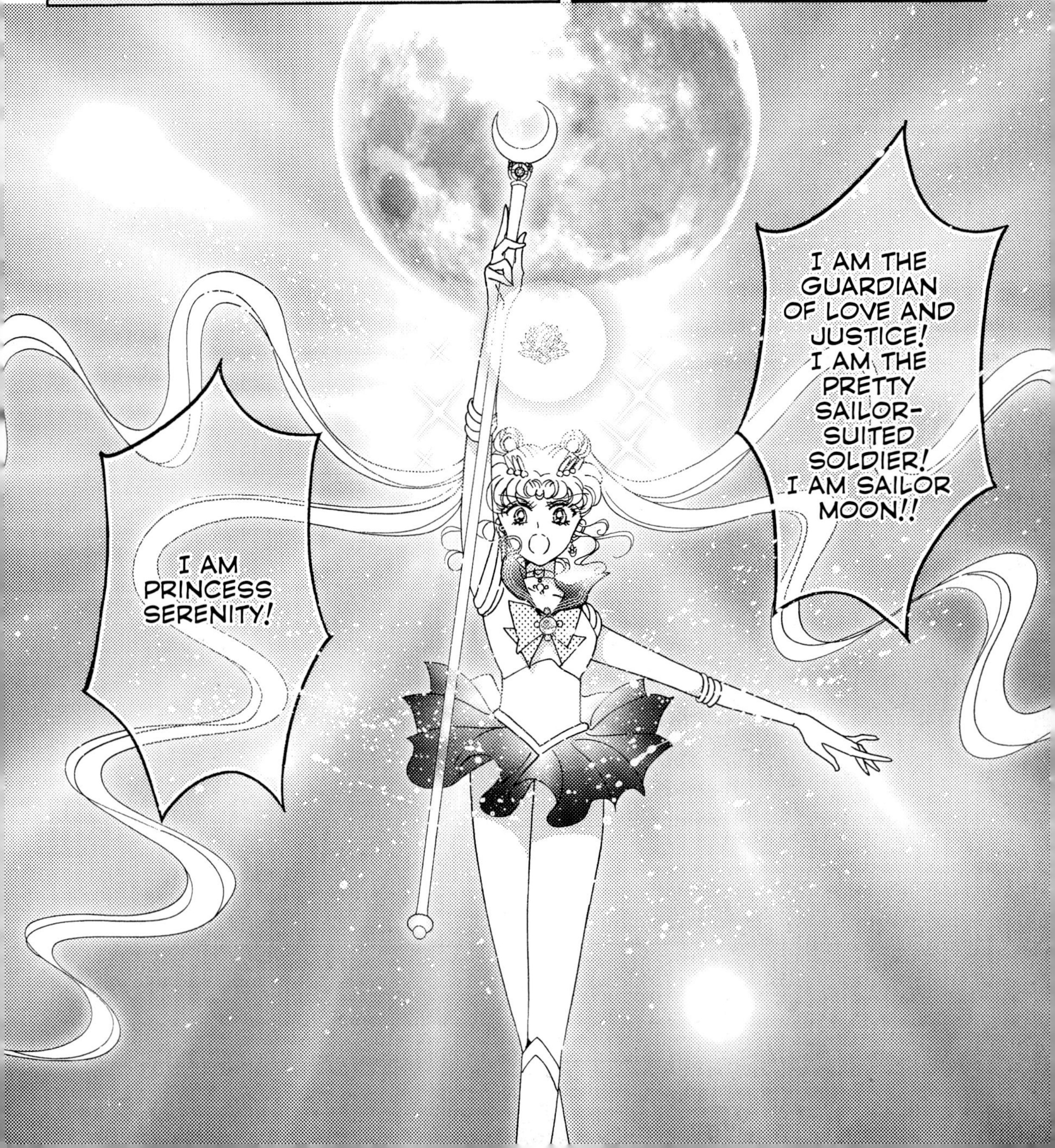
I AM THE GUARDIAN OF LOVE AND JUSTICE! I AM THE PRETTY SAILOR-SUITED SOLDIER! I AM SAILOR MOON!!
I AM PRINCESS SERENITY!

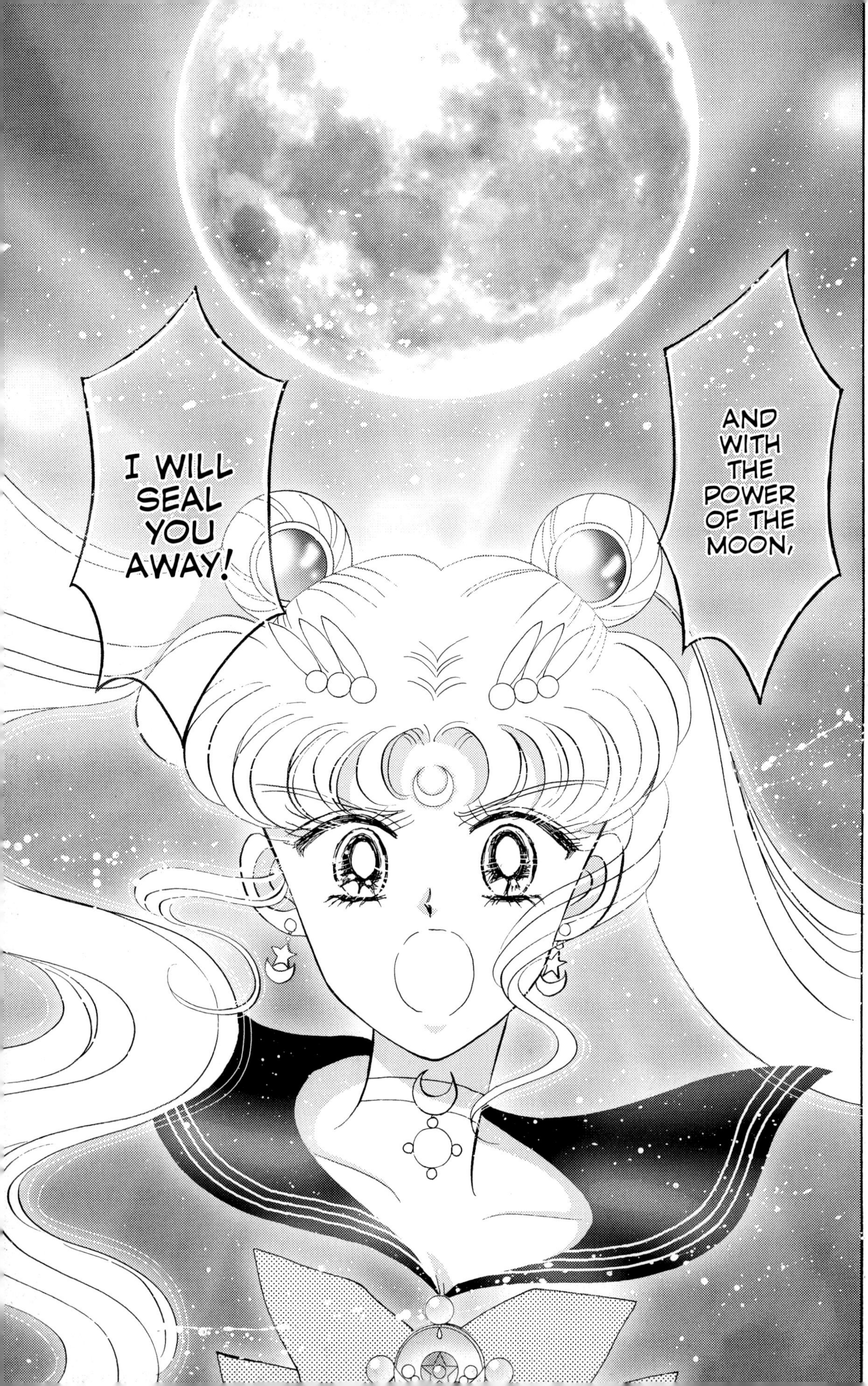
AND WITH THE POWER OF THE MOON,
I WILL SEAL YOU AWAY!

Pretty Guardian

Sailor Moon

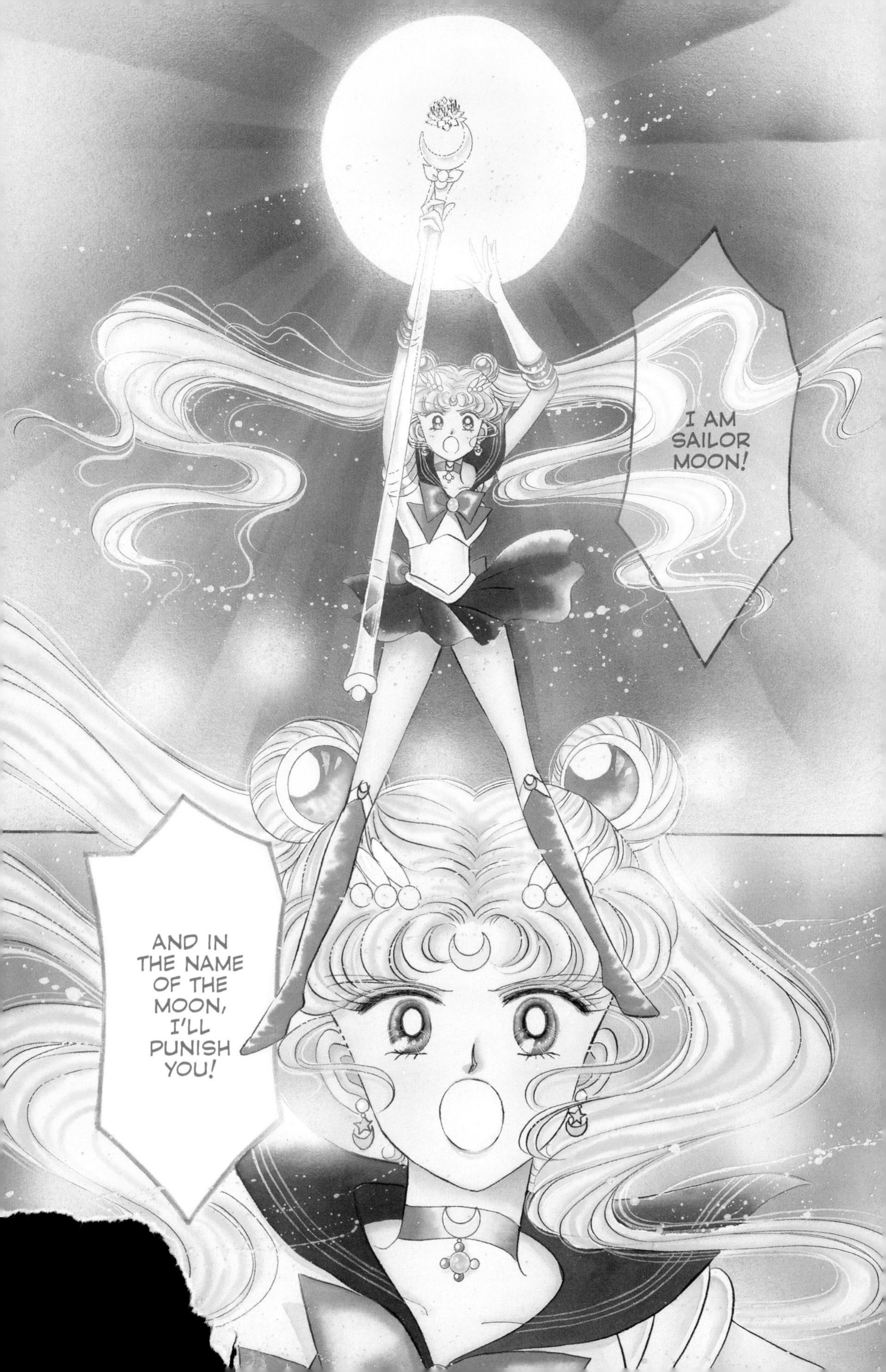
I AM SAILOR MOON!
AND IN THE NAME OF THE MOON, I'LL PUNISH YOU!

# An Ending and a Beginning: La Petite Étrangère

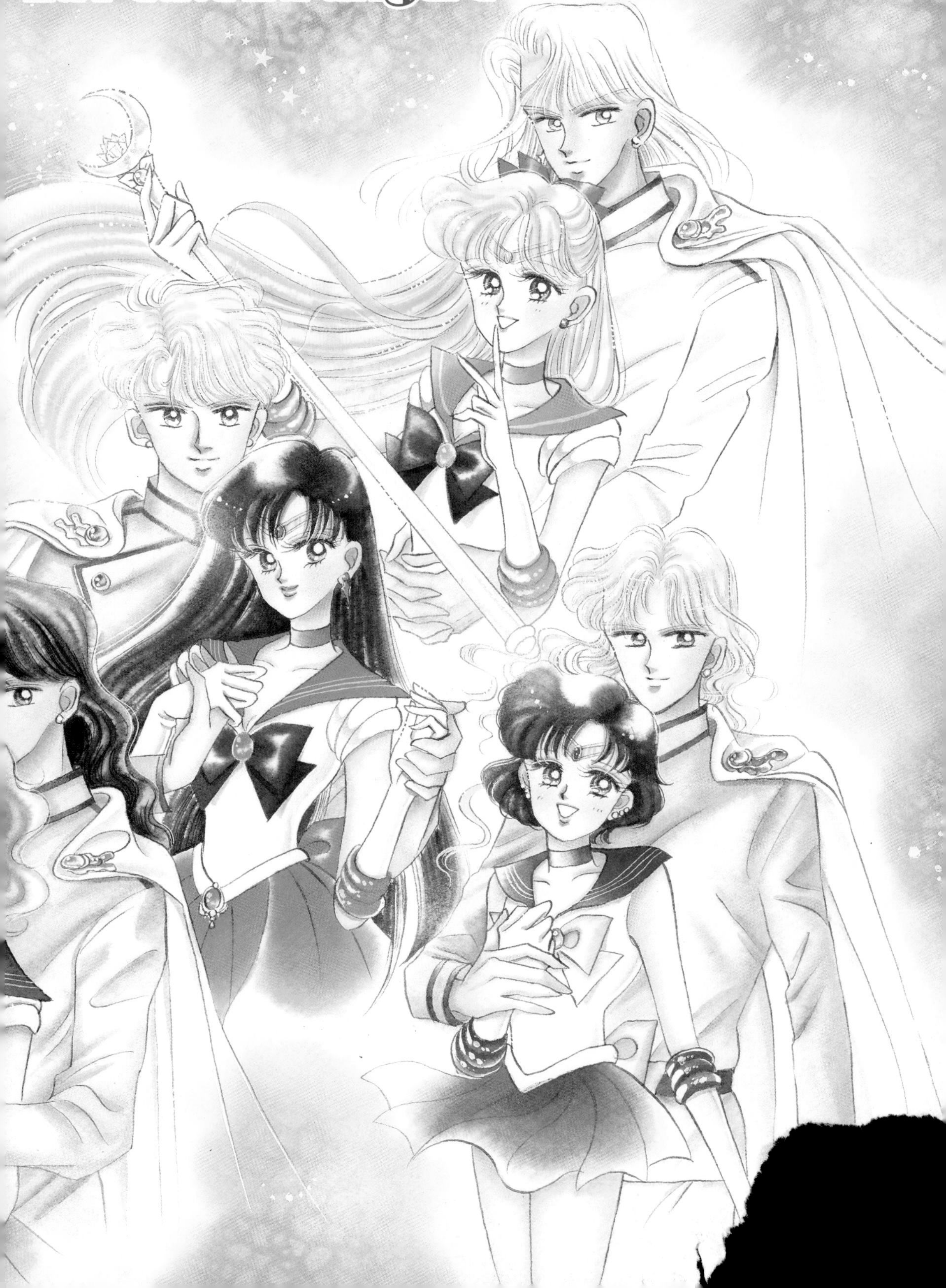

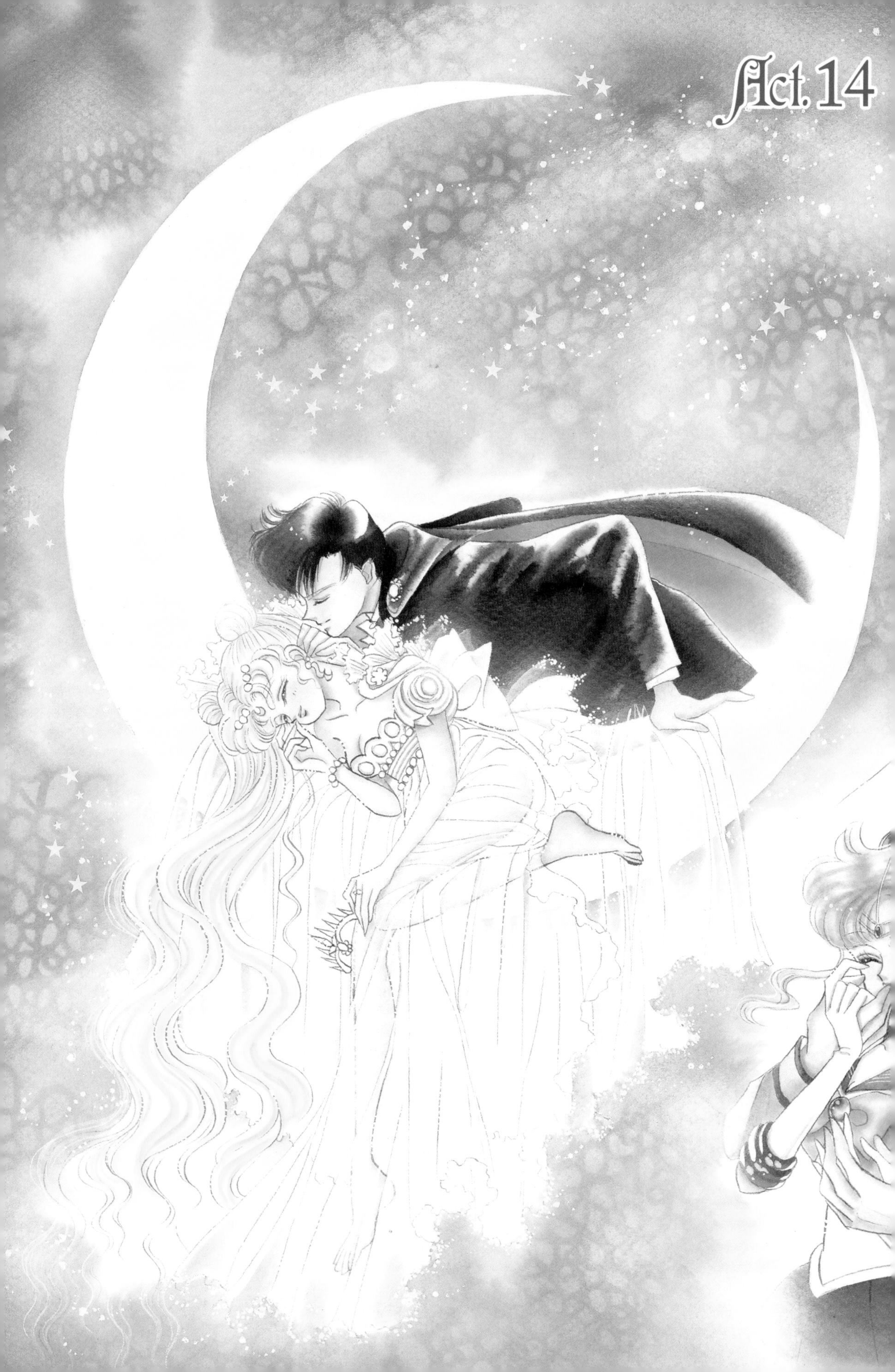
Act. 14

Pretty Guardian Sailor Moon

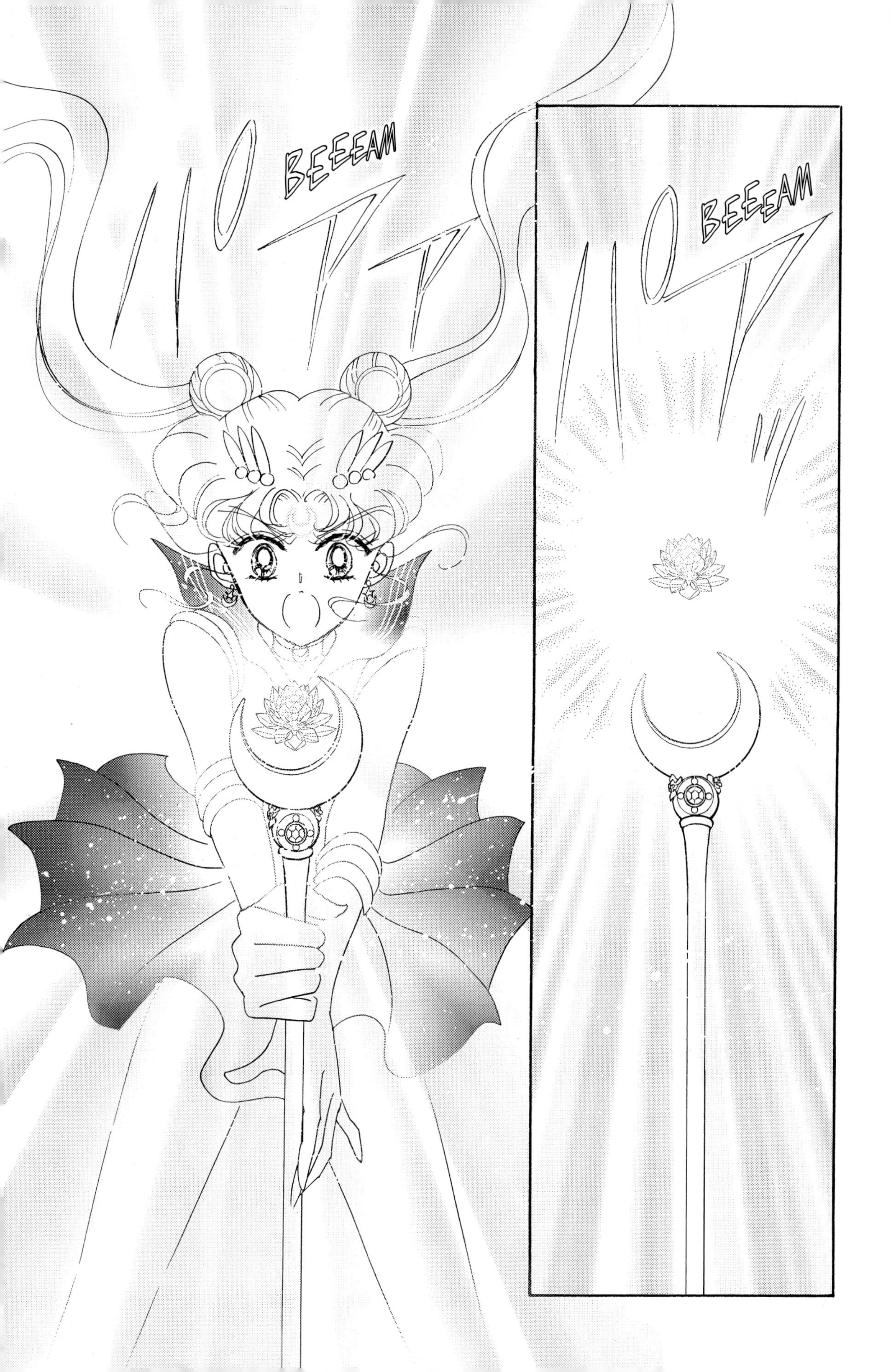
BEEEAM
BEEEAM

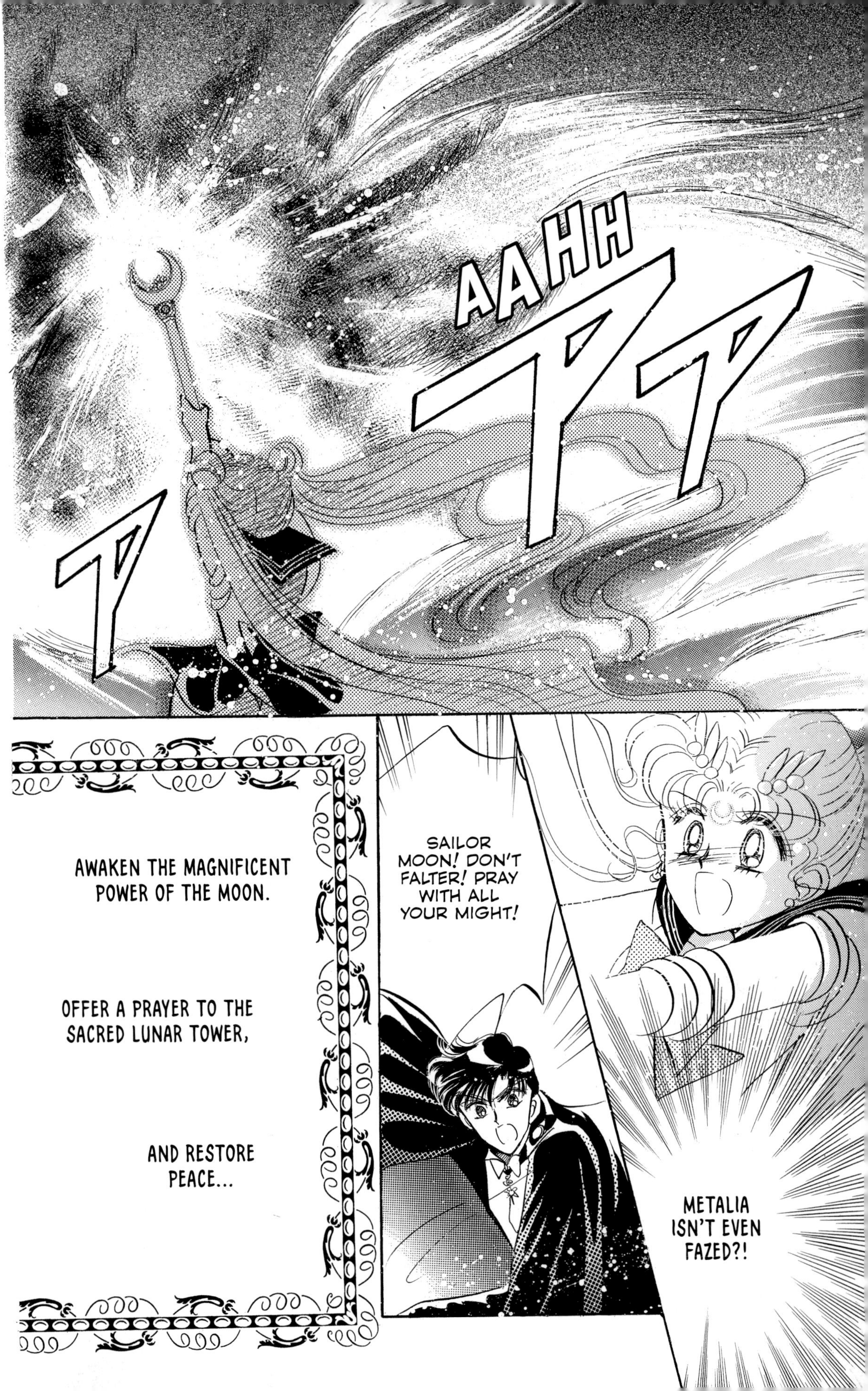
AAHH
METALIA ISN'T EVEN FAZED?!
SAILOR MOON! DON'T FALTER! PRAY WITH ALL YOUR MIGHT!
AWAKEN THE MAGNIFICENT POWER OF THE MOON.
OFFER A PRAYER TO THE SACRED LUNAR TOWER,
AND RESTORE PEACE...

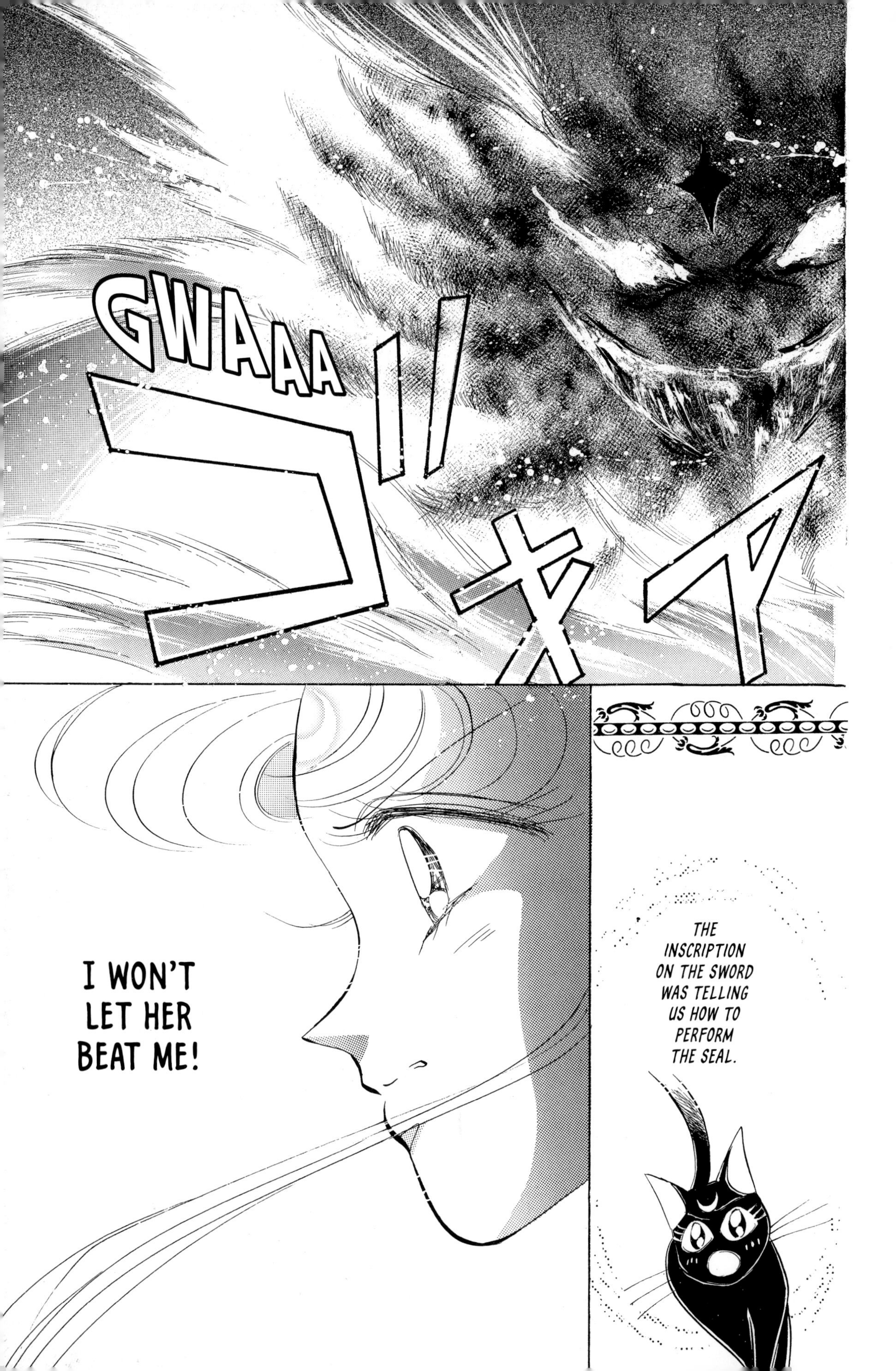
GWAAA
THE INSCRIPTION ON THE SWORD WAS TELLING US HOW TO PERFORM THE SEAL.
I WON'T LET HER BEAT ME!

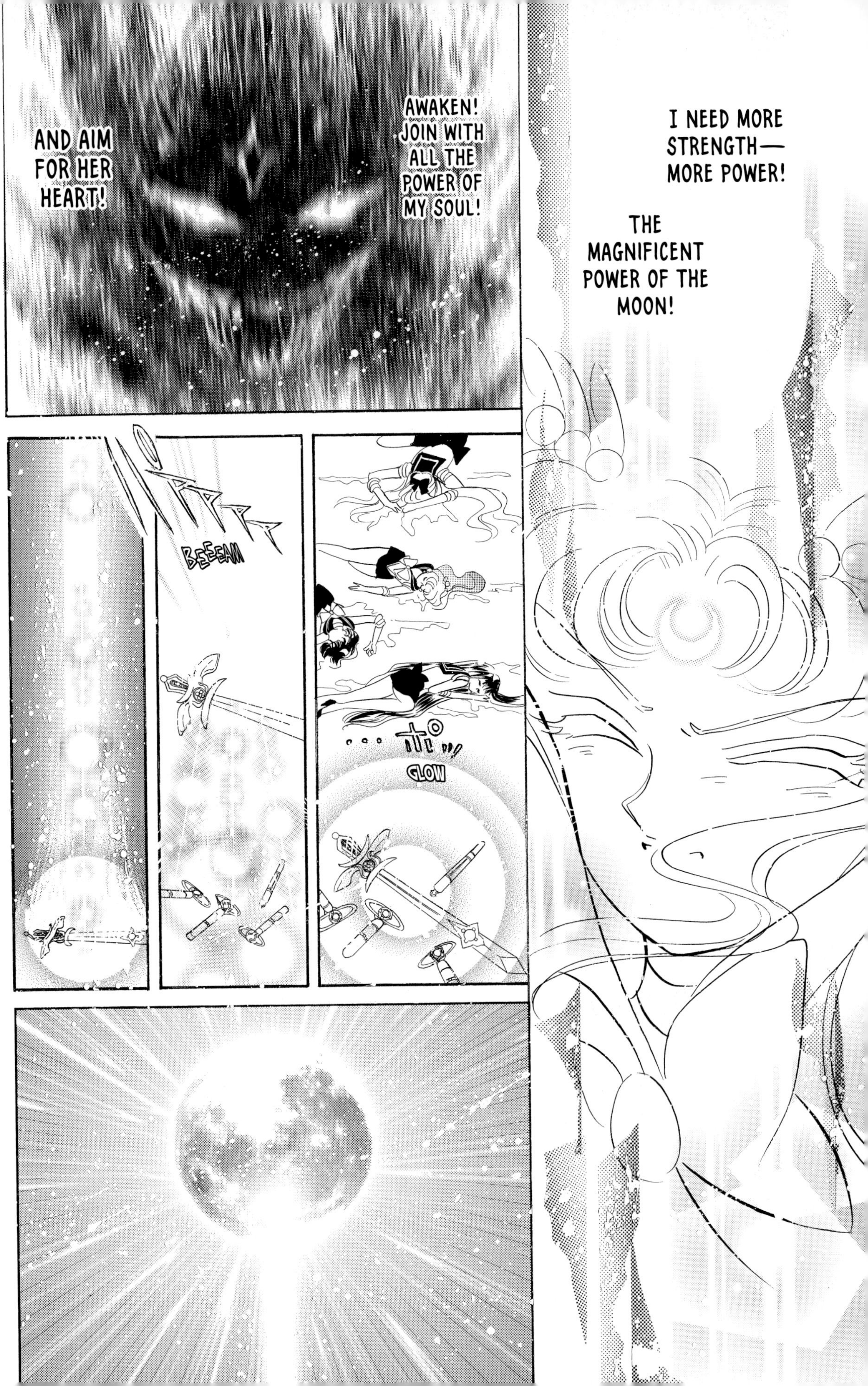
I NEED MORE STRENGTH— MORE POWER!
THE MAGNIFICENT POWER OF THE MOON!
AWAKEN! JOIN WITH ALL THE POWER OF MY SOUL!
AND AIM FOR HER HEART!
GLOW
BEEEAM

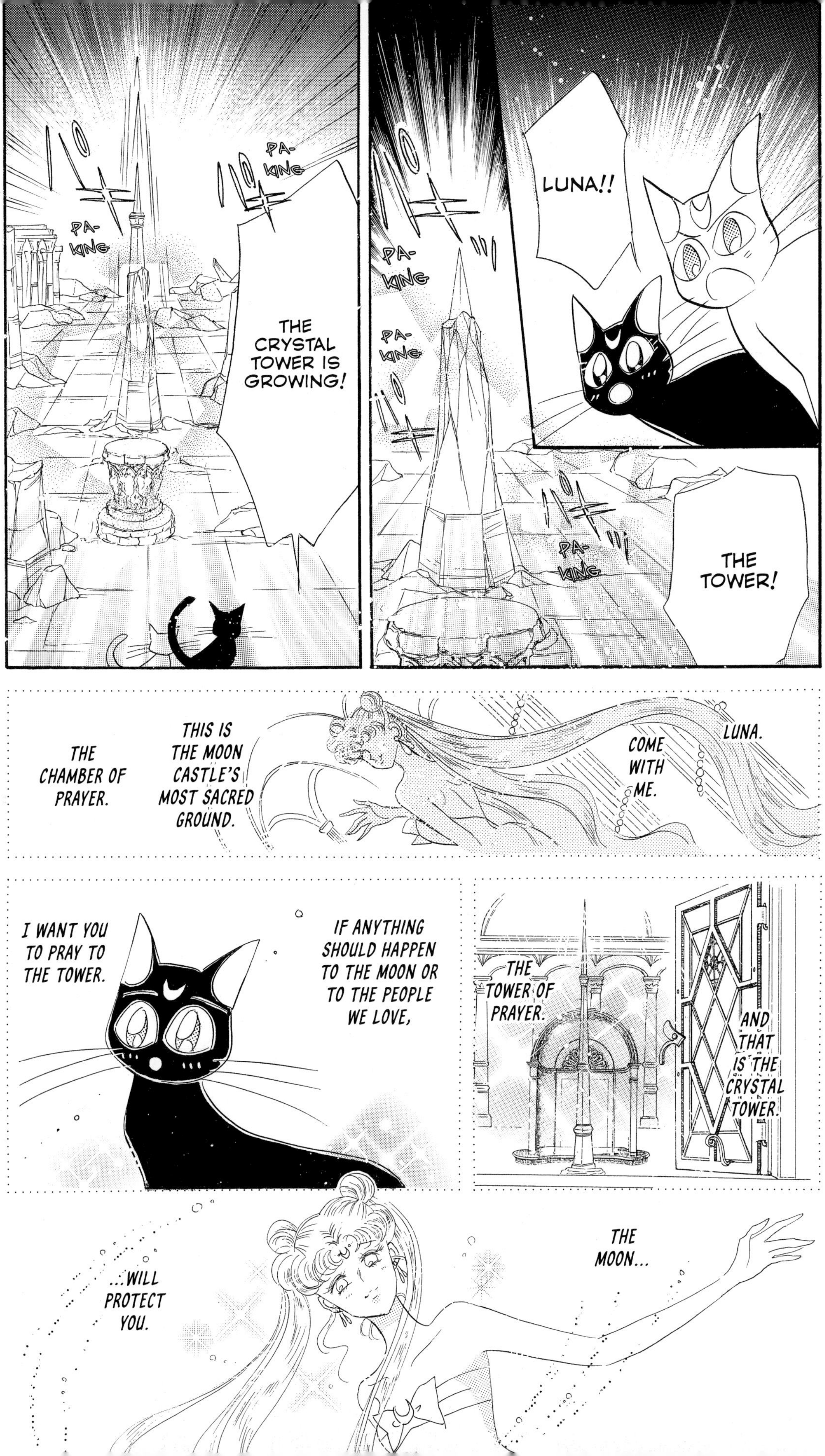
LUNA!!
PA-KING
PA-KING
PA-KING
THE TOWER!
PA-KING
PA-KING
PA-KING
THE CRYSTAL TOWER IS GROWING!
LUNA.
COME WITH ME.
THIS IS THE MOON CASTLE'S MOST SACRED GROUND.
THE CHAMBER OF PRAYER.
THE TOWER OF PRAYER.
AND THAT IS THE CRYSTAL TOWER.
IF ANYTHING SHOULD HAPPEN TO THE MOON OR TO THE PEOPLE WE LOVE,
I WANT YOU TO PRAY TO THE TOWER.
THE MOON...
...WILL PROTECT YOU.

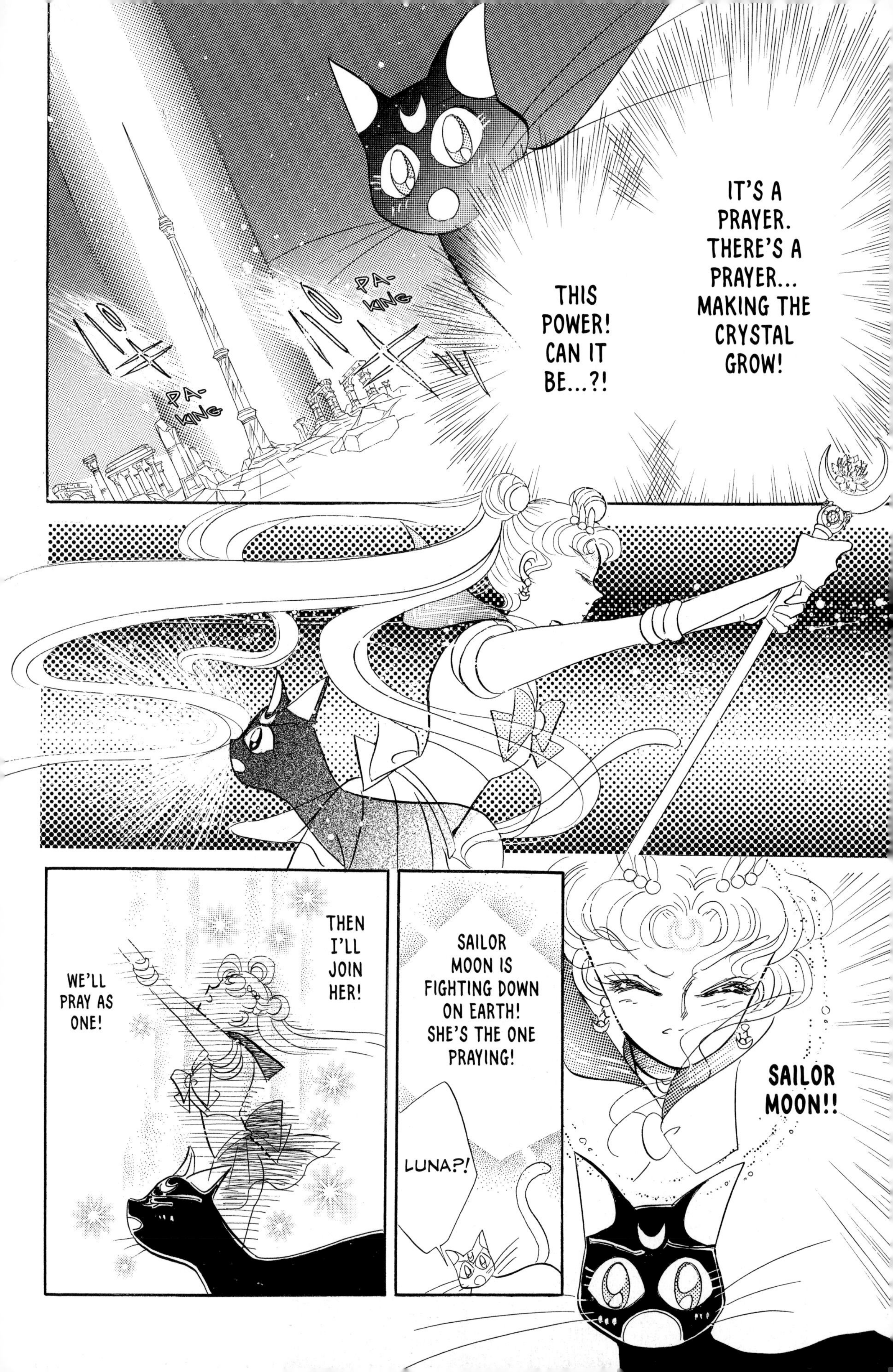
IT'S A PRAYER. THERE'S A PRAYER... MAKING THE CRYSTAL GROW!
THIS POWER! CAN IT BE...?!
PA-KING
PA-KING
SAILOR MOON!!
SAILOR MOON IS FIGHTING DOWN ON EARTH! SHE'S THE ONE PRAYING!
LUNA?!
THEN I'LL JOIN HER!
WE'LL PRAY AS ONE!

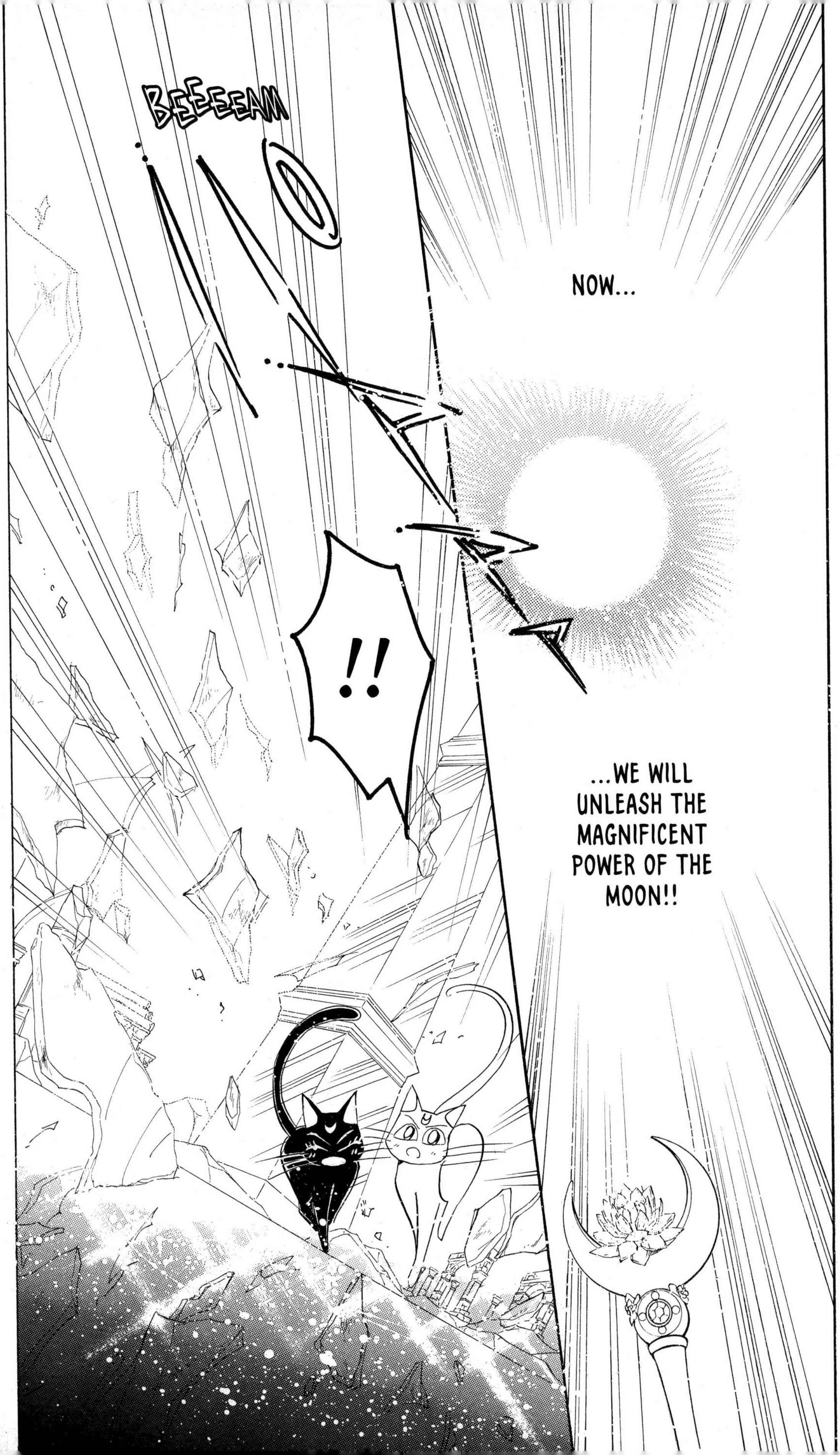
NOW...
...WE WILL UNLEASH THE MAGNIFICENT POWER OF THE MOON!!
BEEEEAM
!!

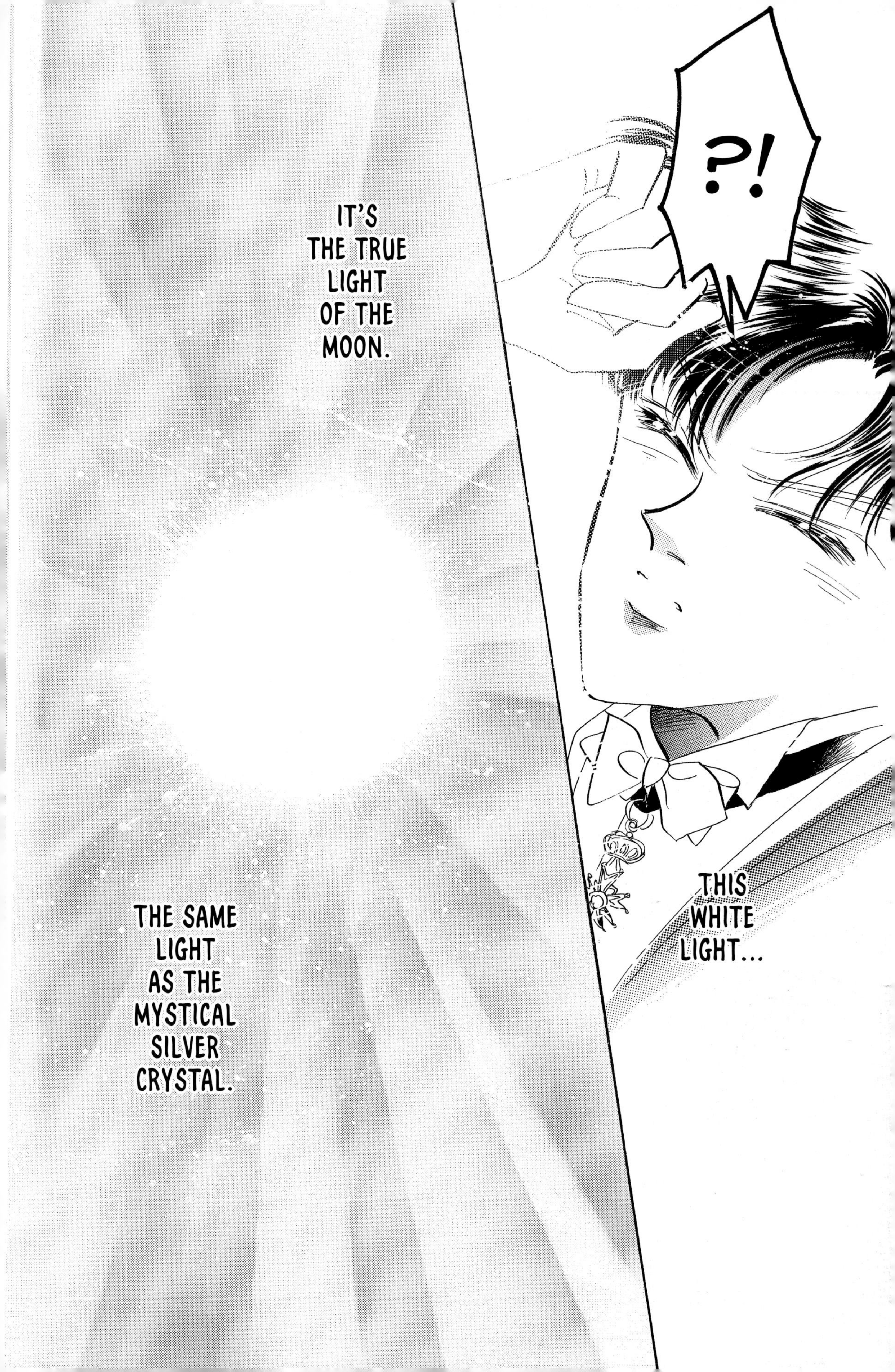
?!
THIS WHITE LIGHT...
IT'S THE TRUE LIGHT OF THE MOON.
THE SAME LIGHT AS THE MYSTICAL SILVER CRYSTAL.

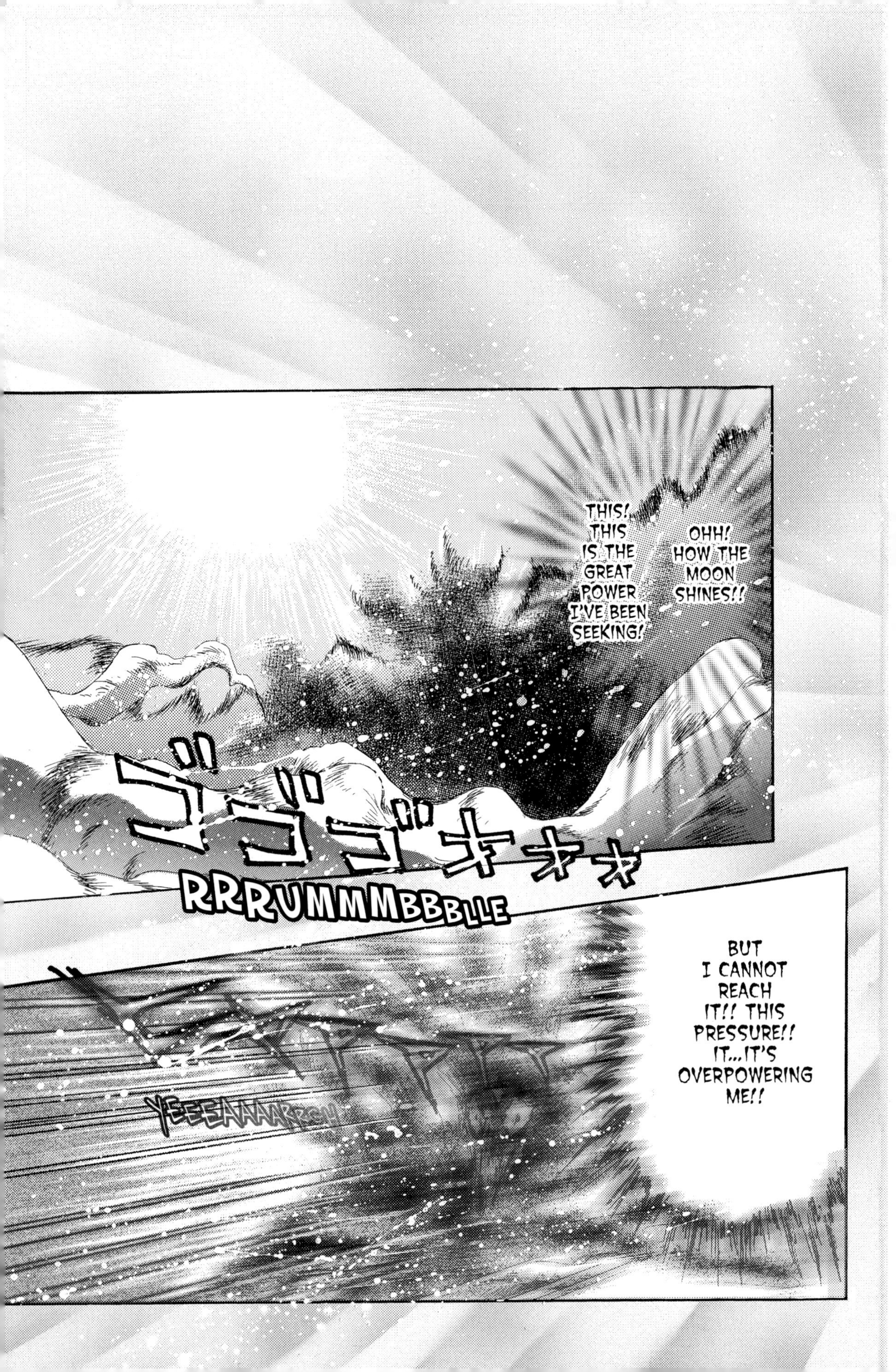
OHH! HOW THE MOON SHINES!!
THIS! THIS IS THE GREAT POWER I'VE BEEN SEEKING!
ゴゴゴオォォ
RRRUMMMBBBLLE
BUT I CANNOT REACH IT!! THIS PRESSURE!! IT...IT'S OVERPOWERING ME!!
YEEEAAAARRGH

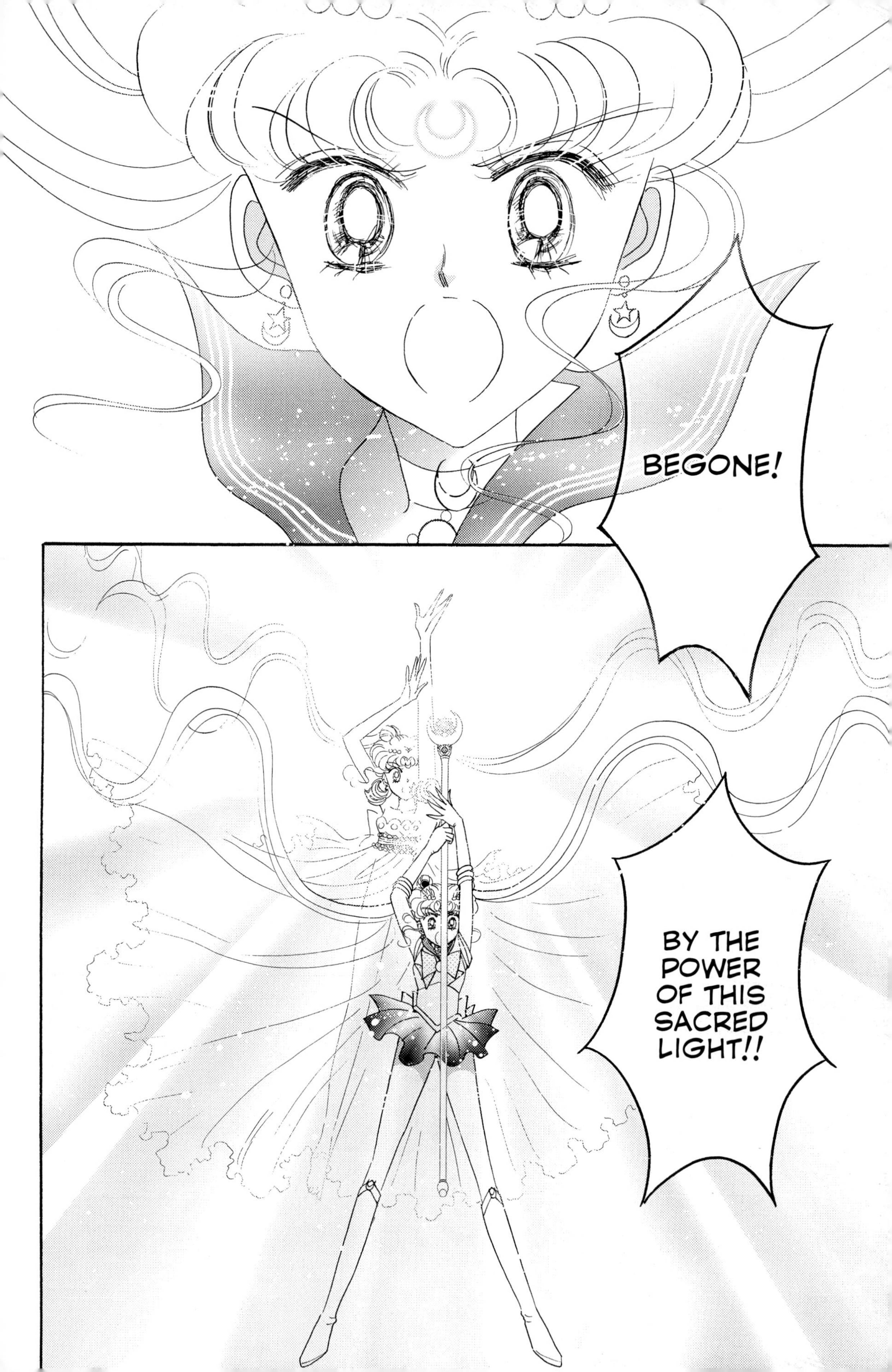
BEGONE!
BY THE POWER OF THIS SACRED LIGHT!!

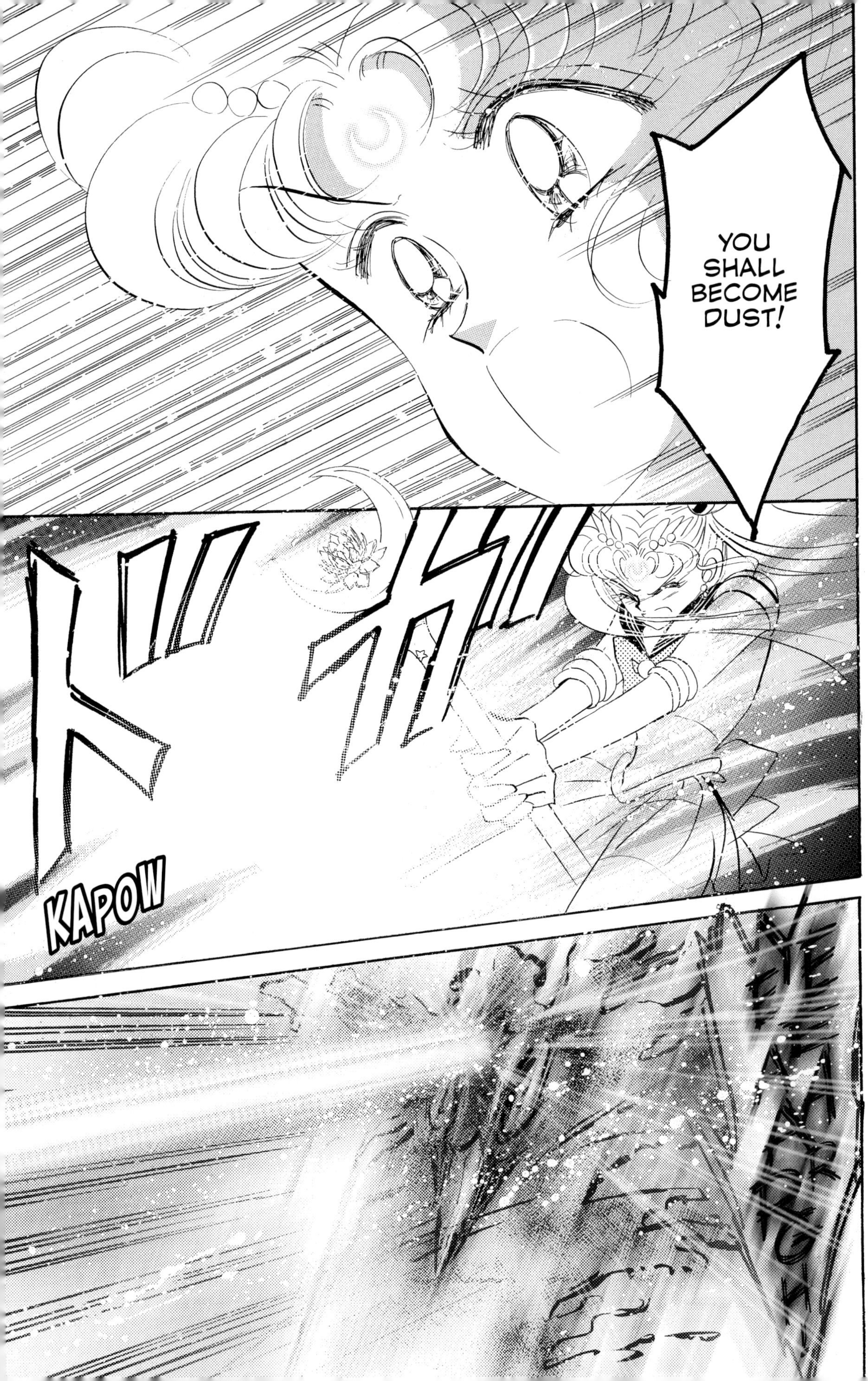
YOU SHALL BECOME DUST!
KAPOW

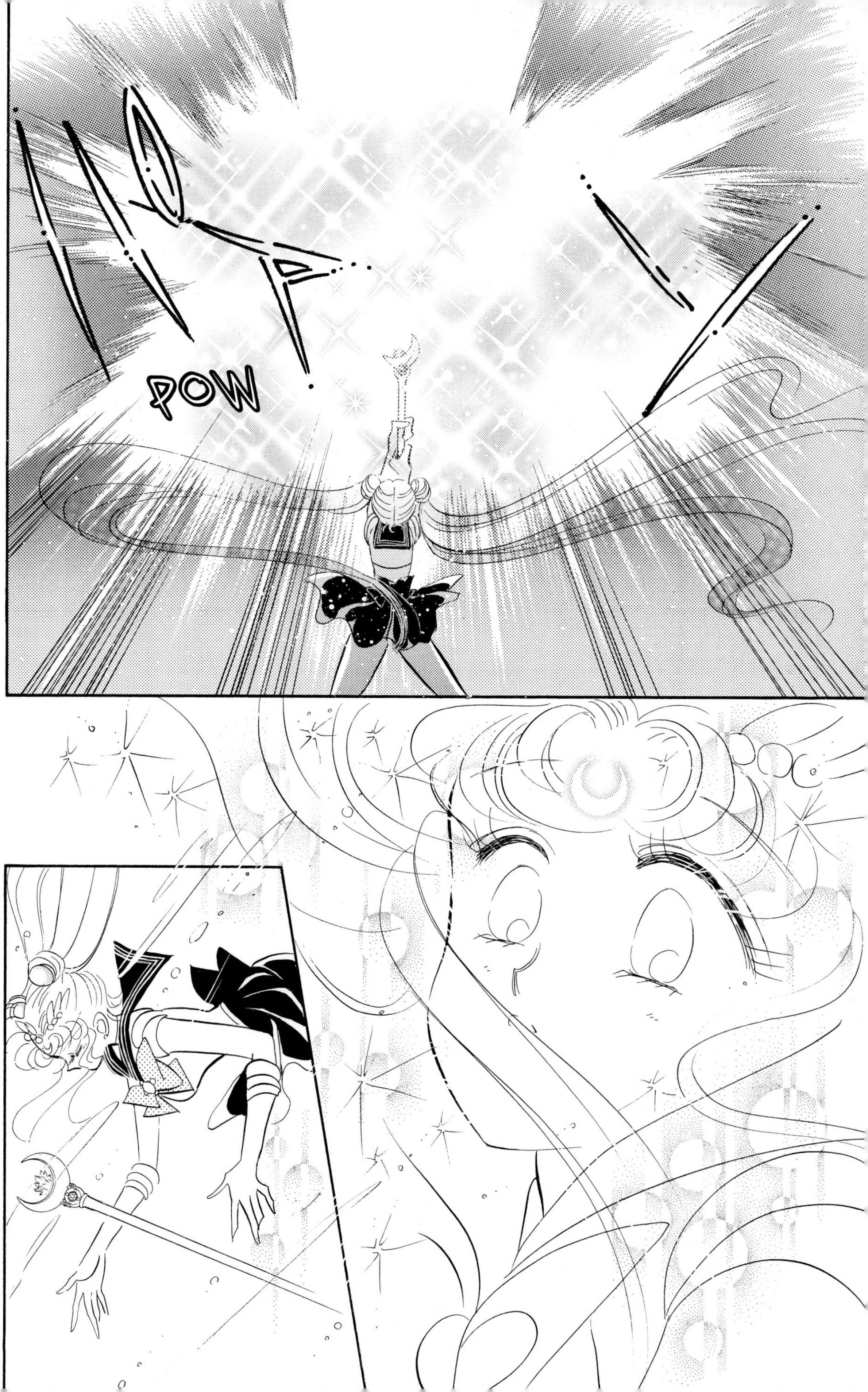
POW

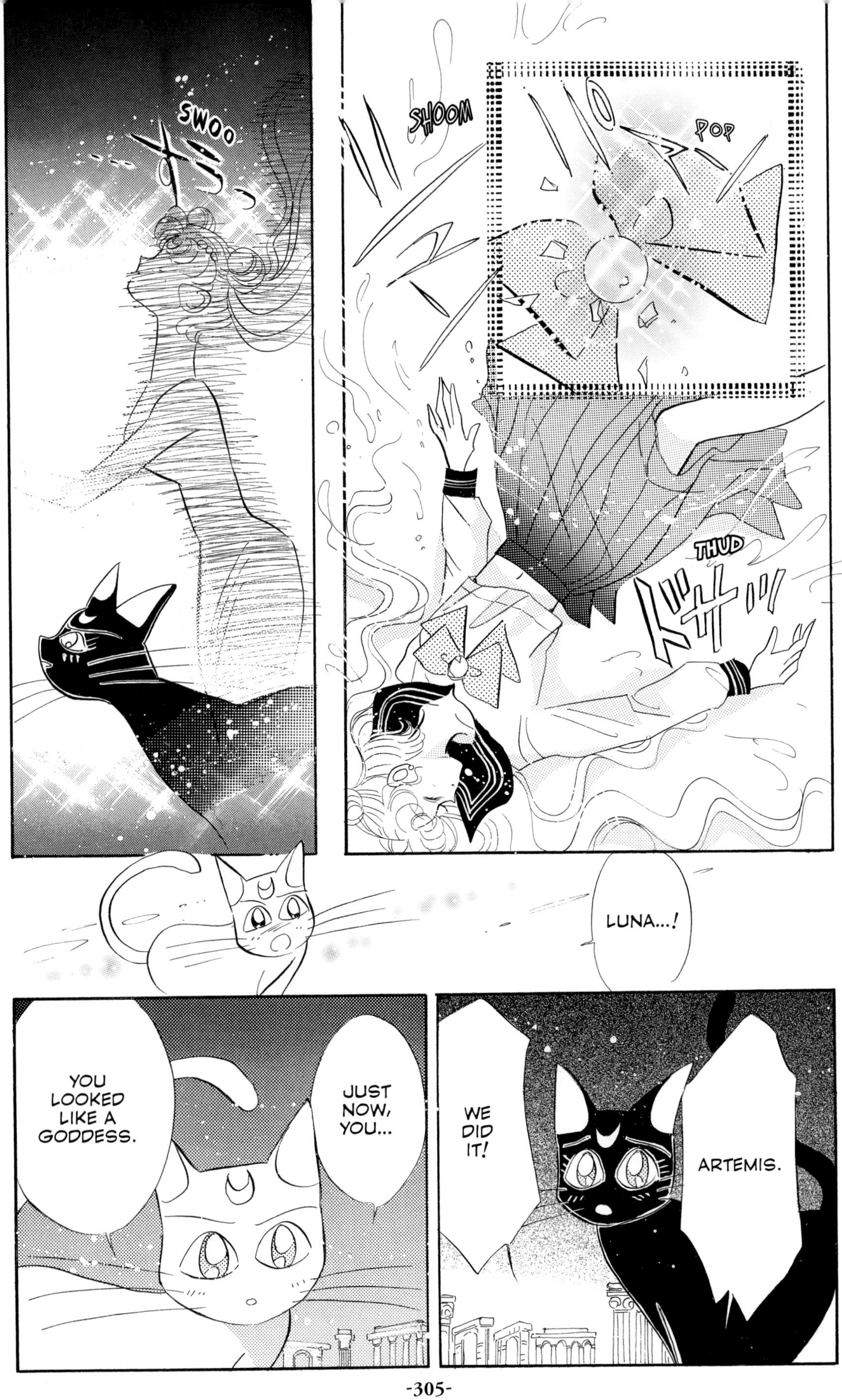
POP
SHOOM
THUD
SWOO
LUNA...!
ARTEMIS.
WE DID IT!
JUST NOW, YOU...
YOU LOOKED LIKE A GODDESS.

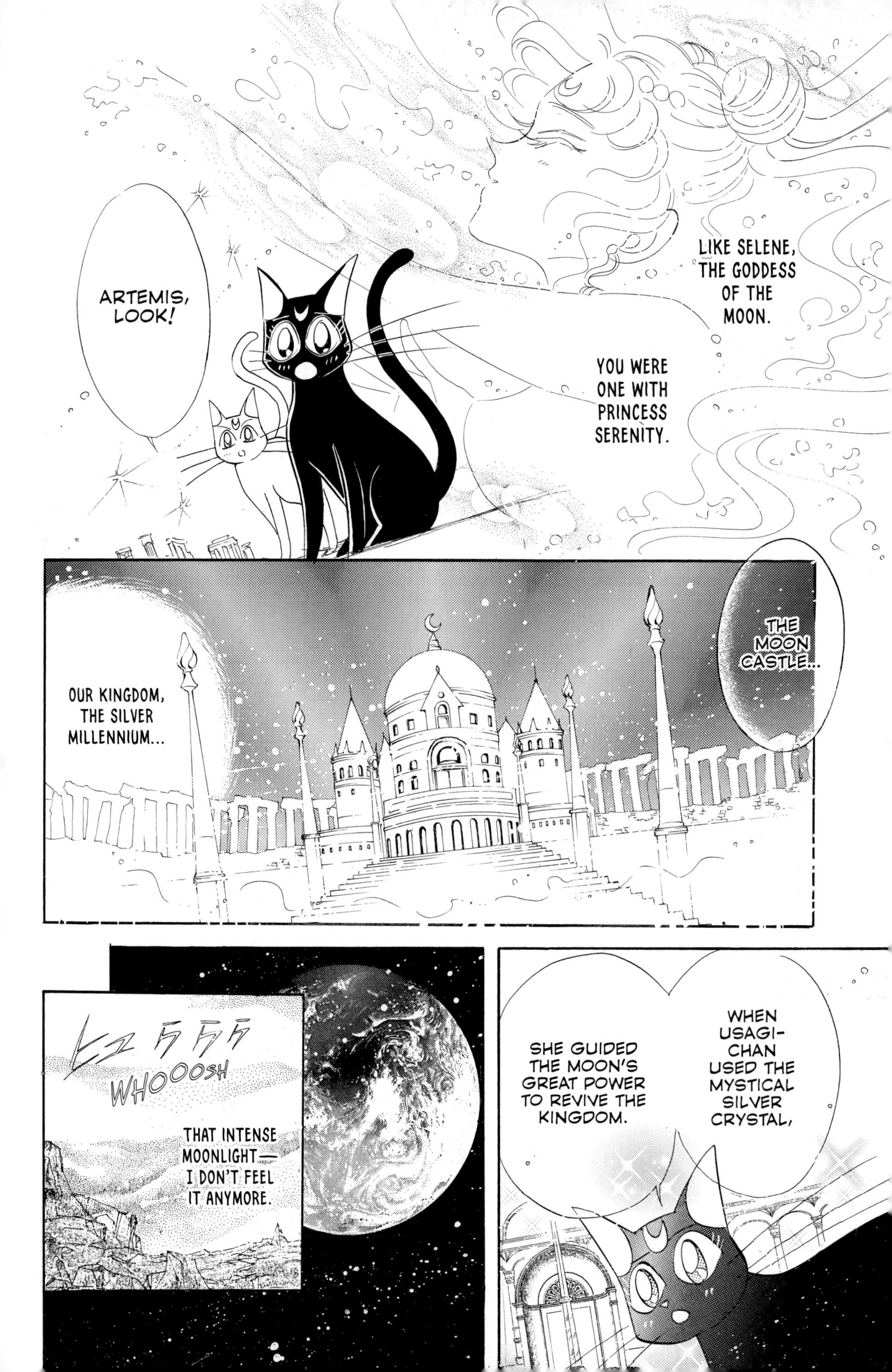
LIKE SELENE, THE GODDESS OF THE MOON.
YOU WERE ONE WITH PRINCESS SERENITY.
ARTEMIS, LOOK!
THE MOON CASTLE...
OUR KINGDOM, THE SILVER MILLENNIUM...
WHEN USAGI-CHAN USED THE MYSTICAL SILVER CRYSTAL,
SHE GUIDED THE MOON'S GREAT POWER TO REVIVE THE KINGDOM.
ヒュラララ
WHOOOSH
THAT INTENSE MOONLIGHT— I DON'T FEEL IT ANYMORE.

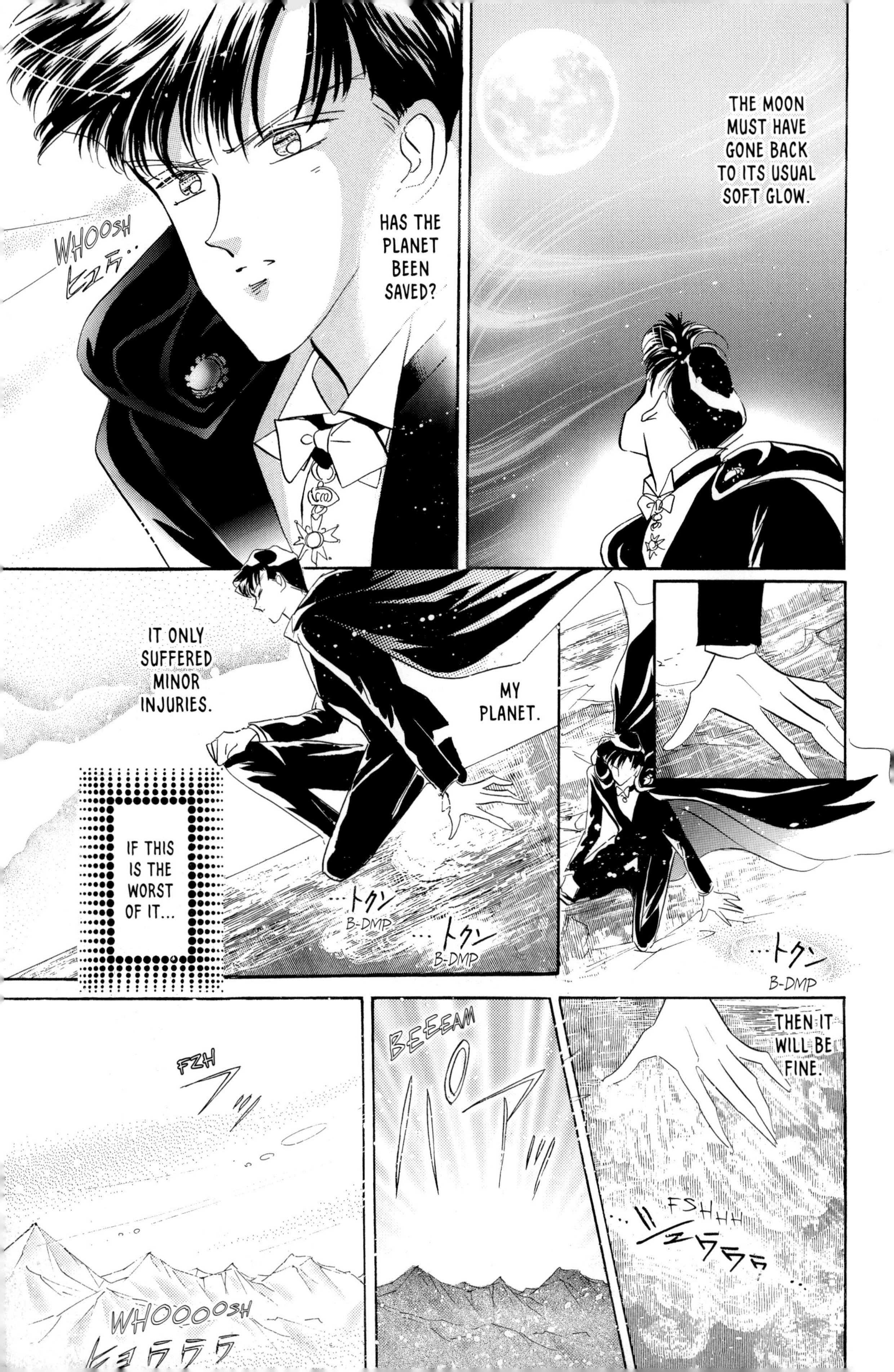

THE MOON MUST HAVE GONE BACK TO ITS USUAL SOFT GLOW.
HAS THE PLANET BEEN SAVED?
WHOOSH
…トクン
B-DMP
MY PLANET.
IT ONLY SUFFERED MINOR INJURIES.
…トクン
B-DMP
…トクン
B-DMP
IF THIS IS THE WORST OF IT…
THEN IT WILL BE FINE.
FSHHH
BEEEAM
パアッ
FZH
フッ
WHOOOOOSH

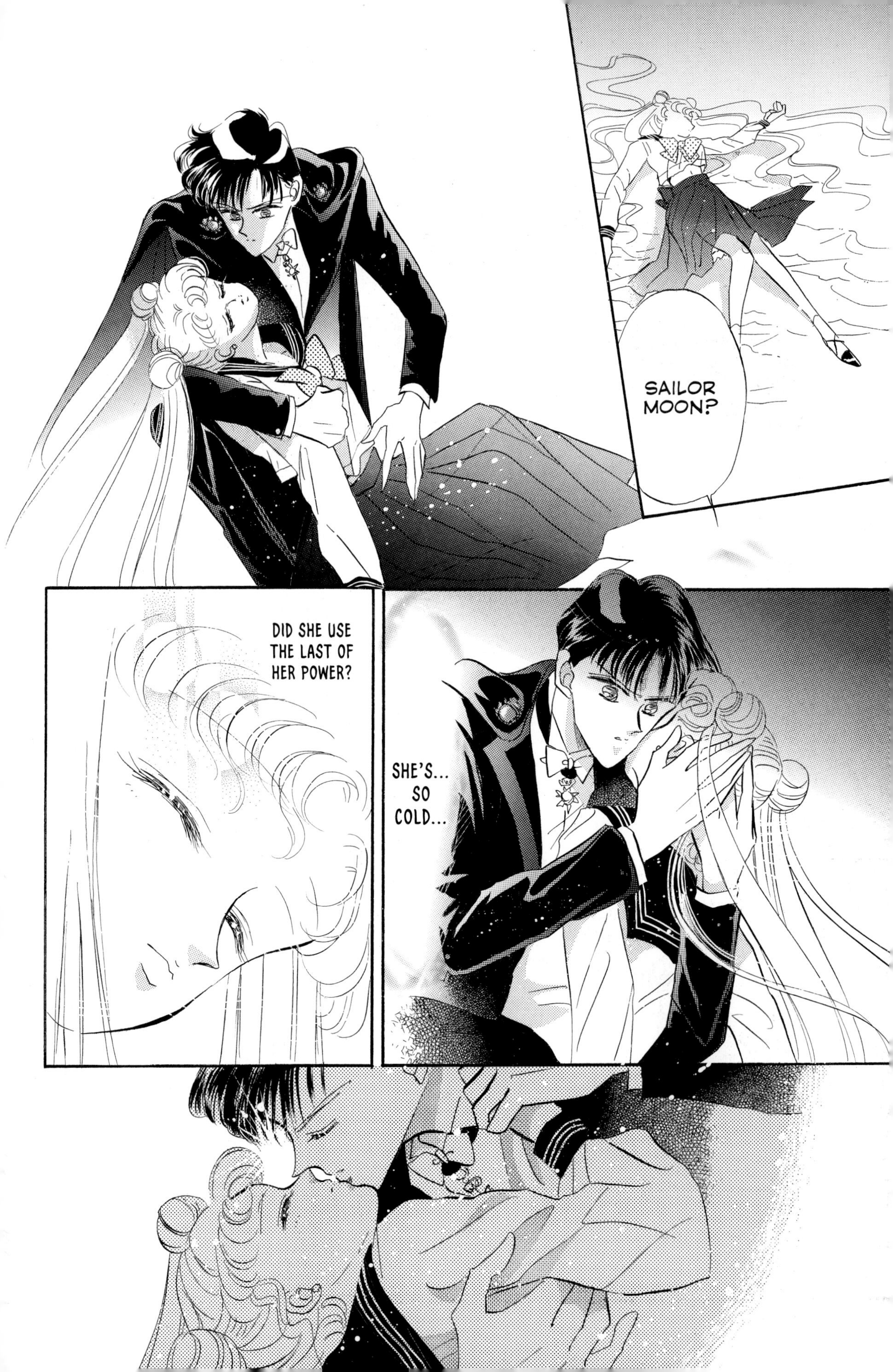
SAILOR MOON?
SHE'S... SO COLD...
DID SHE USE THE LAST OF HER POWER?

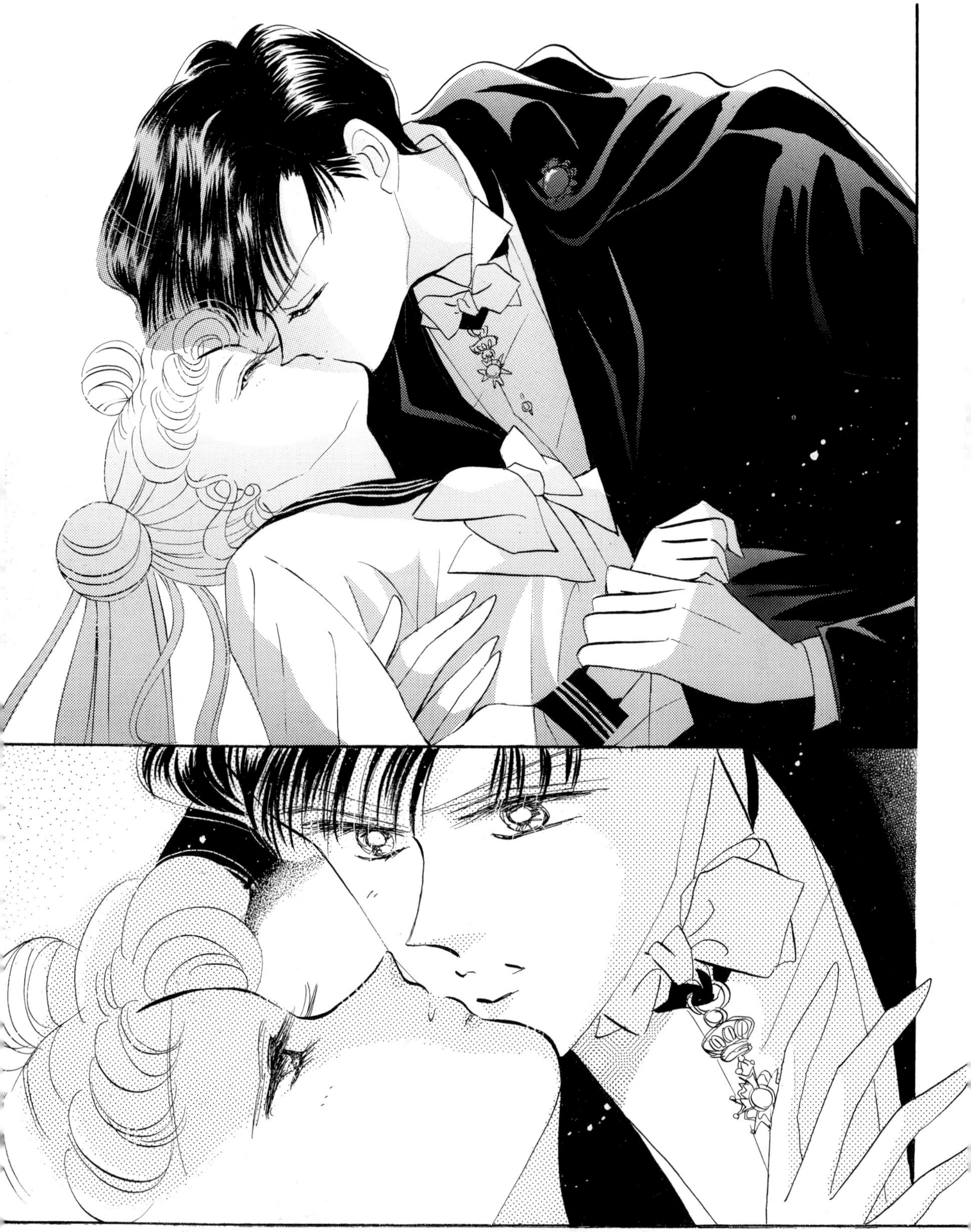

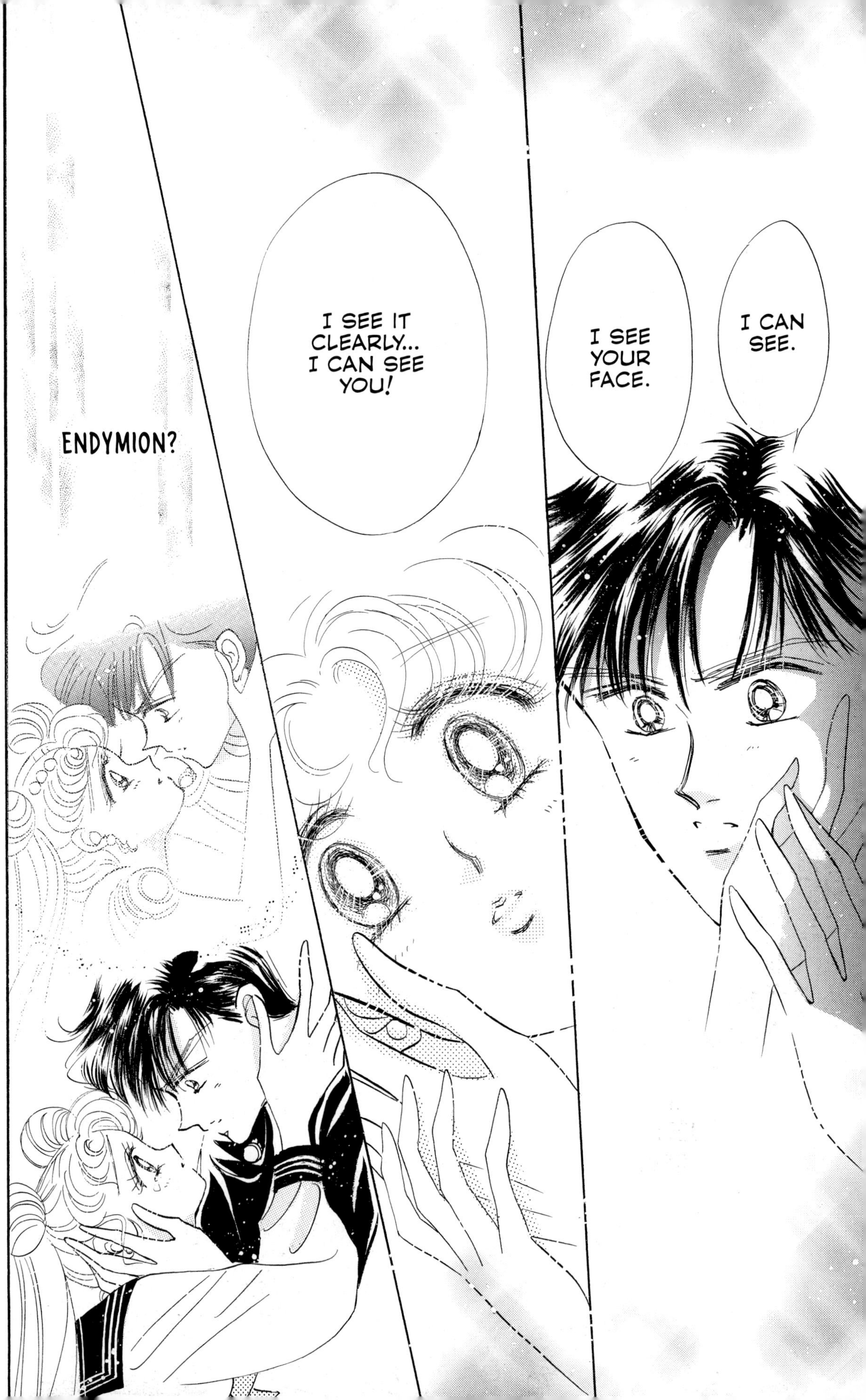
I CAN SEE.
I SEE YOUR FACE.
I SEE IT CLEARLY... I CAN SEE YOU!
ENDYMION?

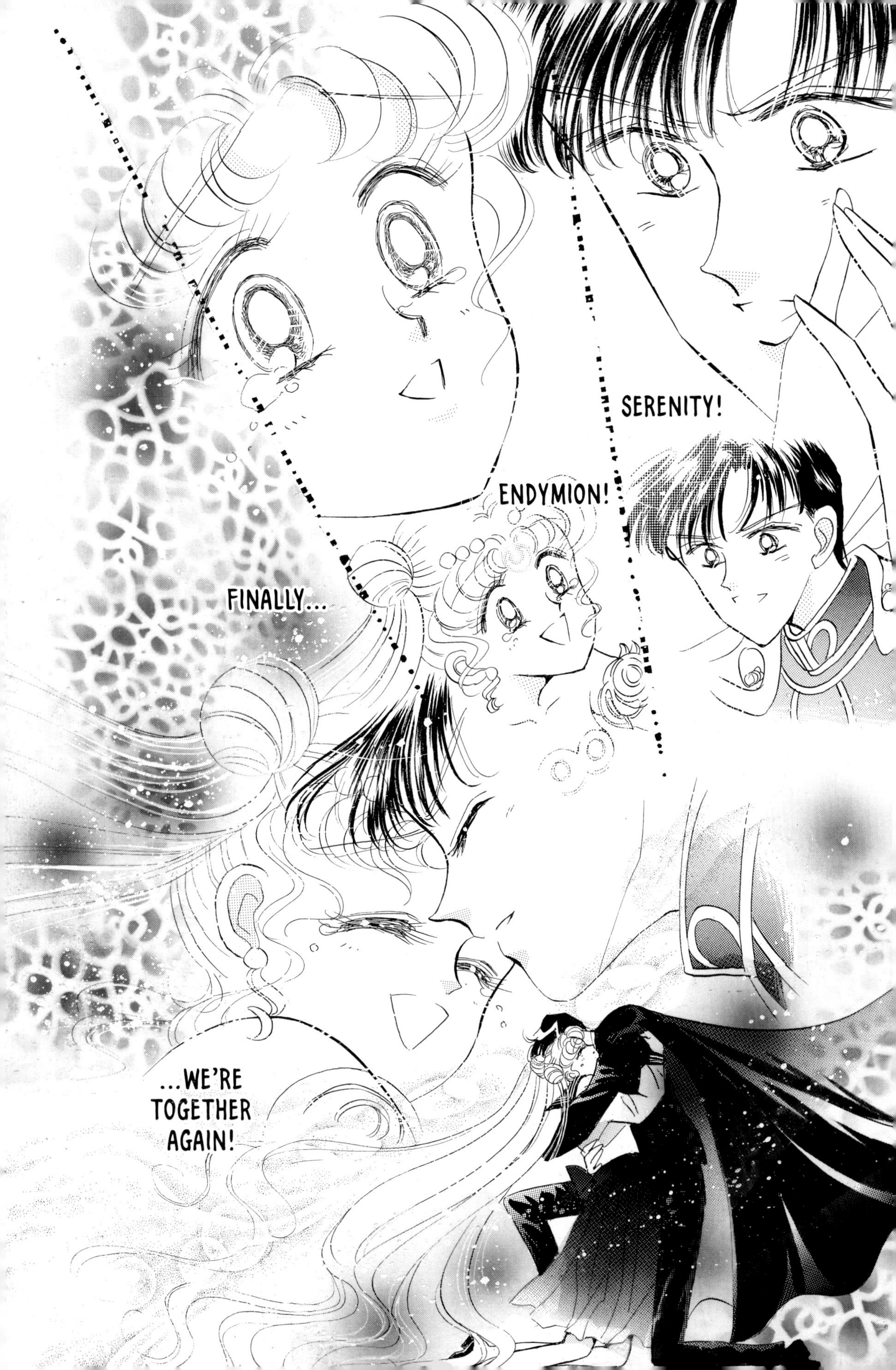
SERENITY!
ENDYMION!
FINALLY...
...WE'RE TOGETHER AGAIN!

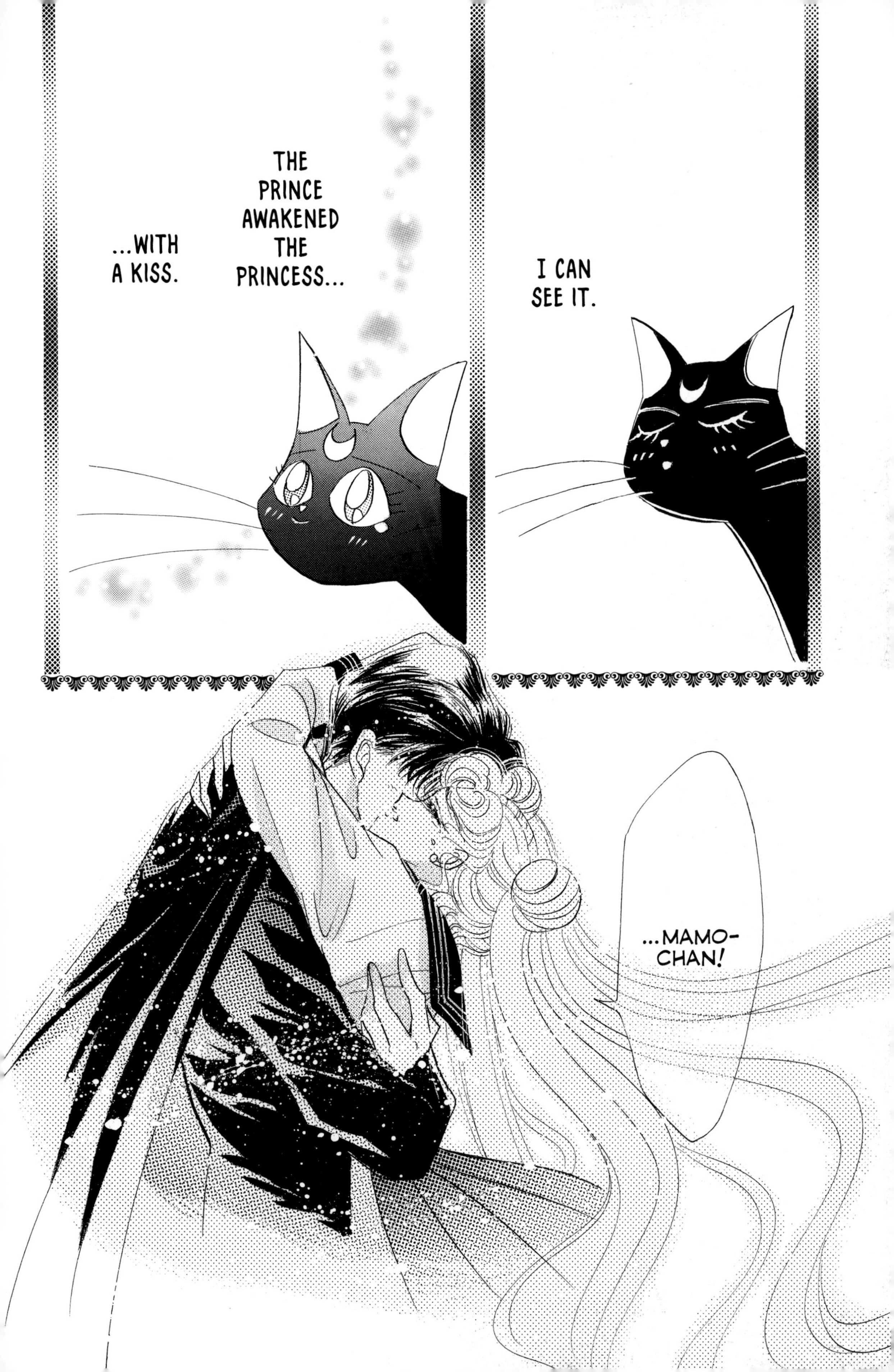
I CAN SEE IT.
THE PRINCE AWAKENED THE PRINCESS...
...WITH A KISS.
...MAMO-CHAN!

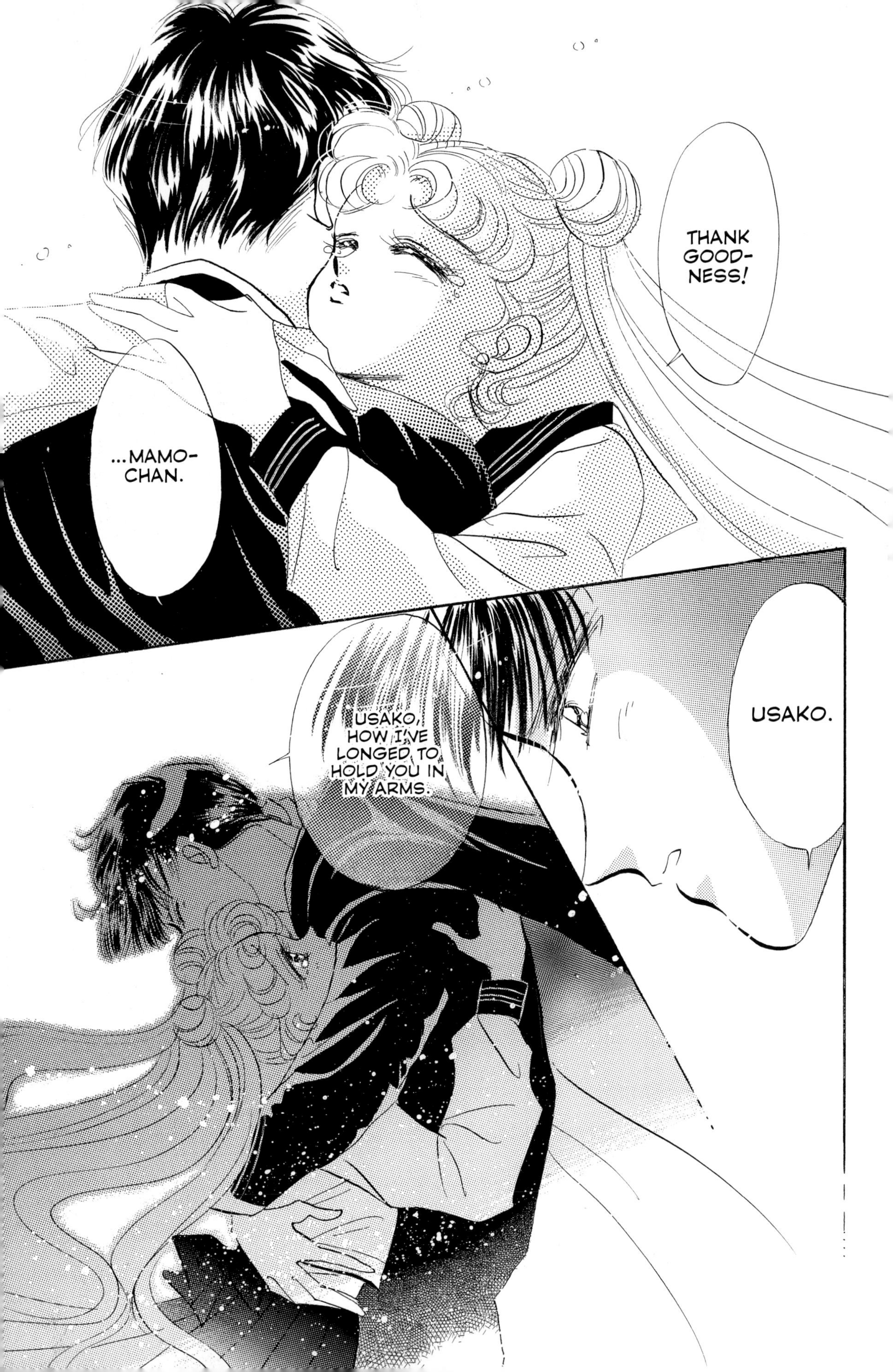
THANK GOODNESS!
...MAMO-CHAN.
USAKO.
USAKO, HOW I'VE LONGED TO HOLD YOU IN MY ARMS.

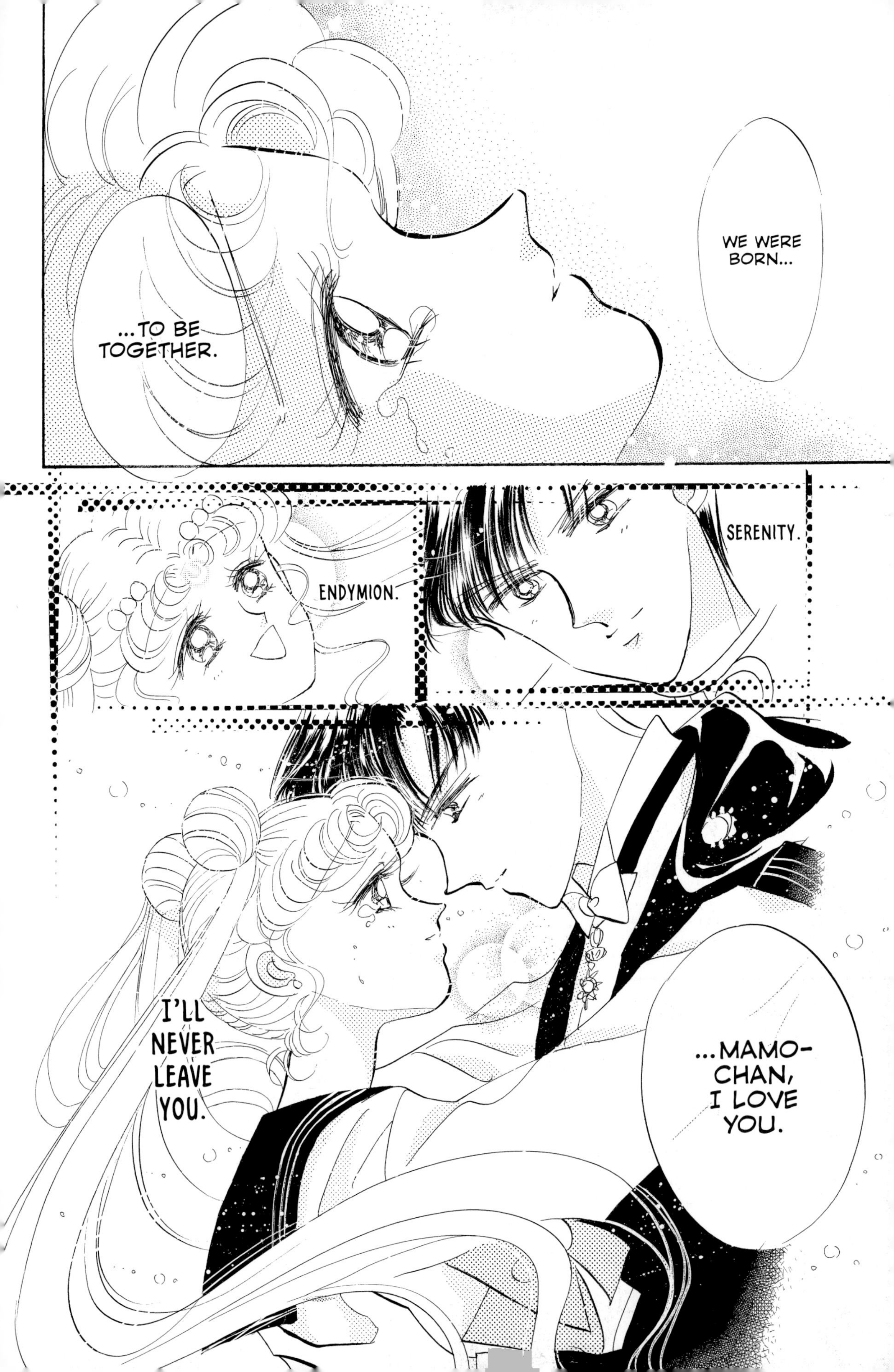
WE WERE BORN...
...TO BE TOGETHER.
SERENITY.
ENDYMION.
...MAMO-CHAN, I LOVE YOU.
I'LL NEVER LEAVE YOU.

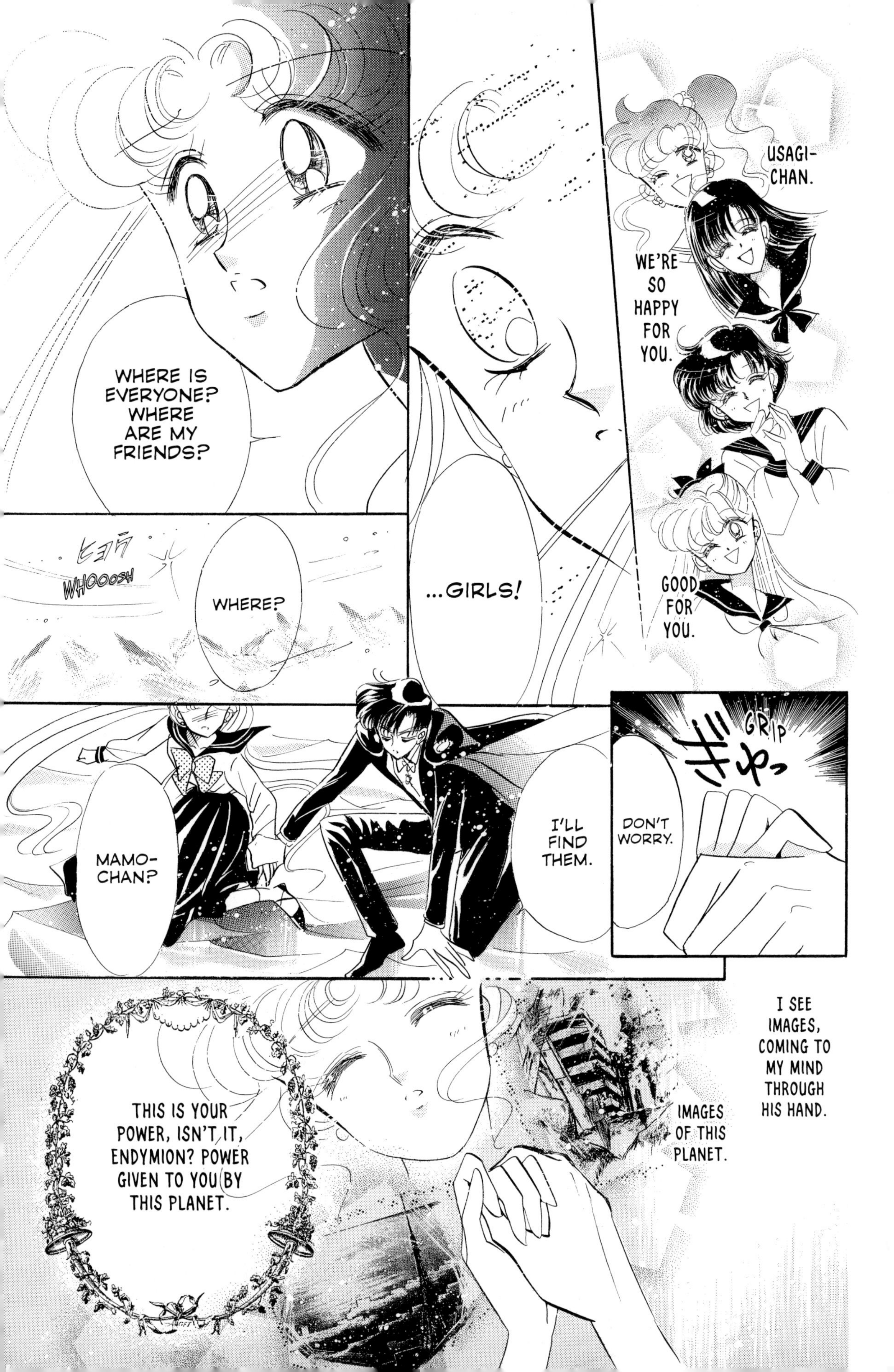
USAGI-CHAN.
WE'RE SO HAPPY FOR YOU.
GOOD FOR YOU.
...GIRLS!
WHERE IS EVERYONE? WHERE ARE MY FRIENDS?
ヒョゥ
WHOOOSH
WHERE?
ぎゅっ
GRIP
DON'T WORRY.
I'LL FIND THEM.
MAMO-CHAN?
I SEE IMAGES, COMING TO MY MIND THROUGH HIS HAND.
IMAGES OF THIS PLANET.
THIS IS YOUR POWER, ISN'T IT, ENDYMION? POWER GIVEN TO YOU BY THIS PLANET.

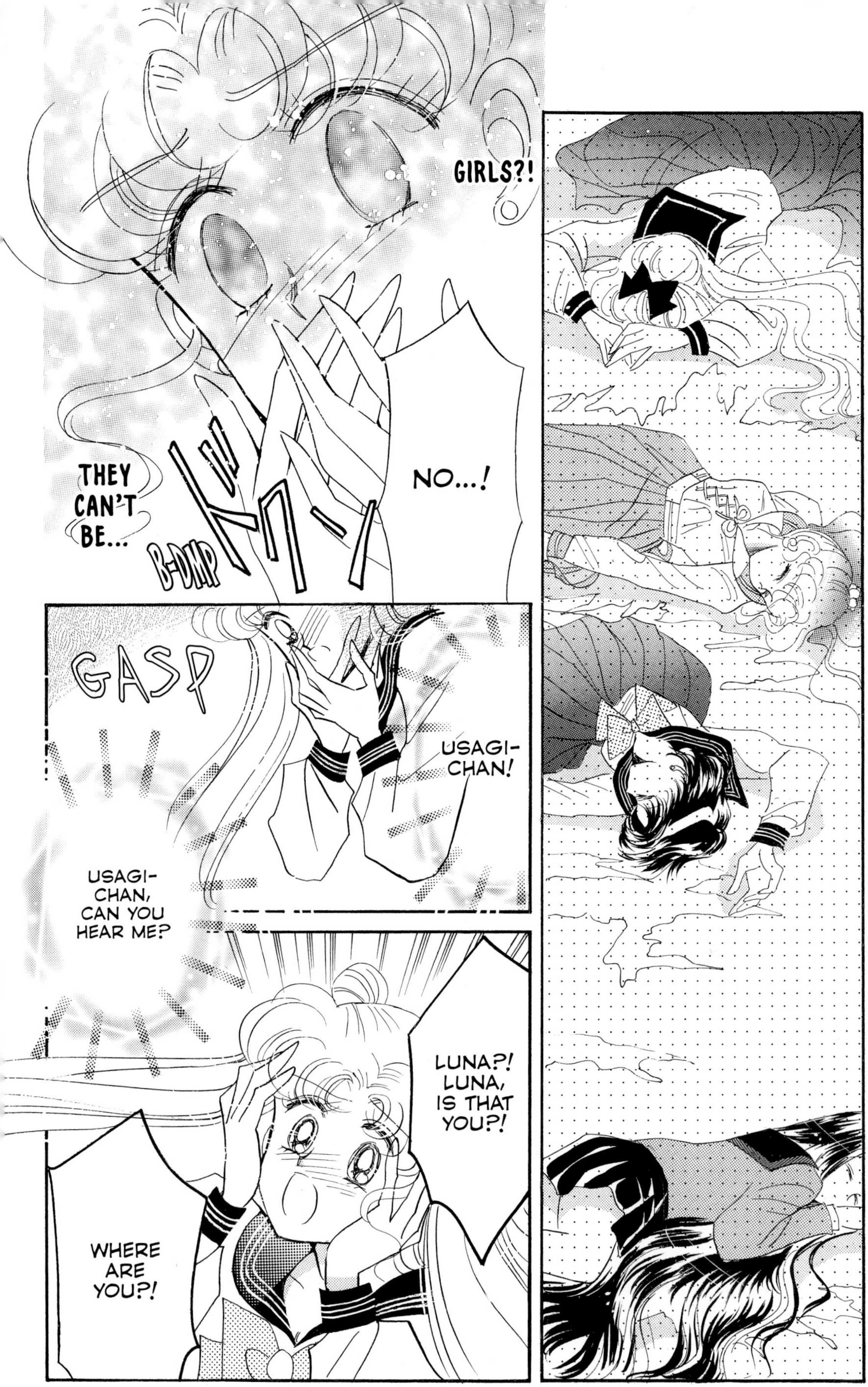
GIRLS?!
NO...!
THEY CAN'T BE...
B-DMP
USAGI-CHAN!
GASP
USAGI-CHAN, CAN YOU HEAR ME?
LUNA?! LUNA, IS THAT YOU?!
WHERE ARE YOU?!

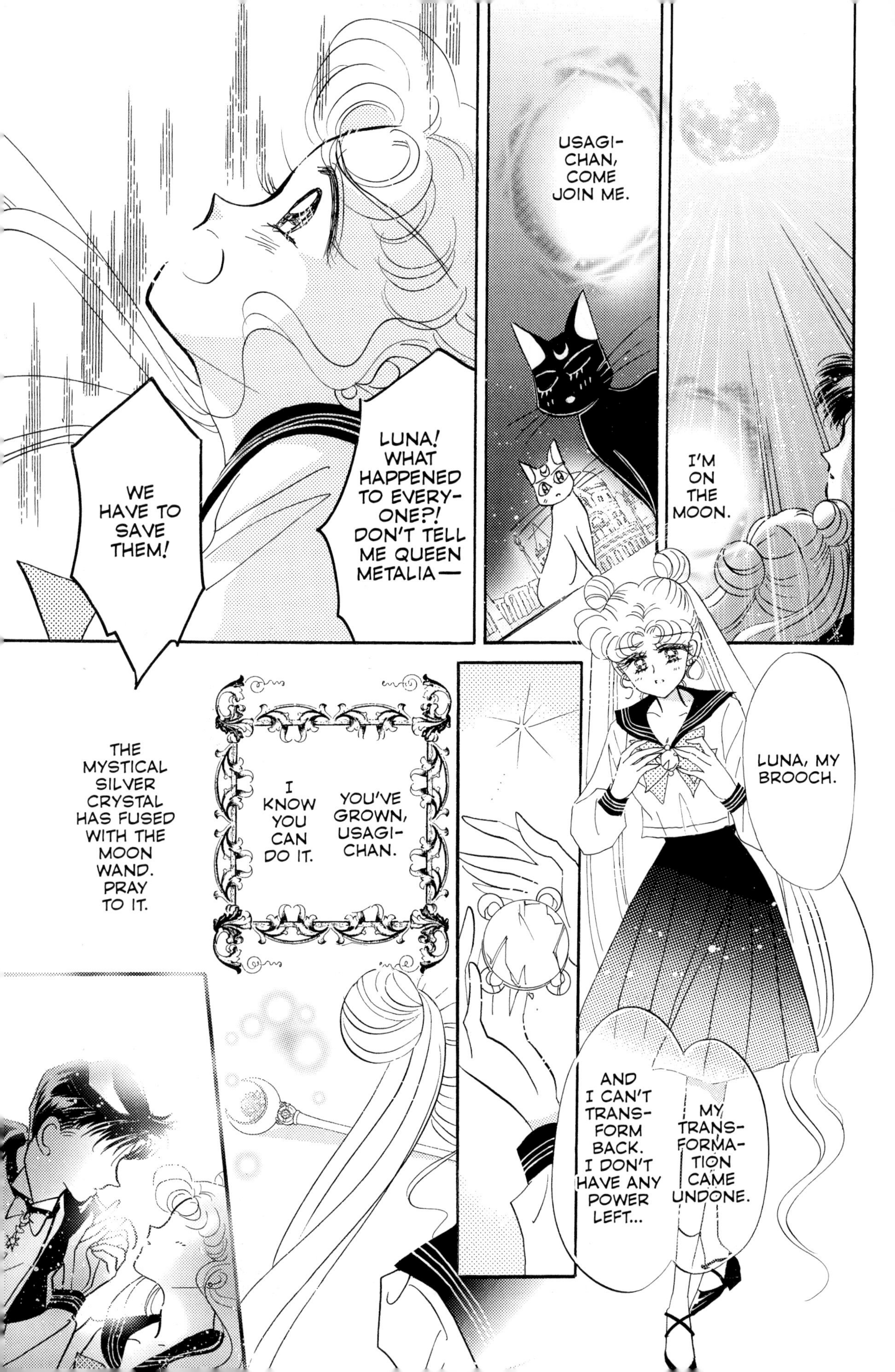
I'M ON THE MOON.
USAGI-CHAN, COME JOIN ME.
LUNA! WHAT HAPPENED TO EVERYONE?! DON'T TELL ME QUEEN METALIA—
WE HAVE TO SAVE THEM!
LUNA, MY BROOCH.
MY TRANSFORMATION CAME UNDONE.
AND I CAN'T TRANSFORM BACK. I DON'T HAVE ANY POWER LEFT...
YOU'VE GROWN, USAGI-CHAN.
I KNOW YOU CAN DO IT.
THE MYSTICAL SILVER CRYSTAL HAS FUSED WITH THE MOON WAND. PRAY TO IT.

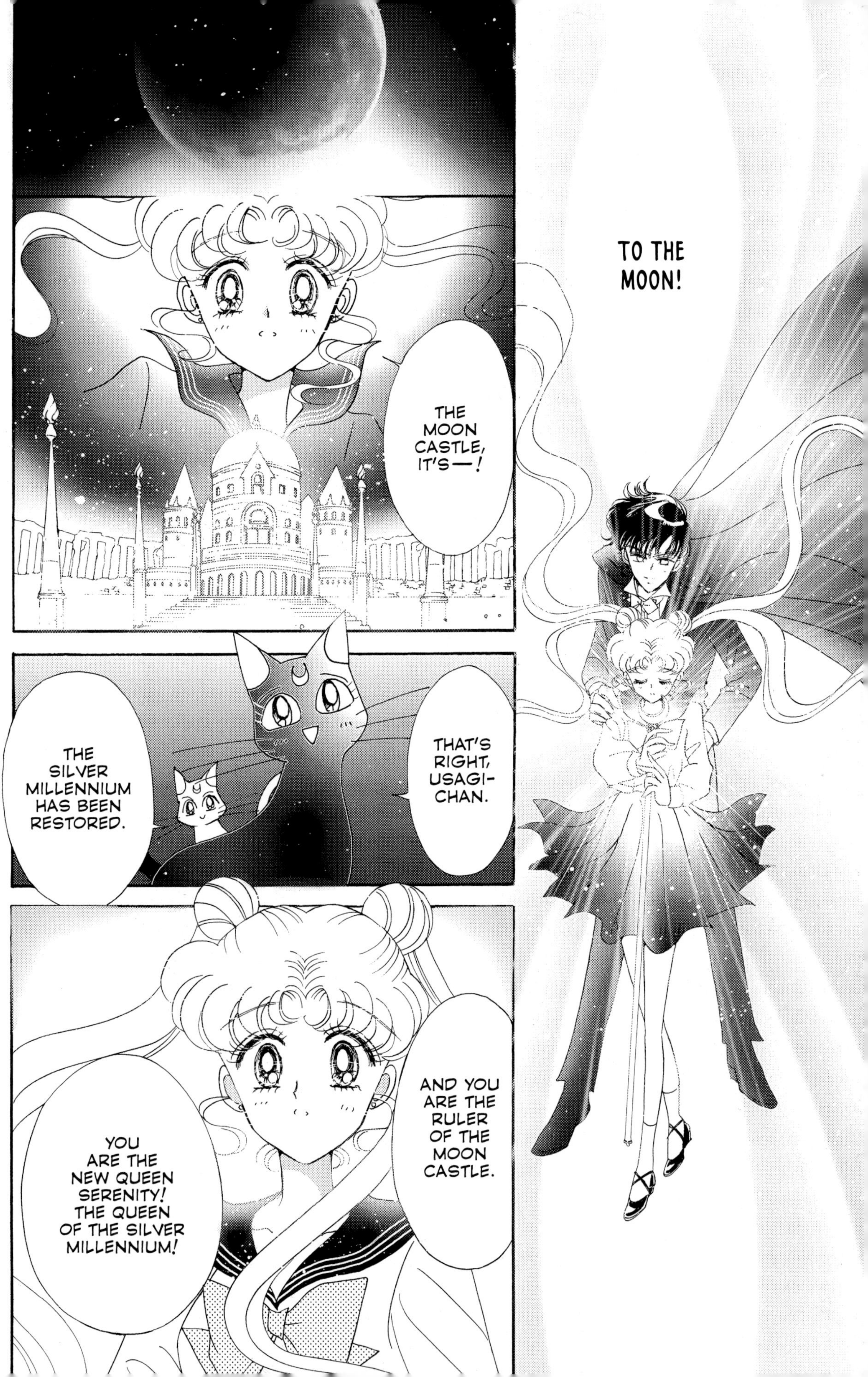
TO THE MOON!
THE MOON CASTLE, IT'S—!
THAT'S RIGHT, USAGI-CHAN.
THE SILVER MILLENNIUM HAS BEEN RESTORED.
AND YOU ARE THE RULER OF THE MOON CASTLE.
YOU ARE THE NEW QUEEN SERENITY! THE QUEEN OF THE SILVER MILLENNIUM!

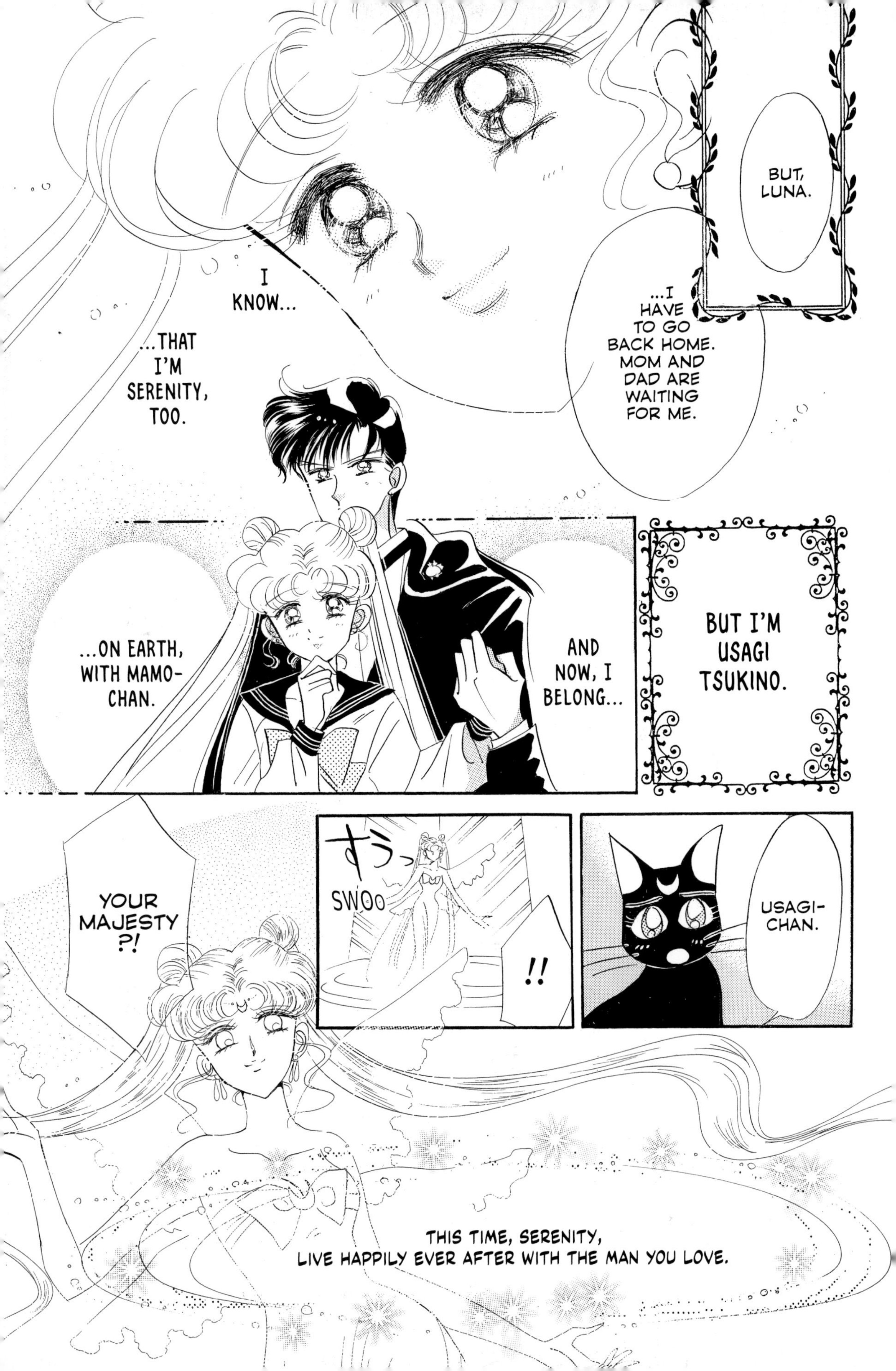

BUT, LUNA.
...I HAVE TO GO BACK HOME. MOM AND DAD ARE WAITING FOR ME.
I KNOW...
...THAT I'M SERENITY, TOO.
BUT I'M USAGI TSUKINO.
AND NOW, I BELONG...
...ON EARTH, WITH MAMO-CHAN.
USAGI-CHAN.
すうっ
SWOO
!!
YOUR MAJESTY ?!
THIS TIME, SERENITY,
LIVE HAPPILY EVER AFTER WITH THE MAN YOU LOVE.

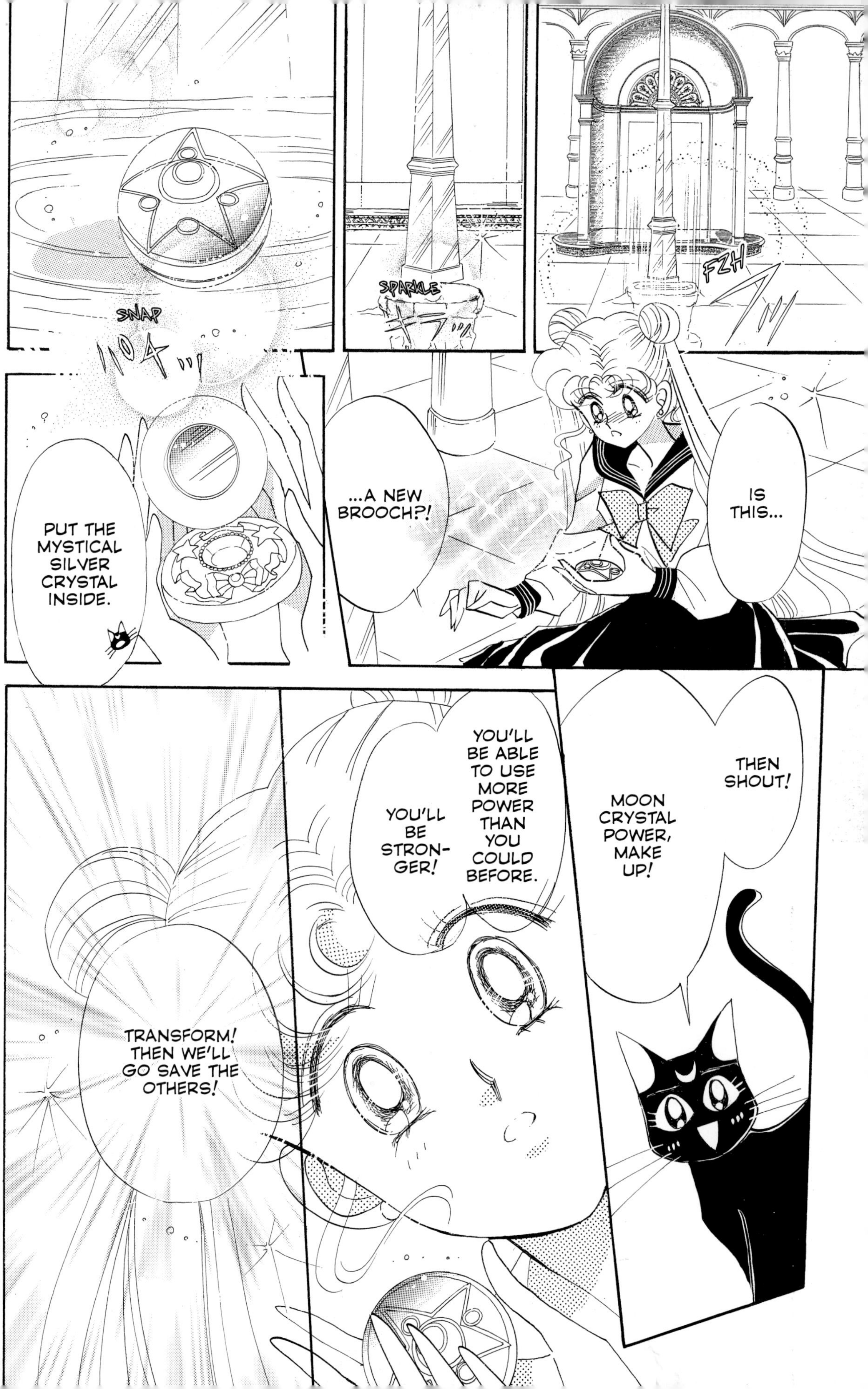
FZH
SPARKLE
SNAP
IS THIS...
...A NEW BROOCH?!
PUT THE MYSTICAL SILVER CRYSTAL INSIDE.
THEN SHOUT!
MOON CRYSTAL POWER, MAKE UP!
YOU'LL BE ABLE TO USE MORE POWER THAN YOU COULD BEFORE.
YOU'LL BE STRONGER!
TRANSFORM! THEN WE'LL GO SAVE THE OTHERS!

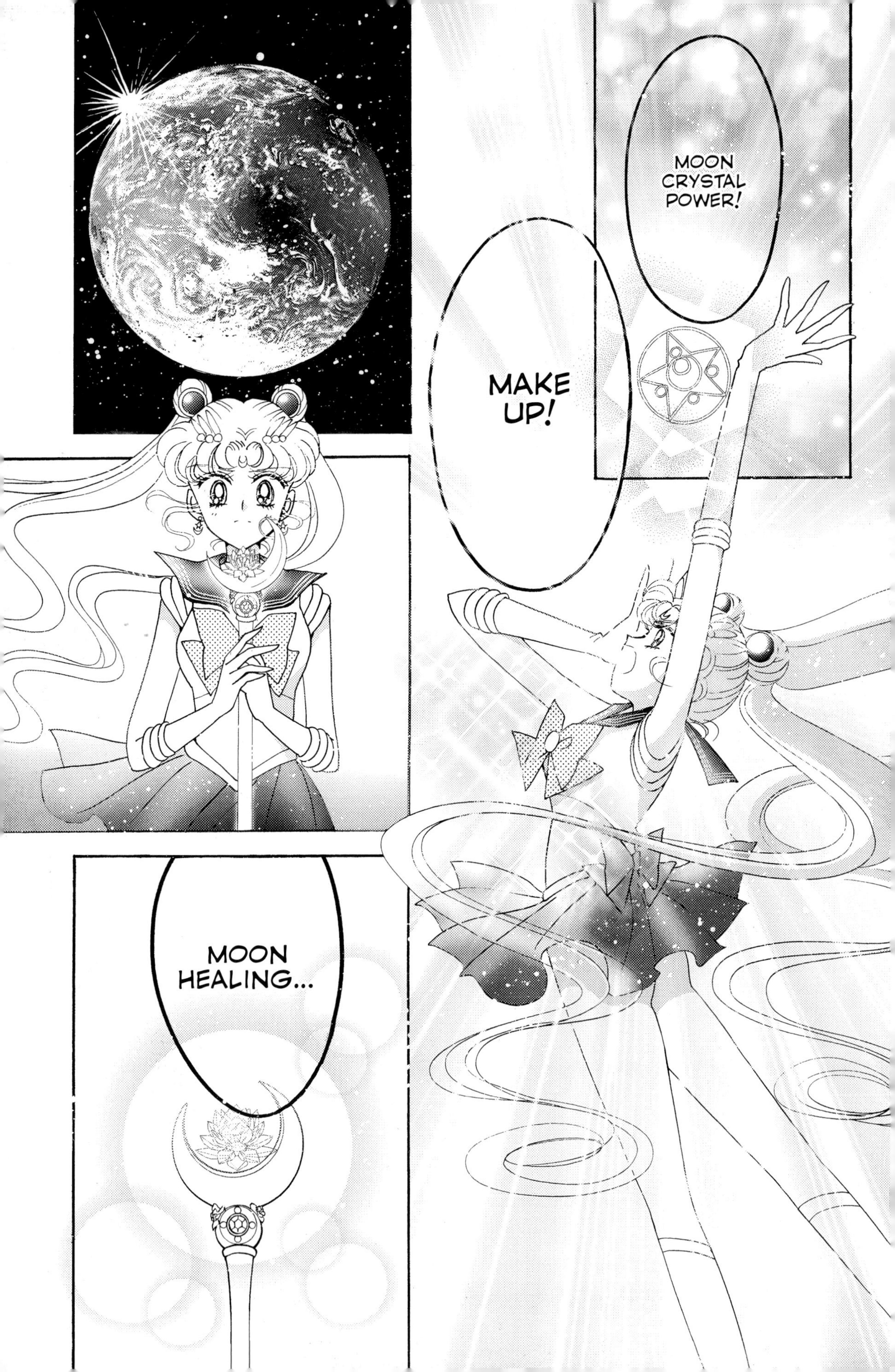
MOON CRYSTAL POWER!
MAKE UP!
MOON HEALING...

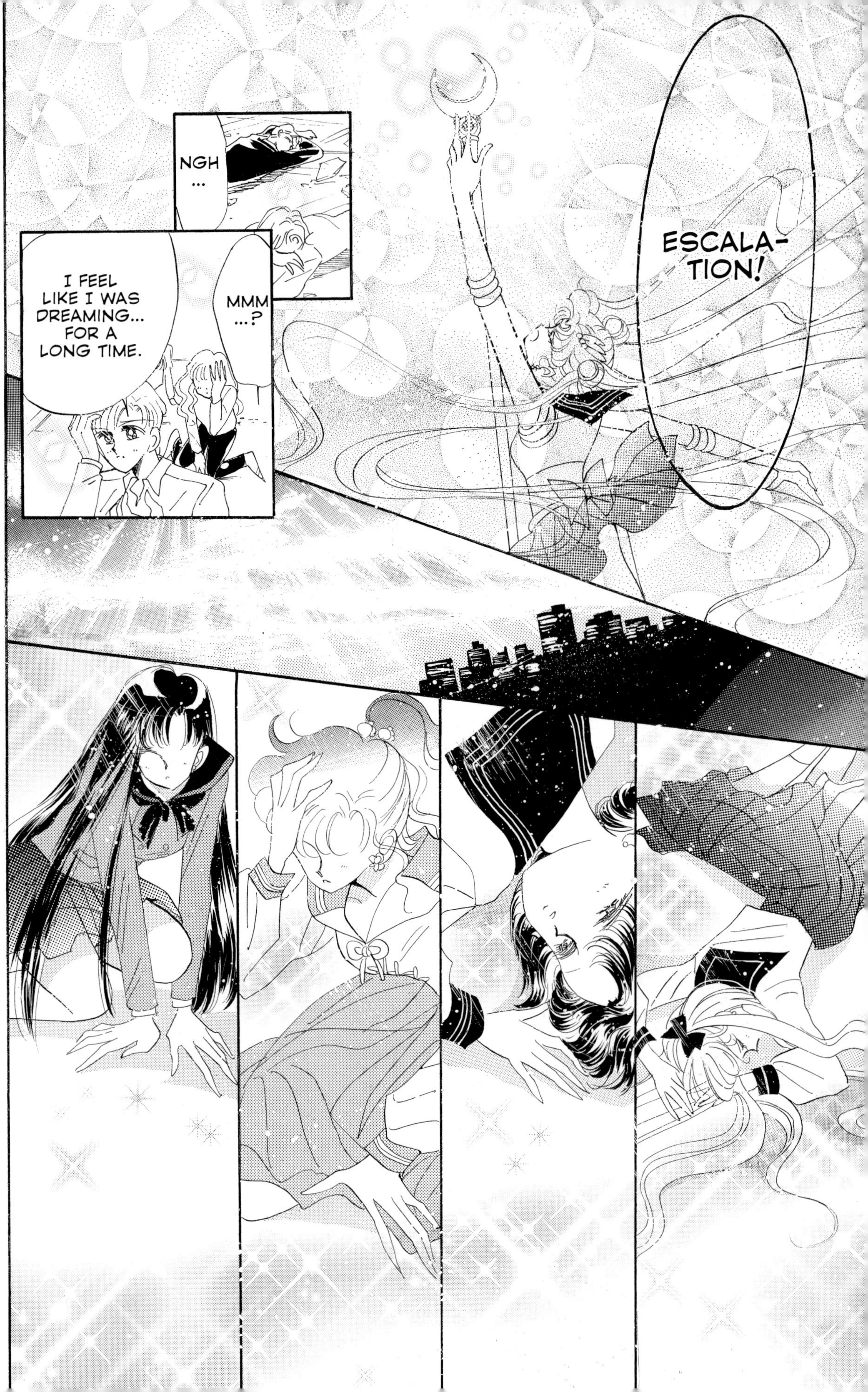
ESCALA-
TION!
NGH
...
MMM
...?
I FEEL LIKE I WAS DREAMING... FOR A LONG TIME.

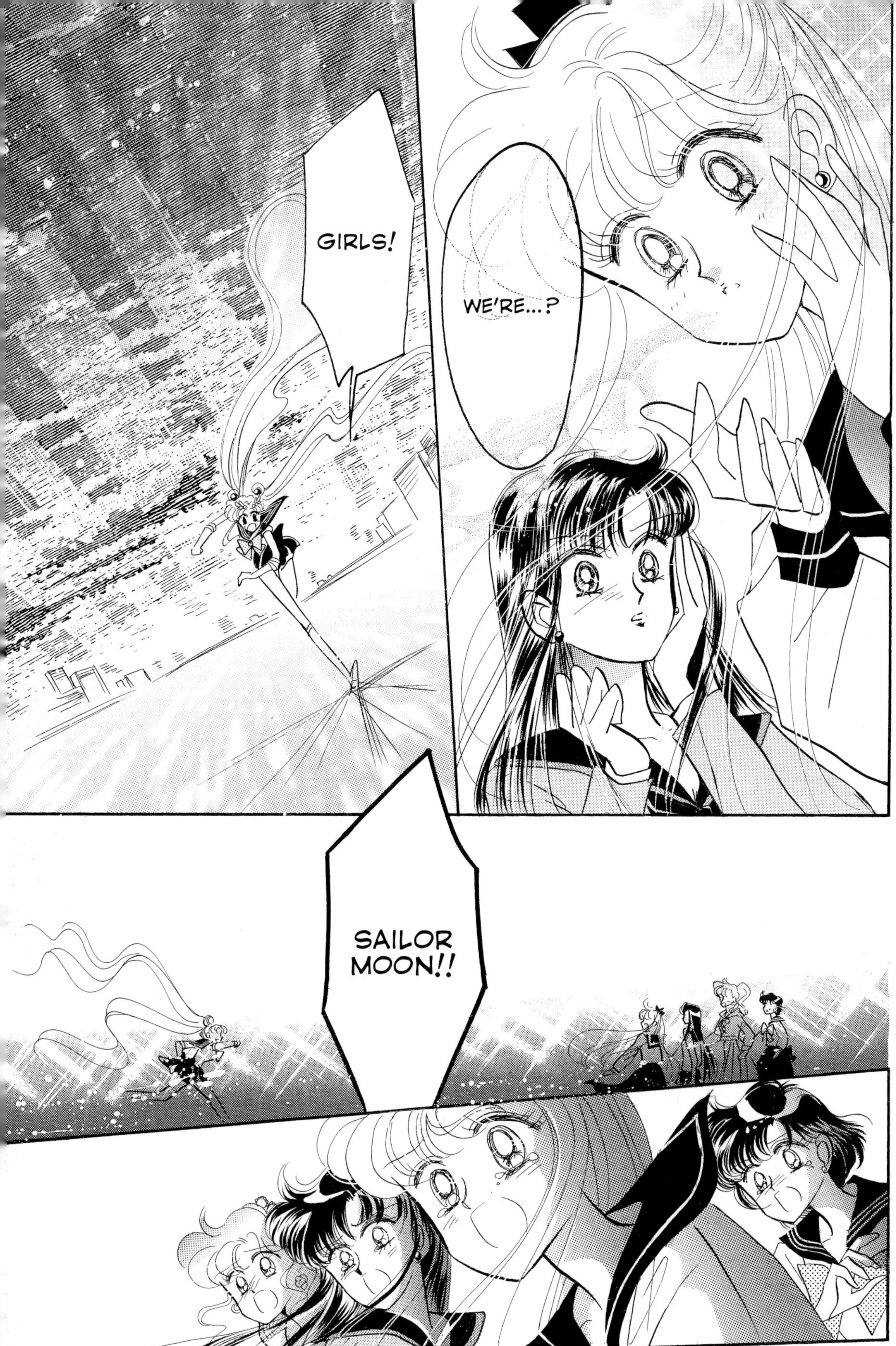
WE'RE...?
GIRLS!
SAILOR MOON!!

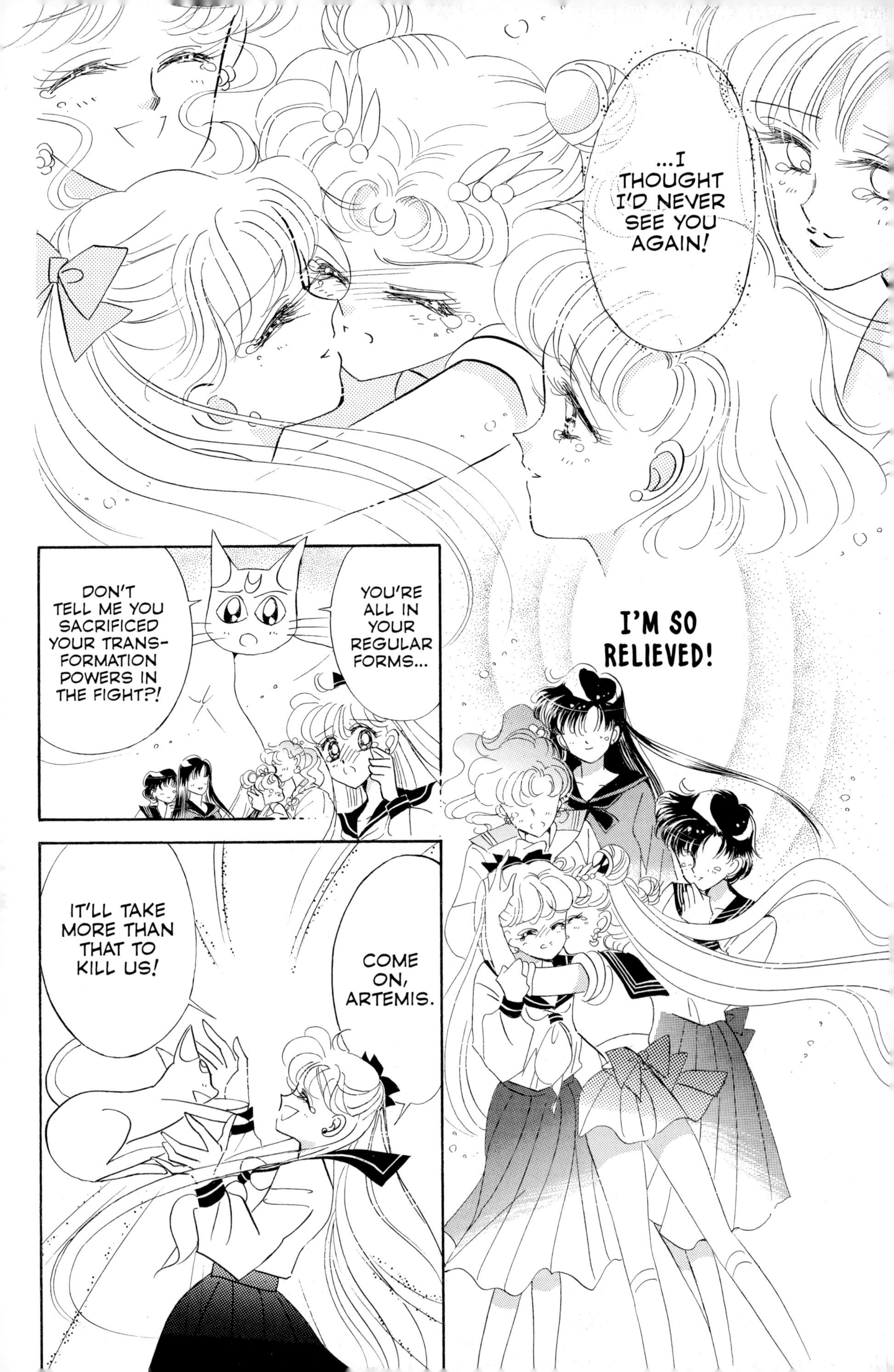
...I THOUGHT I'D NEVER SEE YOU AGAIN!
I'M SO RELIEVED!
YOU'RE ALL IN YOUR REGULAR FORMS...
DON'T TELL ME YOU SACRIFICED YOUR TRANS-FORMATION POWERS IN THE FIGHT?!
COME ON, ARTEMIS.
IT'LL TAKE MORE THAN THAT TO KILL US!

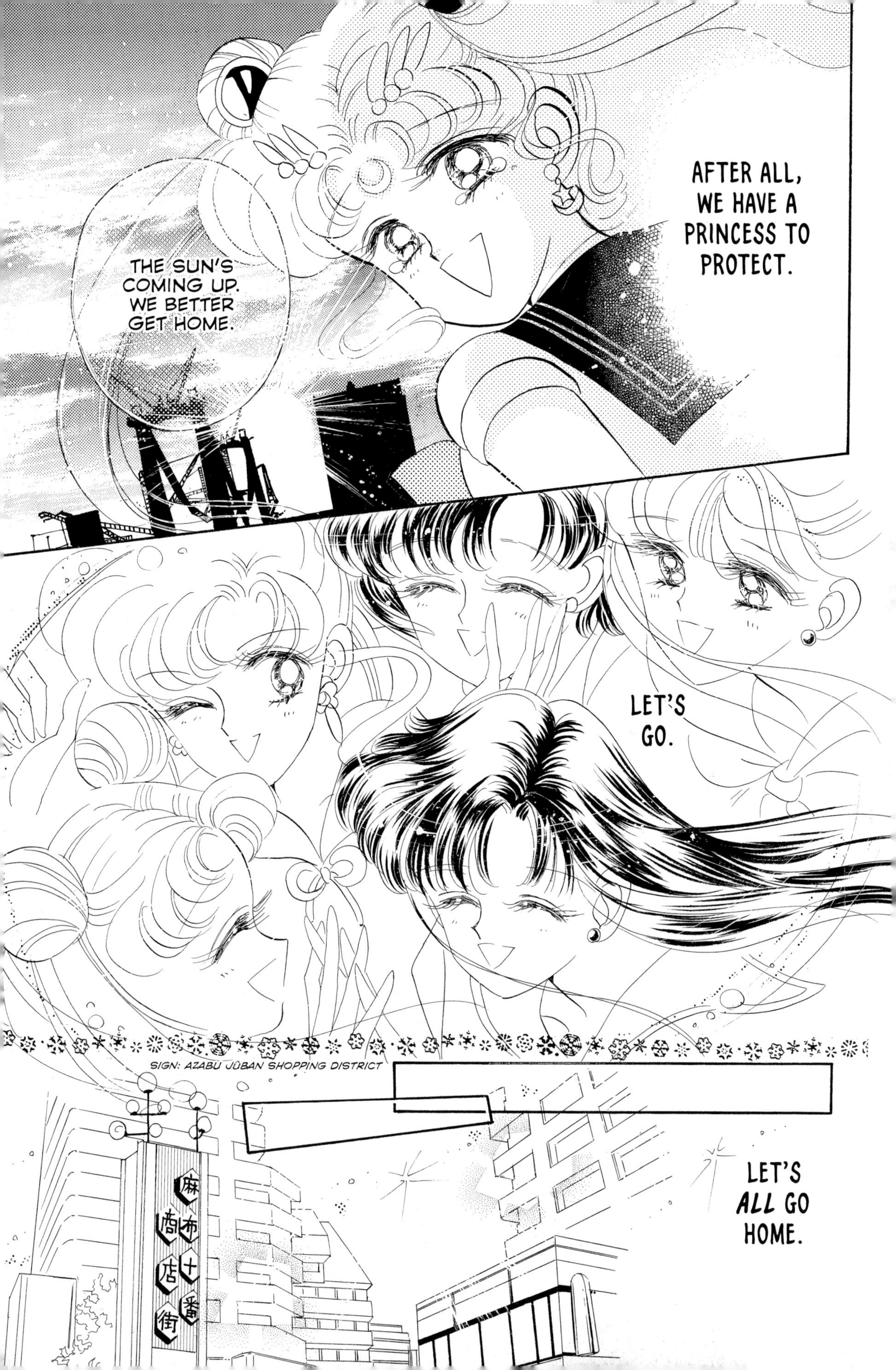
AFTER ALL, WE HAVE A PRINCESS TO PROTECT.
THE SUN'S COMING UP. WE BETTER GET HOME.
LET'S GO.
LET'S *ALL* GO HOME.
SIGN: AZABU JŪBAN SHOPPING DISTRICT
麻布十番商店街

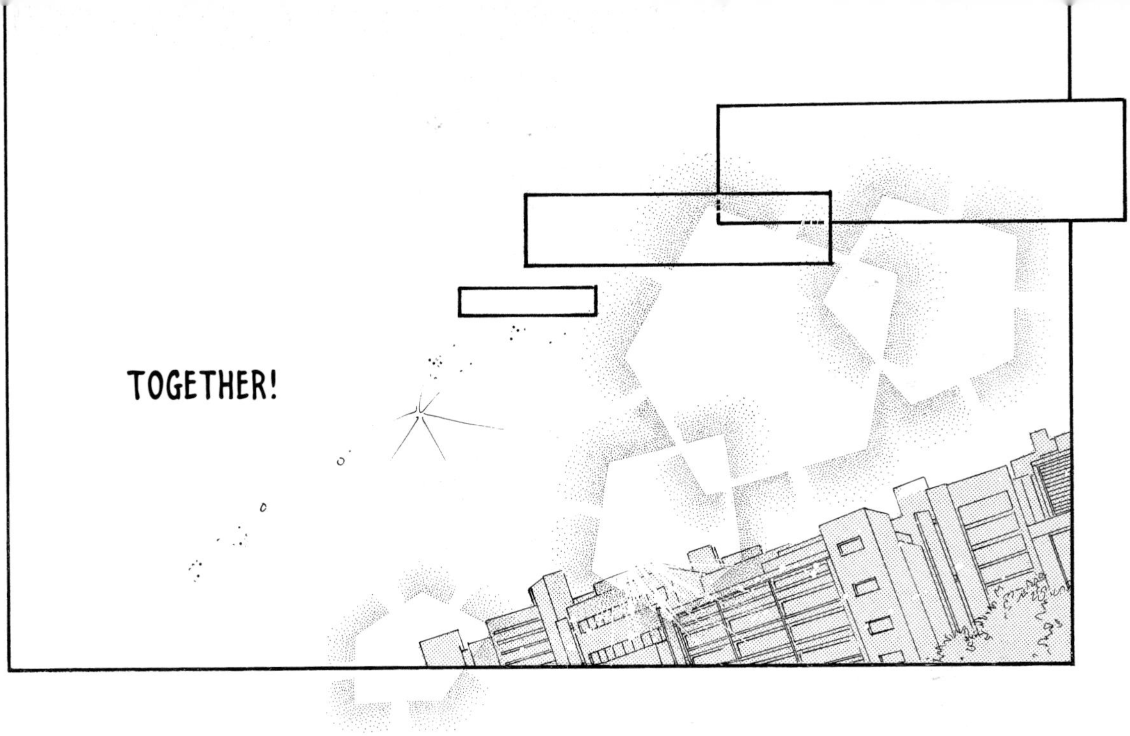
TOGETHER!

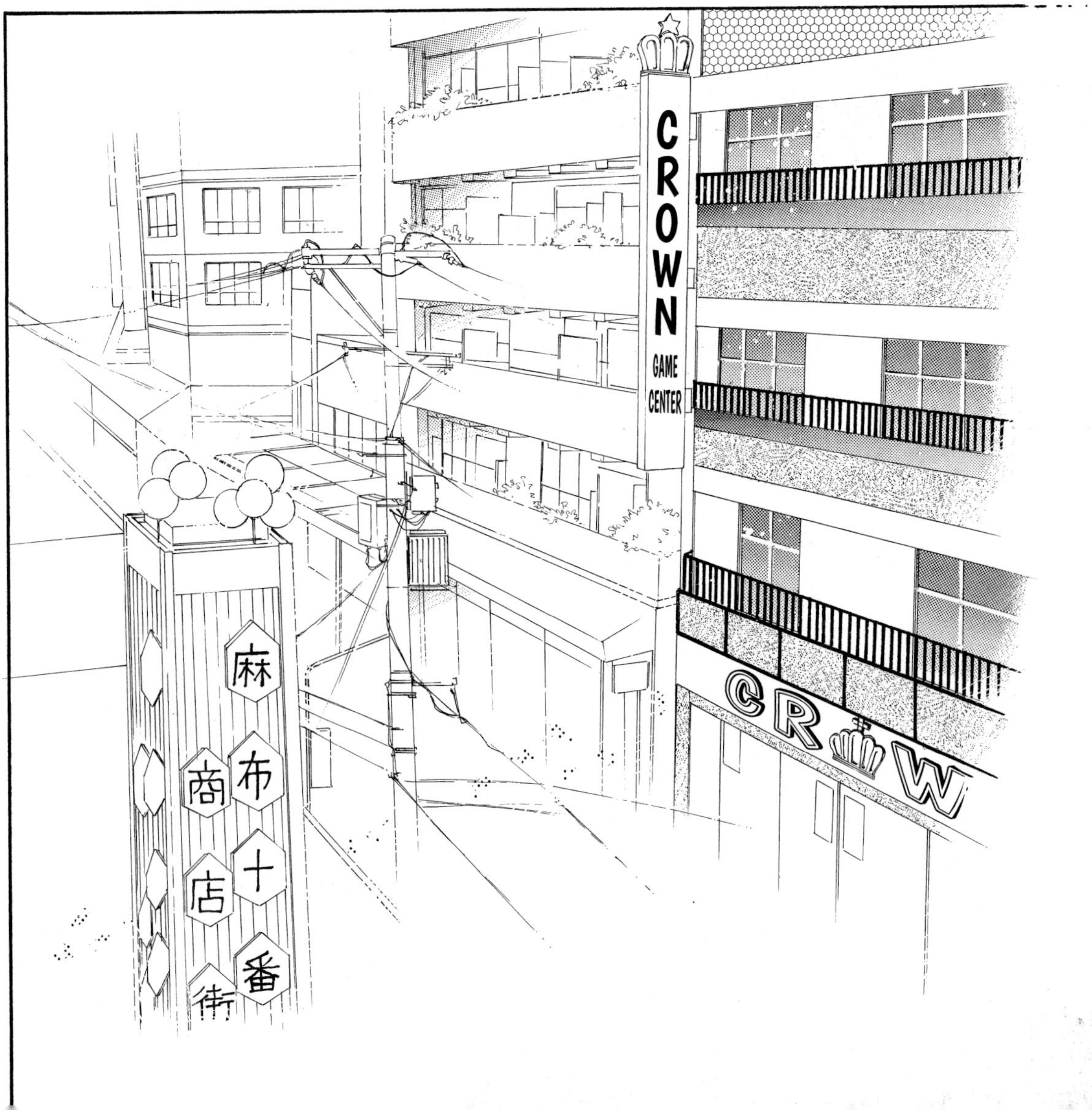
CROWN
GAME CENTER
麻布十番商店街

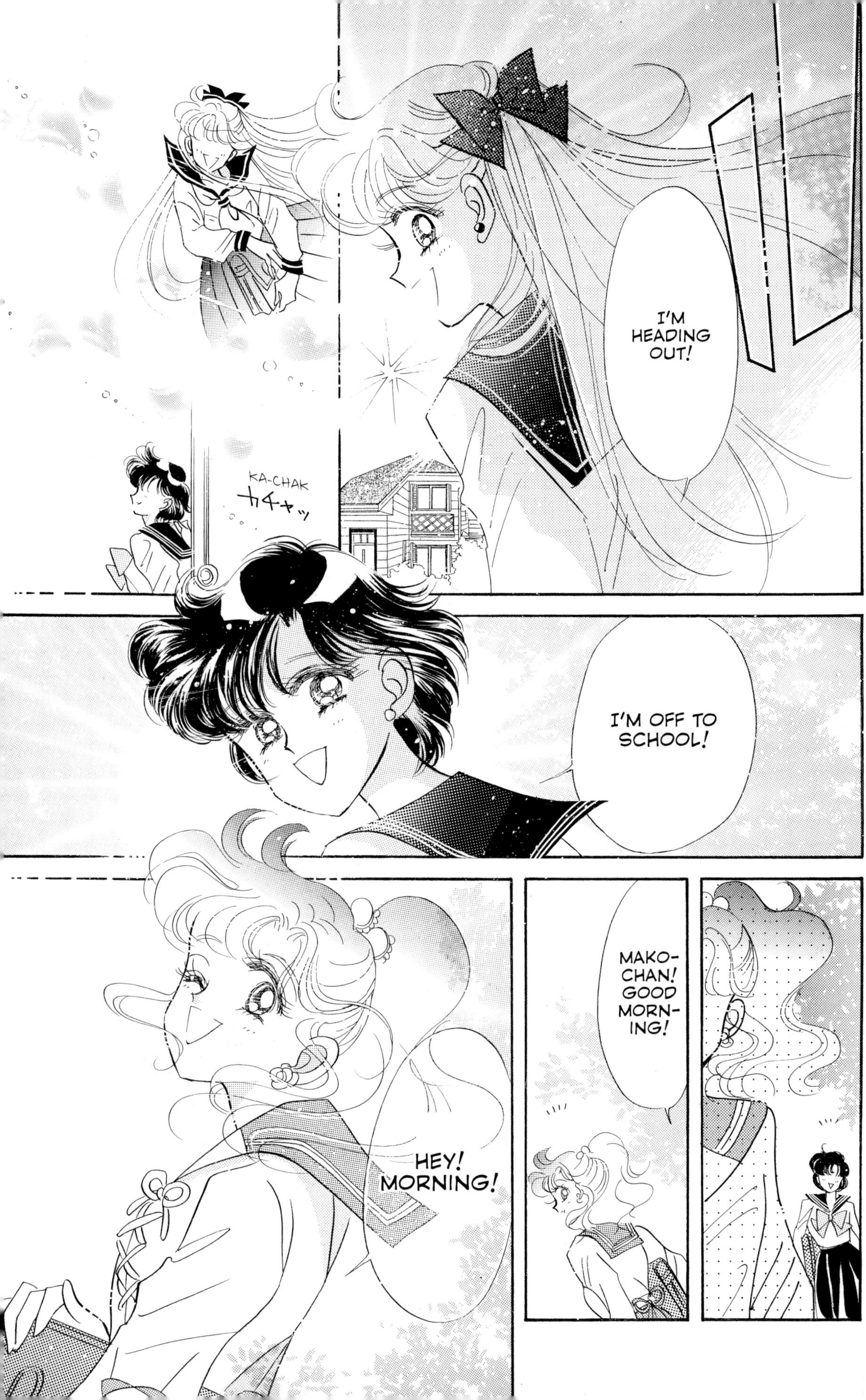

I'M HEADING OUT!
KA-CHAK
カチャッ
I'M OFF TO SCHOOL!
MAKO-CHAN! GOOD MORNING!
HEY! MORNING!

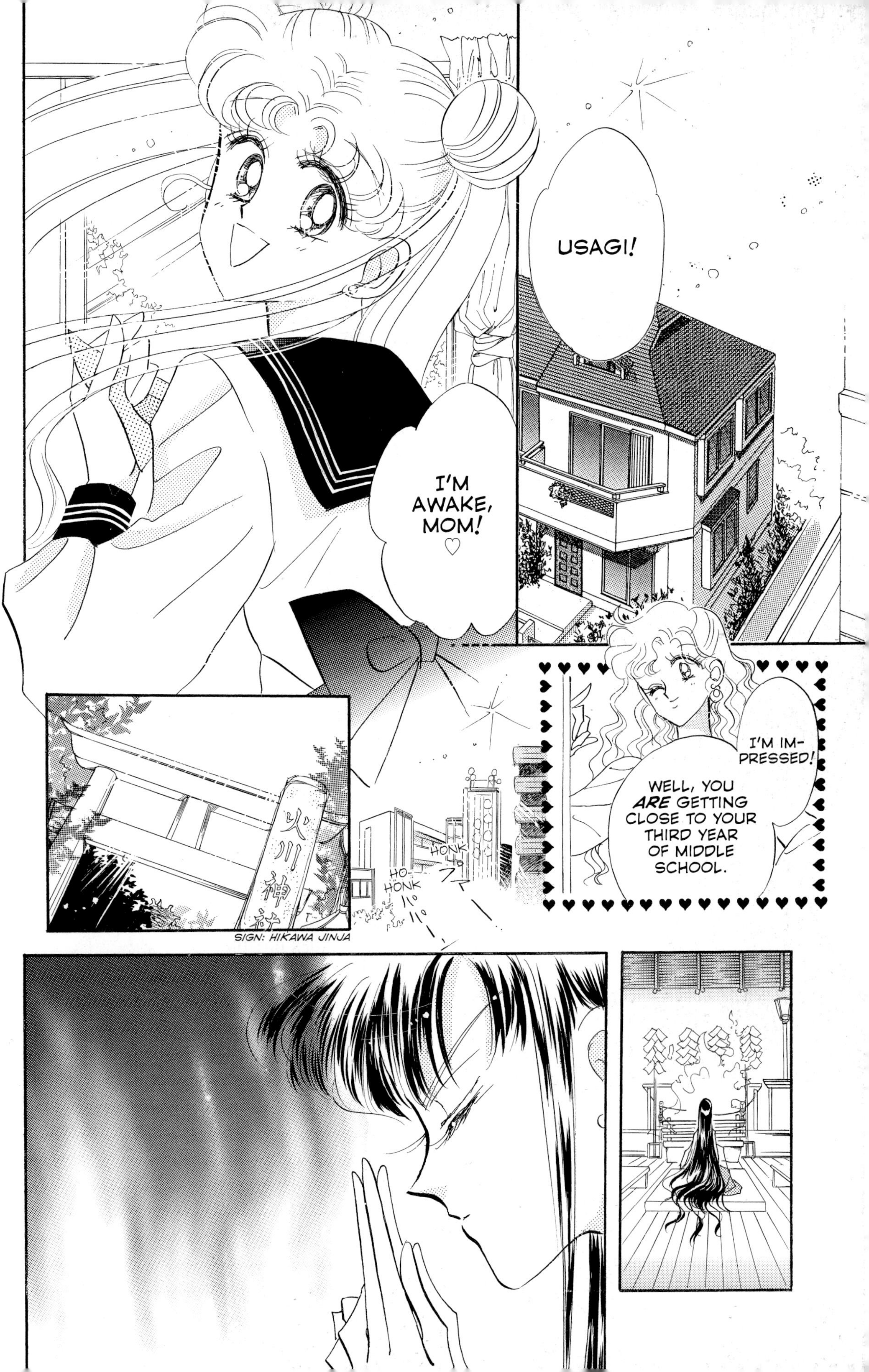
USAGI!
I'M AWAKE, MOM! ♡
I'M IM-PRESSED!
WELL, YOU *ARE* GETTING CLOSE TO YOUR THIRD YEAR OF MIDDLE SCHOOL.
HONK
HO-HONK
火川神社
SIGN: HIKAWA JINJA

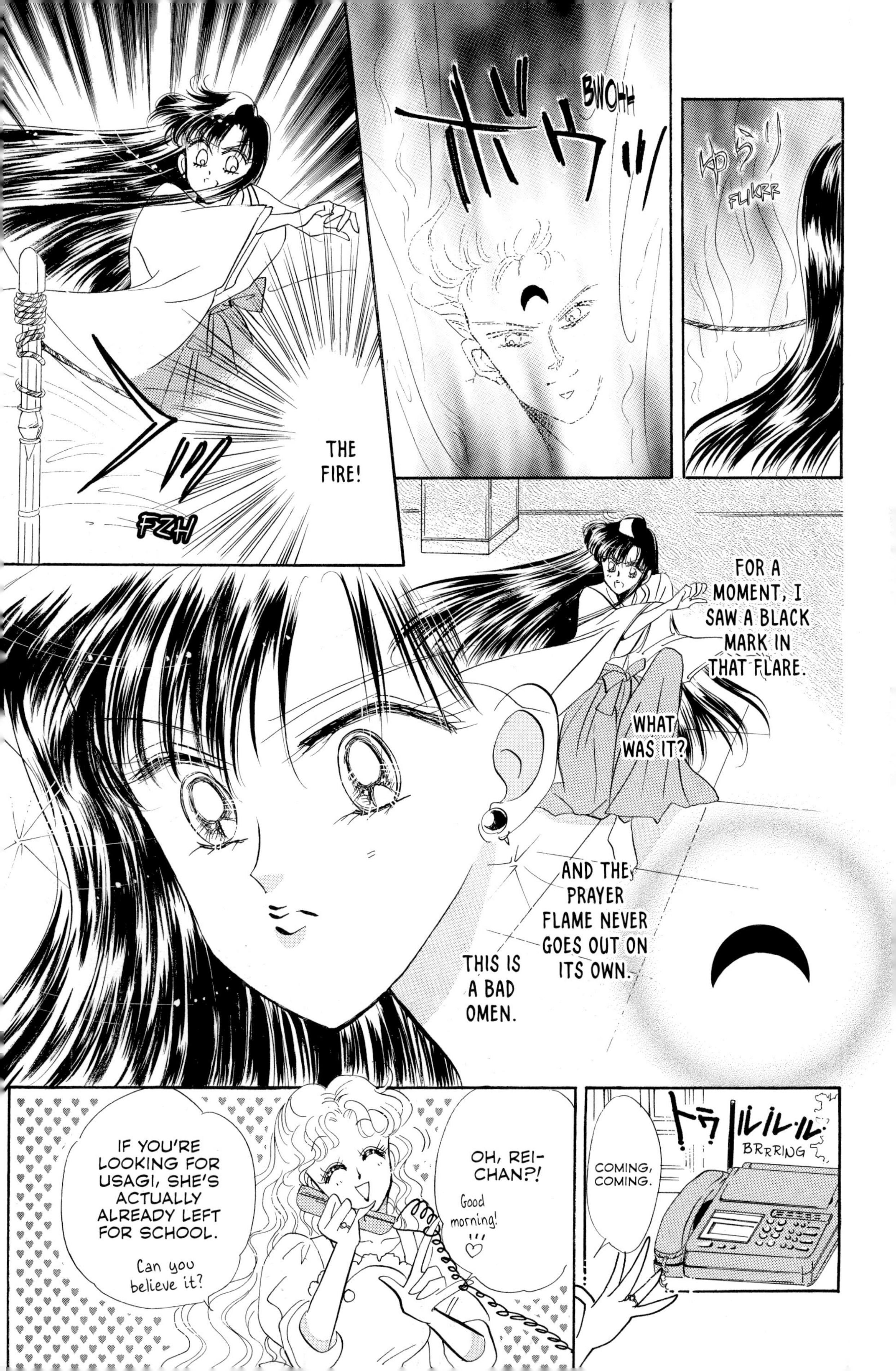
ゆらり
FLIKRR
ボウッ
BWOHH
THE FIRE!
FZH
FOR A MOMENT, I SAW A BLACK MARK IN THAT FLARE.
WHAT WAS IT?
AND THE PRAYER FLAME NEVER GOES OUT ON ITS OWN.
THIS IS A BAD OMEN.
トゥルルル・ル
BRrRING
COMING, COMING.
OH, REI-CHAN?!
Good morning!
IF YOU'RE LOOKING FOR USAGI, SHE'S ACTUALLY ALREADY LEFT FOR SCHOOL.
Can you believe it?

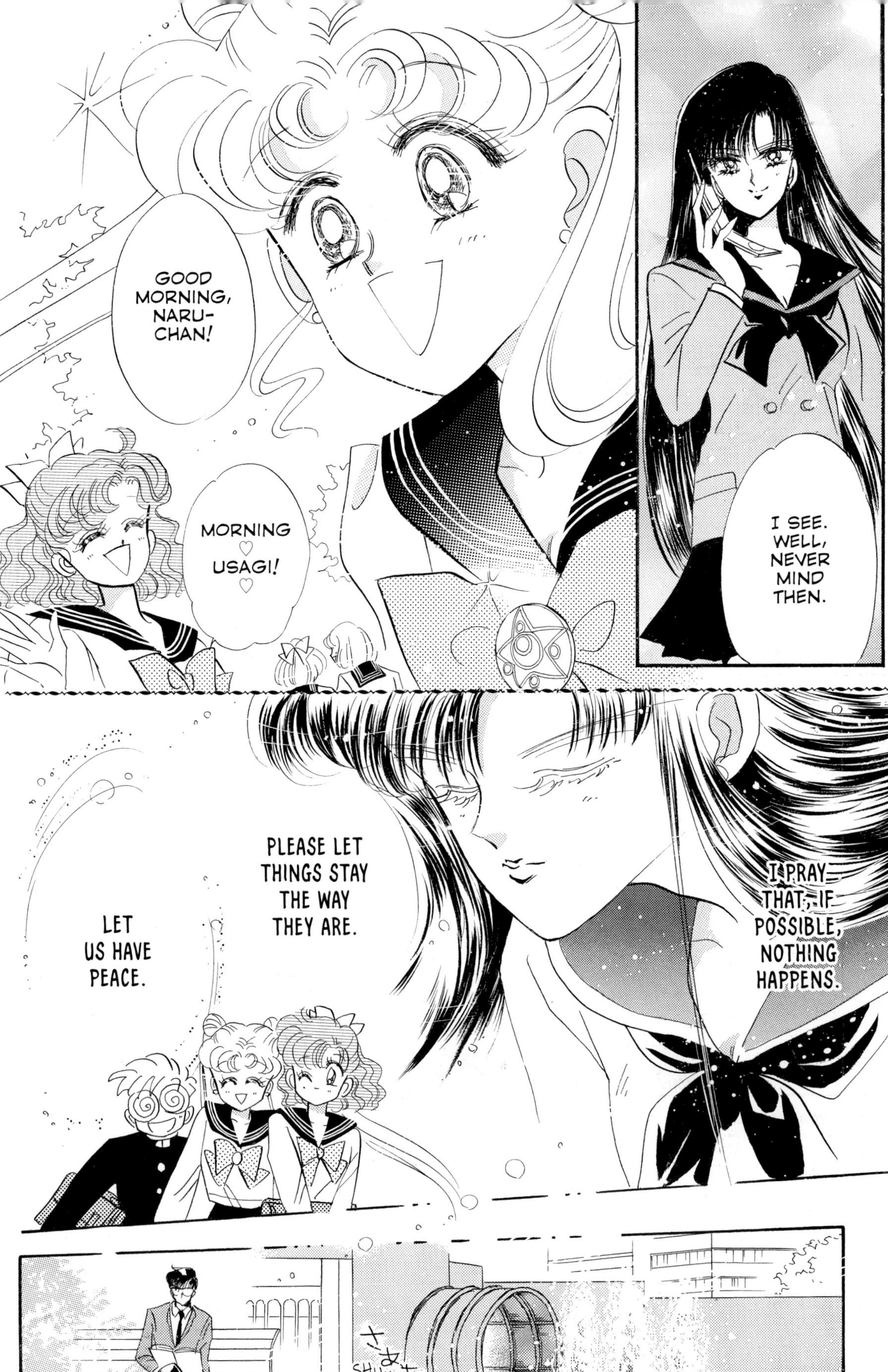

I SEE. WELL, NEVER MIND THEN.
GOOD MORNING, NARU-CHAN!
MORNING ♡ USAGI! ♡
I PRAY THAT, IF POSSIBLE, NOTHING HAPPENS.
PLEASE LET THINGS STAY THE WAY THEY ARE.
LET US HAVE PEACE.
SHHH

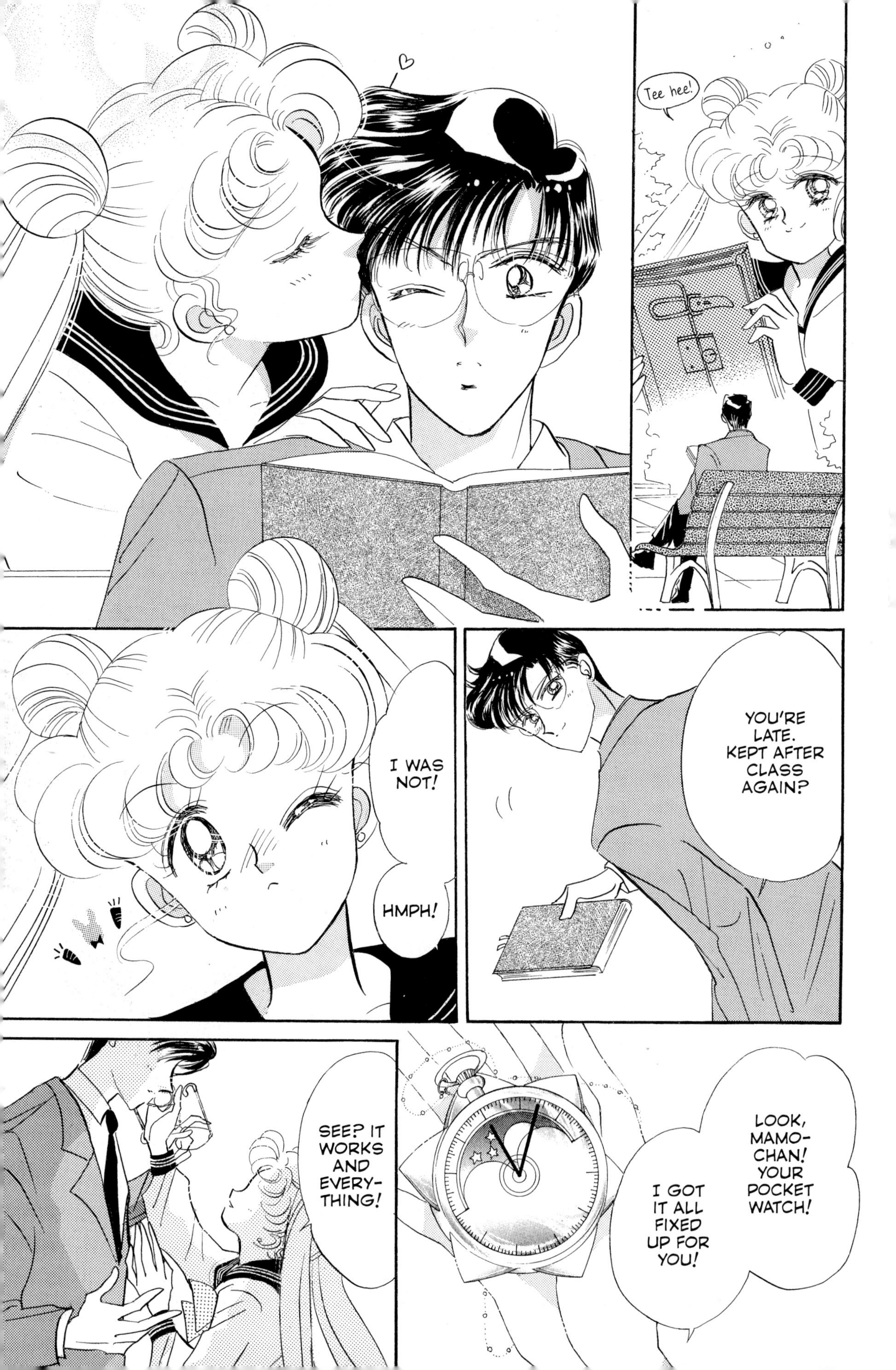
Tee hee!
YOU'RE LATE. KEPT AFTER CLASS AGAIN?
I WAS NOT!
HMPH!
LOOK, MAMO-CHAN! YOUR POCKET WATCH!
I GOT IT ALL FIXED UP FOR YOU!
SEE? IT WORKS AND EVERYTHING!

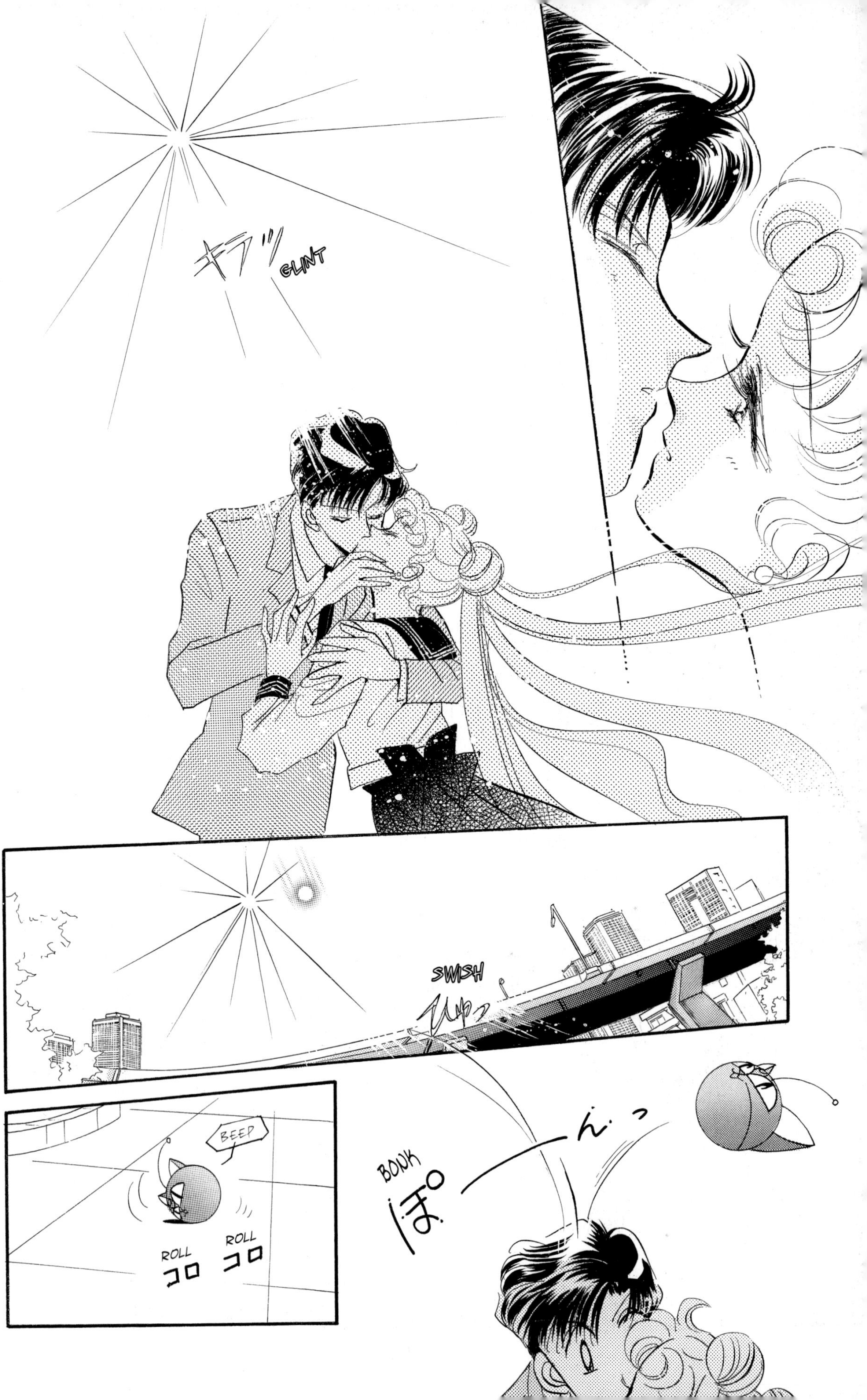

キラッ
GLINT
SWISH
ひゅっ
BONK
ぽ――んっ
BEEP
ROLL
コロ
ROLL
コロ

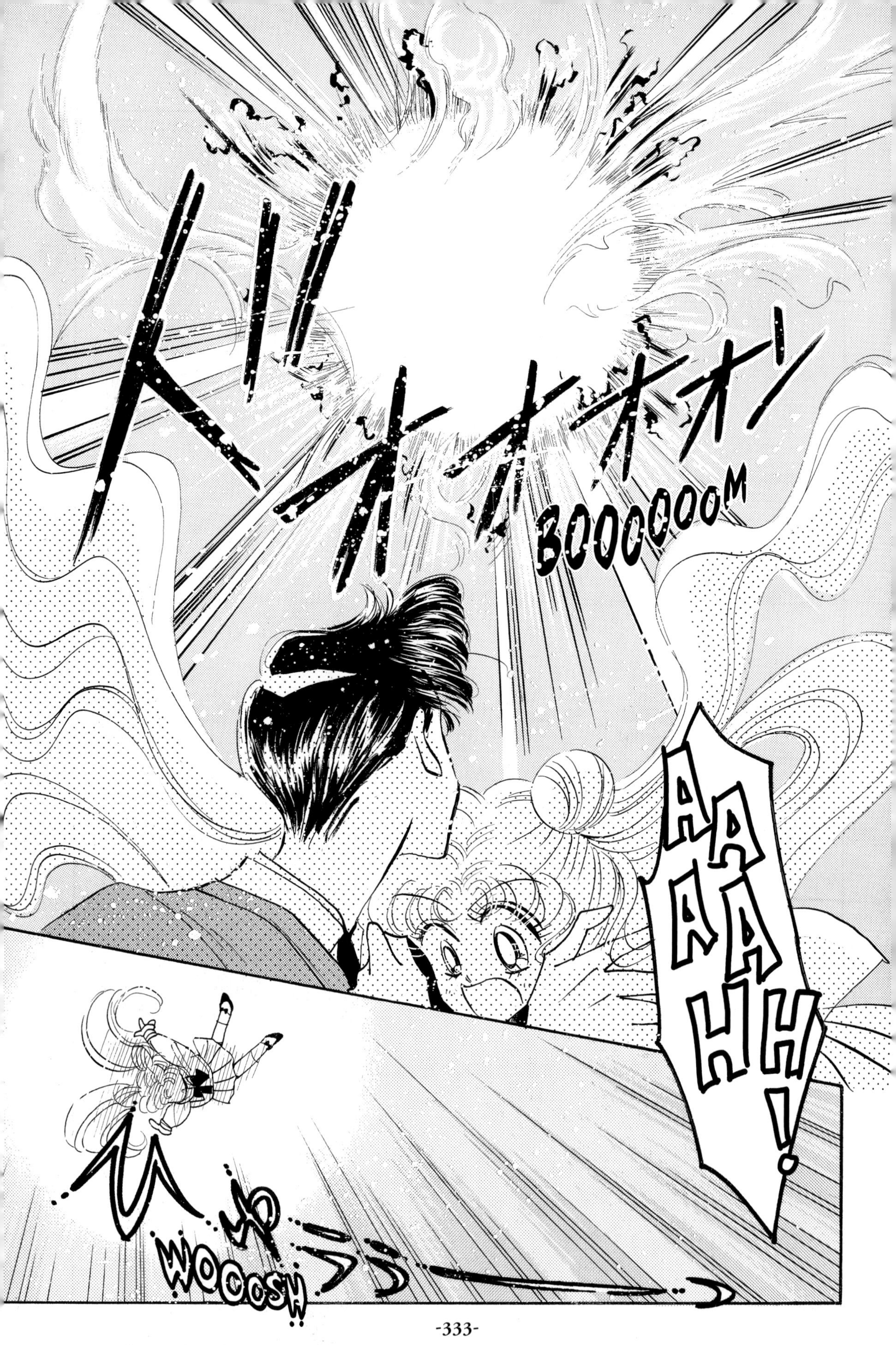
ドオオオン
BOOOOOOM
AAAAAH!
ひゅうう—
WOOOSH

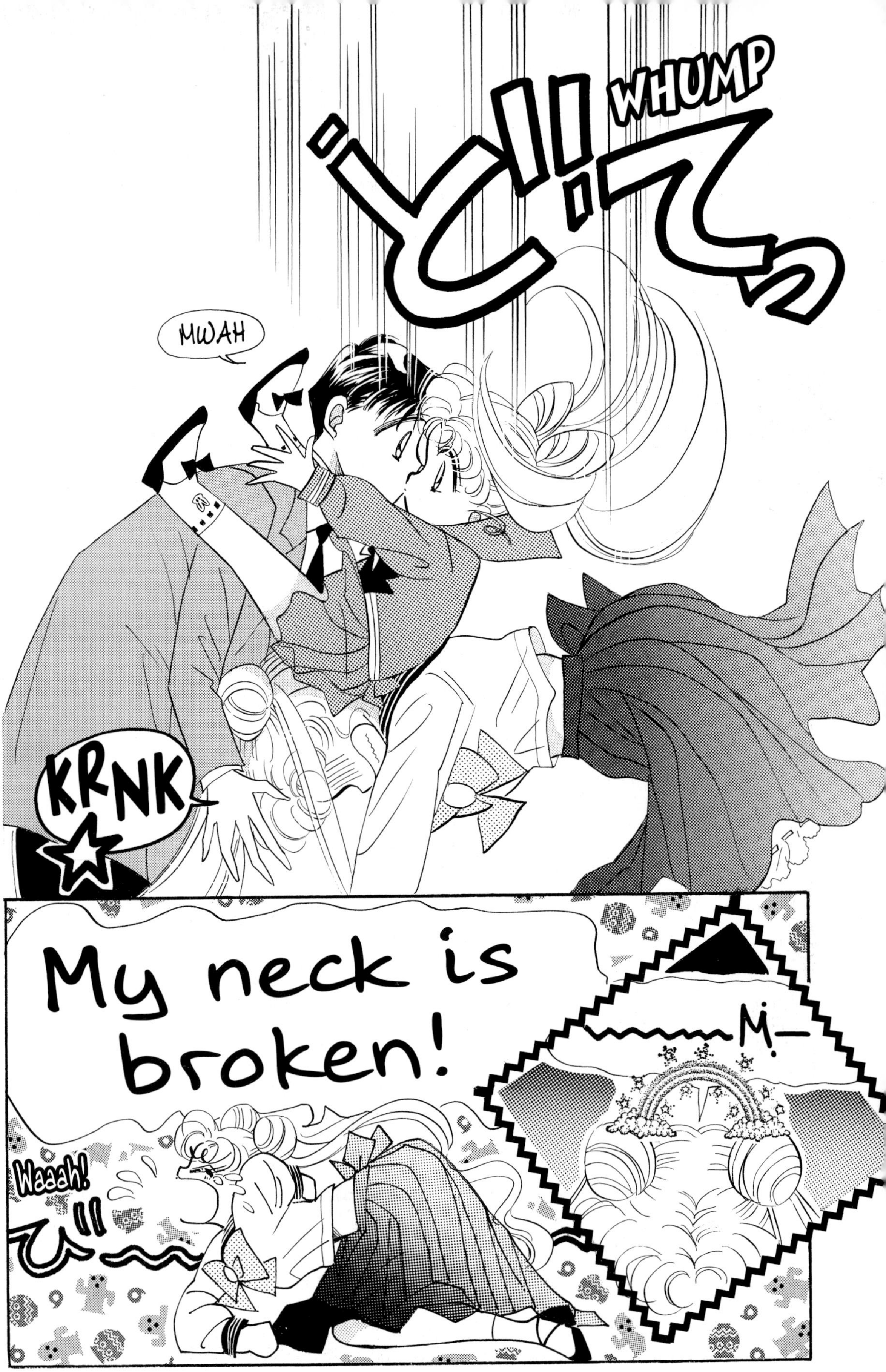

WHUMP
ど!!てっ
MWAH
KRNK☆
M!—
My neck is broken!
Waaah!
び〜〜

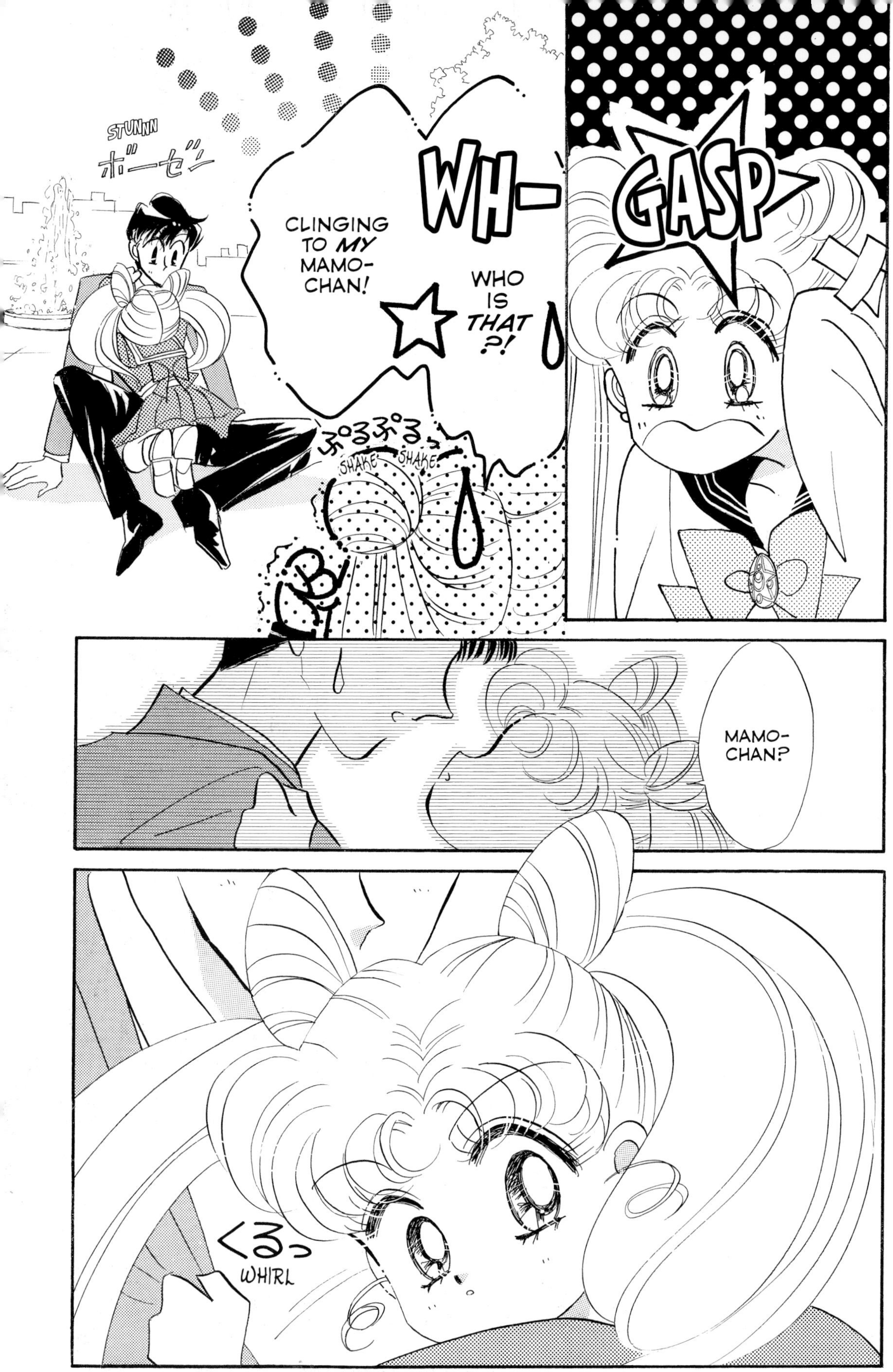
GASP
WH-
WHO IS THAT?!
CLINGING TO MY MAMO-CHAN!
ボーゼン
STUNNN
ぷるぷるっ
SHAKE SHAKE
MAMO-CHAN?
くるっ
WHIRL

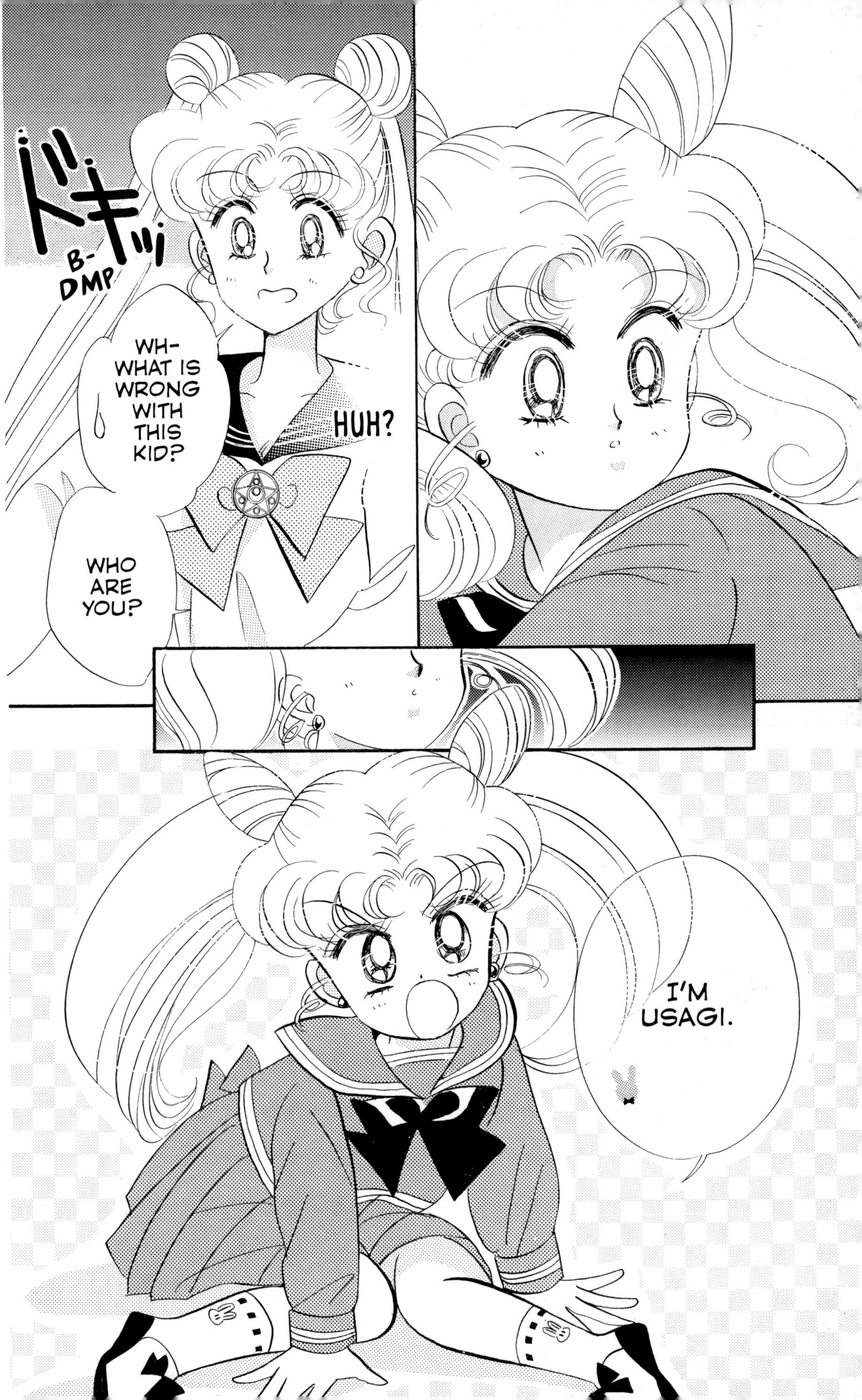

ドキッ
B-DMP
WH- WHAT IS WRONG WITH THIS KID?
HUH?
WHO ARE YOU?
I'M USAGI.

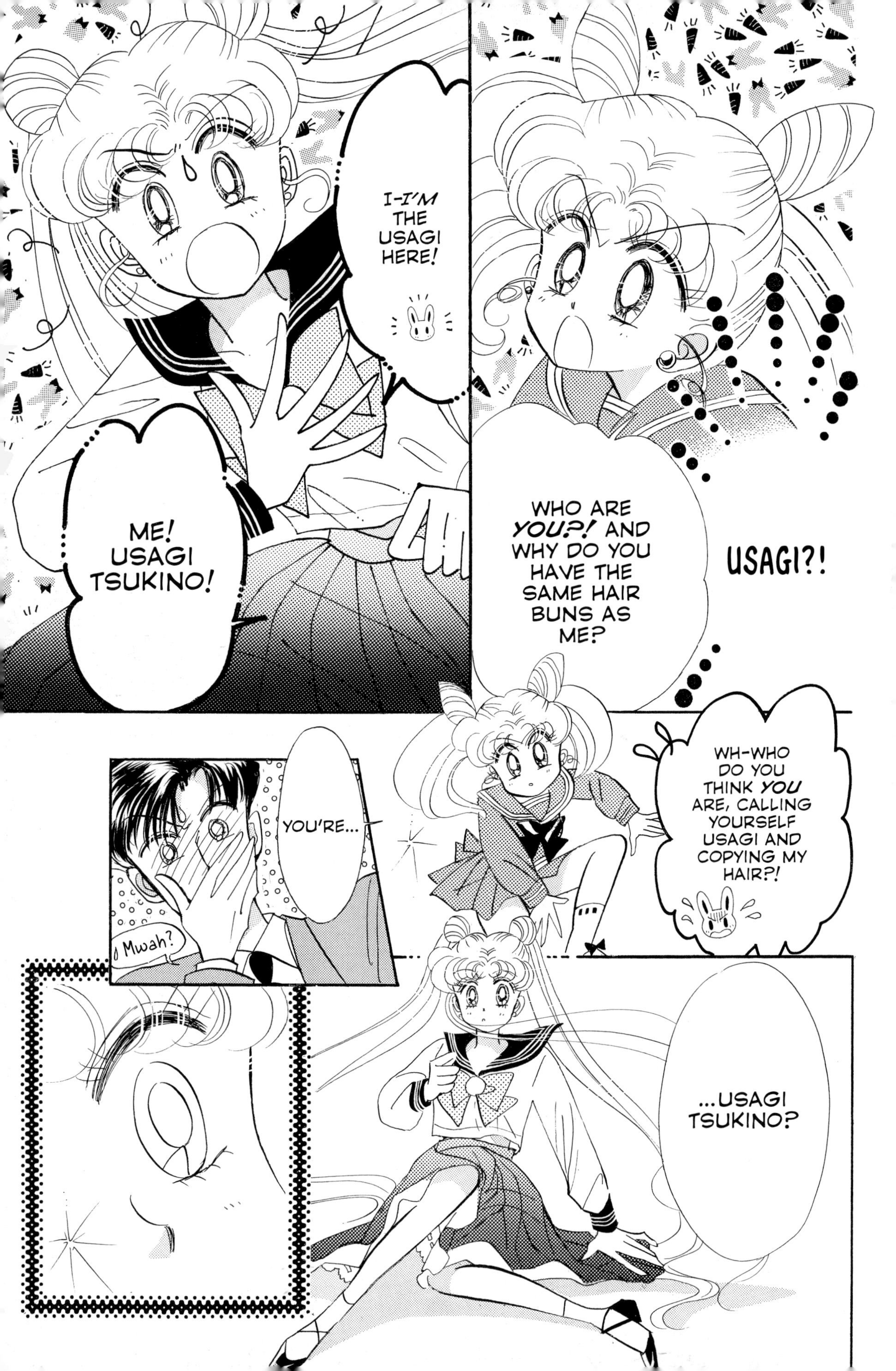
USAGI?!
WHO ARE YOU?! AND WHY DO YOU HAVE THE SAME HAIR BUNS AS ME?
I-I'M THE USAGI HERE!
ME! USAGI TSUKINO!
WH-WHO DO YOU THINK YOU ARE, CALLING YOURSELF USAGI AND COPYING MY HAIR?!
YOU'RE...
Mwah?
...USAGI TSUKINO?

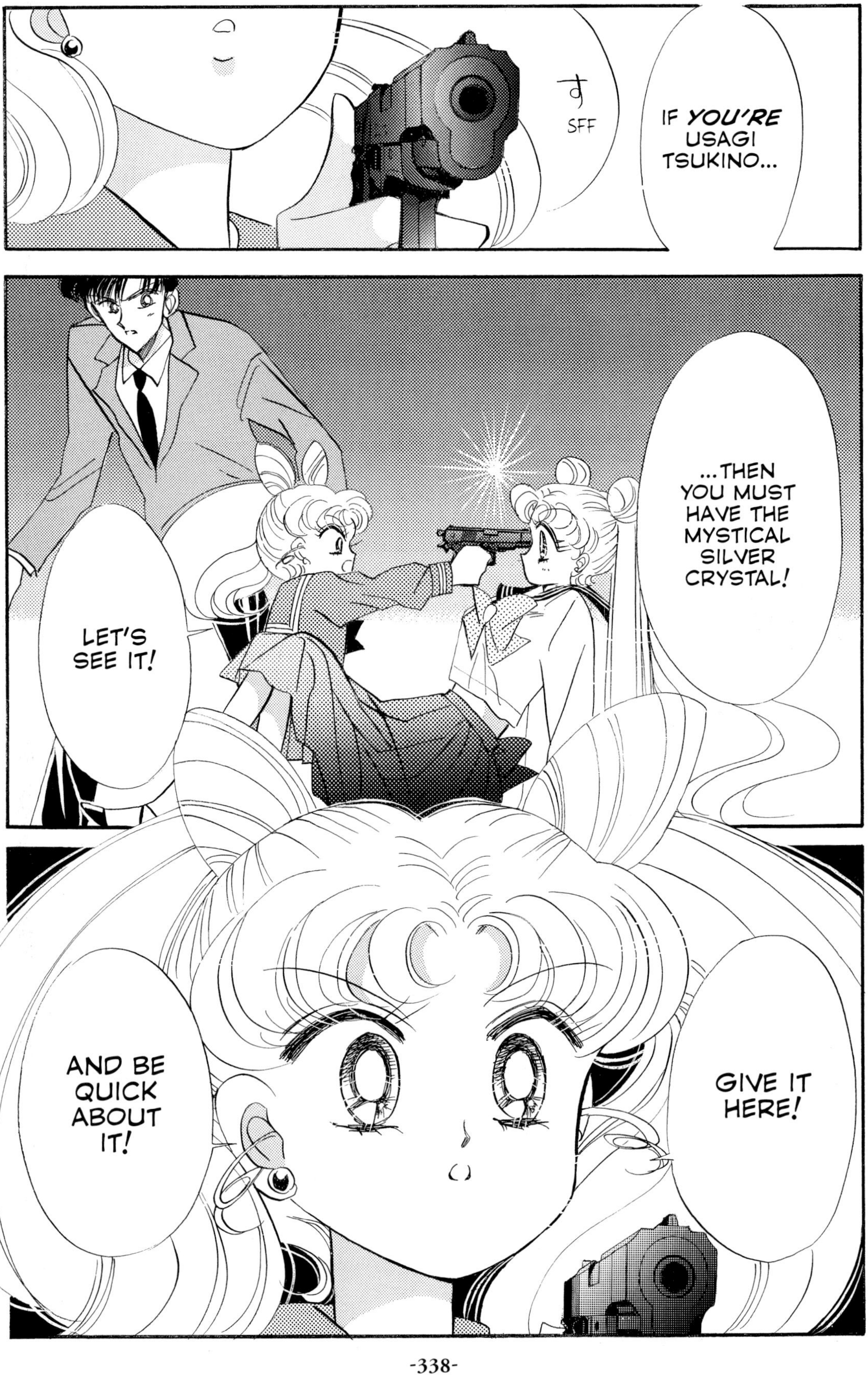
IF *YOU'RE* USAGI TSUKINO...
す SFF
...THEN YOU MUST HAVE THE MYSTICAL SILVER CRYSTAL!
LET'S SEE IT!
GIVE IT HERE!
AND BE QUICK ABOUT IT!

Pretty Guardian
Sailor Moon

# Translation Notes

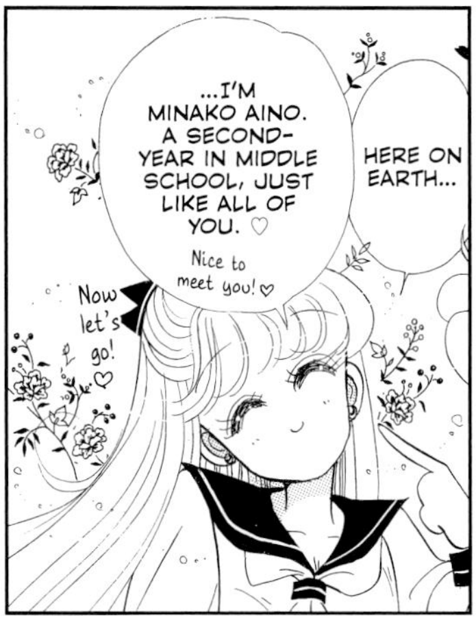
HERE ON EARTH...
...I'M MINAKO AINO. A SECOND-YEAR IN MIDDLE SCHOOL, JUST LIKE ALL OF YOU. ♡
Nice to meet you! ♡
Now let's go! ♡

**Minako Aino, page 15**
According to the pattern established with the other guardians, Minako's surname would be Konno, meaning "of metal," because Venus is *Kinsei*, the gold or metal star. The reader will notice that many of her attacks involve metal. But perhaps because Sailor V existed before the others, her surname, Aino, instead comes from Venus, the goddess of love and beauty, and so means "of love." "Minako" is another bit of wordplay, because the characters representing *mi* and *ko* have alternate pronunciations that would transform this name into *Binasu.* The U would be almost silent, and there is no V in Japanese, so this name would be pronounced similarly to the name Venus.

**Endymion, page 55**
The name Endymion comes from Greek mythology, which tells the tale of a man of surpassing beauty who won the love of the Moon. According to some versions of the myth, the Moon was so enchanted by his countenance that she wished he could remain young and beautiful forever, and as a result, he fell into an eternal slumber.

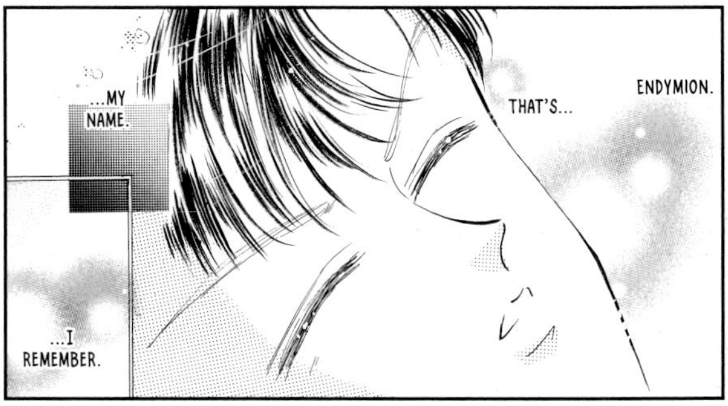
ENDYMION.
THAT'S...
...MY NAME.
...I REMEMBER.

**Moon: Tsuki, page 98**
As with the Tuxedo Kamen chapter in Volume 1, we opted to retain and transliterate the chapter name here. Most of the chapter titles start with the Japanese word or phrase first and then the English second, but here the English word comes first, further highlighting just how foreign both the moon, and the Moon Kingdom, would be.

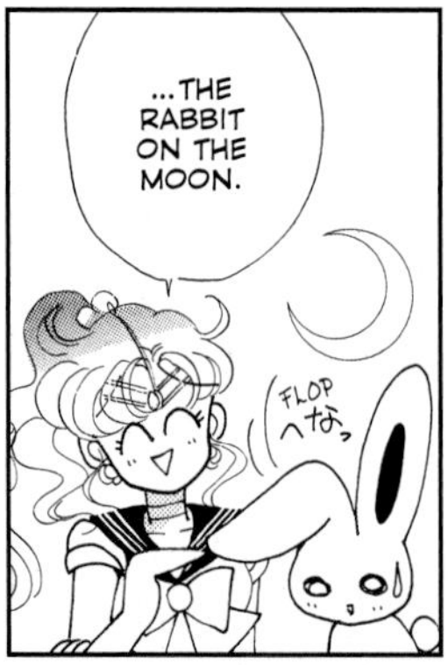
...THE RABBIT ON THE MOON.
FLOP

**Rabbit on the moon, page 112**
As the readers may remember from the notes in Volume 1, Usagi's full name means "rabbit of the moon," or "rabbit on the moon." In the West, traditionally the surface of the moon conjured images of a Man in the Moon, while in many parts of Asia people saw in a rabbit in the craters and mountains of the moon's surface. Beside the rabbit is a mallet, and in the Japanese interpretation, this mallet is used for pounding *mochi* rice cake. As for how the rabbit came to be on the moon, the *Konjaku Monogatarishû* records that a rabbit, a fox, and a monkey came across an old man who had lost his strength and lay dying. Each wanted to help the old man, and the monkey gathered nuts and berries for him to eat while the fox caught some fish in the river. But try as it might, the rabbit could find nothing with which to help the old man. After lamenting its powerlessness, it asked the fox and the monkey to build a fire, and cooked itself for the old man to eat. Touched by this act of self-sacrifice, the old man revealed himself to be the Buddhist deity Śakra and sent the rabbit to the moon so that all would know of its good deeds.

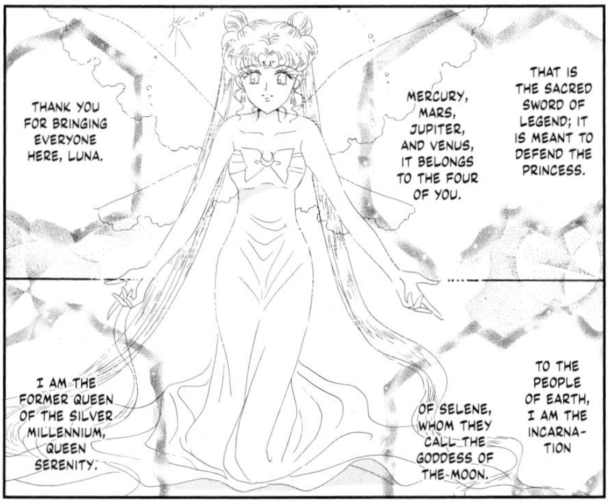
THAT IS THE SACRED SWORD OF LEGEND; IT IS MEANT TO DEFEND THE PRINCESS.
MERCURY, MARS, JUPITER, AND VENUS, IT BELONGS TO THE FOUR OF YOU.
THANK YOU FOR BRINGING EVERYONE HERE, LUNA.
TO THE PEOPLE OF EARTH, I AM THE INCARNATION
OF SELENE, WHOM THEY CALL THE GODDESS OF THE MOON.
I AM THE FORMER QUEEN OF THE SILVER MILLENNIUM, QUEEN SERENITY.

**Selene, page 116**
Selene is a Greek Titan and goddess of the moon, closer to a personification of the moon than her Olympian counterpart Artemis. Because L and R make the same sound in Japanese, and are interchangeable, it is not difficult to make the jump from Selene, goddess of the moon, to Serenity, the sea of which is a prominent location on the moon. Incidentally, the Roman equivalent of Selene is Luna.

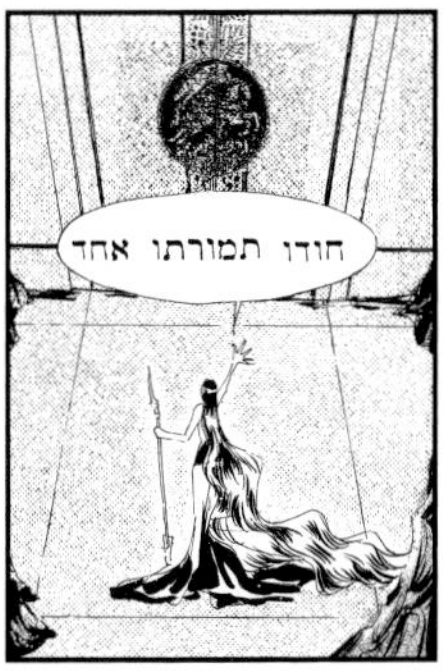
חודו תמורתו אחד

**Beryl's incantation, page 129**
Although written slightly incorrectly, this incantation is the end of a divine name from the Kabbalah. When written correctly, it translates to "His permutation is one." The name has come to be used in Western magic, which would be needed to invoke the presence of Beryl's supreme ruler, Queen Metalia.

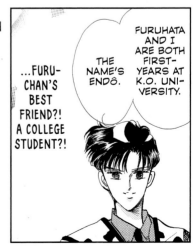

**Condo-million, page 157**

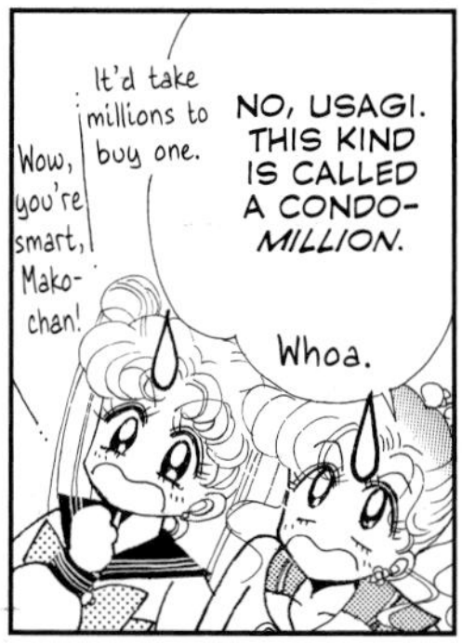
NO, USAGI. THIS KIND IS CALLED A CONDO-*MILLION*.
It'd take millions to buy one.
Wow, you're smart, Mako-chan!
Whoa.

This pun was respectfully borrowed from the previous English edition of this chapter. In Japan, they call condominiums and high-end apartments *manshon*, from the English word for high-end single-family units, "mansion." Of course, *man* is also a Japanese number—ten thousand, to be precise. Ten thousand yen would be about a hundred dollars. In the Japanese version, Makoto rightly points out that you couldn't possibly get such a condo for only 100 dollars, and corrects Usagi by telling her that it's an *oku-shon*, where *oku* means "100 million." 100 million yen is about a million dollars, which seems more like the price range for such a luxury home.

**Endô, page 165**
The name Endô has some interesting, and perhaps cruel, significance. The reader may have already noticed its similarity to the name Endymion, but unfortunately for Usagi, it may also be related to the word *endooi*, which literally means "distant connection," and is used to describe a relationship that is basically nonexistent. In other words, while he looks exactly like her beloved Mamoru, Endô is a complete stranger.

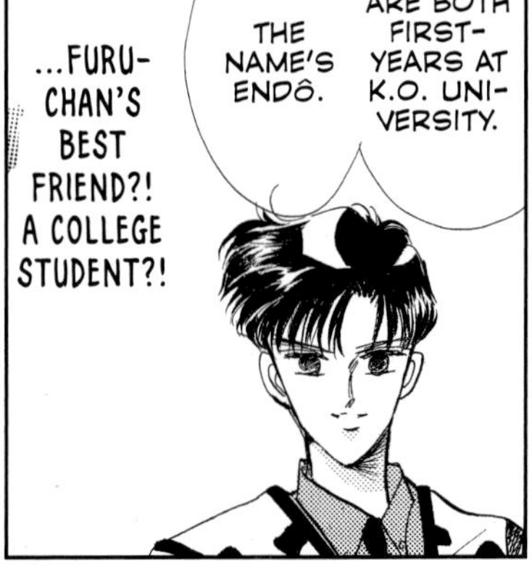
FURUHATA AND I ARE BOTH FIRST-YEARS AT K.O. UNIVERSITY.
THE NAME'S ENDÔ.
...FURU-CHAN'S BEST FRIEND?! A COLLEGE STUDENT?!

**K.O. University, page 165**
Often, manga artists will slightly change or obscure the name of a real-life place in order to fictionalize it. Here, K.O. University is a clever way of "renaming" the very real Keio University, a private and prestigious school located in Mita, a few stops away from Azabu-Jûban.

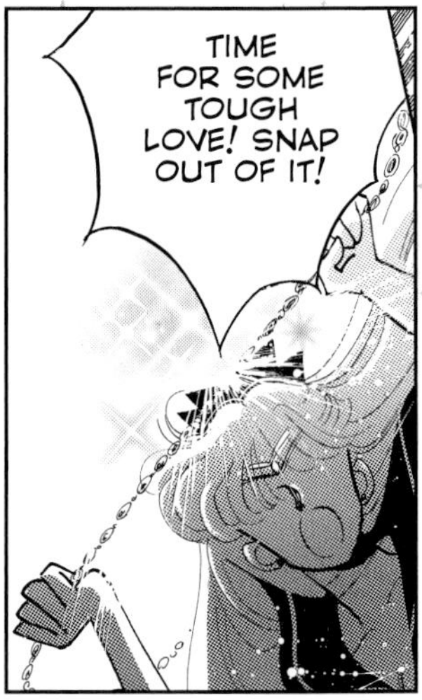
TIME FOR SOME TOUGH LOVE! SNAP OUT OF IT!

**Tough love, page 179**

This particular part of Sailor Venus's arsenal is another pun. The Japanese idiom that equates to the English "tough love" translates more accurately to "love's whip," as in, sometimes you must be cruel in order to be kind. Of course, in the case of Sailor Venus, it is a literal whip, and it is a whip "of love" because Venus is the goddess of love.

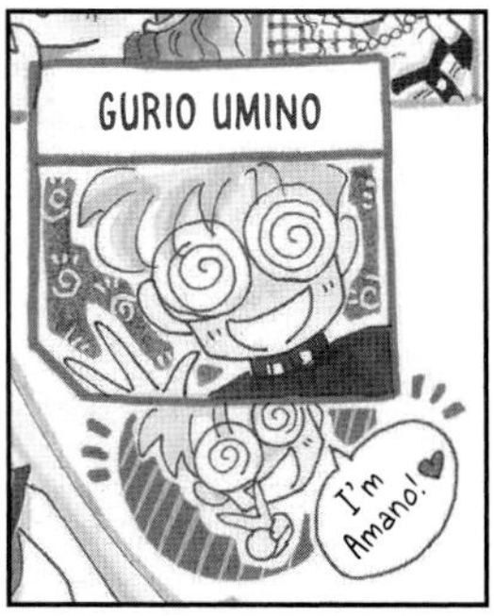
GURIO UMINO
I'm Amano!♥

**Amano, page 193**

Gurikazu Amano is Gurio Umino's doppelgänger who attends Minako's school. Not only do they look alike, but their names seem to be related, as well. Umino means "of the sea," and Amano means "of the sky." The *"guri"* in each of their given names refers to the swirly pattern on their glasses. They must both come from long lines of near-sighted geeks. Readers can learn more about Amano in *Codename Sailor V.*

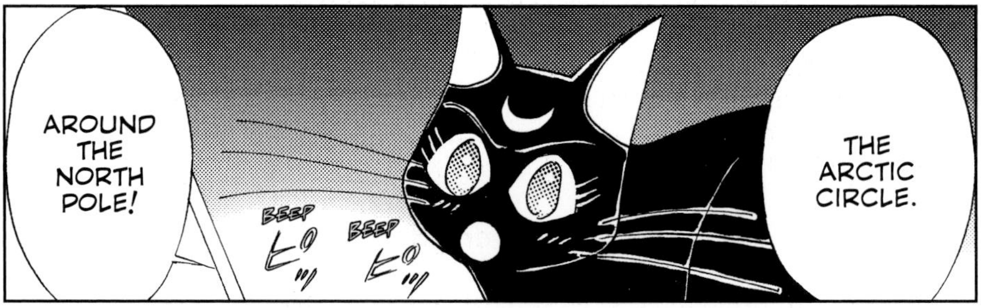
THE ARCTIC CIRCLE.
BEEP
BEEP
AROUND THE NORTH POLE!

**The North Pole, page 214**

The reader may wonder why the Dark Kingdom, or at least its entrance, would have been built so close to Santa's workshop. The answer may be found in Dante's *Divine Comedy,* in which the poet writes of being guided through the three parts of the afterlife: Hell, Purgatory, and Heaven. In the narrative poem, Dante recounts that the entrance to hell is in the North Pole, where Lucifer fell when he was thrust out of Heaven.

A Kodansha Comics Trade Paperback Original
*Sailor Moon Eternal Edition* volume 2 copyright © 2013 Naoko Takeuchi
English translation copyright © 2018 Naoko Takeuchi
First published in Japan in 2013 by Kodansha Ltd., Tokyo.

All rights reserved.

Published in the United States by Kodansha Comics, an imprint of Kodansha USA Publishing, LLC, New York.

Publication rights for this English edition arranged through Kodansha Ltd, Tokyo.

ISBN 978-1-63236-153-0

Printed in Canada.

www.kodanshacomics.com

9 8 7 6 5 4 3 2 1

Translation: Alethea Nibley & Athena Nibley
Lettering: Lys Blakeslee
Editing: Lauren Scanlan
Kodansha Comics edition cover design by Phil Balsman

11/18